Contents

✿ Contents

Workplace Law
Handbook 2012:

Er
hu

Edi

ISBN 978-0-7494-6623-7

Published in association with
Workplace Law
110 Hills Road
Cambridge
CB2 1LQ
Tel. 0871 777 8881
Fax. 0871 777 8882
Email info@workplacelaw.net
www.workplacelaw.net

Design and layout by Workplace Law and Amnet Systems Ltd.
Printed and bound by Oriental Press, Dubai.

Cover design by Gary Jobson.

Publisher's note

Every possible effort has been made to ensure that the information contained in this book is accurate at the time of going to press, and the publishers and authors cannot accept responsibility for any errors or omissions, however caused. No responsibility for loss or damage occasioned to any person acting, or refraining from action, as a result of the material in this publication can be accepted by the editor, the publisher or any of the authors. Readers should be aware that only Acts of Parliament and Statutory Instruments have the force of law and that only the courts can authoritatively interpret the law. The views expressed in the *Workplace Law Handbook 2012: Employment law and human resources* are the contributors' own and not necessarily those of the publishers.

First published in Great Britain in 2011 by Kogan Page Limited in association with Workplace Law.

120 Pentonville Road	1518 Walnut Street, Suite 1100	4737/23 Ansari Road
London N1 9JN	Philadelphia PA 19102	Daryaganj
United Kingdom	USA	New Delhi 110002
www.koganpage.com		India

ISBN: 978 0 7494 6623 7

British Library Cataloguing-in-Publication Data

A CIP record for this book is available from the British Library.

Contents

Comment ...

Virtual reality

Alex Davies, Workplace Law

The way we consume information has changed radically in the past few years, shifting away from traditional printed words on paper to online newspapers, tailored RSS news feeds, homemade video clips shared on the internet to, at its most radical, condensed 'tweets' in which information of importance is refined to just 140 characters. The result is a transient glut of information, constantly evolving, and instantly forgettable. It's true that once something has been said on the internet, it can't be unsaid – however, I'd argue that due to the colossal size of the internet it's also very hard to find! Useful information can very easily be buried, never to be retrieved. That's why I think there is still a place for a traditional reference book, to be placed on a shelf or a desk, within easy reach.

That said, we're not luddites, and appreciate the potential and opportunity that new media can bring. *Workplace Law Magazine*, our bi-monthly magazine for members, will see its last printed edition in December, to be replaced by an entirely digital version in the New Year, offering enhanced features and an easy to use online platform. The launch of our new website in the New Year will also offer more user-friendly content, better search functionality and more content for subscribers. And, to keep the *Handbook* bang on trend, you will also find this publication available as a Kindle edition, as well as an online version, available to Workplace Law's premium members.

Alex Davies is the Project Manager at Workplace Law. She has a degree in Publishing and has worked on a variety of business titles in a range of roles. She has edited the *Workplace Law Handbooks* for the past five editions and enjoys putting together this ever-expanding title whilst cruising the inland waterways of France on her 104-year-old barge.

Whilst on the subject of new media, WPL TV, our online media centre, is growing, with weekly news updates, online seminars, case studies and interviews. Workplace Law also has a YouTube channel, with a wealth of content waiting to be viewed.

All of this is compiled by our expanding team at Workplace Law – our family of consultants and practitioners who are passionate about their subjects and helping our clients achieve not only compliance, but excellence. People are a company's most vital asset, and what the influx of social media has demonstrated most of all is that people are exactly that – social – and there are now so many ways we can reach out, share knowledge, learn and innovate. We like to think that when a client chooses Workplace Law, they are putting their trust in us to help them keep up to date with what's important, in an efficient, responsible, and engaging way.

The law is constantly changing, and this year has seen the end of the default retirement age, changes to agency workers regulations, the introduction and extension of two major pieces of legislation – the Equality and the Bribery Act – and lots more. In the week we went to Press, the Government announced its decision to extend the qualification period for the right to claim unfair dismissal from one to two years, as well as the controversial move to implement fees for an employee taking their employer to Tribunal. These two very employer-focused moves followed the Government's Resolving workplace disputes consultation (p.172) and demonstrate its commitment to saving businesses money and time away from their core activities.

> "In the face of such measures it's easy to forget that an employer's most valued asset is its people, and in austere times the temptation to cut costs is high on the agenda."

In the face of such measures it's easy to forget that an employer's most valued asset is its people, and in austere times the temptation to cut costs is high on the agenda. But people are what will keep a company afloat during stormy weather, and knowing how to manage and utilise them to their greatest potential is the key.

Which brings me back to social media, and the changing way we consume information. Keeping all members of a company informed and up to speed on the changing nature of the workplace is vital to boost morale, team-build and spot potential problems before they escalate out of control. This new edition of the *Employment Law and Human Resources Handbook* features new chapters on mediation (p.300), psychometric testing (p.415) and appraisals (p.40) – all methods that can be used to keep employers in touch with their staff's changing needs – as well as topical comment pieces on recent threats to the modern workplace, such as super-injunctions (p.542), organising holiday (p.22) and whistleblowing (p.555), to keep employers aware of the procedures they need to have in place to manage and protect their operations effectively.

The *Handbook* also contains a brand new 'At a glance' section (p.12), which provides a quick and easy reference point for the key information you need to know over the next 12 months, as well as the usual varied mix of comment pieces, case reviews and chapters to cover all aspects of the modern, dynamic workplace.

As the editor for the past five editions, I'm always keen to hear your views, and in keeping with the social media theme, I'm happy to hear them via any method available. Follow me on @AlexDaviesWPL and keep an eye out for our other consultants' social media presence, throughout the book. See you in the virtual world…

A. Davies.

@AlexDaviesWPL

About Workplace Law

Workplace Law specialises in employment law, health and safety and environmental management. We help clients achieve excellence by easing the burden of compliance and providing valuable best practice solutions.

Operating nationally from offices in Cambridge and London, we are an established market leader in the provision of information, training, consultancy and support to employers. Through our recruitment arm we place competent professionals in permanent and interim positions with UK employers.

With a 15-year pedigree of excellence, we are trusted by employers throughout the UK to help them get to grips with the law and regulation of managing people and their working environment.

Workplace Law is the specialist advisor to the British Institute of Facilities Management (BIFM) on employment law, health and safety and premises management, and a market leader in the facilities management (FM) and education sectors.

Our specialist services

Workplace Law specialises in supporting employers by providing three core services.

Educating our clients through the provision of an award-winning membership and online information service, and through the delivery of recognised training programmes by classroom, e-learning and blended learning study. Licensed by the CIPD, IEMA, IOSH and NEBOSH, we are one of the UK's leading information and training providers.

Supporting our clients by providing bespoke advice and consultancy, by telephone, online and on-site support throughout the UK. We offer a range of solutions to suit your needs, from one-off projects to indemnified annual support contracts.

Resourcing talent for our clients through our sister company, Workplace Law Career Network, which specialises in the permanent and interim placement of competent professionals in the areas of health, safety and environment (HSE), facilities management, and human resources.

Our specialist subject areas

Workplace Law specialises in three core areas of compliance.

Workplace Law Human Resources
Workplace Law Human Resources specialises in HR and employment law. We are an established training provider, licensed by the Chartered Institute of Personnel and Development (CIPD) to provide accredited training programmes. We provide advice and support for employers on recruitment, performance management, discrimination and dismissal, including representing you in Employment Tribunal proceedings.

Workplace Law Health and Safety

Workplace Law Health and Safety specialises in health and safety management and compliance. We are an established training provider, licensed by IOSH and NEBOSH to provide accredited health and safety training programmes via classroom and e-learning study modes. We provide advice and support on health and safety strategy and systems such as HSG 65 and OHSAS 18001, in addition to CDM and fire safety compliance.

Workplace Law Environmental

Workplace Law Environmental specialises in environmental management and compliance. We are an established training provider, approved by the Institute of Environmental Management and Assessment (IEMA) to provide certified courses at foundation level. Our specialist consultancy work includes environmental auditing, advice on environmental management systems, including ISO 14001, BREAAM and energy efficiency assessments, and compliance with environmental regulations.

Workplace Law Career Network

Workplace Law Career Network is a leading professional services firm specialising in the recruitment of personnel in facilities management, building services, health and safety, and human resources.

We provide permanent recruitment and interim management solutions for employers. Part of Workplace Law, the firm draws on a wide range of resources to offer enhanced support to candidates and clients.

Candidates have access to CIPD-accredited training and updated information through the award-winning Workplace Law service.

Enhanced services for clients include psychometric testing, assessment centres, and advice on employment law, including fair recruitment, TUPE and restructuring and redundancy support.

Workplace Law Career Network provides national coverage, operating from offices in Cambridge and London.

How we do it

Clients trust us to deliver value to their business, challenging the status quo to constantly improve the services we provide.

We do this with energy, enthusiasm and endeavour, to make our community a better place to live and work.

T. +44 (0)871 777 8881
F. +44 (0)871 777 8882

Workplace Law
110 Hills Road
Cambridge
CB2 1LQ

At a glance

Chloe Harrold and Pam Loch, Loch Associates

Time off work

Statutory holiday entitlements

Workers are entitled to a minimum of 5.6 weeks' paid annual leave, which can include bank holidays (equivalent to 28 days for full-time employees).

A worker who begins part way through the leave year is entitled to a pro-rata statutory holiday entitlement for that year.

Parental leave

Ordinary Maternity Leave	26 weeks
Additional Maternity Leave	26 weeks
Ordinary Adoption Leave	26 weeks
Additional Adoption leave	26 weeks
Ordinary Paternity Leave	Two weeks
Additional Paternity Leave	26 weeks
Parental leave	13 weeks for each child (unpaid) up to the child's fifth birthday (18 weeks and up to the18th birthday if disabled)

Working time limits

Adults	Adult workers cannot work more than an average of 48 hours per week over a 17-week period.
Young workers	May not work over eight hours per day or 40 hours per week (these hours cannot be averaged).
Child workers (compulsory school age	During term time, a child may not work more than 12 hours per week including a maximum of two hours on a school day or Sunday and a maximum of five hours on a Saturday for 13-14 year olds, or eight hours on a Saturday for 15-16 year olds.
	Child workers may not work for more than one hour before school.
	During school holidays, a 13-14 year old may work a maximum of 25 hours per week including up to five hours on a weekday or a Saturday and up to two hours on a Sunday.
	During school holidays, a 15-16 year old may work up to a maximum of 35 hours per week including up to eight hours on a weekday or a Saturday and up to two hours on a Sunday.

Payments

Payments for time off work

Types of payment	From April 2011	Maximum period
Statutory Sick Pay (standard rate)	£81.60 per week	28 weeks in any period of incapacity
Statutory Maternity Pay (SMP) (earnings related)	90% of employee's normal weekly earnings	Six weeks
SMP (prescribed rate)	£128.73 per week or 90% of employee's normal weekly earnings if lower	33 weeks
Statutory Paternity Pay (SPP)	£128.73 per week or 90% of employee's normal weekly earnings if lower	Two weeks' ordinary paternity leave; 26 weeks' additional paternity leave
Statutory Adoption Pay (SAP)	£128.73 per week or 90% of employee's normal weekly earnings if lower	39 weeks

National minimum wage

Type	From October 2011
Employee aged 21+	£6.08 per hour
Employee aged 18-20	£4.98 per hour
Employee aged 16-17	£3.68 per hour
Apprentice aged below 19 or in first year of apprenticeship	£2.60 per hour

Income tax

Allowances	From April 2011
Personal allowance for under 65s	£7,475
Personal allowance for ages 65-74	£9,940
Personal allowance for ages 75+	£10,090
Income limit for age-related allowances	£24,000
Blind person's allowance	£1,980

Taxable bands

Bands	From April 2011
Basic rate (20%)	£0 – £35,000
Higher rate (40%)	£35,001 – £150,000
Additional rate (50%)	Over £150,000

Redundancy

Statutory redundancy pay is calculated based on length of continuous employment, age and weekly pay (up to a maximum of £400).	
Each full year of service under the age of 22	0.5 weeks' pay
Each full year of service aged 22-41	One week's pay
Each full year of service aged 41+	1.5 weeks' pay
The maximum payment is 30 weeks' pay or 12,000.	

Statutory notice periods

Employment length	Notice
Between one month and two years	One week's notice
Between two and 12 years	One week's notice
12 years or more	12 weeks' notice

Allowances for jury service

Jury service normally lasts for ten days and employers are not liable to pay salary. The employee will usually be given a Certificate of Loss of Earnings from the Court and the employer should ensure they complete the relevant section.

Loss of earnings, benefit or other financial loss	Maximum daily allowance
Up to and including four hours in the first ten days of jury service	£32.47
More than four hours in the first ten days of jury service	£64.95
Up to and including four hours on the 11th and up to the 200th day of jury service	£64.95
More than four hours on the 11th and up to the 200th day of jury service	£129.91
Up to and including four hours on the 201st and all subsequent days	£114.03
More than four hours on the 201st and all subsequent days	£228.06

Employment Tribunal limits and rates

Type of payment	Minimum from February 2011	Maximum from February 2011
Limit on a week's pay for certain purposes including redundancy and basic award for unfair dismissal	No minimum	£400
Unfair dismissal basic award	No minimum	£12,000
Unfair dismissal compensatory award	No minimum	£68,400 (with limited exceptions)
Unfair dismissal additional award	Lower of 26 weeks' pay or £10,400	52 weeks' pay, up to £20,800
Unlawful discrimination	No minimum	No maximum
Statutory redundancy	No minimum	£12,000
Breach of right to be accompanied	No minimum	Two weeks' pay, up to £800
Breach of contract	No minimum	£25,000
Collective redundancy – failure to inform and consult	No minimum	13 weeks' actual pay
Failure to give a statement of particulars of employment	Two weeks' pay, up to £800	Four weeks' pay, up to £1,600
Breach of Flexible Working Regulations	No minimum	Eight weeks' pay, up to £3,200

Tribunal statistics
- A total of 218,100 claims were received during 2010-11 (8% less than 2009-10).
- There were falls in both single and multiple claims by 15% and 4% respectively.
- There has been a fall in the following claims:
    - Unfair dismissal claims (from 57,400 to 47,900)
    - Unauthorised deductions (from 75,500 to 71,300)
    - Breach of contract (from 42,400 to 34,600)
    - Equal pay (from 37,400 to 34,600)
    - Race discrimination (from 5,700 to 5,000)
    - Discrimination on the grounds of sexual orientation (from 710 to 640)
- There has been a rise in the following claims:
    - Sex discrimination (from 18,200 to 18,300)
    - Working time (from 95,200 to 114,000 – due to a group of airline industry claims)
    - TUPE – failure to inform and consult (from 1,800 to 1,900)
    - Part-time working (from 530 to 1,600)
    - Age discrimination (from 5,200 to 6,800)
- Overall, 32% of claims were withdrawn, 12% were successful at Tribunal, 9% were unsuccessful at hearing and 29% were conciliated by ACAS.
- The ET has a target of hearing 75% of its single accepted claims where the hearing begins within 26 weeks. It currently has a 59% success rate, down 6% on last year.

Absence management

Anna Youngs, Mills & Reeve

Key points
- Keep accurate absence / attendance records.
- Monitor absence data.
- Consider whether the Equality Act applies in relation to disability discrimination.

Legislation
- Access to Medical Reports Act 1988.
- Equality Act 2010.

Absence problems

Although employers expect a certain amount of absence, high levels of absence can be disruptive, and expensive. Absence-related dismissals or disciplinary sanctions can lead to expensive Tribunal claims and therefore it is important that employers handle absence carefully. The treatment of absences will depend on a number of factors, including whether the absence is:

- persistent, frequent, short-term absence;
- long-term absence;
- sickness related; and/or
- unauthorised absences (including lateness).

Employers are liable to pay employees statutory sick pay for certain periods. There may be an underlying cause for the absence, which could be sickness related, related to the employee's personal or domestic circumstances, or could be due to a problem in the workplace. Establishing the cause may enable employers to work out a solution and manage absence more effectively.

The following gives a brief overview of some of the issues that arise in this complicated area of employee management.

Monitoring absence levels

Monitoring absence will assist in assessing how much working time is lost, and whether there are particular employees who have more time off than others. Monitoring also assists the employer to get to the cause of absences, and highlight any problems in any particular department or relating to any type of work.

Absence should be monitored by keeping detailed attendance records, showing when, and why, any individual employee has been absent and the duration of the absence (this will include a record of whether the absence was authorised).

Reducing absence levels

Employers should implement an absence management policy, which sets out how they will monitor absence, and what will happen as a result of employee absenteeism.

Most employers have trigger points for different stages of the absence management procedure. Some employers calculate 'working time lost'; others use the 'Bradford Factor', which is a long-standing HR tool.

The triggers and the procedure should be applied consistently, and at each stage the

- The average rate of absence in 2009 was 6.4 days per employee, a decline from 6.7 days in 2007 and a further step in a long-term downward trend, which is to be expected in a cold climate.
- Absence levels across the public sector stood at an average of 8.3 days' absence per employee in 2009, compared to 5.8 days in the private sector.
- Long-term absence (20 days or more) accounted for a fifth of all time lost, despite only accounting for a tenth of absences.
- On average, employers believed that 15% of absence was not genuine, equating to 27 million working days at a cost of £2.52bn.
- In 2009, the average cost of sickness was £595 per employee.

The HSE has since commissioned the Health and Safety Laboratory (HSL) to carry out a further but more extensive nationwide survey of sickness absence across the industry in 2010–12. The HSE refers to estimates that sickness absence costs the UK economy around £12bn annually and results in over 200 million lost working days.

Source: CBI/AXA Absence Survey 2010.

employee should be given an opportunity to explain their absences.

One tool that many employers have found to be effective in reducing absence levels is a return to work interview, where some gentle quizzing of the employee about the reason for the absence, how they are feeling, what support they may need, etc. is undertaken. It is not clear why this is so effective but some speculate that the reduction in absenteeism may be because some employees fear having to face a manager on their return to explain about their absence.

Other steps that can be taken to reduce absences include:

- induction and training for employees;
- training managers and supervisors to manage absence effectively;
- ensuring that the absence policy covers the provision of medical or self certificates to cover sickness absence;
- involving occupational health as appropriate, especially if there is no medical certificate to support self-certified absences;
- undertaking risk assessments in respect of any recurring causes of absence (including stress risk assessments if applicable); and
- keeping in contact with absent employees and throughout any process consult with the employee.

In all cases of sickness absence the employer should have an up-to-date report on the employee's medical condition. This may be a GP report, specialist advice, an Occupational Health report, etc. The employer should not just ask for a 'report' but ask specific questions on diagnosis and prognosis in the employee's / employer's circumstances.

ACAS recommends that in all cases the employee should be told what improvement is expected and be warned of the likely consequences if no improvement occurs. If there is no improvement, ACAS recommends that employers take into account the following factors before deciding upon appropriate action:

- Performance;
- Likelihood of change in attendance levels;
- Any improvement already made;
- The availability of suitable alternative work (if appropriate); and
- The effect of past and future absences on the business.

Historically, an employee's length of service has been taken into account with their employment history when looking at appropriate sanctions for absenteeism, but this should not be a major factor given that the Equality Act 2010 may render this discriminatory on the grounds of age.

Equality Act 2010

Where the reason for absence is ill heath, employers must consider whether the provisions of the Equality Act 2010 relating to disability are applicable. This is not just the case for long-term absences, as a disability within the meaning of the Equality Act could result in an employee taking frequent short periods of absence.

Employers must consider whether there are any reasonable adjustments that can be made for a disabled employee. This may include adjusting the way in which a sickness absence policy is applied to a disabled employee.

Disability discrimination is one of the most complex areas of law. Many employers shy away from dismissing or disciplining an employee who has a disability, fearing a claim of disability-related discrimination. This depends on the facts of the case, but employers should tread carefully and be able to 'justify' their decisions as set out in the Equality Act. In any event, adjustments must have already been considered prior

to any sanction being carried out and, where reasonable, adjustments should be made. Employers are advised to consider a wide range of adjustments and keep a record of those considered. Where an adjustment is not made, the employer should keep a note of why that adjustment was not considered to be reasonable. For more on this subject see 'Discrimination' (p.126).

Dismissals in this context are hard to get right, but that does not mean that it cannot be done. Absence due to ill health and inability to undertake duties of the role due to ill health can fall within the fair reason for dismissal of 'capability', but of course a proper and fair process must be undertaken, along with consideration of the Equality Act (see also 'Dismissal' (p.146) and 'Sickness' (p.470)).

If monitoring absence or discussions with the employee reveal an underlying medical condition, employers should:

- get an up-to-date medical opinion to determine the extent of the condition, its likely duration and whether the levels of absence are likely to decrease to an acceptable level;
- consider, in light of any medical report(s) and other information whether the illness may amount to a disability under the Equality Act; and
- if the employee may be disabled, look at what reasonable adjustments can be made.

Note: Dismissal or disciplinary action in respect of maternity-related absence is highly likely to amount to sex discrimination.

Infertility treatment and elective surgery

There is no statutory right for an employee to take time off work in connection with infertility investigations or treatment. Time off for medical appointments in connection with infertility treatment can be dealt with in the same way as time off for any other medical appointment. Many employers deal flexibly and informally with dental or doctors appointments.

However:

- A woman has special protection (and will not need a male comparator for the purposes of a sex discrimination claim) from the point immediately before implantation of fertilised ova. At the point of implantation the woman is regarded as being pregnant, and will have the usual rights afforded to pregnant women. If the treatment is unsuccessful the woman's protection will end two weeks after the end of the pregnancy, which begins after the pregnancy test taken two weeks after implantation.
- A worker could bring a sex discrimination claim on the basis of direct discrimination (for example, a request by a worker of the opposite sex for time off in similar circumstances would have been granted) or indirect discrimination (for example, a woman could argue that rejecting the request places women at a disproportionate disadvantage). An employee could also bring a claim for constructive unfair dismissal in these circumstances.
- If an employee becomes ill as a result of or during infertility treatment, the employer's normal sick pay regime applies.

In relation to elective surgery, if employers do not want to pay contractual sick pay for time off for elective surgery, then their contracts and policies need to be entirely clear on this point. Employers should nonetheless consider any representations that the employee wishes to make on the point, in case a potential discrimination

claim is revealed. SSP would still be payable in any event.

Dealing with unauthorised absence or lateness

Where absence is unauthorised and is not sickness-related, absence should be treated as a conduct issue. The Tribunals will look at the very least for the following steps to have been taken (as well as compliance with the statutory ACAS Code on disciplinary and grievance procedures and the employer's own policy) before dismissal:

- A fair review of the attendance record and reasons for absence;
- An opportunity for the employee to have made representations; and
- Targets for improvement and warnings of dismissal if attendance does not improve.

If an employer believes that an employee has extended their annual leave through sickness absence, rather than actually being sick, a reasonable investigation must be carried out before taking disciplinary action.

Dealing with short-term certified sickness or uncertified absence

Short-term sickness absence can be dealt with as a capability issue. Special care must be taken if the employee could have a disability (as set out above).

If considering dismissal, check and consider the following:

- Employee's prognosis and whether absence levels are likely to decrease and if so in what time-frame.
- Whether the employee's attendance record has improved.
- The effect of the absences on the business, and whether temporary cover can address this.

■ A thorough investigation (taking into account the above) will be required before dismissal.

■ A hearing will be required and, if the outcome is dismissal, an appeal must be offered.

Dealing with long-term sickness absence

If an employee has been off on long-term sickness absence, the risk that they have a 'disability' is increased.

■ Consider the employee's prognosis and whether absence levels are likely to decrease and if so in what time-frame.

■ Employee consent will be needed to get a medical opinion from a doctor appointed by the employer or the employee's own GP. If the employee refuses permission, employers must take action based on the information available to them.

■ Consider reasonable adjustments to the job or working arrangements, which may include finding an alternative role, or a phased return for the employee.

■ Consider whether the absence is caused in whole or in part because of a failure to make reasonable adjustments. If the employer has failed to meet the duty to make reasonable adjustments, dismissal is likely to be unfair and discriminatory. Employers may need to seek advice as to what adjustments would be reasonable and what can be taken into account when

determining whether an adjustment is reasonable.

■ Consider whether the job can be covered by other employees or temporary replacements and how long the job can reasonably be kept open.

■ Be clear about sick pay arrangements and keep the employee informed.

■ A thorough investigation (taking into account the above) will be required before dismissal.

■ A hearing will be required and, if the outcome is dismissal, an appeal must be offered.

Ill health retirement may be an option, and should be explored prior to an ill health dismissal, but this would not prevent an employee from making a Tribunal claim, so consultation is again key.

The ACAS Advisory Booklet, *Managing Attendance and Employee Turnover,* gives further detailed advice about how to manage different types of sickness absence – see *Sources of further information.*

See also: Disciplinary and grievance procedures, p.121; The Equality Act, p.191; Leave, p.294; Medical records, p.304; Occupational health, p.374; Sickness, p.470.

Sources of further information

ACAS Code of Practice on Disciplinary and Grievance Procedures:
www.acas.org.uk/CHttpHandler.ashx?id=1047

ACAS guide: Discipline and grievances at work:
www.acas.org.uk/index.aspx?articleid=2179

ACAS: Managing attendance and employee turnover:
www.acas.org.uk/index.aspx?articleid=1183

EHRC: www.equalityhumanrights.com/advice-and-guidance/information-for-employers/

HSE: www.hse.gov.uk/sicknessabsence/index.htm

Organisations are increasingly recognising the significant costs associated with high levels of absence, alongside the disruption to their business on a day-to-day basis.

Increased discrimination legislation has left many employers unsure of how to deal with persistent short-term and long-term absence. Many managers feel ill equipped to effectively deal with absence, which requires continual commitment and focus to manage effectively.

Most managers would agree that a certain level of absence is acceptable, but they are often unsure of how to deal with absence when it becomes 'unacceptable' and specifically how they should draw that distinction.

Workplace Law can help, with our knowledge and experience of implementing absence management policies, by implementing an absence management system to suit your business.

We can also train your managers, provide one-off support for a specific absence issue or case, provide ongoing support and give your managers the confidence to effectively manage absence across the organisation. This will enable a reduction in your absenteeism, reduce your financial risks, improve employee morale and increase productivity, amongst other benefits. Visit www.workplacelaw.net for more information.

Comment ...

Overcoming the hurdles

Jonathan Exten-Wright, DLA Piper

The countdown to London 2012 is on. The UK will host the Olympic Games for a record third time from 27 July to 12 August 2012, and the Paralympic Games from 29 August to 9 September 2012. Although the majority of the impact will be felt in London, with events taking place nationwide and blanket coverage on television and radio, widespread Olympic-mania is expected.

However, competing requests for annual leave and disruption to transport networks look likely to pose significant issues for employers. By getting off the starting blocks early, employers can be prepared for the Games and avoid potential headaches.

It is likely that there will be an influx of requests for time off during the Games which fall during school summer holidays when holiday absence is at its peak. Many requests could clash and leave employers with a risk of being short staffed.

Just like at any other time, it is important to balance competing requests fairly while looking after business needs. It is advisable to manage staff expectations early. If you intend to prevent people from taking holiday when they want it, acting quickly will avoid disruption from unhappy staff and minimise dissatisfaction – particularly given the limited opportunities to resell tickets.

Check your employment contracts. Is there a right to decide when holiday is taken,

Jonathan Exten-Wright practises employment law on behalf of public and private companies. He is experienced in senior executive issues and boardroom disputes, injunctive proceedings, in central and local government transactions, contracting-out / outsourcing, private finance initiatives, mergers and acquisitions, and sales of businesses, trade union recognition and negotiations, works councils and collective consultation, redundancy and change programmes, contract variation and discrimination. In addition, Jonathan advises on partnership and LLP disputes.

and to refuse holiday requests where there is a business need? Failing that, the Working Time Regulations allow employers to specify when leave can and cannot be taken by giving notice in writing.

Decide how you intend to ration holiday amongst staff and make sure the process is well-publicised and non-discriminatory. Options include:

- First-come, first-granted basis;
- Drawing names out of a hat; or
- Offering some other benefit to unsuccessful employees – such as priority over booking holiday for the

Queen's Diamond Jubilee in June 2012 (which will create a four-day weekend) or Christmas.

Write to staff at the earliest opportunity, explaining the need for adequate cover at all times, that you expect to be inundated with holiday requests, and that there is no automatic right to take time off. Explain any deadlines for submitting holiday applications and what selection process will be implemented where dates are over-subscribed.

Some employers expect the Games to be a quiet period and might prefer employees to take time off then than in busy periods. Employers can encourage staff to make the most of the Olympics by taking a period of holiday around that time.

Employers could also offer to consider applications for unpaid leave over the period of the Games. This stance should be communicated to employees as soon as possible so that staff can take it into account when planning their holidays for 2012, but it should be made clear that a skeleton staff will need to be retained. It would be sensible to set a deadline by which such holiday requests should be submitted in order to plan which requests can be granted.

> "For organisations in and around London, it is inevitable that there will be disruption to employees' normal commute to work as a result of increased tourism during the Games. The Government is encouraging employers to adopt flexible working policies to reduce the pressure on public transport during peak times. Allowing employees to start work later, or stagger start and finish times, may minimise disruption. This also offers an opportunity to test whether home working is viable for your organisation."

If you find that too few staff have requested holiday during the Games, employers can require employees to take their statutory holiday (5.6 weeks per year) at a time suitable to the business under the Working Time Regulations, provided the employment contract does not state anything to the contrary. In order to do this, written notice of at least twice the duration of the leave must be given (e.g. at least four weeks' notice if requiring an employee to take two weeks' holiday).

While from a legal perspective an employer is generally in a strong position to require employees to take statutory leave, this may not always be a sensible commercial option.

Given the impact on employee relations, it would not be worth exercising this power where an employee has already planned to take a bulk of holiday at another time – for example, if they are getting married. Nor would it be appropriate if taking leave would cause problems with childcare or caring arrangements, as this could give rise to discrimination claims.

For organisations in and around London, it is inevitable that there will be disruption to employees' normal commute to work as a result of increased tourism during the

Games. The Government is encouraging employers to adopt flexible working policies to reduce the pressure on public transport during peak times. Allowing employees to start work later, or stagger start and finish times, may minimise disruption. This also offers an opportunity to test whether home working is viable for your organisation.

No matter how much flexibility is afforded, some employees will still be required to travel at peak time and may face transport delays. While lateness is potentially a disciplinary issue, where staff are genuinely try to get to work on time employers should avoid being heavy-handed given the short period of time for which the problem is likely to exist, unless there is significant disruption for their organisation.

Offering some flexibility to employees is likely to discourage unauthorised absence during popular events. Employers could, for example:

- allow staff to work flexibly or swap shifts so that they can catch major events like the Opening Ceremony;

- host workplace screenings of major events; or
- allow employees to listen to commentary via radio or online live streaming.

Policies should be reviewed to ensure that they adequately deal with the issues that are likely to arise out of the Games. These are likely to include absence management, disciplinary and holiday procedures, and any policies relating to equal opportunities. Internet use to follow events is also likely to be a significant issue. There is no obligation on an employer to allow the use of the internet during working hours to keep track of Olympic events. However, employers should decide their policy on this in advance and ensure that it is communicated to employees before the Games and is consistently enforced.

Where existing policies do not adequately deal with all of the issues likely to arise, it may be worth putting in place a specific sporting events policy, which will allow the employer to outline its expectations of employees. This will assist both employers and employees to plan ahead and facilitate open communication.

Agency and temporary workers

Amanda Trewhella, Pitmans

Key points

- An agency worker is a worker who has a contract with a recruitment agency to work for one or more of their clients, or end user companies, on temporary assignments.
- Usually the recruitment agency will pay the agency worker but the end user company will have day-to-day management of the worker.
- The main legal issue in relation to agency workers is whether they are employees, and if so, whether they are an employee of the agency or the end user company. They will be entitled to benefit from increased employment rights if they are employees.
- The treatment of agency workers when compared with permanent staff will be regulated by the Agency Workers Regulations 2010 from 1 October 2011. Agency workers will benefit from increased employment law protection.

Legislation

- Employment Agencies Act 1973.
- Fixed-Term Employees (Prevention of Less Favourable Treatment) Regulations 2002.
- The Conduct of Employment Agencies and Employment Business Regulations 2003.
- Employment Act 2008.
- Agency Workers Regulations 2010.

Overview

An agency worker is someone who has a contract with an employment agency to provide work to a hiring company, usually for a short period of time. They will be paid by the employment agency.

The rights an agency worker has will depend upon whether they are an employee of either the agency or the hiring company, or whether they are not an employee at all and are a worker.

All agency workers are likely to be deemed 'workers' and therefore have the following employment rights (whether or not they are employed):

- Anti-discrimination (if they work under a contract personally to do any work);
- Equal pay;
- National minimum wage;
- Whistleblowing protection;
- Rights to breaks and a maximum working time limit under the Working Time Regulations; and
- Paid annual leave.

Employed or self-employed?

If an agency worker is an employee they will be entitled to enhanced employment rights in the same way as permanent employees, for example unfair dismissal, redundancy payments and maternity and paternity rights.

Section 230 of the Employment Rights Act 1996 defines an employee as:

'An individual who has entered into, or works under, a contract of employment' and states that a contract of employment is *'an express (whether oral or written) or implied contract of service (or apprenticeship)'.*

> **Facts**
> - There are approximately 1.3 million agency workers currently in the UK job market.
> - Currently 40 to 45% work over 12 weeks on each assignment.
> - It is expected to cost UK business £1.8bn per year in increased costs to comply with the Agency Workers Regulations 2010.

In deciding whether someone is an employee the irreducible minimum requirements considered by the courts are:

- *Personal service* – does the individual undertake to provide their own skill and work?
- *Mutuality of obligation* – does the individual undertake to provide their own skill and work in return for consideration (a wage)?
- *Control* – was there a sufficient degree of control to enable the individual to be called a servant?

Agency workers can often find it difficult to show that they are employees of either the agency or the end user company because the company receives the benefit of the individual's work and has day-to-day control over their activities, whereas it is the agency who pays them. If an agency exercises considerable control over the individual the Tribunal may hold that the worker is an employee of the agency for the whole relationship (including between assignments). This is known as an umbrella contract.

Tax treatment

An agency worker may be an employee of the employment agency for tax purposes. Legislation provides that agency workers will be taxed as employees if they are required to supply their services personally, and if they are subject to a right of direction, supervision or control by the end user company. In those circumstances the employment agency would generally be deemed to be the employer and will therefore be responsible for deducting tax and National Insurance contributions under the PAYE scheme. The HMRC VAT staff hire concession used to permit employment businesses to avoid charging their clients VAT and other payments and benefits provided to agency workers. However, this concession was withdrawn from 1 April 2009. From that date employment agencies have been expected to account for VAT on the full amount of the value of the supply, including costs such as remuneration, National Insurance contributions and pension contributions in respect of agency workers.

Fixed-term employees

If an agency worker is employed on a temporary contract the Fixed Term Employees (Prevention of Less Favourable Treatment) Regulations 2002 should be borne in mind. These Regulations prevent less favourable treatment in comparison to permanent employees.

However, many employment rights do not kick in until an employee has a minimum period of service. To claim unfair dismissal, one year's continuous service is generally required (although as of April 2012 this period will be extended to two years); for redundancy payments two years' service are required and statutory maternity pay is payable only if an employee has worked continuously for the employer for 26 weeks on the 15th week before her expected week of childbirth.

Umbrella company arrangements

Some temporary workers work under an umbrella company arrangement. In such a situation the worker is an employee of the umbrella company, but is not a director or shareholder of the umbrella company or involved in the running of the company in any way.

In an umbrella company arrangement it is the worker themselves, and not the umbrella company, who sources the temporary work. The worker may do this through an employment agency or directly with a client company.

The purpose of the umbrella company will be to handle all pay and tax matters for the worker. The umbrella company will invoice the client for the worker's services, who will forward the remainder of the payment to the worker after deducting a weekly or monthly fee and tax and National Insurance contributions.

Standards for employment agencies

The relationship between the agency worker and the agency is regulated by the Employment Agencies Act 1973 and the Conduct of Employment Agencies and Employment Business Regulations 2003 ('the Conduct Regulations').

The Conduct Regulations require agencies to ensure that workers are properly matched to, are suitable and can legitimately work for their clients. Agencies must agree certain terms with the agency worker before providing any services to them.

The Employment Agencies Act 1973 prohibits employment agencies from charging work-seekers for finding work for them.

Agency Workers Regulations 2010

The Agency Workers Regulations 2010 came into force on 1 October 2011. The Regulations are intended to give effect to the Temporary Agency Workers Directive 2008/104/EC, which was published on 5 December 2008, and for which EU Member States had until 5 December 2011 to implement its provisions.

It was felt that agency workers required protection in the same way that fixed-term workers and part-time workers are currently. During the consultations that have taken place over the past three years the Government has tried to produce regulations that protect agency workers while maintaining the flexibility required by companies in the use of temporary workers.

The Government department of Business, Innovation and Skills published final guidance to the Regulations on 3 June 2011, a copy of which can be found on the BIS website: www.bis.gov.uk.

The purpose of the guidance is to advise and inform and it is supplementary to the legislation. Although it is not mandatory to follow the guidance, it will be wise to follow it as far as possible as it is likely that the Tribunals will refer to the guidance when considering claims under the Regulations.

The objective of the Regulations is to give agency workers the entitlement to the same basic employment and working conditions as a company's permanent employees.

The new Regulations do not affect the current protection afforded to agency workers and do not change the employment status of agency workers.

Agency and temporary workers

Who do the Regulations apply to?

The Regulations do not apply to recruitment consultancies that place individuals into permanent roles with third parties.

The Regulations apply to agency workers who are assigned to do temporary work for hirers through temporary work agencies.

An agency worker is defined in the Regulations as being someone who:

- *is supplied by a temporary work agency to work temporarily for and under the supervision and direction of a hirer; and*
- *has a contract with the temporary work agency which is either:*
    - *a contract of employment with the agency; or*
    - *any other contract with the agency to perform work or services personally.*

The Regulations do not apply to those who are:

- genuinely self-employed;
- employed under a managed service contract;
- in-house temporary staffing banks; and/or
- on secondments.

A hirer is defined in the Regulations as follows:

'A person engaged in economic activity, public or private, whether or not operating for profit, to whom individuals are supplied, to work temporarily for and under the supervision and direction of that person.'

Access to collective facilities

From 1 October 2011, all agency workers have the right to be treated no less favourably than comparable permanent employees or workers in relation to

'collective facilities and amenities', unless the less favourable treatment can be objectively justified. This is the only area of the Regulations where failure to follow the Regulations can be justified. Liability for failure to provide this access will be solely on the hirer, as the agency has no role in providing these rights.

Regulations state that collective facilities include:

- canteen or other similar facilities;
- childcare facilities; and
- transport services.

This list is non-exhaustive and further examples are provided in the guidance as follows:

- Workplace crèche;
- Transport services to include local pick up and drop offs, transport between sites but not company car allowances or season ticket loans;
- Toilet or shower facilities;
- Staff common room;
- Waiting room;
- Mother and baby room;
- Prayer room;
- Food and drinks machines; and
- Car parking.

The concept of collective facilities does not extend to any off site facilities or benefits in kind which are not provided by the hirer, such as subsidised access to an off site gym. The right is to equal, not better, treatment. Agency workers should not therefore be given enhanced access rights when compared with permanent employees. For example, if there is a waiting list for access to childcare facilities an agency worker will be entitled to join the list but not to jump the queue.

Comparators

If they wish to make a claim regarding access to collective facilities, the worker would need to show that they have been treated less favourably when compared to a comparator.

Both the comparator and agency worker must be:

- working for and under the supervision and direction of the hirer;
- engaged in the same or broadly similar work, having regard to whether they have a similar level of qualifications of skills;
- at the same establishment (or if no comparable worker, a different establishment); and/or
- an employee of the hirer (or if no comparable employee, a worker of the hirer).

If there is no comparator, there is no entitlement to equal treatment in relation to facilities.

Justification of less favourable treatment

Not providing facilities can be justified on objective grounds, which could include cost, but this is unlikely to be sufficient if it is the only factor. Practical and organisational considerations could be a factor.

Access to employment vacancies

From the start of their assignment, agency workers have the right to be told of any permanent vacancies of the hirer in order to be given the same opportunity as a comparable employee to apply.

The hirer can inform the agency worker *'by a general announcement in a suitable place in the hirer's establishment'*. A suitable place may be a notice board or on the company's intranet. They must be informed as to where to find the information, which could be explained during a worker's induction.

This right does not apply in relation to the redeployment of permanent employees

to roles in the context of a redundancy exercise or restructuring. These don't count as 'vacancies' for the purposes of the Regulations.

This provision does not curtail an employer's freedom as to how to treat applications for jobs.

Rights following a qualifying period

The right to equal treatment regarding terms and conditions

The right to equal treatment with regard to basic working and employment conditions does not apply until the agency worker has completed a qualifying period of 12 weeks.

This period was agreed between the Confederation of British Industry and the Trades Union Congress.

To qualify, an agency worker must have worked in the same role, whether on one or more assignments, with the same hirer for 12 continuous calendar weeks.

The Regulations are not retrospective; therefore time spent on an assignment prior to 1 October 2011 does not count for the purposes of the qualifying period. Therefore, for existing agency workers these rights will not kick in until 24 December 2011.

Calculating the qualifying period

Breaking continuity
Continuity will be broken, and the agency worker will have to start counting the 12 weeks again, when:

- the agency worker starts a new assignment with a new hirer;
- the agency worker remains with the same hirer but starts a new, substantively different, role; and/or
- there is a break of over six calendar weeks between assignments.

Suspension of continuity

Continuity will not be broken if the following breaks take place, however the weeks during the break will not count towards the 12-week qualifying period. The clock is simply paused and resumed again after the break:

■ Break of no more than six weeks.
■ Up to 28 weeks due to sickness / injury.
■ Any break for the purposes of taking leave – including annual leave.
■ Up to 28 weeks for jury service.
■ Planned shutdown by the hirer (e.g. closing for Christmas).
■ Break caused by a strike, lock out or other industrial action.

Continuity during a break

Continuity will continue to accrue (for the intended or likely duration of the assignment) where a break is due to:

■ pregnancy, childbirth or maternity (for up to 26 weeks after childbirth); and/or
■ taking maternity, adoption or paternity leave.

When is continuity broken?

The 12-week qualifying period must be restarted when an agency worker stops working for one hirer and starts an assignment with a new hirer, or commences a substantively different role with the same hirer.

Group companies

Where a hirer is part of a larger group, and each company has its own legal identity, the qualifying period restarts when the agency worker moves between the various companies. However, there are anti-avoidance provisions that prevent a series of assignments from being structured so as to prevent the agency worker from completing the qualifying period, which are dealt with below in more detail.

Substantively different roles

An agency worker's continuity will be broken if:

■ they start a new role with the same hirer;
■ the work or duties that make up the whole or main part of that new role are substantively different to the previous role; and
■ the temporary work agency has informed the agency worker in writing of the type of work the agency worker will be required to do in the new role.

The guidance lists several characteristics that help to establish whether duties are substantively different:

■ Are different skills and competencies used?
■ Is the pay rate different?
■ Is the work in a different location / cost centre?
■ Is the line manager different?
■ Are the working hours different?
■ Does the role require extra training or a specific qualification?
■ Is different equipment used?

The right to equal treatment

After completion of the 12-week qualifying period an agency worker is entitled to:

'the same basic working and employment conditions as they would have been entitled to for doing the same job had they been recruited by the hirer:

■ *other than by using the services of a temporary work agency; and*
■ *at the time the qualifying period commenced.'*

The basic working and employment conditions are the relevant terms and conditions that are ordinarily included in the contract of employees or workers of the hirer (or associated documents such as a company handbook or collective agreement).

Relevant terms and conditions are those terms relating to:

- pay;
- duration of working time;
- night work;
- rest periods;
- rest breaks; and
- annual leave.

Specific provision is also made in relation to pregnant and nursing mothers for paid time off for antenatal appointments, to be paid by the temporary work agency.

If, due to health and safety reasons, a pregnant woman or nursing mother is unable to continue with an assignment the agency must provide alternative work or must pay them for the period that the original assignment was due to last.

The terms and conditions covered by the Regulations are those which are 'ordinarily included'; therefore one-off arrangements will not be an appropriate point for comparison.

The definition of pay

The guidance states that pay includes:

- basic pay;
- overtime pay;
- shift or unsocial hours allowances or risk payments for hazardous duties;
- payment for annual leave;
- bonuses or commission payments which are directly attributable to the amount or quality of the work done by the individual; and
- vouchers or stamps with a monetary value but which are not provided through a salary sacrifice scheme, such as luncheon vouchers or childcare vouchers.

Pay related rights that are linked to long-term reward and retention are excluded, which includes the following:

- Contractual sick pay.
- Occupational pensions (although this will of course change from next year when the pension auto enrolment provisions come into force).
- Contractual maternity, paternity or adoption pay.
- Redundancy pay (statutory and contractual).
- Notice pay (statutory and contractual).
- Payments linked to financial participation schemes (such as share ownership schemes).
- Bonuses not linked to the contribution of the individual.
- Benefits in kind given as a loyalty incentive, such as where building society staff are given a reduced rate mortgage.
- Payments that require an eligibility period of employment or service.
- Overtime payments where the agency worker has not fulfilled qualifying conditions required of someone directly recruited.
- Payment for time off for trade union duties.
- Guarantee payments.
- Advance in pay or loans, such as season tickets.
- Expenses, such as accommodation and travel expenses.

Bonuses

The key question as to whether the agency worker will be entitled to a bonus provided to permanent employees will be whether the bonus is directly attributable to the amount or quality of work done. If it is for another reason, such as to encourage loyalty or to reward long-term service, it will be outside of the scope of the right to equal treatment.

Bonus payments that would be included are:

- commission payments linked to sales;
- bonuses payable to all staff who meet specific individual performance targets; and

■ bonuses payable on the basis of individual performance over a given period.

Bonus payments that would be excluded are:

■ bonuses determined by the overall performance of the company, given to workers who have been with the hirer for a number of years, and not based on individual performance;
■ bonuses determined by the overall performance of the part of the organisation where the agency worker has worked, where there is no recognition of individual contribution; and
■ bonuses designed to reward loyalty and service to the organisation, and not based on individual performance.

The agency worker should have the same opportunity to achieve a bonus, but will not necessarily receive the same amount as a permanent employee. The bonus could be calculated on a pro rata basis.

Comparators

The guidance suggests that it is unnecessary for an agency worker to look for a specific comparator in relation to the right to equal treatment in respect of terms and conditions because it will be possible to identify the appropriate basic working and employment conditions without one.

Deemed compliance defence

A hirer will be deemed to have complied with the equal treatment provisions where an agency worker is working under the same relevant terms and conditions as an actual employee comparator and those relevant terms and conditions are ordinarily included in the contracts issued to employees in the comparator's position.

For an employee to be used as a comparator both the employee and agency worker must be:

■ working for and under the supervision and direction of the hirer; and
■ engaged in the same or broadly similar work having regard, where relevant, to whether they have a similar level of qualification and skills; and
■ based at the same establishment, or if there is no such employee, a different establishment.

Anti-avoidance provisions

The Regulations contain specific anti-avoidance provisions to prevent temporary work agencies and hirers from structuring assignments to prevent the worker from acquiring equal rights.

A prohibited structure of assignments will occur when an agency worker has:

■ completed two or more assignments with the hirer; or
■ completed at least one assignment with the hirer and one or more earlier assignments with hirers connected to their current hirer; or
■ worked in more than two roles during an assignment with the same hirer and on at least two occasions has worked in a role that was not the 'same role' as the previous role.

The provisions will also apply when the most likely explanation is that the hirer or temporary work agency intended to prevent the agency worker from being entitled to the right to equal treatment.

Hirers are connected where one hirer has control of the other or a third person has control of both hirers.

To decide whether there has been such a structure of assignments the following non-exhaustive list of factors will be taken into account by the Tribunal:

■ Length of the assignments;
■ Number of assignments with the hirer or any connected hirer;

- Number of times the agency worker has worked in a new role with the hirer; and
- The period of any break between assignments with the hirer or any connected hirer.

Tribunals can make an additional award of up to £5,000 where a hirer and/or agency are found to have breached this provision.

Derogations from the Equal Treatment Principle (the Swedish Derogation Principle)

In limited circumstances a contract may be entered into between an agency and an agency worker where it is agreed that the right to equal treatment with regards to pay (only) will not apply.

However, this regulation only applies where:

- the agency worker has a permanent contract of employment with the agency; and
- the contract was entered into before the first assignment started; and
- in periods between assignments the agency pays the worker a minimum of 50% of their basic pay while on assignment, and this must not be less than the national minimum wage.

It is unusual for an agency worker to be permanently employed by an agency and to receive pay between assignments, and this is therefore likely to be rarely used.

Liability and remedies

Automatic unfair dismissal

Agency workers who are employees cannot be dismissed on certain grounds such as making allegations, giving evidence, asserting rights or bringing proceedings in connection with the Regulations.

As with other claims for automatic unfair dismissal, there is no qualifying period for this type of claim.

Right not to be subjected to a detriment

A claim can be brought against the agency and/or hirer if the worker suffers a detriment on certain grounds such as bringing proceedings, giving evidence in proceedings or asserting rights in connection with the Regulations. A dismissal is not counted as a detriment for the purposes of this claim.

Breach of rights of access to employment or facilities

Only the hirer can be liable for a claim for failure to provide access to vacancies or on site facilities.

Right to equal treatment in relation to employment conditions

The temporary work agency will be responsible for any breaches of rights in relation to an agency worker's basic working and employment conditions to the extent it is responsible for the infringement.

The temporary work agency will have a defence if it can show that it took 'reasonable steps' to obtain relevant information from the hirer about its basic working and employment conditions and acted reasonably upon that information.

The hirer will be responsible for any breach to the extent that it is responsible for the infringement.

Temporary work agencies and hirers cannot be jointly and severally liable for any breach.

Either party can be named by the worker in a claim either at the outset or joined later and the Regulations allow the Tribunal to identify the degree to which any party in a 'chain' of relationships is responsible for any infringement.

Right to receive information

If an agency worker believes that either the hirer or temporary work agency has infringed their rights under the Regulations they may make a written request for a written statement containing information relating to the treatment.

The Regulations set out a procedure for a worker to obtain this information from either the hirer or temporary work agency.

Failure to respond to such a request is not unlawful in itself but if the worker subsequently brings proceedings, the Tribunal can draw adverse inferences against any party who fails to respond to a request or provides an evasive or inadequate response.

Remedies

The remedies available to agency workers making the above claims are:

- a declaration as to the worker's rights;
- compensation;
- recommendations for action to be taken, which if not followed can lead to a further award of compensation.

Injury to feelings

It appears that the Tribunal may make an award for injury to feelings for claims of suffering a detriment, as the Regulations list claims to which compensation shall not include compensation for injury to feelings – and this is the only claim not to be included.

The general time limit for bringing a claim under the Regulations is three months.

Compensation

The compensation payable by an agency or hirer will be that which is 'just and equitable' having regard to the extent of their responsibility. There will be no statutory cap on the amount that can be awarded. The legislation states that the minimum amount awarded must be two weeks' pay.

An additional award of up to £5,000 will be awarded if the anti-avoidance provisions are breached.

Factors taken into account by the Tribunal

When considering the level of compensation that an agency worker should be awarded, the Tribunal will take into account the following:

- Nature of the breach;
- Financial loss suffered by the worker; and
- Expenses they have reasonably incurred as a result.

See also: Employment status, p.174; Fixed-term workers, p.218; Self employment, p.465.

Sources of further information

Agency Workers Regulations 2010: www.workplacelaw.net/news/display/id/34518

The Workplace Law website has been one of the UK's leading legal information sites since its launch in 2002. As well as providing free news and forums, our Information Centre provides you with a 'one-stop shop' where you will find all you need to know to manage your workplace and fulfil your legal obligations.

It covers everything from the latest Employment Tribunal cases to redundancy law, as well as detailed information in key areas such as equality and diversity.

You'll find:

- quick and easy access to all major legislation and official guidance, including clear explanations and advice from our experts;
- case reviews and news analysis, which will keep you fully up to date with the latest legislation proposals and changes, case outcomes and examples of how the law is applied in practice;
- briefings, which include in-depth analysis on major topics; and
- WPL TV – an online TV channel including online seminars, documentaries and legal updates.

Visit www.workplacelaw.net for more information.

Alcohol and drugs

Mandy Laurie, Dundas & Wilson

Key points
- There are legal obligations on employers to ensure a safe and healthy workplace for their employees.
- Employees have a right to work in a safe and healthy workplace and they have responsibilities for their own wellbeing and that of their colleagues.
- Having clear guidelines regarding the use of alcohol and drugs in the workplace will assist employers in achieving regulation in this area.

Legislation
- Misuse of Drugs Act 1971.
- Disability Discrimination Act 1995 and 2005.
- Equality Act 2010.

Legal obligations on employers and employees

The Misuse of Drugs Act 1971 makes it illegal for any person knowingly to permit drug use on their premises except in specified circumstances (e.g. when they have been prescribed by a doctor).

Regulation of alcohol and drugs in the workplace

It is important that employers regulate the use of alcohol and drugs in the workplace because failure to do so can lead to:

- poor performance and reduced productivity;
- lateness and absenteeism;
- low morale and poor employee relations; and
- damage to the company's reputation and customer relations.

The detrimental effects of drug and alcohol misuse in the workplace can be seen in the following statistics:

- A survey carried out by Alcohol Concern found that nearly two-thirds of employers have suffered problems in the workplace as a result of employee alcohol abuse.
- The after effects of alcohol and drug abuse can have a serious impact on employee performance. According to a survey conducted by YouGov for PruHealth, every day in the UK around 200,000 workers turn up to work with a hangover.
- In early 2004 the HSE published a report into the scale and impact of illegal drug use by workers, which found that 29% of working respondents under 30 admitted to drug use in the previous year.

Alcohol and drug misuse by employees are two problems that increasing numbers of employers face. It is therefore essential that employers have policies and procedures to deal with such problems. What's more, because the topic touches on so many legal issues, such as privacy, conduct, performance, and disability discrimination, it's important to ensure any policies or procedures are tailored to fit with the working environment.

Facts

- In the UK, up to 14.8 million working days are lost each year as a result of alcohol-related absence.
- A survey carried out by Norwich Union Healthcare found that 77% of employers consider that alcohol represents a significant threat to the wellbeing of staff.
- According to a survey by the Chartered Institute of Personnel Development (CIPD), 43% of employers do not have alcohol policies. It also showed that the vast majority of employers (84%) do not offer health awareness programmes for staff.

Sources: CIPD, HSE, Institute of Alcohol Studies, TUC.

Employment policies and procedures

Policies on alcohol and drugs in the workplace should:

- set out the legal obligations behind the policy and summarise the aims of the policy;
- be clear as to whom the policy applies;
- make clear what will be considered to be alcohol and drug misuse and any specific rules / exceptions, e.g. in relation to prescription medicines or a dependency;
- set out the disciplinary action that will be taken following a breach of the policy or cross refer to the disciplinary policy;
- provide advice as to where help can be obtained and details of any support that the employer will provide;
- assure staff that any alcohol or drug problem will be treated in strict confidence; and
- encourage employees to come forward and ask for help.

The ACAS guidelines on 'Health, Work and Wellbeing' provide information on producing alcohol and drug policies (see *Sources of further information*).

In addition to ensuring that there is a drug and alcohol policy in place, employers should consider the following:

- Putting in place procedures to find out if an employee has an alcohol- or drug-related problem, e.g. alcohol / drugs screening or medical examinations.
- Testing and searching is an invasion of privacy, and employers should take into account the nature of their business before imposing such a requirement; i.e. routine testing is only likely to be proportionate in safety critical industries. Further, if employers wish to impose the right to search or test for drugs, this should be referred to in their policy, included in the contract of employment if possible, and consent should be obtained from the individual before carrying out testing / searching in the individual situation. An employer cannot require an employee to take a test / undergo a search, but if they refuse to do so, the policy should state whether disciplinary action will follow.
- Seeking to support the employee in the event that medical advice determines that they have an alcohol- or drug-related problem.
- Ensuring managers receive appropriate training to implement the

Case study

Sinclair v. Wandsworth Council (2007)

Mr Sinclair worked for the Council. He was caught drinking on duty. The Council agreed to put disciplinary proceedings on hold if he would agree to a referral to the Occupational Health Service. Reluctantly, he agreed to the referral. The Council held a disciplinary hearing and issued Mr Sinclair with a final written warning for his drinking on duty.

Mr Sinclair was caught drunk at work again four weeks later. He was suspended, pending an investigation. He lied during the investigation about drinking and about Occupational Health having referred him for counselling. At the disciplinary hearing, Mr Sinclair said he was cooperating with Occupational Health. He asked that the hearing be suspended. The Council refused. Mr Sinclair had been drunk at his place of work. As he already had a final written warning, he was dismissed.

Mr Sinclair unsuccessfully appealed his dismissal. He then brought a claim before the Employment Tribunal for unfair dismissal.

The Tribunal decided that the dismissal was unfair because the Council had not given its alcohol policy to Mr Sinclair or to his managers, despite the wording of the policy which said it should be circulated to them.

The Council had failed to tell Mr Sinclair what he needed to do to avoid disciplinary proceedings, as obliged under the Council's policy. Mr Sinclair had erroneously believed he was doing enough. The Council should have made it clear to Mr Sinclair what he had to do to halt the proceedings against him.

Despite the problems and risks caused by employees being drunk in the workplace, care must be taken when managing these issues. Mr Sinclair was found guilty of being drunk at work twice (and dismissal was found to be a reasonable response), but his dismissal was ultimately found to be unfair because the Council's alcohol policy had not been followed.

When dealing with any instances of alcohol-related misconduct, you should first take into account any relevant policies the employer has in place and follow the appropriate procedure. Although it is a difficult issue for managers and HR to deal with, any issues arising due to an employee's alcohol problems should be addressed in an up-front, but understanding, manner.

policy and to ensure that it is applied consistently.

- Considering placing the employee on alternative duties until they have combated their alcohol- or drug-related problem.

- Considering the application of the Equality Act 2010 with regard to whether an employee may be considered to have a disability. Under the Equality Act, addictions such as alcohol are excluded. But addiction can also be a symptom of a disability; for example, depression caused by an alcohol addiction could be considered a disability even where the alcohol addiction itself is not. Focus should be on the effects of the condition and not the cause. Therefore, where there is a link with depression or a condition that might amount to a disability, it is critical for employers to obtain medical input and, if an employee is disabled, make reasonable adjustments to alleviate the substantial disadvantage. That may mean putting a disciplinary issue on hold, or, if the conduct is sufficiently serious, applying a lower level of warning.

■ Considering disciplinary action where an employee under the influence of alcohol or drugs places either himself or others at risk in the workplace.

■ Considering dismissal on grounds of capability or for some other substantial reason, where there is an ongoing problem and there appears to be no other alternative. A dismissal on capability grounds may be fair where an employee's performance falls below an acceptable standard, or where an employee is absent through ill health because of an alcohol- or drug-related problem. A fair procedure should always be followed.

■ Considering reporting any criminal activity to the police. However, there is no obligation for an employer to do so.

■ Considering their attitude to 'off-duty' drinking, particularly in light of the law on harassment under the Equality Act 2010. Under the Act, employers will be liable for discriminatory comments made by customers or clients towards staff, provided a customer (not necessarily the same one) does this on three or more occasions. It is therefore advisable to amend policies to refer to employees' conduct at such events and hospitality, and what they should do if customers harass them.

In all cases of dismissal, employers should ensure that they follow the ACAS Code of Practice on Disciplinary and Grievance Procedures – See '*Disciplinary and grievance procedures*' (p.121) for more details.

See also: Mental health, p.308; Monitoring employees, p.358; Private life, p.404; Smoking, p.478; Stress, p.500.

Sources of further information

ACAS – Health, work and wellbeing: www.acas.org.uk/CHttpHandler.ashx?id=854

As an employer, you are committed to providing a safe working environment for your employees. You are also committed to promoting the health and wellbeing of your employees. Alcohol and substance misuse can be detrimental to the health and performance of employees and may pose a potential risk to safety in the workplace and the welfare of other employees. Workplace Law's **Drug and Alcohol Policy and Management Guide v.2.0** policy is designed to help protect employees from the dangers of alcohol, drug and other substance misuse and to encourage those with a drug or alcohol problem to seek help. For more information visit www.workplacelaw.net.

Appraisals

Suzanne McMinn, Workplace Law

Key points
- Make sure that your appraisal process reflects the culture and values of your organisation. What's important to the success of your business should be reflected within your appraisal objectives.
- Take time to train managers in how to conduct appraisals; a badly managed appraisal can be counterproductive and de-motivate employees.
- Appraisals should not only be a review of the past but also a look to the future in terms of individuals' potential, objectives and development needs.
- An effective appraisal process is reviewed and updated regularly throughout the year, not just at appraisal time.

Legislation
- Equality Act 2010.

Introduction

Not all organisations have an appraisal process and there are many reasons as to why this is the case. But those who invest the time and resources into creating and maintaining an effective appraisal process will reap the rewards of having a workforce that is motivated, well developed, has a clear career plan mapped out and understands where their contribution makes a difference. Where management time is at a premium and the focus is on outputs rather than managing people and their careers, it is easy to let appraisals be seen as something that has to be tolerated in order to keep the HR department from chasing you. But appraisals have come a long way in recent years and now they are much more focused on integrating the needs of the business into tangible objectives for people to work towards, and look at how these have been achieved through individuals' behaviour.

Setting objectives

Most employees need to know what their contribution is to the success of the organisation, that they are working in the right direction, and that they are valued for the work they do. By setting clear business objectives that are aligned to the needs and success of the business, this helps not only the business strive ahead, but also ensures that employees are on track with their efforts and shows that the success or failure of the organisation can be down to individuals' contribution, or lack of it.

Once the business plan has been set for the year, showing what the focus is in terms of turnover, acquisitions, growth, etc. these should then be filtered down to each department so that departmental objectives can be set. Now that each department is accountable for its contribution this needs to be cascaded to individuals in the form of individual objectives within the appraisal process.

During the appraisal review, managers will often discuss the new objectives and hopefully gain the employees' agreement as to what their individual contribution will be for the following year. Alongside this process discussions will take place regarding training and development or managerial support that will facilitate the employee meeting these objectives. By linking the individuals' objectives to the business plan it ensures that each employee is doing the right thing at the right time to the best of their abilities.

SMART objectives
To get the best from setting objectives you should always look at setting them in a SMART format.

- Specific.
- Measurable.
- Achievable.
- Realistic.
- Time-bound.

Using this format ensures that employees are clear on the objective that has been set, and allows managers to clearly assess what contribution they have made.

Specific
You should assess what is needed to be completed, why, and who is involved.

Measurable
This is the way in which you will assess if the objective has been achieved.

Attainable
The attainable element looks at how achievable the objective is. It should be stretching enough to keep the employee's interest but not so extreme that it will never be reached. When looking at this area you should look at how the objective can be achieved; this way you will be able to review any issues or problems that would stand in the way of making it achievable.

Realistic
The overall goal of the objective is that it needs to be realistic. The employee needs to be able to assess with their manager if there are issues that would make the objective unworkable. You should ask if the objective is relevant and worthwhile.

Time-bound
With any objective there needs to be a time-bound element, to ensure that the employee is focused on getting the task completed by the target date. The sensible question to ask with this area is, When?

Preparation
Prior to the actual appraisal meeting both the manager and the employee should have prepared fully for the meeting. In preparing you should look to fully review the objectives that were set and understand what the employee has done to achieve them. When reviewing objectives you should not just look at outputs but also the way in which the objective has been achieved, the behaviours exhibited and the work that was done towards them. Sometimes the way that an employee goes about something says more about them than the fact that they did or did not achieve it.

Reviewing the objectives is just one part of the preparation that needs to take place; you should also look to gather information from colleagues, customers, direct reports on their work and behaviours during the appraisal period. Also gather any customer complaints or praise that has been received, as this can be used as objective information to support any feedback that you provide.

Ensure that the employee has prepared, get them to consider how they feel they have achieved against the objectives, look at what they would like to focus on during the next appraisal period, review any training or development areas, and be ready to discuss career progression and next steps within your organisation.

The appraisal meeting
Once both parties have prepared, the actual appraisal meeting needs to take

place. When setting a diary date, try to make sure that it's not cancelled, because if you do cancel it can look like you don't value the importance of the appraisal meeting to the employee. Set enough time aside to have a full discussion and ensure that you have an area where you will not be disturbed.

At the start of the meeting look to review the objectives that were set previously, understand what the employee has done to try and achieve them, and how they went about it. Towards the end of the appraisal process you should look to set and agree new objectives for the next appraisal period.

Ensure that you provide constructive feedback on any areas of concern or where performance / behaviours went well. Don't shy away from addressing issues – managers need to address problems. You need to understand how they happened in order to gain the employee's agreement that they don't happen again. In doing this you may uncover an area for development.

In the meeting, take the opportunity of reviewing the job description and the duties outlined within it. Often it is the case that employees do many tasks that don't fall within their remit. You need to understand if their job description needs updating or if it is the employee who needs to refocus their efforts on the tasks that are required.

Take the opportunity to motivate your employee, talk to them about the direction of the business, and where they fit in. If they have done a good job, thank them for it and recognise the effort that they have given. Managers don't often get the chance to speak to their employees about the business, so take the chance to do this and empower the employee to own their objectives and contribution.

Don't use the appraisal process as a disciplinary meeting. Nothing that is discussed in the appraisal should be a surprise, so don't use it to highlight issues that you have not brought to the employee's attention previously.

Ensure that the discussions look at behaviour and performance. You can't change somebody's personality, so ensure that the meeting does not look at personal issues. Keep the meeting professional and deal with issues supported with objective information.

Throughout the meeting ensure that you take notes of action points, key issues or concerns, development needs, and objectives that have been agreed. This way when you complete the appraisal form you will have a good grasp of what was discussed and agreed.

A good appraisal meeting will have a good mix of listening and questioning on the part of the line manager to understand and clarify the situation. The employee should take the opportunity to feedback on their performance, highlight any concerns or issues that they have had, and discuss any development needs. Managers should not shy away from seeking feedback on how they are doing in terms of management style, support, etc. Use the meeting to ask employees on what more or less they would like from their manager and then, more importantly, act on the feedback that you receive.

Ongoing review

There was a time when appraisals took place every 12 months, and just before the meeting managers and employees alike would dust off the old appraisal form and update it just before the meeting. After the meeting they would 'file' the new appraisal form away and the same cycle would follow.

The appraisal process has evolved significantly now and there are real benefits to be had for organisations and employees alike when following a proactive appraisal process. Rather than leave them year on year, review the objectives regularly, and if they need changing or removing, do so. The needs of the business change throughout the year and so should the objectives to reflect these changes.

Managers' toolkit

To assist managers in conducting good appraisals they should look to have the following skills and documents to get the best from the meeting and their employees.

Skills

- Ability to provide constructive feedback.
- Good listening skills.
- Motivated and able to motivate.
- Good communicator.
- Able to understand the business focus and filter these to individual objectives.
- Approachable and open to feedback.

Documents

- Competency framework.
- Job description.
- Objectives.
- Training plans.
- Previous and current appraisal form.

Benefits of appraisals

Recognising that appraisals can take a lot of time and effort in preparing, conducting and the continual review process for both the manager and the employee, aside of this there are great number of benefits that can be gained for both parties.

It offers a conduit for continuous discussion that is focused on the needs of the business and the individual, which in turn improves performance and motivation. The appraisal process allows managers to develop and identify potential in employees, which can filter into succession planning. Where development and training needs are identified it can help organise the training plans for an organisation. The opportunity for open and honest discussions will allow for two-way constructive feedback, allows both parties to address work issues, and gaining agreement on how these can be solved.

See also: Disciplinary and grievance procedures, p.121; Dismissal, p.146; Employment disputes, p.168; Mental health, p.308; Monitoring employees, p.358; Personnel files, p.392; Private life, p.404; Training, p.520.

Sources of further information

Annual appraisals are one technique available to managers to enable them to successfully manage and motivate their teams. However, it is vital that managers are trained to deliver appraisals consistently across the organisation or their time is wasted and the benefits are lost. Workplace Law's **Appraisal Training for Managers** course can be tailored to your requirements so that it reflects your own appraisal system and job roles. Visit www.workplacelaw.net for more information.

Benefits schemes

Roger Byard, Cripps Harries Hall LLP

Key points

- Employers use benefits to attract, retain and provide incentives for employees.
- Commonly they are provided as part of an overall strategy designed to achieve defined business objectives.
- Such benefits take many forms, offering both financial and non-financial rewards, and go to make up an employee's total reward.
- The benefits employers make available to employees have seen considerable enlargement in recent years. These now range from traditional occupational pensions and sick pay, to flexible working and voluntary arrangements. Many employers offer flexible benefit schemes under which employees are given a sum of money to buy those benefits that reflect their circumstances at the time. However, by offering employees cash to buy their own benefits, employers shift the burden of responsibility to make an informed choice to employees, which may not always be appropriate.
- Although the age of an employee can affect which benefits they prefer, the top five desired benefits usually include pensions, bonuses, flexible working, final salary pensions and extended holiday entitlement.
- Some benefits have tax advantages, the most obvious being a pension, although for higher earners there are currently restrictions that make pension provision less attractive. Voluntary benefits, which use an employer's bargaining power to negotiate discounts on products and services for employees, promote the employer's reputation for providing a good place to work.
- The value of employee benefits can be difficult to assess. In a recent study, less than half of the employees surveyed had evaluated what the benefits package was worth to them. However, the cost to the employer to provide and administer the benefits should not be underestimated.
- The effect of age discrimination legislation (introduced in 2006) on employee benefits appears to be minimal, although there is evidence that benefits providers have modified their products to make the level of benefits less age-related.

Legislation

- Equal Pay Act 1970.
- Social Security Contributions and Benefits Act 1992.
- Employment Rights Act 1996.
- Data Protection Act 1998.
- National Minimum Wage Act 1998.
- Income Tax (Earnings and Pensions) Act 2003.
- Finance Act 2003.
- Pensions Act 2004.
- Civil Partnerships Act 2004.
- Work and Families Act 2006.
- Employment Equality (Age) Regulations 2006.
- Pensions Act 2008.
- Equality Act 2010.

Types of benefit

Financial benefits

These benefits include sick pay, pensions, company cars, bonuses, share option schemes, income protection insurance, medical insurance, life assurance and sports benefits.

Non-financial benefits

These include flexitime, homeworking and discount schemes.

Tax-advantaged benefits

These include salary sacrifice, pensions, childcare vouchers, bicycle loans, season ticket loans up to £5,000, and eat and drink at work schemes.

Particular benefits

Pensions

Employees can save as much as they like in any pension scheme. Income tax relief is available on their own contributions to a pension scheme. However, for the tax year 2011-12 onwards the total annual amount that an employee and employer can contribute to an individual pension account ('annual allowance') will be limited to £50,000. Further special restrictions on high earners (annual incomes of £130,000 or more) limit the relief on their contributions to 20%. Employers are usually able to offset the contributions they make against corporation tax. There is a saving of both employers' and employees' National Insurance contributions on payments made into a pension scheme. As an encouragement to employees to contribute to their personal pension provision, employers often offer to match what their employees pay in, up to certain limits.

In October 2012, the Government will introduce a new pension scheme. Previously known as 'Personal Accounts' the scheme has been branded the National Employment Savings Trust (NEST). Employers will be required to automatically enrol employees over 22 in a 'qualifying workplace pension scheme'. Many existing schemes are likely to meet the qualifying criteria. Compulsory

Case study

In *Swann v. GHL Insurance Services UK Limited* (2008) a flexible benefits package available to staff was held to not be discriminatory. The benefits scheme provided an option to join a private health insurance scheme whose premiums were calculated according to age and gender. However, the Tribunal was satisfied that the employer had good intentions with regard to the scheme. It had sought professional advice and questioned employees about what benefits they would like to receive.

employer and employee contributions are to be phased in between October 2012 and 2017. While it will depend on the size of the company, all UK employers will be required to contribute a minimum of 3% of an employee's earnings into a pension (provided they do not opt out). Employees will be required to pay a personal contribution of 4%. The Government will top up the contribution by a further 1% (making 8% in total) through tax relief. See '*Pensions*' (p.387) for more details.

Salary sacrifice

The employer agrees to provide a benefit in exchange for the employee giving up part of their gross annual salary to optimise tax efficiencies. Where, for example, an employee makes a sacrifice of part of their pay, and the employer makes an equivalent contribution to their pension, the employee saves on income tax at their marginal rate. Both employer and employee save on National Insurance contributions. A salary sacrifice is a change to terms of employment and should be put in writing. There are pitfalls. For lower-paid employees, care needs to be exercised as it might impact on the minimum wage. The Equality Act 2010 requires employers to continue to provide non-cash contractual benefits to employees throughout statutory maternity leave. HMRC guidance states that statutory maternity pay cannot be sacrificed and that benefits will continue

even if an employee is not in receipt of any salary that could be sacrificed (see '*Childcare provisions*,' p.75).

Healthcare and other risk benefits

These benefits include occupational sick pay (where employers pay more than is provided under the statutory sick pay scheme), and are typically insurance-based, such as private medical insurance (including counselling services), critical illness insurance, permanent health insurance and life assurance. The attraction of these benefits is the lower cost to employees of securing the protection that is achieved through economies of scale. Benefits such as insurance cover for death in service and income protection retain a moral or paternalistic element to them. Recent years have seen the insurance market harden in relation to these particular benefits. Premiums have increased substantially and the products offered are more often time limited. This is set to continue and prompts questions about the business rationale for employers continuing to provide them.

An increasing number of employers are offering other health benefits, such as reduced cost dental care, an in-house GP service, physiotherapy and fitness programmes. The percentage of companies that believe dental benefits improve employee morale has risen from

51% in 2008 to 67% in 2010. More and more employers are promoting health awareness among their employees, with some even offering on-site massage therapy.

Company cars or cash allowance and travel loans

Company cars are commonly provided to enable an employee to do their job (e.g. a sales representative) or as a recognition of status. HMRC has always taxed the provision of this benefit. The basis for taxation is now referable not only to the make and engine size but also its environmental impact. The shift to environmental taxation has reduced the value of this benefit and as a result there is a trend for employers to offer as an alternative a cash sum by way of an annual allowance to employees who supply their own vehicle for business use.

Loans to employees to purchase season tickets to use public transport is a benefit employers based in city centres have offered for many years but which is seeing increased take-up as towns become more congested.

Since 1 January 2011, Regulation 31 of the National Minimum Wage Regulations 1999, which lists the payments that are ignored when calculating a worker's pay for National Minimum Wage purposes, was amended to specifically include travel expenses.

Introducing or changing employee benefits

■ Identify the business goals that the introduction or modification of benefits are intended to support.
■ Consult with employees, to learn what benefits would be most valued.
■ When these have been identified, thoroughly research the market for the best products.

■ Promote the introduction of the benefits by raising employees' awareness of the benefits on offer and their value to them, according to their own circumstances, by good and effective communication.
■ Secure the employee's agreement to the introduction of, or changes to, the benefits, and record them in writing as a variation to the terms of employment.

The Equality Act 2010

The key provisions of the Equality Act 2010, which consolidated the law relating to discrimination and equality, came into effect in October 2010. Although the Act will not have a major impact on employee benefits, one of its provisions means that employers cannot prevent employees from disclosing information about their pay and benefits. By 2013, the Act will make it possible for the Government to require all employers with more than 250 staff to report their gender pay gap.

Age discrimination

Since 1 October 2006 it has been unlawful to discriminate against employees on the ground of their age. Decisions made or policies applied that are based on age-related factors could give rise to discrimination. Employee benefits are most likely to be affected by indirect discrimination since they may constitute a 'policy, practice or criterion' that disadvantages a group of people who are defined by their age. This means that employee benefits that are provided by reference to length of employment would be discriminatory as younger workers are likely to have shorter periods of employment. For example, it is common practice for employers to reward employees with an additional day's holiday after a number of years of employment. This would be unlawful unless it could be justified. However, the legislation provides an important exemption for service-related benefits and allows an employer to use a service-related criterion when determining eligibility to benefits of up to five years.

On 6 April 2011 the Default Retirement Age procedure, which provided it was followed, allowed employers to compulsorily retire employees aged 65 or over lawfully, was abolished. This means that after 1 October 2011 an employee cannot be retired relying on a default retirement age unless their employer can objectively justify a particular retirement age for that employee. Interestingly, the amending regulations stipulate that an employer is not required either to provide or to continue to provide insurance-related benefits to employees who are aged 65 or over. Presumably this is a recognition that the cost of doing so may be both significant and disproportionate.

To justify discrimination, an employer would need to show on an objective basis that they are pursuing a legitimate business aim in a proportionate way. The few cases on the point have shown that for employers to satisfy this test, the offending policy must be the least discriminatory option and that they have had proper consultation with employees before it was introduced.

Conclusion

- Employee benefits offer a wide range of financial and non-financial rewards by which employers may attract, retain and incentivise employees.
- It is important that an employer looking to introduce or change benefits has identified clear business goals and analysed how the benefits will affect their employees.
- For the value of benefits offered to be fully appreciated it is essential that there is effective communication with employees.
- Employers need to be alert to changes in the market for benefit products and sensitive to anti-discrimination legislation.

See also: Childcare provisions, p.75; Expenses, p.200; Flexible working, p.221; Pensions, p.387.

Sources of further information

HM Revenue & Customs: www.hmrc.gov.uk

BIS: www.bis.gov.uk

Employee Benefits Research Institute: www.ebri.org

Pension Guide: www.thepensionservice.gov.uk

Employee Benefits: www.employeebenefits.co.uk

CIPD: www.cipd.co.uk

Bribery

Valerie Surgenor, MacRoberts LLP

Key points

- The UK Bribery Act 2010 entered into force on 1 July 2011, and is generally considered to be one of the toughest bribery regimes worldwide.
- There are four offences under the Act – bribing another person, accepting a bribe, bribing a foreign public official, and failure to prevent bribery.
- Individuals who are found guilty of a bribery offence under the Act will face up to ten years' imprisonment and an unlimited fine.
- Companies that are found guilty of the corporate offence of failing to prevent bribery will have to pay an unlimited fine, and directors associated with a bribery offence could be disqualified.
- All companies should be concerned about the corporate offence of failing to prevent bribery. The offence will have a significant impact on the operation and management of companies connected to the UK, both in terms of compliance and non-compliance.

Legislation

- Public Interest Disclosure Act 1998 ('the Whistleblowers Act').
- Public Contracts Regulations 2006.
- The Bribery Act 2010.
- Bribery Act 2010: Statutory Guidance by Ministry of Justice 2011.

Why the Bribery Act 2010 has been introduced

The UK Bribery Act 2010 (the Act) has been introduced to replace the outdated Prevention of Corruption Acts 1889-1916, and entered into force on 1 July 2011.

The reason for the introduction of the new UK bribery legislation is that the UK has been under pressure to reform its bribery laws since 1998 when it ratified the Organisation for Economic Cooperation and Development Bribery Convention (the OECD Convention). Despite having over ten years to address the issue, until the introduction of the new Act, the UK had failed to make its bribery laws compliant with the requirements of the OECD

Convention. The UK was therefore not in line with international standards and was receiving harsh criticism as a result.

The UK's legislation prior to the new Act was considered to be complex, fragmented and, accordingly, ineffective. Despite the fact that vast sums of money are spent on bribery, which in turn causes huge amounts of damage to the global economy, the UK was not well equipped to deal with the problem.

Whilst the US has been successfully prosecuting bribery cases under the Foreign Corrupt Practices Act 1977 (the FCPA) for some time, the UK's Serious Fraud Office (SFO) has struggled. In particular, the UK received significant criticism for its investigations of the *BAE Systems* case. The case involved the sale of overpriced military radar to Tanzania. Whilst the US authorities successfully imposed the considerable fine of $400m on BAE to settle bribery accusations, the SFO was only able to secure a fine of £30m for the offence of failing to keep proper accounting records. The fact was that whilst the US had robust anti-corruption laws, which would have allowed them to effectively prosecute BAE for bribery, the UK laws were not sufficient, which meant that they were forced to accept a lesser fine by way of a plea bargain.

The UK's efforts in prosecuting bribery further pale in comparison to the recent *Siemens* case, where the strength of the US and Germany's anti-corruption laws meant that combined penalties of £1bn were imposed on Siemens for bribery activities.

The new UK Act certainly provides (in wording taken directly from the Bribery Act 2010) 'a more effective legal framework to combat bribery in the public or private sectors'. It aims to 'help tackle the threat that bribery poses to economic progress and development around the world' and illustrates that the UK is making a major effort to comply with its obligations to tackle bribery under the OECD Convention. Although the Act is similar to other countries' anti-bribery regimes, for example the US, the UK Act is now generally considered to be one of the toughest bribery regimes worldwide.

The offences

- *Bribing another person.* Section 1 of the Act provides that a person is guilty of bribery where that person 'promises or gives a financial or other advantage to another person' to 'induce a person to perform improperly a relevant function or activity' or 'to reward a person for the improper performance of such a function or activity'.
- *Accepting a bribe.* Section 2 of the Act provides that a person is guilty of bribery where that person 'requests, agrees to receive or accepts a financial or other advantage intending that, in consequence, a relevant function or activity should be performed improperly'.
- *Bribing a foreign public official.* Section 6 of the Act provides that a person is guilty of bribery where that person bribes a foreign public official ('F') and the person's intention is to 'influence F in F's capacity as a foreign public official' and to 'obtain or retain… business' or 'an advantage in the conduct of business'.
- *Failure to prevent bribery.* Section 7 of the Act provides that a commercial organisation ('C') is guilty of bribery where 'a person… associated with C bribes another person intending… to obtain or retain business for C, or… to obtain or retain an advantage in the conduct of business for C'.

Relevant function / activity

Section 3 of the Act provides that the functions / activities listed below are relevant functions / activities (for the purposes of the offences of bribing / being bribed), provided that the person performing the function / activity is expected to perform it in good faith; or impartially; or is in a position of trust by virtue of performing it:

- Any function of a public nature;
- Any activity connected with a business;
- Any activity performed in the course of a person's employment; and/or
- Any activity performed by or on behalf of a body of persons (whether corporate or unincorporated).

Improper performance

As set out in Section 4 of the Act, a relevant function or activity is performed improperly if it is performed in breach of a relevant expectation, i.e. that the activity is performed in bad faith; not impartially; or the person performing the function or activity misuses their position of trust.

Extra-territoriality

The Act has extra-territorial application (Section 12), which means that an act of bribery does not need to take place in the UK to be caught under the Act. It is sufficient that the person who commits the bribery offence has a close connection with the UK, for example, they are a British citizen.

In terms of the corporate offence, there is no requirement for the individual who commits the bribery offence to have a close connection with the UK. It is also irrelevant whether the conduct which forms the offence is carried out in the UK or abroad. All that is required for a company to be covered by the Act is for them to have been incorporated in the UK or to carry on a business, or part of a business, in the UK. This is of particular significance for international companies with a UK presence. For example, they may not have a UK office but if they employ UK citizens then the Act will be applicable. It will also apply to the actions of foreign agents who are employed by UK companies.

Penalties for committing bribery

Individuals who are found guilty of a bribery offence under the Act will face up to ten years' imprisonment and an unlimited fine.

Companies that are found guilty of the corporate offence of failing to prevent bribery will have to pay an unlimited fine. The aforementioned cases of *BAE* and *Siemens* illustrate the level of fines imposed by other countries and therefore give companies some indication of the potential impact of the new UK bribery legislation.

Directors and senior managers of companies may face prosecution if they are aware of any bribes but fail to take action to prevent them. Furthermore, a director associated with a bribery offence may be disqualified from acting as a director for up to 15 years.

A bribery conviction could be very damaging to your company's reputation and may result in problems with business relationships going forward. Furthermore, companies that are guilty of failing to prevent bribery may be banned from public procurement under Section 23 of the Public Contracts Regulations 2006. A conviction would have to be declared on a 'pre-qualification questionnaire' or an 'invitation to tender'. For some companies this could be severely damaging.

Defences to bribery

The defence to the corporate offence is to show that the company had 'adequate procedures' in place to prevent the bribery. Claiming that you were unaware of the occurrence of bribery or that you did not realise certain conduct was contrary to the Act will not constitute a defence. Once it has been established that bribery has been committed, the burden of proof for utilising the defence of 'adequate procedures' rests with the company, i.e. the company must provide satisfactory evidence that this defence is applicable.

The only other defence to bribery is where the conduct was necessary for 'the proper exercise of any function of an intelligence service, or… the armed forces when engaged on active service'.

How companies can ensure compliance with the Act

All companies should be concerned about the corporate offence of failing to prevent bribery. The offence will have a significant impact on the operation and management of companies connected to the UK, both in terms of compliance and non-compliance.

The Ministry of Justice has issued statutory guidance (the Guidance) on the Act in order to assist companies in becoming and remaining compliant. It sets out further information on what constitutes 'adequate procedures' and also provides guidance on other key matters for companies, including the meaning of 'persons associated', hospitality and facilitation payments.

Other helpful guidance includes the Quick Start Guidance, which was issued by the Ministry of Justice to assist smaller companies in establishing an anti-bribery regime. In addition the guidance on 'adequate procedures' issued by Transparency International is particularly helpful as it includes various checklists that will assist companies in establishing and maintaining an anti-bribery regime.

Adequate procedures
The Guidance on 'adequate procedures' is not a 'checklist' or a 'one size fits all' approach but sets out principles that *must* form the basis of any anti-bribery framework. The principles are as follows:

- Proportionate procedures;
- Top-level commitment;
- Risk assessment;
- Due diligence;
- Communication (including training); and
- Monitoring and review.

Proportionate procedures
It is essential to have proportionate policies and procedures in place to prevent bribery occurring within your company and also to deal with any breaches that do occur. It is also vital that these policies and procedures are properly implemented and regularly reviewed.

All companies should have an anti-bribery policy, which is communicated and accessible to all staff. The policy should include, for example:

- a statement making it clear that bribery is prohibited;
- a statement explaining why bribery is prohibited;
- an undertaking by the company to conduct itself in a suitable manner;
- guidance on procedures that should be followed by staff if they are faced with a bribery scenario or become aware of any instances of bribery, i.e. whistleblowing procedures;
- details of the company's position on gifts and hospitality. This will depend on the industry in which you operate; the nature of your business; and will also vary between staff members, depending on their position within the business, for example, senior members of sales teams may be a particular risk. It would be helpful to provide examples of acceptable and unacceptable conduct;
- due diligence procedures;
- risk assessment procedures; and
- enforcement procedures.

The key when implementing procedures and policies is proportionality. Companies should ensure that the model they have selected is an appropriate means, for their business, of achieving compliance with the Act.

Top-level commitment
Companies must show that there is a culture of commitment against bribery from the top down. It is advisable for the CEO of a company to make a personal statement supporting the business' anti-bribery regime. Furthermore, senior officers and directors must be fully on board with the company's bribery regime and must be aware of any issues that arise (policies, training, amending contracts (including employment contracts); how companies deal with suppliers / customers / contractors and so on will all form part of this). It is also advisable to appoint a senior officer to oversee and audit the bribery regime.

Risk assessment

Companies are encouraged to adopt a risk-based approach to prevent bribery. The first step in adopting an anti-bribery regime should be for companies to assess their risks. Questions to be considered are as follows:

- What size is your company?
- Is it a UK or international company?
- Do the countries in which the company operates pose a higher risk of bribery?
- Does the industry in which you operate pose a higher risk of bribery?
- Have you carried out due diligence in respect of your employees and agents?
- Are your employees appropriately trained for the job they are carrying out?
- Do your customers pose a higher risk of bribery?
- Have you had any problems with corrupt activities in the past?

These questions are simply examples of how detailed risk assessments must be. The idea is to obtain a complete picture of exactly what kind of problems your company may run into, as this will give you a better understanding of how to mitigate your risk.

The results of a risk assessment will vary between companies, depending on the perceived risk of bribery in their respective markets. Companies will have different responses to the questions considered in a risk assessment, and therefore will have different bribery policies. It becomes clear that the risks faced by a large multinational company will be very different to those of a small UK company. Although a small local company will not have a huge amount of resources to implement a bribery regime, it is unlikely that they will require as extensive a regime as a large multinational company.

Some companies may be thinking that they already have an anti-corruption regime in place and therefore don't need to do anything. For example, some companies may currently be subject to the US Foreign Corrupt Practices Act as they have associations with the US. However, the UK Act is not the same as the FCPA and is considered to be more restrictive. The best course of action, therefore, is to first undertake a risk assessment and then determine what further action the company must take to become compliant with the UK law.

Due diligence

If companies are not aware of exactly who they are instructing or dealing with, it can present a significant risk. Due diligence requirements will depend on the particular risks open to your company, for example, companies that operate in high risk areas will require robust procedures. As the requirements for each company will differ there is no set checklist but you may want to consider carrying out due diligence in respect of the following:

- Employees – from the recruitment process, to any training necessary to enable them to perform their role correctly, and examining expense accounts of key employees to check that the activity is appropriate;
- Instruction of third parties or potential business partners, for example contractors, suppliers or agents – e.g. obtaining references and/or conducting a personal assessment prior to entering into a contract; and/or
- Assets or companies you intend to purchase.

It may be helpful to put together checklists as part of the due diligence procedure. This would be helpful in showing compliance with the Act should a company's conduct be called into question.

Please note that companies cannot contract out of their obligations under the Act by including clauses, warranties or indemnities in contracts. The obligation is on companies themselves to do all that they can to prevent bribery occurring in connection with their company.

Communication (including training)

Simply having policies in place is not sufficient to invoke the defence of 'adequate procedures'. Companies must take steps to ensure that the policies are communicated to relevant employees / agents, that the policies are adhered to and enforced, and that any necessary training is conducted.

Training should be specifically tailored for different employees' requirements. For example, individuals who operate abroad or who are involved in negotiating contracts would require more extensive training than administrative staff, whereas cash room staff would require specific training to ensure that potential bribery payments are flagged up.

Monitoring and review

When introducing bribery policies and procedures it is important to ensure that these are reflected in any existing contracts, for example, employee and supplier contracts. Once a company's regime is established and fully implemented, it should be monitored and reassessed on an ongoing basis to ensure that it remains effective. If there are any problems, necessary changes should be made to ensure compliance. Where changes are made to your regime, these should again be reflected in relevant contracts.

'Associated persons'

Under the new corporate offence, where any person associated (as set out in Section 7 of the Bribery Act 2010) with a company, i.e. an employee, agent or any other party, commits a bribery offence, the company is held responsible for failing to prevent bribery. Whilst the scope of 'persons associated' is undoubtedly broad, the Guidance provides that this is intentional to ensure it covers all persons who are potentially capable of committing bribery on behalf of a company.

This means that companies risk falling foul of the Act even though they have not consented to the bribery offence in question and may in fact have no knowledge of it at all.

Companies will therefore have to keep a much closer eye on, and exercise a greater level of control over, employees and company agents. As discussed above, carrying out due diligence would be helpful both in mitigating the risk and illustrating that a company has taken all appropriate measures to prevent the occurrence of bribery.

Facilitation payments

Facilitation payments are prohibited under the Act. These are nominal payments made to government officials to accelerate routine action, rather than to influence the official to act improperly. Whilst such payments are distinguished from bribery and accepted practice under some anti-corruption regimes, for example the US Foreign Corrupt Practices Act 1977, facilitation payments are not authorised under the UK Act.

Companies may therefore be forced to turn down work where facilitation payments are common practice. The Guidance states that companies should establish a policy on the action to be taken by employees or foreign agents if facilitation payments are demanded and that the policy is effectively communicated to all staff and agents.

Corporate hospitality

Prior to the Guidance being published, there was some fear among companies about the impact the Act would have on corporate hospitality. However, the Guidance clearly states that hospitality is permitted.

It states:

'Bona fide hospitality and promotional, or other business, expenditure which seeks to improve the image of a commercial organisation, better to present products and services, or establish cordial relations, is recognised as an established and important part of doing business and it is not the intention of the Act to criminalise such behaviour. The Government does not intend for the Act to prohibit reasonable and proportionate hospitality and promotional or other similar business expenditure intended for these purposes. It is, however, clear that hospitality and promotional or other similar business expenditure can be employed as bribes.

'Where the prosecution is able to establish a financial or other advantage has been offered, promised or given, it must then show that there is a sufficient connection between the advantage and the intention to influence and secure business or a business advantage. Where the prosecution cannot prove this to the requisite standard then no offence under Section 6 will be committed. There may be direct evidence to support the existence of this connection and such evidence may indeed relate to relatively modest expenditure. In many cases, however, the question as to whether such a connection can be established will depend on the totality of the evidence which takes into account all of the surrounding circumstances. It would include matters such as the type and level of advantage offered, the manner and form in which
the advantage is provided, and the level of influence the particular foreign public official has over awarding the business. In this circumstantial context, the more lavish the hospitality or the higher the expenditure in relation to travel, accommodation or other similar business expenditure provided to a foreign public official, then, generally, the greater the inference that it is intended to influence the official to grant business or a business advantage in return.'

The guidance cites the following examples of what may or may not be considered reasonable.

'The provision by a UK mining company of reasonable travel and accommodation to allow foreign public officials to visit their distant mining operations so that those officials may be satisfied of the high standard and safety of the company's installations and operating systems are circumstances that fall outside the intended scope of the offence. Flights and accommodation to allow foreign public officials to meet with senior executives of a UK commercial organisation in New York as a matter of genuine mutual convenience, and some reasonable hospitality for the individual and his or her partner, such as fine dining and attendance at a baseball match are facts that are, in themselves, unlikely to raise the necessary inferences.

'However, if the choice of New York as the most convenient venue was in doubt because the organisation's senior executives could easily have seen the official with all the relevant documentation when they had visited the relevant country the previous week then the necessary inference might be raised. Similarly, supplementing information provided to a foreign public official on a commercial organisation's background, track record

and expertise in providing private health care with an offer of ordinary travel and lodgings to enable a visit to a hospital run by the commercial organisation is unlikely to engage Section 6. On the other hand, the provision by that same commercial organisation of a five-star holiday for the foreign public official which is unrelated to a demonstration of the organisation's services is, all things being equal, far more likely to raise the necessary inference.'

The intention of the Act was not to prevent companies from getting to know their clients by taking them to dinner or sporting events. The main issue for companies to be aware of with hospitality is proportionality: the expenditure on events should be appropriate to the size of the company and the market in which it operates.

Prosecution of offences

Prosecutorial discretion

The Guidance provides that prosecution is a matter for the prosecuting authorities; however, it does say that the key factors are sufficiency of evidence and whether prosecution is in the public interest.

Joint guidance has been issued by the Director of the Serious Fraud Office and the Director of Public Prosecutions, regarding the prosecution of offences under the Act. However, this guidance is only applicable to England and Wales, not Scotland. The prosecutorial guidance provides that the key factors in deciding whether to prosecute are as specified in the Guidance but it also gives examples of evidential considerations and public interest factors that would be useful for companies to consult when undertaking a risk assessment of their business. For example, prosecution of an offence will be in the public interest where it was premeditated, involved persons in position

of authority or trust, and is likely to attract a significant sentence.

Self reporting

An initiative has been launched by the Lord Advocate Frank Mulholland QC to encourage companies to 'self-report' any potential bribery incidents to the Crown Office's Serious and Organised Crime Division (SOCD).

Companies will have a period of 12 months, i.e. until 30 June 2012, to take advantage of this initiative. Reports have to be made through a solicitor and must meet certain criteria. The SOCD will consider what action is appropriate, in the public interest, but it is likely that self-reporting will result in more lenient penalties. Furthermore, the SOCD can refer any less serious matters to the Civil Recovery Unit (CRU) for civil settlement, which means that companies would escape the criminal penalties under the Act.

The benefit of self-reporting is that it would allow companies to identify any weaknesses in the business and move forward with a clean slate and hopefully a more effective bribery regime. In July 2011 MacMillan Publishing agreed an £11.1m civil recovery order in the High Court, after having voluntarily referred itself to the Serious Fraud Office for investigations into an alleged bribe. In March 2010, MacMillan Publishing referred to the SFO concerns over payments made by part of its education business, Macmillan Education, in an unsuccessful bid to secure a multi-million dollar contract in Southern Sudan. Neill Blundell, Partner and Head of Fraud at law firm Eversheds, commented:

"Whilst the Civil Recovery Order is significant, MacMillan have escaped a criminal prosecution and none of their employees are to be prosecuted."

First case

The Act is not retrospective and therefore it will not apply to any incidents of bribery that occurred before the Act came into force on 1 July 2011. The first case under the new Act took place in October 2011, in which a former Magistrates' Court administrative officer admitted taking a £500 bribe to 'get rid' of a speeding charge.

Concluding comments

All companies must act now to ensure that they do everything possible to enable them to rely on the defence of 'adequate procedures' and thus limit their potential liability under the corporate offence.

As discussed above, there is no set form for an anti-bribery regime. Companies must assess their own risk and establish a regime that is appropriate to their business needs. As long as the six principles set out in the Guidance are adhered to, companies should be well placed to defend any bribery allegations.

Whilst many companies may see the introduction of the Act as a hassle and expense that they don't need, the benefits should be remembered. As the Guidance states, the Act has the potential to 'create a level playing field, helping to align trading nations around decent standards'.

See also: Employment contracts, p.164; Monitoring employees, p.358; Whistleblowing, p.551.

Sources of further information

The Bribery Act 2010:
www.workplacelaw.net/news/display/id/34668

Ministry of Justice Guidance on the Act:
www.justice.gov.uk/guidance/docs/bribery-act-2010-guidance.pdf

Ministry of Justice Quick Start Guidance on the Act:
www.justice.gov.uk/guidance/docs/bribery-act-2010-quick-start-guide.pdf

Transparency International Guidance on 'Adequate Procedures':
www.transparency.org.uk/working-with-companies/adequate-procedures

Self Reporting Guidance:
www.copfs.gov.uk/Publications/2011/07/Guidance-approach-Crown-Office-and-Procurator-Fiscal-Service-Reporting-Businesses-Bribery-Offences

Bribery Act 2010: Joint Prosecution Guidance of the Director of the Serious Fraud Office and the Director of Public Prosecutions:
www.cps.gov.uk/legal/a_to_c/bribery_act_2010/

OECD – Good Practice Guidance on Internal Controls, Ethics and Compliance:
www.oecd.org/dataoecd/5/51/44884389.pdf

Bullying and harassment

Debbie Fellows, Anderson Strathern

Key points

- Ensure that a formal statement or policy exists and is supported by senior management.
- Issue a clear statement that bullying and harassment is totally unacceptable.
- Investigate alleged incidents thoroughly and immediately.
- Provide access to counselling and advice for recipients, where practicable, or consider giving time off for these activities.
- Make appropriate use of grievance and disciplinary procedures, or introduce a harassment procedure.
- Train your managers to increase knowledge and awareness.

Legislation

- Protection from Harassment Act 1997.
- Offences (Aggravation by Prejudice) (Scotland) Act 2009.
- Equality Act 2010 (see 'The Equality Act', p.191).

What is bullying and harassment?

Bullying is an abuse or misuse of power that may be characterised as offensive, intimidating, malicious or insulting behaviour intended to undermine, humiliate, denigrate or injure the recipient.

Harassment, in general terms, involves unwanted conduct that has the purpose or effect of violating a person's dignity or creating an offensive, intimidating or hostile environment. It is unlawful if it is related to age, sex, sexual orientation, disability, religion or similar philosophical belief, nationality, ethnic origin, race or any personal characteristic of the individual, and may be persistent or a single incident. Further, if the individual can show that the conduct has created a hostile and degrading environment for them, it will not matter that the harassment related to another individual. An example of this could be where somebody has been

offended by sexist remarks made about or to another person.

The key element is that the actions or comments are viewed as demeaning and unacceptable by the recipient.

In Scotland, the perpetrators of harassment may face increased penalties for harassment offences under the criminal law, which may be treated as aggravated where the harassment is on grounds of disability, sexual orientation or transgender identity in terms of the Offences (Aggravation by Prejudice) (Scotland) Act 2009.

How can bullying and harassment be recognised?

It is good practice for employers to give examples of what is unacceptable behaviour in the workplace. These may include:

- spreading malicious rumours or insulting someone (particularly on the grounds of race, sex, disability, sexual orientation, religion or belief, or age);
- ridiculing or demeaning someone – setting them up to fail;

Case study

Munchkins Restaurant Ltd and another v. Karmazyn and others (2010)

This case concerned Miss Karmazyn and three other claimants who were waitresses working for Munchkins Restaurant Ltd, which was run by the controlling shareholder, Mr Moss. The claimants were all migrant workers from Europe with one, two, three and five years' service. They alleged that throughout their employment they were made to wear short skirts and subjected to talk of a sexual nature by Mr Moss, including talk about sexually explicit photographs that were lying around in the restaurant. The claimants alleged that Mr Moss regularly asked them questions about their sex lives. The claimants sometimes asked Mr Moss questions about his love life as they found this made him easier to handle.

The women had, on occasions, attempted to complain to Mr Moss but he became angry when they did so. When the women complained about Mr Moss' behaviour to the male manager, he replied that nothing could be done. The claimants resigned and brought claims for sexual harassment and constructive dismissal.

An Employment Tribunal upheld the claims. Mr Moss and the company were made jointly and severally liable for the discrimination and harassment awards. Each waitress was awarded £15,000 for injury to feelings, plus an award of £1,000 for aggravated damages to reflect the 'inappropriate and excessive' way in which the case had been conducted.

The respondents appealed on several grounds, including perversity, in that no reasonable tribunal could have concluded that the waitresses could have put up with such intolerable behaviour, if it existed, for such a length of time. The respondents contended it was also perverse of the Tribunal to find that the conduct was unwanted when some of the conversations were initiated by the women.

The EAT rejected the argument that it was perverse for the Tribunal to find that the conduct had been unwelcome, given that the claimants themselves engaged in talk of a sexual nature and sometimes initiated it. It had been entitled to accept the evidence of the claimants that this was a tactic used to divert attention away from their own sex lives. Further, it was not perverse for the Tribunal to find that there were grounds for constructive dismissal where the claimants had put up with allegedly 'intolerable' conduct day after day for several years. Regard should be had to the fact that these were migrant workers, with no certainty of continued employment, who were under financial and sometimes parental pressure. The EAT compared the situation of these women to the battered wife who puts up with violence even though it is unwelcome, commenting that "Putting up with it does not make it welcome". The EAT concluded that it was "not completely beyond the scope of reason to think that women in this particular situation should behave as they did".

> **Case study – *continued***
>
> This case casts doubt on the well-established principle that the employee must always act quickly in response to a breach, or else be taken to have affirmed the contract. It also adopts a very tolerant approach to the question of why the employee delayed in resigning.
>
> Further, this case provides a warning to employers that 'banter' and 'horseplay' that appears to be mutual may in fact be unwanted conduct and any complaint needs to be thoroughly investigated.

- copying memos that are critical about someone to others that do not need to know;
- exclusion or victimisation;
- unfair treatment;
- unwelcome sexual advances – touching, standing too close, displaying offensive materials even generally;
- making threats or comments about job security without foundation;
- deliberately undermining a competent employee by overloading and constant criticism;
- blocking or refusing promotion or training opportunities; and
- threatening behaviour, violent gestures or physical violence.

Why do employers need to take action?

Not only is bullying and harassment unacceptable on moral grounds, but it could cause serious problems for an organisation, including:

- poor morale and poor employee relations;
- loss of respect for managers and supervisors;
- poor performance;
- lost productivity;
- absence;
- resignations;
- damage to company reputation; and

- tribunal and other court cases and awards of unlimited compensation.

The legal position

Employers are generally responsible in law for the acts of their employees, unless it can be shown that the employer took such steps as were reasonably practicable to prevent the employee carrying out the bullying and harassment ('the reasonable steps defence'), which has proven to be a high test to meet.

Further, employers will be liable for the harassment of its employees by third parties, such as customers or visitors, under certain circumstances. The Equality Act 2010 states that an employer will be treated as harassing an employee where a third party harasses the employee in the course of the employee's employment; the employer failed to take such steps as would have been reasonably practicable to prevent the third party from doing so; and the employer knew that the employee had been harassed in the course of their employment on at least two other occasions by a third party (whether or not the third party was the same person on each occasion). Therefore, employers will not be able to ignore acts of harassment, simply because they are due to the actions of customers or other non-employees.

Facts

- The Government has estimated that employers' failure to tackle the root cause of bullying in the workplace costs the UK economy £13.75bn a year.
- According to HSE reports, bullying costs employers 80 million working days and up to £2bn in lost revenue every year.
- Workers experience psychological symptoms as a result of bullying, including anxiety, irritability, depression, withdrawal, and lowered self-esteem, and physical symptoms such as disturbed sleep, lethargy, stomach disorders and headaches.
- One in ten employees experience workplace bullying and harassment according to conciliation service, ACAS, and a survey by the union, Unison, reports that more than a third of employees said they were bullied in the past six months; double the number a decade ago.
- According to HSE reports, 87% of employees have taken sick leave as a result of bullying.
- The CIPD reports that mediation skills are not widely used in training to manage bullying at work (17%), although this rises to 25% in the public sector.
- 44% of smokers reported an increase in smoking as a result of bullying and 20% of drinkers reported an increase in drinking alcohol.
- The Chartered Management Institute (CMI) reports that a lack of management skills is the factor most commonly cited as contributing to bullying in the workplace.

This mirrors a provision that was introduced into the Sex Discrimination Act 1975 in 2008 and has been extended by the Equality Act 2010 to all strands of discrimination.

Employees who suffer bullying and harassment in the workplace may bring a variety of claims against an employer, including:

- a claim of unfair constructive dismissal (based on the employer's breach of the implied terms of trust and confidence);
- a claim for harassment under the Equality Act 2010 (i.e. a claim that the harassment is on grounds of sex, race, disability, sexual orientation, religion or belief, or age); and
- in more extreme cases, including personal injury, a claim can be brought in the civil courts based on

either negligence or a breach of a statutory duty, such as the duty to provide a safe place and system of working under the Health and Safety at Work etc. Act 1974.

Employers can be vicariously liable under the Protection from Harassment Act 1997 for bullying by their employees, if it constitutes harassment under this Act and it satisfies the appropriate tests. In order to bring a successful case under this Act there must be a course of conduct consisting of two or more instances, the conduct must constitute harassment (e.g. cause harm to others) and the perpetrator must have known / ought to have known that the conduct amounted to harassment. According to the judgment of the Court of Appeal in *Sunderland City Council v. Conn (2008),* what crosses the boundary between unattractive and even unreasonable conduct, and conduct that is oppressive and unacceptable, may well depend on the context in which the conduct occurs. What might not be harassment on the factory floor or in the barrack room might well be harassment in the hospital ward and vice versa. The touchstone for recognising what is not harassment for the purposes of the Act will be whether the conduct is of such gravity as to justify the sanctions of the criminal law. In respect of a claim under this legislation there is no 'reasonable steps defence' available.

What should employers do?
- Ensure there are in place up-to-date equal opportunities / harassment policies, coupled with commitment from senior management.
- Supplement policies with training for managers and employees.
- Set a good example.
- Maintain fair procedures.
- Ensure complaints are handled confidentially, fairly and sensitively.

Formulating a policy
- Include in the policy a clear statement that bullying and harassment will not be tolerated.
- Give examples of unacceptable behaviour.
- State that bullying and harassment may be treated as disciplinary offences.
- Outline the steps you will take to prevent bullying and harassment.
- Outline the responsibilities of supervisors and managers.
- Give reassurance of confidentiality for any complaint.
- Ensure protection from victimisation.
- Refer to grievance procedures (informal and formal), including a timescale for action.
- Refer to disciplinary procedures, including a timescale for action.
- Include provisions for counselling and support.

How should employers respond to a complaint?
There are four basic options:

1. *Informal approach*. In some cases, people are unaware that their behaviour is unwelcome. Sometimes a 'quiet word' can lead to greater understanding and an agreement that the unwelcome behaviour will stop.
2. *Counselling*. This can provide a vital and confidential path for an informal approach and sometimes the opportunity to resolve the complaint without the need for formal action. Other options include employee assistance programmes funded by the employer.
3. *Grievance procedures*. If the employee does not wish his/her complaint to be dealt with informally (or the informal approach has failed) the complaint should be fully investigated and dealt with in terms of the grievance procedure.
4. *Disciplinary procedures*. Where the outcome of the grievance procedure is that the complaint of bullying and harassment is upheld, the employer may consider disciplinary action against the perpetrator in accordance with the disciplinary procedure.

It is important to follow a fair procedure with regard to both the complainant and the person accused. See *'Disciplinary and grievance procedures'* (p.121) for more information.

What should be considered when imposing a penalty?
Action taken must be reasonable in the circumstances. In some cases, counselling or training may be more appropriate than disciplinary action. When a penalty is imposed, consider the employee's general disciplinary record, action in previous cases, any explanations or mitigating circumstances, and whether the penalty is reasonable.

Written warnings, suspension or transferring the bully or harasser are examples of suitable disciplinary penalties. Suspension or transfer can only be used if permitted in the employee's contract of employment, so check it carefully before imposing this.

When gross misconduct has occurred, dismissal without notice may be appropriate.

Finally, review your harassment and bullying policy on a regular basis to ensure that it remains effective.

See also: Disciplinary and grievance procedures, p.121; Discrimination, p.126; Employment disputes, p.168; The Equality Act, p.191; Mental health, p.308; Stress, p.500.

Sources of further information

Equality and Human Rights Commission: www.equalityhumanrights.com

Employers should have a clear record of the policy and procedures for disciplinary matters to provide clear guidance to employees on the procedure that will be followed by their employer. Workplace Law's **Non-contractual Disciplinary and Grievance Policy and Management Guide, v.4.0** helps employers comply with their obligations, with a view to minimising allegations of unfair treatment. For more information visit www.workplacelaw.net.

Carers

Gareth Edwards, Veale Wasbrough Vizards

Key points

- Caring has an important role in society and workplaces need to accommodate carers.
- The law has improved considerably in providing support and assistance to working carers.
- It is in employers' interests to help carer employees.
- Caring can be difficult and stressful and there is evidence to suggest that one in every five carers has to give up their paid employment to be a full-time carer. Becoming a carer can often happen overnight; for example, if a relative is injured in an accident, or is diagnosed with a serious illness. Therefore, the nature of caring is unpredictable and changeable.

Legislation

- Employment Rights Act 1996.
- Maternity and Parental Leave Regulations 1999.
- Employment Framework Directive (2000/78/EC).
- Employment Act 2002.
- Work and Families Act 2006.
- Equality Act 2010.

Definition of a carer

A 'carer' is usually defined as someone who, without pay, looks after and provides help and support to a partner, child, relative, friend or neighbour, who could not manage without their help or support. This caring responsibility could be necessary due to age, physical or mental illness, addiction, sickness or disability.

Providing support for employee carers

It is increasingly important for employers to be aware of the difficulties carers face, and provide support to employee carers. Employee carers have to juggle their work commitments with their other responsibilities. Many employers need educating in the issues working

carers face and how they can assist them. The question of why employers should work to assist carers is simple to answer. Most carers tend to be over 30 and consequently are in their prime employment years. Employees in this age range are often the most experienced and valuable.

Organisations derive benefit from retaining their existing staff, as it reduces the need to recruit and retrain and provides stability. There are many other benefits to providing such support, including lower turnover of staff, reduced absence rates, higher levels of morale and greater productivity.

Carers and the law

Flexible working

The right to request flexible working was initially introduced in 2003 under the Employment Act 2002 and has since been modified and extended by various regulations. Originally only carers of children under the age of six (or disabled children under the age of 18) qualified for the right. The Work and Families Act 2006 extended the right to carers of adults. In

> **Facts**
>
> - It is estimated that there are approximately six million carers in the UK, of which three million are employees.
> - This equates to one in seven of the workforce having some form of caring responsibilities in addition to their employment.
> - It is estimated that over the next three decades the total number of carers in the UK will increase from six million to nine million, and this will obviously impact on the workforce.

April 2009 the right was further extended to those responsible for children up to and including the age of 16.

Only certain employees qualify under the legislation. The right applies to employees who have been continuously employed for 26 weeks and who fall into one of the following categories:

- Have a child under 17 or a disabled child under 18 and are responsible for the child as a parent / adoptive parent / guardian / foster parent or holder of a residence order, or are the spouse, partner or civil partner of one of the categories listed or are applying to care for the child; or
- Are a carer who cares, or expects to be caring, for a spouse, partner, civil partner or relative who lives at the same address and who is over the age of 18.

Many carers do not fall within the statutory definition of those who are entitled to apply for flexible working. The application to work flexibly must be made in writing and the employee may request a change to the hours they work, a change to the times they are required to work, and to work from a different location. These three categories enable a wide range of possible working patterns. Upon receipt of the application, the employer has a legal duty to consider the request seriously and objectively and it can only object on specified business grounds. The following procedure must be followed:

1. The employee submits a written application.
2. The employer and employee must meet within 28 days of receipt of the application to discuss the matter.
3. The employer must provide the employee with written notification of its decision within 14 days of the meeting.
4. If the employer accepts the request, both parties will need to meet again to consider what arrangements will need to be put in place. An accepted request normally amounts to a permanent variation to the employee's contract of employment.
5. If the request is rejected, the employee has the right to appeal in writing within 14 days.
6. Within 14 days of receiving the written appeal the parties must again meet and the outcome should be notified to the employee within 14 days of the meeting.

This process can take up to 14 weeks but it should be noted that an employee can only make one request a year under the legislation. The employee is entitled to be accompanied at all meetings by a workplace colleague. There are limited circumstances in which an employee may lodge a claim in the Employment Tribunal for failure to follow the procedure, but such cases are rare. Employers should note that employees have a statutory right not to be subjected to detriment or be dismissed for making, or proposing to make, an application for flexible working.

Employers should also note that the refusal of an application for flexible working could form the basis of a discrimination claim by the employee. Claims could include discrimination by association following the introduction of the Equality Act (see Case study). Employers therefore need to be able to show they are acting consistently and are able to justify objectively their decision.

Emergency time off

The Employment Rights Act 1996 gave employees the right to 'reasonable time off' to deal with any unexpected emergencies that arise in relation to 'dependants'. A dependant is classified as a husband, wife, partner, child or parent of the employee. It also includes someone living with the employee as part of the family.

In the case of illness or injury, it also includes a person who relies on the employee for assistance. It is unlawful for an employer to penalise an employee for taking time off for genuine reasons. The right is intended to cover genuine emergencies only and is unpaid.

There is, as yet, no limit set on the number of times an employee can be absent from work exercising this right. However, it should be noted that this right is generally for unforeseen circumstances. If an employee knows in advance that he/she will need time off, he/she should ask for leave in the usual way. This could involve the employee taking annual leave, or some other type of leave, e.g. compassionate leave, if the employer provides it (see 'Leave', p.252).

This right is available for all employees, regardless of length of service.

An employee can make a complaint to the Employment Tribunal if he/she considers that he/she has been unreasonably refused time off, suffered a detriment for taking or seeking to take time off, or been dismissed for taking or seeking to take time off.

Parental leave

Parental leave is available to employees who have one year's continuous service and have, or expect to have, parental responsibility for a child. Employees can take 13 weeks' unpaid leave in total for each child and the leave must be taken before the child's fifth birthday or before the fifth anniversary of the date of placement in respect of an adopted child. Parents of disabled children can take up to 18 weeks in total, which must be taken before the child's 18th birthday.

Parental leave should only be used for the purpose of caring for a child. Leave may be taken in short or long blocks. Employers and employees can agree their own procedures for taking parental leave and the legislation encourages this.

However, the legislation does provide a default scheme that will apply automatically where there is no other agreement in operation. Employees have the right to bring a claim in the Employment Tribunal if their employer prevents or attempts to prevent them from taking parental leave and they are also protected from victimisation, including dismissal, for taking it.

EU proposals to increase parental leave from three months to four months have been introduced and member states have until 8 March 2012 to put this into place. We wait further to hear exact

Case study

Prior to the case of *Coleman v. Attridge Law* (2009) and the Equality Act 2010, support and assistance to working carers was ambiguous and inadequate. However, these two milestones and the principle of discrimination by association that they introduced and enshrined have now improved the protection available for carers. This improvement began with *Coleman* and the decision of the European Court of Justice (ECJ) in June 2008. The ECJ extended the ban on employment discrimination beyond the disabled, to their carers or those with close connections. The English courts subsequently held that the Disability Discrimination Act 1995 could be interpreted so as to prohibit associative direct discrimination.

The ECJ's ruling was significant and dramatically strengthened the employment rights of carers as they now could not be treated less favourably in connection with their caring responsibilities. Employers needed to be careful that they did not discriminate against employees who care for disabled people, or they would risk facing a disability discrimination claim. There is no limit on the amount of compensation that can be awarded if discrimination is proven.

The principle in *Coleman* has been incorporated in to statute and expanded with the Equality Act 2010 coming into force on 1 October 2010 (see '*The Equality Act*,' p.191). Section 13 of the Equality Act states:

'*A person (A) discriminates against another (B) if, because of a protected characteristic, A treats B less favourably than A treats or would treat others.*'

This advances the *Coleman* principle to cover age (where someone cares for an elderly dependant) as well as disability, as both are 'protected characteristics'.

It is therefore unnecessary under the Act for a person to have a protected characteristic themselves. A person can be discriminated against by association with a person who has a protected characteristic. For working carers this is a substantial shield to protect them from discrimination.

The Act also extends to harassment, Section 26 providing that:

'*A person (A) harasses another person (B) if:*

a) A engages in unwanted conduct related to a relevant protected characteristic, and

b) the conduct has the purpose or effect of (i) violating B's dignity, or (ii) creating an intimidating, hostile, degrading, humiliating or offensive environment for B.'

The conduct need only relate to a protected characteristic. Again, the person, a carer for example, need not possess that characteristic themselves.

details. However, employers should not be alarmed; parental leave remains unpaid and it is expected that few employees will take up this additional benefit.

How employers can help

It is evident from the above that only certain employees are entitled, under law, to request certain types of leave and flexible working. Carers who look after friends and families who do not live at the same address are often excluded. Accordingly, employers could consider going beyond the statutory minimum. There are a variety of actions employers can take to help carer employees. An easy first step would be to consult with employees and produce a carer-friendly policy.

Employers should investigate a full range of flexible working options, including part-time work, job sharing, flexi-time, homeworking, etc. It may be that employees who do not fall within the statutory definition, or those that do not have any caring responsibilities, become resentful towards those who work flexibly, and therefore employers should consider whether it would be appropriate and practical to allow all employees to request to work in a flexible manner.

In particular, employers should try and act promptly in responding to any requests. The use of a trial period may also be a sensible option, to allow both parties to decide if a variation is workable. In addition, some carers may only need to work flexibly at certain times, depending on the circumstances, and employers should aim to be as accommodating as possible.

The rights to emergency time off work and parental leave do not carry with them any right to payment, but employers may consider it appropriate for this to be

paid. In addition, employers may want to investigate introducing measures such as planned leave for situations where people may need to provide nursing care for a short period, or allow a longer lunch break to enable a worker to visit the person they care for.

Other practical support would be to allow the employee access to a telephone or give him/her parking near work to allow him/her to get in and out of work more easily.

National Carers Strategy

In June 2008 the Prime Minister launched the National Carers Strategy. The Strategy sets out a ten-year vision, including a set of commitments on some of the important issues surrounding carers. Many consider the Strategy to be an important step forward in recognising the needs of carers, and it includes a focus upon carers in employment.

In relation to employment matters, the Government has stated that it will be funding an awareness campaign to ensure that both employers and employees are aware of their rights. Furthermore, the Government will be undertaking a review of who is entitled to request flexible working rights, due to the fact that many carers do not fall within the statutory definition of a carer and therefore miss out. The Strategy has also committed £38m of additional funding to support carers in returning to work.

The Coalition Government has said that the vision from the last strategy in 2008 will remain, but that a new action plan will outline the 'key activities upon which the Government can focus' (from April 2011) to 'ensure maximum value for money in the context of the current economic climate'.

A further strategy was published by the Department of Health in November 2010 identifying the actions the Government proposes to take over the next four years to ensure the best possible outcomes for carers and those they support. This includes:

- supporting those with caring responsibilities to identify themselves as carers at an early stage, recognising the value of their contribution and involving them from the outset, both in designing local care provision and in planning individual care packages;
- enabling those with caring responsibilities to fulfil their educational and employment potential;
- personalised support, both for carers and those they support, enabling them to have a family and community life; and
- supporting carers to remain mentally and physically well.

See also: Childcare provisions, p.75; Discrimination, p.126; The Equality Act, p.191; Family-friendly rights, p.206; Flexible working, p.221; Homeworking, p.243; Leave, p.252; Pregnancy and maternity, p.400.

Sources of further information

National Carers' Strategy: www.carersuk.org; www.dh.gov.uk

Department for Business, Innovation and Skills: www.bis.gov.uk

Direct Gov: www.directgov.co.uk

CCTV monitoring

Lisa Jinks and John Macaulay, Greenwoods Solicitors LLP

Key points

- Employers should note that most CCTV systems will be covered by the Data Protection Act 1998 (the DPA). They should therefore familiarise themselves with the requirements of the DPA and the Information Commissioner's CCTV Code of Practice.
- Before installing a CCTV system, an impact assessment should be carried out to assess whether the use of CCTV is justified or whether another, less intrusive solution (such as improved lighting in a car park), could achieve the same objectives.
- A policy regarding the use of CCTV systems by camera operators and retention of images should be implemented.
- Warning signs should usually be posted, and the organisation must ensure it is able to comply with data subject access requests for images.

Legislation

- Data Protection Act 1998.
- Human Rights Act 1998.

CCTV in the UK

Increasingly, CCTV has become the principal method of carrying out surveillance of areas that may be accessed by the public as well as becoming commonplace in many workplaces in a variety of industries.

While CCTV has an obvious crime-prevention role in the high street and in places such as shops and car parks, its use in the workplace as a means of observation of staff is both less obviously beneficial, and considerably less accepted. Employers who use CCTV in the workplace need to ensure that doing so does not affect overall levels of trust in the employment relationship. Employers are advised to bear in mind the Information Commissioner's CCTV guidance, which recognises the special considerations that apply in the workplace to assist employers to comply with their legal obligations.

Data Protection Act 1998

The DPA is the major legal control over CCTV surveillance in the UK, both within and outside the workplace. Most images recorded by CCTV systems will constitute 'personal data' for the purposes of the DPA, for example, where someone is identifiable from the images captured, or where other information relating to a living individual is caught, such as car registration numbers.

This is a change from the Information Commissioner's original view that most CCTV images would not be covered by the DPA, and reflects the fact that systems are becoming far more technologically advanced.

Furthermore, some of the data recorded by CCTV may constitute 'sensitive personal data' under the DPA, for example, where the images relate to the commission or alleged commission of an offence. In these circumstances, the DPA applies more stringent processing guidelines that must be complied with.

Employers using CCTV systems should also be aware that they must be able to respond to data subject access requests under the DPA. Data subjects – i.e. those individuals about whom the data relates – have the right to see data held about them, and in the CCTV context, this will generally be the right of those recorded by cameras to see a copy of any such recording. Such 'subject access requests' must be complied with within a statutory time period unless one of the limited exemptions in the DPA applies (see 'Data protection', p.101).

To assist employers to comply with the DPA, the Information Commissioner has issued two pieces of guidance. The first relates specifically to CCTV in the workplace, with the second of more general application, relating to all workplace 'monitoring' – see Sources of further information.

Human Rights Act 1998

Under Article 8 of the Human Rights Act 1998 (HRA) everyone has 'the right to respect for his private and family life, his home and correspondence'.

It is arguable that workers' right to privacy under Article 8 may be compromised by some use of CCTV, particularly in areas where there is a legitimate expectation of privacy – toilets or private offices, for example. Employers should bear in mind

the provisions of the HRA when using CCTV systems, although compliance with the DPA and various Information Commissioner's Codes of Practice will likely lead to compliance with the HRA as well.

Code of Practice for users of CCTV

The Information Commissioner published a revised CCTV Code of Practice in January 2008. It sets out the measures that should be adopted in order to ensure that a CCTV scheme complies with the DPA and provides guidance on good practice.

The Code of Practice applies to most CCTV and other systems that capture images of identifiable individuals, or information relating to individuals, for specific purposes including monitoring their activities or potentially taking action against them (for example, as part of a disciplinary or criminal investigation). Note that the Code does not apply to the covert surveillance activities of law enforcement agencies or the use of conventional cameras (not CCTV) by the media or for artistic purposes such as filmmaking.

Although the Code should be considered in its entirety, Appendix 3 is specifically aimed at employers who use CCTV to monitor their workers, and supplements the Employment Practices Code guidance on monitoring employees (see below).

The full text of the Code should be considered by employers, but the main practical requirements are summarised in the following paragraphs.

Impact assessments

Employers should conduct an impact assessment before installing and using CCTV to assess whether the objectives of monitoring can be achieved by a less intrusive means. The guidance lists a number of questions that companies should consider before installing CCTV, such as:

- What are the problems the use of CCTV will address?
- Can CCTV realistically deal with those issues?
- How will the system work in practice, and who will manage it?
- What are the views of those who will be surveyed? Can the impact on them be minimised?

Under the DPA, organisations must notify the Information Commissioner of purposes for which they process data (see *'Data Protection,'* p.101). Such notification should cover data collected through CCTV and so organisations should be clear about the purposes for which they need CCTV and ensure the Information Commissioner is informed of these.

In some cases, it may be appropriate to install CCTV specifically for workforce monitoring, provided this is justified and properly impact-assessed. Workers should normally be made aware that they are being monitored, but, in exceptional circumstances, covert monitoring may be used as part of a specific investigation, for example, where there is reason to suspect criminal activity or equivalent malpractice, and the decision to use covert recording is taken by senior management having considered the intrusive effects on innocent workers.

Cameras and listening devices should not be installed in private areas such as toilets and private offices, except in the most exceptional circumstances where serious crime is suspected. This should only happen where there is an intention to involve the police, not where it is a purely internal disciplinary matter, and again should be considered properly by senior management prior to authorisation.

Camera positioning and signage

Cameras should be positioned in such a way that they are only able to monitor areas intended to be covered by the CCTV scheme. The operators of the equipment must be aware that they may only use the equipment in order to achieve the purpose as notified to the Information Commissioner. For example, if the aim of the CCTV is to prevent and detect crime, it should not be used for monitoring the amount of work done, or compliance with company procedures.

Clearly visible and legible signs of an appropriate size should be used to inform the workers (and, if appropriate, the public) that they are entering a zone with CCTV coverage. Such signs should detail the identity of the person or organisation responsible for the scheme, its purpose, and details of who to contact regarding the scheme. The contact point should be available during office hours, and workers staffing the contact point should be aware and understand the relevant policies and procedures.

Where CCTV is used to obtain evidence of criminal activity, signage may not be appropriate. However, the Code sets out tight controls over the use of CCTV in these circumstances, and employers should bear in mind the potential preventative effect of CCTV that would be negated where no signage is used.

Image quality

Images captured by CCTV equipment should be as clear as possible to ensure that they are effective for the purposes intended. Cameras should be properly maintained and serviced, and capable of recording with a high resolution. If dates and times are recorded, these should be accurate. Consideration must also be given to the physical conditions in the camera locations (e.g. infrared equipment may need to be used in poorly lit areas). No sound should accompany the images except in limited circumstances. Images should not be retained for longer than necessary and, while they are retained, access to and security of the images must be tightly controlled in accordance with the DPA. Disclosure of images from the CCTV system must be controlled and the reasons for disclosure must be compatible with the purposes notified to the Information Commissioner. All access to or disclosure of the images should be documented.

Employment Practices Code

Part Three of the Information Commissioner's Employment Practices Code on Monitoring at Work sets out the general guidelines for employee monitoring. Employers considering the use of CCTV in the workplace must consider this Code, even where the purpose is not specifically to monitor employees – for example, CCTV systems in shops designed to prevent shoplifting will inevitably also capture workers.

The Code stresses the need for proportionality – any adverse impact of monitoring must be justified by the benefits to the employer and others. Continuous monitoring of particular workers is only likely to be justified where there are particular safety or security concerns that cannot be adequately dealt with in other, less intrusive, ways. All employees and visitors to organisations should be made aware that CCTV is in operation and of the purposes for which the information will be used.

British Standards Institution

The British Standards Institution has issued Code of Practice BS 7958:2009 *Closed circuit television (CCTV): management and operation* to assist CCTV operators' compliance with the DPA (and other applicable legislation) and to ensure that CCTV evidence can be used by the police to investigate crime. The Code is particularly useful where CCTV systems are used in public places, or have a partial view of a public place, and may therefore be of use to workplace managers.

Conclusion

Workplace managers responsible for CCTV use should familiarise themselves with the relevant Information Commissioner's Codes of Practice, as well as the underlying legislation. The main points to consider are:

- An initial assessment should be carried out before installing the CCTV system.
- Clear guidelines for use should be established before the system 'goes live', and these should be communicated to all staff who use, and those who may be caught by, the system.
- Warning signs alerting people to the presence of CCTV, and containing relevant information should normally be put in place.
- CCTV images should be handled in accordance with the requirements of the DPA, in particular those relating to storage and security.
- Employers should ensure they are able to comply with data subject access requests.

See also: Data protection, p.101; Monitoring employees, p.358.

Sources of further information

Information Commissioner: www.ico.gov.uk

CCTV Code of Practice: Revised Edition 2008: http://bit.ly/4wioW

Employment Practices Code: June 2005:
http://bit.ly/1HLK49

BS 7958:2009 *Closed circuit television (CCTV): management and operation:*
www.bsigroup.co.uk

Childcare provisions

Kirstie Allison and Lizzie Mead, Berwin Leighton Paisner LLP

Key points

- According to the Government initiative, Every Child Matters: Sure Start (a programme aiming to increase the availability of childcare), an increasing number of employees in UK workplaces have responsibility for the care of children.
- A number of family-friendly rights are granted to such individuals, of which employers must be aware.
- As well as having to comply with the legal and statutory obligations, employers are now increasingly being encouraged to support Government-driven initiatives that assist employees and workers to meet their childcare needs.

Legislation

- Family-friendly legislation.

The so-called family-friendly legislation now encompasses a wide variety of rights (granted to employees but not workers) that employees may exercise in order to assist them with their childcare needs. By way of summary, these rights currently include:

- maternity leave and adoption leave of up to 52 weeks (statutory maternity pay and statutory adoption pay are payable (subject to eligibility) for 39 weeks);
- ordinary paternity leave of either one or two consecutive weeks, for which statutory paternity pay is payable;
- additional paternity leave of up to 26 weeks if the relevant individual's spouse or partner returns to work without using their full maternity or adoption leave entitlement (this will be paid if their spouse or partner returns to work with at least two weeks' maternity or adoption pay remaining);
- unpaid parental leave of up to 13 weeks for each child up to the child's

fifth birthday (or 18 weeks' leave in the case of a disabled child up to the child's 18th birthday) or within five years of placement for an adopted child (or the adopted child's 18th birthday, if sooner);

- for employees caring for certain adults the right to request a flexible working arrangement;
- for parents of children under the age of 17 (or 18 if disabled) who have responsibility for the child's upbringing, the right to request a flexible working arrangement; and
- the right to take reasonable unpaid time off work to deal with emergencies involving dependants.

There has been considerable discussion about other proposed changes to further extend the family-friendly legislation, in particular by extending the period for which statutory maternity pay and statutory adoption pay are payable, from 39 weeks to 52 weeks, extending the right to request flexible working to all employees and introducing a new system of shared 'parental leave'.

> **Facts**
> - All three- and four-year-olds are entitled to 15 hours' free early education per week in nurseries, playgroups, pre-schools, children's centres or at their childminders, for 38 weeks a year.
> - In 2010, 38% of all three- and four-year-olds in England were enrolled in non-school education settings in the private and voluntary sector, such as local playgroups.
> - In 2010, 66.5% of women with children were in employment but only 29% worked full-time.
>
> *Sources: Government Department for Education, National Statistics.*

Workplace nurseries and employer-supported childcare

Government-driven and trade union-backed initiatives such as the Sure Start Strategy are seeking to encourage greater employer-supported childcare through various voluntary schemes. Under these schemes, employees sacrifice a portion of their salary to be paid towards childcare costs, or their employer may offer childcare support on top of their salary. There are tax incentives available to both employer and employee. The schemes include the following:

- *Workplace nurseries.* This is where the employer is wholly or partly responsible for funding and managing the provision of childcare facilities (either a workplace nursery or an in-house / on-site holiday play scheme) on work premises. For small employers, this can be done jointly with other companies. In respect of this cost, the employer is exempt from employer's National Insurance Contributions (NICs) and the employee is exempt from employee's Class 1 NICs and income tax. In April 2005, this exemption was widened so that if you allow another employer's staff who work on your premises to use your childcare facility, they will benefit from the exemption also.

- *Childcare vouchers.* These are paper or electronic vouchers issued to employees to pay childcare providers for forms of childcare. There are tax incentives and savings available to both employer and employee, which were extended in April 2005. Currently, the first £55 a week or £243 a month of childcare vouchers paid for by the employer is exempt from NICs for employers, and from income tax and NICs for employees, provided that access to the scheme is available to all employees and that the vouchers are used to pay for registered or approved childcare (for eligible children) only.

- *Enhanced employee rights.* An increasing number of employers are opting to provide enhanced maternity, paternity, adoption and parental leave rights over and above the statutory minimum levels, extra statutory emergency leave to deal with a sick child or problems with childcare, and career breaks or sabbaticals.

Childcare vouchers and maternity leave

Since 2008, women going on maternity leave have been entitled to benefit from the terms and conditions of employment that would have applied to them had they been at work throughout the whole of their maternity leave, except those relating to 'remuneration'. Remuneration is defined within the Maternity and Parental Leave etc. Regulations 1999 as 'sums payable to the employee by way of wages or salary'. It is generally considered that, as they are non-transferrable and cannot be converted into cash, childcare vouchers are benefits rather than remuneration. HMRC has issued guidance to support this view. As a result, an employer has to provide childcare vouchers (together with other benefits) to employees throughout maternity leave even though, unlike other benefits, they are often funded by way of salary sacrifice. This is a potentially significant cost and as such in May 2009 the British Chambers of Commerce warned its members to carefully consider the costs risks before offering childcare vouchers to employees.

The benefit to employers is that if vouchers are funded through a salary sacrifice arrangement, the employer's NICs bill is reduced as it is paying NICs on a lower salary. The cost implications will depend on whether an employer is able to offset any of the cost against maternity pay. If an employer only pays its employees

SMP, it cannot offset any of the cost of the vouchers against this and any attempt to do so will be void. If an employer pays contractual maternity pay in excess of SMP, it will be able to deduct the cost of providing the vouchers against this if a policy allows it to be done. It is also theoretically possible to draft a maternity pay policy that allows an employer to further discount any maternity pay at the beginning of leave (if it is at a higher rate) to fund future vouchers during the unpaid or SMP period. However, this has not been tested.

Since the British Chambers of Commerce warning in 2009, there has been considerable debate around whether employers would be better off withdrawing childcare vouchers as a benefit. If employees have a contractual right to receive the benefit this is likely to cause its own problems.

See also: Carers, p.64; Children at work, p.80; Family-friendly rights, p.206; Flexible working, p.221.

Sources of further information

Early Years Education: www.education.gov.uk

Right to request flexible working: www.direct.gov.uk/en/Employment/Employees/Flexibleworking/index.htm

Comment ...

Pregnancy and work – the law and the reality

Baroness Margaret Prosser of Battersea OBE, EHRC

In 2005, the Equal Opportunities Commission estimated that 30,000 women each year are forced out of their jobs simply for being pregnant or taking maternity leave. While the laws relating to work and pregnancy have been in place for decades, the experiences of many pregnant women in the workforce would indicate that while the law says one thing, the reality is often different.

It is a well established principle that unfavourable treatment on the grounds of pregnancy or maternity leave amounts to automatic direct sex discrimination. The Equality Act 2010 confers 'protected status' on women from the start of their pregnancy until the end of their maternity leave.

The Act also provides that special (i.e. more favourable) treatment of women in connection with pregnancy or childbirth cannot be regarded as unlawful discrimination against men.

Some employers and commentators struggle with these provisions, seeing them as unwarranted and burdensome. However, robust legal protection is necessary if the negative effects of having children on women's employment opportunities are to be mitigated. There is ample evidence of women's vulnerability to unfavourable treatment, including demotion, dismissal and redundancy, as a result of pregnancy or taking maternity leave.

On 5 December 2006, Margaret Prosser was announced as Deputy Chair of the Equality and Human Rights Commission. Previously Deputy Secretary General of the Transport and General Workers Union, Margaret was President of the TUC, an Equal Opportunities Commissioner and active International Trade Unionist, chairing the World Women's Committee of the International Chemical and Energy Workers' Union.

In 2004 Margaret was asked by the Prime Minister to chair the Women and Work Commission, looking at the continuing reasons for the gender pay and opportunities gap. The WWC reported in 2006 and Margaret continues to work with trade unions, the business lobby and NGOs to promote its recommendations.

Earlier this year, the Commission released a report on the experience of workers in the meat processing industry. The inquiry uncovered frequent breaches of the law in meat processing factories –

some of which supply the UK's biggest supermarkets – and the agencies that supply workers to them. A quarter of those people interviewed for the inquiry said they had witnessed mistreatment of pregnant workers, such as the instant dismissal of agency workers if they reported being pregnant. Pregnant women were also made to continue doing work that posed risks to their health and safety, including heavy lifting and extended periods of standing. A number of women also reported miscarriages due to a lack of adjustments being made at work to accommodate their pregnancies.

Despite finding their experience in the workplace distressing and degrading, nearly one-third of workers endured this treatment without complaint both because of fears that they would lose their jobs as a result and that it would reduce their chances of securing stable employment.

The Commission also conducted an inquiry into the experience of women working in the UK finance sector, which found negative management attitudes towards women, particularly in relation to pregnancy and maternity leave, which adversely affected their career progression.

"Robust legal protection is necessary if the negative effects of having children on women's employment opportunities are to be mitigated. There is ample evidence of women's vulnerability to unfavourable treatment, including demotion, dismissal and redundancy, as a result of pregnancy or taking maternity leave."

The Commission recently funded the case of Geraldine Furbear, whose claims of pregnancy discrimination and unfair dismissal against her former care home employer were upheld. During her probationary period, Ms Furbear was denied time off for her antenatal appointments, was refused permission to use a lift in the building and, at times, was forced to lift patients. She was also put under pressure to work weekends against her doctor's advice. She was dismissed shortly after.

The Employment Tribunal found the care home had dismissed her for reasons that clearly related to her pregnancy.

In the current economic climate there is concern that women's vulnerability to redundancy, reorganisation and other workforce changes has increased. Women who are pregnant or have just had a baby who feel they have been discriminated against are often unlikely to have the energy, inclination or means to pursue a claim in the Employment Tribunal. Those cases that do reach the Tribunal bear testament to the disparity between what the law says and what the reality often is.

Children at work

Nicola McMahon, Charles Russell LLP

Key points

- A child is a person not over compulsory school age (i.e. up to the last Friday in June in the academic year of his/her 16th birthday). A young person is a person who has ceased to be a child but is under 18.
- The employment of children in the UK is subject to limitations regarding the number of hours that they can work. Children also have a number of special rights and protections in the workplace, justified on health and safety grounds. It is important for all employers of children to be aware of the legal framework.
- The general principle, subject to exceptions, is that a child under 14 may not work.
- Any organisation employing a child of compulsory school age must inform the Local Education Authority in order to obtain an employment permit for that child. Without one, the child may not be covered under the terms of the employer's insurance policy. (This does not apply, however, in respect of children who are carrying out work experience arranged by their school.)

Legislation

- Children and Young Persons Act 1933 (as amended).
- Children and Young Persons Act 1963 (as amended).
- Employment Rights Act 1996 (as amended).
- Education Act 1996 (as amended).
- Children (Protection at Work) Regulations 1998-2000 (implementing the provisions of the EC Directive on the Protection of Young People at Work (94/33/EC)).
- Working Time Regulations 1998.
- Management of Health and Safety at Work Regulations 1999.
- Working Time (Amendment) Regulations 2002.
- Equality Act 2010.

In addition, the United Nations Convention on the Rights of the Child (for these purposes, all persons under 18) provides that Member States have an obligation to protect children at work, set minimum ages for employment, and regulate conditions of employment.

Key restrictions on the employment of children

No child may be employed to carry out any work whatsoever (whether paid or unpaid) if s/he is under the age of 14. This is subject to some specific exceptions, e.g. in relation to children working for their parent / guardian, or in sport, television, the theatre or modelling. In the case of a child who is 14 or over, s/he may not:

- do any work other than light work;
- work in any industrial setting, sea-going boat, factory or mine (subject to very specific exceptions);
- work during school hours on a school day;
- work before seven a.m. or after seven p.m.;
- work for more than two hours on any school day;
- work for more than 12 hours in any week during term-time;

> **Case study**
> *Addison v. Ashby* (2003)
>
> This case involved the issue of whether or not newspaper delivery boys and girls below school-leaving age (16 in the UK) were entitled to be paid during their statutory annual leave.
>
> The National Federation of Retail Newsagents (NFRN), which supported a couple who own a newsagents' shop, argued that current laws entitle workers aged under 16 to annual leave, but this should be unpaid as they are too young to qualify for paid leave.
>
> The EAT ruled in favour of the NFRN, which represents 22,000 members nationwide operating approximately 30,000 outlets and employing 192,000 newspaper deliverers, and agreed that children in England and Wales aged under 16 were covered by the Children (Protection at Work) Regulations 1998, which give young workers the right to two consecutive weeks' unpaid leave.
>
> The EAT ruled that the Working Time Regulations 1998 give young workers the right to paid annual leave only if they are over school-leaving age.
>
> The case affects millions of people who have their newspapers delivered, and who faced the prospect of having to pay more for the delivery service if the extra cost had been imposed on newsagents. "Many newsagents would have had to pass on the cost to their customers or cease deliveries," said Colin Finch, National President of the NFRN.
>
> Helen Brooks of Charles Russell, which represented the NFRN, said: "This is an important decision as it clarifies the scope of the Working Time Regulations 1998, and clearly affects the majority of newsagents and their customers nationwide."

- work more than two hours on a Sunday;
- work for more than eight hours on any day s/he is not required to attend school (other than a Sunday) (or five hours in the case of a child under the age of 15);
- work for more than 35 hours in any week during school holidays (or 25 hours in the case of a child under the age of 15);
- work for more than four hours in any day without a rest break of at least one hour;
- work without having a two-week break from any work during the school holidays in each calendar year; or
- work without an employment permit, issued by the education department of the local council, and signed by the employer and one of the child's parents.

In addition, each Local Authority has specific, additional by-laws regulating the employment of children in its area.

Work experience

Guidelines were issued by the DTI (now BIS) in 2007 regarding work experience placements in the television industry, and these are now regarded as being applicable in various industries. The main points of note in the guidelines are:

- a written document should detail the framework of the work experience placement;
- placements should be for a fixed period of time (ideally between two weeks and a month);
- placements should not entail more than 40 hours' work per week;
- before starting the placement, specific learning objectives should be agreed between the child on the placement and the provider of the placement; and
- no unpaid volunteer should be under an obligation to comply with an employer's instructions.

Entitlement to holidays and time off

Under the Working Time Regulations 1998, all adult employees are entitled to at least 5.6 weeks' paid annual leave. In the case of *Addison v. Ashby* (2003), however, the Employment Appeal Tribunal ruled that this entitlement does not apply to a child. The Children and Young Persons Act 1933 provides that a child is entitled to two consecutive weeks without employment during a school holiday; however, this period of time is unpaid.

National minimum wage and sick pay

The national minimum wage for young workers, aged under 18 but above the compulsory school age, but who are not apprentices, is (as of October 2011) £3.68 per hour and is reviewed in October of each year. There is no national minimum wage for children still of compulsory school age. In England and Wales, a person is no longer of compulsory school age after the last Friday of June of the school year in which their 16th birthday occurs.

The Statutory Sick Pay Regulations specify that workers aged 16 or over are entitled to receive statutory sick pay (SSP). Under 16s are not entitled to SSP.

Age discrimination

As a result of the Equality Act 2010, it is unlawful to discriminate against any person on the grounds of age. This applies to discrimination against young as well as older people. The lower age limit of 18 has also now been removed, meaning that under 18s have the same rights as older workers and can bring unfair dismissal and discrimination claims.

> *See also*: Childcare provisions, p.75; Minimum wage, p.342; Work experience, internships and apprenticeships, p.558; Young persons, p.571.

Sources of further information

Worksmart – children's work rights: www.worksmart.org.uk/rights/childrens_work_rights

DirectGov: www.direct.gov.uk/en/Parents/ParentsRights/DG_4002945

Children's Legal Centre – a charity providing advice and information for young people: www.childrenslegalcentre.com/Legal+Advice/Child+law/childemployment/

Compromise agreements

Camilla Beamish, Cripps Harries Hall LLP

Key points

- After declaring that any agreement to exclude or limit the operation of the Employment Rights Act 1996 is void, Section 203 then sets out the circumstances in which an employer can enter into a contract which compromises an employee's statutory employment rights and which it describes as a compromise agreement. Similar provisions appear in most employment-related legislation, thus making it possible for almost all claims arising out of statutory employment rights to be compromised.
- Should an employee subsequently bring a claim in the Employment Tribunal (ET) in respect of a claim that has been compromised, the compromise agreement will serve as clear evidence that a settlement has been agreed and will operate to prevent the claim from going any further. A compromise agreement is the only lawful way for an employee to waive their statutory employment rights.
- There are benefits for both the employer and employee in entering into such an agreement. The employer can be confident that the risk of an employee bringing a claim is slight. Compromise agreements can save time if the employer does not want to follow lengthy disciplinary / consultation procedures. The employee is given bargaining power, certainty and, more importantly, a compensation package. Compromise agreements offer both parties a clean break.
- For the agreement to be recognised as legally binding, it must comply with the six conditions contained in the Act (*see below*). A compromise agreement cannot be used to contract out of all statutory claims. There are exceptions which are outlined below.

Legislation

- Trade Union Reform and Employment Rights Act 1993.
- Section 203 Employment Rights Act 1996.

Introduction

A compromise agreement can be an effective tool for an employer who wants to terminate an employee's employment where the dismissal is likely to give rise to an employment claim. As part of the agreement, the employee will promise not to bring any claims against their employer and in return will receive a compensation package (which they will usually be able

to negotiate and which will include a monetary payment).

A compromise agreement can be likened to an 'insurance policy' for the employer, since once the employee has entered into the agreement the likelihood that they will bring a claim is minimised and if the employee does bring a claim, the compromise agreement can be used to stop the proceedings going any further.

The use of compromise agreements is flexible. They can be negotiated before an employee has commenced a claim, or during ET proceedings. A compromise

> **Facts**
> - A recent survey showed that 80% of employers made use of compromise agreements to protect their business against employment claims from former employees.
> - More than half of employers who used compromise agreements believed that they helped to reduce employment claims. A third of employers reported an increase in their use of compromise agreements, although on average an employer will not use more than six in any one year.
> - On 27 January 2011 the Department for Business, Innovation and Skills (BIS) launched a consultation on wide-ranging reforms to the Employment Tribunal system, one of the principal aims being to achieve the earlier resolution of disputes without the need for tribunals. It is seeking information about the use of compromise agreements, the costs of using them and the advantages and disadvantages of them. At the time of writing, the Government was still considering responses, although the results are expected by the end of 2011.
>
> *Sources: Employment Review. Resolving workplace disputes – public consultation.*

agreement can be used to settle multiple claims an employee might have against their employer.

For a compromise agreement to be valid it must comply with the following conditions:

1. The agreement must be in writing.
2. The agreement must relate to a 'particular complaint' or 'particular proceedings'.
3. The employee must have received legal advice from a relevant independent adviser on the terms and effect of the proposed agreement and its effect on the employee's ability to pursue any rights before an Employment Tribunal.
4. The independent adviser must have a current contract of insurance, or professional indemnity insurance, covering the risk of a claim against them by the employee in respect of the advice.
5. The agreement must identify the adviser.
6. The agreement must state that the conditions regulating compromise agreements have been satisfied.

'Particular complaint' or 'particular proceedings'

- A 'particular complaint' relates to claims brought under the Equality Act 2010, Equal Pay Act 1970, Sex Discrimination Act 1975, Race Relations Act 1976, Employment Relations Act 1999, Disability Discrimination Act 1995, Working Time Regulations 1998, Employment Equality (Sexual Orientation) Regulations 2003, Employment Equality (Religion or Belief) Regulations 2003 and Employment Equality (Age) Regulations 2006.
- 'Particular proceedings' relates to claims brought under the Trade Union and Labour Relations (Consolidation) Act 1992, Employment Rights Act 1996 (ERA 1996), National Minimum Wage Act 1998, Transnational Information and Consultation of Employees Regulations 1999,

Case studies

Gibb v. Maidstone and Tunbridge Wells NHS Trust (2010)

This Court of Appeal (CA) decision held that a compromise agreement that included a provision to pay a £250,000 severance package was not, contrary to the view of the High Court, irrational, nor was the NHS Trust acting beyond its powers by entering into it. The High Court should not be drawn into acting more as an auditor than as a judge.

Rose Gibb was employed as Chief Executive of the Maidstone and Tunbridge Wells NHS Trust from April 2004 to September 2006, during which time several outbreaks of clostridium difficile at Maidstone Hospital occurred, which resulted in the deaths of approximately 90 patients. The Healthcare Commission investigated the outbreaks and the measures taken to control and to respond to them and produced draft reports, which were shared with the Trust. The final report recommended that the Trust's board should review its leadership in light of significant failings, in order to ensure that it was able to discharge its responsibilities to an acceptable standard. Prior to the publication of the final report, and in anticipation of public reaction, the Trust had decided to encourage or, if necessary, force Ms Gibb to step down.

The Trust and Ms Gibb negotiated a settlement (to be recorded in a compromise agreement) which gave her approximately £75,000 as payment in lieu of notice and £175,000 as compensation. Ms Gibb agreed to the termination of her employment and undertook not to pursue any claims and not to make any statement potentially damaging to the Trust. When, following the intervention of the Secretary of State, the Trust refused to pay her the promised £175,000, Ms Gibb accused the Trust of 'unjustly enriching' itself and brought a claim to enforce the agreement. The High Court accepted the Trust's argument that it was ultra vires for the Trust to agree the payment and stated that it was 'irrationally generous'.

The CA allowed Ms Gibb's appeal and said that that the judge should not have been concerned to reach his own conclusions as to what financial prudence might require. The financial question was one which should rest with the NHS Trust.

Although the High Court erred in its decision on this occasion, the case highlights that, until a compromise agreement is in place, neither party is bound by what has been negotiated. It also identifies a risk for employees particularly of public bodies that a compromise agreement may be invalid if the employer exceeds its powers when agreeing the terms.

Fixed-Term Employees (Prevention of Less Favourable Treatment) Regulations 2000, Part-Time Workers (Prevention of Less Favourable Treatment) Regulations 2000, Information and Consultation of Employees Regulations 2004, Occupational and Personal Pension Schemes (Consultation by Employers and Miscellaneous Amendment) Regulations 2006 and Companies (Cross-Border Mergers) Regulations 2007.

An agreement that seeks to exclude all possible claims an employee might take to the ET will be void. For example, an agreement, the terms of which stated that the settlement was in 'full and final settlement of any claims you may have against this company,' was not enforceable (*Sutherland v. Network Appliance Ltd* (2001)).

It is important to note that there are certain statutory claims that cannot be contracted out of. A compromise agreement cannot be used to contract out of:

- the Human Rights Act 1998;
- the Data Protection Act 1998;
- claims for failure to inform / consult under the Trade Union and Labour Relations (Consolidation) Act 1992 or the Transfer of Undertakings (Protection of Employment) Regulations 2006;
- a claim for damages for personal injury; and
- a claim in relation to accrued pension rights.

A practical way to deal with potential personal injury claims is to ask the employee to warrant in the compromise agreement that they are not suffering from any form of personal injury and are not aware of any circumstances that could give rise to a personal injury claim.

Hinton v. University of East London (2005) is authority that particular proceedings should be identified in the agreement. Mummery L J said:

"It is good practice for the particulars of the nature of the allegations and of the statute under which they are made or the common law basis of the alleged claim to be inserted in the compromise agreement in the form of a brief factual and legal description."

Therefore it is not sufficient to merely identify the particular statute; the agreement must identify the particular sections of the statute or provide a description of the claim.

If proceedings have already commenced in the ET, then the agreement should give details of the specific claim(s).

In *Hilton UK Hotels Ltd v. McNaughton* (2005), the EAT held that the statutory claims contained in the compromise agreement only covered claims the employee believed she had against the employer, not potential claims the employee had been unaware of at the time of the agreement.

However, the case did not exclude the possibility that an agreement may seek to waive claims not within the employee's contemplation. An agreement seeking to do this must be completely open and unequivocal.

A compromise agreement can be negotiated directly between the parties after proceedings in the ET have commenced. An alternative method of negotiating a settlement is for the parties to use an ACAS Conciliation Officer who will mediate the discussions and record the terms agreed in a compromise agreement using form COT3.

Relevant independent adviser

To ensure there is no suggestion of undue influence by the employer and also to ensure the employee is aware of what they are agreeing to, it is a statutory requirement for the employee to seek independent legal advice before signing the agreement. This provision provides protection for both the employer and employee. A relevant adviser may be one of the following:

- A qualified lawyer – a solicitor or barrister who holds a current practising certificate.
- Officers, officials, employees, or members of an independent trade union who have been certified in writing by the trade union as competent to give advice and as authorised to do so on behalf of the trade union.
- If he/she works at an advice centre either as an employee or volunteer and has been certified by the centre as competent to give advice and as authorised to do so on its behalf.
- Those specified in an order made by the Secretary of State. This covers Fellows of the Institute of Legal Executives.

Because it is to the employer's advantage to secure a compromise agreement it is usual for the employer to make it a term of the agreement that they will make a contribution to the employee's legal fees incurred obtaining legal advice on the terms of the agreement. The amount of the contribution will depend on the individual facts of the case.

It is standard practice for the employee to acknowledge in the compromise agreement that they have received independent legal advice. Although there is no requirement for an independent adviser to provide a certificate, it is accepted practice that they will do so. A certificate

provides the best evidence that this condition has been met by the employee.

Due to a probable drafting error in Section 147(5) of the Equality Act 2010, a person who is party to the contract or the complaint, or someone who is acting for that person in relation to the contract or the complaint, cannot be a relevant independent advisor. This is a contradiction in terms and effectively rules out anyone who is advising the employee about a possible claim and/or the terms of a compromise agreement. The Government has issued a statement to say that the position is as it was previously but until this drafting anomaly is rectified, when discrimination is raised as an issue between the parties, employers may wish to consider using a COT3 agreement instead. Alternatively employers could seek to defer the payment of compensation under the compromise agreement, in so far as it relates to discrimination claims, until after the three-month time limit for bringing claims has expired.

Tax

The main financial provisions contained in compromise agreements usually relate to payments due to the employee on termination of employment and an additional compensatory sum. The former include payments in lieu of notice, holiday pay and bonus payments (if applicable). These payments will be taxed as employment income and will usually be paid by the employer through the payroll.

By virtue of an HMRC concession, the first £30,000 of a payment of compensation for loss of employment is free of tax.

A statutory redundancy payment is free of tax but, if paid, will be counted as part of the £30,000 concession.

Before 6 April 2011 employers making a payment to a former employee after Form

P45 had been issued needed to deduct tax at basic rate only on any excess over £30,000. However, this practice has now ended and since 6 April 2011 any payment made after the P45 has been issued has been subject to a new 'OT' code which will require higher rate tax to be deducted if the employee had a higher rate code when in employment. The effect is to make sure all the tax due to HMRC is collected at the time of payment. This change will mean that employers need not withhold termination payments until after the P45 is issued. Indeed, employers may be best advised to deduct the tax from the termination payments through the payroll before the P45 is issued.

Any contribution towards the employee's legal costs will be tax-free and not treated as a taxable benefit, provided that:

- the fees are paid directly to the employer's legal adviser;
- the costs are incurred in connection with the termination of the employee's employment; and
- the payment is made under a term of the compromise agreement.

Payments for any new promises made by the employee (such as new restrictive covenants) are taxable at the employee's marginal rate.

What terms should be included?
A compromise agreement typically will include the following:

- Definition of terms;
- Termination of employment date;
- Where notice is given any provisions relating to garden leave;
- Payment in lieu of notice, unused holiday and any further benefits;
- Compensation package;
- Return / retention of the employer's / company's property;
- An agreed form of reference;

- An agreed statement for announcement of the employee's departure;
- Confidentiality of the employer's information;
- The treatment of existing restrictive covenants and the introduction of new ones if appropriate;
- Confidentiality of the terms of agreement;
- Commitment not to make derogatory statements about the other party;
- Waiver of employment claims by the employee;
- Payment of contribution to legal fees by the employer;
- Identification of the relevant independent adviser; and
- A statement that the agreement complies with the provisions of the Act.

It is good practice for an employee's adviser to ensure that any personal injury claims or claims arising out of employment pension benefits are expressly excluded from the settlement.

Where there is a breach of a compromise agreement it can be enforced:

- by way of a claim for breach of contract in the civil courts; and/or
- as a contract claim in an Employment Tribunal, provided the compromise agreement is made before termination subject to the limit on the value of the claim (£25,000).

'Without prejudice and subject to contract'
Negotiations with a view to reaching a settlement are usually conducted 'without prejudice and subject to contract'. These words are intended to enable non-binding and legally privileged discussions and negotiations to take place between the parties and their advisers until such time as the parties are agreed on all points and formally consent to an agreement coming into effect. Draft compromise agreements

and relevant correspondence should always be marked 'without prejudice and subject to contract'.

The moment an employer raises with an employee that it is intended to terminate their employment 'with a compromise agreement' it is almost certain that the implied term that the employer will act in such a way as to maintain the trust and confidence between employer and employee will have been breached. Should negotiations not lead to an agreement the employee could treat such a discussion as a repudiatory breach of contract by the employer. Employers should be aware that any discussions with an employee about the termination of their employment (as opposed to discussions about an offer of compensation) may be admissible as evidence at an ET hearing and will not be excluded even if the employer said they were 'without prejudice'. Conversations that are a genuine attempt to settle will be treated as privileged and only then if they are expressed to 'without prejudice'.

Conclusion

- Compromise agreements can provide an effective way to avoid litigation when there is a risk that an employee may bring a claim against their employer, especially in the context of the termination of their employment.
- A compromise agreement ensures a clean break for both parties. The advantage for the employer is that they are able to draw a line under an employee's departure and be protected from future claims. The advantage for the employee is the certainty of the financial sum received in return for their agreement not to bring a claim.
- The agreement must satisfy all of the six conditions identified in the ERA 1996, otherwise it will not be effective as a compromise agreement (it will still be a binding contract as far as common law claims are concerned).
- A compromise agreement may not be sufficient to waive rights of which the employee was unaware at the time or were not within the employee's contemplation.
- The maximum tax-free compensation payment that can be agreed is £30,000.
- The *Gibb* case is authority that a public body cannot rely on the irrationality of its own financial decision to escape making an agreed compensatory payment to an employee. The Court should not be drawn into acting as an auditor.
- Case law highlights the emphasis the Tribunals place on tailoring the compromise agreement to fit the facts and circumstances of each case.

See also: Disciplinary and grievance procedures, p.121; Dismissal, p.146; Employment contracts, p.164; Employment Tribunals, p.179; References, p.434; Restrictive covenants and garden leave, p.441

Sources of further information

CIPD: 'Tribunal claims, settlement and compromise': www.cipd.co.uk/EmploymentLaw/FAQ/_Tribunal/Tribunal.htm

ACAS: www.acas.org.uk

Contract disputes

Rupert Choat, CMS Cameron McKenna

Key points

As disputes are expensive and time-consuming, it is advisable to manage them by:

- including appropriate dispute resolution provisions in contracts;
- anticipating disputes in record-keeping practices; and
- handling disputes effectively.

Legislation

- Arbitration Act 1996.
- Housing Grants, Construction and Regeneration Act 1996.

Dispute resolution provisions in contracts

Wherever possible, when drafting any pro-forma contracts and when negotiating contracts, it is advisable to consider the various dispute resolution methods available and to include clauses providing for the chosen method(s). Some 'picking and mixing' of methods is possible.

Negotiation

Discussions invariably occur before any dispute goes to formal proceedings. Even if formal proceedings are commenced, negotiation remains one of the most effective ways of resolving disputes.

It may help to discuss disputes on a 'without prejudice' basis, so that what is said cannot be referred to later in any formal proceedings. This can promote a frank exchange of views.

Some contracts provide for a structured approach to discussions. For instance, a dispute may be required to be considered initially by those at project level. If this is unsuccessful within a specified time, the dispute may go to board or principal level.

The contract might make compliance with this procedure a precondition to the commencement of any formal proceedings.

Court proceedings

Generally, unless the contract otherwise provides (e.g. by providing for arbitration), the courts can decide the parties' disputes. Proceedings are started by issuing a claim form.

The Civil Procedure Rules govern court proceedings.

The courts deal with disputes according to their value and complexity. Directions are given to the parties to prepare their dispute for trial. Directions usually provide for the production of statements of case, disclosure of documents, exchange of witness statements and expert reports (if necessary).

Court proceedings are public.

Arbitration

Parties to a contract can agree that their disputes will be resolved by arbitration rather than by the courts. This can be done either in the contract or 'ad hoc' once a dispute arises.

The Arbitration Act 1996 governs arbitration.

> **Facts**
> - About 90% of court cases are settled before trial.
> - Mediation saves UK business over £1bn a year in wasted management time, damaged relationships, lost productivity and legal fees.
> - There are approximately 1,500 adjudications a year. About 5% of decisions are enforced with the courts' help. Few are invalid or treated as not finally resolving the dispute.

Generally the parties decide who the arbitrator(s) will be or, failing that, a nominating body decides. The parties can agree the procedure for the arbitration by which the dispute will be decided. They might agree on a procedure similar to court proceedings or they might opt for the dispute being decided on paper without a hearing.

Arbitration is a confidential process.

One disadvantage of arbitration is that third parties cannot be joined in the arbitration without the consent of all concerned. This is not the case with court proceedings.

Adjudication

The Housing Grants, Construction and Regeneration Act 1996 empowers a party to a 'construction contract' to refer any dispute arising under the contract to adjudication. The option to go to adjudication exists in addition to the right to go to court or arbitration (whichever is applicable).

Adjudication is rough and ready but usually cheaper than court proceedings or arbitration. The appointed adjudicator is required to reach a decision within 28 days of the dispute being referred to him (subject to extensions). The adjudicator's decision is temporarily binding pending the outcome of any subsequent court proceedings or arbitration.

There is some uncertainty as to the extent to which facilities management contracts are construction contracts. To avoid confusion it is usually sensible to provide expressly for adjudication in such contracts.

Alternative dispute resolution (ADR)

Parties to a contract can agree that their disputes will be resolved by any of a number of forms of ADR. This can be done either in the contract or 'ad hoc' once the dispute arises. The parties may agree that ADR is a precondition to court proceedings or arbitration.

- One method of ADR is mediation. The parties (or an appointing body of the parties' choice) appoint the mediator, whose role is facilitating the resolution of the dispute. The mediator has no decision-making powers, although the parties can empower him to opine on where the merits lie in their dispute. The mediation is held 'without prejudice'. The process is non-binding. Any party can withdraw at any time, and there is no guarantee of a resolution at the end of the mediation.
- Early neutral evaluation involves a third party, who is usually a lawyer, assessing the merits of the dispute and advising the parties of his views in a, usually, non-binding manner. This might help the parties to settle between themselves.
- Another method of ADR is expert determination. It is particularly suited to disputes that turn on technical

rather than legal issues. A third party expert is appointed to reach a decision on the dispute. The parties agree a (usually short) timetable that may allow them to make submissions to the expert. The parties may agree that the expert's decision will be final and binding or that it will be subject to review by the courts or arbitration.

Record keeping
Good documentary records tend to help in resolving disputes and may reduce any legal costs you incur.

Bear in mind that in court and arbitration proceedings you will invariably be directed to disclose to the other party relevant documents under your control (including documents that are prejudicial to your case). Disclosable documents will include emails and other electronic documents. Documents are generally disclosable even if they contain confidential information.

It is advisable to retain documents for between six and 15 years after the matter to which they relate ends (depending upon the nature of the contract).

Handling disputes
When a dispute arises, try to address it early rather than allowing it to escalate.

If it is not possible to resolve the dispute by discussion, check the contract to see which dispute resolution method(s) apply. Consider also whether you want to suggest another method not provided for by the contract (e.g. mediation). In some cases statute may dictate that a certain dispute resolution method applies even if it is not specified in the contract (e.g. adjudication in construction contracts).

It invariably favours a party during any formal proceedings if they have behaved reasonably in conducting the dispute (especially if the other party has not). For instance, if a party unreasonably refuses a proposal to mediate a dispute, that party may later incur a costs penalty.

Remember that even if you win the dispute, you will not recover all of your legal costs and will find it difficult to recover compensation for management time spent in handling the dispute.

> *See also*: Employment contracts, p.164; Employment disputes, p.168; Mediation, p.300.

Sources of further information

Civil Procedure Rules: www.justice.gov.uk/civil/procrules_fin/index.htm

Arbitration Act 1996: www.workplacelaw.net/news/display/id/32378

Housing Grants, Construction and Regeneration Act 1996, Part II (as amended by the Local Democracy, Economic Development and Construction Act 2009, Part 8): www.workplacelaw.net/news/display/id/35434

Adjudication case summaries:
www.law-now.com/law-now/zones/LN_Adjudication.htm

Contractors

Hayley Overshott, Kennedys

Key points

- Contractors are not normally employees of a business, but have a contract to provide agreed services. This is known as a contract for services, which is in contrast to a contract of service, e.g. a contract of employment.
- The employment status of contractors has both tax and employment rights implications.

Legislation

- Employment Rights Act 1996 (ERA).

Overview

It is important for anyone hiring a contractor to understand the distinction between employees and contractors so that their legal rights and obligations are clear. Contractors will not normally be considered employees of a business. Instead, they might be self-employed, an agency worker or an employee of another business. Contractors have more control over the type of work they do and how they do it, whereas employees normally have less control over what they do but instead benefit from employment rights that contractors do not. Employees and contractors are also treated differently for tax purposes.

The distinction between employees, workers and contractors is not clear-cut. It is possible that a contractor may actually be considered to have an employment relationship with a business and be categorised as either a worker or (although unlikely) an employee.

In what circumstances could a contractor be an employee or a worker?

Under Section 230(1) of ERA 1996, an employee is 'an individual who has entered into or works under a contract of employment'. A contract of employment is defined in Section 230(2) of ERA 1996 as 'a contract of service or apprenticeship, whether express or implied, and (if it is express) whether oral or in writing'. There is no statutory definition of 'contract of service,' but, generally speaking, under a contract of service a person agrees to serve another.

It is unlikely that a contractor would be found to be an employee of the business that has hired them. However, while the requirements for an 'employee' are hard for a contractor to meet, the bar is set lower for a 'worker' and it is therefore possible that a contractor could be classified as a worker in some situations.

Under Section 230(3) of ERA 1996 a worker is an individual who has entered into or works under a contract of employment, or any other contract whereby the individual undertakes to do or perform personally any work or service for another party to the contract. The definition of a worker is very wide and will include employees as well as those individuals who provide personal services under a contract, provided the other party to that contract is not a client or customer. Therefore, where an individual is on balance a contractor but there are some factors that point towards

Case studies

There have been a number of recent cases where the Courts have grappled with the employment status of contractors. The difficulties lie in the fact that each case turns on its own particular facts and there are a range of factors (as set out above) that may point towards an employment relationship in varying degrees. A few key cases are set out below.

In the case of *Redrow Homes (Yorkshire) Limited v. Wright, Roberts and others* (2004), the Court of Appeal rejected the argument that bricklayers engaged on a sub-contracted basis were not workers because there was no contractual obligation to perform work personally. It held that they were workers because there was a mutuality of obligation and the scheme of payment pointed in the direction of contracts with individual bricklayers to do the work personally.

In reaching this decision, the Court upheld the earlier judgment in *Byrne Bros Ltd v. Baird* (2002), where it was found that while building labourers had been designated as sub-contractors in the contracts, they were in fact workers because they were personally required to perform work and services.

A situation where the Court found that contractors do not qualify as workers came in the recent case of *MPG Contracts Ltd v. England* (2009). In this case the Court held that a contractual term allowing a building contractor to veto substitutes found by its sub-contractors did not impede the sub-contractors' rights of substitution. It was therefore held that there was no contract for personal services, and so the contractors were not 'workers' within the meaning of the Working Time Regulations.

In circumstances where self-employed sole traders perform their services personally as part of a business, as in the case of *Bacica v. Muir* (2006), the Court has held that such persons would not qualify as workers.

The Court of Appeal in *Protectacoat Firthglow Limited v. Szilagyi* (2009) held that when assessing whether express contractual provisions should be disregarded when determining an individual's status, 'The question is always what the true legal relationship is between the parties. If it is asserted that the contractual document does not represent or describe the true relationship, the court or tribunal has to decide what the true relationship is.'

This reasoning was upheld by the Supreme Court when dismissing the appeal in the case of *Autoclenz Ltd v. J Belcher and Ors* (2011). The case involved car valeters who signed agreements stating they were self-employed and in the circumstances were found to be employees. The Court clarified that contracts relating to work or services can be very different to commercial contracts, as written documentation may not accurately reflect the reality of the relationship between the parties. In every case the question to be determined is 'What was

Case studies – *continued*
the true agreement between the parties?' The focus of the Tribunal's enquiry must be to discover 'the actual legal obligations of the parties'. This involves examining all the relevant evidence, including the written terms, evidence of how the parties conducted themselves in practice and the expectation each party had of the other.

an employment relationship, it is possible they could qualify as a worker.

Employment Tribunals look at various factors when determining if an employment relationship exists. The factors to be considered when determining whether an individual is a contractor involve the same factors that arise when deciding if someone is an employee. The following should be considered:

- *Personal service.* Is there an obligation to perform work personally? If there can be no substitution of the individual and the nature of the duties cannot be delegated then this would indicate worker status.
- *Mutuality of obligation.* Is there an obligation on the employer to provide work and an obligation on the individual to accept that work? If the employer provides specified work to the individual and the individual has to accept that work, then this would indicate worker status.
- *Control.* Is there overall control over the contractual relationship, such as the power to terminate and to subject the individual to disciplinary procedures? If the contractor is controlled in the manner in which they carry out their tasks, in that they are told what days to perform their work, their working hours, they use equipment provided by the employer and are subject to the employer's rules and policies, this would indicate worker status.

None of these factors on its own is definitive. Consideration should also be made to the surrounding circumstances when determining the nature of the relationship, such as:

- *Economic reality of the situation.* Where the individual is considered to be in business on their own, they are unlikely to be considered to be a worker. Similarly, the tax status of the individual may be considered, i.e. there are no PAYE or National Insurance contributions administration for contractors.
- *Integration.* Where an individual is seen as an integral and involved part of the business, this can help to demonstrate their status as a worker. Long periods working for one business may be more likely to signal an employment relationship, as would inclusion of an individual into any company benefit schemes.

Employment rights
Contractors will generally have no employment rights. However, in some circumstances where a contractor may fall under the definition of a worker, they will have some employment rights and, if in the unlikely event they are found to be an employee, they will have the full range of employment rights.

Workers' rights are becoming more wide-ranging and at present cover the areas set out below:

- Protection against unlawful deduction from wages.
- Working Time Regulations, i.e. the right not to work more than 48 hours per week, the right to rest breaks and the right to paid annual leave.
- Right to minimum wage.
- Protection for making a protected disclosure.
- Protection under the Data Protection Act 1998.
- Right to receive equal pay.
- Right not to be discriminated on the grounds of sex, race, disability, religion or beliefs, and sexual orientation, and not to be victimised for alleging discrimination.
- Right as a part-time worker not to be treated less favourably.

If a business wishes to make sure that a contractor engaged to do a job does not bring an employment claim, it would be helpful to the business if the contractual documentation expressly states that the contractor is not an employee or worker, although the label given to the relationship by the parties will not be decisive. If the relationship has changed over time, it is possible that a Tribunal might find that someone who started work as a contractor has subsequently become a worker or even an employee.

A business hiring a contractor should ensure that the contract is not personalised, that it contains substitution provisions and that it does not contain mutuality of obligation. The business needs to ensure that the contractor is not treated on a day-by-day basis as an employee. This means that, for example, contractors should not be entitled to any employee benefits.

If there are any factors that may point to an employment relationship existing, then the business should be careful that the contractor is not denied their worker, or, in some cases, their employee, rights. While determination of employment status remains highly subjective, businesses should err on the side of caution when engaging contractors.

See also: Employment status, p.174; Part-time workers, p.382; Self-employment, p.465.

Sources of further information

See www.inlandrevenue.gov.uk/manuals/esmmanual/index.htm for an employment status manual.

Workplace Law's ***Working with contractors 2008: Special Report*** is essential reading for those involved in the appointment of contractors for work activities. It is designed to provide workplace managers with everything they need to know to ensure they, and the contractors they employ, meet their duties under employment law. For more information visit www.workplacelaw.net.

Criminal records

Howard Lewis-Nunn, Rochman Landau LLP

Key points

- Other than in some excepted situations, employees or applicants are not obliged to disclose their past or 'spent' convictions once the appropriate period of time for their conviction has elapsed. The appropriate length of time before the conviction is spent depends on the nature of the sentence.
- Sentences of imprisonment for more than 30 months are never spent.
- Individuals can be required to disclose spent convictions when applying for jobs in certain sectors, where trust is a particular concern.
- The Coalition Government has simplified the system by merging the Independent Safeguarding Authority's roles into those of the CRB.

Legislation

The principal legislation dealing with the disclosure of spent convictions is the Rehabilitation of Offenders Act 1974. Various amendments have been made by Regulations, chiefly to identify sectors of work where employers are entitled to know about spent convictions. Criminal records are also classed as 'sensitive personal data' under the Data Protection Act 1998 and so employers will be required to obtain the individual's explicit consent before making use of such information.

Rehabilitation of Offenders Act 1974

The Act provides that, unless there is an express exception, once a conviction has been spent an individual is a 'rehabilitated person'. The Act sets out a tariff for the timescales after which various sentences are classed as spent. Sentences exceeding 30 months, for life, or at Her Majesty's Pleasure, are never spent.

Once a conviction is spent, an individual is not required to give any details and is treated as if he had not been convicted. Any requirement that imposes an obligation (whether legal or contractual) on an individual to disclose information is deemed not to require disclosure of spent convictions or any related matters and he is not required to answer any questions in a way that will reveal his spent convictions. He shall not be prejudiced in law for any failure to disclose his spent convictions. An employer may still ask for disclosure of current (i.e. unspent) convictions.

Consequently, unless an exception applies, an employer has no valid grounds for refusing to employ someone or dismissing him for possessing or failing to disclose a spent conviction. A dismissal on these grounds is likely to be unfair. However, it is not clear what remedy could be pursued for a refusal to employ someone, as an individual must have one year's employment in order to claim unfair dismissal (two years' from April 2012).

Exceptions

A number of occupations have been identified where spent convictions must be disclosed and an individual may therefore be dismissed or excluded from employment because of a spent conviction. The professions include barristers, solicitors, accountants, teachers, police officers, healthcare professionals, officers of building societies, chartered psychologists, actuaries, registered foreign lawyers, legal executives, and receivers appointed by the Court of Protection. More recently, the exempted occupations have been widened to include anyone who would have access to persons under the age of 18 or vulnerable adults (this includes the elderly and mentally impaired). Firmss employing individuals in any of these occupations are entitled to ask about spent convictions and the potential employee is required to give details.

Criminal Records Bureau

The Government established the Criminal Records Bureau (CRB) as a central point for employers to obtain details of potential employees' or volunteers' criminal convictions. This system is only available to organisations within the categories of employment that are exempt under the Rehabilitation of Offenders Act 1974, and in particular those working with persons under 18 or vulnerable adults.

Two types of disclosure certificate can be obtained at present – Standard and Enhanced Disclosure. Both Standard and Enhanced Disclosure provide details of all convictions including spent convictions as well as cautions, reprimands and warnings held on the police national computer. Standard disclosures will be required for those entering professions or occupations specified in the Exceptions Order, i.e. the legal or accountancy professions.

Employers will be able to employ someone barred from working in a regulated or controlled activity, provided they have appropriate safeguards in place. An example of a controlled activity might be caseworkers and administrators within social services or healthcare settings who have access to sensitive records. The Government is proposing to narrow the definition of a regulated activity.

Enhanced Disclosures are the highest level of check available. In addition to the information supplied by Standard Disclosure, it will provide any information stored about the person on lists (containing details of people who have been considered unsuitable to work with children or vulnerable adults) maintained by the ISA. It will also contain 'relevant' information held on local (as opposed to national) police force records. Enhanced Disclosures are the highest level of check, and are available for certain positions that involve work most closely and regularly with children and vulnerable adults and for those working in licensing and for judicial appointments.

The threshold for what is relevant and proportionate is relatively low. In the case of *R (on the application of John Pinnington) v. Chief Constable of Thames Valley Police* (2008) it was sufficient that the Chief Constable reasonably believed that the allegations disclosed might be true and might be relevant to the post applied for by the applicant. It is therefore up to the employer what it does with the information. Whilst the courts have advised against employers operating a blanket policy of requiring a clean check, employers are likely to be reluctant to take risks if information is disclosed. The results of any check would have to be considered very carefully in the context of the overall application and the post applied for. Details of the disclosure are provided to the registered body making the application and the individual who is the subject of the application. In limited situations the CRB may provide the employer only with additional information that is not to be disclosed to the individual.

Basic disclosure

Scotland operates its own separate criminal records checking system called Disclosure Scotland. Under this scheme, basic disclosure can also be obtained for any individual living in any part of the UK. Basic disclosure contains only convictions considered unspent under the Rehabilitation of Offenders Act. It is possible to obtain a basic disclosure even where the work is not covered by the CRB exemption and therefore a standard or enhanced disclosure is not available. For example, employees of solicitors and barristers are not covered by the CRB disclosure exemption (only the lawyers are).

The Independent Safeguarding Authority

The role of the ISA has been radically reduced. It is no longer necessary for individuals wishing to work with children or vulnerable adults to register with the ISA. The ISA's responsibilities are limited to maintaining lists of those individuals banned from working with children or vulnerable adults.

Obtaining disclosure

In order to apply for disclosure, employers who are entitled to use the service must either be registered with the CRB or apply through an 'Umbrella body', which is registered. Umbrella bodies can be used by any employer that does not wish to register itself directly with the CRB. Registered bodies are required to abide by the CRB's Code of Practice. Umbrella bodies are required to ensure that their clients abide by the Code also. The CRB may audit the user in order to ensure compliance.

The Code's key requirements:

■ Registered users must have a written policy on the recruitment of ex-offenders to be given to all job applicants. Umbrella bodies must ensure that their clients have a policy in place and provide a model one to the client if necessary.

■ All applicants who will be subject to a CRB request must be informed of the use to which the disclosure information will be put.

■ Where a position will require a CRB check the application form should state that a disclosure request will only be made in the event of a successful application, and if a conviction is disclosed this will not necessarily mean that the offer of employment is withdrawn.

■ The contents of the disclosure should be discussed with the individual before any offer is withdrawn. The existence of the Code should be brought to their attention and the employer's policy on the treatment of ex-offenders made available.

■ Only authorised personnel should have access to the disclosure, which includes storing it securely. There should be a written policy on secure storage of disclosure records. It is a criminal offence to pass it on to unauthorised persons.

■ Disclosure should not be kept for longer than is necessary and should be securely destroyed.

■ Umbrella bodies are required to ensure that their clients observe the Code and that they are in one of the exempt categories under the Rehabilitation of Offenders Act 1974 who can ask about convictions.

Portability

Some individuals may hold more than one position that requires a CRB check, and so organisations may be tempted to accept the disclosure results for a previous position if it is sufficiently recent. This is known as portability. The CRB does not support this and so organisations that re-use disclosure results do so at their own risk. However, as part of a risk assessment, unless there is a legal requirement for the employer to carry out its own check, a check carried out by another organisation may be relied on. One risk to relying on previous CRB checks is that they will not reveal whether any additional information was provided to the employer that was not disclosed to the individual. In deciding whether to make a fresh check the following factors should be considered:

- Is there a legal requirement to obtain a check?
- Is the existing check at the same level required for the new post?
- Is the position for which the check was obtained similar to the new post?
- Have all the checks the organisation needs been carried out?
- Has the identity of the person holding the check been authenticated?
- Is the applicant still living at the same address to which the check relates?
- Has the applicant given consent to contact the organisation that carried out the previous check?
- Is the check more than six months' old?

Where a previous check is being relied on, steps should be taken to confirm the authenticity of the check, such as contacting the person who countersigned the certificate for the applying organisation to confirm the registration number and that the details match. The new employer should ask the previous employer if there is any additional information of which they are aware. While they cannot provide the details they can confirm or deny its existence. If there does appear to be further information, a new check is advisable; however, there may be difficulties in explaining to the applicant why a fresh application is required.

Overseas applicants

Disclosure from the CRB will have limited information on overseas convictions and so records for anyone who has spent a substantial amount of time outside of the UK may not be complete. It is possible to carry out the equivalent of a CRB check in some countries and the CRB can provide guidance on this. The employer can also ask the individual to obtain the equivalent disclosure where he is resident overseas.

Future changes

The Coalition Government has already implemented a number of changes, such as halting the Vetting and Barring Scheme and removing the requirement to register with the Independent Safeguarding Authority. The Government is in the process of implementing its changes.

See also: Data protection, p.101; Interviewing, p.275; Personnel files, p.392; Recruitment and selection, p.420; Vetting, barring, blacklisting and social engineering, p.534.

Sources of further information

Criminal Records Bureau: www.direct.gov.uk/crb

Disclosure Scotland: www.disclosurescotland.co.uk

National Association for the Care and Resettlement of Offenders (NACRO): www.nacro.org.uk

Data protection

Lisa Jinks and John Macaulay, Greenwoods Solicitors LLP

Key points

- The Data Protection Act 1998 (DPA) is the principal piece of legislation in the UK governing personal data, and includes restrictions on processing data, gives data subjects certain rights, as well as creating eight legally enforceable 'data protection principles' with which organisations must comply.
- It is vital that companies understand the DPA and how it applies to them, particularly in light of the Information Commissioner's relatively recently introduced power to fine organisations up to £500,000 for serious breaches, not to mention the business implications that stem from adverse publicity surrounding data protection breaches.

Legislation

- Data Protection Act 1998.
- Freedom of Information Act 2000.
- Privacy and Electronic Communications (EC Directive) Regulations 2003.

How does the Data Protection Act apply to your company?

The DPA regulates the 'processing' of 'personal data' held on a computer, intended to be held on a computer, or held in paper form in a 'relevant filing system' by a 'data controller'. An understanding of these defined terms is crucial to understanding the obligations imposed by the DPA.

'Personal data'

This is defined as information that relates to living individuals who can be identified from it (whether from the data on its own or when used in conjunction with other information in the possession of, or likely to come into the possession of, the data controller). This may therefore include details such as a postal address or email address, as well as facts and opinions held about an individual or images of them.

The Information Commissioner's Data Protection Code of Practice looks at all the elements of the definition in greater detail and provides useful examples of what is caught by the definition and what is not – for example, truly anonymous data such as aggregated statistics will not be regulated by the Act.

The DPA also provides that some data is to be regarded as sensitive personal data and can only be processed under stricter conditions, which generally includes the need to obtain 'explicit' consent from the data subject. Such data includes information on racial or ethnic origin, political opinions, religious or other beliefs, trade union membership, health, sex life, and criminal proceedings or convictions.

'Processing'

The DPA defines this widely as 'obtaining, recording or holding information or data or carrying out any operation or set of operations on the information or data'. Organisations that hold personal data are very likely to fall within the scope of this definition by doing anything with the data, including simply storing it. Processing may only be carried out in accordance with the data protection principles (*see below*).

'Data controller'

A data controller is someone who determines how and for what purpose personal data is processed. Obligations in the DPA fall mainly on data controllers, who are likely to be companies or other organisations rather than individuals, such as a workplace manager. Certain obligations also fall on 'data processors', i.e. those who process personal data on behalf of a data controller (such as third party storage companies). The EU Article 29 Working Party has produced some guidance on the meaning of data controllers and data processors, which contains some specific examples from the experience of EU data protection authorities (see *Sources of further information*).

'Relevant filing system'

The key elements of this definition are that there must be a set of information, e.g. a grouping together of things with a common theme or element. It follows that a mere list of names is unlikely to satisfy this definition. The set of information must be structured, by reference either to individuals or to criteria relating to individuals, and specific information relating to an individual must be readily accessible. Recent case law has suggested that this definition is to be interpreted narrowly and that (a) files need to indicate clearly at the outset whether personal data is held within them; and

(b) there must be a sufficiently sophisticated and detailed means of readily indicating whether and where in an individual file or files specific criteria or information can be located. The ICO has published a list of FAQs on relevant filing systems, giving examples of what may constitute such a system (see *Sources of further information*).

Data controllers' responsibilities

Anyone processing personal data as a data controller must comply with the eight data protection principles contained in the DPA. These say that data must:

1. be fairly and lawfully obtained and processed;
2. be processed for limited purposes and not in any manner incompatible with those purposes;
3. be adequate, relevant and not excessive;
4. be accurate and where necessary kept up to date;
5. not be kept for longer than necessary;
6. be processed in line with the data subject's rights;
7. be secure; and
8. not be transferred to countries outside the EEA without adequate protection.

Fair and lawful processing

The first data protection principle underpins all the others, requiring that the processing of data is fair and lawful. The

Act states that, in order to ensure fairness, data controllers must ensure that:

- certain information is readily available to individuals (e.g. the name of the data controller and the purposes for which the data will be processed). The ICO has issued a Privacy Notices Code of Practice (June 2009) to help data controllers meet this requirement (see *Sources of further information*);
- certain pre-conditions are met to justify the processing of personal data. At least one condition in Schedule 2 of the Act must be met for any processing of personal data and, for sensitive personal data, at least one condition in Schedule 3 must also be met; and
- the individuals must not be misled or deceived as to the purposes for which their data will be processed.

The most common Schedule 2 conditions, one of which must always be met, are:

- Consent from the data subject (which must be freely given, specific and informed);
- The processing is necessary for the performance of any contract to which the data subject is party;
- The processing is necessary for compliance with any other legal obligation to which the data controller is subject; and
- The processing is necessary for the purposes of the legitimate interests of the data controller (except where it is unwarranted by reason of prejudicing the rights of the data subject).

Other Schedule 2 conditions apply in limited circumstances, such as where processing is ordered by the Secretary of State.

At least one Schedule 3 condition must be met in addition to a Schedule 2 condition where 'sensitive personal data' is processed. The most commonly relied

upon condition is that the processing 'is necessary in order to perform any rights or obligations imposed or conferred by law' on the employer in connection with employment – this would cover situations where the processing is necessary to comply with health and safety requirements, to check an entitlement to work in the UK, and not to discriminate on the grounds of the various protected characteristics.

Processing data for specified purposes

This principle requires that data is only obtained for a specific and lawful purpose, and is not further processed for purposes that are incompatible with the original purpose (for example, data collected for payroll purposes cannot then be passed on to marketing agencies).

In practice, this requires data controllers to be clear about why they are collecting data and what will be done with such data once it is collected. If, once data is collected, it is needed for another purpose, the data controller must inform the data subject and take steps to ensure that such use is fair as if it was being collected for the first time.

The 'lawful' collection requirement under this principle will require data controllers to comply with the other data protection principles – in particular the first principle (i.e. fairly and lawfully obtained and processed) – as well as the requirement to notify the Information Commissioner of processing (see '*Notification*' below).

Information standards

The third, fourth and fifth principles state that personal data must be:

- adequate, relevant and not excessive;
- accurate and, where necessary, kept up to date; and
- kept for no longer than necessary.

These three principles overlap to a certain degree and, read together, make it clear that data must be kept up to date and in a proportionate manner. Organisations should regularly review the data they hold to ensure that these principles are complied with – it may be that, when collected, data was adequate or relevant, but since then it has become out of date or is no longer necessary.

Individuals' rights

Data subjects – i.e. those about whom a data controller holds data – have the following rights under this sixth principle:

- A right of access to a copy of the personal data held about them ('subject access');
- A right to object to processing that is likely to cause or is causing damage or distress;
- A right to prevent processing for direct marketing;
- A right to object to decisions being taken by automated means;
- A right in certain circumstances to have inaccurate personal data rectified, blocked, erased or destroyed; and
- A right to claim compensation for damages caused by a breach of the Act.

In relation to subject access, data controllers should be aware that generally an individual has a right to be provided with copies of all information held about that individual within 40 days of a written request being made. Although there are limited grounds for withholding certain information, systems should be structured so that requests can be met as easily as possible.

Specific rules apply in relation to direct marketing, whether it is carried out by email, post, telephone, fax, or SMS messaging, and data controllers will also need to consider the impact of the Privacy and Electronic Communications (EC Directive) Regulations 2003. Legal advice should be sought if organisations are carrying out direct marketing campaigns.

Information security

The DPA requires that 'appropriate technical and organisational measures [are] taken against unauthorised or unlawful processing of personal data and against accidental loss or destruction of, or damage to, personal data'.

In practice, this seventh principle involves implementing policies and procedures on data security, as well as taking physical and technical steps to prevent unauthorised access to, or accidental loss of, data. The precise steps taken will depend on an analysis of the risk to a particular organisation – which will depend on its size, sector and nature of the data held – and a balancing act between that risk and the cost and technical feasibility of taking certain measures. For more on this subject, see 'IT Security' (p.282).

Transferring personal data abroad

The eighth principle holds that personal data can only be transferred to a country outside the EEA if:

- the EU Commission has made a finding of adequacy in respect of the third country, which currently exists in relation to countries such as Australia, Canada and Switzerland, and to those organisations in the USA that are registered under the 'Safe Harbor' scheme;
- an assessment of adequacy has been made by the data controller itself following the guidelines set out in the Act;
- there is no general adequacy but the parties have put in place adequate safeguards such as the use of

Commission-authorised standard contracts or binding corporate rules; or

■ one of the limited derogations to the eighth principle applies (e.g. the individual has consented to the transfer or the transfer is necessary for the performance of a contract between the data controller and the individual).

Notification

Most data controllers will need to notify the Information Commissioner, in broad terms, of the purposes of their processing, the personal data processed, the recipients of the personal data processed and, if relevant, any transfers of data overseas. This information is made publicly available on a register. However, under the DPA, data controllers must comply with the data protection principles, even if they are exempt from the requirement to notify.

An annual notification fee of £35 is payable, unless the organisation has an annual turnover of over £25.9m and has more than 250 members of staff (or if the organisation is a public authority with more than 250 members of staff), in which case the fee rises to £500. Notification can be made via the ICO website or through the post, with payment required at the time of notification.

Enforcement and remedies

Data controllers can commit criminal offences under the Act, including:

■ failure to notify the Information Commissioner either of the processing being undertaken or of any of the changes that have been made to that processing; and
■ failure to respond to an information notice or breaching an enforcement notice issued by the Information Commissioner.

Individuals can also commit criminal offences if they obtain, disclose or sell personal data without the consent of the data controller. The Ministry of Justice has consulted on the possible introduction of custodial sentences for breaches of the DPA, although such penalties are not expected to be introduced in the near future.

The Information Commissioner now also has a power to impose monetary penalties of up to £500,000 for serious and deliberate breaches of the DPA that cause substantial damage or distress, or where the data controller knew or ought to have known that there was a risk of serious breach that would be likely to cause substantial damage or distress, and failed to take reasonable steps to prevent this.

The ICO also has the following powers:

■ To issue enforcement notices and require undertakings for breaches of the DPA, which will require organisations to acknowledge and remedy such breaches.
■ To carry out an assessment (with the organisation's consent) as to whether the organisation's processing of personal data follows good practice.
■ To issue an information notice on a data controller for the purpose of determining whether the controller has complied with or is complying with the data protection principles.
■ The power of entry and inspection, on application to a judge, where there are reasonable grounds for suspecting an offence under the Act has been committed or the data protection principles contravened.

The ICO also has the power to spot check public authorities for compliance with the DPA without their consent, and has used this power, for example, by carrying out checks on the Department for Work and Pensions and the DVLA.

Individuals who have had their personal data processed otherwise than in accordance with the DPA may claim compensation for any damage or distress caused, such as where a security breach puts sensitive personal data in the public domain. They may also obtain a court order for the rectification, blocking, erasure or destruction of inaccurate data. In addition, in some cases, the court may order a data controller subject to such an order to notify third parties to whom the data has been passed of such rectification, blocking, erasure or destruction.

Employment Practices Code

The Information Commissioner has issued a Code of Practice to help employers to comply with their data protection obligations with respect to their dealings with their workers. The Code gives employers specific guidance on:

- recruitment and selection processes;
- how best to keep employment records;
- the monitoring of employees at work (see 'Monitoring employees', p.358); and
- issues relating to workers' health.

In addition, the Code provides information about workers' rights under the Act (see Sources of further information).

Freedom of Information Act

The Freedom of Information Act 2000 (FOIA) gives individuals the right to request information from a public authority. On receipt of the request, the authority is obliged to:

- tell the individual whether or not it holds the information; and (where applicable)
- provide the individual with the information requested (or provide a reason why the information will not be provided).

Note, however, that the FOIA applies to data held that is of general interest, rather than personal data. Where individuals request data about themselves through a FOIA request, public authorities will generally consider the request as a subject access request under the DPA.

See also: CCTV monitoring, p.70; Criminal records, p.97; IT security, p.282; Medical records, p.304; Monitoring employees, p.358; Personnel files, p.392; Private life, p.404; Vetting, barring, blacklisting and social engineering, p.534; Confidential waste, p.545.

Sources of further information

Further information on Freedom of Information may be found on the Ministry of Justice website: www.justice.gov.uk

ICO guidance on personal information:
www.ico.gov.uk/for_the_public/your_personal_information.aspx

ICO Data Protection Guide: http://bit.ly/rrNFfp

ICO Employment Practices Code:
www.ico.gov.uk/for_organisations/topic_specific_guides/employment.aspx

ICO Privacy Notices Code of Practice: http://bit.ly/q1o8V5

EU Article 29 Working Party: Guidance on the meaning of data controllers and data processors (WP 169, 16 February 2010):
http://ec.europa.eu/justice_home/fsj/privacy/docs/wpdocs/2010/wp169_en.pdf

Workplace Law's *Data Protection Policy and Management Guide v.4.0* has been published to help employers understand and meet their obligations under data protection legislation and to provide clear guidance for employers on their responsibilities when handling sensitive personal data. For more information go to www.workplacelaw.net.

Directors' responsibilities

Rachel Farr and Lorraine Smith, Taylor Wessing

Key points

- Company directors are primarily responsible for the management of their companies and, generally, their duties are owed to the company. However, they also owe duties to the owners as a whole. In addition, they have responsibilities in respect of the company's employees and its trading partners, and under statute these duties may be supplemented or modified by a company's articles of association. Furthermore, many directors will be subject to service agreements (contracts of employment) which may augment these duties.
- Directors are responsible for ensuring that the company complies with the various requirements imposed upon it by law.
- Although generally the company is liable for any failure to comply with legal requirements, in certain circumstances the directors can be held personally liable where the default was due to their neglect or connivance.

Legislation

- Health and Safety at Work etc. Act 1974.
- Company Directors Disqualification Act 1986.
- Insolvency Act 1986.
- Value Added Tax Act 1994.
- Management of Health and Safety at Work Regulations 1999.
- Companies Act 2006.
- Corporate Manslaughter and Corporate Homicide Act 2007.
- Health and Safety (Offences) Act 2008.
- Bribery Act 2010.

Directors' duties under the Companies Act 2006

The Companies Act 2006 (CA 2006) codifies certain key duties of directors. It sets out a statutory statement of seven general duties:

1. A duty to act in accordance with the company's constitution and only to exercise powers for the purposes for which they are conferred.

2. A duty to act in a way which a director considers, in good faith, would be most likely to promote the success of the company for the benefit of its members as a whole.
3. A duty to exercise independent judgement.
4. A duty to exercise reasonable care, skill and diligence.
5. A duty to avoid conflicts of interest.
6. A duty not to accept benefits from third parties.
7. A duty to declare to the other directors an interest in a proposed transaction or arrangement with the company.

These duties are (apart from the duty to exercise reasonable care, skill and diligence) all fiduciary duties. They are expressed to replace the previous common law duties but continue to be interpreted by reference to the case law in this area.

These duties are owed to the company and only the company can enforce them, although shareholders can make a claim by statutory derivative action on behalf of

> **Facts**
> - There has been an increase of 14% in the number of large firms with a board level director responsible for health and safety, rising from 73% to 87%.
> - The HSE research report, 'Health and Safety Responsibilities of Company Directors and Management Board Members,' indicates that 82% of companies involved in the research have appointed a person responsible at board level, 42% of which are nominated as 'Director' of health and safety.
> - In 2011, Cotswold Geotechnical Holdings Limited was fined £385,000 (equivalent to 250% of its annual turnover) for corporate manslaughter, the first conviction of its kind. Following the decision, the company entered into liquidation.
> - HSE research demonstrates 61% of directors or managers agree or strongly agree that individuals' belief they could be imprisoned constitutes an essential or important argument for enforcement to have a deterrent effect.

the company. CA 2006 has extended the common law derivative action, making it easier for shareholders to bring a claim on behalf of the company against directors and others for negligence, default, breach of duty or breach of trust, where a prima facie case is disclosed and the court gives permission for the claim to continue.

Duty to act in accordance with the company's constitution and only to exercise powers for the purposes for which they are conferred

A director must act in accordance with the company's constitution, which, for this purpose, includes resolutions or decisions made by the company in accordance with its articles of association, as well as the articles of association themselves.

Duty to act in a way a director considers most likely to promote the success of the company for the benefit of its members as a whole

In fulfilling this duty, directors must have regard to a statutory non-exhaustive list of factors, namely:

- the likely consequences of any decision in the long term;
- the interests of the company's employees;
- the need to foster the company's business relationships with suppliers, customers and others;
- the impact of the company's operations on the community and the environment;
- the desirability of the company maintaining a reputation for high standards of business conduct; and
- the need to act fairly as between members of the company.

This duty has extended and replaced the common law duty on directors to act in good faith and in the best interests of the company.

The decision as to what will promote the success of the company, and what constitutes such success, is one for a director's good faith judgement. For a commercial company, 'success' will usually mean a long-term increase in value.

Duty to exercise independent judgement

This duty is likely to be most relevant where a director wishes to bind himself to a future course of action which might be seen as 'fettering the discretion' of the director to make future decisions. It is not infringed by a director acting in a way authorised by the company's constitution or acting in accordance with an agreement duly entered into by the company that restricts the future exercise of discretion by its directors.

Duty to exercise reasonable care, skill and diligence

A director must exercise reasonable care, skill and diligence. The standard expected of him is not only the general knowledge, skill and experience he has (for example, a particular expertise in financial matters), but also the general knowledge, skill and experience that may reasonably be expected given his position and responsibilities to the company.

Duty to avoid conflicts of interest

A director must not use information gained by him as a director to further his own interests (unless he has the consent of the company to do so, as outlined below), nor must he seek to apply company assets for his own gain. For example, a director must not receive commission on a transaction between the company and a third party or offer to take up, on a private basis, work offered to the company.

A director must disclose any direct or indirect personal interests in a contract and will have to account for any profit made unless he complies with the requirement for disclosure before the contract was entered into.

These requirements for avoiding conflicts of interest and declaring interests in contracts are dealt with in specific statutory duties, as set out below.

A director must not, without the company's consent, place himself in a position where

there is a conflict, or possible conflict, either directly or indirectly, between the duties he owes the company and either his personal interests or other duties he owes to a third party. That applies, in particular, to the exploitation of property, information or opportunities, and whether or not the company could take advantage of the property, information or opportunity. There is no breach if the situation cannot reasonably be regarded as likely to give rise to a conflict of interest.

This duty does not apply to a conflict arising in relation to a transaction or arrangement with the company. In that situation, it is the duty to declare an interest in a proposed or existing transaction or arrangement with the company which applies (*see below*).

The duty to avoid conflicts of interest continues to apply after a person ceases to be a director as regards the exploitation of any property, information or opportunity of which he became aware when he was a director.

The company's consent can be obtained in advance by board authorisation (unless the company's constitution prevents this) but will only be effective if the quorum and voting majority are met without counting the director in question or any other interested director. For a private company incorporated before 1 October 2008, the board can only do this if the shareholders have previously approved the board giving such authorisations. For a public company, whenever incorporated, the board can only do this if authorised by the articles.

The shareholders themselves can also authorise conflicts of interest that would otherwise be a breach of this duty. To some extent, a company's articles can also contain provisions for dealing with conflicts.

Duty not to accept benefits from third parties

A director has a duty not to accept benefits from third parties, except where the benefit is not likely to give rise to a conflict of interest (in fact, most directors' service agreements will have an express prohibition on accepting benefits or 'kickbacks' from any third party, irrespective of whether or not a conflict of interest might arise).

Benefits conferred by the company, its holding company or subsidiaries, and benefits received from a person who provides the director's services to the company, are excluded. See 'Bribery' (p.49).

Duty to declare an interest in a transaction or arrangement with the company

A director has a statutory duty to declare the nature and extent of any direct or indirect interest in a proposed transaction or arrangement with the company. No declaration is needed where:

■ the director is not aware of the interest or the transaction in question (unless he ought reasonably to be aware of it);
■ it cannot reasonably be regarded as likely to give rise to a conflict of interest;
■ the other directors are already aware of it (or ought reasonably to be aware); or
■ it concerns terms of his service contract being considered by the board or a board committee.

A director also has a statutory obligation (although not a fiduciary duty) to declare any direct or indirect interest in an existing transaction or arrangement with the company.

Duties to employees

While a director owes no common law duty to consider the interests of the workforce,

and a director's duties are owed to the company, CA 2006 recognises the principle that the interests of the workforce fall within the wider picture of the interests of the company, as the interests of employees are one of several matters that directors must have regard to when satisfying their duty to act in the way they consider to be most likely to promote the success of the company.

Directors must comply with employment law in dealings with employees. In some circumstances, directors personally can be sued for unfair work practices such as race, sex, disability and other discrimination. Directors must ensure the company complies with any new employment laws.

Health and safety issues

A company has various obligations to fulfil under the Health and Safety at Work etc. Act 1974 (HSWA) and the Management of Health and Safety at Work Regulations 1992 (MHSWR).

The most important of these are as follows:

■ A duty to ensure, so far as is reasonably practicable, the health, safety and welfare of its employees. The size of the company and the activities that are carried on by it will be taken into account when assessing what is reasonably practicable.
■ A duty to carry out a risk assessment and implement procedures to minimise any risks that are highlighted.
■ A duty to provide (and periodically revise) a written health and safety policy, to implement it and to bring it to the attention of employees.

These are the company's responsibility, but the directors would be breaching their duties to the company by failing to take the appropriate measures. Furthermore, directors can be prosecuted under Section 37 of HSWA where the offence committed by the company occurred with their consent or connivance or through neglect on their part. If found guilty, directors can be sentenced to up to two years in prison. In addition, the Corporate Manslaughter and Corporate Homicide Act 2007 means the company is liable where a death is caused as a result of a gross breach of a duty of care and the way in which the company's activities were organised or managed by senior management constitutes a substantial element of that breach.

It is wise for directors to ensure they have health and safety systems in place. The HSE provides comprehensive guidance on this issue.

Financial responsibilities

Accounts

CA 2006 requires directors to maintain accounting records that:

- show the company's transactions and its financial position;
- enable the directors to ensure that accounts required under CA 2006 comply with the CA 2006 requirements;
- contain entries of all receipts and payments, including details of sales and purchases of goods, and a record of assets and liabilities; and
- show stock held at the end of each year.

Records must be kept at the company's registered office (unless the directors specify a different location) and be retained for a period of six years for a public company or three years for a private company.

The directors of a public company must lay its annual report and accounts before a general meeting (usually the AGM) and then file them with the Registrar of Companies within six months of the end of the company's financial year. Private companies do not have a statutory requirement to lay their accounts before the company in general meetings but they must file them with the Registrar of Companies within nine months of the end of the company's financial year.

Statutory returns, including the annual report and accounts, the annual return (including a statement of capital) and notice of changes to directors and secretaries, must be filed with the Registrar of Companies on time.

Failure to comply with these requirements renders the company liable to a penalty and directors liable to a fine.

Directors are also responsible for filing tax returns.

Financial management

Directors must exercise prudence in the financial management of the company. In the event of insolvency, directors can find themselves personally liable to creditors where it can be shown that they acted outside of their powers or in breach of their duties or were engaged in wrongful or fraudulent trading. The latter offences will be committed where a director continues to incur liabilities on behalf of the company where he knows or ought to have known that the company was, or inevitably would become, insolvent, or there was no reasonable prospect of repaying debts.

Directors have an obligation not to approve accounts unless they give a true and fair view of the financial position of the company (or of the companies included in the group accounts, to the extent that this concerns members of the company).

Bribery Act 2010

The Bribery Act 2010 (BA 2010) came into effect on 1 July 2011. It is of fundamental importance to all commercial organisations that either operate or are registered in the UK. BA 2010 has reformed the criminal law to provide a modern and comprehensive scheme of bribery offences to enable courts and prosecutors to respond more effectively to bribery, wherever it occurs. It is a far-reaching piece of legislation with some provisions that are more extensive than equivalent laws elsewhere, including the US Foreign Corrupt Practices Act (FCPA). It applies to bribery in both the private and the public sectors and makes illegal the bribery of another person, being bribed, and the bribery of a foreign public official (see 'Bribery', p.49).

Adequate procedures to prevent bribery by a corporate organisation

An offence under BA 2010 is committed by a commercial organisation when a person 'associated' with it (i.e. performs services for it) bribes another person and that bribe is intended to obtain or retain business for the commercial organisation or retain an advantage in the conduct of the organisation's business. It is a defence to this offence if the company can show it had adequate procedures in place to prevent such bribery taking place, which must include:

- *Proportionate procedures* – the procedures an organisation should take must be proportionate to the risks they face. The Adequate Procedures Guidance suggests, for example, that factors such as an organisation's size and the nature and complexity of its business will influence the response required.
- *Top level commitment* – this requires top level management, including directors to ensure that the organisation's staff and those who do business with or for the organisation understand that bribery is never acceptable.
- *Risk assessment* – this requires organisations to assess the nature and the extent of their exposure to external and internal risk of bribery. This assessment needs to be periodic, informed and documented.
- *Due diligence* – this is about knowing who you do business with; the Adequate Procedures Guidance recommends organisations undertake a proportionate and risk based approach to due diligence in respect of persons who will perform services for and on behalf of the organisation.
- *Communication* (including training) – the Government believes the communication of bribery policies and procedures will deter bribery by enhancing awareness of the organisation's procedures and its commitment to their proper application. Training should be used to raise awareness about the threats posed by bribery in general and the sector areas in which the organisation operates.
- *Monitoring and review* – an organisation should monitor the effectiveness of the procedures they put in place and make improvements where necessary.

In order to show adequate procedures, the board of directors will be expected to take responsibility for the matters above.

Individual directors' liability

If a corporate body (of any kind) or a Scottish partnership commits an offence under BA 2010 then a senior officer, including a director, can be personally liable for the same offence if he or she has consented or connived in the commission of the offence. 'Senior officer' is defined widely and includes director, manager, company secretary or similar officer of the corporate body or a partner of the Scottish partnership. Such a senior officer must have a close connection to the UK as defined in Section 12(4) – such as British citizenship, British Overseas citizenship, or being ordinarily resident in the UK.

If found to have committed an offence under BA 2010, a senior officer may be liable to a maximum penalty of ten years' imprisonment and/or an unlimited fine.

Other duties

Directors must maintain various statutory books including:

- a register of members;
- a register of mortgages and charges;
- a register of debenture holders; and
- a register of directors.

The statutory books are to be kept either at the company's registered office, or at a single alternative location (subject to certain criteria being met).

An annual return must be filed with the Registrar of Companies within 28 days of the anniversary of either its incorporation or the made-up date of the company's previous annual return.

Directors must ensure that minutes are taken at board meetings, giving a record of all decisions taken.

Checklist: practical steps for directors

All directors should:

- ensure that they are fully aware of their duties under CA 2006 and that their board processes reflect these duties;
- check the company's articles of association to establish the scope of their powers;
- ensure that minutes are maintained;
- be alert to conflicts of interest between the company and themselves as individuals;

- always comply with employment law;
- ensure that the company operates a comprehensive system for assessing and minimising health and safety risks;
- keep informed about the company's financial position – ignorance will not save them from facing personal liability in certain circumstances;
- be very clear about what their service agreements require of them – often their obligations in such agreements will be more onerous than their statutory or common law obligations; and
- make sure that the company obtains insurance to protect them against facing personal liability.

Directors' indemnities

Companies are prohibited from exempting a director from any liability he may incur in connection with any negligence, default, breach of duty or breach of trust by him in relation to the company, unless the provision constitutes a 'qualifying third party indemnity provision' (QTPIP). For the indemnity to be a valid QTPIP the director must not be indemnified against:

- liability the director incurs to the company or a group company;
- fines imposed in criminal proceedings or by regulatory bodies such as the FSA;
- legal costs of criminal proceedings where the director is convicted;
- legal costs of civil proceedings brought by the company or a group company, where judgment is given against the director; or
- liability the director incurs in connection with applications under Sections 661 or 1,157 CA 2006 for which the court refuses to grant the director relief.

Companies can therefore indemnify directors against liabilities to third parties, except for legal costs of an unsuccessful defence of criminal proceedings or fines imposed in criminal proceedings or by regulatory bodies.

Companies can pay a director's defence costs as they are incurred, even if the action is brought by the company itself against the director.

The director will, however, be liable to repay all amounts advanced if he is convicted in criminal proceedings or if judgment is given against him in civil proceedings brought by the company or an associated company.

Companies can now also provide slightly wider indemnities to directors of corporate trustees of occupational pension schemes against liability incurred in connection with the company's activities as trustee of the scheme. This is known as a 'qualifying pension scheme indemnity provision' (QPSIP).

A QTPIP or QPSIP must be disclosed in the directors' report in each year that the indemnity is in force and a copy (or summary of its terms) must be available for inspection by shareholders. The QTPIP or QPSIP must also be retained by the company for at least one year after its expiry. Departing directors may also ask for such policies to be retained after their termination as part of exit negotiations.

See also: Bribery, p.49.

Sources of further information

Institute of Directors: www.iod.uk

Health and Safety Executive: www.hse.gov.uk

Disability legislation

Dave Allen and Steve Cooper, BYL Group

Key points

- The DDA and various parts of associated legislation were repealed on 1 October 2010 by the Equality Act 2010.
- The Disability Discrimination Act 1995 (DDA 1995) brought in many rights for disabled people in terms of challenging the discrimination they faced in employment, access to services, transport and education. These rights were subsequently extended by several measures, including the Special Educational Needs and Disability Act 2001 and the Disability Discrimination Act 2005.
- The Equality Act 2010 imposes duties on all those that provide goods and services and public, voluntary and community sector organisations that are aimed at protecting people from discrimination on the basis of protected characteristics (formerly grounds).
- The Act seeks to protect people from discrimination on the grounds of race, sex, sexual orientation, disability, religion or belief, being a transsexual person, having just had a baby, being pregnant, being married or in a civil partnership and age. In effect, everybody will have some form of protection under the Act.
- The Act aims to not only make the existing law stronger in some areas but also to simplify the previous requirements and bring them together in one place.

Legislation

- Equality Act 2010.

Duties

The governing statute is the Equality Act 2010, together with supporting Regulations and Codes of Practice.

Key rights and duties imposed on employers and service providers by the Act are:

- not treating persons covered by the Act less favourably than others;
- not subjecting people to harassment;
- a right to use positive action in recruitment and promotion; and
- a ban on asking job applicants questions about their health or disability until the applicant has been offered a job.

Protection is given to carers from suffering from discrimination or harassment due to their caring duties. The provisions also apply to certain associations that have rules and a selection process for members and have more than 25 members.

A staged implementation of the provisions of the Act was put into place, as the Government has decided not to bring provisions on gender pay gap information, combined discrimination and public sector duties regarding socio-economic inequalities into force, so certain sections remain inactive. The staged implementation is now complete and all of the other provisions are now in force.

Facts

- It is estimated that disabled people spend around £50bn a year on goods and services.
- There are over two million disabled people in employment in the UK.
- Although 79% state that disabled people still face many barriers to museums, libraries and archives, many (67%) agreed that more disabled people use their services than five years ago.
- Among those establishments that were aware of having employed disabled people, 42% felt that there were advantages to doing so. This compared with only 24% of those who were not aware of having employed disabled people.
- Just over one-third of establishments (36%) report a specific approach to actively encouraging the employment of disabled people.
- 78% of disabled people think that the assumption that disabled people need more support from their colleagues and managers prevents employers from employing disabled people.
- 23% of employees think the fact that their company has never employed a disabled person before might prevent their company employing a disabled person.

The parts that came into force on 1 October 2010 make provisions in respect of:

- protection against discrimination, harassment and victimisation;
- protection against discrimination due to a perceived protected characteristic;
- protection against discrimination due to an association with someone with a protected characteristic;
- a new concept of discrimination arising from disability (due to a court ruling on the previous definition);
- protection against indirect discrimination due to disability;
- harmonisation of the thresholds for the duty to make adjustments for disabled people;
- questions about health and disability, which cannot be asked of prospective employees until they have been offered a post;
- protection against harassment for employees;
- pay secrecy clauses – which are unenforceable;
- Employment Tribunals, which have been given powers to make recommendations to benefit the wider workforce;
- claims for gender pay discrimination where there is no comparator;
- sex, religion or belief, pregnancy and maternity and gender reassignment provisions extended to private clubs;
- voluntary positive action provisions;
- application of a uniform definition of indirect discrimination;
- clearer protection for breastfeeding mothers;
- detriment model for victimisation protection; and
- a new definition for gender reassignment.

The parts that came into force in April 2011 make provisions in respect of:

- Duty for Public Sector equality; and
- Positive action for recruitment and promotion.

Premises

A disabled person should not be put at a disadvantage due to the nature of the premises of the organisation. Reasonable steps, which can include the need to make an auxiliary provision, have to be taken to prevent this happening. This can result in the need to make physical changes to the premises and its features or the provision of auxiliary aids.

A person is held to be disabled if they have a physical or mental impairment that has a substantial long-term adverse effect on their ability to carry out normal day-to-day activities. 'Long-term' is considered to be for more than 12 months or for the rest of the person's life. In the case of some impairments, such as cancer and HIV, the person is deemed to be disabled from the point of diagnosis, and some conditions, such as addiction to alcohol and seasonal allergic rhinitis, are not considered to be an impairment.

There is a duty on landlords and managers of let premises (both commercial and residential) to consider requests from a tenant or occupier and to make reasonable changes to the premises and respond to such requests within 42 days. If a response is not received within 42 days the permission is deemed to have been refused and an application to the County Court will be needed. The provisions also extend to the need to consider altering the lease to allow tenants to make alterations within their demise in order to carry out whatever work is needed to meet their obligations. The landlord cannot unreasonably withhold consent but may attach appropriate conditions to the consent, such as requiring the person carrying out the work to apply for statutory approvals and for having his reasonable costs paid. If the landlord refuses permission for the work to be carried out or refuses to alter the lease, an alternative means of meeting the requirement will need to be sought or an application will need to be made to the County Court in respect of the landlord's refusal.

Physical features

Physical features of buildings can create barriers for disabled employees and people who need to access the goods and services of the organisations occupying those premises. The Act places an obligation on the owners and occupiers of buildings to make reasonable adjustments to overcome these barriers. It may not be necessary to remove the feature providing that reasonable means of allowing a disabled person to avoid it can be employed. If this cannot be done then the feature will need to be removed or changed so that it does not create a barrier.

Physical features that fall within this requirement are not just those that form part of the fabric of the building itself: the approach from and exit to the perimeter of the site, furniture, fittings, fixtures, machinery and even colour scheme can all be included for consideration.

The test for discrimination is whether disabled employees or customers are placed at a substantial disadvantage when compared to non-disabled employees or customers. However, in the case of employees there is no requirement to anticipate the needs of future employees, only to accommodate the needs of those currently in employment and to ensure that potential employees are not placed at a disadvantage. In the case of employees the extent to which the employee is willing to cooperate with the adjustments that are to be made can be taken into account.

Providing that the feature being considered was constructed in accordance with the accessibility requirements that existed in Building Regulations at the time of construction there is no need to alter it for up to ten years after it was constructed for people accessing the goods and services on offer. If the feature is being considered in light of the needs of an employee this exemption does not apply.

Auxiliary aids

Reasonable steps, which may depend on the size and resources of and cost to the business or organisation, will need to be taken to ensure that aids are incorporated into the premises to assist disabled people to gain access to the goods and services provided. Examples of aids are induction loops and portable ramps and could include assisting a person in a wheelchair by reaching goods that are too high for them.

See also: Discrimination, p.126; The Equality Act, p.191.

Sources of further information

The Home Office: http://homeoffice.gov.uk/equalities

Equality and Human Rights Commission: www.equalityhumanrights.com

EHRC Disability Equality Duty Code of Practice: www.equalityhumanrights.com/advice-and-guidance/public-sector-duties/guidance-and-codes-of-practice/codes-of-practice/index.html

Cit·i·zen·ship
sit-*uh*-*zuh*n-ship

– noun

the character of an individual viewed as a member of society; behaviour in terms of the duties, obligations, and functions of a citizen

'When the story of these times gets written, we want it to say that we did all we could, and it was more than anyone could have imagined.' Bono

Disciplinary and grievance procedures

Pinsent Masons Employment Group

Key points

- Rules and procedures for handling disciplinary and grievance situations should be set out in writing.
- Disciplinary and grievance policies do not normally form part of the employment contract. However, employers must provide employees with certain information about these policies and this information will often be included in the employment contract or written statement of employment particulars.
- The ACAS Code of Practice on Disciplinary and Grievance Procedures (the ACAS Code – see *Sources of further information*) is intended to help employers and employees resolve disciplinary and grievance issues in the workplace. It applies to misconduct and poor performance issues.
- Unreasonable failure to comply with the ACAS Code may result in compensation being adjusted by up to 25%.
- The statutory disciplinary and grievance procedures, which used to apply to disciplinary and grievance situations, were repealed from 6 April 2009.

Legislation

- Employment Rights Act 1996.

Written procedures

Procedural fairness in the workplace is essential if employers are to avoid falling foul of employment protection laws.

Best practice requires that an employer should have a written procedure to deal with disciplinary and grievance issues, carefully drafted to take into account the advice set out in the ACAS Code.

The written procedure should either be provided to each employee individually or be readily available to them, e.g. on the employer's intranet. The written procedures will commonly be contained in the employee handbook.

The written procedure should be incorporated in such a way as not to be a part of the employment contract, so that it can more easily be changed from time to time. This can be done by making express provision for the employer to amend it.

If the procedure is incorporated in such a way that it does form part of the employment contract, the employee may sue the employer or seek to obtain an injunction or interdict for failure to follow it.

Statement of employment particulars

Every employer is obliged to provide to each employee within two months after the beginning of the employee's employment

Case studies

Sodexho Defence Services Ltd v. Steele (2009)

The claimant was dismissed for gross misconduct for stealing substantial amounts of money. At the end of each day, before the money was bagged up, it was counted by two members of staff in an office in which there was CCTV. Between April and July, about £10,000 went missing and on each occasion the claimant was responsible for bagging up the money.

The investigation carried out by the employer led it to the conclusion that the claimant had turned off the CCTV tape, which recorded the counting and bagging process, since there was footage of the claimant approaching the camera, which then ceased to operate.

The claimant and another employee were both suspended. During the disciplinary hearing, the claimant admitted that she bagged and sealed the money bags. She accepted that she should have kept the tape running, given that she was counting the money at the time.

The Tribunal held that the dismissal was unfair because the employer "wholly irrationally" failed to pursue disciplinary action against the other employee who was cashing up at the time, even though that employee had since left employment.

The EAT overturned this decision and substituted a finding of fair dismissal commenting that "any employer was fully entitled to take the view that the claimant was guilty and the investigation... was entirely adequate".

This case highlights that Tribunals should not substitute their own views for that of employers in disciplinary investigation cases and should instead apply the range of reasonable responses test.

---

a written statement that specifies (among other things):

- any disciplinary rules and any disciplinary or dismissal procedures applicable to the employee (or a reference to a document setting out such rules, which is accessible to the employee);
- a person to whom the employee can apply if dissatisfied with any disciplinary decision;
- a person to whom the employee can apply to seek redress of any grievance; and
- the manner in which any application should be made.

Disciplinary and grievance procedures are generally structured in a tiered system, so that if the grievance is not resolved or there is a recurrence of misconduct or

---

> **Facts**
> - The average employer has had to handle an average of three tribunal applications over the past year.
> - Employers have to manage on average 30 formal disciplinary cases a year and nine grievance cases.
> - Disciplinary and grievance cases take up on average 10.5 days in management, HR staff and in-house lawyers' time, per case.
> - Preparing for a tribunal hearing takes up 12.8 days in human resource, line management and in-house lawyers' time.
> - There has been a slight decrease in the number of Employment Tribunal claims, from 236,100 in 2009/10 to 218,100 in 2010/11.
>
> *Source: CIPD, Tribunals Service.*

continued poor performance, the next step of the procedure is taken.

Grievance procedure

A grievance is a complaint, concern or problem that an employee raises with their employer. Employers should follow the ACAS Code when dealing with grievances.

In a grievance procedure, there will ordinarily be provisions for making several attempts to resolve a grievance. These will start with an informal approach and then lead to a requirement for the grievance to be put in writing and then to a right of appeal.

A failure to raise the grievance in writing does not prevent an employee bringing a subsequent Tribunal claim, based on the grievance, but they may recover less compensation if the failure to do so was unreasonable.

Each attempt to resolve the grievance typically involves a higher level of management for the employee to approach, usually working directly up the line of management responsibilities. On a practical note, when preparing such a procedure, care should be taken to avoid

an open-ended series of hearings coming from the one grievance, which could lead to very senior managers becoming involved.

On the other hand, the procedure should make provision for employees to be sure that their grievance is being considered properly by the employer and not dismissed at a junior manager level. Employees should also be able to bypass a particular manager if that manager is personally involved in the grievance (e.g. where s/he is alleged to have harassed an employee).

Upon receipt of a written grievance, the employer should hold a meeting without unreasonable delay and investigate the complaint. If the matter requires further investigation, the employer should consider adjourning the meeting and resuming it after the investigation has taken place.

The employee is usually entitled to bring a companion (a fellow worker or trade union representative) to the grievance meeting.

Once the employer has come to a decision, it should confirm its decision in writing without unreasonable delay and at the same time tell the employee that they have a right of appeal.

The appeal should be in writing and should (where possible) be heard by someone who has not previously been involved in the matter.

Again, the employee is usually entitled to bring a companion to the appeal meeting. The employer should inform the employee of the result of the appeal without unreasonable delay. If the employee brings a Tribunal claim without appealing, any compensation may be reduced.

Disciplinary procedure

The ACAS Code also applies to disciplinary and dismissal procedures.

Whereas the statutory dismissal and disciplinary procedures (DDPs) applied to dismissal for nearly any reason, the ACAS Code applies only to 'disciplinary situations'. This includes misconduct and poor performance, but excludes dismissals on grounds of redundancy or the non-renewal of a fixed-term contract.

An Employment Tribunal will take account of the provisions of the ACAS Code and the extent to which an employer has complied with them when determining whether a fair procedure was followed and therefore whether a dismissal is unfair.

If an employee brings a successful claim for unfair dismissal or another type of claim (e.g. relating to discrimination, breach of contract, working time, detriment and deduction from wages) arising out of dismissal or disciplinary action for misconduct or poor performance, the level of compensation awarded to the employee can be affected if either party failed to follow the Code. It may go up or down by 25%.

The employer must investigate potential disciplinary issues without unreasonable delay in order to establish the facts. If paid suspension is necessary during the investigation, this should be as brief as possible and kept under review.

The employer should inform the employee of the allegations / issues in writing. Any written evidence, including any witness statements, should normally be given to the employee. The employee should be informed of the time and place of the disciplinary hearing and informed of their right to bring a companion (either a fellow worker or a trade union representative).

At the hearing:

- the employer should explain the allegations and go through the evidence;
- the employee should be allowed to set out their case and answer the allegations; and
- the employee should have a reasonable opportunity to ask questions, present evidence, call witnesses and raise points about information provided by witnesses.

The employer should inform the employee of the decision in writing without unreasonable delay. If misconduct or poor performance is established, a dismissal would usually only be appropriate if a written warning and a final written warning have already been given. Gross misconduct can justify dismissal for a first offence, but not without following the disciplinary procedure.

The employee can appeal (in writing) if they feel that the disciplinary action against them is unjust. The appeal should be heard without unreasonable delay by a manager who (where possible) has not previously been involved. The employee can bring a companion to the appeal hearing. The employer should inform the employee in writing of the result of the appeal as soon as possible. If an employee brings a Tribunal claim without raising an appeal, any compensation may be reduced.

See also: Dismissal, p.146;
Employment disputes, p.168;
Employment Tribunals, p.179;
Mediation, p.300.

Sources of further information

ACAS: www.acas.org.uk

ACAS – Code of Practice on Discipline and Grievance:
www.acas.org.uk/CHttpHandler.ashx?id=1041

Employers should have a clear record of the policy and procedures for disciplinary matters to provide clear guidance to employees on the procedure that will be followed by their employer. Workplace Law's ***Non-Contractual Disciplinary and Grievance Policy and Management Guide v.4.0*** helps employers comply with their obligations and can also act as a checklist for managers, in relation to the steps that should be taken, with a view to minimising procedural irregularities and allegations of unfair treatment. For more information visit www.workplacelaw.net.

Discrimination

Pinsent Masons Employment Group

Key points

- Employment legislation makes it unlawful to discriminate because of sex, gender reassignment, marriage or civil partnership, pregnancy or maternity, race, disability, sexual orientation, religion or belief and age.
- Discrimination will usually be direct or indirect, but can also arise due to harassment and victimisation.
- Workplace managers need to act to avoid discrimination at all stages of employment – job adverts, recruitment, the provision of benefits, terms and conditions of employment, promotion and dismissal – to avoid claims for unlimited compensation being made.
- The Equality Act 2010 harmonises and strengthens existing discrimination laws and makes some significant changes to discrimination law. The majority of the employment provisions are now in force.

Legislation

- Human Rights Act 1998.
- Part time Workers (Prevention of Less Favourable Treatment) Regulations 2000.
- Fixed Term Employees (Prevention of Less Favourable Treatment) Regulations 2002 (as amended).
- Equality Act 2010.

Equality Act

The Equality Act 2010 was passed on 8 April 2010. It has two main purposes – to harmonise discrimination law and to strengthen the law to support progress on equality. The core provisions of the Equality Act came into force on 1 October 2010 and further provisions came into force on 1 April 2011. The Equality Act repealed previous discrimination legislation and brought it under one roof. Most discrimination legislation is now contained in the Equality Act. The Sex, Race and Disability Discrimination and Equal Pay Acts have been repealed in their entirety, and the Sexual Orientation and Religion / Belief Regulations and the Age

Discrimination Regulations have also been revoked. However, the Part-time Workers Regulations and Fixed-term Employees Regulations are untouched by the Act and remain in force.

Overall, the Equality Act harmonises various concepts and irons out previous anomalies, so there is a standard definition of direct discrimination, indirect discrimination, harassment, objective justification, victimisation, occupational requirement, and so on. For the most part, these concepts apply to all of the protected characteristics, although some anomalies remain. For example, indirect discrimination now covers disability and gender reassignment (but not pregnancy and maternity leave); and the job-specific genuine occupational qualifications (which used to apply in relation to sex, gender reassignment and nationality) were removed and replaced with the common occupational requirement defence.

The Equality Act also made some significant changes to the law including:

Facts

- Age discrimination occurs across the age range, although it is most common at the younger and older age ranges, particularly under 25 and over 50. In a recent CIPD survey, 59% of respondents reported that they had been disadvantaged by age discrimination at work.
- Women who work full-time earn 13% less than men who work full-time, based on median hourly earnings, and 17% less based on mean hourly earnings.
- 64% of gay men and lesbians reported experience of sexual orientation discrimination in the workplace. Nine per cent said that this resulted from an instruction or encouragement by a boss.
- There are currently 1.3 million disabled people in the UK who are available for and want to work.
- Only half of disabled people of working age are in work (50%), compared with 80% of non-disabled people.
- 83% of workers claim that the impact of indirect / unintentional discrimination on them was just as damaging as if it had been direct and/or intentional. Consequently, 76% feel that both forms of discrimination should be treated as equally serious.
- The latest statistics from the Employment Tribunal Service reveal that cases of discrimination on the grounds of sex and age have both increased in 2010/11 from 2009/10, with a sharp increase (by nearly a third) in age discrimination cases.

- Prohibiting direct discrimination based on perception and association across all the protected characteristics (except marriage and civil partnership status). This means that a person is able to claim direct discrimination even if they themselves do not have the relevant protected characteristic, but they nevertheless suffer less favourable treatment 'because of a protected characteristic'. This might occur, for example, where a woman is treated less favourably than another employee because of her husband's race or her child's disability. Note that harassment based on perception and association is also prohibited, although (oddly) the harassment provisions do not cover the protected characteristics of pregnancy and maternity or marriage and civil partnership. It is still possible to bring claims related to those characteristics as direct discrimination claims.

- Permitting positive action – this allows an employer to recruit or promote someone from an under-represented or disadvantaged group, where it has a choice between two or more candidates who are 'as qualified as each other'.
- Introducing changes to disability discrimination laws by prohibiting pre-employment health enquiries and introducing two new types of discrimination:
  - Discrimination arising from disability (replacing disability-related discrimination); and
  - Indirect disability discrimination.
- Permitting the Government to pass laws dealing with gender pay reporting. For private sector employers, it contains a power to issue regulations requiring employers

with 250 or more employees to publish pay data to show if there are differences in the pay of male and female employees. The Government has not implemented this provision yet as it prefers to work with businesses to develop a voluntary scheme for gender pay reporting in the private and voluntary sector. Public sector employers are required to publish by 31 December 2011 and annually thereafter information on their gender pay gap, ethnic minority employment rate and disability employment rate.

- Allowing Employment Tribunals to make recommendations that benefit the wider workforce where an employer is found to have discriminated. This compares with the previous position where they could only make a recommendation that benefited the claimant. Although recommendations are not binding, a failure to comply could result in an inference of discrimination in subsequent discrimination proceedings.

- Introducing the right to bring direct discrimination claims based on a combination of two (but no more than two) protected characteristics. (Pregnancy and maternity, and marriage and civil partnership are excluded for these purposes.) This means that a person could claim that they have been discriminated against because they are a black woman. However, a person who brings a 'combined' discrimination claim will still be able to bring claims based on each of the single protected characteristics at the same time. This provision is not yet in force and no date has been set for it to come into force.

For more on the Equality Act, see p.191.

Discrimination – overview
The law prohibits discrimination and harassment on a number of different grounds in all facets of employment, including recruitment, contractual terms, working conditions, promotions, transfers, dismissals and training.

An employer must not discriminate against employees on the basis of sex, gender reassignment, marital or civil partner status, pregnancy or maternity, race, disability, sexual orientation, religion or belief and age.

Discrimination laws protect, among others, agency workers, freelance workers, consultants, partners and directors as well as employees (including former employees and applicants for employment).

Generally, discrimination can be split into four categories – direct, indirect, harassment and victimisation:

Direct
Direct discrimination is based on the concept of less favourable treatment. This is where a decision or action is taken because of a distinctive characteristic – e.g. preferring a male applicant to a female applicant. It is unlawful to discriminate both because of the victim's own characteristics and because of another person's characteristics (for example, discrimination against an employee because of her husband's race). This is often referred to as discrimination based on association or associative discrimination. It is also unlawful to discriminate because of a person's perceived characteristics (for example, discrimination against someone based on a perception, because you think that the individual is older than he or she actually is). The Equality Act 2010 covers direct discrimination based on perception and association across all the protected characteristics (except marriage and civil partnership status).

Case study

Seldon v. Clarkson, Wright and Jakes (2010)

This age discrimination case considered whether a compulsory retirement age of 65 can be objectively justified.

S, a partner at a law firm, was compulsorily retired from the partnership at the end of the year following his 65th birthday in accordance with the partnership deed. S wished to continue working for the firm after his retirement but his proposal was rejected. Following his compulsory retirement he commenced Tribunal proceedings, claiming that he had been directly discriminated against on grounds of age.

The Court of Appeal ruled that an employer can justify direct age discrimination by relying on an employer's individual objectives and self-interest, as long as the objectives are consistent with the Government's approach to the default retirement age. Therefore, in this case, a compulsory retirement age of 65 for partners was potentially justifiable by reference to the partnership's legitimate aims. These were:

- that senior solicitors are given the opportunity of partnership after a reasonable period;
- facilitating workforce planning; and
- creating a congenial and supportive firm culture by limiting the need to expel partners by way of performance management, thus allowing people to retire with dignity.

This case demonstrates that a compulsory retirement age can be justified by reference to workplace planning aims, collegiality and to provide employment prospects for young people. As a result of this case, it is possible that employers may find it possible to justify having a compulsory retirement age, now that the default retirement age has been abolished, if they tread carefully. Employers need to look closely at their need to have a retirement age and then at how to justify it. See '*Retirement*' (p.445).

There is no justification defence in cases of direct discrimination, except in cases of discrimination because of age, part-time worker status, and fixed-term employee status. However, there may be other defences available, such as occupational requirements. For further information on possible defences to direct discrimination, see below.

Indirect

This occurs where a practice that appears to treat people equally nevertheless adversely affects some groups more than others. An employer's apparently neutral provision, criterion or practice (PCP) has the effect of putting a particular group at a disadvantage compared to other groups. For example, where an employer insists on a wide mobility clause in its contract of employment, this could be interpreted as discriminating against women, as they are more likely to be the 'second earner' and therefore less able to relocate. Indirect discrimination is often less easy to spot than direct discrimination.

Indirect discrimination can be justified if the employer is able to show that its PCP meets a legitimate aim (a real business need) and is a proportionate means of achieving it. The burden is on the employer to prove justification, and it is for the Tribunal to decide whether the treatment was justified. The Tribunal must carry out a balancing exercise to evaluate whether the employer's legitimate business needs are sufficient to outweigh the impact on the workforce generally and the claimant in particular, and ask whether the employer's aims could reasonably be achieved by less discriminatory methods.

Harassment

This involves unwanted conduct related to a protected characteristic that has the purpose or effect of violating a person's dignity or creating an offensive, intimidating or hostile environment. Harassment can never be justified.

An employer can also be liable for harassment by third parties (such as customers and suppliers) if the employer fails to take reasonable steps to prevent the third party harassing one of its employees in the course of his/her employment. The employer will only be liable if the employer knows the employee has been harassed in the course of his/her employment on at least two previous occasions by a third party. This applies to all of the discrimination strands (except for pregnancy and maternity, and marriage and civil partnership).

Victimisation

The prohibition on victimisation is intended to ensure that victims and witnesses are not deterred from speaking out against discrimination or harassment for fear of reprisals. Victimisation occurs where an individual is subjected to a detriment because he/she has threatened to bring discrimination proceedings, given evidence or information in connection with such proceedings, or makes some genuinely held allegation of discrimination. For example, a prospective new employer can be liable for victimisation if it refuses to employ someone who has given evidence against a previous employer in a discrimination case. Victimisation can never be justified.

Defences

In addition to the 'justification' defence mentioned above, different exceptions or defences can apply for each discrimination strand to an act of direct or indirect discrimination that is otherwise unlawful (although it is not possible to detail here all the exceptions comprehensively). Exceptions include:

- It may be lawful to discriminate if having a particular characteristic is an occupational requirement and is a proportionate means of achieving a legitimate aim. For example, where being of a particular religion or belief is an occupational requirement for the job in question, it may be lawful for employers to refuse to offer employment to an applicant who is not of that religion or belief. For instance, if the vacancy was for a priest or similar spiritual leader, it would be lawful to refuse employment to a candidate who was not of the relevant faith. Occupational requirement defences are available for most strands of discrimination.
- Where the discrimination is a consequence of a legal requirement or where issues of national security are involved, then discrimination will not be unlawful.

■ Also, employers may not be liable for the discriminatory acts of their employees if they can show that they took such steps as were reasonably practicable to prevent the employee from doing the act. For example, if an employer can show that it has a diversity policy in place, that it makes it employees aware of the policy and its implications, that it regularly trains all its employees in diversity issues and that it deals effectively with complaints under the policy, it may be able to establish the defence.

Burden of proof

Claims for discrimination, harassment and victimisation in employment must be brought in the Employment Tribunals within the relevant time limit. The task of proving a discrimination case lies initially on the claimant. However, once a claimant has established a 'prima facie case', the burden of proof (in most cases) then formally shifts to the respondent employer to prove that its treatment of the claimant was not discriminatory.

Compensation

Employment Tribunals have unlimited scope to compensate affected individuals, not only for pure financial loss but also for injury to feelings. There is no limit to the amount of compensation that can be awarded in a successful case. Such cases can involve significant management time and legal costs, which are usually not recoverable.

Impact of the Human Rights Act 1998

The Human Rights Act 1998 came into force on 2 October 2000 and requires the Courts and Tribunals to interpret UK law in a way that is compatible with the European Convention on Human Rights.

It includes, in Article 9, a right to freedom of conscience, thought or religion. This could widen the scope of the current laws on discrimination on grounds of race or religion or belief.

Further, other relevant provisions provide the right not to be subjected to inhuman or degrading treatment and the right to respect for private life and freedom of expression (which could include the right to wear certain clothes at work, linked to religion).

Moreover, Article 14 of the Convention provides that all of the rights contained within the Convention shall be secured without discrimination on any ground such as sex, race, colour, language, religion, political or other opinion, national or social origin, association with a national minority, property, birth or status. This could potentially widen the concept of discrimination beyond the scope of the discrimination legislation currently in force in the UK. However, the impact of this in the workplace has been fairly limited to date.

Sex discrimination

The Equality Act 2010 prevents direct discrimination, indirect discrimination, harassment and victimisation in all facets of employment.

The Equality Act covers:

■ *Direct discrimination* – Directly treating another person less favourably because of sex. Direct sex discrimination cases often occur where an employer fears that a married woman will want to take time out for a family. The comparison that is used is between the person claiming discrimination and another person with similar skills and qualifications, and the test is generally whether the person would have been treated the same but for his or her sex. Discrimination based on perception and association are also covered.

- *Indirect discrimination* – Whereby a PCP is applied that disadvantages people of a particular sex, without justification. The concept of a PCP is very broad. For example, it may be broad enough to include informal work practices such as a long-hours culture, which would be seen as having a greater impact on women as they tend to have primary childcare responsibilities. Making decisions on the assumption that women will stay at home and men will go out to work is also liable to lead to claims of discrimination. Indirect discrimination will not be unlawful if the employer is able to show that its PCP meets a legitimate aim and is a proportionate means of achieving that aim. It requires an objective balance to be struck between the discriminatory effect of the PCP and the reasonable needs of the employer. So, where female employees are refused requests to return part-time or to job-share after a pregnancy, workplace managers will need to be able to justify why the job has to be done on a full-time basis or by one person.

- *Harassment* – This covers subjecting someone to harassment related to sex (for example, where male workmates place tools on a high shelf to make them hard to reach by a female engineer) or harassment of a sexual nature (such as sexually explicit comments or conduct with sexual overtones).

- *Victimisation* – This covers victimising someone because they have made or intend to make a complaint or allegation or have given evidence against someone else in relation to a complaint of sex discrimination.

- *Discrimination because of gender reassignment* – It is direct discrimination to treat a person less favourably because they intend to

undergo, are undergoing, or have undergone gender reassignment.

- *Discrimination against married people because of their marital or civil partner status* – This covers direct and indirect discrimination against married people of either sex because of their marital or civil partner status. There is no parallel protection for unmarried people. Discrimination based on perception and association are not covered, however.

- *Discrimination because of pregnancy or maternity leave* – If a woman is disadvantaged because she is pregnant or on maternity leave, this will be discriminatory. For example, a female RAF officer won a place on a training programme but she was unable to attend due to pregnancy. The Ministry of Defence (MoD) refused to allow her to attend the same course in the following year, although there would have been no practical difficulty in allowing her to do so. The failure of the MoD to allow her to take the course was found to be directly discriminatory because of pregnancy.

Sex discrimination may be permitted in certain limited circumstances, for example where a person's sex may be an occupational requirement for a job. Examples include where a man or woman is needed for decency or privacy or where for reasons of authenticity or realism being of a particular sex is necessary to perform a particular acting role.

Where discrimination or harassment has been committed by an employee, the employer will usually be liable unless it has taken reasonable steps to prevent such conduct from taking place. The offending employee may also be liable.

Race discrimination
The Equality Act 2010 prohibits direct discrimination, indirect discrimination,

harassment and victimisation in vocational training and all facets of employment. Discrimination is prohibited if it is carried out because of race, i.e. because of colour, race, nationality, ethnic or national origins.

The Equality Act covers:

- *Direct discrimination* – Treating another person less favourably than others because of race. Examples in the context of race discrimination would be not promoting someone because he is Indian or not employing a Sikh because he might not 'fit in' with white workers. Discrimination based on perception and association are also covered.
- *Indirect discrimination* – Applying a PCP that disadvantages people of a particular racial group, without justification. For example, a rule that employees or pupils must not wear headgear could exclude Sikh men and boys who wear a turban, or Jewish men or boys who wear a yarmulke, in accordance with practice within their racial group. The employer would have to justify the need for the rule.
- *Harassment* – This covers subjecting someone to racial harassment. Many of the high awards of compensation in discrimination cases arise out of complaints about harassment. For example in *Yeboah v. Hackney LBC* an award of £380,000 was made to a senior black African employee who suffered a prolonged campaign of harassment.
- *Victimisation* – This covers victimising someone because they have made or intend to make a complaint or allegation or have given evidence against someone else in relation to a complaint of race discrimination. Thus, a white woman who is dismissed for complaining about race discrimination against a black employee can claim victimisation.

Race discrimination may be permitted in certain limited circumstances – for example, if there is an occupational requirement for the worker to be of a particular ethnic origin in order to do the job. Grounds upon which it may be claimed there is an occupational requirement include:

- being of a particular race is a requirement for authenticity in a dramatic performance or other entertainment, or for authenticity purposes as an artist's or photographic model;
- the work is in a place where food or drink is consumed by the public and a particular race of person is required for authenticity (e.g. Chinese or Indian restaurants); or
- the job holder provides his or her racial group with personal services promoting their welfare (e.g. an Afro-Caribbean nursery nurse in an Afro-Caribbean area) where those services can be more effectively provided by a person of that racial group.

Where discrimination or harassment has been committed by an employee, the employer will usually be liable unless it has taken reasonable steps to prevent such conduct from taking place. The offending employee may also be liable.

Disability discrimination

The Equality Act 2010 prohibits discrimination against people with disabilities in terms of services provided to them as members of the public as well as in the field of employment rights.

Workplace managers should take care in avoiding disability discrimination in advertisements, recruitment, terms and conditions of employment, benefits provided to staff, dismissals and victimisation.

The Act prohibits several different types of discriminatory behaviour, of which the third and fourth below have no parallel in other discrimination legislation:

1. Direct discrimination.
2. Indirect discrimination.
3. Discrimination arising from disability.
4. Failure to comply with a duty to make reasonable adjustments.
5. Victimisation.
6. Harassment.

It also prohibits employers from asking pre-employment health questions, except for specific purposes.

Each of these is considered independently below.

Direct discrimination

This occurs where an employer treats a disabled person less favourably because of disability than he would a person not having that disability. For example, direct discrimination will occur where an employer fails to employ a person because he has a facial disfigurement (which amounts to a disability) solely because he will be uncomfortable working with him. Discrimination based on perception and association are also covered.

Indirect discrimination

This occurs where persons sharing the same disability as the claimant are put at a particular disadvantage by a PCP applied by the employer. Indirect discrimination can be justified where the employer is able to show that its PCP meets a legitimate aim (a real business need) and is a proportionate means of achieving it. For example, an employee with depression might argue that their employer's absence management policy indirectly discriminates and the employer would then need to justify why it could no longer support the employee's absence.

Discrimination arising from disability

It is unlawful to treat someone unfavourably 'because of something arising in consequence of' their disability, for example their sickness absence.

It is not necessary to consider how a comparator would have been treated. An employer is able to justify the treatment where it is a proportionate means of achieving a legitimate aim. The Act makes it clear that an employer will not be liable if it did not know, and could not reasonably be expected to have known, of the disability. An example of where discrimination arising from a disability might occur is where an employer dismisses an employee who has been off sick for a long time – in such a case the reason for the treatment is the sickness (which arises from the disability) but is not the disability itself. The employer would then need to justify its decision to dismiss by showing that it was a proportionate means of achieving a legitimate aim.

Failure to comply with a duty to make reasonable adjustments

This occurs where an employer fails to make 'reasonable adjustments' to the physical nature of its premises or to any PCP to ensure that disabled people are not placed at a substantial disadvantage, or fails to take reasonable steps to provide an auxiliary aid where this would avoid the employee being placed at a substantial disadvantage. Failure to make a reasonable adjustment will constitute discrimination. The only defence is that the adjustment was not a reasonable one to make, although the duty does not apply where the employer does not know and could not reasonably be expected to know of the employee's disability. Factors that may be taken into account in assessing the reasonableness of the adjustment include:

- how effective the step will be in ameliorating the disadvantage and the practicability of taking the step;
- the costs to the employer of making the adjustment and the financial and other resources available to the employer; and/or
- the nature of the employer's activities and the size of the undertaking.

Examples of what may be regarded as reasonable adjustments are:

- changing building structure (e.g. by introducing ramps, lowering switches or panels, moving doors and widening entrances) – but remember most people affected by the Equality Act are not in a wheelchair;
- permitting different working hours (e.g. to deal with tiredness or medical treatments);
- providing specialist or modified equipment (e.g. computer screens or adapted / different chairs); and
- providing training (e.g. for use of specialist equipment or extra training for someone whose disability may make him/her slower).

Victimisation

This is subjecting a person to a detriment because they have threatened to bring disability discrimination proceedings, given evidence or information in connection with such proceedings, or made some genuinely held allegation of disability discrimination.

Harassment

It is unlawful to harass an employee for a reason relating to disability, by engaging in unwanted conduct that has the purpose or effect of violating the person's dignity, or creating an intimidating, hostile, degrading, humiliating or offensive environment for him or her.

The case of *Coleman v. Attridge Law* held that where a person is discriminated

against because of their association with a disabled person, rather than because of their own disability, they are protected because the discrimination law was interpreted as extending to associative discrimination. This applies equally to harassment under the Equality Act.

Pre-employment health questions

The Act prohibits an employer from asking questions about a job applicant's health before offering them work or before including them in a pool of candidates from whom a post will be filled when a vacancy arises. The purpose is to prevent disabled candidates being screened out without being given the chance to show they have the skills and competencies for the job. It was also thought that pre-employment health questionnaires deter disabled people from applying for a job in the first place.

Employers may still make health-related enquiries where they are necessary:

- to establish whether the job applicant will be able to comply with the requirement to undergo an assessment (e.g. an interview or selection test) to test their suitability for the work;
- to determine whether the employer has a duty to make reasonable adjustments in respect of the interview and recruitment process;
- to establish whether a candidate will be able to carry out a function intrinsic to the work concerned;
- to monitor diversity in applications for jobs;
- to enable the employer to take positive action (see above); and
- to establish whether a job applicant has a particular disability, where having a disability is an occupational requirement.

Simply asking a question about health will not amount to disability discrimination but could lead to an Employment Tribunal drawing an inference of discrimination requiring the employer to prove that no discrimination has in fact occurred. However, the EHRC will be able to investigate the use of prohibited questions and take enforcement action, even where no discrimination can be shown to have taken place.

Meaning of 'disability'

There are no duties or liabilities to an individual if there is no 'disability' as defined in the legislation. It is therefore important that there is an understanding that not all medical conditions constitute disability.

For a disability to exist, there needs to be a physical or mental impairment that has a substantial and long-term adverse effect (i.e. lasts or is likely to last, 12 months, or is likely to recur) on the person's ability to carry out 'normal day-to-day activities'.

In 2005, the definition of disability was extended to cover people with cancer, multiple sclerosis and HIV from the date of diagnosis.

The EHRC Code of Practice on Employment provides guidance and there is also guidance, issued by the Secretary of State, on matters to be taken into account in determining questions relating to the definition of disability, to which workplace managers should refer. See Sources of further information.

Schizophrenia, claustrophobia, epilepsy, back injuries, depression, blindness, arm pains and dyslexia have all been found to constitute 'disabilities'. However, each of these cases has been decided on the level of disability of an individual.

The legislation is very specific on the subject of substance abuse, and excludes

alcohol, nicotine or substance dependency as a disability. Again, however, caution is needed as the effects of the abuse could result in physical disabilities (e.g. liver damage), which would be covered by the law.

If an employee is ill, particularly where that illness is long-term and a dismissal is contemplated, the disability discrimination legislation needs to be considered carefully and specialist advice taken as this area is fraught with potential issues.

Sexual orientation discrimination

The EC Equal Treatment Framework Directive sets out an anti-discrimination 'principle of equal treatment' in the context of sexual orientation, and this is now implemented through the Equality Act 2010.

'Sexual orientation' covers orientation towards persons of the same sex (gays and lesbians), the opposite sex (heterosexuals), and the same and opposite sex (bisexuals).

The Act prevents direct discrimination, indirect discrimination, harassment and victimisation in all facets of employment:

■ *Direct discrimination* – Less favourable treatment than others because of their actual or perceived sexual orientation or because of association. For example, while being interviewed, a job applicant says that she has a same-sex partner. Although she has all the skills and competencies required of the job holder, the organisation decides not to offer her the job because she is a lesbian.
■ *Indirect discrimination* – Whereby a PCP is applied that disadvantages people of a particular sexual orientation and which is not objectively justified as a proportionate means

of achieving a legitimate aim. An example would be that a policy or practice aimed at employees with children would put homosexual employees at a particular disadvantage if it could be shown that they were less likely than heterosexual employees to have children. The employer would then have to show that the policy or practice favouring employees with children was a proportionate means of achieving a legitimate aim.

- *Harassment* – Conduct related to sexual orientation that violates dignity or creates an intimidating, hostile, degrading, humiliating or offensive environment. An example in a sexual orientation context is that a male worker who has a same-sex partner is continually referred to by female nicknames, which he finds humiliating and distressing.

- *Victimisation* – This would be subjecting a person to a detriment because of something done in connection with the Act. For example, a worker gives evidence for a colleague who has brought an Employment Tribunal claim against the organisation of discrimination because of sexual orientation. When that worker applies for promotion her application is rejected even though she is able to show she has all the necessary skills and experience. Her manager maintains she is a 'troublemaker' because she had given evidence at the Tribunal and therefore should not be promoted.

Exceptions may be made in very limited circumstances:

- If there is an occupational requirement for the worker to be of a particular sexual orientation in order to do the job. For example, an organisation advising on and promoting gay rights may be able to show that it is essential to the credibility of its chief executive, who will be the public face of the organisation, that they should be gay. The sexual orientation of the holder of that post may therefore be an occupational requirement.

- Where the employment is for purposes of an organised religion an employer may apply a requirement relating to sexual orientation for limited specified reasons, such as the leader of a faith or of an establishment such as a mosque or temple, for example in order to comply with doctrines of the religion.

- On the grounds of national security or positive action.

Where discrimination or harassment is made out an employer may not be held liable if it has taken reasonable steps to prevent such conduct from taking place.

Religion or belief discrimination

The EC Equal Treatment Framework Directive sets out an anti-discrimination 'principle of equal treatment' in the context of religion or belief and this is now implemented through the Equality Act 2010.

The Act prevents direct discrimination, indirect discrimination, harassment and victimisation in all facets of employment.

The Act defines religion or belief as meaning 'any religion, or religious or philosophical belief'. Non-believers have the same rights as believers under the Act.

The Act prohibits:

- *Direct discrimination* – Less favourable treatment than others because of religion or belief. For example, at interview it becomes apparent that a job applicant is a Hindu. Although the applicant has all the skills and competencies required of the job, the organisation decides not to offer him the job because he is a Hindu.

Discrimination based on perception and association are also covered.

- *Indirect discrimination* – Whereby a PCP is applied that disadvantages people of a particular religion or belief and which is not objectively justified as a proportionate means of achieving a legitimate aim. Research conducted by the Home Office suggests that the most common areas where employers may be required to accommodate religious observance and practice in order to avoid indirect discrimination are dress codes, break policies, recruitment and job applications, flexible work schedules, leave for religious holidays and social and training events.

- *Harassment* – This covers conduct related to religion or belief that violates dignity or creates an intimidating, hostile, degrading, humiliating or offensive environment. For example, an employee is continually teased about her partner's religious convictions. She finds such teasing to be distressing and offensive and complains to her line manager who fails to address the matter, claiming it to be harmless banter. The employee has a potential claim for harassment on the grounds of religion or belief, even though it is not her own religion or belief that it the subject of the teasing.

- *Victimisation* – This covers subjecting a person to a detriment because of something done in connection with the Act. A common example is where someone is disciplined at work or is merely passed over for promotion because they have raised a complaint against their employer in the Employment Tribunal. It is not necessary that proceedings have been brought. Informal complaints of unlawful discrimination made to management, or the provision of information supporting such complaints, will suffice.

Exceptions may be permitted in certain limited circumstances:

- If there is an occupational requirement for the worker to be of a particular religion or belief having regard to the nature or context of the work.

- To comply with the religious- or belief-based ethos of the organisation. For example, a faith-based care home may be able to show that being of a particular faith is a genuine requirement of its carers because they are required to carry out their duties in a manner that fulfils both the physical and spiritual needs of its patients. However, they may not be able to justify a similar requirement for their maintenance or reception staff whose jobs do not require them to provide spiritual leadership or support to the patients.

- Special rules apply if the job is for a head teacher in a denominational school.

- Special rules apply to Sikhs working on building sites, as Sikh men are exempted from the requirement to wear safety helmets while on a construction site.

- 'Positive action' may be permitted in the form of targeted advertising or training to address existing inequalities or to allow an employer to recruit or promote someone from an under-represented or disadvantaged group, where it has a choice between two or more candidates who are 'as qualified as each other'.

- Cases involving national security.

Where discrimination or harassment has been committed by an employee, the employer will usually be liable unless it has taken reasonable steps to prevent such conduct from taking place. The offending employee may also be liable.

Age discrimination

Age legislation is required to comply with the EC Equal Treatment Framework

Directive and this is implemented in the UK through the Equality Act 2010.

The Act prevents direct discrimination, indirect discrimination, harassment and victimisation in vocational training and all facets of employment. It covers employees, applicants for employment and former employees. The Equality Act prohibits:

- *Direct discrimination* – Where a person is treated less favourably because of age without objective justification. For example, setting an upper and lower age limit for a particular job (whether formally or informally) may be direct discrimination against a person outside the age band. Discrimination based on association and perception is also covered. Age discrimination is one of only a few cases where direct discrimination may be justified (*see below*).

- *Indirect discrimination* – Where a PCP has a greater impact on workers in one age group compared to those in another and is not objectively justified. These are not always easy to spot because there is no overt less favourable treatment – everyone appears to be treated the same. However, restricting a post to 'recent graduates' is likely to discriminate indirectly against a worker over 30, since most recent graduates are likely to be in their 20s.

- *Harassment* – Where a person is subjected to unwanted conduct related to age that has the purpose or effect of violating their dignity or creating an intimidating, hostile, degrading, humiliating or offensive environment. Examples of this include intentional bullying, but it can also be unintentional, subtle and insidious, e.g. nicknames, teasing, inappropriate jokes that are not malicious in intent, but that are upsetting. Harassing behaviour may be targeted at an individual or may consist of a general culture that appears to tolerate, for example, the telling of ageist jokes. Harassment is judged from the perception of the victim, although unintentional harassment is subject to the test of reasonableness.

- *Victimisation* – An employee who complains in good faith of alleged age discrimination or harassment, or who supports another employee in such a complaint, must not be subjected to a detriment because they have complained / supported a complaint. Employees are protected from acts of victimisation even if the complaint turns out not to be upheld.

Unusually, the age discrimination laws permit employers to justify objectively both direct and indirect discrimination. However, this is not straightforward. The law says that an employer must be pursuing a 'legitimate aim' (for example, encouraging loyalty, rewarding experience, employment planning or maintaining health and safety) and the means of pursuing the same must be 'proportionate'. In practice, this means that the benefit of a discriminatory practice to an employer must be sufficient to outweigh the discriminatory effect. If there are two ways of achieving a similar aim, the less discriminatory way must be chosen.

Age discrimination may be permitted in certain limited circumstances:

- An employer might be able to rely on an occupational requirement for an employee to possess a characteristic related to age. A characteristic related to age could be wrinkles, baldness, greying hair or (in the case of men) an unbroken voice. This provision will be relevant for acting jobs.
- 'Positive action' might be allowed in the form of targeted advertising or training to address existing inequalities or to allow an employer to recruit or promote someone from an

under-represented or disadvantaged group, where it has a choice between two or more candidates who are 'as qualified as each other'.

- An employer might be able to award benefits based on length of service and may be able to cease insurance cover at age 65 or state pension age, if higher, for example private medical insurance or permanent health insurance.
- Cases involving national security.

Default retirement age

The default retirement age (DRA), which allowed employers to compulsorily retire employees at or over the age of 65 was abolished with effect from 6 April 2011. However, provisions were put in place to allow retirements which were already underway to continue.

However, the abolition of the DRA does not prevent employers from having a compulsory retirement age, as long as they have legitimate aims for having one – in relation to those employees to whom it applies – and both the chosen retirement age and the process for implementing it are a proportionate means of achieving those legitimate aims. See 'Retirement' (p.445).

See also: Carers, p.64; Disability legislation, p.116; Employment Tribunals, p.179; Equal pay, p.184; Equality Act, p.191; HIV and AIDS, p.234; Part-time workers, p.382; Pregnancy and maternity, p.400; Recruitment and selection, p.420; Retirement, p.445; Stress, p.500.

Sources of further information

Equality and Human Rights Commission: www.equalityhumanrights.com

Government Equalities Office: www.equalities.gov.uk/equality_act_2010.aspx

The EHRC Code of Practice on Employment: www.equalityhumanrights.com/uploaded_files/EqualityAct/employercode.pdf

Guidance on matters to be taken into account in determining questions relating to the definition of disability: www.equalityhumanrights.com/uploaded_files/EqualityAct/odi_equality_act_guidance_may.pdf

Equal Opportunities policies are becoming ever more important in today's increasingly multicultural, multiracial society. The purpose of Workplace Law's **Equal Opportunities Policy and Management Guide v.4.0** is to set out the obligations on both the employer and the employee to treat all people with equal dignity and respect within the workplace. The aim is to create a pleasant and harmonious working environment for all.

The Policy sets out and explains the rights of each employee. A well-drafted Equal Opportunities policy combined with good management will ensure your organisation meets its legal obligation to provide a non-discriminatory work environment and persuade employees that an equal opportunities policy at work is for the benefit of the whole workforce. For more information visit www.workplacelaw.net.

Case review

Accommodating faith – what is reasonable?

Amanda Trewhella, Pitmans

Discrimination on the grounds of religion or belief has been a hot topic in employment law recently. Despite the fact relatively few discrimination claims are brought on these grounds (880 in the year to March 2011 out of 218,100 claims accepted by the Employment Tribunals) they gain substantial media interest.

Many recent cases involve indirect discrimination on the grounds of religion or belief, where the employer is seeking to show that a religiously discriminatory provision, criteria or practice is objectively justified, in relation to areas such as dress code, food and time off for prayers and religious holidays.

Cherfi v. G4S Security Services Limited (2010)

Mr Cherfi worked as a security guard for G4S from 2005 and, as a Muslim, would regularly leave the site on Friday lunchtimes in order to attend Friday prayers at a local Mosque.

In October 2008 G4S was informed by its client that it must have a minimum number of security guards on duty at all times or would be at risk of losing the contract.

Mr Cherfi was therefore informed that he could no longer leave the site on Friday lunchtimes. In order to accommodate Mr Cherfi's religion, G4S gave him alternative options. It suggested that he use an on-site prayer room, or gave him the option of working a Monday to Thursday

Amanda Trewhella is a solicitor who has been part of Pitmans' employment team since 2009. Amanda is an employment law specialist with experience of advising on all aspects of the employment relationship, from recruitment and the drafting of HR policies and employee handbooks through to advising on business reorganisations, disciplinary and grievance procedures and drafting and negotiating compromise agreements and severance packages. She has advised on the bringing and defending of a variety of Employment Tribunal claims, including unfair dismissal, breach of contract, flexible working, whistleblowing and discrimination claims.

pattern or to work Saturdays or Sundays instead of Fridays. However, Mr Cherfi did not wish to use these alternative options.

Instead Mr Cherfi stopped working Fridays, by taking them as sick leave, annual leave or authorised unpaid leave and in March 2009 G4S informed Mr Cherfi that the arrangement could not continue.

Mr Cherfi claimed indirect religious discrimination on the basis that G4S was requiring him to remain on-site during Friday lunchtimes which placed him, as a Muslim, at a particular disadvantage.

The Tribunal held that, although Mr Cherfi was placed at a disadvantage by not being allowed to attend Friday prayers, the requirement that he must remain on-site was a proportionate means of achieving the legitimate aim of meeting the operational needs of the business.

The Tribunal found that:

- G4S would suffer financial penalties and be at risk of losing the client contract if it failed to ensure that the requisite number of security guards were on site.
- Given this, G4S could only run its business properly and on a sound financial basis by engaging security guards workings shifts of at least eight hours.
- G4S had offered Mr Cherfi weekend work so that he would not suffer financially if he chose not to work on Fridays. It had not pressured him into working weekends.
- Although the provision preventing Mr Cherfi from attending prayers in congregation, there was a prayer room available to him on-site.

When Mr Cherfi appealed to the Employment Appeal Tribunal, the EAT upheld the Tribunal's decision and stated (obiter) that an employer can rely upon cost alone to justify a policy which may otherwise be held to be discriminatory.

Dhinsa v. Serco and another (2009)
Mr Dhinsa was a trainee prison officer at a prison run by Serco. Mr Dhinsa is an Amritdhari (or baptised) Sikh and is therefore required by his religion to wear a kirpan, which is a small, ceremonial knife or dagger warn in a sheath under clothing.

The Prison Service policy bans the wearing of a kirpan, except for Sikh chaplains, and Mr Dhinsa was informed of this shortly after his training.

Serco suggested alternative ways to accommodate Mr Dhinsa's religion. It suggested that he wear a replica kirpan or temporarily work in the gatehouse, to which the ban may have been temporarily disapplied.

When Mr Dhinsa refused to remove his kirpan he was dismissed and brought claims for indirect race and religion discrimination, which were rejected by the Employment Tribunal.

In relation to the religious discrimination claim, the Tribunal agreed that the ban from wearing a kirpan did put Amritdhari Sikhs at a particular disadvantage when compared with other employees. However, it found this to be a proportionate means of achieving the legitimate aim of securing the safety of staff, prisoners and visitors.

The factors that the Tribunal took into account were:

- There was no breach of Article 9 of the European Convention on Human Rights – the right to freedom of religion. It has been established in case law that where a person is free to find alternative work which is compatible with their religious view there is no breach of Article 9.
- The overall discriminatory impact of the ban was small; it affected only 10% of the Sikh group and only two Sikhs within the prison service had been adversely affected.
- Statistics from 2008 showed nearly 16,000 assaults in prisons, of which

over 3,000 were against staff and over 200 with a knife or blade. This was a medium security prison holding a number of violent offenders, and the consequences of assault with a kirpan could be serious if not fatal.

- Although the Prison Service allows Sikh chaplains to carry kirpans, they are in a very different role to prison officers, and are seen more as father figures. As such, they are unlikely to come into conflict with prisoners.
- Ligature knives, which are used in the event of a prisoner trying to hang himself, are the only knives permitted to be carried by prison officers. They are attached to the prison officer by a chain, and their design makes them virtually impossible to be used as a weapon.
- Although some prisoners have access to other tools that may be used as weapons, these are strictly controlled.
- There is a public interest in ensuring public confidence in the prison system, especially prison security and the safety of visitors and staff.
- Serco did not apply the policy 'blindly' but had spoken to another prison and a police constabulary about their approach to the kirpan, had discussed the possibility of temporary alternative work with Mr Dhinsa, and had sought clarification from representatives of the Prison Service as to what solutions (if any) might be available.
- To have breached the policy would have resulted in a financial penalty as well as undermining their own credibility as a contracted out service provider of prison services.

This case is a good example of where the Tribunal has carried out a thorough balancing act to assess whether the provision in question was proportionate.

Ladele v. London Borough of Islington (2009)
Ms Ladele was a registrar employed by the Council. She refused to carry out civil partnership ceremonies because same-sex relationships are against her religious views, as a Christian.

Ms Ladele had disciplinary action taken against her and was found to be guilty of gross misconduct on the basis that her actions breached the Council's 'Dignity For All' policy and was discriminatory against the gay community.

Ms Ladele brought a claim for religious discrimination, which failed. The Tribunal held that the Council had a legitimate aim in providing effective services relating to civil partnerships and that, as a public authority employer, it was committed to promoting equal opportunities.

Ms Ladele appealed to the EAT and then the Court of Appeal, which approved the Tribunal's decision in that, having established that providing a non-discriminatory service was a legitimate aim, the Council was entitled to require all registrars to perform the full range of civil partnership services.

Ms Ladele has now appealed to the European Court of Human Rights and a decision is awaited.

McFarlane v. Relate Avon Ltd (2009)
Mr McFarlane, a Christian, was a counsellor with Relate, and similarly to Ms Ladele, refused to counsel couples in a single-sex relationship.

When Mr McFarlane was dismissed and brought a claim for religious discrimination the Employment Appeal Tribunal held that it was not necessary for Relate to show that it had considered all other possible ways of achieving its legitimate aim of providing the full range of counselling services to all sectors of the public. Mr McFarlane's claim therefore failed.

Mr McFarlane has also appealed to the European Court of Human Rights together with Ms Ladele and a decision is awaited.

These two cases show that if an employee refuses to comply with principles that are fundamental to the employer's ethos, the employer does not have to compromise those principles by making or considering arrangements to accommodate the employee's request.

In these types of case, it appears that a balancing exercise between the employer's need and the employee's individual rights is not the appropriate test where the belief involves discrimination against other individuals with a characteristic protected by the discrimination legislation under the Equality Act 2010.

Eweida v. British Airways Plc (2010)
Miss Eweida is a Christian who wished to wear a two-inch high cross on a necklace visibly as a symbol of her faith. However, British Airway's dress code for uniformed staff forbade the wearing of visible jewellery.

The policy stated that *'any accessory or clothing item that the employee is required to have for mandatory religious reasons should at all times be covered up by the uniform'*, unless this is *'impossible to do given the nature of the item and the way it is to be worn'*. Therefore, for example, Muslim hijabs and Sikh turbans were allowed to be on show, but Sikh bangles were required to be hidden by sleeves, unless the uniform was short-sleeved.

Miss Ewieda claimed indirect religious discrimination. The Employment Tribunal dismissed her claim on the basis that the policy did not put Christians at a particular disadvantage. It was decided that the wearing of a cross was a personal decision of Miss Ewieda and was not a requirement of Christian faith or scriptures, according to a number of Christian witnesses and the views of the Christian Fellowship.

The Court of Appeal upheld the Tribunal's decision because Miss Eweida had failed to provide evidence of other Christians who felt disadvantaged because they could not openly wear the cross. Therefore she failed to show the necessary degree of group disadvantage.

Miss Eweida has now appealed to the European Court of Human Rights and a decision is awaited.

Azmi v. Kirklees Metropolitan Borough Council (2007)
Mrs Azmi was a bilingual support worker in a junior school. Mrs Azmi is Muslim and wore a veil which covered her head and face except her eyes when in the presence of adult males. She did not, however, wear the veil during her interview, nor when she attended training prior to the commencement of her job, and she did not advise the school that she wished to wear a veil.

Mrs Azmi was asked to remove the veil while she was teaching as the head teacher at the school, who observed her when teaching, concluded that pupils could not obtain the visual clues they needed because they could not see her facial expressions. Also, Mrs Azmi's diction was not as clear or loud as it would have been without her veil. When she refused to remove the veil she was suspended.

Mrs Azmi claimed direct and indirect religious discrimination, but failed in her claims. The Employment Appeal Tribunal held that the instruction to remove her veil while teaching was a proportionate means of achieving the legitimate aim of providing the best quality education to the children.

Williams v. Five Rivers Child Care Consortium Limited (2005)

Mr Williams was a classroom carer who did not eat pork for religious reasons. The Claimant brought a claim for religious discrimination because pork was served on the menu in the kitchen, and he claimed that there was a lack of choice provided that was appropriate to his religion.

Mr Williams was unsuccessful in his claim, the Tribunal finding that the serving of pork together with an appropriate alternative was an appropriate means of achieving the legitimate aim of the employer's need to provide a varied menu at reasonable cost.

Fugler v. MacMillan-London Hairstudios Limited (2004)

Mr Fugler was a Jewish employee who requested a day's holiday from his employer for Yom Kippur, which fell on a Saturday that year. Given that Saturday was the busiest day for the hair salon, Mr Fugler was refused holiday on that day.

The Employment Tribunal found that this provision put Jewish people at a disadvantage, and that the employer was not justified in refusing Mr Fugler's request, as they had failed to consider whether its staffing needs could have been met in some other way on this occasion.

It appears from the cases that it can be fairly easy for employers to justify not being able to accommodate employees in terms of their religious beliefs, provided they can show an objective reason.

The Equality and Human Rights Commission (EHRC) has made an application to intervene in two cases going before the European Court of Human Rights – Nadia Eweida and Shirley Chaplin against the United Kingdom and Lillian Ladele and Gary McFarlane against the United Kingdom.

EHRC believes that the law in this area has been interpreted too narrowly and that the courts have set the bar too high for individuals to prove discrimination, with the result that freedom of religion or belief is being compromised.

The EHRC has suggested that clearer legal principles and the provision of 'reasonable accommodations' for workers wishing to manifest their religion or belief would help employers to determine what can be justifiable in religion or belief cases, and avoid the need to resort to litigation.

The decision of the European Court of Human Rights is awaited.

Dismissal

Pinsent Masons Employment Group

Key points

- Employers must give employees adequate notice in accordance with their contract of employment in order not to breach the contract and become liable for wrongful dismissal.
- Regardless of whether there is a breach of contract, dismissals will be unfair unless:
  - the dismissal is for one of a list of five potentially fair reasons allowed by law;
  - the employer acts reasonably in dismissing the employee; and
  - the employer has followed a fair procedure.
- In some circumstances, the ACAS Code of Practice on Disciplinary and Grievance Procedures must be complied with. If it is not, and an employee wins an Employment Tribunal case, Employment Tribunals have discretion to increase awards by up to 25% where the employer unreasonably fails to comply with the Code.

Legislation

- Employment Rights Act 1996.
- National Minimum Wage Act 1998.
- Working Time Regulations 1998.
- The Equality Act 2010.

What is dismissal?

A number of key employment law rights arise when a 'dismissal' takes place.

Dismissal is an act of the employer that occasions a termination of the employment relationship.

For a dismissal to be lawful, an employer must have a reason allowed by law, follow the correct procedure and, if necessary, give adequate notice. If this is not done, it is likely to lead to a claim for unfair and/or wrongful dismissal.

A resignation – although an act of the employee, not the employer – can also constitute a 'constructive dismissal' where it is in response to a fundamental breach of contract by the employer.

Dismissal can also include the expiry and non-renewal of a fixed-term contract.

Employees have the right to be provided with a written statement setting out the reasons for their dismissal under Section 92(1) of the Employment Rights Act 1996 (ERA), and this document may be used in evidence in any subsequent Tribunal proceedings.

Notice

Dismissal by an employer can be with or without notice. The amount of notice required will usually be set out in the employment contract and a contract of employment can be for a fixed term or for an indefinite period. If the contract is for an indefinite period, the contract should also contain provisions relating to the period of notice to be given by the employer or the employee. If the contract of employment is silent about the notice period, 'reasonable' notice must be given, the length of which will vary depending on the employee's circumstances and industry norms.

In any event, the following statutory minimum notice must be given by an employer:

- An employee who has been continuously employed for one month or more but less than two years is entitled to not less than one week's notice.
- An employee who has been continuously employed for two years or more but less than 12 years is entitled to one week's notice for each year of continuous employment.
- An employee who has been employed for 12 years or more is entitled to not less than 12 weeks' notice.

These minima will override any agreement to a shorter notice period. However, the parties may agree to notice periods longer than the statutory minimum.

Generally, once notice has been given it cannot be withdrawn, save by mutual consent.

The employer may make a payment in lieu of notice if it wishes to do so and if the contract provides for it. Payment in lieu of notice clauses (commonly referred to as 'PILON' clauses) are attractive for employers as they provide for a swift termination of the employment relationship, given that the employer will often not wish to have the employee serve out a notice period for reasons related to the protection of goodwill. PILON clauses work on the principle that an employee will be content to agree to early termination, provided that the employee receives the remuneration to which the employee would otherwise be entitled.

Failure by an employer to give notice in accordance with the terms of the contract will leave the employer liable to pay damages for wrongful dismissal to the employee in respect of salary and other benefits that would have fallen due in the notice period. If there is a PILON clause in the employee's contract, there will be no breach of contract if notice money is paid instead of the employee working out his notice.

The tax treatments of these two types of payment are different. As the PILON payment is contractual, the employee will be liable for income tax, whereas the former is treated as damages and may generally be free of tax up to £30,000.

Serious or gross misconduct can justify summary dismissal of an employee, i.e. immediate dismissal of an employee without notice. What constitutes gross misconduct may vary according to the particular circumstances of the employer and the work the employee is carrying out. Acts of gross misconduct, such as theft, fraud, physical violence, serious negligence or serious breach of health and safety regulations, will result in a serious breach of contractual terms, and examples of such conduct will usually be given in an organisation's disciplinary procedure.

Unfair dismissal

For a dismissal to be lawful an employer must have a reason allowed by law, follow the correct procedure and, if necessary, give adequate notice. If this is not done, it is likely to lead to a claim for unfair or wrongful dismissal.

Save for certain special cases (see below), employees must have one year's continuous service (at the date the dismissal takes effect) in order to have the right to claim that they have been unfairly dismissed (although see below for recent changes). A fair dismissal has two elements:

1. The employer's reason to dismiss must be one of a list of potentially fair reasons (Section 98(1), ERA).

2. Even if a fair reason exists, it must have been reasonable in all the circumstances for the employer to dismiss the employee (Section 94(4) ERA). In other words, the employer must follow a fair procedure.

Potentially fair reasons for dismissal

- *Lack of capability or qualifications.* Capability is skill and ability to do the job. This is most often relevant for poor performance or physical incapability such as injury or sickness. Lack of qualifications could involve a practical qualification necessary to do the job, which may be lost during employment (e.g. a driver losing a driving licence).
- *Conduct.* In other words, misconduct on the part of the employee.
- *Redundancy.* For the purposes of the ERA, an employee who is dismissed shall be taken to be dismissed by reason of redundancy if the dismissal is wholly or mainly attributable to the fact that his employer has ceased or intends to cease to carry on the business for the purposes of which the employee was employed by him, or to carry on that business in the place where the employee was so employed, or where the requirements of that business for employees to carry out work of a particular kind, or for employees to carry out work of a particular kind in the place where the employee was employed by the employer, have ceased or diminished or are expected to cease or diminish.
- *Continued employment would breach legislation.* For example where, if the employment continued, either the employer or the employee would be in breach of health and safety laws.
- *'Some other substantial reason'.* In some ways this is a catch-all to allow Tribunals to respond to the circumstances of individual cases. It can cover a multitude of cases

including dismissals by reason of a reorganisation, and dismissals in order to effect changes in terms and conditions of employment.

Having determined that a potentially fair reason exists for the dismissal, the employer must be able to show that it has acted reasonably in all the circumstances in dismissing the employee for that reason. Has the employer followed a fair and proper procedure? This involves taking into consideration different factors depending on the reason for the dismissal (*see below*). Tribunals will take account of the size and administrative resources of the employer when determining whether the employer acted reasonably. The question of fairness is closely linked to disciplinary procedures and the need to follow a fair procedure in disciplining and dismissing the employee.

What is appropriate in terms of procedure will vary, depending on the reason for the dismissal. The employer must follow a fair and reasonable procedure and the Tribunal will look at whether the decision to dismiss the employee and the procedures followed fell within the band of reasonable responses expected of reasonable employers.

Note: On 3 October 2011 the Government announced the qualification period for the right to claim unfair dismissal will be extended from one to two years as of 1 April 2012. It claims this will see the number of unfair dismissal claims drop by around 2,000 a year.

Some key procedural points that workplace managers should follow for the most common dismissals are as follows.

Capability
- Tell the employee precisely why his performance is poor and what is needed to improve it.

- Give the employee a reasonable opportunity to improve.
- Before dismissal, except in cases of gross negligence or during a probationary period, the employee must be given at least two warnings and told that a failure to improve within a reasonable timescale will lead to dismissal.
- A fair procedure should be followed, which includes ensuring that the employee knows the case against them and has an opportunity to state their case before decisions are taken.
- Consider whether training is needed or if an alternative job can be offered.
- The decision to dismiss must be within the range of reasonable responses of a reasonable employer.
- Provide the employee with the right of appeal against dismissal.
- The ACAS Code of Practice on Disciplinary and Grievance Procedures (see *Sources of further information*) must be complied with. If not, and an employee wins an Employment Tribunal case, Employment Tribunals have a discretion to increase awards by up to 25% where the employer unreasonably fails to comply with the ACAS Code.

Long-term sickness

- Investigate the true medical position and prognosis for recovery (usually through a medical report).
- Consult with the employee.
- The employee should be aware of the reasons for the proposed dismissal and have an opportunity to state their case before a decision is taken.
- The decision to dismiss must be within the range of reasonable responses of a reasonable employer, having regard to the prognosis for a return to work and the impact of the absence on the business.
- It will typically be unfair to dismiss an employee for long-term ill health

before contractual sick pay has expired. Where an employee is in receipt of, or has the prospect of receiving, benefits under a PHI Scheme, generally dismissing in these circumstances will be unfair and amount to wrongful dismissal.
- The employer should consider all reasonable adjustments to the job or work environment that could aid a return to work. There may also be a requirement to offer any available suitable alternative employment to an employee who is 'disabled' under the Equality Act 2010.
- The ACAS Code of Practice on Disciplinary and Grievance Procedures does not apply to dismissals for long-term sickness absence.

Conduct

- The question is whether the employer has reasonable grounds to believe the employee is guilty of misconduct.
- Carry out a full investigation.
- Inform the employee of all the allegations in advance of disciplinary meetings.
- Put all the evidence of misconduct to the employee.
- The employee must have an opportunity to put his case on the evidence.
- Dismiss only on the evidence put to the employee. The decision to dismiss the employee must be within the range of reasonable responses of a reasonable employer.
- Provide the employee with a right of appeal against dismissal.
- The ACAS Code of Practice on Disciplinary and Grievance Procedures must be complied with. If not, and an employee wins an Employment Tribunal case, Tribunals have a discretion to increase awards by up to 25% where the employer unreasonably fails to comply with the Code.

Individual redundancy

Although a potentially fair reason for dismissal, redundancy can give rise to unfair dismissals where there is a failure to follow a fair procedure. Fair and proper procedures are based on:

- giving the employee advance warning of the potential redundancy situation;
- if selection is necessary, using selection criteria that are as objective as possible and ensuring any selection process is carried out fairly in accordance with the criteria and that the criteria are fairly and consistently applied. Employees must understand how the criteria have been applied to them and be allowed to make representations about their selection.
- considering alternative employment and taking reasonable steps to investigate alternative employment opportunities for employees at risk of dismissal;
- the employer taking a decision to dismiss for reasons of redundancy only after proper consultation has taken place;
- allowing the employee time off to look for alternative jobs;
- continuing to look for alternative jobs for the employee within the organisation;
- giving employees the right of appeal against dismissal (in appropriate cases).

The ACAS Code of Practice on Disciplinary and Grievance Procedures does not apply to redundancy dismissals, although these continue to be covered by unfair dismissal law. For collective redundancies see 'Redundancy' (p.429).

Unfair dismissal remedies

Employees have three months after the date of dismissal in which to bring a claim before an Employment Tribunal.

Alternatively, employers and employees can decide to place the dispute before an ACAS-appointed arbitrator under the ACAS Arbitration Scheme. The scheme is devised to provide a quicker, cheaper and, where possible, more amicable resolution to this type of dispute. Remedies available to both the Tribunal and an ACAS arbitrator include re-engagement or reinstatement, both of which are imposed only rarely. More usually, compensation is awarded. This falls under two heads:

1. *Basic award.* Calculated by reference to salary, age and length of service, subject to a maximum, which was increased on 1 February 2011 to £12,000.
2. *Compensatory award.* Designed to reimburse the employee for actual losses and is at the discretion of the Tribunal, subject to a maximum, also increased on 1 February 2011, and now set at £68,400.

Automatically unfair reasons

Detailed provisions exist for unfair claims that do not require one year's continuous service and where dismissal for that reason will be automatically unfair.

The most important are dismissals for:

- membership of a trade union or for participating in trade union activities;
- taking part in protected industrial action;
- taking action on specified health and safety grounds (including leaving premises due to danger);
- asserting statutory rights against the employer;
- pregnancy or related reasons;
- holding the status of a part-time worker or a fixed-term employee;
- reasons connected with rights under the Working Time Regulations 1998 or National Minimum Wage Act 1998;
- exercising a right to be accompanied by a union representative or fellow

worker at a disciplinary or grievance hearing;

■ asserting rights under the 'whistleblowers' legislation;
■ taking leave for family reasons;
■ making a flexible working application;
■ refusal of Sunday working by shop and betting employees;
■ performing certain functions as a trustee of an occupational pension scheme;
■ performing certain functions as an employee representative under TUPE or collective redundancy legislation; and
■ selection for redundancy for any of the above reasons.

Dismissal for the following reasons will be automatically unfair but the employee will still need one year's service to bring the claim:

■ Dismissal because of a spent conviction; and
■ Certain dismissals in connection with a TUPE transfer.

Wrongful dismissal

A wrongful dismissal occurs where the dismissal is not implemented in accordance with the terms of the contract (typically, a failure to comply with the notice period).

A court will not generally order an employer to reinstate an employee or to take an employee back once wrongfully dismissed. In any event, such a remedy is rarely practicable. However, in rare cases an employee acting swiftly may be able to persuade a court to issue an injunction requiring the employer to perform the contract in accordance with its terms (although the employer may subsequently dismiss the employee lawfully in accordance with the terms of the contract). A wrongful dismissal is therefore effective, though the employer will be required to compensate the employee for loss caused, applying the principles that govern compensation for breach of contract. These seek to put the employee in the position he or she would have been in had the dismissal not been wrongful. The simple measure of compensation is notice pay plus value of benefits less remuneration earned from alternative employment during what would otherwise have been the notice period.

See also: Disciplinary and grievance procedures, p.121; Mediation, p.300; Notice periods, p.369; Redundancy, p.429.

Sources of further information

ACAS – Code of Practice on Discipline and Grievance: www.acas.org.uk/CHttpHandler.ashx?id=1041

Employers should have a clear record of the policy and procedures for disciplinary matters to provide clear guidance to employees on the procedure that will be followed by their employer. Workplace Law's **Non-Contractual Disciplinary and Dismissal Policy and Management Guide, v.4.0** can also act as a checklist for managers, in relation to the steps that should be taken, with a view to minimising procedural irregularities and allegations of unfair treatment. For more information visit www.workplacelaw.net.

Dress codes

Jackie Thomas, Berwin Leighton Paisner LLP

Key points

- Employers seek to apply dress codes to their employees for many reasons. In doing so, however, it is important that employers consider any potentially discriminatory implications as dress codes have historically been challenged under both the Sex Discrimination Act 1975, the Race Relations Act 1976 and, more recently, the Employment Equality (Religion or Belief) Regulations 2003. These characteristics are now all protected under the Equality Act 2010.

- Furthermore, since the European Convention on Human Rights has been incorporated into UK law by way of the Human Rights Act 1998, it may also be possible to challenge the application of a dress code on the basis that it infringes the employee's human rights.

- To avoid potential liability, employers should ensure that the policy applies evenly to both men and women, and that any requirements imposed are reasonable when balancing the rights of the employee and the requirements of the employer's business.

- Factors that may be relevant include:
  - whether the employee has contact with the public;
  - whether the dress code is necessary for performance;
  - health and safety; and
  - illegality.

Legislation

- Human Rights Act 1998.
- Equality Act 2010.

The Equality Act came into force in October 2010. It is a consolidating Act, which brings together the old, separate discrimination legislation (for example, the Sex Discrimination Act 1975 and the Race Relations Act 1976) into one new Act. While the new Act does change the law in some respects (see '*The Equality Act*', p.191), it is unlikely to have an effect on existing case law on dress codes.

In what situations will an employer seek to enforce a dress code?

Dress codes are used in the workplace for a number of reasons. Firstly, dress codes may be applied for reasons of food hygiene or other safely related reasons. Secondly, employers may require employees to wear a uniform in order to signify their status (for example, a ticket inspector). Finally, they are also used by many employers merely as a way of ensuring that their employees are dressed appropriately (where the employees concerned come into contact with the employer's clients or customers).

The impact of sex discrimination legislation on dress codes

The Equality Act provides that it is discriminatory for an employer to treat an employee less favourably than it would treat an employee of the opposite sex. This amounts to direct discrimination and the

Facts

- 64% of those employers operating a dress code policy relax their dress codes rules at times, while just under a third (31%) do not.
- 66% of UK companies and public sector bodies found that while standards of dress are becoming less formal, the policing of what is and is not acceptable clothing for the office is being tightened up.
- A significant minority of employers (27%) say that while their dress code policy is observed, it still has to be policed.
- More than two-thirds (67%) of dress code policies now have the force of the employment contract behind them.
- Most employers (73%) say enhancing the external image of the company is the most common reason for having a dress code.
- Fewer than one in ten employers involve their staff in devising the organisation's dress code.
- Employees have to wear a uniform or overalls at less than half of organisations (46%).
- Two-thirds of companies support people in meeting the dress codes of their religion.
- Only around one in ten employers with a policy impose restrictions on religious dress or jewellery.

employer cannot defend such a claim on the grounds that the treatment is justified.

There are numerous cases of employees claiming that their employer's dress code is directly discriminatory. Examples include provisions of policies that prevented female employees from wearing trousers or that prevented male employees from having long hair. Interestingly, two Tribunals simultaneously considered whether it was discriminatory for a policy to require a male employee to wear a tie; each Tribunal reached conflicting conclusions – in one case (*Department for Work and Pensions v. Thompson*, 2003) finding that such a policy was discriminatory, and in the other (*Blaik v. The Post Office*, 2003) concluding that the employer's policy was acceptable.

The reasoning for this conflict is that Tribunals will not directly compare the treatment of men and women in respect of each requirement of the dress code. The crucial issue will be whether, when viewed as a whole, the policy treats men and women in a generally equivalent manner in order to enforce a 'common principle of smartness'.

In fact, this principle was expressly reaffirmed by the EAT in relation to the appeal of the Thompson case, in which the Tribunal had found the dress code to be discriminatory. The EAT held that the policy did require women to dress to an equivalent level of smartness (despite the fact that they did not do so in practice) and so the Tribunal should properly have considered whether the requirement for a man to wear a collar and tie with no specific requirements for what a woman should wear was in itself discriminatory. The Tribunal had not considered this point and so the matter was remitted to a fresh Tribunal.

Potential race discrimination claims

It is also possible for claims to arise if an employer's policy has a disparate impact on a particular racial group. This type of claim is an 'indirect discrimination' claim and is therefore capable of being justified by the employer. Broadly, justification involves demonstrating that the policy is a proportionate means of achieving a legitimate aim.

An example that resulted in a claim was a policy that required a Sikh to shave his beard for health and safety reasons. The employee claimed that this amounted to indirect discrimination (in that it was more difficult for Sikhs as a racial group to comply). However, the Tribunals held that the employer's actions were justifiable as the policy was in place for reasons of food hygiene. To the extent that such a requirement could not be justified it would be discriminatory.

Historically, such claims were limited by the fact that the Race Relations Act did not prevent discrimination on the grounds of religious belief unless the individual could also be said to fall within a particular racial group; however this loophole was closed by the introduction of the Employment Equality (Religion or Belief) Regulations 2003. (This distinction is no longer relevant under the Equality Act.)

This issue also arose in the *Azmi v. Kirklees Metropolitan Council* case, which held that the refusal by a school to permit a Muslim teaching assistant to wear a veil did not amount to either direct or indirect race discrimination. The Tribunal and the EAT both found that this treatment did not amount to direct discrimination (on the basis of the correct comparator being a person who wore a face covering but was not Muslim). They went on to find that it was not indirect discrimination because the treatment could be justified.

Another recent case, *Eweida v. British Airways plc*, saw a female member of BA's check-in staff challenge BA's policy that prevented the wearing of non-uniform items. The policy excluded 'mandatory' religious items; for example, turbans. However, Miss Eweida wished to wear a cross on the grounds that she was a devout Christian. BA refused on the basis that this was not mandatory for Christians. Miss Eweida lost her case at both the Tribunal and the EAT on the basis that the policy did not result in group disadvantage, merely subjective disadvantage for the employee. Interestingly, however, the Tribunal and EAT both held that the policy would not have been objectively justifiable had the group disadvantage been established.

The case was also appealed to the Court of Appeal. Again, BA was successful with the Court finding that group disadvantage meant that employees other than Miss Eweida had to be affected and that Miss Eweida could not rely on human rights arguments as wearing a cross was not a mandatory part of her religion. Further, despite succeeding, BA still changed its policy, potentially as a result of significant unfavourable press generated by the case. This demonstrates that, particularly for large, public organisations, the interaction between dress codes and religious beliefs is problematic if an employer misjudges its position and does not correctly balance business needs and employee rights.

Recent developments

The issue has also been considered recently in a public law case, *G v. Head Teacher and Governors of St Gregory's Catholic Science College*, which concerned the uniform policy of a school that prevented boys (but not girls) from wearing their hair in cornrows. The policy was found by the High Court not to be directly discriminatory on the grounds of sex; however, it was found to be indirectly discriminatory on grounds of race. The High Court held that family and social customs can be part of ethnicity for the purposes of the Equality Act and, in this instance, the school had failed to objectively justify its policy.

Human rights issues

As well as being potentially discriminatory, it is also possible for a dress code to infringe an employee's human rights. The European Convention on Human Rights has now been incorporated into UK law by the HRA. Of the rights it enshrines, Article 10 (the right to freedom of expression), Article 9 (freedom of thought, conscience and religion) and Article 14 (prohibition on discrimination) are all relevant when considering dress codes.

In the case of most private sector employers, employees will not be able to bring a claim directly under the HRA but the employees of Public Authorities may be able to do so. Further, since the Tribunals are required to construe existing laws in a way that is compatible with these rights, future claims based on discrimination legislation may also need to take into account these rights when balancing the needs of the employer with the rights of the employee. As seen above, Miss Eweida sought to utilise arguments based on Article 9 in the UK Courts but was not successful. The outcome may well have been different, however, if the case had involved a mandatory religious symbol. Importantly, Miss Eweida's case is now one of four cases involving the rights of Christians being considered by the European Court of Human Rights and, in June 2011, the UK Government was asked to comment on whether the law has resulted in the breach of the applicants' human rights.

See also: Discrimination, p.126; The Equality Act, p.191; Human rights, p.248.

Sources of further information

Equality and Human Rights Commission: www.equalityhumanrights.com

Driving at work

Kathryn Gilbertson, Greenwoods Solicitors LLP

Key points
- Employers need to manage the use of both the company car driver and the person using his own vehicle for business using risk assessments and a driving for work policy.
- Working time rules apply to drivers.
- Motorists can be prosecuted for driving while using a handheld mobile phone. Employers may also be prosecuted if they require their employees to use their mobile phones while driving.
- If a work vehicle is used as a workplace by more than one person it must be smoke-free at all times.

Legislation
- Road Traffic Act 1988.
- The Road Transport (Working Time) Regulations 2005.
- The Health Act 2006.
- Road Safety Act 2006.
- The Smoke-Free (Vehicle Operators and Penalty Notices) Regulations 2007.
- The Highway Code.

These lay down certain rules and restrictions (e.g. speed limits) and are normally enforced by the police and the courts. While the driver of the vehicle will primarily be held responsible for any offence, employers may also be liable, for instance in setting schedules that are so tight that the driver would consistently be breaking the speed limits if he attempted to meet them. The Magistrates Act 1980 may also be relevant to employers in England and Wales who aid, abet, counsel or procure an offence. Employers are responsible for ensuring their company vehicles are properly taxed and insured.

Working time
The Road Transport (Working Time) Regulations 2005 cover mobile workers who will, in the main, be drivers and accompanying crew involved in road transport activities in a vehicle that is required by EU laws to have a tachograph (Council Regulation 3821/85 on recording equipment in road transport). The Regulations include the following provisions:

- A mobile worker's working time shall not exceed an average 48-hour working week, typically calculated over a four-month reference period;
- A maximum of 60 hours may be worked in a single week (provided that the average working week does not exceed 48 hours);
- There is a ten-hour limit for night workers over a 24-hour period;
- Workers cannot work more than six consecutive hours without taking a break. If working between six and nine hours, a break of at least 30 minutes is required. If working over nine hours, breaks totalling 45 minutes are required. Each break may be made up of separate periods of not less than 15 minutes each.
- The Regulations now affect self-employed drivers. Other drivers who fall outside the scope of the new Regulations, such as drivers of smaller

---

Facts

- According to RoSPA, 1,857 people were killed in road accidents in 2010.
- Company drivers who drive more than 80% of their annual mileage on work-related journeys have 50% more accidents than similar drivers who do no work-related mileage.
- Every week around 200 road deaths and serious injuries involve someone at work.
- About 300 people are killed each year as a result of drivers falling asleep at the wheel.
- Around four in ten tiredness-related crashes involve someone driving a commercial vehicle.

---

vehicles or drivers exempt from the EU Drivers Hours Rules, are covered by the WTR; for example, the 48-hour average working week and the need for adequate rest. However, unlike the WTR, employees covered by the new Regulations cannot 'opt out'.

- Employers must monitor working time and should do what they can to ensure the limits are not breached. Records need to be kept for two years. Generally speaking, annual leave / sick leave cannot be used to reduce the average working time of a mobile worker. For each week of leave that is taken, 48 hours' working time must be added to their working time; for each day's leave, eight hours must be added to working time.

- If no employer exists, the agency, employment business or even the worker themselves should monitor working time.

For further guidance on working time issues see 'Working time' (p.564).

Mobile phones

Motorists can be prosecuted for driving while using a handheld mobile phone. Drivers committing this offence will be liable to pay a fixed penalty or a fine on conviction in court. The offence also attracts three penalty points. The Regulations apply in all circumstances other than when the vehicle is parked, with the engine off. This means that the prohibition applies even if a vehicle has paused at traffic lights, stopped in a temporary traffic jam, or is in very slow-moving traffic.

The definition of 'handheld' means a mobile phone or other device that is held at some point during the course of making or receiving a call or fulfilling some other interactive communication function. An interactive communication function includes sending or receiving oral or written messages, facsimile documents, still or moving images, or accessing the internet. Hands-free products, which do not require drivers to significantly alter their position in relation to the steering wheel in order to use them, have not fallen foul of the change in the law.

Employers' liability

The Regulations also created an offence of 'causing or permitting' another person to drive while using a handheld phone or other similar device. Employers may, therefore, be prosecuted if they require their employees to use their phones when driving. The DfT has stated that employers cannot expect their employees

Case studies

R v. Melvyn Spree (2004)

This case illustrates a combination of working time and dangerous driving that resulted in a manslaughter conviction for the company director. Melvyn Spree, a road haulage director, was jailed for seven years after one of his lorry drivers fell asleep at the wheel and killed three motorists. It was held that Melvyn Spree, a director of Keymark Services, encouraged and enabled his drivers to work dangerously long hours, through fraudulent record-keeping and tachograph tampering. Melvyn Spree's fellow director, Lorraine March, was also jailed for conspiracy offences and Keymark Services was fined £50,000 for manslaughter.

Police investigations had found that the driver, Stephen Law, was partway through an 18-hour shift when the accident occurred. The police also discovered systematic abuse of working hours' restrictions. Drivers were rewarded with a profit-share scheme. Melvyn Spree showed drivers how to jam tachographs and to keep false records of working times that demonstrated legal compliance.

R v. Knapman and Legg (2005)

In December 2005, Raymond Knapman, Partner at R&D Drivers, was prosecuted for manslaughter but acquitted after it could not be established that a fatal accident involving the deaths of two lorry drivers was caused by excessive hours or a heart attack by one of the drivers. However, Knapman was subsequently charged with eight counts of obtaining property by deception due to consistently requiring drivers to work excessive hours. Knapman pleaded guilty to the offences and to a breach of Section 3(2) of the Health and Safety at Work etc. Act for failing to ensure the health and safety of persons not in his employment and was sentenced to two-and-a-half-years' imprisonment in January 2006.

to make or receive mobile phone calls while driving. This must be reflected in the company's health and safety policy and risk management policy. Employers will not be liable simply for supplying a telephone or for telephoning an employee who was driving. However, employers must send a clear message to employees that they are forbidden to use their handheld mobile phones while driving and their employer will not require them to make or receive calls when driving.

Employers should inform their staff that, when driving, handheld mobile phones should be switched off, or, if switched on, the calls should be left to go through to voicemail, and that a safe place to stop should be found to check messages and return calls. Company policy should specify that using a handheld phone or similar device while driving is a criminal offence and will be treated as a disciplinary matter. Hands-free kits are widely available and the use of these kits is still legal. However, employers should be aware that this does not mean that drivers will be exempt from prosecution altogether if they use hands-free kits. Dangerous and careless driving can still be committed as separate offences under the Road Traffic Act 1988. Research shows that using a hands-free phone while driving distracts the driver and increases the risk of an accident. Therefore, many businesses have banned them outright. Employers who install hands-free kits should balance the commercial advantage of this with the potential risk of future liability, were an employee to cause an accident while speaking on the phone and driving.

- Switch off the phone while driving and let it take messages.
- Alternatively, leave the phone switched on and let the calls go into voicemail.
- Alternatively, ask a passenger to deal with the call.
- Find a safe place to stop before turning off the engine and picking up the messages and returning calls.

Smoking

All enclosed public places and workplaces must be smoke-free. These include company cars and hire vehicles. If a work vehicle is used as a workplace by more than one person it must be smoke-free at all times. The legislation does not extend to private vehicles.

If a private vehicle is used for work and the employee doesn't ever use it with others, it is permissible to smoke in that vehicle. There is no guidance available at present with regard to vehicles when used for primarily private journeys but sometimes used for business together with others.

Owners or managers of smoke-free premises will be guilty of an offence if they fail to prevent people from smoking. 'No smoking' signs must be displayed in all work vehicles. Managers should as a matter of good practice require that vehicles be smoke-free.

Conclusion

It is essential that there is a driving at work policy and risk assessment in place so that compliance with health and safety and working time legislation can be seen to be actively implemented and ongoing. This will not only assist in any HSE investigations but will also help to protect against any civil claims.

See also: Smoking, p.478.

Sources of further information

INDG 382 Driving at work – managing work-related road safety: www.hse.gov.uk/pubns/indg382.pdf

Managing Occupational Road Risk – The RoSPA Guide: www.rospa.org.uk

Workplace Law's ***Driving at Work Policy and Management Guide v.5.0*** helps you cover yourself and your staff and ensure that your employees keep to the highest standards of safe driving at work. If your business hasn't already got a driving at work policy in place, or your current policy is not up-to-date, this is an essential publication. The policy highlights the issue of liability should prosecution occur following a driving at work accident, and who might face prosecution as a result. Visit www.workplacelaw.net for more information.

Employee consultation

Suzanne McMinn, Workplace Law

Key points

- The Information and Consultation of Employees Regulations 2004 (ICER or 'the Regulations') came into force in April 2005. Depending on the number of employees employed in the undertaking, the Regulations applied at different stages:
  - Undertakings with 150 or more employees from 6 April 2005;
  - Undertakings with 100 or more employees from 6 April 2007; and
  - Undertakings with 50 or more employees from 6 April 2008.
- Therefore, all undertakings with 50 or more employees are now subject to the Regulations.
- The Regulations provide a statutory basis for reaching agreement on the process of keeping employees informed and consulted about matters affecting their employment.
- The request to negotiate an agreement is triggered where either the employer starts the process and wishes to negotiate an existing agreement or introduce a new one, or there is a valid employee request. Therefore, there is no automatic obligation on any employer to do anything under the Regulations.
- Where there is a valid pre-existing agreement in place, the employer may ballot the workforce to determine whether they endorse the employee request or whether they are happy with the existing agreement.
- If the workforce does not endorse the request, the pre-existing arrangement continues.
- If negotiations fail to lead to agreement, the 'default provisions' will apply.
- If there is no employee request or the employer does not commence negotiations, there is no obligation to establish an information and consultation (I and C) agreement.

Legislation

- Information and Consultation Directive (2002/14/EC).
- Information and Consultation of Employees Regulations 2004.

Introduction

ICER came into force in April 2005 and implemented the EU Information and Consultation Directive. These Regulations are aimed at providing a statutory basis for keeping employees informed and consulted about employment issues that affect them in the workplace. This is a significant piece of legislation, which can affect the management of industrial relations in the UK, particularly for employers who are not used to dealing with issues on a collective basis.

The Regulations have been implemented on a phased basis, depending on the number of employees in the particular undertaking, and the last phase was introduced on 6 April 2008. Now all undertakings in the UK with 50 or more employees are potentially affected by the Regulations.

ICER applies to both public and private undertakings carrying out an economic activity, whether or not operating for gain. It is the number of employees employed by an individual undertaking that is relevant, not those employed by a subsidiary or parent company.

Pre-existing agreements

If there is a valid pre-existing agreement and fewer than 40% of employees in an undertaking make a request for an I and C body, an employer may (but is not obliged to) ballot its workforce to see whether it endorses the request for a new body.

Where a ballot is held, and 40% of the workforce and a majority of those who vote endorse the employee request for a new I and C body, the employer is obliged to negotiate a new agreement (as set out below).

Where fewer than 40% of the workforce or a minority of those voting endorse the employee request for a new agreement, the employer will not be under an obligation to negotiate a new I and C agreement.

ICER sets out the conditions that need to be satisfied to be a valid pre-existing agreement. These include that it must be in writing, cover all the employees of the undertaking, have been approved by them, set out how information is given, and how the employees' views on this information will be sought.

The agreement must have been in place before an employee request under ICER was made.

Negotiating an I and C agreement under ICER

There are two ways to trigger negotiations for an I and C agreement:

1. If a valid request under ICER has been made by at least 10% of the employees in an undertaking (subject to a minimum of 15 and a maximum of 2,500 employees); or
2. If the employer initiates the process itself.

Any disputes about the validity of employee requests will be dealt with by the Central Arbitration Committee (CAC).

An employer must initiate negotiations for an agreement as soon as reasonably practicable and within three months at the latest. During this three-month period, the employer must:

- make arrangements for its employees to appoint or elect negotiating representatives; and
- inform employees in writing of the identity of the representatives who have been elected and then invite those representatives to enter into negotiations to reach an ICER agreement.

Negotiations for reaching an agreement may last for up to six months, which is extendable by agreement. If a negotiated agreement is not reached, the 'default model' will apply (*see below*). There is a further six-month period for an employer to set up the necessary consultation body or reach a negotiated agreement.

Criteria for a negotiated ICER agreement

A negotiated agreement must comply with certain criteria. It must:

- be in writing and dated;
- cover all employees in the undertaking or group of undertakings;
- be signed by or on behalf of the employer;
- set out the circumstances in which employers will inform and consult – ICER gives employers and employees the freedom to agree on the subject matter, method, frequency and timing of information and consultation best suited to the employer's particular circumstances;
- provide either for the appointment or election of I and C representatives or for information and consultation directly with employees; and
- be approved by the employees.

Duration of agreement

Once a negotiated agreement is in place, there is a three-year moratorium on making further requests.

The 'default model'

If negotiations to reach an agreement fail, the 'default model' will apply. Employers have a further six months to facilitate the election of representatives. This must be via a ballot with one employee representative per 50 employees, subject to a minimum of two and a maximum of 25. If an employer fails to arrange this, it may be subject to a penalty fine of up to £75,000.

Information must be provided to I and C representatives at an appropriate time on:

1. the recent and probable development of the undertaking's activities and economic situation;
2. the situation, structure and probable development of employment within the undertaking and on any anticipatory measures envisaged, in particular where there is a threat to employment; and
3. decisions likely to lead to substantial changes in work organisation or in contractual relations (including those covered by existing legislation in the area of collective consultation on collective redundancies and business transfers).

In respect of the second and third issues, the representatives must be consulted as well as informed.

Other factors

Protection of confidential information

There is a statutory duty of confidentiality on all I and C representatives in respect of information the employer discloses to them. However, they can challenge this duty before the CAC. Employers need not disclose information where to do so would 'seriously harm the functioning of the undertaking or be prejudicial to it'.

Compliance and enforcement

A complaint may be made to the CAC that an employer has failed to establish a negotiated agreement or has failed to inform and consult with employees in accordance with a negotiated agreement or the default model. This must be done within three months of the failure. These compliance mechanisms do not apply to pre-existing agreements. The CAC may make a declaration and an order requiring the defaulting party to take such specified steps as are necessary to comply with the I and C agreement within a specific period of time. There is a maximum penalty of £75,000 for the employer's failure.

Where an employer is under information and consultation obligations arising from TUPE or collective redundancy legislation, it is excused from the obligations to consult under ICER, provided it notifies I and C representatives of this. I and C representatives are entitled to reasonable paid time off work during normal working hours and have the right not to be dismissed or suffer any detriment.

Practical steps for employers

Now that the Regulations have come into force for all undertakings with 50 or more employees, employers essentially have the option to either:

- negotiate a voluntary I and C agreement;
- negotiate an I and C agreement with employee representatives once a request has been made; or

- do nothing and allow the default provisions in ICER to apply.

The advantages to an employer of negotiating a voluntary agreement are that it is seen to be proactive, it can seize control of the process and a more flexible agreement may result. The default model is much less flexible with set categories of information and consultation and a predetermined number of representatives. In preparation and in order to determine which option to follow, employers should:

- carry out an audit of any existing information and consultation processes;
- assess the likelihood of employees making an ICER request or other improvements to existing information and consultation structures;
- develop a strategy for dealing with any request – e.g. how to run internal elections, what the organisation is willing to 'consult' with employee representatives about;
- educate and train management in dealing with employees collectively, particularly where trade unions are likely to be represented on the consultation body;
- consider improving on existing consultation bodies / procedures; and
- consider what competitors are doing.

See also: Employment disputes, p.168; Trade unions, p.516; TUPE, p.523.

Sources of further information

BIS – Information and consultation:
www.berr.gov.uk/employment/employment-legislation/ice/index.html

ACAS – Information and consultation: www.acas.org.uk/index.aspx?articleid=1017

Employment contracts

Chris McDowall, Anderson Strathern

Key points

- A contract of employment can be created very simply. It is not required to be in writing. However, statutory requirements impose minimum obligations on employers to issue a written statement confirming the main particulars of employment.
- Employers can seek to regulate the employment relationship and comply with legal obligations by providing a more extensive written contract.
- Once contractual terms have been created, they cannot be changed unilaterally. Whether they are in writing or not, any proposed changes require to be handled appropriately to avoid claims of breach of contract and constructive unfair dismissal.

Legislation

- Copyright, Designs and Patents Act 1988.
- Data Protection Act 1988.
- Employment Rights Act 1996.
- Working Time Regulations 1998.
- Employment Act 2002.
- Equality Act 2010.

Introduction

A contract of employment is created when one party accepts an offer of employment from another. Although a written contract is not required in order to create an employer–employee relationship, it is a statutory requirement and good practice to record the terms of the employment in writing. This can often be done by issuing the proposed contract, or a statement of the main contractual terms that will apply, with the offer of employment. The employee should be asked to sign a copy of the written contract to clearly signify acceptance of its terms.

It should be noted, however, that a written term in a contract of employment could be rendered void if it seeks to avoid or restrict certain statutory rights, or is deemed to be contrary to public policy.

Certain terms are implied into every contract by law, such as the implied duty of trust and confidence or the duty to take care of health and safety. Other terms are also incorporated into the contract, such as the obligation of equal pay or as a result of a collective agreement.

Providing written terms: the compulsory elements

Section 1 of the Employment Rights Act 1996 (ERA) places a statutory duty on employers to provide employees with particulars in writing of certain fundamental contractual terms. Since 1 October 2004 employers have been able to provide these in the form of a written contract, although they can still be provided in a simple statement of employment particulars.

The main requirements are as follows:

- Where an employee begins employment, the employer must give the employee a written statement of particulars of employment (Section 1(1), ERA).
- The written statement may be given in instalments but shall not be given later than two months after

commencement of employment (Section 1(2), ERA).

- The written statement shall contain names of the employer and employee, the date when the employment commenced and the date when the period of continuous employment commenced (Section 1(3), ERA).
- The written statement is required to contain details of all of the following particulars as at a date not more than seven days before the date of the statement (Section 1(4), ERA):
  - Scale or rate of remuneration, or method of calculating remuneration;
  - The intervals at which remuneration is paid;
  - Any terms and conditions relating to normal hours of work;
  - Any terms and conditions relating to entitlement to holidays, including public holidays and holiday pay (the latter sufficient to calculate the precise amount payable), incapacity for work due to sickness or injury, and the provision of sick pay;
  - Length of notice required to terminate employment;
  - Title of the job the employee is employed to do or a brief description of it;
  - The duration of the employment if it is not permanent;

- The place or places the employee is required to work at;
- Any collective agreements that affect the terms of employment;
- Where the employee is required to work outside the UK, the length of that period and the currency he will be paid in and any additional remuneration or benefits payable to him as a result; and
- Whether there is a contracting-out certificate in force for the purposes of the Pensions Schemes Act 1993, stating that the employment is contracted out.

The written statement must also contain a note specifying any disciplinary rules applicable to the employee or referring the employee to an easily accessible document containing that information (Section 3, ERA). The note must contain details of to whom the employee can apply if dissatisfied with a disciplinary decision or for the purposes of seeking redress of any grievance. These requirements apply to all employers. Employers who fail to comply with these requirements now risk financial penalties of between two and four weeks' pay if relevant Employment Tribunal claims are made.

Any changes to the compulsory elements of the statement of terms and conditions should be notified to the employee in writing within one month of the change.

Providing written terms: other important issues

Many employers will employ written contractual terms to exercise control over other important issues. Which issues will be appropriate will always depend on the individual circumstances of the particular contract. Some examples of these additional terms are as follows:

- Probationary period permitting the employer to terminate the contract, normally within the first few months of employment, on minimal notice.
- Data protection terms, designed to give fair notice of the purposes for which data processing will be carried out, for compliance with the Data Protection Act 1988.
- Restrictions on acceptance of other work during employment.
- Flexibility clause (e.g. requirements to work overtime, undertake other duties, mobility clauses).
- The ability to put employees on lay-off or short-term working.
- Confidentiality terms, which give the employee notice of the types of information to be regarded as confidential during and after employment.
- Authority for deductions from wages (e.g. overpayments of holiday pay or expenses).
- Garden leave terms, designed to allow the employer to require the employee to stay away from work, often used to protect business interests during notice periods.
- Intellectual property terms, which set out ownership of copyright of work created during employment and assign rights to it.
- Restrictive covenants, which impose restraints post-employment on competition, solicitation of customers

and significant employees and the use of trade secrets of the employer.
- Payment in lieu of notice clause, to allow the employer to dismiss an employee immediately without adhering to the notice period provided for in the contract. If this term is not expressly written into the contract, the employer will be unable to make a payment to the employee in lieu of notice, without being in breach of contract.
- Opt-out arrangements under the Working Time Regulations 1998. While this is often included in the contract and therefore signed before the contract begins or during the probationary period, there is an argument that such consent is not freely given. If an employee's working time will or could exceed the working time limits, considerations should be given to asking the employee to sign a separate opt-out agreement after the end of the probationary period.
- Many of these clauses will be subject to legal restrictions in relation to enforceability and it is essential that they are drafted in a manner that will be legally compliant.

Altering terms and conditions of employment

Once established, contractual terms can be varied but only if the consent of *both* parties to the proposed variation is achieved. This can sometimes involve employers 'buying out' existing terms with a compensatory financial payment.

One practical way employers have sought to get around this is to have a provision within the contract that gives the employer a contractual right to vary the contractual terms upon giving notice to the employee, the idea being that the employee has already given consent to future changes by the employer to their contractual terms by agreeing to such a provision in the contract. While this can be a useful provision for employers, caution still needs to be shown in how they seek to implement it. Any discretion should not be exercised capriciously. Furthermore, the courts will generally apply any ambiguity in such provisions in favour of the employee and will, where appropriate, give them a narrow interpretation. Accordingly, very general contractual provisions to vary tend to only be effective for reasonable and/or minor amendments.

If consent is not forthcoming, the only potentially valid alternative to 'force through' the change is to serve appropriate notice that the contract is being terminated and, at the same time, offer a new contract, containing the new terms, to take effect immediately upon termination.

However, such an approach can give rise to claims of unfair dismissal, so, before taking such action, careful analysis is advised. If the original contract is not brought to an end effectively, breach of contract claims may ensue following any change. If the breach is fundamental, this can lead to a claim that the employee has been constructively unfairly dismissed.

See also: Data protection, p.101; Flexible working, p.221; Holiday, p.240; Leave, p.252; Notice periods, p.369; Personnel files, p.392; Probationary periods, p.412; Restrictive covenants and garden leave, p.441; Retirement, p.445; Staff handbooks, p.494.

Sources of further information

ACAS: www.acas.org.uk

UK Department for Business, Innovation and Skills: www.bis.gov.uk

All employers are required to issue employees with a written statement of certain terms of employment. Workplace Law's *Employment Contract and Management Guide, v.5.0* has been published to help employers ensure that they comply with their requirements under law and to provide a clear record of the agreement between employer and employee. The policy also comes with a 20-page Management Guide containing helpful notes on the policy and alternative provisions for employers. Visit www.workplacelaw.net for more details.

Employment disputes

Tina Maxey, Steeles Law

Key points

- Most claims brought against a company by job applicants, employees, workers and ex-employees (and also contractors and agency workers) are brought in an Employment Tribunal. Sometimes claims may be brought in the County Court or High Court.

- The Employment Tribunal has jurisdiction to hear most employment-related litigation (dismissal, discrimination, working time, TUPE). It is a relatively less expensive forum than other civil courts and is less formal. Historically, each party has met its own legal costs, although Tribunals are more frequently making costs awards in particular circumstances.

- Breach of contract claims arising or outstanding on termination of employment can be brought in the Employment Tribunal if they are for £25,000 or less. Breach of contract claims where the possible damages are above £25,000 should be brought in the County or High Courts.

- The County and High Courts are more formal and expensive. It is possible to get costs awards against the losing party.

- Mediation is an increasingly popular option for employers and employees as a means of avoiding having to go to Court or to an Employment Tribunal. The ACAS Code of Practice (introduced in April 2009) encourages employers to consider using independent third parties to resolve workplace disciplinary or grievance issues, such as external mediators.

- Since April 2009, the Employment Tribunal has offered a Judicial Mediation scheme. Suitable cases for Judicial Mediation will be identified as part of the normal Tribunal process and with agreement of the parties.

- The Advisory, Conciliation and Arbitration Service (ACAS) is the Government's conciliation service and is responsible for conciliating between the parties in cases brought in the Employment Tribunal. This is entirely separate from Judicial Mediation.

- It is also possible to use ACAS as an arbitrator in a dispute if it is an unfair dismissal case.

Legislation

- Employment Tribunal: Employment Tribunals (Constitution and Rules of Procedure) Regulations 2004 and Employment Tribunals (Constitution Rules of Procedure) (Amendment) Regulations 2008.
- County / High Court: Civil Procedural Rules.
- Employment Act 2008.

Proceedings brought in the Employment Tribunal

The Tribunal's procedural regulations are governed by the 'overriding objective,' which is to enable Tribunals to deal with cases justly, such as ensuring the parties are on an equal footing, saving expense, dealing with the case in ways that are proportionate to the complexity of the issues, and ensuring the case is dealt with expeditiously and fairly.

A case is started when the employee, known as the 'claimant,' presents the Tribunal with a written application in the appropriate form known as the claim form (or ET1).

There are distinctive time limits for lodging claims in the Employment Tribunal – these are normally three months from the date of the termination of the employee's employment, or the act being complained of. The time limits are strictly enforced. However, in certain circumstances, a claimant may apply for an extension of time to submit a claim.

The employer is 'the respondent' and must submit a defence known as a 'response form' (or ET3) within the 28-day limit, as advised by the Tribunal.

After the response form is received by the Employment Tribunal, the case will be prepared for a hearing. To do so, a number of tasks must be undertaken by both parties – disclosure of documents, requests for additional information, and exchanging witness statements. Sometimes these matters will be ordered by the Employment Tribunal in correspondence or following a case management discussion.

Sometimes there may be issues that would be dealt with at a pre-hearing review (e.g. in complex discrimination cases). After the full hearing, usually presided over by an employment judge and two lay wing members, judgment is made either orally or in writing or both. A judgment might deal with both liability and remedy, or it might only deal with the question of liability, in which case if the claimant is successful the remedy is decided by the Employment Tribunal at a separate remedies hearing. Either party may appeal the decision to the Employment Appeal Tribunal. Again, strict time limits apply.

The Employment Tribunal does not normally order that the unsuccessful party pay the costs of the winner. However, there is an increasing trend towards the Tribunal making costs orders. The Employment Tribunal and EAT statistics for 1 April 2009 to 31 March 2010 demonstrated that in 88 cases the Tribunals awarded costs in favour of the claimant, and in 324 cases the Tribunal awarded costs in favour of the respondent. The maximum award was £13,942 and the average award was £2,288.

The Tribunal can order costs in certain circumstances such as where:

- a party or his representative has acted vexatiously, abusively, disruptively, or otherwise unreasonably in bringing or conducting the proceedings, or the bringing or conducting of proceedings has been misconceived;
- the hearing was adjourned at the request of one party; or
- a party has not complied with a Tribunal's directions order (e.g. to supply documents or particulars).

The Employment Tribunal can also make wasted costs orders and preparation time orders.

The Tribunal only has the power to award up to £10,000 in costs without ordering a detailed assessment. If the costs are above £10,000, the bill of costs claimed will then be subject to a detailed assessment by the County Court

Settlement via the Advisory, Conciliation and Arbitration Service (ACAS)

There is a statutory provision for ACAS conciliation, conducted via conciliation officers, in most employment claims, including every claim for unfair dismissal or unlawful discrimination. An ACAS officer can conciliate between the parties at any point from the ET1 being submitted to the hearing taking place, or generally where there is a workplace dispute that could turn into an Employment Tribunal claim. The ACAS officer has no duty to advise on the merits of the claim and will not enter into lengthy discussion on legal points.

The ACAS officer will contact each party (by letter or telephone) at the start of proceedings in the Employment Tribunal. He or she can negotiate between the parties towards a settlement. A settlement agreement reached through ACAS is binding and effective. It is normally recorded on a 'COT3 form'.

ACAS has also set up an arbitration scheme for unfair dismissal cases and claims under the flexible working legislation as a form of alternative dispute resolution (*see below*). This is different from conciliation in that ACAS provides an independent arbitrator who hears the evidence and decides the case for the employer and employee. As an arbitrator, ACAS can award the same level of payments as a Tribunal against employers.

County Court and High Court

Employment disputes can also give rise to a civil action that is heard in either a County Court (if it is a small claim or if it is not a complex matter) or the High Court. The High Court will not hear a claim whose value is £25,000 or less (or less than £50,000 where personal injury damages are involved). There are three tracks:

1. Small claims (under £5,000);
2. Fast track, for claims between £5,000 and £25,000; and
3. Multi-track, for claims above £25,000.

The main types of civil actions relating to employment are wrongful dismissal / breach of contract or injunctions to stop employees joining a competitor, setting up in competition, or disclosing confidential information.

The High Court sits at the Royal Courts of Justice in London as well as at some major court centres around the country. Most employment-related civil actions are heard in the Queen's Bench Division of the High Court.

The parties can appeal a decision of the High Court to the Court of Appeal and in certain rare circumstances on to the Supreme Court (formerly the House of Lords) or European Court of Justice.

Alternative dispute resolution

Alternative dispute resolution encompasses many methods for parties avoiding going to Court and settling legal disputes through other means. Mediation is one of those means; arbitration is another.

Mediation is used in employment-related claims very successfully because:

- it can be a cost saving for both parties;
- it is less intimidating than a Court or Tribunal;
- it does not involve lengthy trials or hearings; and
- it focuses less on the legal issues and so can be a lot less complex.

Arbitration is used in more complex commercial cases and international cases and is not generally used in domestic employment disputes apart from the new ACAS arbitration scheme mentioned above.

There are a number of bodies that provide alternative dispute resolution, such as the Centre for Effective Dispute Resolution (CEDR), the ADR Group and In Place of Strife (see *Sources of further information*). Also, many barristers' chambers provide mediation services.

The ACAS Code of Practice

In April 2009, ACAS issued a new Code of Practice on handling discipline and grievance. The Code only applies to misconduct issues, poor performance and grievances. It does not apply to individual redundancies or the non-renewal of fixed-term contracts, but in either of these circumstances employers should still follow a fair procedure, in accordance with other legislation or case law as appropriate. Employment Tribunals can take the Code into account and increase awards by up to 25% for unreasonable failure of an employer to comply with any part of it. Similarly, an employee's unreasonable failure to comply may result in a decrease of their award by 25%. ACAS has also published a guide to complement the Code, which provides detailed advice to employers on practical aspects of disciplinary and grievance issues in the workplace.

Proposals for reform

On 27 January 2011 the Government issued a consultation paper setting out proposed reforms to the Employment Tribunal system, with the aim of reducing the number of claims. The key proposed changes include:

- Extending the qualifying period for employees to be able to bring a claim for unfair dismissal from one to two years.
- Encouraging early dispute resolution through mediation or by requiring all claims to be lodged with ACAS in the first instance, in order to allow pre-claim conciliation.
- Tackling weak and vexatious claims by, for example, requiring claimants to pay a fee for lodging a claim and giving judges more powers to strike-out a claim.
- The Government is also considering giving Tribunals the power to penalise employers that have breached an individual's rights, with a 'fine' of up to £5,000 payable to the Exchequer.

The consultation ended on 20 April 2011, although the Government has yet to issue its response. In view of the wide ranging nature of the changes, it is unlikely any changes will take place before April 2012.

> See also: Disciplinary and grievance procedures, p.121; Dismissal, p.146; Employment Tribunals, p.179; Mediation, p.300.

Sources of further information

Centre for Effective Dispute Resolution: www.cedr.co.uk/

ADR Group: www.adrgroup.co.uk

ACAS – Code of Practice on Discipline and Grievance:
www.acas.org.uk/CHttpHandler.ashx?id=1041

In Place of Strife: www.mediate.co.uk/

Government Consultation on resolving workplace disputes:
www.bis.gov.uk/Consultations/resolving-workplace-disputes?cat=open

---

Comment ...

Resolving workplace disputes

Shaun Hogan, Blandy & Blandy

On 20 April 2011 the consultation period closed on the Government's wide-ranging and potentially quite radical reforms to the Employment Tribunal system. We must now wait whilst the Government reflects on the responses received and develops firm amendments to the Tribunal process. However, a quick round up of responses to the consultation includes, amongst others, the following proposals.

Increasing the qualifying period for unfair dismissal claims

The Government has proposed increasing the minimum length of service for an employee to bring an unfair dismissal claim from one to two years. This would see a return to the position that applied from 1985 to 1999 and, according to the Government, would result in approximately 3,700-4,700 less claims per year, while stimulating the economy by removing a barrier to job creation.

Critics argued that few employers would be persuaded to hire merely on the basis they have a further year in which to dismiss without fear of facing an unfair dismissal allegation. Most consider 12 months is long enough to establish whether to dismiss. With a long service requirement, many claimants would instead focus their attention on spurious discrimination and whistleblowing claims (as these have no qualifying service limits) and so it remains unclear whether the number of claims would fall. *On 3 October 2011, the Government announced the two-year qualifying period would indeed be introduced from 1 April 2012.*

Shaun Hogan joined Blandy & Blandy in 2008 as a trainee solicitor and is now a newly qualified Solicitor in the Employment team. He studied law at the University of Reading before completing his LPC at the College of Law in Guildford where he was awarded the Michael Fellingham Memorial Prize for the highest mark in the private client elective.

Fees, fines and deposits

A lot of attention has been drawn to the introduction of a fee-based system whereby a claimant must pay to submit their claim, although the Government indicated this would be the focus of a separate consultation. The justification for a fee is to discourage weak and vexatious claims, but Unions have argued that a fee may deny access to justice for low paid workers at a time when they may have no source of income. The level of fee would need significant consideration along with the further use of the existing power to order a claimant to pay a deposit of up to £500 (which itself may be increased to £1,000 under the proposals).

Of great concern to employers, particularly small employers, is the proposed introduction of a fine payable by the employer if a claimant is successful at a full Hearing. The fine would be additional to any damages awarded and would equate to 50% of the Tribunal award (subject to a minimum of £100 and maximum of £5,000). It would be paid to the Exchequer, presumably as a method of funding the £2bn of savings the Ministry of Justice is required to make over the next four years. *On 3 October 2011, George Osborne confirmed that, for the first time ever, a fee for taking a case to a Tribunal will be introduced. Litigants will only get the fee back if they win. Osborne did not specify amounts in his speech but it is understood that workers will face a £150 to £250 charge to make any Employment Tribunal application and a further £1,000 for starting a hearing.*

> "Of great concern to employers, particularly small employers, is the proposed introduction of a fine payable by the employer if a claimant is successful at a full Hearing."

In his Review of Civil Litigation Costs, Lord Justice Rupert Jackson highlighted there is less incentive to accept a reasonable offer in an Employment Tribunal claim than in the civil courts. This is because there is no equivalent to a 'Part 36 offer', whereby a party that fails to better a settlement offer is at risk of having to pay the other party's costs. The consultation proposes that formal offers could be backed by penalties for failing to accept reasonable offers. The penalty could be in the form of an uplift or reduction in any compensation awarded and could point towards vexatious or unreasonable action triggering a costs award.

Mediation and settlement offers

ACAS currently offers a voluntary pre-claim conciliation service to help parties resolve disputes early. Statistics suggest that although it is rarely used, the service is relatively successful. The consultation encourages conciliation by requiring a claimant to submit details of their claim to ACAS. There would then be a one-month period in which the parties could engage in conciliation, during which the time limit for submitting a full claim to the Tribunal would be put on hold. The change would undoubtedly decrease the number of claims going to Tribunal but may increase the costs, as ACAS resources would have to be bolstered to cope with the increased workload.

On the whole, the reforms will be welcomed by employers as the majority seek to make it more difficult for employees to submit and/or pursue weak claims. If all the proposals were to be implemented we would see quite a dramatic change in how parties pursue and defend claims.

Various proposals look to front load the system by requiring the parties to enter conciliation and provide information (e.g. a statement of loss) at an earlier stage, thereby helping to reduce the number of hearings. Much more emphasis would be placed on settling claims and parties would have to be much more realistic about the strengths and weaknesses of their cases.

Employment status

Sarah Lee, BPE Solicitors LLP

Key points

- Given that distinct rules exist for employees, workers and the self-employed, determining employment status is an important but sometimes complex exercise. There are a number of factors that can be taken into account in determining employment status (which are explored more fully below), although none of these is definitive.
- The Employment Rights Act 1996 defines 'employee' and 'worker' as follows:
  - An 'employee' is an individual who has entered into or works under a contract of employment (also known as a contract of service).
  - A 'worker' is an individual who has entered into or works under a contract of employment or any other contract under which the individual undertakes to perform work or services personally for another party to the contract who is not a client or customer of the individual.
- On the contrary, a self-employed individual operates under a 'contract for services', under which they agree to provide services to another.
- However, what the parties call themselves and the contract under which they operate is not the decisive factor. If there is a dispute, Employment Tribunals will look beyond the terms used by the parties and will examine the true nature of the relationship. For example, an individual engaged as a 'casual worker' or 'consultant' may, in fact, be deemed to be an employee by an Employment Tribunal.

Legislation

It is important to determine employment status, as certain legal rights only apply if an individual is an employee, although, increasingly, statutory rights are also being granted to workers.

The main legal rights in question can be found in the following legislation:

- Social Security Contributions and Benefits Act 1992.
- Trade Union and Labour Relations (Consolidation) Act 1992.
- Employment Rights Act 1996.
- National Minimum Wage Act 1998.
- Public Interest Disclosure Act 1998.
- Working Time Regulations 1998.
- Employment Relations Act 1999 and 2004.

- Part-Time Workers (Prevention of Less Favourable Treatment) Regulations 2000.
- Employment Act 2002 and 2008.
- Fixed-Term Employees (Prevention of Less Favourable Treatment) Regulations 2002.
- Conduct of Employment Agencies and Employment Businesses Regulations 2003.
- Transfer of Undertakings (Protection of Employment) Regulations 2006.
- Equality Act 2010.

Basic categories

There are three main types of employment status:

1. Employee.
2. Worker.
3. Self-employed.

Case studies

Autoclenz Ltd v. Belcher and ors (2009)

In this case, a group of car valets had terms and conditions stating and indicating that they were self-employed – for example, their terms and conditions allowed them to provide a substitute. However, the Court of Appeal said that they were, in reality, employees.

It stated that the law in this area was as set out in *Firthglow Ltd (t/a Protectacoat) v. Szilagyi*. Following that case, a Tribunal must consider whether or not the words of the written contract represent the true intentions or expectations of the parties. In the *Autoclenz* case, the Tribunal held that no one seriously expected the valets to provide a substitute, and that the valets were expected to turn up every day and do the work provided (despite the terms and conditions to the contrary). The Court of Appeal concluded that there was the necessary mutuality of obligation to conclude that the car valets were workers and, furthermore, the necessary control to establish that they were employees.

Secretary of State for Business, Enterprise and Regulatory Reform v. Neufeld and anor (2009)

In this case the Court of Appeal confirmed that a shareholder and director of a company can also be an employee.

In this case, Mr Neufeld was a controlling shareholder and director of a company that became insolvent. When the company became insolvent, he was denied payments from the National Insurance Fund on the basis that his 90% shareholding was not compatible with employee status.

Mr Neufeld lost at the Employment Tribunal, which found that, although he worked under what appeared to be a genuine employment contract, the fact that he gave personal guarantees for the company, lent it money and controlled it indicated that, in reality, he was not an employee. The Employment Appeals Tribunal allowed his appeal, and the Secretary of State took the matter to the Court of Appeal for guidance on this area.

The Court of Appeal made it clear that a shareholder and director of a company can also be an employee, even if his or her shareholding gives him or her total control of the company.

Employees

There are three essential elements in a contract of employment:

1. There must be mutuality of obligation between the employer and the employee, i.e. the employer is obliged to provide work to the employee, and the employee is obliged to perform that work.

2. The contract must impose an obligation on the employee to

perform the work personally, i.e. the employee is not permitted to provide a substitute.

3. The worker must expressly or impliedly agree to be subject to the control of the employer to a sufficient degree to make the employer 'master'.

Other factors that go towards demonstrating the existence of a contract of employment are:

- remuneration by way of payment of wages or salary;
- payment during absence through holiday or sickness;
- tools or equipment required to perform the job are provided;
- being subject to the 'employer's' internal rules and procedures, e.g. a disciplinary procedure;
- membership of the company pension scheme; and
- a prohibition on working for other companies or individuals.

Employee checklist

If the answer is yes to all or many of the following questions, the individual is likely to be an employee:

- Does the 'employer' have to provide the worker with work, and does the worker have to perform it?
- Does the worker have to perform the work personally?
- Can the 'employer' tell the worker what work to do, and where, when and how to do it?
- Is the worker paid by way of wages or salary?
- Is the worker paid when absent due to holiday or sickness?
- Does the 'employer' provide the tools or equipment the worker requires to do their job?
- Is the worker subject to the 'employer's' internal rules and procedures?

- Is the worker a member of or permitted to join the company pension scheme?
- Is the worker prohibited from working for other companies or individuals?

Workers

'Workers' are creatures created by statute in recent years. They fall somewhere between an employee and the genuinely self-employed. Where an individual does not meet the higher threshold of being an employee, they may still qualify as a 'worker'.

Worker checklist

The key requirements for establishing 'worker' status are that:

- there is mutuality of obligation;
- the individual has to perform work or services personally and cannot send a substitute (although in some cases a limited right to provide a substitute will not prevent an individual being a 'worker'); and
- the individual is not undertaking the work as part of their own business (e.g. if the 'employer' is actually one of their clients).

Self-employed individuals

Self-employed people are usually identified by the fact that they are in business for themselves and provide a service to multiple clients. Self-employed people are generally more independent than workers. They have far greater control over how and when to deliver the services and who delivers it. They will usually be better able to protect their own commercial interests, although they will bear any financial risk from the business they operate.

Self-employed checklist

If the answer is yes to all or many of the following questions, the individual is likely to be self-employed:

- Can the individual refuse work offered by the 'employer'?
- Can the individual provide a substitute to perform the work for them, e.g. can they sub-contract the work?
- Can the individual decide what work to do, and where, when and how to do it?
- Does the individual regularly work for a number of different people?
- Does the individual bear a financial risk and also have an opportunity to profit from the work?
- Does the individual submit an invoice for their services, rather than being paid through the payroll?
- Does the individual provide the main items of equipment they need to perform their job, not just the small tools that many employees provide themselves?

Legal consequences of the distinction

Employees

Employers and employees have obligations that are implied into the contract between them, e.g. the mutual duty of trust and confidence. There are no such obligations for workers or the self-employed.

An employee enjoys the following rights (subject to satisfying any relevant qualifying conditions):

- To benefit from all contractual entitlements.
- Right to receive written particulars of employment.
- Right to receive an itemised pay statement from an employer.
- National Minimum Wage.
- Protection against unlawful deduction from wages.
- Right to be given a statutory minimum period of notice.
- Statutory Sick Pay.

- Remuneration during suspension on medical grounds.
- Guarantee payments.
- Protection against unfair dismissal.
- Statutory redundancy pay.
- A minimum period of paid holiday.
- Right to specified minimum rest breaks.
- Right not to work more than 48 hours on average per week (or to opt out of this right if the employee chooses).
- Right to request time off for study or training.
- Time off for emergencies involving dependants.
- Time off for jury service and some public duties.
- Statutory maternity, paternity and adoption leave and pay.
- Time off for antenatal care.
- Right to request flexible working.
- Protection against unlawful discrimination (including race, sex, disability, age, religious belief, sexual orientation, part-time and fixed-term status).
- Equal pay.
- Protection for 'whistleblowing'.
- Protection for their health and safety.

This list is not exhaustive.

In addition, only employees are covered by the ACAS Code of Practice on Disciplinary and Grievance Procedures, and only employees will be automatically transferred to any purchaser of their employer's business under the Transfer of Undertakings (Protection of Employment) Regulations 2006.

Workers

Workers enjoy the following core rights:

- To benefit from all contractual entitlements.
- To receive the National Minimum Wage.
- Protection against unlawful deductions from wages.

- A minimum period of paid holiday.
- Right to specified minimum rest breaks.
- Right not to work more than 48 hours on average per week (or to opt out of this right if the worker chooses).
- Protection against unlawful discrimination (including race, sex, disability, age, religious belief, sexual orientation, part-time and fixed-term status).
- Protection from 'whistleblowing'.
- Protection for their health and safety.

Self-employed individuals

Self-employed individuals are not generally covered by employment legislation, because they are, in effect, their own boss.

However, they will benefit from protection for their health and safety (under the employer's common law duty of care in respect of occupiers' liability) and, in some cases, protection from discrimination. This is because discrimination law protects those who are 'in employment'. Anti-discrimination legislation defines 'employment' as 'employment under a contract of service… or a contract personally to execute any work'. Therefore, if a self-employed individual is under an obligation to provide services personally, rather than simply providing services, they may have protection from discrimination.

The rights and responsibilities of self-employed individuals would be set out by the terms of the contract they have with their client.

The Construction Industry Scheme

The Construction Industry Scheme (CIS) is a set of rules for contractors and sub-contractors in the construction industry. The rules were originally introduced by HMRC to tighten up on the status of employees and sub-contractors, given the differences in tax and National Insurance contributions.

Under CIS, contractors are required to:

- register with the scheme;
- check sub-contractors' employment status (to ensure that they are properly self-employed and not an employee);
- verify sub-contractors, i.e. check whether they are registered with HMRC, so that the contractor knows whether to pay them gross or after making a deduction from their payment;
- pay sub-contractors in the right way, making deductions if necessary;
- pay deductions made from sub-contractors' payments over to HMRC;
- give sub-contractors deduction statements; and
- send monthly returns to HMRC.

See also: Contractors, p.93;
Employment contracts, p.164;
Fixed-term workers, p.218;
Part-time workers, p.382;
Self-employment, p.465; Work experience, internships and apprenticeships, p.558.

Sources of further information

Inland Revenue: www.inlandrevenue.co.uk

HM Revenue and Customs – Construction Industry Scheme: www.hmrc.gov.uk/cis

---

Employment Tribunals

Anna Youngs, Mills & Reeve

Key points
- Parties do not have to be legally represented, but representation is of assistance in more complex cases, particularly discrimination issues.
- Use only the prescribed forms to issue or respond to a claim.
- Follow the Tribunal's Orders.
- Consider settlement via compromise agreement/ACAS conciliation/judicial mediation.

Legislation
- Employment Tribunals Rules of Procedure 2004 (which are set out at Schedule 1 of the Employment Tribunals (Constitution and Rules of Procedure) Regulations 2004) as amended.

Introduction to proceedings in the Employment Tribunals
The Employment Tribunals are less formal than the other Courts of England and Wales. The idea is that anybody can bring or defend a claim, without necessarily seeking legal advice. That said, employment issues are notoriously complex, particularly where discrimination is alleged and in such cases legal advice is likely to be needed.

The Employment Tribunals Rules of Procedure 2004 (the Rules) set out the way in which proceedings must be lodged and conducted. This chapter will highlight some general practice points for conducting proceedings.

The Overriding Objective
The Overriding Objective is a principle that runs throughout our litigation system. The Objective is to enable the Courts and Tribunal to deal with cases justly. This must be considered when making applications to the Tribunal and when conducting Tribunal proceedings in general, because the Tribunal will make its decisions in accordance with the Overriding Objective.

The Overriding Objective is set out at Regulation 3 of the Employment Tribunals (Constitution and Rules of Procedure) Regulations 2004, which states that dealing with a case justly includes, so far as practicable:

- ensuring that the parties are on an equal footing;
- dealing with the case in ways that are proportionate to the complexity or importance of the issues;
- ensuring that it is dealt with expeditiously and fairly; and
- saving expense.

Using the prescribed form
There are set forms that must be used when bringing (form ET1) and responding (form ET3) to a claim in the Employment Tribunal. If the correct form is not used, the claim or response will not be accepted. The current forms can be downloaded from the Employment Tribunals' website (www.employmenttribunals.gov.uk). There are some sections on the form that are marked with a star (*). These sections must be answered, or the claim or the response will be rejected.

> **Facts**
> - In 2009/10, 236,100 claims were made to the Employment Tribunals Service (an increase of 56% compared to 2008/09); in 2010/11 the number of claims reduced by 8% to 218,100.
> - 484,300 cases still remain outstanding within the Tribunal system (20% more than the previous year).
> - The average award for unfair dismissal was £8,924 in 2010/11.
> - The average award for race discrimination in 2010/11 was £12,108 and the highest award was £62,530.
> - The average award for sex discrimination was £193,911 in 2010/11, and the highest award was £289,167.
> - The average award for disability discrimination was £14,137 in 2010/11, and the highest award was £181,083.

Time limits

Strict time limits apply in the Employment Tribunals. When a claim is sent to the employer, the Tribunal will state on the accompanying letter the date by which they must respond.

Failure to respond by that deadline is likely to result in a default judgment being entered in favour of the claimant, unless the employer has applied for and received an extension of time (which should not be relied upon as a given). Any such application for an extension must be made prior to the deadline expiring.

The claimant also has to comply with time limits. Generally claims must be lodged within three months of either the date of dismissal, or the last act complained of, although there are some exceptions and variations. Due to the various discretions that can be exercised by the Tribunal, it is worth seeking legal advice.

Management of the case

Once the claim has been received and the response has been accepted, the next step is for the Tribunal to set down directions for the future conduct of the case. This is usually done at a Case Management Discussion. These directions will set dates by which the following must have been done:

- Exchange of documents. All relevant documents within your possession or control, whether or not they help your case, help your opponent's case, or damage either case.
- Agree a 'bundle' of documents. The bundle should contain all documents relevant to the matters in issue. The claimant is responsible for preparing the bundle, but many respondents take on this responsibility as they have more resources and generally have more documents in their possession.
- Exchange of witness statements. This is usually done by way of mutual or simultaneous exchange, but may be done by sequential exchange if the claimant's case is not clear from their claim form or any further particulars of claim.
- Date and length of the hearing.

Parties may also be required to agree a chronology, statement of agreed facts and statement of issues that the Tribunal must determine, although even if the Tribunal does not order a statement of issues, it is important that you know what the issues are so that you can focus your case effectively.

An important document is the schedule of loss. The Tribunal will require the claimant to serve a schedule setting out what financial losses they have suffered. This is usually ordered at the earliest stage in the hope of promoting settlement. If this is not ordered by the Tribunal, employers should certainly ask for one. This will help you assess the cost effectiveness of resisting the claim.

Documents that do not have to be disclosed or included in the Bundle

'Without prejudice' documents, which generally take the form of negotiations between the parties, should not be included in the Bundle.

Documents that attract legal advice or litigation 'privilege' (which is the right not to disclose) do not have to be disclosed:

- Legal advice privilege protects communications passing between lawyer and client created for the purpose of giving or receiving advice. This type of privilege is not confined to advice about legal rights and obligations but it will not arise unless the advice is given in a relevant legal context.
- Litigation privilege protects documents created for the dominant purpose of gathering evidence for use in proceedings if they are made:
    - confidentially;
    - between a lawyer and a client, a lawyer and his agent or a lawyer and a third party; and
    - for the dominant purpose of conducting or aiding the conduct of actual litigation or litigation that is reasonably in prospect.

The Tribunal has powers to award costs or even to strike out a claim for failure to comply with an Order.

The hearing

In full hearings, where the merits of a claim are to be decided, the Tribunal panel will be made up of three people:

- A legally qualified Employment Judge (who sits in the middle of the panel and is addressed as 'Sir' or 'Madam').
- Two lay members – one who has an employee background, such as someone from a Union, and one who has an employer background.

The idea is that there is a balanced panel,who will make a balanced decision. As the Tribunal is a civil court, liability will be determined on the 'balance of probabilities', which means, for example, whether it is more likely than not that the dismissal was unfair.

There are differing rules as to which side goes first, depending on the type of claim. The Tribunal will assist unrepresented parties with procedure as far as possible, but as a rule of thumb, where discrimination is alleged, the claimant's case will be heard first (as the claimant must prove facts out of which discrimination could be inferred), and in unfair dismissal cases, the respondent will go first.

Whichever side goes first, the procedure is the same for the witnesses. Using the claimant's witness as an example:

- the witness may have to read their statement aloud (bear this in mind when drafting statements);
- the claimant's representative may be able to ask some questions;
- the other side will then cross-examine the witness;
- the Employment Judge or the panel members may ask some questions; and

- the claimant's representative will have the opportunity to ask further questions to clarify points made by the other side.

After all the evidence from both sides is heard, each side will make 'submissions' about their case. This is an opportunity for each side to put forward their best points, address any damage done to their case by the other side, and highlight the weaknesses in the other side's case.

Top tips for witnesses
- Don't avoid answering a question.
- If you don't know or don't remember, say so (but don't use this as a get out!).
- Don't fill silences by talking (this is where the most damage is commonly done!).
- Familiarise yourself with your witness statement and read documents relevant to your evidence.

The judgment
The Employment Judge may give an oral judgment on the day. If s/he does this, s/he will only provide a full written judgment if you ask for one. A party must have a written judgment if you think you have grounds for appeal. If you win, you may be able to get costs from the other side. Costs are not given automatically in the Tribunal. Refer to the rules for the circumstances in which you can apply for costs and the time limits for doing so. The Tribunal has a booklet on Tribunal Judgments that it sends out with the written judgment, which should be of use.

Costs or expenses orders may be made if:

- a hearing or pre-hearing review is postponed;
- in bringing or conducting the proceedings, a party has been misconceived or if the party or his representative has acted vexatiously,

abusively, disruptively or otherwise unreasonably; and/or
- a party has not complied with an order or practice direction.

The Tribunal may also make preparation time orders and wasted costs orders as appropriate.

Withdrawal by the claimant
If the claimant withdraws their claim at any stage, this ends the proceedings. However, it does not necessarily prevent them from re-issuing fresh proceedings. Therefore, upon receipt of a notice of withdrawal it is advisable for respondents to apply to the Tribunal for the claim to be 'dismissed' pursuant to Rule 25(4) of the Rules. This prevents the claimant from being able to re-issue the proceedings. An application should be made within 28 days from the date that the notice of withdrawal is sent to the parties by the Tribunal. Current practice (although not set out within the Rules) is that the claimant (or their representative) should be copied in to the application and given time to object (some Tribunals currently say that the claimant should be given 14 days to object).

ACAS and conciliation
An ACAS officer is assigned to each case in order to try to assist the parties to conciliate or settle the case. ACAS' services are free and confidential, and therefore settling a claim through ACAS can avoid unwanted costs and publicity. Litigation risk is avoided if a case settles, and an ACAS settlement can include things that a Tribunal would not be able to consider; for example, an agreed reference can be consideration for a settlement, but the Tribunal cannot order an employer to provide a reference. This is a key negotiation point (but when providing references employers must consider their duty of care to both the employee and to future employers).

There is a procedure set out in Rule 25A of the Rules regarding dismissal of proceedings following an ACAS settlement.

Judicial mediation

A Judicial mediation pilot scheme commenced in July 2006, and judicial mediation is now available throughout England and Wales. The aim is to encourage resolution of disputes without having a full Employment Tribunal hearing (and therefore will normally be appropriate for cases where there is an ongoing relationship between the parties). The intention is to save time and costs.

Suitable cases are identified by an Employment Judge, normally at a Case Management Discussion. If the parties agree to judicial mediation, the Tribunal proceedings will be stayed and the case will be referred to a full-time Employment Judge who is trained in mediation. The Employment Judge will not make a decision in the case or give what is effectively a judgment in the case.

The mediation will be in private, and will be confidential. The Employment Judge who mediated the case will not be involved further in the case if the mediation is not successful and it proceeds to a hearing. The mediation files and Tribunal hearing files will be kept completely separate so that the parties can speak freely in mediation.

Recent developments

On 3 October 2011 the Government announced, as from April 2013, claimants will, for the first time, have to pay a fee if they wish to bring a claim in an Employment Tribunal. The fee will be refundable if the claimant wins. It proposes to consult on the level and structure of fees.

See also: Disciplinary and grievance procedures, p.121; Discrimination, p.126; Dismissal, p.146; Employment disputes, p.168; Mediation, p.300.

Sources of further information

Tribunals Service: www.employmenttribunals.gov.uk

Tribunals Service – EAT: www.employmentappeals.gov.uk

ACAS: www.acas.org.uk

Workplace Law can provide information and advice to employers who have received an Employment Tribunal claim, or who are aware a claim is likely to be lodged, on the services we can provide in this area. Through our network of associates, we have access to experienced Tribunal lawyers who can defend your case on your behalf, and our experienced HR team will ensure they are fully briefed. Our HR consultancy team has extensive experience in supporting clients throughout the entire tribunal claim process, and Jayn Bond, Head of Human Resources at Workplace Law, has served as a Lay Member on the East London Employment Tribunal Panel since 2005, and has a wealth of experience in dealing with all matters 'tribunal'. Visit www.workplacelaw.net for more details.

Equal pay

Siobhan O'Neil, MacRoberts

Key points

- The principle of equal pay originates from Article 141 of the Treaty of Rome (previously Article 119). Article 141 and, later, the Equal Pay Directive, underpinned the rights in Europe to equal pay between men and women. The UK implemented these EU provisions by the Equal Pay Act 1970 (EPA).

- The EPA has now been repealed and the provisions largely replicated in the Equality Act 2010 (EA).

- The EA gives the right to equal pay to men and women, although for ease of reference the presumption in this chapter is that a woman is the affected employee.

- The EA implies an equality clause into any employment contract that does not already include one. This provision applies to all terms and conditions of employment and not only to pay but, for example, sick pay provisions. Any term in a contract that purports to limit or exclude any provision of the EA is unenforceable (with the exception of a COT3 agreement or a compromise agreement).

- The implied equality clause modifies the contract of employment in any situation where a woman is engaged in like work to a man, on work rated as equivalent to work done by a man, or on work of equal value to that done by a man, unless her employer can justify the difference in pay due to a material factor that is not sex.

- Equal pay questionnaires can be served before a claim is issued at the Employment Tribunal to establish facts that are material to a potential claim. If the employer fails to respond to the questionnaire, or the employer's response is evasive, the Tribunal is entitled to draw adverse inferences from the employer's failure.

Legislation

- Treaty of Rome, Article 141.
- Equal Pay Directive (75/117/EEC).
- Equal Pay Act 1970 (repealed as of 1 October 2010 by the Equality Act 2010).
- Sex Discrimination Act 1975 (repealed as of 1 October 2010 by the Equality Act 2010).
- Data Protection Act 1998.
- Equal Pay Act 1970 (Amendment) Regulations 2003 (repealed as of 1 October 2010 by the Equality Act 2010).
- Equal Pay (Questions and Replies) Order 2003.
- Employment Tribunals (Constitution and Rules of Procedure) Regulations 2004.
- Employment Equality (Sex Discrimination) Regulations 2005 (repealed as of 1 October 2010 by the Equality Act 2010).
- Occupational Pension Schemes (Equal Treatment) (Amendment) Regulations 2005 (repealed as of 1 October 2010 by the Equality Act 2010).
- The Equality Act 2010.
- The Equality Act 2010 (Obtaining Information Order) 2010.

Facts

- Women who work full-time earn, on average, 15.5% less per hour than men working full-time. For women who work part-time, the gap in pay relative to full-time men is 34.5% per hour.
- The full-time gender pay gap has narrowed in recent years and was lower in 2010 than in any previous year.
- It is possible to infer from national statistics that an average woman working full-time from age 18 to 59 would lose around £360,000 in gross earnings over the course of her working life, as compared to an equivalent male.
- The scale and direction of the gender pay gap varies according to age. For example, in 2010 the full-time gender pay gap for the 22-29 age group was only 0.9% compared to 20.1% for those in the 40-49 age group.
- The trend in the full-time gender pay gap by occupational group has been consistent in recent years. In 2010 the widest gaps were for managers and senior officials and skilled trades, and the narrowest gaps were for sales and customer service and professional occupations.
- In 2010 the full-time gender pay gap was much lower in Northern Ireland and Wales than in England and Scotland. This reflects the fact that the average male earnings in Northern Ireland and Wales are well below the UK average.
- In the four decades since the Equal Pay Act came into force, major changes in the UK's economy and society have increased the opportunities available to women. It has become more socially acceptable for women to work. Currently 70% of women of working age are in employment, compared to 56% in 1971.

Sources: Equality and Human Rights Commission and National Statistics.

Like work, work rated as equivalent and work of equal value

Like work

A woman is employed on like work with a man if the woman's and man's work is of the same or a broadly similar nature. Employers need to consider the nature and extent of the differences between the work and the frequency with which such differences occur. For example, a cook in a director's dining room was held to be engaged on like work with the assistant chefs of the company's factory canteen.

Work rated as equivalent

An objective job evaluation study can be carried out in respect of a woman's and man's work, and the woman's job is rated for equivalence on the basis of the demand made in terms of matters such as skill or effort required, or level of responsibility. A woman can compare herself to a man who is rated at the same level or lower than her in the job evaluation study. Where a woman raises a rated as equivalent claim, any back pay awarded (see '*Remedies*,' below) should reflect only the period when the job evaluation scheme was in place (although the employee could also raise an equal value claim in respect of the period prior to the job evaluation study).

Work of equal value

A woman's work may be of equal value to a man's in terms of the demands made on her, even if it is not like work or rated as equivalent. A woman may therefore potentially still claim equal pay with a man, even if he is doing a different job. For example, a female cook employed as a canteen assistant succeeded in a claim for equal pay with a male skilled tradesman. Where work is claimed to be of equal value, an independent expert is often appointed to determine the issue.

Appropriate comparator

A person making a claim under the EA must select a comparator, that is, a person of the opposite sex whose terms and conditions can be compared for the purpose of determining equality. There is one limited exception to the requirement to cite a comparator and that is in pregnancy-related cases where:

■ a pay rise that the woman would have been entitled to had she not been on maternity leave is not taken into account in calculating her maternity pay; and
■ contractual bonuses are missed during a period of time before or after her maternity leave.

The comparator cannot be hypothetical. In the case of *Walton Centre for Neurology v. Bewley*, the EAT held, overturning previous case law, that a claimant cannot compare herself to her successor. The choice of comparator under the EA is limited by the requirement for the comparator to be employed by the same employer or associated employers. However, under Article 141, the scope for comparison is wider and the ECJ has established that it may not be limited to the same employer. The important factor is whether the relationship between the two employers is sufficiently close and, in particular, whether the disparity in terms and conditions can be attributed to a 'single source'. In the case of *Robertson v. Defra* (2005), the Court of Appeal held that the Crown was not the 'single source' responsible for determining pay and conditions with the

effect that the claimants could not compare themselves with employees in different departments within the Civil Service.

In the recent case of *North and Others v. Dumfries and Galloway Council* (2011) the Court of Session concluded that Lady Smith of the EAT had erred in law where she held that a female equal pay claimant must show 'a real possibility' of her chosen male comparator being employed at her establishment in the job he carries out at the other establishment, or in a broadly similar job. In that case the EAT had overturned a Tribunal that had held that a group of claimants who worked as classroom assistants, support for learning assistants and nursery nurses were in the same employment for the purposes of the EPA as their comparators who were groundsmen, refuse collectors, refuse drivers and leisure attendants. This was despite the fact the claimants were each based at particular schools and the comparators (with the exception of leisure attendants) were based at depots but worked at a variety of locations across the geographical area covered by the Council. The Tribunal had relied on the case of *British Coal Corporation v. Smith and Others* (1996), in which the House of Lords held that a claimant can satisfy the 'same employment' test by showing that male comparators at her establishment share common terms and conditions with male comparators at other establishments.

The EAT held that the Tribunal had misapplied *British Coal* and that to be 'in the same employment' must have a basis in reality; there must be a real possibility that the male comparator could be employed at the same establishment as the woman, carrying out the same, or broadly similar, job to the one he does at his current establishment. However, even having demonstrated that there was such a possibility, there was a further need to provide evidence that the male comparator's employment at the woman's establishment would have broadly similar terms and conditions.

The Court of Session considered that this requirement imported a test that went beyond what was stated in the legislation, case law or the European Community Treaty and would place an additional burden on equal pay claimants. In delivering the judgment Lady Paton stated that:

"if it can be shown that, no matter how unlikely the employment of the male comparator at the female claimant's establishment, the comparator would (or could be assumed to) remain on broadly the same terms and conditions of employment as other members of his class of employee, then the *British Coal* hypothesis would be satisfied, and the claimant and the comparator would be shown to be 'in the same employment'." (Paragraph 42)

Unfortunately the law in this area cannot be regarded as settled just yet. The claimants are appealing the decision in *North* and the appeal will be heard by the Supreme Court later this year. Similarly, a decision is awaited by the Court of Session in the recently heard appeal of *Wilkinson and Others v. Edinburgh City Council*. In that case, contrary to its decision in *North*, the EAT had held that female claimants and their male comparators, who were all employed by the Council, were indeed employed at the 'same establishment' for the purposes of the EPA.

Meaning of 'pay'

The scope of the EA is not limited to 'pay' in the usual sense of the word. In this context, the word 'pay' can generally be regarded as meaning 'terms and conditions'. For example, the EA covers ex-gratia perks, redundancy pay and pension contributions.

In one case, the Court of Appeal took the unusual approach of aggregating the employees' basic pay, fixed bonuses and attendance allowances in order to work out an overall hourly rate for the purposes of comparison. The Court of Appeal clarified that an employee cannot pick and choose terms from the comparator's contract for comparison.

Material Factor (MF) defence

An employer can defend an equal pay claim by establishing that the variation between the woman's contract and the man's contract is due to a material factor that is not the difference of sex; for example, qualifications or performance. The courts, both at a European and national level, have accepted that economic reasons can constitute 'material factors'. An example would be where an employer recruits a new female employee and offers her more advantageous terms and conditions than an existing male employee carrying out a similar role, on the basis that the job market is such that competitive terms and conditions are essential to recruit quality employees.

In the case of *Cadman v. Health and Safety Executive* (2006), the ECJ confirmed that where the difference in pay can be attributed to length of service, it will usually be justifiable unless 'the worker provides evidence capable of raising serious doubts in that regard'.

There has been confusion surrounding whether it is sufficient for an employer to demonstrate that there is a reason for the disparity in terms and conditions that are not related to gender or whether the employer has to go one step further and objectively justify the difference. Domestic case law has held that the employer will not be required to justify objectively any difference in pay unless the claimant has shown there to be a potentially indirectly discriminatory reason for the difference. The European Court of Justice, however, has held that an employer must objectively justify any difference in pay, even where the claimant has failed to establish that the difference in pay is potentially indirectly discriminatory.

In the case of *Sharp v. Caledonia Group Services* (2006), the EAT preferred the ECJ's approach. This decision was appealed to the Court of Appeal, but the case settled before the appeal was heard. However, *Middlesbrough Borough Council v. Surtees and Others* (2007) adds significant weight to the argument that objective justification is only required where the explanation being put forward for the difference in pay is tainted by sex.

The case of *West Midlands Police v. Blackburn* (2009) is an interesting example of a Tribunal misunderstanding the purpose of the MF defence. The claimants were police officers who received less than their male comparator who was employed on like work. The reason for the disparity in pay was that the comparator worked shifts involving night work and received a special payment (effectively a bonus) for this, but the claimants did receive similar special payments because they did not work at night due to childcare responsibilities.

The Tribunal held that it was a legitimate objective to reward night work, but that the Chief Constable could have paid the claimants as though they had done night work even though they had not. It would not have been a significant expenditure and would have eliminated the discrimination. The EAT upheld the Chief Constable's appeal and held that the Tribunal had misunderstood the nature of the justification defence and had erred in concluding that the differential was not reasonably justified.

Elias P stated that:

"The payment of money to compensate for the economic disadvantages suffered by those who have childcare responsibilities is not what the Equal Pay Act requires. Nor is the assessment of the employer's ability to pay sums of this kind a task which Parliament could conceivably have expected Tribunals to do." (Paragraph 46.)

The Court of Appeal subsequently held that the analysis of objective justification, aims and means in the judgment of the EAT was correct.

Implied equality clause

If the employer cannot justify the difference in pay, the implied equality clause operates so that:

- any contractual term that is less favourable to a woman is modified to become as favourable as the corresponding term in the man's contract; and
- any beneficial term in a man's contract that is not included in the woman's contract is included into the woman's contract.

To give a simple example, if a man is paid £500 more per month than a woman for like work, the equality clause will entitle the woman to that extra £500 per month.

Remedies

These are:

- back pay (limited to six years, or five in Scotland from the claim date), representing the difference in pay between the woman and the 'equal' or 'equivalent' employee, with interest; and
- the same level of pay or benefits as her comparator for the future (if the complainant remains in the same job).

The EAT previously confirmed that a claim under the EPA could not include an element for non-pecuniary losses (e.g. injury to feelings).

Procedure

As with discrimination claims, cases can be brought while the employee is still employed. In the standard case, claims must be brought at any time during employment or within six months of leaving employment.

An individual may submit equal pay questionnaires to the employer, either before a claim is made to the Tribunal or within 21 days of such a claim being lodged. Employers are not obliged to answer these questionnaires, but the Tribunal may draw an adverse inference if a questionnaire is not answered deliberately and without reasonable cause in an eight-week window from it being served, or where the reply is evasive or equivocal. This includes an inference that the equality clause has been breached. An employer may be reluctant to disclose certain information when responding to the questionnaire on the basis that it may result in a breach of the Data Protection Act 1998 (DPA). That may be appropriate in some cases; however, if the Tribunal subsequently issues an Order compelling the employer to disclose the information, and the processing can be deemed 'fair,' it will have no liability under the DPA.

Pay protection

Consideration was given to the justification of pay protection arrangements, introduced by Local Authorities in order to preserve the position of disadvantaged (predominantly male) workers, following the introduction of job evaluation schemes in the case of *Redcar and Cleveland Borough Council v. Bainbridge and Ors*, and *Surtees and Ors v. Middlesbrough Borough Council* (2008).

The Court of Appeal held that, on the facts of these cases, the Councils' pay protection schemes were *prima facie* discriminatory and therefore could not be justified. The Court did go on to say, however, that even though such arrangements may be found to be discriminatory, they might nevertheless be justified in some circumstances.

Those circumstances will depend on the facts of each case and consideration may be given to whether the employer had an awareness that the introduction of a particular pay protection scheme would directly or indirectly discriminate against certain groups of workers, usually women. The Court further stated that the employer's motivation in introducing the scheme can be taken into account when the Employment Tribunal is considering whether or not the scheme can be justified.

We have indeed seen an Employment Tribunal in the north of England find a six-and-a-half-year period of pay protection, introduced by *Agenda for Change*, to be non-discriminatory in *Hartley v. Northumbria Healthcare NHS Foundation Trust*. Critical to the Tribunal's reasoning was the proposition that, in assessing justification, an Employment Tribunal is entitled to give weight to approval by the trade unions in the collective bargaining process. During the introduction of *Agenda for Change*, the 15 trade unions involved went directly to their memberships for a vote on the job evaluation study and the pay and grading changes, with 13 of the 15 voting in favour of the changes. As the Employment Judge noted, some of those unions voting in favour were composed mainly of women members. Another factor was that there was no clear evidence of historical discrimination which the pay protection would be perpetuating.

The EA includes a new term that attempts to clarify the position regarding pay protection schemes and includes a provision that can make them lawful. Section 69(3) states that the long-term aim of reducing inequality between men's and women's pay is always to be regarded as a legitimate aim for the purposes of justifying pay practices that indirectly discriminate against women. Therefore, short-term pay protection schemes introduced with the aim of removing long-term inequalities in pay may be capable of being objectively justified, provided that their use is a proportionate way of achieving that aim.

Recent legislation

The Equality Act 2010 came into force on 1 October 2010. The Act largely replicates previous equal pay legislation, with a few exceptions. The key changes are as follows:

- The 'Genuine Material Factor' defence has become the 'Material Factor' defence. The reasoning behind this is that the word 'genuine' did not add anything to the meaning of the defence.

- It is now possible to rely on a hypothetical comparator in relation to sex discrimination claims (which can be brought under Section 13 of the EA). Under the old legislation there had to be an actual comparator. This means that an employee who can show evidence that they would have received better remuneration from their employer if they were of a different sex may have a claim, even if there is no one of the opposite sex doing equal work in the organisation. Previously this was not possible under the EPA. Indirect sex discrimination claims still require an actual comparator.

- Pay secrecy clauses are now unlawful. An employer cannot prevent employees from discussing their pay for the purpose of establishing whether differences exist.

See also: Discrimination, p.126; The Equality Act, p.191; Minimum wage, p.342.

Sources of further information

Equality and Human Rights Commission: www.equalityhumanrights.com

Equal Opportunities policies are becoming ever more important in today's increasingly multicultural, multiracial society. The purpose of this type of policy is to set out the obligations on both the employer and the employee to treat all people with equal dignity and respect within the workplace. The aim is to create a pleasant and harmonious working environment for all.

Workplace Law's *Equal Opportunities Policy and Management Guide v.4.0* sets out and explains the rights of each employee. A well-drafted Equal Opportunities policy, combined with good management, will ensure your organisation meets its legal obligation to provide a non-discriminatory work environment and persuade employees that an equal opportunities policy at work is for the benefit of the whole workforce. For more information visit www.workplacelaw.net.

The Equality Act

Heidi Thompson and Tar Tumber, Workplace Law

Key points

The Equality Act 2010 was introduced on 1 October 2010 and distils and extends previous legislation in order to provide a more consistent and effective legal framework for preventing discrimination. Its key provisions include the following:

- *Harmonisation and extension of discrimination law.* The prohibition in directly or indirectly discriminating 'because of a protected characteristic' covers age, disability, sex, gender reassignment, sexual orientation, race, religion or belief and, in many but not all instances, marriage and civil partnerships. Disability-related discrimination was replaced with a prohibition on discriminating against a disabled person by treating them unfavourably where that treatment is not a proportionate means of achieving a legitimate aim.
- *Discrimination by perception.* The prohibition of an employer treating one employee or group of employees less favourably than others for a reason that would mean the treatment would be unlawful discrimination if it were true. Previously disability, gender reassignment and sex were not covered under perception.
- *Discrimination by association.* The prohibition in an employment context refers to an employer treating one employee or group of employees less favourably than others as a result of their association with a person against whom it would be unlawful to discriminate. Previously age, disability, gender reassignment and sex were not covered under association.
- *Pre-employment health questionnaires.* This now prohibits employers asking job applicants questions about their health and whether they have a disability prior to offering work to the applicant.
- *Positive action in recruitment and promotion.* On 6 April 2011 this provision came into force and enables employers to pick someone for a job from an under-represented group when they have the choice between two or more applicants who are 'as qualified' as each other – but they must not have a policy of doing that in every case.
- *Equal pay.* The Act incorporates provisions to cover previous equal pay and sex discrimination law, with the aim of reflecting key decisions in equal pay case law and avoiding any gap or overlap between provisions.
- *Dual discrimination.* It was proposed that a clause outlawing discrimination on the basis of two (and no more) protected characteristics was to be inserted in the Act. This would have enabled, for example, someone who claims they have been specifically discriminated against because they are an Asian woman, rather than just because of their race or gender, to claim for this combination of characteristics. However, this has not come into force and is currently unlikely to do so.
- *Recommendations by Tribunals.* The Act aims to widen Tribunals' powers to enable wide-ranging recommendations to be made applying across the workplace, such as re-training staff.
- *Specific duties for public bodies to adhere to.* Ensuring equal opportunities for all backgrounds within the community.

Legislation

- Employment Act 1989.
- Employment Rights Act 1996.
- Human Rights Act 1998.
- Employment Relations Act 1999.
- Part-time Workers (Prevention of Less Favourable Treatment) Regulations 2000.
- Employment Rights Act 2002.
- Fixed-term Employees (Prevention of Less Favourable Treatment) Regulations 2002 and 2008.
- Employment Act 2008.
- Equality Act 2010.

Overview

The Equality Act 2010 (the Act) received Royal Assent on 8 April 2010 and came into force on 1 October 2010. It consolidates all existing anti-discrimination legislation, i.e. legislation banning discrimination (direct and indirect) on the grounds of sex (including equal pay), race, disability, religion or belief, sexual orientation and age. The main aim of the Act is to reconcile some of the differences and discrepancies in current anti-discrimination legislation and strengthen the law to support progress on equality. The Act applies to England, Wales and Scotland, but not to Northern Ireland. The Act will be implemented in stages, from 1 October 2010, although the exact timetable is currently unclear, pending further clarity from the Coalition Government.

Types of discrimination

Direct discrimination

Direct discrimination occurs when someone is treated less favourably than another person because of a protected characteristic they have or are thought to have (*see Perceptive discrimination below*), or because they associate with someone who has a protected characteristic (*see Associative discrimination below*).

Associative discrimination

This already applied to race, religion or belief and sexual orientation and now under the Act is extended to cover age, disability, gender reassignment and sex. This is direct discrimination against someone because they associate with another person who possesses a protected characteristic. For example, someone is bypassed for promotion because their manager is aware they have a dependant who is disabled. The manager therefore bypasses the employee, as they believe the employee will be too busy looking after their dependant to concentrate on the role. This would be discrimination against the employee because of their association with the disabled person.

Perceptive discrimination

This form already applied to age, race, religion or belief and sexual orientation and was extended to cover disability, gender reassignment and sex. This is direct discrimination against an individual because others think they possess a particular protected characteristic. It applies even if the person does not actually possess that characteristic. For example, someone is denied an opportunity because they look much younger than they actually are; this could be discrimination on the perception of a protected characteristic, in this case age (*see below*).

Indirect discrimination

This already applied to age, race, religion or belief, sex, sexual orientation and marriage and civil partnership and is now extended to cover disability and gender reassignment. Indirect discrimination can occur when a condition, rule, policy or even a practice in the company applies to everyone but particularly disadvantages people who share a protected characteristic. Indirect discrimination can be justified if the employer can show that it acted reasonably in managing its business, i.e. that it is 'a proportionate means of achieving a legitimate aim'.

Harassment

Harassment is 'unwanted conduct related to a relevant protected characteristic, which has the purpose or effect of violating an individual's dignity or creating an intimidating, hostile, degrading, humiliating or offensive environment for that individual'. Harassment applies to all protected characteristics except for pregnancy and maternity and marriage and civil partnership. Employees are now able to complain of behaviour that they find offensive, even if it is not directed at them, and the complainant need not possess the relevant characteristic themselves. Employees are also protected from harassment because of perception and association.

Third party harassment

This already applied to sex and is now extended to cover age, disability, gender reassignment, race, religion or belief and sexual orientation. The Equality Act makes employers potentially liable for harassment of employees by third parties, such as customers or clients. However, the employer is only liable when harassment has occurred on at least two previous occasions, the employer is aware that it has taken place, and has not taken reasonable steps to prevent it from happening again.

Victimisation

Victimisation occurs when an employee is treated badly because they have made or supported a complaint or raised a grievance under the Equality Act, or because they are suspected of doing so. An employee is not protected from victimisation if they have maliciously made or supported an untrue complaint.

Protected characteristics

The Equality Act continues to protect the same groups that were protected by previous discrimination legislation; however, these are now called 'protected characteristics' and are summarised as follows.

Age

The Act protects people of all ages. However, different treatment because of age is not unlawful direct or indirect discrimination if it can be justified, i.e. by demonstrating that it is a proportionate means of meeting a legitimate aim.

Age is the only protected characteristic that allows employers to justify direct discrimination.

Disability

The Act details a new definition, making it easier for a person to show that they are disabled and protected from disability discrimination. Under the Act, a person is disabled if they have 'a physical or mental impairment which has a substantial and long-term adverse effect on their ability to carry out normal day-to-day activities,' which would include things like using a telephone, reading a book or using public transport. As with the previous legislation, the Act places a duty on the employer to make reasonable adjustments for staff to help them overcome that disadvantage.

The Act further includes a new protection that states that it is discrimination to treat a disabled person unfavourably because of something connected with their disability (e.g. a tendency to make spelling mistakes arising from dyslexia). This is unlawful where the employer is or should be aware that the person has a disability.

Additionally, indirect discrimination now covers disabled people. This means that a job applicant or employee could claim that a particular rule or role requirement disadvantages people with the same disability – unless this can be justified, it would be deemed unlawful.

Gender reassignment
A new definition is provided under the Act – a transsexual person is someone 'who proposes to, starts or has completed a process to change his or her gender'. The Act no longer requires a person to be under medical supervision to be protected – so a woman who decides to live permanently as a man but does not undergo any medical procedures would be covered. It is discrimination to treat transsexual people less favourably for being absent from work because they propose to undergo, are undergoing or have undergone, gender reassignment than they would be treated if they were absent because they were ill or injured.

Marriage and civil partnership
The Act continues to protect employees who are married or in a civil partnership against discrimination. Single people are not protected.

Pregnancy and maternity
A woman maintains her protection against discrimination on the grounds of pregnancy and maternity during the period of her pregnancy and any statutory maternity leave to which she is entitled. During this period, pregnancy and maternity discrimination cannot be treated as sex discrimination.

Race
For the purposes of the Act, 'race' includes colour, nationality and ethnic or national origins.

Religion or belief
Under the Act, religion includes any religion. It also includes a lack of religion, so employees or jobseekers are protected if they do not follow a certain religion or have no religion at all. Additionally, a religion must have a clear structure and belief system. Belief means 'any religious or philosophical belief or a lack of such belief'. To be protected, a belief must satisfy various criteria, including that it is a weighty and substantial aspect of human life and behaviour. Denominations or sects within a religion can be considered a protected religion or religious belief. Humanism is a protected philosophical belief but political beliefs would not be protected.

Discrimination because of religion or belief can occur even where both the discriminator and recipient are of the same religion or belief.

Sex
Both men and women continue to be protected under the Act.

Sexual orientation
The Act continues to protect bisexual, gay, heterosexual and lesbian people.

Potential impact on recruitment and selection activities
The Equality Act, whilst harmonising previous legislation, and protecting the same groups, also extends and strengths particular aspects of equality law. One such area is recruitment and selection.

Health questionnaires
A provision in the Act now makes it potentially discriminatory, on the ground of disability, for employers to ask applicants questions about their health or disability prior to making a decision on whether or not to proceed with applications or offer employment. It is also potential discrimination for employers to require applicants to complete a medical questionnaire or undergo a medical examination prior to deciding whether or not to select them.

An employer will be able to make enquiries about an applicant's health if there is a justifiable reason for doing so, for example to:

■ establish whether or not it will be under a duty to make reasonable adjustments in the recruitment process;
■ establish whether or not the applicant would be able to carry out an 'intrinsic' function of the work, i.e. heavy lifting;
■ monitor diversity;
■ support positive action; or
■ identify suitable applicants for a job where there is a genuine occupational requirement for the post holder to be disabled.

However, the rejection of an otherwise suitable applicant, following enquiries about health or disability, will be potentially discriminatory on the ground of disability. An applicant does not have recourse through the Employment Tribunal if they believe the employer is acting unlawfully by asking prohibited questions, but can complain to the Equality and Human Rights Commission to undertake investigations.

Positive action to increase diversity

As with previous equality legislation, the Equality Act will allow employers to take positive action where employees or job applicants who share a particular protected characteristic suffer a disadvantage connected to that characteristic, or if their participation in an activity is disproportionately low. For example, job adverts can currently be aimed at people from different racial backgrounds, women, or other groups, where the employer wishes to make their workforce more diverse.

This positive action permits measures such as recruiting or promotion and training to alleviate the disadvantage or reduce

their under-representation. Specifically in recruitment, the positive action may only be taken where applicants (or employees) are equally qualified, and that act of treating the person more favourably because of their protected characteristic remains lawful. However, the employer must not maintain a policy of positive action in every situation.

For example, an employer needs a new person for one of its senior roles – all other senior roles are undertaken by men. Through the recruitment process, two applicants are right for the role, and equally qualified: one male and one female applicant. The employer can use positive action to offer the role to the female, because it will make the employer's senior employee group more diverse. However, the employer cannot give the role to the female applicant if the male applicant is better for the position.

In reality this could be a tricky principle to apply without having one party of the two 'equally qualified' applicants aggrieved by reason for their non-selection, and employers will need to manage the situation sensitively.

Potential impact on equal pay claims

Despite years of legislation to reduce the pay gap, significant differences remain in salaries paid to males and females. Therefore the Equality Act will build on the existing framework by introducing two key changes:

■ Firstly, a claimant who can show evidence that they would have received better remuneration from their employer if they were of a different sex, may have a claim even where there is no one of the opposite sex undertaking equal work in the organisation.

■ Secondly, the Act makes it unlawful for employers to prevent or restrict employees from discussing pay (so-called pay-gagging) to establish whether pay differences are linked to protected characteristics.

It was previously considered that there may be a requirement for organisations employing 250 or more employees to publish pay differences between male and female employees, and fines were proposed to be imposed where such requirements were not met. However, the Government has decided that it will not implement the reporting measures at this time as it is currently working on how best to support increased transparency on a voluntary basis. The Government has confirmed it is monitoring the success of this practice and retains the option to making such reports compulsory.

Extra powers for Tribunals

The Equality Act also has implications for Tribunals, namely by extending their powers: it will therefore be possible for Tribunals to make recommendations in discrimination cases, not only in relation to individual claimants, but also in relation to the wider workforce, in order to prevent similar types of discrimination from re-occurring. This also applies where the complainant ceases to work for the employer.

Impact on public bodies

Single equality duty

On 5 April 2011 the new public sector Equality Duty came into force. The Equality Duty replaced the three previous duties on race, disability and gender, bringing them together into a single duty, and extends it to cover age, sexual orientation, religion or belief, pregnancy and maternity, and gender reassignment (in full). The aim of the Duty is for public bodies to consider the needs of all individuals in their

day-to-day work, in developing policy, in delivering services, and in relation to their own employees. The Duty requires public bodies to have 'due regard' to the following three aims:

1. To eliminate discrimination, harassment, victimisation and any other conduct prohibited by the Act.
2. To advance equality of opportunity between people who share a relevant protected characteristic and those who don't.
3. To foster good relations between people who share a relevant protected characteristic and those who don't (which involves tackling prejudice and promoting understanding).

Having 'due regard' involves consciously thinking about the three aims of the Duty as part of any decision-making process and before reaching a decision.

In particular this will involve:

■ removing or reducing disadvantages suffered by people who share a protected characteristic and which are connected to that characteristic;
■ taking steps to meet the different needs of people who share a particular characteristic which are different from the needs of those without the characteristic; and
■ encouraging people who share a particular characteristic to participate in public life or other activity where participation by such people is disproportionately low.

The Act is not prescriptive about exactly what public bodies need to do to comply with the Duty, but one example of how it could be put into practice could be a local council providing special meals through its meals on wheels service for people who need to eat special food because of their religion.

To comply with the Duty, public bodies will need to assess the effect of their proposed decisions on different groups, will need to have sufficient data available to them to do so, and will have to consider proportionate ways of mitigating any detrimental impact.

It may help public bodies demonstrate compliance if they:

- keep a written record of the equality considerations they have taken into account;
- ensure their decision-making includes a consideration of the actions that would help to avoid or mitigate any negative impacts on particular protected groups; and
- make sure their decision is based on relevant evidence (as the Duty includes some new protected characteristics it may be necessary for public bodies to gather additional data to cover the gaps in its existing information).

See also: Discrimination, p.126; Equal pay, p.184; Employment Tribunals, p.179; Recruitment and selection, p.420; Staff handbooks, p.494.

Sources of further information

ACAS: www.acas.org.uk

The Equalities and Human Rights Commission: www.equalityhumanrights.com

The Government Equalities Office: www.equalities.gov.uk

Direct Gov: www.direct.gov.uk

Shoosmiths – Briefing note:
http://myinfo.shoosmiths.co.uk/reaction/pdfs/Briefing_note.pdf

Comment ...

The view from HR

Jayn Bond, Workplace Law

The biggest change in HR and employment law in the last year has undoubtedly been the Equality Act. This has harmonised all the discrimination legislation and introduced new definitions driven by recent case law. It has made it much easier to explain the law to managers. Third party discrimination and the detail around disability is really important.

The biggest change next year will most likely be changes to the Employment Tribunal system. The consultation has finished now so we wait and see. As one myself, I hope that Lay Members will not be sidelined as I genuinely believe that we contribute positively to the whole process. There are occasions when I am sitting that I feel that if I had not been there then the outcome may have been very different for one of the parties. In a good way of course!

If I had to pinpoint the worst thing that has happened to me professionally this year, I'd say meeting other HR professionals in Tribunals or in interviews who aren't as well versed in the law as I feel they should be. It is vital that HR professionals provide a quality and trusted service to their employers. Some of the actions or knowledge illustrated by some of the people I have met almost made me ashamed to be in the same profession.

However, successfully managing a large number of Employment Tribunal claims for our clients so that we reached a satisfactory conclusion – mainly prior to

Jayn Bond is a Chartered Fellow of the CIPD with over 20 years' experience in HR. She is commercially aware and has a pragmatic approach to her work that is underpinned with an in-depth knowledge of employment legislation and best practice. Jayn is Head of HR at Workplace Law and Course Director for our accredited CIPD certificate level courses. Jayn has been advising Chief Executives, Managing Directors and Senior Managers of SMEs, local authorities and not-for-profit organisations at both strategic and operational level for a number of years. Jayn has served as a Lay Member on East London Employment Tribunal Panel since 2005.

the Tribunal – has been the highlight. In a growing number of cases, we have found that by not conceding early in the process it has become clear that the claimant was not expecting to have to take any further action before achieving a payout – so when faced with having to produce documents and witness statements they have either withdrawn or the claim has been struck out.

Also, in many cases, we have been able to divert the continuous trail of emails / correspondence from the claimant away from the client to ourselves, and this has significantly reduced our clients' stress levels!

If I could introduce one bit of legislation, it would be that parties in a Tribunal must settle by a week before the hearing at the latest, or go ahead. Particularly as a lay member I find it frustrating that all the action happens in the last few days and then the Tribunal is cancelled at the last minute!

The HR team's greatest achievement this year – what we are most proud of – is successfully delivering the new CIPD certificate courses in the face of continuous change. We started the new courses 12 months before the majority of providers and then became a victim of our own success! The initial courses enabled the CIPD to review the format and, as a result, they made a number of changes. This meant that we had to revise our courses on an ongoing (almost daily) basis, but it all settled down again from September 2011.

Over the next year, I can see that there will be a need to retain and motivate staff once the economy picks up. So I would like to see a more positive side to our roles, rather than continually focusing on redundancies and dismissals. HR is not all about employment law, but is also about encouraging people to be employers of choice and developing their staff teams.

> **"I wish I had a pound for every time someone asked me...**
>
> **...Surely the Tribunal won't look at this case?"**

There is also likely to be an increasing need to be flexible as an employer, and so our roles will be to encourage creative thinking in companies.

I think the demise of the retirement age may cause many people problems – I'm not sure if companies have got their heads around the fact there is no longer a retirement age. With the current financial problems it may well be that employees just simply do not want to give up work as they cannot afford the drop in income. So this will present management issues, and managers will have to get used to performance managing everyone effectively.

I love problem solving for managers. Making a confused complex employee issue appear more understandable always gives me job satisfaction. Supporting managers through a stressful situation is a positive part of my job, and one that I always feel makes the biggest contribution.

@JaynBondWPL

Expenses

Pam Loch, Loch Associates Employment Lawyers

Key points
- Under general tax law, some expenses payments are taxable remuneration.
- Expenses payments include:
  - advance payments and reimbursements, including all kinds of travelling and entertaining;
  - allowances related to specific expenses, for example based on mileage or calculated by referring to a fixed scale;
  - round sum allowances for entertaining and other expenses;
  - amounts made available to the employee in respect of expenses and paid away by the employee; and
  - expenses paid by the employee by means of a credit card in the employer's name.
- Employers should have a clear expenses policy in place and enforce its provisions consistently. 95% of those surveyed in 2008 said that their employer never queried or rejected an expense claim for being too high.
- The majority of expenses are taxable and an effective policy can help to ensure compliance with HMRC.
- Employees who breach an expenses policy may risk disciplinary action, including dismissal.
- Employers who do dismiss for breach of the expenses policy should ensure this is the main (or preferably only) reason for dismissal.

Legislation
- Income Tax (Earnings and Pensions) Act 2003 (ITEPA).
- Bribery Act 2010.

Background

Reclaiming the cost of horse manure, moat cleaning and repairing a portico on expenses by MPs became the hot topic of conversation in 2009 by drawing attention to the potential opportunities for employees to abuse expenses. The public horror that 'our' money had been abused by MPs to purchase these goods and services fuelled the fire of anger, in no small part due to three Labour MPs being investigated for expenses fraud in January 2010 who were arguing that they should not be prosecuted because their suspect claims were covered by parliamentary privilege relating to a 320-year-old law. This was later ruled against in June 2010 when several MPs stood trial, accused of fiddling their expenses. Lord Hanningfield was sentenced to nine months' imprisonment on 1 July 2011 for his £14,000 worth of falsely claimed expenses and former MP, Elliot Morley, was jailed for 16 months for a £31,000 fraud.

The 'expenses scandal' continues to attract media attention and with the introduction of the Bribery Act this has also led to many more general conversations about expenses; what you can and can't claim and what employers can do to protect their business from illegitimate expense claims. Employers also need to be aware of the tax implications of expenses, and what is and isn't taxable can be a confusing area.

> ### Case studies
>
> Employers should be aware of cases highlighting the approach Employment Tribunals may take in assessing whether an unfair dismissal has taken place. Early 2009 saw the case of *Thompson v. Brick Services Limited* in which an employee was dismissed for submitting a false expenses claim. The employee argued he had asked a hotel receptionist to add £27 to a receipt to cover drinks he had bought personally, which he considered to be a legitimate business expense. The Tribunal heard evidence that Brick Services Ltd had been putting pressure on Mr Thompson for some time to agree less favourable terms and conditions of employment, which he refused to do. The Tribunal found that the employer had used the expenses claim as an excuse to dismiss the employee without conducting a full and impartial investigation, and the dismissal was found to be unfair.
>
> In the case of *East Lancashire Coachbuilders v. Hilton*, Mr Hilton was dismissed on the grounds of gross misconduct after taking his wife on a business trip to Mexico and claiming her fare as well as his own. The Tribunal found that whilst the employer could reasonably have treated Mr Hilton's conduct as justifying immediate dismissal, the real reason for his dismissal was for other reasons. Because the employer's main reason for dismissal was for matters other than the expenses issue (which was essentially used as a smokescreen), the conclusion was that there was an unfair dismissal.

In most organisations, expenses are monitored very closely, with rigid policies and numerous controls in place to ensure compliance with procedures to avoid abuse taking place. The employee's contract of employment will usually set out that expenses are payable, but only if the expense is incurred in accordance with the expenses policy.

Expenses policies

What takes place inside the average organisation as far as expense claims are concerned can have a serious impact on the bottom line and affect budgets across all departments. Often this isn't due to employees submitting questionable claims but rather because no one has taken a close look at how expenses are being managed inside the organisation. The expense policy should clearly set out

what is regarded as an expense by the organisation and provide employees with an upper limit. It can be difficult to set out specific examples and usually there will be a generic reference to what is covered and then it is over to accounts, HR, or whoever is given the responsibility to approve expenses. Key to avoiding suspicion or confusion is making sure that all expenses are fully documented.

The person who approves expenses plays an important role. Not only must they interpret how the policy applies but they must resist the pressure that can be placed on them to agree that something is a legitimate expense.

In some sectors there is far less rigidity, and expenses policies may have limited application. One could take the view that this is not really an issue to be

> **Facts**
>
> - A 2007 survey conducted by YouGov found that a third of employees admit fiddling expenses. This echoes research in 2008 from GlobalExpense, a leading expense management provider, showing that many employees say they will exaggerate their expenses claims from their employer if they get into financial difficulties.
> - The Global Expense Employee Expenses Benchmark Report 2009 estimates that British businesses are losing around £2bn each year for wrongly-approved employee expense payments.
> - According to the same report, around 11% of all employee expense claims should not be paid as the items are not covered by company policy, but managers approve the payments anyway.
> - The expenses of employees earning less than £8,500 p.a. generally will not be taxable.
> - After the end of the tax year employees may need to complete and file key expenses and benefits forms depending on the type of employee, i.e. director / employee. A form P11D or P9D needs to be filed for each employee who has received expenses and benefits during the tax year, and one form P11D(b) to declare the overall amount of Class 1A National Insurance contributions (NICs) due on all the expenses and benefits provided. All of these forms must be submitted to HMRC by 6 July and are likely to be required to be submitted online.

concerned about, as it only impacts on the organisation itself. However, that is not the case. Expenses are generally a tax-deductible business expense, as long as it is not for entertaining clients or customers. Therefore, HMRC also has certain rules that apply to ensure there is no abuse of the tax system.

An abuse of an organisation's expenses policy usually results in disciplinary action being taken and ultimately could lead to an employee being dismissed. Despite the potential risks, however, some employees will stretch the boundaries of expenses for the sake of securing extra funds that are not taxable.

For example, some employees will arrange a meeting in a city they would like to spend the weekend in to be able to reclaim the cost of the travel. In other instances, personal and business expenses become closely entwined – visits to lap dancing clubs being one example.

However, tax implications are now not the only concern that employers need to ensure is a foremost concern. The Bribery Act came into force on 1 July 2011 and with it came the corporate offence of bribery. A company will be held liable if an 'associated person' (employee, worker, consultant or possibly even sub-contractor, for example) offers or accepts a bribe. Liability for the corporate offence is strict – it doesn't matter whether the company knows about an associated person's unlawful behaviour or not. If a company takes no measures to prevent bribery, then they will be at huge risk of conviction and an unlimited fine.

Preventative measures

So what can an employer do when an employee is caught cheating the expenses policy, and how can an employer protect itself from being liable for the corporate offence of bribery? Employers who discover an employee abusing their expenses policy will want to take action against that employee. Depending on the degree of dishonesty and abuse involved, the employer may often feel that an unacceptable breach of trust has taken place and dismissal is the only option.

Employers should always investigate fully before taking any disciplinary action – it may be the case that an employee has simply misunderstood the policy and the employer discovers that a review of the policy wording is required to make it clearer. Where there is a clear expenses policy in place and an obvious case of dishonesty or fraud involved in obtaining funds as expenses has taken place, summary dismissal following an investigation for gross misconduct may well be a reasonable response.

There is a complete defence against the corporate offence of bribery if a company can prove that it had adequate procedures in place designed to prevent associated persons engaging in such conduct. What constitutes adequate procedures will depend on the company and the bribery risks involved. As a general guide,

companies should follow one or more of the following steps to provide themselves with the complete defence that will otherwise be unavailable:

1. *Assess risk* – develop and carry out a risk assessment to identify the bribery risks your business faces.
2. *Policy and procedure* – ensure you have appropriate bribery prevention policies and procedures in place.
3. *Communication and awareness* – ensure all workers are aware of the law concerning bribery and the measures in place to prevent bribery.
4. *Due diligence* – carefully vet your associated persons.
5. *Enforcement* – ensure suspected incidents of bribery are strictly investigated and sanctioned.
6. *Top level commitment* – ensure senior managers are involved in setting bribery prevention measures.
7. *Monitor and review* – monitor the effectiveness of the measures you put in place and review and update policies as appropriate.

See also: Bribery, p.49; Disciplinary and grievance procedures, p.121; Dismissal, p.146.

Sources of further information

In its Money, Tax and Benefits section, Directgov online has some useful guidance on tax on company benefits: www.direct.gov.uk.

Business link and the HMRC website provide useful practical advice for businesses in relation to a wide range of topics, including business expenses: www.businesslink.gov.uk   www.hmrc.gov.uk

The Ministry of Justice has produced a helpful quick start guide for commercial organisations to help them understand the procedures which can be put in place to prevent bribery: www.justice.gov.uk

Facilities management contracts

Marc Hanson, Berwin Leighton Paisner LLP

Key points

- Like all other forms of contract, a facilities management contract is essentially a legally binding and enforceable bargain between two parties.
- Each party contributes something to the bargain; the facilities management contractor – the provision of certain services; and the client – payment for those services.

Negotiation

For a contract to be legally binding, there must be an offer from one party, an unconditional acceptance of that offer by the other party, and consideration provided by each party for the promise made by the other party. A client's invitation to tender is not usually an 'offer' – it is usually no more than an offer to negotiate.

A facilities management contractor's tender to carry out the services will, usually, amount to the initial 'offer'.

When the client accepts the facilities management contractor's tender and each party gives consideration, then, provided both parties have an intention to be legally bound, a legally enforceable contract will come into place. Offers and acceptance can be made in writing, orally or by conduct.

It is of course unusual for facilities management contractors' tenders to be accepted without qualification by a client. There may be areas of extensive negotiation, e.g. in relation to scope of services and fees. Every time each party provides any revised proposals, then each revised proposal will take effect as a 'counter-offer'.

When eventually all outstanding points have been agreed, one party will invariably 'accept' the other party's final 'offer'.

When does the contract start?

The process of negotiating a facilities management contract can be protracted. In many cases, services may be provided to the client and payment may be made without any form of contract having been signed. Where relationships subsequently deteriorate, it can be extremely difficult to establish whether there was ever a binding contract in place and, if there was, on what terms it was made.

Whether a binding contract exists in such circumstances will depend on whether the parties managed to agree all the key terms of the contract and whether the terms of the alleged contract included all terms that would be essential for a contract to exist. It would be unlikely that there was a contract agreed if key elements of the contract were still outstanding; for example, if the exact scope of the services was undecided or if a price had not been agreed. However, a contract can still come into effect where certain points in the contract terms are still to be agreed, provided that the key elements have been finalised and agreed.

Scope of contracts

When drafting facilities management contracts, it is important to ensure that they cover the complete understanding and agreement between the parties. As such, it is necessary to include not only a list of the services to be provided by the supplier but also a mechanism for dealing with changes to the services and also any details as to what equipment or facilities are to be provided to the supplier by the client in relation to the services.

Payment

Careful thought needs to be given as to how payment to the facilities management contractor will be structured. Will it be on the basis of a lump-sum price, by prime cost or by reference to a schedule of rates? If the price is to adjust, then a mechanism needs to be set out allowing for this, detailing the circumstances in which adjustments will be made. Careful consideration also needs to be given to any mechanism to be included in the contract that would allow the contract price to be adjusted to reflect performance or non-performance by the supplier of the services.

Service levels

Service levels should be included in the contract against which the performance by the supplier can be assessed. Consideration needs to be given as to how poor performance is dealt with and whether the liability of the supplier under the contract is to be limited in any way.

Duration

The duration of a facilities management contract is of critical importance, and this should be clearly stated in the contract, together with the circumstances in which it can be extended or terminated by either party.

Facilities management contracts should also address other key areas such as compliance with statutory requirements, transfer of undertakings provisions, insurance requirements and provisions dealing with dispute resolution.

See also: Contract disputes, p.90; Contractors, p.93; TUPE, p.523.

Sources of further information

Workplace Law's **Facilities Management Contracts 2008** follows the success of two editions of the *Guide to Facilities Management Contracts*. Now fully updated, it provides an introduction to contract law as it relates to FM contracts, and a guide to common contractual law provisions. This extended publication looks at new areas of law including amendments to the Construction Act, amendments to CDM Regulations, revised TUPE Regulations, revised EU Procurement law, dispute resolution procedures, and European standards for facilities management. For more information visit www.workplacelaw.net.

Family-friendly rights

Pinsent Masons Employment Group

Key points

- All pregnant employees are entitled to 52 weeks' maternity leave, consisting of 26 weeks' ordinary maternity leave and 26 weeks' additional maternity leave.
- Pregnant employees may also be entitled to statutory maternity pay during their maternity leave for up to 39 weeks.
- Qualifying employees may take 52 weeks' adoption leave when they adopt a child, consisting of 26 weeks' ordinary adoption leave and 26 weeks' additional adoption leave.
- Qualifying employees are entitled to take up to two weeks' paternity leave, which must be taken within eight weeks of the date of childbirth or placement of an adopted child.
- There is a new right to additional paternity leave and pay. However, this only affects parents of babies due on 3 April 2011 or later.
- Working parents are entitled to take unpaid parental leave in order to care for a child, generally up to 13 weeks in respect of each child before the child's fifth birthday.
- Employees have the right to take a reasonable amount of 'time off for dependants' leave to deal with emergency situations affecting their dependants.
- The flexible working legislation can be used to request a variation of the time, hours or place of work, and provides a statutory framework for considering that request.

Legislation

- Sex Discrimination Act 1975.
- Statutory Maternity Pay (General) Regulations 1986.
- The Social Security Contributions and Benefits Act 1992.
- Employment Rights Act 1996.
- Maternity and Parental Leave etc. Regulations 1999.
- Flexible Working (Procedural Requirements) Regulations 2002.
- Flexible Working (Eligibility, Complaints and Remedies) Regulations 2002.
- Paternity and Adoption Leave Regulations 2002.
- Statutory Paternity Pay and Statutory Adoption Pay (Administration) Regulations 2002.
- Work and Families Act 2006.
- Additional Paternity Leave Regulations 2010.

Key concepts

- 'Childbirth' means the birth of a living child or a still birth after 24 weeks of pregnancy.
- 'Expected week of childbirth' (EWC) is the week from Sunday to Saturday in which childbirth is expected to occur, confirmed on a MAT B1 certificate given to the employee by the employee's doctor.
- 'Qualifying Week' is the 15th week before the EWC.
- 'Ordinary maternity leave' (OML) refers to 26 weeks' leave available regardless of length of service to all

employees who give birth (but not the self-employed or individuals meeting the statutory definition of 'worker').

- 'Additional maternity leave' (AML) follows immediately after the end of OML and lasts for up to another 26 weeks, regardless of length of service.
- 'Keeping in touch days' (KIT days) are days on which women may do paid work during maternity leave for up to ten days without bringing their OML or AML to an end.
- 'Statutory maternity pay' (SMP) is available during maternity leave for up to 39 weeks.

Maternity

Maternity leave

All pregnant employees, regardless of length of service, are entitled to 52 weeks' statutory maternity leave, consisting of 26 weeks' OML and 26 weeks' AML.

An employee must notify her employer no later than the end of the Qualifying Week of:

- the fact that she is pregnant;
- the EWC; and
- the date when she intends her OML to start.

Pregnant employees have a right to reasonable paid time off during working hours for antenatal care, regardless of hours worked or length of service. There are also workplace health and safety duties for expectant mothers requiring employers to assess workplace risks posed to mothers, alter the employee's working conditions or hours to avoid risk and, in certain circumstances, offer suitable alternative work on terms not 'substantially less favourable' or suspend on full pay. See 'Pregnancy and maternity' (p.400).

The employee can decide to commence her maternity leave on any day; however,

the earliest date she can do so is the 11th week before the EWC. Any pregnancy-related absence (i.e. sick leave) from the fourth week before the EWC will trigger OML and statutory maternity pay (SMP), as will childbirth itself.

Once the employer knows the date the employee wishes to start her maternity leave, it has 28 days to notify her of the date when it will end. If the employee changes her start date the employer has 28 days from the start of her maternity leave to notify her of the new end date.

Maternity pay

The employee needs 26 weeks' continuous service at the end of the Qualifying Week and must meet a minimum earnings criterion to qualify for SMP. SMP is calculated on the basis of average earnings during an eight-week period ending with the Qualifying Week. SMP is payable for up to 39 weeks and is calculated as follows:

- First six weeks: SMP is paid at 90% of the employee's average weekly earnings;
- Remaining 33 weeks: SMP is paid at the prescribed rate set by the Government for the relevant tax year, currently £128.73 per week.

Many employers provide a contractual right to maternity pay that exceeds the SMP entitlement.

During OML and AML, an employee benefits from all of their terms and conditions of employment, except remuneration (i.e. wages or salary).

Employers may make 'reasonable contact' with employees on maternity leave to discuss an employee's return to work or to keep the employee informed of work developments. In addition, women may do paid work during maternity leave for up to ten days (called 'keeping in touch' or 'KIT' days) without bringing their OML or AML to an end. This could include attending a conference, undertaking training or attending a team meeting.

It is up to the employee to decide how much of her maternity leave entitlement she wants to take. The minimum amount is the two weeks' compulsory maternity leave after the birth. The maximum period of maternity leave is 52 weeks.

The expected date of the employee's return will be at the end of her AML. If she has not told her employer that she wants to return at a different time, there is no need for her to provide any further notice. If, however, she wishes to return to work before the end of her maternity leave, she must give her employer eight weeks' notice of her return date.

Returning to work

If the employee takes only OML, she will be entitled to return to the same job on the same terms and conditions. After AML, if there is some reason why it is not reasonably practicable for the employee to return to the same job, she is entitled to return to a suitable alternative job with terms and conditions no less favourable than they would have been had she not been absent.

If a redundancy situation arises during an employee's maternity leave, and it is not practicable for the employer to continue to employ her in her existing role, the employee is entitled to be offered a suitable alternative vacancy. This gives the employee on maternity leave priority over other employees at risk of redundancy. If the employee unreasonably refuses the offer, she will lose her right to a redundancy payment.

An employee who has a child under the age of 17, or a disabled child under the age of 18, has the right to request a flexible working pattern. Employers must give proper consideration to any requests and are obliged to follow a statutory procedure. The employer may refuse the application only on certain grounds. If an employer refuses to allow a woman to work part-time, or to change her working pattern, this may lead to a claim for unlawful indirect sex discrimination.

Adoption

Adoption leave

Adoption leave and pay has many similarities with the maternity leave and pay regime. Qualifying employees may take 52 weeks' statutory adoption leave when they adopt a child. It is split into 26 weeks' ordinary adoption leave (OAL) and 26 weeks' additional adoption leave (AAL).

An employee is entitled to OAL if he or she:

- is the child's adopter;
- has 26 weeks' qualifying service;
- has been matched with a child for adoption;
- has notified the adoption agency of agreement to the adoption going ahead; and
- has complied with various notification and evidential requirements (*see below*).

The employee must tell his employer of the date the child is expected to be placed with him for adoption and the date on which the leave will begin. This notice must be given no more than seven days after the employee has been told by the adoption agency of a match, or as soon as reasonably practicable, and the employer may request that the employee provides evidence of the match.

An employee can begin OAL on the date the child is placed with him for adoption or a predetermined date no more than 14 days before the expected placement date. The employee may change the start date for his or her adoption leave, giving the employer 28 days' notice. The employer must then notify the employee of the date on which their leave will end. This will normally be 52 weeks from the intended start of their adoption leave.

Adoption pay

As with maternity leave, all the employee's terms and conditions continue to apply during adoption leave, except those relating to remuneration. Employees may also be entitled to statutory adoption pay during their leave for up to 39 weeks. It is calculated at the prescribed rate currently of £128.73 per week, or 90% of normal weekly earnings, if lower.

If the employee wishes to return to work before the end of AAL, he or she must give at least eight weeks' notice. Employees have a right to return to the same job on the same terms and conditions after adoption leave or, in some cases, a suitable alternative job.

Note: The rules relating to adoptions from overseas are different.

Paternity

Paternity leave

Employees are entitled to either one whole week or two consecutive weeks' statutory paternity leave (SPL).

The one- or two-week period of leave must be taken between the date on which the child is born and eight weeks after that date. The two-week SPL entitlement cannot be taken as two separate periods of one week: the entitlement to paternity leave is only to one period of leave. It is for the employee to choose whether that period is to be for one or two weeks.

The eligibility criteria are:

- Continuous employment for a period of not less than 26 weeks ending with the Qualifying Week;
- The employee is the father of the child or is married to, is the civil partner of, or is the partner of the child's mother;
- The employee will have responsibility for the child's upbringing (if the employee is the child's biological father) or have the main responsibility (other than that of the child's mother) for the child's upbringing (if the employee is married to, the civil partner of, or the partner of the child's mother).

The eligible employee will also need to satisfy the notification and evidential requirements (see below).

The employee must give their employer in writing by the Qualifying Week details of their intention to take paternity leave, confirming:

- the EWC;
- the length of the period of SPL that the employee intends to take (i.e. either one week or two consecutive weeks); and
- the date on which the employee wishes to commence their SPL.

Paternity pay

Statutory paternity pay for up to two weeks is available and is the prescribed rate of currently £128.73 per week (or 90% of normal weekly earnings, if lower). Employees are also entitled to benefit from their usual contractual terms during their period of SPL, except for remuneration. The employee must be treated by the employer as if they were not absent. An employee who has exercised their right to take SPL has the right to return to the same job that they were employed to do immediately prior to taking the leave.

The statutory minimum standards apply as the default position. Employers are free to provide enhanced paternity leave and pay.

There are also provisions that deal with fathers who are adopting, which are largely the same as those outlined above.

Additional paternity leave and pay

There is a new right to additional paternity leave and pay. This only affects parents of babies due on 3 April 2011 or later.

Generally, fathers can take up to six months' leave to care for a child, if the child's mother returns to work without exercising her full entitlement to maternity leave. Any period taken during the mother's maternity pay period will be paid; any leave taken after the mother's maternity pay period expires will be unpaid.

The eligibility requirements for additional paternity leave (APL) are largely the same as for statutory paternity leave (SPL), which is now referred to as 'ordinary' paternity leave (OPL). The key addition to be eligible to take APL is that the mother must return to work having not exhausted her entitlement to statutory maternity leave. Only if the mother declines to take a proportion of OML and/or AML will the father's right to take APL be triggered.

Parents will be required to self-certify their entitlement. The employee must give the employer:

- a leave notice – a written notice setting out the child's week of birth, the child's date of birth and the start and end dates for the employee's APL period;

- an employee declaration – a written declaration, signed by the employee, confirming that the purpose of the APL is to care for the child, that he is the child's father, or married to or is the partner or civil partner of the child's mother, and that he will have the main responsibility (with the child's mother) for bringing up the child; and

- a mother declaration – a written declaration by the child's mother, setting out their name, address, National Insurance number and the date on which they intend to return from maternity leave.

The earliest that APL can be taken is 20 weeks from the child's date of birth. The minimum period that may be taken is two weeks and the maximum period is 26 weeks. APL can only be taken in multiples of complete weeks and must be taken in one block. APL must be completed before the child's first birthday.

An employee must give their employer a minimum of eight weeks' notice of their intention to take APL. The employer must then confirm the employee's entitlement to APL within 28 days.

Additional statutory paternity pay (ASPP) will be available where the APL is taken during the mother's maternity pay period. ASPP will be paid at the lesser of the standard statutory maternity pay rate, which is £128.73, or 90% of the father's average earnings. In order to claim ASPP the mother must report the start date of her maternity pay period to the father's employer.

Like mothers on maternity leave, the father's contract of employment will continue throughout APL, and fathers / partners will have a right to all their terms and conditions of employment, except for remuneration. Fathers on APL will be also entitled to up to ten KIT days for the purposes of work or training without the loss of ASPP and without bringing the leave period to an end. A father taking APL will also be entitled to the same right to return to work as a mother returning after OML – the right to return to the same job on the same terms and conditions as before the APL began.

The Regulations have provisions that deal with fathers who are adopting, which are largely the same as those outlined above.

Parental leave

Parental leave is unpaid leave available to working birth and adoptive parents, and to anyone who has parental responsibility for a child. To take parental leave, an employee must have been continuously employed for a period of not less than one year.

The leave can only be for the purpose of 'caring for a child'; however, the scope is wide. Examples are spending more time with a young child, accompanying a child during a stay in hospital, checking out new schools, settling a child into new childcare arrangements, and enabling a family to spend more time together.

The right applies in respect of each child. An employee with one qualifying child can normally take 13 weeks' leave (increased to 18 weeks in the case of a child entitled to a disability living allowance). An employee with two children would therefore be entitled to 26 weeks' leave in total.

The parental leave must be taken:

■ before the child's fifth birthday; or
■ before the child's 18th birthday in the case of a child entitled to a disability living allowance; or
■ before the fifth anniversary of the date of placement in the case of an adopted child.

Employers may contractually agree to vary their employees' parental leave entitlements and the way in which they are exercised. However, in the absence of an appropriate agreement, the legislation automatically imposes a default scheme in schedule 2 of the Maternity and Parental Leave etc. Regulations 1999.

In general, under the default scheme, 21 days' notice must be given by employees (and so the leave cannot be used to deal with emergencies involving the child; however, *see below*). More than four weeks' parental leave for each child cannot be taken per year. Employees must also take the leave in multiples of a week, although these restrictions do not apply if the child is in receipt of disability living allowance.

An employer can postpone the leave where the operation of its business would be disrupted. The postponement can be for up to six months. However, the employer cannot postpone leave that has already been postponed once. If leave is unreasonably postponed, the employee may make a claim to a Tribunal.

If the employee takes parental leave for four weeks or fewer, the employee enjoys the same right to return to work as someone returning from OML. For periods of more than four weeks, the employee enjoys the same right as someone returning from AML.

On 8 March 2010 the EU Council of Ministers adopted a new Parental Leave Directive, which replaces the current Parental Leave Directive. The new Directive increases parental leave entitlement from three to four months. Member states have two years to implement it. It is thought that the increase is unlikely to have a major impact in the UK, given parental leave is unpaid.

Time off for dependants

Employees have the right to take a reasonable amount of unpaid time off work to deal with emergency situations affecting their dependants.

A 'dependant' is generally defined as a spouse, civil partner, child or parent (but not grandparent) of the employee, or a person who lives in the same household as the employee (excluding tenants, lodgers, boarders and employees).

The situation must fall within one of the following categories:

- To provide assistance if a dependant falls ill, gives birth, is injured or assaulted;
- To make care arrangements for the provision of care for a dependant who is ill or injured;
- In consequence of the death of a dependant;
- To deal with the unexpected disruption, termination or breakdown of arrangements for the care of a dependant; and/or
- To deal with an unexpected incident, which involves the employee's child during school hours.

The right to time off applies to all female and male employees (not workers or the self-employed), irrespective of their length of service, or whether they work full-time or part-time or are employed on a permanent, temporary or fixed-term basis.

The employee must tell their employer, as soon as reasonably practicable, the reason for their absence and how long they expect to be away from work. The employee is not required to produce any evidence of their need to take time off. See 'Leave' (p.252).

New system of shared parental leave

A Government consultation launched in May 2011, *Modern Workplaces*, seeks views on proposals for a system of genuinely flexible parental leave that will give parents choice and facilitate truly shared parenting, helping both parents to retain their attachment to the workplace.

The proposals are as follows:

- 18 weeks' maternity leave will be retained around the time of the birth and reserved exclusively for mothers. It will be available in one continuous block and the current statutory maternity pay (SMP) and maternity allowance (MA) arrangements for this period will be retained, as well as existing arrangements for two weeks' ordinary paternity leave and pay for fathers.
- The remaining 34 weeks of existing maternity leave will be reclassified as parental leave, and this will be available to either parent on an equal basis (similar provisions will apply for adopters and same-sex couples):
  - Four weeks of paid parental leave will be exclusively reserved for each parent – able to be taken concurrently if parents wish. However, this will not reduce mothers' overall leave rights: if a family still wishes the mother to take the full 52 weeks' leave, she can do so. An additional four weeks of paid leave will therefore be provided to the father so that the mother will still be able to take her full 52 weeks;
  - The remaining 30 weeks of parental leave will be available to either parent – 17 weeks will be paid and 13 weeks will be unpaid. The weeks can be broken in blocks between parents; and

- 21 weeks of maternity pay will be reallocated as parental pay – the existing system of SMP and MA will be replicated with statutory shared parental pay.
- The Government is seeking views on allowing employees to take leave on a part-time basis or allowing leave to be broken into two or more shorter periods between which parents could return to work (with employer agreement).
- The existing right to unpaid parental leave beyond the first year of the child's life will be incorporated into the new scheme and the consultation also considers whether to extend the limit for taking unpaid parental leave beyond the child's fifth birthday – to either age eight, 12, 16 or 18.

- Fathers may be given the right to unpaid leave to attend antenatal appointments.
- The new provisions will supersede those recently introduced for additional paternity leave and pay.

The proposed changes are to be introduced in April 2015, although the Government says that this date is subject to 'affordability'.

See also: Carers, p.64; Discrimination, p.126; Flexible working, p.221; Leave, p.252; Pregnancy and maternity, p.400.

Sources of further information

Template adoption, maternity and paternity policies are available as electronic downloads from Workplace Law. Visit www.workplacelaw.net or call 0871 777 8881 for further details.

BIS – Work and Families:
www.berr.gov.uk/employment/workandfamilies/work-families-history/index.html.

Fit notes

Sophie Applewhite and Chloe Harrold, Loch Associates Employment Lawyers

Key points

- Officially known as a Statement of Fitness for Work, the fit note was introduced on 6 April 2010.
- This followed the recommendations of a major review carried out by Dame Carol Black, National Director for Health and Work, in response to growing concerns that the sick note system wasn't working.
- Employers had complained that the sick note system was too inefficient, as all it required GPs to do was state whether an employee on sick leave for longer than seven calendar days was 'unfit for work'.
- The fit note is designed to enable a gradual return to work for employees who have been on long-term sick leave, as well as cutting the cost of sickness absence to employers.
- It provides for two outcomes – a patient can be declared 'unfit for work', or 'may be fit for work'. GPs can then advise employers on ways that employees can be helped – by a reduction in hours, for example, changes to duties, or an adaptation to their working environment.

Legislation

- Social Security (Medical Evidence) and Statutory Sick Pay (Medical Evidence) (Amendment) Regulations 2010.

Introduction

The 'fit note' regime was introduced on 6 April 2010, despite concerns raised during consultation that stakeholders would not have sufficient time to familiarise themselves with the new rules.

The main changes to the pre-existing 'med 3' sick note regime include:

- The fit note allows a GP to select one of two options: 'You are not fit for work' or 'You may be fit for work taking account of the following advice'. It was hoped that this option would facilitate discussion between the employer and employee about suggested changes on return to work.

- The fit note lists four standard changes that could be made to an employee's work environment to help accommodate their return to work. The fit note also gives doctors the opportunity to detail alternative changes should this be appropriate.
- Within the first six months of absence, the maximum duration a fit note can be issued for is three months. After the first six months, a fit note can be issued for 'any clinically appropriate period'.
- If an employer is unable to facilitate a change or an adjustment, the detail given on the fit note is sufficient evidence that the employee has a condition that prevents him or her carrying out the role. It is not necessary for the doctor to issue a revised fit note.

The fit note is designed to enable a gradual return to work for employees who have been on long-term sick leave, as well as cutting the cost of sickness absence to employers. Importantly it does not alter the current self certification regime and employees are still entitled and required to self-certify for the first seven days of sickness absence.

Reaction to the regime

Concerns were initially expressed regarding the practicality of doctors providing a detailed assessment in respect of an employee's workplace when they have no knowledge of the workplace in question. Doctors are not specifically trained in occupational health and will only have the patient's explanation of their role and the workplace to rely on. This may not be comprehensive enough for the doctor to provide a proper assessment and, if so, employers may struggle to implement measures that are not detailed enough to apply to specific workplaces. Research published by the DWP six months after the introduction of the fit note suggested that a staggering 89% of GPs had not received training in health and work within the past 12 months.

There have also been concerns that employees are being forced to return to work before they are ready, which may cause their health to deteriorate. This could arise from a misunderstanding of the employee's role and workplace on the part of the doctor. It is yet to be established if a doctor would be liable for the employee's deterioration in health in this situation.

Statistics published in July 2010 by the DWP showed that three-quarters of applicants for Employment and Support Allowance (ESA) made between October 2008 and November 2009 were found either fit for work or ceased their application before assessment was completed. Chris Grayling, Minister for Employment, stated that:

'The vast majority of people who are applying for these benefits are being found fit for work. These are people who under the old system would have been abandoned on incapacity benefits'.

Under the new fit note regime, it was hoped that applicants for ESA will now be given specific support and suggestions to assist with their return to work. However, DWP research carried out six months after the introduction of the fit note suggested that only 23% of GPs felt their knowledge of the benefits system was up to date.

Facts

- On introduction it was estimated that the fit note would save £240m within ten years.
- Six months on, 70% of GPs believed the fit note had made a positive difference in helping their patients back to work.
- Six months on, 48% of GPs stated that the fit note resulted in them increasing the occurrences of recommending a return to work.
- The UK economy lost 190 million working days to absence in 2010, an average of 6.5 days per employee, an increase on 6.4 days in 2009.

Source: Department for Work and Pensions (DWP), Confederation of British Industry and Pfizer Absence and Workplace Health Survey.

A positive result?

Early indications were that the implementation of the fit note regime would do little to convince doctors and employers that it will assist in reducing long-term absences. Doctors indicated that they would feel forced to take on an occupational health role and employers would be expected to facilitate suggestions from doctors that did not reflect an understanding of the practicalities of specific workplaces.

However, the DWP research suggests that in fact GPs consider fit notes to have made a positive difference. Almost half of the GPs surveyed said the fit note regime has made them more likely to suggest a return to work as an aid to recovery.

However, at a welfare reform conference in March 2011, Lord Freud criticised the effectiveness of the regime. The Welfare Reform Minister stated that many GPs are refusing to complete the fit notes and that there is an inherent contradiction in requiring GPs to complete fit notes. GPs are supposed to be advocating the health of their patient, but instead are required to become 'policemen' by completing the fit note. Lord Freud went on to suggest that many long-term sickness absences are linked to the workplace environment itself, making it very difficult for doctors to establish the real barrier to a recovery and return to work.

Employers have also criticised the fit note regime for a more fundamental reason – that it fails to address the issue of illegible doctors' handwriting. Although there were hopes that the fit note would become electronic by the end of 2010, this has not transpired, and Lord Freud stated that although there were plans to establish an e-fit note, he could not elaborate on when this might happen.

Conclusion

Despite the encouraging results of the DWP six-month GP survey, figures concerning sickness absence show an increase for 2010. It may be that the impact of fit notes will be more long-term and that with some finessing of the regime, greater effectiveness will follow.

The DWP has invited members of the Chartered Institute of Personnel and Development to provide feedback on fit notes intended to survey the success of the scheme, from an employer's point of view. Responses are invited from organisations in the private, public and voluntary sectors that have had at least one fit note since last April. It will be interesting to see how the results of this compare to the survey of GPs carried out.

The DWP has also commissioned an independent review into Britain's 'sickie' culture to be led by David Frost, Director General of the British Chamber of Commerce, with results expected to be available in late 2011. The review will have a wide-ranging remit, although with a focus on getting people back to work quickly it is envisaged that a key part of this will be an examination of the fit note regime, how it is working, and any improvements that can be made.

The fit note regime is still in its early stages but its operation so far appears to have gone slightly better than expected when first introduced. It remains to be seen whether fit notes will stand the test of time and further scrutiny.

See also: Absence management, p.16; Alcohol and drugs, p.36; Health surveillance, p.231; Mental health, p.308; Occupational health, p.374; Stress, p.500.

Sources of further information

The Department for Work and Pensions website has a page dedicated to the fit note which provides a 'fit note explained' guide and provides links for further information for healthcare professionals, employers and to employees and patients: www.dwp.gov.uk/fitnote

Organisations are increasingly recognising the significant costs associated with high levels of absence, alongside the disruption to the business on a day-to-day basis. Increased discrimination legislation has left many employers unsure of how to deal with persistent short-term and long-term absence. Many managers feel ill equipped to effectively deal with absence, which requires continual commitment and focus to manage effectively.

With our knowledge and experience of implementing absence management policies and practices across all sectors, Workplace Law can help by implementing an absence management system to suit your business.

We can also train your managers, provide one-off support for a specific absence issue or case, provide ongoing support and give your managers the confidence to effectively manage absence across the organisation. This will enable a reduction in your absenteeism, reduce your financial risks, improve employee morale and increase productivity, amongst other benefits. Visit www.workplacelaw.net for more information.

Fixed-term workers

Pinsent Masons Employment Group

Key points

- Legislation introduced in 2002 provides statutory protection for fixed-term employees.
- The Regulations state that fixed-term employees have the right not to be treated less favourably than comparable permanent employees because they are employed on a fixed-term basis, unless the different treatment can be objectively justified.
- Employees cannot agree to waive their right to bring a claim for unfair dismissal as part of a fixed-term contract.
- After four years on successive fixed-term contracts, employees will be regarded as permanent.
- Workplace managers should take care in using fixed-term contracts, and should not assume that they provide employers with any greater protection than they would have in relation to employees on other forms of contracts.

Legislation

- Employment Rights Act 1999.
- Fixed-term Employees (Prevention of Less Favourable Treatment) Regulations 2002.

Who has fixed-term contracts?

Fixed-term contracts are found mainly in sectors such as education, the media, healthcare and public administration. Often they are used when someone is required only for a specific task or project, for maternity cover, or where demand for the role is not clear and the employer would like to carry out a trial before committing to a permanent position.

What is a fixed-term contract?

The Regulations define a fixed-term contract as a contract of employment that will terminate:

- on the expiry of a specific term;
- on the completion of a particular task; or
- on the occurrence or non-occurrence of any other specific event other

than the attainment by the employee of a bona-fide retiring age in the establishment for an employee holding the position held by him.

Who is covered?

The Regulations apply only to 'employees' rather than a wider category of workers.

There are a number of categories of employees that are specifically excluded from the scope of the Regulations, namely:

- employees working under contracts of apprenticeship;
- agency workers contracted to perform work for an end user company through a temporary work agency;
- people employed on training schemes supported by the Government or an EU institution;
- people employed on work experience placements of one year or less that they are required to attend as part of a higher-education course; and
- serving members of the armed forces.

Less favourable treatment

Fixed-term employees have the right not to be treated less favourably than comparable permanent employees as regards the terms of their contract; and to not be subjected to any other detriment by an act, or deliberate failure to act, of the employer. Common examples of less favourable treatment are exclusion from a pension, bonus, PHI scheme or gym membership.

It is open to an employer to objectively justify any less favourable treatment.

Fixed-term employees can compare their employment conditions to a comparable permanent employee in order to assess whether they are being treated less favourably. If, overall, the terms of the fixed-term employee's contract, taken as a whole, are at least as favourable as those of the permanent employee, the employer will be able to justify the differences.

The right not to be treated less favourably includes a right not to be treated less favourably in relation to the opportunity to secure any permanent position in an organisation. An employer will be required to objectively justify any difference in the availability of internal permanent vacancies between fixed-term and permanent employees.

Successive fixed-term contracts

After four years on successive fixed-term contracts (discounting any period before 10 July 2002) an employee shall be regarded as a permanent employee, unless a further fixed-term contract can be objectively justified. This includes instances where the original contract has been renewed or extended, or where an entirely different contract has been entered into after the expiry of the original contract. It does not cover instances where there has only ever been one fixed-term contract, whatever its duration, if it has never been renewed or extended.

Termination of employment

Failure to renew a fixed-term contract on its expiry constitutes a dismissal for the purposes of employment legislation. In such circumstances, workplace managers should take care to avoid the possibility of a claim for unfair dismissal or redundancy being brought by a fixed-term employee (see 'Dismissal', p.146). Whether the dismissal was fair or unfair will be determined by whether or not the employer can show that it acted reasonably in not renewing the contract.

Historically, employers tried to get around this problem by including clauses in fixed-term contracts where the employee agreed to waive his right to bring a claim for unfair dismissal due to the expiry and non-renewal of the contract. However, since October 1999 it has not been possible to do this. In addition, the waiver of redundancy rights in fixed-term contracts was made unlawful from 1 October 2002.

Agreements purporting to contract out of the right to receive a statutory redundancy payment which were entered into or renewed after 1 October 2002 are now deemed to be invalid. Fixed-term employees will therefore be entitled to receive a statutory redundancy payment, provided they have at least two years' continuous service and the reason for the non-renewal of their contract is redundancy.

By virtue of the Regulations, a dismissal will be automatically unfair if the reason for the dismissal is that the employee has brought proceedings against the employer under the Regulations, or requested from the employer a written statement of reasons for less favourable treatment or otherwise done anything under the Regulations in relation to the employer or any other person. No qualifying period of employment is required for such a claim.

ACAS Code
The ACAS Code of Practice on Disciplinary and Grievance Procedures expressly states that it does not apply to fixed-term contracts. However, this does not mean that employers can ignore procedural issues when not renewing a fixed-term contract, for example, in situations where non-renewal is influenced by conduct, performance or discrimination.

Enforcement
Under the Regulations, a fixed-term employee may bring a complaint to an Employment Tribunal that he has suffered less favourable treatment, not been informed of available vacancies, or suffered a detriment. The complaint must be brought within three months of the date of the act complained of. Time can be extended where the Tribunal considers this to be just and equitable.

Where an employee believes he has been subject to less favourable treatment from his employer he has the right to submit a written request for a written statement of the reasons for such treatment. The employer must respond within 21 days, providing full reasons for the actual difference in treatment, or a denial with an explanation if the difference is wrongly perceived by the employee. A failure to reply to such a request, or an evasive

or equivocal reply, will allow the Tribunal to draw adverse inferences about the employer's actions.

A fixed-term employee who feels that the renewal of their contract has triggered the successive fixed-term contract provision of the Regulations can write to their employer requesting a statement of variation of their contract in order to reflect the change to permanent status. Again, the employer must respond within 21 days, providing a full explanation if they are seeking to assert that the employee remains on a fixed-term contract. Adverse inferences can be drawn if the employer fails to respond or provides an evasive response. Further, the Tribunal can also make a declaration that the employee has permanent status.

Compensation
Compensation is unlimited but should bear some connection to the financial loss suffered by the employee. Compensation cannot generally include an award for injury to feelings. Fixed-term employees can also seek a declaration of permanent employment status. Additional compensation may be awarded if an employer fails to comply with a Tribunal recommendation.

See also: Benefits schemes, p.44; Employment contracts, p.164; Flexible working, p.221; Part-time workers, p.382.

Sources of further information

Business Link – Fixed-term workers: http://bit.ly/nbeiVJ

Flexible working

Mark Kaye, Berwin Leighton Paisner LLP

Key points

- Since 6 April 2003 employers have been under a legal obligation to consider applications for flexible working.
- Parents of young children have the right to submit a request to their employer to allow them to work 'flexibly', by changing hours, changing days or working from home. The change, if agreed, will be a permanent change to the employee's terms and conditions.
- The right applies to parents of children aged 16 or under (or under the age of 18 if disabled) with more than 26 weeks' service who have responsibility for the child's upbringing and make the request to enable them to care for the child and where the employee is the 'carer' of an adult relative or someone living at the same address.
- Carers of adults also have the right to make a request to work 'flexibly' on condition that the person in need of care is a spouse, civil partner or relative of the employee or lives at the same address as the employee.

Legislation

- Employment Act 2002.
- Work and Families Act 2006.

The law

The procedure for making a flexible working request is as follows:

- The employee makes a written, signed and dated request, specifying the change requested and proposed date from which it should apply. The request should also state what effect (if any) the employee thinks the change will have on the employer and how any such effect may be dealt with.
- The employer must either agree to the request in writing or hold a meeting to discuss the application with the employee within 28 days of the application being made.
- The employer must notify the employee in writing of its decision within 14 days of the meeting (which may include detailing any compromise agreed in the meeting).

- Any refusal must specify the grounds (*see below*) with a sufficient explanation for the refusal.
- The employee has the right of appeal against any refusal within 14 days of receiving the employer's notification.
- The employer must hold a meeting with the employee within 14 days of receiving the notice of appeal in order to discuss the appeal.
- The employer must give the employee notice of its decision in writing within 14 days of the appeal meeting. If the appeal is dismissed, grounds of the dismissal must be provided by the employer.

The following are permitted reasons for refusing a request:

- Burden of additional costs.
- Detrimental effect on ability to meet customer demand.
- Inability to reorganise work among existing staff.
- Inability to recruit additional staff.
- Detrimental impact on quality.

> **Case study**
> *Shaw v. CCL Ltd* (2008)
>
> In this case the EAT held that a rejection of a request for flexible working could amount to sex discrimination and also constructive dismissal.
>
> Following six months of maternity leave, Mrs Shaw requested to work on a part-time basis. She submitted a flexible working request, stating that she did not want to work more than 100 miles from home or stay away from home overnight on business.
>
> Her request was rejected and Shaw resigned, claiming sex discrimination and constructive dismissal.
>
> The EAT held that the Tribunal had erred in looking separately at the issues of discrimination and constructive dismissal and considered that the reason for her resignation was because of the way she had been treated, which the Tribunal had found to be discriminatory.
>
> The EAT further held that, as any act of discrimination is a breach of the implied term of trust and confidence, she was entitled to resign and treat herself as constructively dismissed.

- Detrimental impact on performance.
- Insufficiency of work during the period the employee proposes to work.
- Planned structural changes.

These allow an employer to refuse a request, for example, where the employee wishes to change his days or hours from peak periods to quiet times or where the operational needs of the business require staff at a particular time. For example, a bartender who asked to change his hours to work from 11 a.m. to five p.m. could have his request turned down on the grounds that customer demand is highest in the evening.

An employee can complain to a Tribunal that the ground given did not fall within one of the permitted reasons, or that the employer's decision was based on incorrect facts. However, the Tribunal cannot question the commercial validity of the employer's decision or substitute its own view on the employer's business reason. The Tribunal's role is to determine whether the employer has given serious consideration to a request to work flexibly and whether the employer has complied with the statutory procedure.

If the employee's complaint is successful, the Tribunal can either order that the employee's request is reconsidered or award up to eight weeks' pay, subject to the statutory cap, currently £400, making the maximum award £3,200. It is worth noting, however, that these rights exist independently of other employment rights and therefore an employee can bring a sex discrimination claim, for example, arising out of the same facts as a claim under the flexible working provisions, and could potentially be successful in one claim and fail in the other.

Facts

- According to the CBI Employment Trends survey (2009), more than two-thirds of employers have increased flexible working (45%), whilst 13% intend to, and 11% were considering it.
- 91% of employers approve all flexible working requests.
- Over six million employees have the right to request flexible working (2.65m of these are carers of adults, 3.6m are parents of children under six and disabled children).
- 92% of employers believe that people work best when they can balance their work and the other aspects of their lives. 92% of employers said they would consider a request to change a working pattern from any employee.
- Over 700,000 employees and self-employed people work from home. In all, 2.2 million people are involved in some form of flexible working.

Practical guidance for employers

- Treat requests for flexible working seriously.
- Follow the statutory procedure.
- If the request cannot be accommodated, identify the reason and provide an explanation.
- Allow the employee to appeal.
- Consider if a refusal to allow the employer's request for flexible working could give rise to a claim such as indirect sex discrimination.

See also: Carers, p.64; Employment contracts, p.164; Family-friendly rights, p.206; Homeworking, p.243; Pregnancy and maternity, p.400.

Sources of further information

Workplace Law's *Flexible Working Policy and Management Guide, v.4.0*, has been fully revised and updated to take into account the changes in the law. For more details visit www.workplacelaw.net.

Workplace Law's *Guide to Flexible Working 2008* provides information on the formal legislative right to request to work flexibly, but also considers working patterns in a wider sense. It covers the reasons why some employers are looking to introduce flexible working into their workplace, explores different flexible working patters, including their benefits and disadvantages, and provides detail on the formal legislative right to request. It also looks at the employment and non-employment legal issues that surround flexible working and the necessary amendments that need to be made to an employee's contractual terms and conditions if a flexible working pattern is agreed. Finally, it gives practical advice in relation to drafting and implementing a flexible working policy. For more information visit www.workplacelaw.net.

Freedom of information

Pinsent Masons Employment Group

Key points
- The Freedom of Information Act 2000 (FOIA) gives individuals a statutory right to see a huge amount of information held by government departments and public bodies. The Data Protection Act 1998 has traditionally provided individuals with a right of access to information held about themselves; and now FOIA extends this right to cover information about third parties as well as any other information that may be held by the Public Authority, including about private companies that have public sector contracts.
- Under FOIA, anyone of any nationality, and living anywhere in the world, can make a written request for information, and expect a response within 20 working days. The Public Authority will be obliged to meet that request, subject to a number of specified exemptions and certain practical and financial constraints.
- FOIA has imposed a substantial burden on those responsible for administering freedom of information (FOI) requests in Public Authorities. However, it is not only Public Authorities that have been affected by the Act. Whilst the primary impact of the Act is on Public Authorities, it has had a knock-on effect on private companies dealing with Public Authorities.

Legislation
- Data Protection Act 1998.
- Freedom of Information Act 2000 (FOIA).

Some FOI examples
The following are all examples of requests that could be made to a Public Authority in the HR context – whether you disclose the information depends on the circumstances of each case, and each request has to be treated individually. In some cases, an exemption may apply. One of the exemptions that is most common in an HR context is the exemption that protects personal data about individuals. This exemption requires a balancing act between freedom of information and protection of privacy.

- Aggregated information about salary and overtime levels of senior employees.

- Summary information about the number of grievances and disciplinaries dealt with by an organisation.
- Witness statements relating to a grievance.
- CCTV footage of an incident in the workplace.
- A copy of HR policies, for example on sickness, discrimination, IT use, etc.

Remember that if an individual asks for information about themselves, this is treated as a request under the Data Protection Act 1998, but if a request is for information about someone other than the requestor then FOIA applies, subject to privacy considerations.

Other relevant exemptions include information provided in confidence by a third party and information whose disclosure would prejudice the commercial

> **Facts**
>
> - Individuals or organisations have the right to request information from any Public Authority, for any reason.
> - Requests must generally be responded to within 20 working days.
> - Public Authorities could receive requests from employees or former employees or for information about employees or former employees – some of this will overlap with the Data Protection Act 1998.
> - Public Authorities must also provide information proactively through a Publication Scheme.
> - Private companies contracted by Public Authorities should be aware that their information may be caught too, and should know about the Freedom of Information Act 2000 (FOIA).

interests of any party. Some exemptions are subject to an additional public interest test.

What does this mean for public sector employers?

The public sector employer is to a large extent caught between a rock and a hard place. Whilst the aim of FOIA is to increase openness in the public sector, and disclosing information about decisions and activities of employees may promote this, it is recognised that employees also have legitimate concerns over privacy and rights to have those concerns respected. With this delicate balancing act, how should the public sector employer deal with requests made by third parties about their employees? They should consider the following factors.

Consider your publication scheme

The Information Commissioner has issued a model publication scheme for all Public Authorities to follow. This includes organisational information and contacts, policies and procedures, etc. There should already, therefore, be some HR-related information in the public domain and the Authority should ensure that its employees are aware of what this is and that it is regularly reviewed and maintained. Authorities are encouraged to be open and transparent and so it may be helpful to include standard policies in the scheme, along with information about key individuals in the organisation. This should be coupled with comprehensive training for all staff who handle disclosure requests.

Implement policies

The public sector employer should draw up a policy setting out how it intends to deal with requests for employee information, to provide a clear view of how information will be dealt with under the Act. This policy should be made available to all employees and ideally be published on the publication scheme for all to see. Policies could cover what types of information and in what circumstances information will or will not generally be disclosed, and also what issues will be considered in determining whether to disclose employee information. Issuing this policy will help the Authority meet its Data Protection Act obligations to employees. Remember, it is not just personal data that may be requested but any information, including HR policies and procedures.

Know your information

Records management is important. Try to know what personal data you have and have clear filing and records management practices so that information is easy to find. This will also be useful in dealing with subject access requests under the Data Protection Act. Consider separating or flagging information at the point of collection or creation of information which is not exempt from third party requests and other information.

Raise awareness

One potential factor to consider when determining whether information should be disclosed is what the employee was told when the information was collected. With this in mind, the Authority could consider alerting new employees to the potential for disclosure of employee information under the Act by including a notice on induction. Including FOIA as part of new employees' training would provide them with a greater understanding of the Authority's obligations under the Act, and also the relevant exemptions, and they could be given a basic information sheet to use as a checklist for FOIA compliance.

It is important to give notice of, or consult the employee about, any proposed disclosure and certainly where there is any doubt as to whether the information should be disclosed.

Impact on private sector employers

Although it may seem that FOIA will only be relevant to Public Authorities, in practice it will also have an effect on the private sector. While there are limited circumstances where a private company may be deemed a Public Authority for the purposes of the Act (and therefore required to disclose information that it holds), the more concerning effect of the Act relates to information that private sector businesses hand over to the public sector.

Most Public Authorities contract with private sector companies for the provision of goods and services on a regular basis. Many of these contracts contain sensitive information (about HR, commercial or financial issues), which the private sector company would rather not be disclosed. However, all of this information is held by Public Authorities and, in theory, is accessible by anyone requesting it.

Moreover, the Protections of Freedoms Bill, currently at the committee stage of the House of Commons, will allow for an extension of FOIA to cover more bodies receiving public funding (such as the Association of Chief Police Officers, the Financial Services Ombudsman, and higher education admissions body, UCAS; and also all companies wholly owned by any number of public authorities). It is possible that further extensions will be made to include fostering organisations, private prisons, utility companies, etc.

Protecting interests

What can private sector businesses do to protect their interests? They may consider the following factors.

Put in place clear internal policies

Make it clear which individuals are authorised to release information to Public Authorities and identify individuals to liaise with Public Authorities with regard to monitoring the information once the Authority has it. Raise awareness within the organisation of the risk that any information disclosed to a Public Authority may potentially end up being disclosed to a member of the public or a competitor.

Manage information that is provided to Public Authorities

Identify which customers may be Public Authorities and review what information is provided to them. Record what information is provided to aid monitoring of this. If information is particularly sensitive, consider whether it is really necessary to disclose it or whether it can be redacted or anonymised.

Confidential information

Amend standard terms and conditions used for dealing with Public Authorities to include drafting to minimise the impact of the Act. Blanket confidentiality clauses are no longer likely to be accepted by Public Authorities or by the Information Commissioner. Consider segregating confidential and non-confidential material to reduce the risk of inadvertent disclosure, and to increase the likelihood of the confidentiality exemption applying.

Consider negotiating a clause in the contract that provides a right to be notified about, and make submissions in relation to, an information request that may contain employee / commercially sensitive information. This is important as it is the Authority's decision whether to disclose and, similarly, if a decision made by the Information Commissioner is unfavourable to you, it will be the decision of the Authority, not you, as to whether to appeal. There is no obligation on the Authority to consult any interested third parties. Be aware that information that is passed to

Public Authorities may contain employee information such as CVs, experience, etc. Thought should be given to consulting any affected third parties prior to releasing the information. Consider providing induction training on FOIA, amending your data protection notices, and alerting employees when their information may be disclosed.

Use the Act to your advantage

Consider what types of information might be available from the public sector to assist your business and make use of your own rights to access that information. Training employees about the Act will increase your effectiveness in this area.

Both public and private sectors are increasingly being affected by obligations imposed by the Act, albeit in different ways. What is clear is that it is essential for both sectors to implement policies, training and raise awareness within their organisations as to how the Act should be dealt with within their individual business.

See also: Data protection, p.101; Intellectual property, p.252.

Sources of further information

Ministry of Justice: www.justice.gov.uk/guidance/freedom-of-information.htm

Information Commissioner's Office: www.ico.gov.uk

Guidance on access to information about public sector employees: http://bit.ly/ncIe09

When should salaries be disclosed: www.ico.gov.uk/upload/documents/library/freedom_of_information/practical_application/salaries_v1.pdf

When should names be disclosed: www.ico.gov.uk/upload/documents/library/freedom_of_information/practical_application/whenshouldnamesbedisclosed.pdf

Gangmasters

Jonathan Exten-Wright, DLA Piper

Key points

- In lay terms, a gangmaster is a person who organises and oversees the work of casual manual labourers whose services are often supplied to businesses operating in sectors such as agriculture and food processing.
- Until 2004, people knew little of gangmasters and their work. However, the death that year of at least 21 Chinese cockle pickers at Morecambe Bay brought gangmasters into the public eye. The incident highlighted that, in some instances, gangmasters were exploiting labourers, who were often migrant workers. They were being required to work long hours in dangerous or unhygienic conditions and were being deprived of various employment rights, including being paid less than the national minimum wage.

Legislation

As a result of the Morecambe Bay tragedy, the Gangmasters (Licensing) Act 2004 came into force in April 2005. The Act, together with supplemental secondary legislation:

- introduced a licensing scheme for gangmasters;
- created an offence of operating without a licence;
- created an offence of engaging the services of an unlicensed gangmaster;
- created an offence of using false documentation; and
- established the Gangmasters Licensing Authority (GLA) to operate the licensing scheme, set licensing conditions, and maintained a register of licensed gangmasters. The GLA also enforces criminal offences under the Act.

Licensing scheme

The Act prohibits a person from acting as a gangmaster unless they are licensed to do so by the GLA. For the purposes of the Act, a gangmaster is an individual or business that:

- supplies labour to someone operating in one or more of the licensable sectors, which are agriculture, forestry, horticulture, shellfish gathering and food or drink processing and packaging;
- uses labour to provide a service to one of the licensable sectors (for example harvesting or gathering agricultural produce); or
- uses labour to gather shellfish.

'Using labour' includes where a worker is retained on an employment contract or a contract for services but also where someone makes arrangements with a worker that requires the worker to follow their instructions and that determines where, when or how the work is carried out.

Applicants for a licence and existing licence holders must comply with the GLA licensing standards in order to be granted and retain a licence. Compliance with the standards is assessed through inspections conducted by a GLA officer. All new applicants for a licence are inspected and existing licence holders can be inspected at random or on the basis of risk assessment.

The licensing standards require that:

- The licence-holder, the person who is the principal authority under the licence, and any person named on the licence, must at all times act in a fit and proper manner. As part of its assessment, the GLA considers the principal authority's competence and capability to hold a licence.
- The licence-holder must comply with PAYE, NI and VAT obligations, must pay the national minimum wage, and must provide workers with itemised pay slips.
- The licence-holder must prevent forced labour and mistreatment of workers. This includes not retaining identity papers, restricting a worker's ability to work elsewhere, or withholding wages.
- A licence-holder who provides accommodation for workers must ensure the property is of adequate quality and properly licenced (if required) and must allow time for the worker to find alternative accommodation when the provision of accommodation by the licence-holder ends.
- Workers must be able to exercise their rights not to be discriminated against and to, for example, rest breaks, maximum weekly working hours, and trade union membership.
- The licence-holder must comply with health and safety requirements including carrying out risk assessments, ensuring proper instruction and training, ensuring adequate and appropriate personal protective equipment, ensuring access to sanitary facilities, washing facilities, drinking water and facilities for rest / consuming food and drink, and only using vehicles and drivers that are properly registered and licenced.
- A licence-holder must not charge workers a fee for work-finding services and must not make finding work conditional on the worker using other services or hiring / purchasing other goods provided by the licence-holder.
- Written terms should be agreed between the licence-holder and any worker and between the licence holder and any labour user. Written records should be kept by the licence holder of workers and of labour users. Licence-holders should only use sub-contractors who also hold a current GLA licence.

Operating without a licence

It is a criminal offence to operate as a gangmaster without a GLA licence, and the maximum potential penalty is ten years in prison and a fine.

Recent information reveals that the GLA has made 12 successful prosecutions under the Act. A significant case involving the prosecution of a dairy farmer for using labour supplied by an unlicensed gangmaster is due before the Courts in autumn 2011. In terms of the power to revoke licences, GLA records show that approximately 110 licences have been revoked between March 2007 and August 2011.

Engaging the services of an unlicensed gangmaster

A business that operates in one of the licensable sectors, for example a food processing company, and is supplied with labour by a gangmaster (a labour user) must only use GLA licensed labour providers. It is a criminal offence for a labour user to use an unlicensed gangmaster, and the maximum potential penalty for this offence is six months in prison and a fine. It will be a defence, however, for a labour user to demonstrate that they took all reasonable steps to ascertain if the gangmaster had a licence and that the labour user did not know, and had no reasonable grounds to suspect, that the gangmaster did not hold a valid licence.

To safeguard against the risk of prosecution, before agreeing to use labour supplied by a gangmaster, a labour user should check the GLA public register, which lists all licence-holders and applicants. The GLA also recommends that labour users should make an 'active check'. Under this system, the GLA retains a record that the labour user has made a check, informs them of any changes to the status of the gangmaster, and informs them if the gangmaster is inspected by the GLA. It will also be useful for labour users to refer to DEFRA's reasonable steps guidance (see *Sources of further information*), which sets out steps to take to verify the status of a gangmaster.

See also: Agency and temporary workers, p.25; Migrant and foreign workers, p.318; Minimum wage, p.342.

Sources of further information

Gangmasters Licensing Authority: http://gla.defra.gov.uk/

DEFRA – Guidance on the steps that a labour user can take to ensure a labour provider is licensed: http://gla.defra.gov.uk/embedded_object.asp?id=1013034

Health surveillance

David Sinclair, Metis Law

Key points
- Employers who expose their employees to certain chemicals, physical agents, materials or ergonomic risks may be required to undertake systematic, regular and appropriate health surveillance on those employees.
- Health surveillance may be either specified in Regulations or covered by the umbrella provisions of health and safety legislation. Employers must offer night workers health assessments.
- Where health surveillance is required, it should be undertaken only by competent people, who in many cases must be medically qualified.
- Employers are required to provide adequate information to employees on health surveillance provisions, results and the records they keep. Records may have to be kept for up to 50 years.

Legislation
- Health and Safety at Work etc. Act 1974.
- Opticians Act 1989.
- Sight Testing (Examination and Prescription) (No. 2) Regulations 1989.
- Health and Safety (Display Screen Equipment) Regulations 1992.
- Manual Handling Operations Regulations 1992.
- Data Protection Act 1998.
- Working Time Regulations 1998.
- Management of Health and Safety at Work Regulations 1999.
- Control of Substances Hazardous to Health Regulations 2002.
- Control of Vibration at Work Regulations 2005.
- Noise at Work Regulations 2005.
- Control of Asbestos Regulations 2006.
- Equality Act 2010.

Specific and non-specific duties

Health and safety regulations can specify mandatory health surveillance – e.g. the Control of Asbestos Regulations and the Noise at Work Regulations – where employers expose their employees to certain biological hazards, chemicals or physical agents (e.g. asbestos, lead, noise, radiation, or vibration). In such circumstances, the relevant regulations will specify the type, level and frequency of the surveillance to be undertaken, along with details on what records are to be kept by the employer and for how long.

Regulation 7 of the Working Time Regulations 1998 imposes a duty on employers to offer night workers a free assessment of their health and capacity to carry out the work they are to be given, prior to them undertaking that work.

In circumstances where there is no specific duty on the employer to carry out health surveillance, the employer has general duties under Section 2 of the Health and Safety at Work etc. Act 1974 and Regulation 6 of the Management of Health and Safety at Work Regulations 1999 to carry out appropriate health surveillance.

This general duty applies where the employer's risk assessments identify that:

- there is an identifiable disease or adverse health condition related to the work;
- there is a valid technique available to detect indications of the disease or condition;
- there is a reasonable likelihood that the disease or condition may occur under the particular conditions of the work; and
- health surveillance is likely to further the protection of the health and safety of the employees concerned.

Health surveillance can only be carried out in the above circumstances where the techniques used to undertake the surveillance pose a low risk to the employee. Employers may need to carry out health surveillance in the following situations:

- Post-accident (or during long-term illness);
- On forklift truck and other machinery operators; and
- On drivers to test for colour blindness.

Employers should be extremely careful in undertaking pre-employment health surveillance, so that if, for example, they require candidates to complete pre-employment health questionnaires, they do not discriminate against disabled candidates in breach of the Equality Act 2010. Employers should seek expert assistance in deciding what surveillance is needed and who is competent to provide that surveillance.

Objectives
The objectives of health surveillance are:

- to protect the health of individual employees by detecting, as early as possible, adverse changes that might be caused by exposure to hazardous substances;

- to help evaluate the measures taken to control exposure to health hazards; and
- to collect, keep, update and use data and information for determining and evaluating hazards to health.

Procedures
There are a number of health surveillance procedures that employers can use:

- Biological monitoring, i.e. taking samples of blood, urine, breath, etc. to detect the presence of hazardous substances;
- Biological effect monitoring, i.e. assessing the early biological effects in exposed workers;
- Clinical examinations by occupational doctors or nurses to measure physiological changes in the body of exposed people, e.g. reduced lung function; and
- Medical enquiries (often accompanied by a medical examination) by a suitably qualified occupational health practitioner to detect symptoms.

Competent people acting within the limits of their training and experience should determine the appropriate level, frequency and procedure to be followed. For most types of health surveillance the appropriate competent person will be a suitably qualified occupational medical practitioner, occupational health nurse or occupational hygienist.

Once health surveillance has been started, it must be maintained throughout the remainder of the employee's period of employment, unless the risks to which the employee is exposed and the associated health effects are rare and short-term.

Display screen equipment
Regulation 5 of the Health and Safety (Display Screen Equipment) Regulations 1992 places a duty on employers to

provide, when requested to do so, an eye or eyesight test to employees who are about to become (or who are already) display screen users. Eye and eyesight tests are defined in Section 36(2) of the Opticians Act 1989 and the Sight Testing Examination and Prescription (No. 2) Regulations 1989, which specify what examinations the doctor or optician should perform as part of the test. Although the employer only needs to provide the eye or eyesight test when requested to do so, he is under a duty by Regulation 7(3) of the DSE Regulations to provide employees with adequate information about the risks to their health and their entitlement under Regulation 5.

Records

Where health surveillance is undertaken in compliance with particular Regulations, those Regulations will state what data is to be collected and the minimum period for which information is to be stored. Other health surveillance records should be kept:

- for the period specified in the Regulations; or
- for three years after the end of the last date of the individual's employment (the date after which the employee cannot normally bring a claim against the employer), whichever is the longer.

Employers will need to provide employees with access to their personal health records and copies of such records may have to be provided to the Enforcing Authorities.

To comply with the employer's duty to provide information to employees (and others who might be affected), employers should provide the appropriate people with the general results of health surveillance, but keep confidential individuals' surveillance data.

Data gathered during health surveillance is regarded as 'sensitive data' within the meaning of Section 2 of the Data Protection Act 1998. As such, all health surveillance data must be processed in accordance with the requirements of that Act. Detailed advice should be sought as to these requirements.

See also: Discrimination, p.126; The Equality Act, p.191; Medical records, p.304; Occupational health, p.374.

Sources of further information

HSE: Understanding health surveillance at work:
www.hse.gov.uk/pubns/indg304.pdf

Workplace Law's *Occupational Health 2008: Making the business case – Special Report* addresses the issues of health at work, discusses the influence of work on health and highlights the business case for occupational health services at work. The Report focuses on the advantages of occupational health services, and the benefits they can provide to a company, in terms of financial savings, increased employee morale, and improved corporate image. For more information visit www.workplacelaw.net.

HIV and AIDS

Robert Dillarstone and Lisa Jinks, Greenwoods Solicitors LLP

Key points

- Employers and employees need to understand what HIV and AIDS are.
- Employers need to be aware of their liability under various employment-related laws as well as health and safety legislation.
- Specific employment issues include discrimination on grounds of disability and/or sexual orientation, unfair / constructive dismissal, and aspects of data protection law.
- Key areas of the employment relationship that need addressing include recruitment, disclosure, medical testing and reasonable adjustments to working conditions.
- Employers should implement an HIV and AIDS policy.

Legislation

- Access to Medical Reports Act 1988.
- Employment Rights Act 1996.
- Data Protection Act 1998.
- Management of Health and Safety at Work Regulations 1999.
- Equality Act 2010.

What are HIV and AIDS and what are the real risks for the workplace?

It is important for employers and employees to understand what HIV and AIDS are, as there are many common misconceptions.

AIDS stands for Acquired Immune Deficiency Syndrome. It is caused by the human immunodeficiency virus (HIV), which attacks the body's natural defence system and leaves it open to various infections and cancers.

HIV is mainly contained in blood. There is a minimal risk of it being contained in other bodily fluids such as urine, saliva and sweat unless these are contaminated with infected blood.

HIV is not spread through normal social interaction such as sharing cutlery or toilets – it is transmitted through sexual intercourse or direct exposure to infected blood through accidental contamination.

The risk of infection at work is very low for the majority of workplaces. The types of occupation where the risk is higher include healthcare, custodial (e.g. prisons), education, emergency services, hair and beauty and plumbing. *Note: The strict requirements on such specialist occupations are beyond the scope of this chapter.*

There is no reason to treat workers with HIV differently from other workers. People who have the virus but have not developed AIDS will not usually be ill and their ability to work will normally be unaffected. There is often a time lag of many years before their ability to do their job will be affected. In many instances this time lag would be longer than people stay in their job on average in ordinary circumstances.

Those who develop AIDS will have severe illnesses inevitably affecting performance and should be treated in the same way as anyone with any other life threatening illness.

> **Facts**
> - There are approximately 86,500 adults in the UK living with HIV.
> - It is not known what proportion of those will progress to AIDS, and the incubation period between infection and onset of AIDS can be very long.
> - During this time, the individual is unlikely to be ill and may not even be aware of the infection.
> - Although there is no known cure for AIDS, HIV symptoms, such as swollen lymph glands, weight loss and minor infections, can be treated with anti-retroviral drugs and enable HIV positive people to lead healthy lives.

Discrimination

Protection from discrimination covers the whole of the working relationship – from recruitment, benefits, promotion and training, dismissal and harassment through to post-termination discrimination, such as the giving of references.

Unlike unfair dismissal claims, there is no financial cap on awards made for discrimination claims, and additional awards can be made for injury to feelings.

Disability discrimination

Under the Equality Act 2010, HIV-infected employees are 'deemed' to have a disability from the point of diagnosis – irrespective of whether they exhibit any symptoms – and are therefore protected from disability discrimination. This contrasts with the previous legal position (pre December 2005) where an employee was only held to be disabled when he was in the symptomatic stages of HIV or had AIDS.

The Equality Act also includes the concepts of associative and perceived discrimination. This means that someone could claim disability discrimination where they are treated as if they had – but did not in fact have – HIV / AIDS, or where they are less favourably treated as a result of a relationship they have with someone with HIV / AIDS.

Reasonable adjustments

One key area of disability discrimination is the duty on employers to make reasonable adjustments to working conditions once they are aware that an employee is HIV positive. In such circumstances, an employer is under a positive duty to take whatever steps are reasonably necessary to prevent the employee from being disadvantaged. For instance, this may require an employer to provide time off for treatment, allocate duties to others and so on.

If an employee requires time off work for an HIV-related reason, the reason for the time off should, as far as possible, be treated in strictest confidence. Managers should not need to know the precise reason for the time off.

Discrimination on grounds of sexual orientation

Dismissal or other detrimental treatment of a worker on the grounds that they are, or are perceived to be, gay is unlawful. This may extend to discrimination or harassment on the basis that a worker is, or is assumed to be, HIV positive.

There is also protection from discrimination for people associated with someone who is HIV positive (for example, they have gay or HIV positive friends). Both perceived and associative discrimination are expressly protected under the Equality Act 2010. In addition to a potential claim for disability or sexual orientation discrimination, a claim for indirect sex discrimination might be brought on the basis that more men than women are HIV positive.

Recruitment, disclosure and medical testing

Medical information is protected under the Data Protection Act 1998 and is classified as 'sensitive personal data'. There are various stringent requirements on the 'processing' of medical information, which include obtaining, holding and disclosing such data.

Pre-employment health questions

One key aspect of the Equality Act 2010 is that it limits the circumstances in which employers may ask pre-employment health-related questions. Previously, employers were able to ask job applicants whether they had a disability, were taking medication, or had a medical condition – even if it had no relevance to the role. This new provision is expected to reduce the barrier to people living with HIV from entering the workplace.

There are various exemptions from the prohibition on asking pre-employment health-related questions. Prior to making an offer of employment, employers are permitted to ask candidates questions that:

■ help the employer to determine whether any reasonable adjustments need to be made for the candidate during the selection process;
■ allow the employer to determine whether the candidate can carry out a function that is intrinsic to the job;
■ monitor diversity amongst the applicants; or
■ allow the employer to take positive action in favour of disabled people.

While asking an applicant pre-employment health questions, other than those that are permitted, will not in itself amount to discrimination against a job applicant, acting on the answers may well do. Furthermore, if the candidate were to subsequently bring a discrimination claim against an employer who had asked pre-employment health-related questions, the burden of proof would shift to the employer, who would be required to demonstrate that no discrimination took place.

Disclosure

Disclosure is one of the main HIV-related issues in the workplace. Employees worry about breaches of confidentiality if they reveal their status to their line manager or HR department.

HIV-positive employees do not have to reveal their HIV status (although it may be a condition of employment in certain higher risk occupations). However, if the employee fails to disclose such information, the employer cannot be expected to make reasonable adjustments. If an employee discloses their HIV status, it is important for employers to handle this in the correct manner by ensuring the information disclosed by the employee is kept confidential. The 'best practice' approach would be to have an HIV / AIDS policy in place so employers are aware of their obligations in situations where an employee discloses their HIV status.

Medical testing

Again, generally, there will be no justification for requiring employees to take an HIV / AIDS test unless the occupation is high risk or the job requires travel to countries asking for evidence of HIV status.

Employers may ask applicants to undertake a medical test, but this is subject to various conditions under data protection principles. Employers must have a legitimate reason as to why they need this information, which outweighs any intrusion to the worker, such as a genuine health and safety reason, and applicants should not be tested unless there is a real likelihood that they will be employed.

The worker must be assured that the results will be treated in strictest confidence. Employers should also respect the right to privacy and should always obtain the worker's consent, particularly before seeking a medical report from the employee's own medical practitioner, under the Access to Medical Reports Act 1988.

Employers cannot insist that an applicant undertakes a medical test, but, if they refuse, the employer can refuse to employ them. It is preferable, wherever possible, to use health questionnaires rather than medical tests, as these are less intrusive. However, in light of the provisions in the Equality Act, pre-employment health questionnaires need to be used with caution.

Note: If the penalty for an existing employee's refusal to consent to testing is dismissal, then the consent is highly unlikely to be considered by an Employment Tribunal to be freely given and will be invalid.

Unfair / constructive dismissal

In extreme cases, workers have been dismissed because of their HIV status. More likely, however, is that an employee with HIV is treated detrimentally, whether by way of harassment, being denied equal benefits and so on.

In addition to any claim for discrimination, such treatment could lead an employee to resign, resulting in a claim for constructive dismissal.

Colleagues may refuse to work alongside an employee with HIV, or pressurise an employer into dismissing that employee. Employers are also responsible for the actions of their staff, and should take steps to deal with such issues, preferably by consulting with and educating such workers but, where necessary, by taking disciplinary action. The 'best practice' approach would be to have an effective HIV / AIDS policy already in place.

Checklist: policy document and implementation

Employers are advised to draw up a policy on HIV and AIDS so that, if a problem arises, this can be dealt with in accordance with the policy. The policy should be developed in consultation with employee representatives. Once finalised, managers should be provided with appropriate training and an employee awareness programme implemented.

The policy will vary depending upon the type of organisation but could include:

- a brief description of HIV and AIDS and how HIV is transmitted;
- the organisation's position on HIV testing;
- an assurance of confidentiality;
- a guarantee that absenteeism or other AIDS-related work issues are to be treated like any other serious illness;
- assurances that colleagues are expected to work normally with such workers and that any refusal to work normally will be dealt with and if appropriate under the disciplinary procedure;
- identifying help available;
- first aid procedures; and
- provisions for overseas travel – the risks of infection through inadequate medical practices as well as sexual encounters.

It is also advisable to make express reference to HIV / AIDS in anti-discrimination and harassment policies. Employers are also advised to review existing pre-employment health questionnaires in recruitment procedures and policies in the light of the Equality Act.

See also: Data protection, p.101; Discrimination, p.126; The Equality Act, p.191; Medical records, p.304; Occupational health, p.374; Recruitment and selection, p.420.

Sources of further information

INDG 342: Blood-borne viruses in the workplace – guidance for employers and employees: www.hse.gov.uk/pubns/indg342.pdf

Equality and Human Rights Commission (EHRC): www.equalityhumanrights.com

National AIDS Trust: Advice for Employers: www.nat.org.uk/Media%20library/Files/Policy/2010/HIV-Work-employers.pdf

Holiday

Pav Clair and Lisa Gettins, BPE Solicitors LLP

Key points

- The Working Time Regulations 1998 came into force in 1998 and implemented the European Working Time Directive.
- Initially, workers were only entitled to three weeks' (15 days') paid leave each holiday year.
- However, following a number of consultations held by the Government, the holiday entitlement was progressively increased over the years and since April 2009 it has been 5.6 weeks (28 days) for full-time workers.

Legislation

The Work and Families Act was introduced in 2006, through which the Government extended workers' annual statutory holiday entitlement from four weeks to 4.8 weeks and then to 5.6 weeks since 1 April 2009 (subject to a maximum of 28 days). The increase was enacted by the Working Time (Amendment) Regulations 2007, which took effect on 1 October 2007.

Public holidays

The 2007 Regulations satisfy the political intention to provide an additional eight days' holiday per year for a full-time worker. However, on closer inspection, the 2007 Regulations are careful not to introduce a right to have public holidays as paid leave. If a worker wishes to take paid annual leave on a public holiday, then the worker must make a request to his/her employer in the normal way and the employer is entitled to refuse any such request as long as it is done in accordance with the procedures set out in the 1998 Regulations.

Problems for employers

Following the introduction of the 2007 Regulations, employers are advised to review their contracts of employment. Existing contracts may contain holiday clauses along the lines of 'Statutory Entitlement plus Bank / Public Holidays'.

An employer whose contracts have the above wording might be confronted by an employee who claims that his paid annual leave is now 36 days, because it includes the Statutory Entitlement of 28 days plus any bank holidays.

The 2007 Regulations cater for this potential problem. Regulation 26a enables an employer to avoid raising the holiday entitlement of such workers beyond 28 days as long as the following provisions are in place:

- A relevant agreement between the employer and the workforce providing that each worker will receive paid annual leave entitlement of 1.6 weeks (eight days) in addition to each worker's current four-week statutory entitlement;
- No provision for payment in lieu of that leave except on termination of employment; and
- Statutory leave cannot be carried over beyond the next leave year.

Carrying over leave entitlement

Employers are often unsure whether or not they are obliged to carry over the remaining annual leave into the next holiday year of a worker who has not exhausted their annual leave.

The 2007 Regulations do allow that the additional entitlement of 1.6 weeks (eight days) can be carried over into the subsequent leave year. This was expressly prohibited by the 1997 Regulations.

Regulation 13a(7) provides that the carry-over of 1.6 weeks can be done by means of a 'relevant agreement'. This is a document by which an employer agrees with its workers to modify particular aspects of the Working Time Regulations.

Therefore for Regulation 13a(7) to have effect, an employer should ensure that it has specific wording in the relevant agreement to carry over of 1.6 weeks' statutory leave.

Small employers will be dismayed by this new Regulation as it will increase their administrative burden. Employers will need to keep track of workers' holiday entitlement, past and present, and distinguish between holidays taken in the previous holiday year and those taken in the current holiday year. However, this carry forward entitlement is not a right for the employees. It only comes into effect if it is expressly agreed between a worker and its employer by means of a relevant agreement. An employer can refuse to agree to a request to carry forward annual leave and insist that the full 28 days' leave is taken in one holiday leave year.

Holiday pay for the long-term sick

Since there is no statutory provision for the legal relationship between long-term sickness and holiday pay, it has been down to the courts to resolve this particular issue.

The most recent developments in this area took place in 2009 following rulings on two

cases by the European Court of Justice. In *Stringer v. HMRC*, the ECJ ruled that holiday entitlement would continue to accrue during a period of long-term sick leave and workers should receive their full entitlement for the holiday year. This was the case even if the sickness lasted for the whole holiday year, in which case it could be carried over if the worker did not have the opportunity to take their leave in time.

The second case of *Pereda v. Madrid Movilidad SA* ruled that workers can take paid holiday during a period of sickness. However, if they preferred not to, then they must be allowed to take their leave at a later date, even if this meant it had to be carried over into the next holiday year.

Whilst the new Regulations are silent, the Government's January 2007 consultation document hinted that it could foresee a situation in which the 2007 Regulations were interpreted so that a worker on long-term sickness absence does receive the benefit of paid holiday entitlement.

Part-time workers

The normal entitlement of 5.6 weeks' holiday a year applies to 'full-time workers'. Where a worker is employed on a part-time basis, their leave entitlement would be calculated pro rata.

The simplest calculations would be where workers simply work less days per week on a permanent basis. For example, a worker working three days a week would only be entitled to 3.36 weeks' (or 16.8 days') holiday a year.

This issue becomes slightly more complicated when workers work irregular shift patterns that change on a weekly basis. In such circumstances, the 'average' working week should be calculated. However, certain difficulties arise in doing so, in particular because there is no statutory provision that provides a formula for carrying out this calculation. Instead, employers should calculate the average working week by first ascertaining how many hours on average the worker works a year and then dividing that by the number of working weeks in a year. BIS uses 48 weeks in its calculations, whereas others argue that it should be 46.4 weeks, once the 5.6 weeks' statutory holiday entitlement has been taken into account. Since there is no set formula, either can be used, although it does appear more sensible to use the 46.4 weeks.

New contracts of employment

The Working Time Regulations apply to workers. However, under the Employment Rights Act 1996 employers are under a duty to give 'employees' a written statement with particulars of employment detailing such things as rates of pay, hours of work and holiday entitlement. The law states that whenever there is a change in detail, the employer is under a duty to provide a written statement containing particulars of that change.

Employers should ensure that they have already provided amended particulars of employment to their employees to update them regarding the increase to 28 days' paid annual leave from 1 April 2009 and if they have not done so, then they should do so as soon as possible.

See also: Agency and temporary workers, p.25; Benefits schemes, p.44; Flexible working, p.221; Leave, p.252; Sickness, p.470.

Sources of further information

The Government's Business Link website has an interactive holiday pay calculator that allows you to work out your employees' annual holiday entitlement: http://bit.ly/3CKJZP

Homeworking

Dale Collins, Bond Pearce LLP

Key points

- Employers have a duty to protect the health, safety and welfare of their employees and other staff members working at an employer's workplace.
- This duty extends to all employees who work either at, or from, their home.
- As a general guide, therefore, employers should treat both the work area and the equipment used in an employee's own home as though they were in the main office. This approach should be reflected in the employer's employment policies and guidelines, as well as in the Home Working Agreement made and signed between the employer and the employee before homeworking is approved.

Legislation

- Health and Safety (Display Screen Equipment) Regulations 1992.
- Data Protection Act 1998.
- Health and Safety (Miscellaneous Amendments) Regulations 2002.

Computer (display) screens

The main legislation relevant to homeworkers (or teleworkers) here is the Display Screen Equipment Directive (90/270/EEC). This is implemented in the UK by the Health and Safety (Display Screen Equipment) Regulations 1992 – as amended by the Health and Safety (Miscellaneous Amendments) Regulations 2002.

This requires that there should be:

- a clear and stable screen, bright and free from glare, which should swivel and tilt easily;
- adequate arrangement of keyboard characters, adjustable keyboard with sufficient space to support the hands and arms of the user;
- sufficient user space to change positions and vary movements, a sufficiently large work desk, a document holder that is adjustable and stable;
- satisfactory lighting conditions;
- minimised glare and reflection at the workstation, and minimisation of radiation levels;
- a work chair that is adjustable in height, including the backrest;
- a footrest available if required; and
- provision to reduce environmental factors to a minimum, including the effects of reflection or glare, noise, heat and humidity.

Computer users can request an eye examination and an eye test from their employer, under Regulation 6 of the Management of Health and Safety Regulations, which require employers to provide users or operators of DSE with an appropriate eye and eyesight test if they request it. The employer has a liability to pay for these tests.

The working environment

Employers should put in place a system for their homeworkers to report accidents or hazards, as there would be in a conventional workplace. Practical experience within the Telework Association

> **Case study**
>
> *Secretary of State for Work and Pensions (Job Centre Plus) and Ors v. J Wilson*
>
> An EAT case from February 2010 considered the question of whether an agoraphobic was entitled to work from home when her usual place of work (near to her home) closed and she was to move to a new site, further away.
>
> Ms Wilson suffered from agoraphobia and had anxiety and panic attacks in new situations which made it difficult for her to work with the public. She worked for Job Centre Plus in a back-office administrative role, which ensured minimal contact with the public. Job Centre Plus accepted that her condition amounted to a disability for the purposes of the Disability Discrimination Act 1995.
>
> The pilot scheme that Ms Wilson worked for closed and the staff would no longer work from offices close to Ms Wilson's home. Prior to the closure of the office Ms Wilson asked if she could work from home when the closure happened. Having considered a number of ways in which Ms Wilson's work could be facilitated, Job Centre Plus advised her that were no vacancies in which it was reasonably possible for her to work from home. Ms Wilson indicated that the only basis upon which she was willing to work (even though she had worked elsewhere in the past) was from home.
>
> In the particular circumstances that existed, it was held that allowing her to work from home would not be a 'reasonable adjustment'.

suggests that the following areas also often need attention.

- There should be a sufficient number of power sockets, avoiding overuse of extension leads, trailing cables and adaptors. Home offices may need rewiring for more sockets – have the homeworker's installation checked by an electrician.
- The use of IT equipment usually requires an additional two power outlets, and one or two telecoms sockets. Safely stowing cabling is important.
- Electrical equipment needs to be checked for safety (e.g. all cable grips in place, no burn marks on plugs or cracked sockets).
- Shelves should be conveniently situated so that when heavy files are placed and replaced there is no risk of stress on the spine or overbalancing.
- Office chairs and tables should all be of the appropriate height and adjustability for long periods of work.
- If the homeworker wears reading glasses, the prescription should be correct for close work. Anyone working with computers should have their eyes tested, and the optician should be informed of the computer work.
- Spotlights and angle-poise-type lamps are generally less tiring than fluorescents in small spaces. Light levels should be about 350 lux.
- Computer screens should be positioned at right angles to windows. Blinds to prevent sunlight making screens hard to read should be installed where needed.

- Temperatures should be as near as possible to 18.5°C. Small home offices can easily overheat because IT equipment generates heat. Temperatures may become uncomfortably hot in summer unless adequate ventilation can be provided.
- Adequate ventilation is also important where equipment such as laser printers may give off ozone or other fumes.
- Psychologically, most homeworkers prefer to be situated so that they can see out of a window if possible, although, as noted above, it is important to avoid problems with glare and reflection on computer screens.
- Rest breaks are vital. There are now a number of software packages that can be set up to remind homeworkers to take frequent breaks and so interrupt their more concentrated work environment.

Tax implications for homeworkers

If you set aside part of the house for the sole use of the business, that part of the house is potentially liable for capital gains tax. The precise implications of this will vary from year to year, and so, particularly if the homeworker is self-employed, it is advisable for him to discuss these with an accountant who will also advise on the proportions of household expenses attributable to home-office use that can be legitimately claimed.

'Business' charges by public utilities

There have been rare instances of power utility companies charging a non-domestic rate. The practical situation is that they would have to know that someone is working from home before any change could be made, and that the exact conditions vary from company to company.

For telephone services, BT does not compel people to use the business rate, but points out that the business service has the advantage of Yellow Pages and Business Pages entries. BT also puts business users on a higher priority for fault correction than residential users. In both cases, compensation is paid if the fault is not repaired within 24 hours.

Insurance

The insurance market has pretty much caught up with the shift to homeworking. It is still the case that a standard home contents policy is unlikely to cover home office equipment, but specific policies targeted at home offices have been produced to replace the plethora of computer, office and home policies previously designed to confuse the homeworker. These new policies also cover important business issues that can affect homeworkers, such as public liability, employee liability and loss of earnings.

Areas particularly to consider include the following:

- Insurance against loss of data (e.g. through virus or malicious attack). Employers should clarify the position on home-stored data with their insurers.
- Public liability or employer's liability insurance if other people work at or visit the homeworker's home office (this is mandatory in the Republic of Ireland). It is also important for employers to ensure that employees other than the homeworker visiting the home office are covered (e.g. managers or those involved in health and safety checks).
- Business interruption insurance, which, in the case of the self-employed or small home-based businesses, would provide compensation for the costs of putting a business back together and other expenditure incurred after an incident.
- Computer breakdown insurance. In some situations this can be cheaper

than holding a maintenance contract and ensures that expensive part replacements are covered. Employers need to check rather than assume that this insurance applies to computers off site.

- Cover off the premises (e.g. for portable computers at the homeworker's home or in transit).

Employment issues

The degree of employment protection available to a homeworker depends on whether they are self-employed or an employee or a worker. However, there are issues that will be relevant to all categories.

Data protection issues and confidentiality

The importance of this depends on the nature of the work but it is likely that the majority of homeworkers will have at home some confidential information belonging to the employer, either on a computer or in another format.

Whilst all employees are subject to an implied duty of confidentiality, most employers will want an express clause on the issue setting out what amounts to confidential information and ensuring that the duty of confidentiality continues post-termination of employment. As ensuring compliance with confidentiality is more difficult for those employees who are not habitually in the office, employers need to address their minds to this issue more closely.

In addition, the Data Protection Act 1998 places additional responsibilities on data controllers, in this instance the employer, to ensure that all personal data is kept in compliance with the data protection principles. Consequently, employers should ensure that homeworkers are trained on the provisions of the Data Protection Act 1998 and what their responsibilities are

under the Act. Compliance with any data protection policy should also be stated in the contract.

Competency, supervision and monitoring

As with all employees, it is important to ensure that homeworkers are appraised and meet their objectives. Whilst working remotely or at separate times to a supervisor may cause some difficulties, nevertheless a suitable system for appraising such employees is important. It is important, not just for employers, but also for the employees, who may feel more vulnerable than their colleagues whose output is more obvious.

Supervision of employees who do not necessarily work either at the same location or the same time as their supervisor is clearly more complicated. However, there are ways of monitoring employees remotely and supervisors should also be encouraged to spend time working with the homeworker, for example by arranging a regular time to meet with the homeworker to discuss issues.

Monitoring of employees should only be done for specific reasons, and employees should be made aware of the amount of monitoring that will take place, the methods for monitoring, and how the information obtained from monitoring will be used and stored. Any monitoring must be proportionate to the objectives to be met (which in themselves must be reasonable) and must be the least intrusive method of achieving those reasonable objectives.

Disabled homeworkers

Employers should look at each individual homeworker to ensure that any duties they may have towards that individual are complied with, such as duties that relate to disabled homeworkers in respect of making reasonable adjustments, and regularly monitoring and reviewing such adjustments going forward.

Flexible working

Since April 2009, all employees with children aged 16 or under, or disabled children under 18, have been able to request to work from home, and employers are under an obligation to consider the request in accordance with the relevant statutory provisions relating to requests for flexible working. (See '*Flexible working*,' p.221.)

See also: Carers, p.64; Flexible working, p.221; IT security, p.282.

Sources of further information

The Telework Association: www.telework.org.uk

The datasheet 'Teleworking' can be downloaded free from the Institution of Occupational Health and Safety's website: www.iosh.co.uk. The datasheet includes a homework premises assessment form and stresses the importance of adequate training and regular reassessment of the risks.

Human rights

Susan Thomas, Charles Russell

Key points

- An employee of a public authority can bring a freestanding claim against their employer directly for a breach of any right provided by the Human Rights Act.
- An employee of a semi-public authority or private employer can only bring a claim under the Human Rights Act that is attached to an existing employment claim.
- All employee policies should be reviewed to ensure any interference with human rights is justifiable.

Legislation

- Human Rights Act 1998.
- European Convention on Human Rights and Fundamental Freedoms.

Application of the Human Rights Act

The Human Rights Act 1998 (the HRA) adopted the European Convention for the Protection of Human Rights and Fundamental Freedoms into UK law on 2 October 2000. Some of the rights and freedoms set out in the Convention relevant to the workplace are:

- Prohibition of slavery and forced labour (Article 4);
- Right to a fair trial (Article 6);
- Right to respect for private and family life (Article 8) (see 'Private Life', p.404);
- Freedom of expression (Article 10); and
- Freedom of assembly and association (Article 11).

The HRA requires public authorities to act in compliance with the Convention. Public authorities include all courts and tribunals, and any person exercising functions of a public nature.

UK courts must interpret legislation in a way that is compatible with the Convention, even to the extent, in some cases, that additional wording is implied, provided that this is compatible with the 'scheme' of the legislation. This means that the HRA affects different types of employers differently.

Public authorities

Employees can bring a claim against a public authority employer directly for a breach of a right set out in the HRA.

Public authority employers include the police, the Government, local authorities, the NHS, and so on.

Semi-public authorities

Private bodies that carry out public functions are also defined as public authorities, but only insofar as they are carrying out their public function.

The relationship between employer and employee would normally be considered to be within the scope of their private function as employer, and any related acts to be outside the scope of their public function. This means that semi-public authority employers are affected by the HRA in the same way as private employers.

Semi-public authorities include privatised utility companies, or a private security

Case studies

Pay v. United Kingdom (2008)

P was employed by the Probation Service, and worked mainly with sex offenders. His employer discovered that he sold bondage and sado-masochism products on the internet, and dismissed him. P brought a claim for unfair dismissal and breach of his rights under Articles 8 and 10 of the Convention (the right to respect for private life, and the right to freedom of expression). The Employment Appeal Tribunal decided that a probation officer, as a professional, had a reputation to maintain, and that P's activities were publicised on a website and in the public domain, and were therefore not part of his private life. This meant that Article 8 was not engaged. There was an interference with P's right to freedom of expression, but this was justified due to the potential damage to the Service's reputation.

Two recent Court of Appeal decisions indicate the potential rise of a right to legal representation at disciplinary hearings as a result of Article 6 (right to a fair trial).

Kulkarni v. Milton Keynes Hospital NHS Foundation Trust (2009)

In this case the Court of Appeal held that a doctor was contractually entitled to be represented at an internal disciplinary hearing by a lawyer instructed by the Medical Protection Society. The CoA decided the appeal by reference to the employment contract but suggested that, had it been required to do so, it would have held that Article 6 of the ECHR was engaged and that, in circumstances such as those of this case (where the employee was facing what was in effect a criminal charge), it implied a right to legal representation in civil proceedings.

R (on the application of G) v. X School and others (2010)

In this case the CoA confirmed that a teaching assistant was entitled to legal representation during disciplinary proceedings for sexual misconduct involving a child. Article 6 ECHR was engaged and, given the seriousness of the charge and its likely effect in ending G's career, this included the right to legal representation.

In both cases it was held that Article 6 may be engaged in disciplinary proceedings where the employee risks losing his or her right to practice their profession, resulting in an implied right to legal representation at disciplinary hearings. Although the first case did not turn on this point, the reasoning was upheld in the second case. In the second case, it was also held that the right to legal representation will apply even where dismissal will not automatically lead to loss of the right of the employee to engage in their profession. As this case concerned a classroom assistant it also established that 'profession' is not limited to the occupations traditionally thought of as the 'professions' (lawyers, doctors etc.). These cases will therefore have significant implications for public sector and possibly even private sector employers.

company exercising public functions in relation to the management of a prison.

Private employers

These are organisations that carry out no public function. The HRA is only indirectly enforceable against such employers, in that an Employment Tribunal's decision about workplace conduct and workplace decisions must be compatible with the HRA. An employee cannot directly bring a claim for breach of the HRA, but may 'attach' a claim that the employer has breached the HRA to an existing employment claim, such as unfair dismissal. Therefore, if an employer were to have unjustifiably breached an employee's human rights in its treatment of the employee in a dismissal situation, a Tribunal might find that the employer's actions made the dismissal unfair.

The Act sets out 'justifications' that an employer may be able to rely on, such as the prevention of crime, or the prevention of infringement of rights of others. Whenever a Convention right is breached by an employer, the breach must not only be justified but must also not go beyond what is strictly necessary.

Equality and Human Rights Commission (EHRC)

The EHRC came into existence on 1 October 2007 and has taken over the functions of the previous equality bodies (such as the Equal Opportunities Commission and the Commission for Racial Equality) and is also responsible for promoting the awareness, understanding and protection of human rights.

Issues for employers

Disciplinary procedures

Disciplinary procedures must now satisfy ACAS' statutory Code of Practice requirements and are therefore likely

to respect the employee's right to a fair trial, incorporating an opportunity to hear and consider the employee's case and a mechanism for appeal.

However, given recent decisions upholding a right to legal representation at disciplinary hearings in certain situations, both public and private sector employers should take advice before refusing legal representation where an adverse finding may affect an employee's ability to practise a profession, even if the loss of such ability is not necessarily automatic.

Dismissal

Any dismissal procedure must also be fair, and any reason given for dismissal must not represent an unreasonable breach of a Convention right. For example, dismissing an employee on the grounds of membership of a political party may lead a Tribunal to find that the dismissal was not fair, since for a Tribunal to uphold such a reason for dismissal would represent an unreasonable breach of the employee's freedom of expression.

Investigating a complaint

The investigation of an employee's complaint or conduct should not involve breach of a Convention right. For example, one individual was awarded £10,000 compensation when her employer tapped her phone without warning during its investigation of her sex discrimination complaint.

However, it was also recently held that the actions of a public sector employer that undertook covert surveillance to track an employee's movements were justified as the employer was investigating the suspected submission of fraudulent timesheets, which is a criminal activity. See 'Monitoring employees' (p.358).

Codes of Conduct

Codes of Conduct should be reviewed to ensure that they do not unnecessarily restrict an employee's Convention rights. For example, provisions on how an employee wears their hair, or whether they wear a nose ring, could raise issues about the way an individual expresses his or her personality in the workplace.

Employee checks

The right to respect for private life may include matters such as moral or physical integrity, so that 'private' in this context means 'personal'. This means that a security check that collects wide-ranging information about a person's personal affairs may go too far.

Also potentially unlawful is the practice of carrying out random drug or alcohol tests, as such testing is likely to entail an invasion of Article 8 – personal privacy. However, such testing could be justified if it was in the interests of public safety; for example, where workers are in high risk situations such as pilots or train drivers.

Employers should also ensure that any procedures such as security checks comply with the requirements of UK data protection legislation (see 'Data protection', p.101).

See also: CCTV monitoring, p.70; Data protection, p.101; Discrimination, p.126; Monitoring employees, p.358; Private life, p.404; Vetting, barring, blacklisting and social engineering, p.534.

Sources of further information

Information Commissioner: www.informationcommissioner.gov.uk

ACAS: www.acas.org.uk

Intellectual property

Ian de Freitas and Toby Headdon, Berwin Leighton Paisner LLP

Key points

- Intellectual property can be a valuable asset. Every business will own intellectual property rights of one sort or another. Intellectual property rights should, therefore, be protected and enforced in order to ensure that they retain their value.
- Use of a third party's intellectual property rights (whether knowingly or otherwise) without their permission can be disastrous: infringement is usually very expensive.
- Copyright, unregistered design rights and database rights arise automatically.
- UK patents, registered trademarks and registered designs are granted by the UK Intellectual Property Office based in Newport, Wales.
- Protection is now provided in all 27 Member States of the European Community (EC) for trademarks by the Community Trade Mark and for designs by the Community design right. Applications for these registered rights are made to the Office of Harmonisation for the Internal Market (OHIM) in Alicante, Spain.
- Internet domain names are administered by a network of private non-governmental registries.
- Intellectual property is territorial in scope and an international protection strategy should be considered.

Legislation

- Registered Designs Act 1949.
- Patents Act 1977.
- Copyright, Designs and Patents Act 1988.
- Trade Marks Act 1994.
- Data Protection Act 1998.
- Human Rights Act 1998.
- Council Regulation (EC) No. 6/2002 on Community Designs.

Copyright

Copyright arises automatically in any:

- original artistic, literary (which includes computer programs), musical or dramatic works;
- sound recordings, films or broadcasts; and
- typographical arrangements in published works,

which have been recorded in some tangible form. Ideas and concepts are not protected by copyright. It is the way that they are expressed or recorded that is protected. For a work to be original, it must not have been copied from another work and it must involve some skill or judgement (however small). Independent copyrights may therefore subsist in two identical works so long as their respective creators did not copy each other or a third party. In this sense, copyright protection does not confer a monopoly.

Broadly speaking, copyright will last for:

- 70 years from the death of the author in the case of literary, dramatic, musical, or artistic works (but only 25 years in the case of industrially-exploited artistic works), and films; and

- 50 years in the case of sound recordings and broadcasts.

As copyright arises automatically, there is no need in this country for the owner to register it. A UK national's copyright will also be recognised in all countries that are signatories to the Berne Convention 1886, the WIPO Copyright Treaty 1996, and the WTO Agreement. The copyright owner will usually be the person who created the work, unless that person was an employee acting in the course of his/her employment, in which case the employer will own the copyright. An independent contractor is not an employee, so the independent contractor will, generally speaking, own any copyright in the work created for the commissioning party. Copyright can be assigned (transferred) or licensed (a permission is given to use it) to a third party.

When engaging an independent contractor to create a copyright work it is important that they assign (or at least licence) the copyright in the work to the commissioning party so that the commissioning party owns the copyright in the work that they have paid for (or, in the case of a licence, they have express permission to use it).

Copyright is infringed by someone copying the whole or a substantial part of a copyright work without the permission of the copyright owner. A substantial part can be quite a small part of the work provided that it is significant qualitatively. So far as proving that copying has occurred, the Court may assume copying has taken place if the similarities are significant and it can be shown that there was an opportunity to copy.

Design rights

Design rights fall into two main categories: unregistered and registered rights. These rights can either be UK-only rights or EC-wide rights.

Unregistered UK design right

Design right protects aspects of the shape and configuration of a design, with certain exclusions for features that are designed to create an interface with or match the appearance of other articles. To qualify for protection, a design must be:

- original (it must be the result of the independent skill and labour of the designer); and
- not commonplace in the relevant design field at the time it was designed.

Unregistered design right protection lasts for ten years, unless the design has not been commercially exploited. In addition, anyone can ask for a licence to copy a design protected by unregistered design right after the first five years of its being put into the marketplace. Owing to the limitations of the UK unregistered design right, designers are strongly advised to consider registering their designs in order to benefit from the greater protection that a registration offers.

UK and Community registered designs

The owner of a registered design can prevent a third party from using a design that is the same as or that creates the same overall impression as the registered design, even if the third party can show that they did not copy the registered design. A registered design can protect aspects of:

- shape and configuration of a design;
- contours and lines;
- texture or materials;
- ornamentation;
- colours; and
- packaging, logos, motifs and typefaces.

Designs can be registered if they:

- are 'new' (that is, they differ from existing designs in the marketplace to a material extent); and
- create a different overall impression from other designs.

A design can be marketed for up to 12 months in order to test the market before making an application for registration without prejudicing the registrability of the design. Since it is the design itself that is protected, once registered, it can be applied to any number of different products. The duration of a registered design is 25 years, renewable

every five years on payment of a fee. The Community registered design allows one registration to be filed for all 27 member states of the EC. The protection given is the same as for the UK.

Unregistered Community design right

This is based on the Community registered design system. Therefore, the same criteria for protection apply. The period of protection is only three years, however, from the date that the design is first made available to the public. Although the term of protection is less favourable than under UK unregistered design right, the sort of designs covered by the Community unregistered right are the same as under the Community registered design. The unregistered Community right may therefore be of use where UK design right fails to protect a design, such as where the shape of a design is commonplace but what makes it new and of individual character is its texture or ornamentation.

Trademarks

A trademark is any sign capable of being represented graphically and which distinguishes goods or services of one business from those of another business. In theory, sounds and smells are registrable as trademarks, although trademarks usually consist of:

- words, designs, letters, numerals (or a combination of these); or
- the shape of goods or their packaging.

Trademarks are territorial in nature and therefore there is a need to seek registration in all countries that may be of interest to the business. Trademarks may be registered through national trademark applications. An international trademark application can cover those countries that are signatories to the Madrid Protocol. A Community Trade Mark application (CTM) will automatically cover the countries of the EC. It is advisable to search the relevant trademarks registers prior to filing an application. The searches should reveal the existence of any prior, identical or similar marks in respect of identical or similar goods or services that may be potential obstacles to the use and registration of the proposed mark. Applications are usually examined for 'distinctiveness' of the mark applied for and in some countries there is an examination for conflicts with existing trademarks (no longer the case in the UK). Once the application has been examined, the application is published and, depending upon where the application has been made, third parties may have the opportunity to file an opposition against the registration of the mark. Once registered, trademarks can be renewed indefinitely. However, a trademark that is not used for a continuous period of five years will be vulnerable to cancellation. A registered trademark is infringed by someone:

- using an identical sign in respect of identical goods or services; or
- using an identical sign in respect of similar goods or services, where there is a likelihood of confusion by the public; or
- using a similar sign in respect of identical or similar goods or services, where there is a likelihood of confusion by the public; or
- using an identical or similar sign in respect of any goods or services where the trademark is well known and the use of the sign takes unfair advantage of, or is detrimental to, the distinctive character or the reputation of the trademark.

Passing off

The identity of a business – its reputation, as well as its name – is generally embodied in its branding. Registering that brand identity as a trademark (or

portfolio of trademarks) will make it easier to protect and enforce its rights in that identity. However, it may be possible for a business to enforce its rights in its unregistered trademarks and associated goodwill by bringing a claim under the law of passing off.

Such actions can be costly as substantial evidence needs to be provided to show:

- the extent of the reputation and goodwill that the business has in the unregistered trademark / branding;
- confusion (or the likelihood of confusion) on the part of the public; and
- the damage suffered by the business as a result of the passing off.

Patents

Patents protect inventions. To be patentable, a patent must:

- be novel;
- involve an inventive step; and
- be capable of industrial application.

A patent will not be granted if the invention is obvious to persons skilled in the field in question or if it has been disclosed to the public prior to the patent application. It is therefore important not to discuss an invention with third parties prior to making an application, unless the discussions are confidential. It is advisable in those circumstances to put a confidentiality agreement in place before such discussions take place. Some things cannot be patented, including some inventions relating to software, business methods, discoveries, and games. To obtain a patent, applications are made to the UK Intellectual Property Office (for a UK patent) with a description of the invention and payment of an application fee. A separate patent is required for each country where protection is needed, although there is a centralised procedure for making multiple applications within Europe (a European patent application under the European Patent Convention). In the UK, patents last for up to 20 years (sometimes 25 years for pharmaceuticals), with annual renewal fees payable on a rising scale.

- As part of the application process, full details of it are published, meaning that some businesses decide not to patent their inventions but instead keep the nature of their invention secret.
- A patent does not give its owner an absolute right to use the invention, if its use infringes someone else's patent, confidential information or design right. Also, it is possible for a patent to be declared invalid following an attack by a third party.
- Like registered design rights, a patent is infringed even if the alleged infringer can prove that their invention was independently developed without copying. In this sense the patent grants a monopoly to the patent holder.
- In most cases, it is the inventor who has the right to apply for the patent, unless he/she was an employee acting within the course of their employment, in which case it is generally the employer who has the right. In such cases, the employer may have to make a compensatory payment to the employee if the patent is particularly valuable.

Database rights

A database is a collection of independent works, data or other materials that are arranged in a systematic or methodical way and are individually accessible by electronic or other means. A database may be protected by copyright and/or a database right. To benefit from copyright protection, a database must be original. A database will be original where, by

reason of the selection or arrangement of its contents, it constitutes the author's own intellectual creation. The copyright expires after 70 years from the end of the year in which the author dies. Where there is a substantial investment in obtaining, verifying or presenting the contents of a database, the maker will own a separate database right. A database right entitles its owner to take action against a person who extracts or reutilises all or a substantial part of the contents of the database. The database right expires after the later of 15 years from the end of the year in which the database was completed or when the database is made available to the public.

There are exceptions to both rights enabling others to make limited use of the contents of a database, although unauthorised use of a database may also give rise to issues under the Data Protection Act 1998.

Domain names

Domain names are available for registration through a number of registries as a 'private' contractual arrangement. Businesses need to think about not just registering domain names for their trading names and brands, but misspellings as well. They should also ensure that domain names are registered in the company's name, not in the name of an employee (as often happens). Following the inception of the Internet, businesses developed significant internet brands which became a target for third parties to infringe. Cybersquatting (the registration of infringing domain names as a blocking tactic or to sell on to brand owners for inflated prices) became a particular problem. However, more importantly, infringing domain names were registered and used to point to third parties' websites, which often sold goods or offered services similar to those provided by the brand owner. Therefore, right holders were forced to protect their brands by taking legal action (usually registered trademark infringement or passing off proceedings) against anyone registering domain names similar to their own.

As a result of the increasing number of court actions involving domain names, the bodies that regulate domain names introduced alternative dispute resolution processes solely for domain name disputes. Nominet, the body that regulates co.uk domains, EURid (the regulator of the .eu domain names) and the World Intellectual Property Organisation (WIPO), which regulates other top-level domains, have put in place separate dispute resolution policies and procedures, enabling internet brand owners to bring quick and cheap actions to prevent third parties from using infringing domain names, without having to resort to formal court proceedings.

Confidence

The law of confidence has been developed by the courts to protect confidential or secret information, such as trade secrets or inventions before a patent is granted. To bring a claim for breach of confidence, a person must demonstrate that:

- the information has the necessary quality of confidence;
- the information has been imparted in circumstances importing an obligation of confidence or be obviously confidential; and
- there must have been an unauthorised use of the information.

A claim for breach of confidence can be defeated if the information has already entered the public domain. The law of confidence will not protect immoral information or where there is a public interest in the disclosure of the information. The Human Rights Act 1998 has had a significant impact on the traditional model

of breach of confidence, having to strike a balance between the right to respect for private and family life and the contrasting right to freedom of expression. This has been seen in several high-profile cases involving celebrities who have argued that a publication has infringed their right to privacy. The current position is that there is no law of privacy in this country, but instead the law of confidence has been adapted by the courts to cover situations where an individual is aggrieved by an invasion of their privacy. This has led to the development of two distinct new limbs of confidentiality: the right of a celebrity to control the use of their image where they trade on such image; and the right of a person to prevent disclosure or further disclosure of private information, even where they may be public figures.

Remedies for infringement of intellectual property rights

The penalties for infringement of intellectual property rights vary depending upon the right infringed, but typically include:

- court orders to stop infringement, including urgent interim injunctions before a full trial takes place;
- damages (such as loss of sales or a payment equivalent to a licence fee to use the intellectual property right) or an account of the profits made from the infringement (whichever is the greater); and
- delivery up or destruction of infringing goods.

For some intellectual property rights, criminal sanctions apply, including fines and custodial sentences.

Groundless threats

Owners of patents, trademarks and registered and unregistered UK and Community design rights must be wary of making anything amounting to a 'groundless threat' to an alleged infringer. An accusation of particular types of infringement that cannot later be substantiated may result in the accuser being sued.

See also: Data protection, p.101; Music licensing, p.363; Private life, p.404.

Sources of further information

The Workplace Law website has been one of the UK's leading legal information sites since its launch in 2002. As well as providing free news and forums, our Information Centre provides you with a 'one-stop shop' where you will find all you need to know to manage your workplace and fulfil your legal obligations.

It covers everything from CDM, waste management and redundancy regulations to updates on the Carbon Reduction Commitment, the latest Employment Tribunal cases and the first case to be tried under the Corporate Manslaughter and Corporate Homicide Act, as well as detailed information in key areas such as energy performance, equality and diversity, asbestos and fire safety.

You'll find:

- quick and easy access to all major legislation and official guidance, including clear explanations and advice from our experts;
- case reviews and news analysis, which will keep you fully up to date with the latest legislation proposals and changes, case outcomes and examples of how the law is applied in practice;
- briefings, which include in-depth analysis on major topics; and
- WPL TV – an online TV channel including online seminars, documentaries and legal updates.

Content is added and updated regularly by our editorial team who utilise a wealth of in-house experts and legal consultants. Visit www.workplacelaw.net for more information.

International employees

Dan Fawcett and Karen Plumbley-Jones, Bond Pearce LLP

Key points

- Employers that send British employees abroad, and British employers that employ foreign nationals abroad, need to be aware of the risk that British employment law may apply but also that there is a risk of being sued by employees abroad in jurisdictions with which they are unfamiliar.

- It is possible to end up with the courts of one country hearing a claim under the law of another. Employers should take steps to avoid this by including choice of law and choice of jurisdiction clauses in employment contracts, although they should be aware that choice of jurisdiction clauses are unlikely to be effective within the EU.

- Unfortunately, the question of which country's courts or tribunals have jurisdiction to hear a claim, and which law applies to that claim, can differ depending on the nature of the claim.

- Employees often have special protection, so efforts by employers to choose the law and jurisdiction that apply to an employment relationship may be overridden.

- Case law in this area continues to develop, and employers should always consider whether specific advice is needed before taking action with regard to internationally-based employees.

Legislation

- Employment Rights Act 1996.
- Working Time Regulations 1998.
- Fixed-term Employees (Prevention of Less Favourable Treatment) Regulations 2002.
- Equality Act 2010.
- Equal Treatment Directive.
- Posted Workers Directive.

Background

In today's increasingly global society, British employees can be posted all over the world to carry out their duties. Employers also increasingly operate from a number of countries and will employ local staff. These kind of global arrangements work fine when things are going well. However, when things go wrong, complex issues are raised as to which country's law and jurisdiction apply to the relationship.

In this chapter we aim to explore some of the key principles when it comes to determining which law and jurisdiction apply to an employment relationship with an international aspect.

Governing law and jurisdiction

Lawyers tend to talk about 'governing law' and 'jurisdiction' and to the uninitiated these terms can be confusing. 'Jurisdiction' means the country in which an employee or employer is entitled to bring a claim. 'Governing law' is the country's law that applies to a claim.

As we will mention later, some claims could theoretically be brought in two or more countries (jurisdictions). In such circumstances, the employer or employee will have a choice as to where to sue and may be guided in that choice by which governing law applies to the employment relationship. Unfortunately, sometimes the country with jurisdiction will not be the same as the country whose governing law applies to a claim. It is possible (although clearly not desirable) to have a dispute where, for example, the Courts / Tribunals of England and Wales have jurisdiction to hear a claim, but the law that applies to it is Spanish law. This will be costly and time-consuming for all involved.

Therefore, to the extent that the parties to an employment relationship can do so, it is sensible to reach agreement at the start of the relationship on which law is intended to apply and which country has jurisdiction.

Can an employer or employee choose the law and jurisdiction that will apply?

Yes and no. The parties to an employment contract are of course free to make whatever choice they want as to law and jurisdiction and it is always advisable to do so. However, both within the legislation that makes up British employment law and within international agreements on law and jurisdiction (in particular within the European Union (EU)) there is special protection for employment rights, which limits the freedom of choice of the parties to an employment contract.

Because this publication is aimed at UK employers, we will concentrate on the position under British employment law and within the EU; if an employer is based within the EU, EU rules are likely to have an impact even if the employee in question is based outside the EU.

Equally, if an employee is based in the EU they are likely to be able to rely on EU rules. However, where neither party has a link to the EU (or if court proceedings are brought outside the EU) then those involved will need local advice on how the

relevant court will decide whether it has jurisdiction and whose law applies.

It is also important for employers to be aware that the rules on which country's courts or tribunals have jurisdiction and what law applies are different depending on the nature of the employment dispute. In this chapter we look at the position for the most common types of UK employment law claims.

Breach of contract claims

Jurisdiction

As mentioned above, the general rule is that the parties to a contract are free to choose which jurisdiction applies. However, within the EU special protection is given to employment contracts under the Brussels Regulation. Largely identical provisions apply between EU member states and Iceland, Switzerland and Norway, for which the Lugano Conventions deal with jurisdiction.

The most important protection for employees is that, within the EU and Lugano Convention countries, a jurisdiction clause will only have effect if it is entered into after a dispute has arisen. Therefore, if an employer is domiciled in the UK, a choice of jurisdiction clause included in an employment contract specifying, for example, that the Tribunals of England and Wales will have jurisdiction, will be ineffective if an employee is based in Germany and has the right to sue the employer there (*see below*).

Under the Brussels Regulation, an employee is entitled to sue his employer either where the employer is domiciled or where the employee habitually works. If an employee does not habitually work in any one member state then the employee can choose to sue his employer in the courts of the place where the business that engaged the employee is situated. These provisions have the effect that an employee working for a branch of a UK company in an EU member state will often have a choice as to the country in which he sues his employer. This could be the UK (where the company is domiciled) or the country in which he works.

'Domicile' means where an employer has:

- its statutory seat (its registered office or its place of incorporation if it does not have a registered office);
- its central administration; or
- its principal place of business.

However, there is a further provision that can catch out international employers who would not, on the face of it, appear to be domiciled in the EU. For employment contracts, an employer can be deemed to be domiciled in an EU member state if it has a branch, agency or other establishment in one of the member states and a dispute 'arises out of the operations of the branch, agency or establishment'. Therefore, a US company with a branch in the UK that recruits and carries out personnel administration for employees who then work outside the UK could be treated as domiciled in the UK.

The position if an employer wants to sue an employee is rather more restricted. An employee can only be sued in the courts of his country of domicile.

In summary, a UK-based employer can generally be sued in the UK by any of its employees working outside the UK as long as the claim is one for breach of an employment contract. However, those employees, if based in the EU, will often have a parallel right to sue the employer in the country in which they work.

Where an employee is based outside the UK but not within the EU or a Lugano

Convention state then whether he can sue a UK employer in the country in which he is based will depend on the approach taken in that country. Local advice should be taken if such a situation arises and it would be advisable to seek local advice before taking any action in relation to such an employee.

Law

Thankfully, the position on choice of law is much more straightforward. The Rome I Regulation, which governs choice of law where an EU member state (other than Denmark) has jurisdiction to hear a dispute, allows parties to an employment contract to choose the law that applies to it. The Rome I Regulation applies to contracts entered into after 17 December 2009 but its predecessor, the Rome Convention, had essentially the same effect and will apply to earlier contracts.

If the parties to a contract have failed to include a choice of law clause then the general rule is that the applicable law will be that of the country in which, or failing that from which, the employee habitually carries out his work. The 'from which' provision only applies to contracts entered into after 17 December 2009 and seems to be intended to deal with mobile employees who travel from a base in a particular country.

However, there is, as ever, a further restriction on the law that applies to employment contracts. It is possible for 'mandatory rules' of a country (laws that cannot be derogated from) to oust the parties' choice of law if that country is:

- where the employee habitually carries out his work;
- the country in which the place of business through which he was engaged is situated; or

- some other country, if it appears from the circumstances as a whole that the contract is more closely connected with that country.

For the purposes of employment law, mandatory rules are likely to be any rights given to employees that cannot be derogated from except by way of a valid compromise agreement. Examples of UK employment law provisions that would be seen as mandatory rules are the right not to be unfairly dismissed and the various discrimination law rights. However, as will be seen below, special rules apply to these rights anyway.

Mandatory rules can also oust the parties' choice of law for contracts that are not classified as employment contracts, such as contracts with self-employed contractors. For such non-employment contracts, the mandatory rules would be either those of the country with jurisdiction to hear the dispute or those of the country with which all other elements of the situation are connected. Businesses should therefore be aware that the issue of mandatory rules ousting an express choice of law is unlikely to be avoided simply by ensuring an individual doing work for them is not classed as an employee.

Identifying which country's mandatory rules apply based on where an employee habitually carries out his work will not always be straightforward. This question has recently been looked at by the European Court of Justice in the context of an employee working in international transport who carried out his work in more than one EU state. The ECJ concluded that the court with jurisdiction to hear such a case would need to look at all the characteristics of the relationship. This could include from where the transport tasks were carried out; where the employee received instructions; where

his work tools were situated; where transport was carried out; where goods were unloaded and where the employee returned to after completion of his tasks. Taking all of those factors into account the Court would determine in which country the employee habitually carries out his work by looking at where he performs the greater part of his obligations to his employer. The Court would then have to apply the mandatory rules of that country. This case illustrates how much the question of what law applies to an employment relationship can come down to the interpretation of the Courts.

In the event that a non-EU country ends up with jurisdiction to hear a dispute, the Rome I Regulation will not apply. If this is the case, it will generally depend on the approach of the courts or tribunals of that country as to which law they will apply and employers would be well advised to seek local advice. It would also be advisable to seek local advice before taking action in relation to an employee if it appears that a non-EU country will end up with jurisdiction to hear any dispute.

Summary

A claim by a UK employer that an employee has breached his employment contract can only be brought in the courts of the state where that person is domiciled. However, an employee who resides within the EU or whose employer resides within the EU can generally choose whether to sue his employer where the employer is domiciled or in the country where the employee habitually carries out his work and a choice of jurisdiction clause will not change this. A choice of law clause will be effective within the EU but can be overridden by 'mandatory rules' of the country with jurisdiction. If no choice of law has been made then the determining factor will normally be where an employee works. Employers should therefore always include choice of law clauses in employment contracts and where there is a possibility of another country's law applying, employers should take local advice before taking action in relation to an employee.

Unfair dismissal

In standard unfair dismissal cases the Employment Tribunal will simply look at where an employee is working when he or she is dismissed. However, there are cases where it is difficult to determine where an employee is working and there have been a number of cases in which employees working outside the UK have argued that they have unfair dismissal rights.

The established principle from the decision of the House of Lords (now the Supreme Court) in *Lawson v. Serco Limited* (2006) was that employees based outside the UK could only rely on UK unfair dismissal law in the following very limited circumstances:

- *Peripatetic (mobile) employees.* The classic example of such an employee is an air steward / stewardess – such an employee can rely on unfair dismissal rights if he/she is 'based' in the UK.
- *Expatriate employees based entirely outside the UK but who were recruited in the UK in exceptional circumstances.* These may include employees posted abroad for the purposes of a business carried on in GB (such as a foreign correspondent of a British newspaper) or employees working for a British employer in what counts as an extra-territorial political or social enclave (such as an overseas military base).
- *A third category where there was an equally strong connection with GB to the above* (although the House of Lords could not think of any examples falling into this category).

Under the above exceptions to the general rule, the key points are where recruitment takes place and where an employee is based and/or the nature of the work they do.

Before *Lawson v. Serco* there was confusing case law on the territorial scope of unfair dismissal rights and this was therefore a welcome decision. Unfortunately, the recent cases of *Ravat v. Halliburton Manufacturing and Services Limited* (2010) and *Wallis v. MoD* (2011) both appear to have created some confusion by extending the principles of *Serco* slightly (with *Halliburton* being particularly problematic).

In the *Halliburton* case, the Court of Session allowed an employee who worked entirely outside the UK to rely on UK unfair dismissal rights. The employee worked on a rotational basis in Libya on a 'one month on, one month off' basis. One of the judges in this case decided that the employee's employment did not fall into any of the established categories in *Serco* but did have a 'sufficiently strong connection' to the UK for him to rely on unfair dismissal rights. The other judge considered that the employee was akin to a peripatetic employee and looked at the fact that contractual matters relating to his employment were dealt with in the UK and that he paid UK tax.

The *Halliburton* case should be treated with some caution because it is a decision of the Inner House of the Court of Session in Scotland, which is below the House of Lords / Supreme Court in the hierarchy of UK courts. Accordingly, it has no binding effect on Courts or Employment Tribunals in England and Wales and will only have persuasive effect. This means that they can consider it as an aide to interpreting the *Serco* decision but ultimately they are bound to follow the decision in

Serco. It may present employers with more difficulties if they have operations in Scotland or recruit employees from Scotland to international assignments. This is because the Scottish Courts and Tribunals may be more minded to follow the *Halliburton* case. However, they are still bound to follow *Serco* and should therefore only use it to interpret the categories set out in *Serco.*

If *Halliburton* is followed by the Scottish Tribunals (or the English ones) then employers wanting to avoid UK unfair dismissal rights applying to overseas employees should ensure that the employment relationship has no link to the UK. *Halliburton* is being appealed to the Supreme Court and that may give clearer guidance.

As mentioned above, the case of *Wallis v. MoD* is another recent example of a case in which employees based outside the UK who did not fall into either of the first two *Serco* categories were held to have unfair dismissal rights. The claimant employees in *Wallis* were married to serving members of the British Armed Forces who had been posted to NATO in Belgium and the Netherlands. The claimant employees were employed by the MOD to teach in NATO schools and had to be UK dependants of members of the Armed Forces to get their jobs. The Court of Appeal held that, although they were not expatriate employees working in a British enclave (the first part of the *Serco* test), they were nevertheless in a closely analogous situation to a British enclave and that they therefore had unfair dismissal rights.

It is clear from *Halliburton* and *Wallis* that UK Courts and Tribunals will extend unfair dismissal protection to employees based outside the UK in special circumstances where there is a strong link between the

employment relationship and the UK. However, overall, the risk of employees based outside the UK being able to bring unfair dismissal claims in the UK should remain low, and this should only be permitted in exceptional circumstances like those outlined in *Serco.*

Other UK statutory employment law rights

Save for discrimination claims (*dealt with in more detail below*) other areas of employment law are likely to be treated in the same way as unfair dismissal claims. For example, there is case law that a claim under the unlawful deductions from wages provisions of the Employment Rights Act 1996 could not be brought in the UK Employment Tribunal when it failed the *Serco* test.

Additionally, the *Serco* test has been applied to determine whether the UK Tribunals can hear claims under the Fixed-term Employees (Prevention of Less Favourable Treatment) Regulations 2002, which protect fixed-term employees from discrimination (and have not been replaced by the Equality Act). However, a further decision on a section of these Regulations that converts successive fixed-term contracts into a permanent contract when they are over four years in length has since been applied to an employee who could not pass the *Serco* test, so there is an argument that these Regulations now apply to any contract governed by UK law. (See *Duncombe and others v. Secretary of State for Children, Schools and Families* (2009).)

It will therefore depend from right to right as to where claims can be brought.

Claims derived from EU law

There may be some additional complications where a claim is derived from EU law. It seems that if UK law applies to a contract then the UK Courts / Tribunals should try to give effect to any rights derived from EU law. For example, if UK law applies to an individual's contract, the UK Courts / Tribunals should allow that employee to claim for unpaid holiday pay and the Working Time Regulations 1998 need to be construed so as to allow the employee to bring that claim in the UK, even if he actually works outside the UK (see *Bleuse v. MBT Transport Limited and another*). The *Bleuse* case was applied in the *Wallis* case mentioned above, in which it was decided that the Employment Tribunal could hear sex discrimination claims brought by the wives of service personnel employed at NATO headquarters in Belgium. They were employed by schools attached to the headquarters and were dismissed when their husbands' service ended. As mentioned above, the Court of Appeal held that there was a sufficiently close connection between their employment and GB for them to come within the scope of domestic unfair dismissal legislation. Additionally, because the Equal Treatment Directive was intended to confer rights on expatriate employees, domestic rules limiting territorial scope (in the Sex Discrimination Act 1975) had to be displaced and the Tribunal also had jurisdiction to hear their sex discrimination claims.

Discrimination law

The Equality Act 2010 came into force on 1 October 2010 and now deals with most areas of discrimination law. However, for reasons explained more fully below, it remains important for employers to understand the position under the pre-1 October 2010 discrimination legislation.

Prior to the Equality Act, UK discrimination legislation had specific clauses dealing with its territorial scope. This meant that UK discrimination laws would apply when:

- the employer had a place of business in GB;
- the work was for the purposes of the business carried on at that establishment; and
- the employee was ordinarily resident in GB:
  - at the time when he applied for or was offered the employment; or
  - at any time during the course of the employment.

Therefore, if an employer had places of business in GB and France and an employee who was normally resident in GB worked from France for the GB-based business, that employee would be able to rely on British discrimination law. Since claims under British discrimination law can only be brought in the British Employment Tribunal system, any such claims would have to be brought in GB and the British Tribunals would have exclusive jurisdiction to hear such claims.

Of course, there are likely to be similar provisions in the discrimination laws of other EU member states and employers would be advised to take local advice where necessary.

The problem with claims in this area is that the definition of work 'wholly or partly in Great Britain' is not straightforward. Principles developed in case law on the question of work wholly or partly in GB include:

- Tribunals should look at the period of employment as a whole and not just when discrimination is alleged to have occurred;
- It is irrelevant where an act of discrimination is alleged to have taken place;
- Tribunals should look at the nature of a job performed in a country and not just time spent in different countries; and

■ 'Partly' simply means more than 'de minimis'.

As for 'ordinarily resident in Great Britain', case law has suggested that this may mean 'a person's abode in a particular place or country which he had adopted voluntarily and for settled purposes, as part of the regular order of his life for the time being, whether of short or long duration'. However, employers should be aware that case law has also decided that it is possible for someone to be ordinarily resident in more than one country at the same time.

Additionally, as mentioned above, if an employee outside Great Britain is based in the EU then the Courts have held that the UK Employment Tribunals need to give effect to European law and such employees should therefore be able to bring discrimination claims.

The Equality Act 2010

Since 1 October 2010 all UK discrimination law (save for specific rights relating to fixed-term and part-time status) has been replaced by the Equality Act 2010, and any claims arising on or after that date will be brought under the new Act. Additionally, where an employee can show that discrimination is a continuing act and that the act began before 1 October 2010 and continued afterwards, the new law will also apply.

The Act is largely designed to harmonise the previous anti-discrimination laws. However, the Act does not contain any provisions on jurisdiction or territorial scope. The Equality and Human Rights Commission Code of Practice on the Act suggests that the Tribunal should look at whether there is a sufficiently close link between the employment relationship and Great Britain. The Code of Practice also states that Tribunals will be able to

consider where the employee lives and works, where the employer is established, what laws govern the employment relationship in other respects, where tax is paid, and other matters it considers appropriate. This clearly gives a Tribunal quite wide discretion in deciding whether the Equality Act applies to a relationship, but further case law under the new Act will have to be seen before it is known how the Courts and Tribunals will interpret this. It is unlikely that the Tribunals will narrow the current scope of discrimination law and they may well therefore carry on following the existing rules. Hence, if an employee would be covered by UK discrimination law under the old rules (as set out above), a Tribunal is likely to apply the Equality Act to him/her.

Additionally, as mentioned above, there is an argument that because the Equality Act implements EU law, the UK Courts and Tribunals will have to take a broad approach to whether it applies to an employment relationship. It is therefore likely that discrimination rights will continue to apply to a wider category of expatriate employees than unfair dismissal rights.

The Posted Workers Directive

Where workers from other EU countries are posted to the UK, the Posted Workers Directive gives them equivalent rights and protections on matters such as minimum holidays and pay as they would get if working in their home state. The full details of this Directive are beyond the scope of this chapter but employers who take on EU Nationals should ensure they are aware of this.

Other factors to consider

As well as considering which jurisdiction and governing law will apply to a relationship when employing someone abroad or sending a UK-based employee abroad, employers should also consider:

- immigration and visa rules;
- the tax and social security position for UK employees posted abroad;
- where an employee is seconded, making it clear what happens at the end of the relationship;
- checking the documentation is up to date when sending an employee abroad (for example, ensuring the employee has been given the additional information required by Section 1 of the Employment Rights Act 1996); and
- if the employee is seconded to a third party organisation, the employer should ensure that they get the commercial terms right, including who is responsible for immigration / visa issues and, potentially, including restrictions on poaching the employee.

Conclusion

Employees working for UK-based employers outside the UK (or nationals of other countries working within the UK) can create a minefield of complications as to which courts should hear disputes that arise from the relationship and which country's law applies. The parties can attempt to use choice of jurisdiction and law clauses to manage the risks of being sued in unfamiliar jurisdictions under foreign law. However, this will not always be effective.

There is also the risk that employers that send British Nationals to work in jurisdictions that give employees little protection could still be caught in the net of British discrimination or unfair dismissal law. If in doubt, employers should seek advice and this could avoid them being involved in costly disputes in foreign lands or, alternatively, ending up with an unfair dismissal claim against them that could have been avoided had they been aware that UK law applied.

See also: Discrimination, p.126; Employment contracts, p.164; The Equality Act, p.191; Migrant and foreign workers, p.318.

Sources of further information

The full text of the Rome I Regulation and Brussels Regulation is available through the Eur Lex website at http://eur-lex.europa.eu/en/index.htm

Comment ...

Drowning in digital distractions

David Lavenda, harmon.ie

You're writing a report when your smart phone rings. Before you've had the chance to say hello, another five emails drop into your inbox – all asking you to do something, now. And that's on top of the text messages, tweets and instant messages, all waiting for you to respond. Does this sound familiar? Well, you're not alone, as virtually every office worker is facing the same pressures – we're drowning in a sea of digital distractions.

According to a recent survey we carried out of more than 500 corporate email users, researching the impact that electronic distractions have on the workplace, employees are interrupted on average at least every 15 minutes. For the majority of people, this means they'll 'waste' at least an hour a day dealing with a variety of distractions, but interestingly the majority are digital.

An independent field study titled 'Disruption and Recovery of Computing Tasks' by the University of Illinois and Microsoft adds that, 'participants spent on average nearly ten minutes on switches caused by alerts, and another ten to 15 minutes (depending on the type of interruption) before returning to focused activity on the disrupted task'.

You don't need me to tell you that the impact of these digital distractions means your employees are having trouble completing work, thinking creatively and generally taking care of the responsibilities you've hired them for.

For the past 20 years, David Lavenda has served as an executive for a number of high tech companies. After completing an undergraduate degree in Physics, advanced studies in Electrical Engineering, and an MBA in Marketing, David co-founded Business Layers, an identity management company, serving as VP Marketing and Product Strategy from its inception until the company's successful sale five years later. Additional stints as VP of Marketing and Product Strategy for several successful high-tech companies followed. David is a technology expert blogger for Fast Company. He is also pursuing advanced studies in STS (Science, Technology, and Society), focusing on the research of online behaviours.

The perceived pressure to stay constantly connected has a lot to do with fear. Our electronic distractions research also showed that a third of survey respondents fear they will lose their competitive edge if they disconnect from their inbox for 30 minutes or less, and 20% felt in danger of losing the upper hand when cut off from email for just five minutes.

The result is many employees are taking drastic action – for example, some are continuing to respond to emails instead of paying attention in face-to-face meetings; others are still communicating when at home in bed.

Beyond managing this personal addiction to staying constantly connected, businesses can take steps to reduce digital distractions to a manageable pace – an immediate requirement for any organisation hoping to make use of the full potential of every employee, while alleviating some of the pressure.

Here are five steps to get you started.

Step one: Create policies to prevent distraction

Everything starts with a policy but, of course, not all policies are good ones. I've heard of organisations enforcing 'no email Fridays'. Rather than solving the problem, all this does is defer the deluge until a later point in time and add additional stress. Another knee-jerk reaction is to completely ban access to social networking tools which, when used correctly, can be beneficial for certain job functions, such as identifying expert resources. Employees are more likely to break the rules rather than face the wrath of a disgruntled customer whose urgent request went ignored.

A better policy would be to disable email alerts, even if for only brief periods of the day, allowing individuals to focus their

efforts rather than fixating on the small pop-up on the screen. Every organisation is different and, if the idea of a blanket policy just isn't practical for your business, then perhaps creating 'best practice guidelines' would be more appropriate.

Don't forget the rules of engagement. If you want 100% attention in face-to-face meetings, then mandate that employees must turn off mobile devices, or the temptation to respond to communications may be too strong.

Another option is to limit the length of emails individuals are allowed to write, the number of recipients included on the distribution list, or the rare circumstances when a 'reply all' is appropriate.

> "The perceived pressure to stay constantly connected has a lot to do with fear. A third of survey respondents feared they would lose their competitive edge if they disconnect from their inbox for 30 minutes or less, and 20% felt in danger of losing the upper hand when cut off from email for just five minutes."

Step two: train your staff to swim

This really is in tandem with creating policies that define what is and isn't acceptable.

Things you could consider are going back to basics with a quick refresher in diary prioritisation. The simple truth is that there is always more than enough work to fill the day, and it's easy to get sidetracked on the latest assignment that lands in your email unless you have clearly defined three or so actions that you're going to take.

Likely, you will also need to train employees on how and when to use the myriad of digital devices, social collaboration and communication tools. There is a strong argument that email is not the right tool for editing documents, because you have to reconcile feedback from multiple parties, which invariably leads to document chaos. Instead, upload it to a collaboration platform like Microsoft SharePoint or Google Docs and share a document link. That way, everyone works on the most current version of the document, without having to reconcile feedback from multiple people in various copies of the document.

And it's not all about work. Something as simple as relaxation techniques can be very effective, and demonstrate your commitment to allowing them to switch off.

Step three: reduce context switch: aggregate typical workflows into a single window

A *New York Times* report, titled 'Attached to Technology and Paying a Price', referenced research that found 'Computer users at work change windows or check email or other programs nearly 37 times an hour'. Primarily this is because the tools needed to complete a job are not organised by business task.

On average, people typically access six to nine platforms to get work done. A task might require people to toggle between their email client, various Microsoft Office applications, instant messenger services, web-based applications such as SAP, the CRM system and file servers such as Microsoft SharePoint.

Rather than relying on a hodge-podge of disparate systems and tools, organisations should consider aggregating collaboration and social channels into their users' familiar work window, such as the corporate email client or CRM system.

Step four: respect employee downtime

Agreed, this one is slightly controversial, but it may be the most crucial. We all talk about family values, respecting staff and

understanding the value of downtime, but the sad reality is few actually practise what they preach. I've been on too many conference calls with people who are on holiday, both within our organisation and external parties, to know that the practice is rife.

There are numerous occasions when something is important but not everything is time-sensitive. Just because you can reach someone doesn't mean that you have to – or that you should.

Instead, develop a strategy for handling all but 'life-threatening' crises so when someone is out of the office, the world doesn't stop turning. This could be a rule that clearly defines what constitutes a crisis that merits reaching out to a person after the office has officially closed.

Step five: set realistic expectations

Many service businesses have created the expectation that people will respond instantaneously to customer requests 24/7. The sad reality is, once you've set such an unrealistic expectation, you've already defeated any possibility of spending quality time resolving problems.

So, if you pride yourself on being a 24/7 business, then you need the right staffing levels to deliver.

No one can tell you what the right steps for your organisation are. However, if your workforce is struggling to deflect digital distractions, then ignoring the problem isn't going to make it easier.

It's time to grab the digital bull by the horns – so to speak – and implement strategies for your organisation that deflect its digital distractions, thusly managing your information overload.

Internet and email policies

Heidi Thompson, Workplace Law

Key points

- Where relevant, employers should have in place a written internet and email policy making employees aware of what, if any, personal usage of the internet and email systems is reasonable.
- This policy needs to be effectively and transparently communicated to employees at the earliest opportunity.
- Employers must take into account the rights of employees (particularly their right to privacy under Article 8 of the European Convention on Human Rights) in assessing how to monitor employees' usage of the internet and email systems, and should make employees aware of what monitoring will take place.

Legislation

- Copyright, Designs and Patents Act 1988.
- Defamation Act 1996.
- Protection from Harassment Act 1997.
- Data Protection Act 1998.
- Human Rights Act 1998.
- Regulation of Investigatory Powers Act 2000.
- Equality Act 2010.

The need for a suitable internet and email policy

It is clear that the advantages to businesses of the internet and email systems are undermined by the greater potential for staff to abuse these facilities. The legal issues that an employer may face as a consequence of staff misusing either the internet or email are also surprisingly broad. For example, these may include email harassment or unauthorised use of computer systems, issues surrounding agency law where employees inadvertently form contracts through email correspondence, intellectual property law in disputes over the downloading or dissemination of material subject to copyright, the law of defamation for libel following comments made about individuals or businesses in emails, and criminal law, where employees download obscene material or are involved in hacking.

In light of these potential pitfalls for employers, setting out employees' rights, responsibilities and limitations on the use of the internet and email systems will help employers prevent any unauthorised or careless use, which may result in one of the legal risks detailed above. Any such policy should also make clear any monitoring or interception that the employer may lawfully undertake and the reasons for this.

Content of the policy

The content of an internet and email policy will largely depend on issues such as the size and nature of the business, and there is no one policy that would be appropriate for all businesses. Whilst model policies are useful, they must be tailored to suit the needs of the organisation and its employees.

> ### Case study
>
> An estate agent who viewed porn and gambled on his work computer lost his case for unfair dismissal. Anthony Stewart was sacked for gross misconduct in 2008 and took Dorset agents Lloyds Property Group to an Employment Tribunal. He claimed unfair dismissal and lost earnings of £45,000.
>
> The inappropriate use of the computer was uncovered when it was being checked for a virus. He was alleged to have spent 'hundreds of hours' on porn and gambling sites over a number of years. Mr Stewart's defence argued that he viewed porn to take his mind off his gambling addiction and that this addiction should be viewed as an illness. Mr Stewart also argued that his employer allowed staff to use the internet for personal use and claimed there was no policy in place that banned employees viewing inappropriate websites. This was rejected by the Tribunal and it ruled in Lloyds Property Group's favour on all eight counts it was challenged on. Despite winning the case, Lloyds Property Group was left with a £10,000 legal bill following the case.

However, a typical internet and email policy should make provision for the following:

- An indication of the extent to which personal use of the internet and email is acceptable, if at all. Employers should be conscious of the fact that employees have a reasonable expectation of some privacy in the workplace and, if personal use of email is prohibited (or monitored), employers are recommended to provide workers with some means of making personal communications that are not subject to monitoring (by telephone, for example).
- An instruction not to share passwords with other employees and to make appropriate arrangements for relevant staff to access work emails when absent.
- A statement that both internet and email use are intended predominantly for business use.
- Advice on email etiquette, including guidance on when staff should add signatures / disclaimers to emails; the use of cc'ing others into emails; guidance on forwarding attachments; and downloading files and software.
- Guidance on what is deemed 'acceptable use', in particular an outline of the types of websites that are considered inappropriate to access from work, particularly those that contain obscene, offensive or pornographic content. This should include a warning to employees not to access, download or disseminate any material that could be construed as offensive in nature.
- A clear statement informing employees that their email and internet usage may be subject to monitoring.
- Details of what may happen if employees breach the policy.

In addition, employers should cross reference any internet and email policy with other relevant policies it has in place. Examples include policies relating to the handling of confidential information, use

Facts

■ The proportion of UK companies with a broadband connection to the internet stands at 97%, with 16% of UK companies suffering from staff misuse of information systems (which rises to 47% of large businesses suffering from staff misuse).

■ The term applied to staff who use their work internet access for personal reasons while maintaining the appearance of working is 'goldbricking'.

Source: BERR 2008 Information Breaches Survey.

and storage of personal data, consultation and communications at work, training, equal opportunities and harassment, and the employer's disciplinary and grievance policies and procedures, which should state what types of misuse would be considered misconduct and/or gross misconduct.

Monitoring

It is essential that any internet and email policy contains a clear statement about how employees' use of the internet and email systems is to be monitored. A failure to do so may lead to claims from employees that the employer is in breach of Article 8 of the European Convention on Human Rights (right to respect for private and family life). If, however, the employer's policy makes clear that monitoring will take place (and what form this monitoring will take), employees cannot have a reasonable expectation of privacy, and this should be sufficient for employers to escape such liability.

It should be noted that, by its very nature, monitoring of employees' internet and email usage is intrusive. Careful consideration should therefore be given to the impact of such monitoring on workplace relations, as it may be interpreted by employees as a lack of trust in staff. Providing employees with clear reasons as to why the monitoring is taking place, together with assurances that it will only be done within the strict limits set out in the policy, should help to allay any concerns employees have in relation to the monitoring of their internet and email activity.

Employers should be aware that monitoring should be proportionate to the legitimate business needs of the organisation. Covert monitoring is likely to be unlawful and should be restricted to circumstances where it is used for the prevention or detection of crime.

The Information Commissioner has provided specific advice on monitoring in relation to data protection issues, which can be found at www.ico.gov.uk.

Communicating and enforcing the policy

It is not only essential for employers to have an adequate internet and email policy in place, but also to ensure that the policy's existence is adequately communicated to employees. Tribunals have found employees to be unfairly dismissed in circumstances where the employer did not make them properly aware of its policy, even when employees had clearly carried out acts of misconduct serious enough to be dismissed, such as accessing and distributing pornographic images.

There is no one particular way in which such employees should be made familiar with the contents of the policy, but communication methods may include:

- via email (although employers may require a read receipt to know that employees have opened and read the email);
- a circular sent to all staff, or to incorporate the policy into a staff handbook (which could then be made available to staff either electronically or in hard copy);
- incorporating the policy into the employee's contract of employment;
- a presentation to staff explaining the system and its use; and/or
- holding training sessions on the new policy.

Additionally, employers may wish to get employees to 'sign off' that they have read and understood the policy.

Self-employed contractors, agency workers or any other individuals working temporarily for the employer should be made aware of the rules regarding the use of email and the internet.

See also: Data protection, p.101; Intellectual property, p.252; IT security, p.282; Monitoring employees, p.358; Private life, p.404; Social media, p.485.

Sources of further information

Information Commissioner's guidance on how to comply with obligations under the Data Protection Act 1998: www.ico.gov.uk

Technological advances in the field of information technology have resulted in many positive benefits for employers. However, the increase in technological advances has also brought with it many employment-related issues. These include harassment, discrimination, and breach of contract issues. Workplace Law's *IT and Email Policy and Management Guide v.3.0* has been designed to alert employers of the potential problems associated with using computer systems, the internet, and email systems within the workplace and to provide certain safeguards. For more information visit www.workplacelaw.net.

Interviewing

Heidi Thompson, Workplace Law

Key points

- Planning and preparation are essential.
- Bear in mind equality and diversity legislation.
- Avoid stereotypical assumptions to minimise the risk of a discrimination claim.
- Be objective – avoid whims or gut instincts.
- Be fair, consistent and transparent.
- Where possible, have a mixed interview panel.
- Be organised – plan out questions in advance.
- Focus on the job description and person specification as the basis for questioning.
- Ask open questions.
- Avoid questions that are not job-related.
- Be able to justify your decisions and record this justification.
- Choose the best person for the job.

Legislation

- Equality Act 2010.

The recruitment and selection process can be a minefield from a legal perspective, particularly in the context of equal opportunities legislation. It is therefore important for interviewers to understand how employment law can impact on the interview process, what potential liabilities can be incurred, and the consequences of getting it wrong.

Overview

Staff are an employer's most important asset and largest investment, but recruitment is a two-way process and is as much about an individual deciding whether he/she wants to work for the employer as it is about the employer deciding which candidate to appoint. The interview is often the first, and a very powerful, impression for both the candidate and the employer.

In order to recruit and retain the best candidates, an interview selection panel needs to gather all the information it needs during the interview process. Time spent at the beginning of the process, identifying precisely what the role is and what skills and experience are needed to fill it, will aid the decision-making process.

Diversity in recruitment

Diversity should be seen as a positive thing, and something to aspire to. There is often a tendency for employers to look for people who are similar to the person already employed in a particular role, but cloning existing staff is unlikely to add value. Interviewers should therefore bear this in mind from the outset. Ideally, employers should also ensure interviewers are trained in both interviewing skills and diversity factors before commencing recruitment practices.

Legal perspective

Equality is not a new concept in employment relationships. The UK is used to the raft of legislation from Europe, including discrimination on the grounds of sex, race, disability, sexual orientation, religion, belief, pregnancy, maternity

> **Case study**
> *Bridges v. SITA (GB) Ltd* (1999)
>
> In this case, the applicant, who had an HGV driving licence, had been interviewed for the post of road sweeper driver / operator. Over and above the driving duties, there was an occasional need for drivers to clamber up on to the top of the vehicles for inspection purposes. The applicant had cerebral palsy, the effect of which was some loss of mobility. He had not been asked about this at the interview, even though it would have been obvious to anyone meeting him that he had a mobility impairment. For his part, the applicant had not volunteered any information about his condition during the interview.
>
> On the second day of his employment, the site manager asked the applicant about his gait, upon which he explained it was as a result of cerebral palsy. Later, the manager noticed that he was having difficulty climbing up on to the vehicle, and formed the view that he was potentially a safety risk. The applicant was immediately dismissed. He subsequently brought a complaint of disability discrimination before an Employment Tribunal.
>
> The Tribunal upheld the claim and ruled that the employer had failed without good reason to comply with the duty under the Disability Discrimination Act 1995, Section 4a to make reasonable adjustments. The employer should have considered what adjustments to its working arrangements or to the vehicle might be possible so as to support the applicant in his work. One option might have been to allocate the inspection duties to another employee, since the need for inspection occurred only occasionally. Alternatively, consideration might have been given to providing a different means of access to the vehicle. There was no justification for the employer's failure to make adjustments, and the dismissal therefore constituted unlawful disability discrimination.

and age. In addition, employers are encouraged to offer flexible working and to address work–life balance issues.

Interview panels should ensure they do not ask questions that expose the employer to potential claims. For example, a panel should not put too much emphasis on the desirability of having qualifications from a UK educational institution, or work experience within the UK, as non-British Nationals will find this more difficult to comply with than British Nationals.

A panel should use the interview to establish the quality of the qualifications and experience. Similarly, if in an interview situation a non-British candidate's spoken English is not as fluent as that of a British National, an employer may not be justified in using this as a criterion for turning down the non-British candidate from all posts; it will depend on whether fluency in spoken English is an essential requirement for the post.

As a further example, if an interview panel knows in advance that a candidate who is coming for interview is disabled, the panel should consider whether any adjustments need to be made to the physical arrangements for the interview or the interview process itself. From a practical point of view, the panel may want to ask, during the interview, whether the disabled candidate has any particular requirements to help him/her fulfil the role, but should not make any decisions about whether or not to employ him/her based on his/her disability, or the effects, without very good reasons for doing so (see *Case study*).

It is imperative to avoid making stereotypical assumptions. If an interview panel gets this wrong, an unsuccessful candidate can bring an Employment Tribunal claim within three months of the act of discrimination (or within such further period as the Employment Tribunal considers just and equitable). The remedies are a declaration of rights, a recommendation and/or potentially unlimited compensation.

The process

As selection is, by its very nature, a subjective process, it is important to consider the process in as objective a way as possible.

The key focuses for the panel during the interview process are:

- to gain all the information needed to decide who is most suitable for the role;
- to ensure that selection is carried out in a fair, objective, consistent and open manner;
- to avoid falling foul of employment legislation; and
- to appoint the right person.

At the outset, a panel needs to decide how to assess the shortlist of candidates in person. The most common method is interviewing (although alternatives include

assessment centres, written testing and psychometric testing, and obtaining references).

For interviewing, the following issues need to be considered early on:

- Will there be one stage or two?
- The make-up of the panel. Where possible, the panel should not be potentially gender- or racially-biased. Instead, there should be a mixed panel if this is feasible.
- Is there going to be a Chair? If so, will he/she have a deciding vote?
- What will the structure of the interview be? Be organised and decide beforehand who will ask what.
- How long will the interview last? This is important for both planning and consistency.
- Ensure that the interview takes place in an appropriate setting, without interruptions.
- Be prepared and know what you are asking for. The panel should meet to discuss the interview beforehand and should be familiar with the job description and person specification.

The format

Interviews can take a variety of forms. One suggested format would be to welcome the candidate, introduce the panel and explain the interview format; acquire information by asking relevant questions; supply information by giving the candidate an opportunity to ask questions; ensure the candidate is aware of the terms and conditions associated to the role; make the candidate aware of the next stage, including when he/she will find out the outcome; and thank him/her for attending.

The purpose

The key purpose of the interview is to assess the candidate's suitability for the post. As an interviewer, you should ask yourself if the candidate can do the job, and what he/she would bring to the job.

The job description and person specification should be used as the basis for areas of questioning and the questions should draw out information about the candidate's knowledge, experience and skills. The interviewer needs to be satisfied with the candidate's evidence, whilst considering the relative importance of each of the selection criteria.

It is usually best to ask all candidates the same basic questions, in order to ascertain whether they are right for the role. However, the panel should feel confident about deviating from the basic questions and to probe further to obtain the evidence needed.

Where possible, interviewers should ask open questions that are experience-based, rather than questions that just require a 'yes' or 'no' answer. Follow-up questions could also include hypothetical situations, to measure thought processes; however, leading questions should be avoided.

Questions asked at interview should be designed to:

- obtain relevant information about the applicant's experience and skills;
- check facts, for example whether a qualification has been obtained;
- test achievement; and
- assess aptitude and potential in relation to the organisation's aims and objectives.

As a general rule, questions that are not job-related should not be asked (e.g. questions related to family, marital status, childcare commitments, age and ethnic origin). Also, assumptions about these issues should not be made. These questions or assumptions could cause a panel to inadvertently discriminate against a candidate, which would then be compounded if the decision is based upon the answer to the question.

Subjective judgement

Although gut instincts should be avoided, interview panels will inevitably also take into account the more subjective aspects of a person's character, attitude and confidence. These are likely to be relevant and so, in many cases, the best thing to do is to include these criteria in the scoring grid, together with a space for writing down any comment that an interviewer feels helps to justify the score given. Care should be taken to ensure that any written comments cannot be construed as discriminatory in any form. Where a number of candidates meet the essential criteria for the job, the likelihood is that the successful candidate will be chosen on the basis of how the panel rated his/her more subjective criteria.

In terms of scoring subjective criteria, it is probably prudent to attach less weight to subjective scores than to objective scores. In reality though, where candidates are otherwise equal, the subjective score is likely to tip the balance in any event.

Considerations with internal candidates

Interviewing an internal candidate, or someone you know, presents its own set of challenges. Interviewers should not make assumptions, but should gather evidence of whether he/she satisfies the selection criteria in the same way as with any other candidate. Interview questions should (still) be objective and probing. Interviewers should steer clear of irrelevant points and keep the interview formal, rather than being tempted to adopt a more informal approach.

Written notes

It is a good idea to take brief notes or use an interview form, as this will act as a reminder when the interviewer comes to make a decision. It is also good evidence of why a particular candidate was or was not selected, particularly where feedback is requested by the candidate at the end of the process. However, interviewers should avoid making copious notes, as this could make it difficult to establish a rapport with candidates. Also, bear in mind that any notes taken, even on scraps of paper, will be discoverable documents in any subsequent legal proceedings. Therefore, it is important to avoid discriminatory comments or comments that could be interpreted as such.

Where notes are not made during the interview, they should be written up as soon after the interview as is reasonably practicable, in order to ensure that the details are recalled accurately. All notes should be returned to Human Resources for storage with the job file and should be kept for at least six months.

Selection

It is crucial to go back to the job description and person specification when deciding which candidate to select for the position. Ideally, each panel member should assess each of the candidates him/herself, where possible immediately after the interview, formulating his/her own view and scoring the candidate before any discussion takes place.

It is helpful to have a standard evaluation form to complete, to ensure consistency in ratings. (In practice, the panel will also take into account information from the application process, any references and so on.) These records should be kept for six months.

Each candidate should then be discussed by the panel in turn. Candidates who do not meet the essential criteria can be eliminated. In terms of the remaining candidates, the panel should not come to a premature decision based on personality / who they like best, but should focus on the (essential and preferred) selection criteria.

The panel should then rank the candidates, in order of preference. Again, a record should be kept of this process. The first choice candidate can then be offered the job, ideally with a time limit for acceptance.

Those deemed unsuccessful can also be informed at this stage. However, it may be prudent to delay informing any reserves of the final decision, in case the first choice declines the offer. It is best practice to keep reserves informed of the situation.

Feedback should be offered to both the successful and unsuccessful candidates, and this should be based on the written notes compiled throughout the interview process, bearing in mind the provisions of the Data Protection Act 1998, which will enable the candidate to ask to see interview notes where they form part of a 'set' of information about the candidate – for instance, the application form, references received and so on, or the full personnel file if the candidate is already working for the organisation.

Future developments

The Equality Act 2010 came into force on 1 October 2010. The Act consolidates all the existing anti-discrimination legislation, i.e. the legislation banning discrimination on the grounds of sex (including equal pay), race, disability, religion or belief, sexual orientation and age. The main aim of the Act is to reconcile some of the differences and discrepancies in the previous anti-discrimination legislation and strengthen the law to support progress on equality.

The Act applies to England, Wales and Scotland but not to Northern Ireland. A provision in the Act makes it potentially discriminatory, on the ground of disability, for employers to ask candidates questions about their health or disability, prior to making a decision on whether or not to proceed with applications or offer employment. It is now also potentially discriminatory for employers to require candidates to complete a medical questionnaire or undergo a medical examination, prior to deciding whether or not to select them.

An employer can only make enquiries about a candidate's health if there is a justifiable reason for doing so, for example to:

- establish whether or not it will be under a duty to make reasonable adjustments in the recruitment process;
- establish whether or not the candidate would be able to carry out an 'intrinsic' function of the work;
- monitor diversity;
- support positive action; or
- identify suitable candidates for a job where there is a genuine occupational requirement for the post holder to be disabled.

However, the rejection of an otherwise suitable candidate, following enquiries about health or disability, will be potentially discriminatory on the ground of disability. In these circumstances, if the employer's actions are challenged in an Employment Tribunal, the onus will be on the employer to satisfy the Tribunal that its decision to reject the candidate was for a reason other than disability.

Positive action

On 6 April 2011 provisions in the Equality Act 2010 related to positive action in recruitment and promotion commenced.

These are voluntary provisions and allow an employer faced with making a choice between two or more candidates of equal merit to choose one that is from a group that is disproportionately under-represented or disadvantaged within the workforce.

Positive action does not allow an employer to appoint a less suitable candidate just because that candidate has a protected characteristic that is under-represented or disadvantaged. Such a decision to take this action would only be possible at the end of the recruitment selection when a 'tie break' situation was encountered between candidates.

In order to determine that a group is disproportionately under-represented or disadvantaged in the workplace, some information or evidence will be required to indicate to the employer that one of those conditions exists. However, it does not need to be sophisticated statistical data or research. It may simply involve an employer looking at the profiles of their workforce and/or making enquiries of other comparable employers in the area or sector as a whole.

See also: Criminal records, p.97 Discrimination, p.126; The Equality Act, p.191; Personnel files, p.392; Probationary periods, p.412; Psychometric testing, p.415; Recruitment and selection, p.420; References, p.434; Staff handbooks, p.494.

ACAS: Advisory booklet – Recruitment and Induction:
www.acas.org.uk/index.aspx?articleid=744

ACAS: Advisory factsheet – Getting it Right – Recruitment and Selection:
www.acas.org.uk/media/pdf/9/3/S06_1.pdf

Assessment centres (ACs) function on the principle that no individual method of selection is particularly good, and no individual assessor infallible; therefore the centre utilises multiple methods in which several assessors assess different candidates. The result – each candidate is assessed by each assessor across several exercises assessing different competencies / criteria.

ACs can be used both for external recruitment campaigns and also when promoting internally. Workplace Law's AC solutions can be used in both instances, and can be resourced through a mixture of your business contacts and Workplace Law assessors; or entirely through Workplace Law – the choice is yours.

Using business simulations, interviews and psychometrics, the Workplace Law AC greatly increases your chances of selecting or promoting the right candidate and reduces the risk and cost of failed recruitment.

The Workplace Law AC offering provides a number of different assessment methods which can be tailored to the needs of the business. The methods include:

- case studies;
- in tray exercises;
- group exercises;
- presentations;
- interviews; and
- psychometric tests – both personality profiling, team fit and individual aptitude.

Visit www.workplacelaw.net for more information.

IT security
Lisa Jinks and John Macaulay, Greenwoods Solicitors LLP

Key points

- Serious breaches of IT security and major losses of customer or employee data regularly feature in the news. Clearly, such breaches of security have a major impact on the organisation affected on a number of levels – from damage to reputation and loss of key intellectual property, to regulatory sanctions, including large potential fines as well as criminal penalties. Employers can take a number of steps to protect their organisation against security breaches:
  - Put a security breach action plan in place;
  - Put security policies in place, implement them and ensure that they are regularly reviewed;
  - Update security software regularly; and
  - Put effective systems administration procedures in place.

- The annual Global State of Information Security Survey by PricewaterhouseCoopers found that, in 2011, although respect for data security was on the rise, the global economic downturn had put a strain on the resources available to combat IT security breaches. However, at a time when privacy issues are more than ever under public scrutiny and data protection penalties have been significantly increased, businesses simply cannot afford to limit their investment in IT security.

Legislation
- Data Protection Act 1998.

Security breaches in the news

Serious breaches of security hit the headlines with alarming regularity, with both public and private sector organisations reporting data protection security breaches to the Information Commissioner frequently. Breaches include the malicious hacking of company websites, the accidental mailing of sensitive personal data to the wrong recipients, and the loss of unencrypted laptops and hard drives with masses of personal data stored.

In the two years running up to January 2010, 818 data security breaches were reported to the Information Commissioner's Office (ICO), with human error accounting for 195 of these. A further 262 breaches were the result of theft, often where the personal information was held on an unencrypted portable device, and 240 of the reported breaches came from within the NHS. As more of these types of cases are reported in the media, most employers do not need to be reminded of the devastating effect on business of such incidents, not least in light of the Information Commissioner's power to fine organisations up to £500,000 for serious breaches of the Data Protection Act 1998 (DPA).

Examples of fines imposed under this power for data security breaches include:

- A fine of £60,000 issued to employment services company, A4e Limited, for the loss of an unencrypted laptop containing personal information relating to 24,000 people who had used community legal advice centres.
- Ealing Council was fined £6,000 following the theft of an unencrypted laptop, which contained personal information, from an employee's home. Issuing the unencrypted laptop to the member of staff was in breach of the Council's own policies.
- A fine of £1,000 was issued to Andrew Crossley, formerly trading as solicitors' firm ACS Law, for failing to keep sensitive personal information secure when his IT system was hacked, allowing details of thousands of alleged illegal file sharers to be leaked on the internet.

In addition, other regulators have the power to punish organisations for security breaches. For example, in 2009, the FSA fined HSBC more than £3m for failing to protect customers' confidential details.

Data Protection Act 1998
The DPA is the principal piece of legislation in the UK governing personal data, and includes restrictions on processing such data, rights for data subjects as well as the eight 'data protection principles' (see *'Data protection,'* p.101).

The seventh of these 'data protection principles', which are legally enforceable, requires organisations that control data to take 'appropriate technical and organisational measures... against unauthorised or unlawful processing of personal data and against accidental loss or destruction of, and damage to, personal data'. 'Personal data' for the purposes of the DPA is defined as data relating to any identifiable living person, provided it is electronically stored (or is part of a 'relevant filing system').

Examples of data that organisations may commonly hold, and that will come within the scope of the DPA, and therefore the seventh data protection principle, include:

- details of employees' salaries and bank accounts held on an organisation's computer system;
- emails about incidents involving named workers;
- managers' notebooks containing notes on named individuals, where there is an intention to put that information in workers' computerised personnel files; and/or
- information about persons external to the organisation, such as clients and customers, suppliers and other contacts whether in databases, emails or otherwise stored.

Breaches of the DPA can leave organisations liable for compensation for any damage or distress caused to individuals (such as where a security breach puts sensitive personal data in the public domain), as well as to potential criminal sanctions for the knowing or reckless disclosure of personal data without consent, and data protection penalties of up to £500,000.

The threats

Companies face a number of security threats. These could involve threats to system availability, integrity or general data losses.

Breach of IT security through human error and organisational failures

Many high-profile incidents of data loss are blamed either on human error or on communication and system failures. Security breaches are increasingly occurring as a result of human error or ineffective procedures, for example as a result of non-encrypted laptops, lost removable media (e.g. disks, USB drives) and a failure to dispose of customer details in a secure way. As many such breaches are not publicised (and there is no legal obligation to report breaches to the ICO other than for public electronic communications service providers) it is difficult to estimate precisely how many businesses are affected by a physical breach of IT security. However, the recent proliferation of remote working and mobile devices (such as laptops, smartphones and tablets) makes the potential for security breaches even higher.

Companies should ensure that they provide training on IT security to all staff, including making sure staff are aware of the possibility of confidence tricks to gain access to premises or passwords, and should promote an organisational culture that seeks to reduce the risk of such activities. For example, companies should seek to develop a culture where unidentified individuals within buildings are challenged, where sensitive information is not provided over the phone, and where there are clear policies on the use and protection of passwords. Many companies now develop IT use policies that put in place clear rules about the use and sharing of passwords. Although these steps cannot guarantee protection, especially as attacks become more sophisticated, greater awareness may reduce the risk of such attacks.

Malicious software

Malicious software may be used in an attempt to attack company networks. Popular malicious installations include key loggers that spring to life if particular websites are visited or programs, such as online games. It is worth noting that malicious software authors are increasingly moving away from the indiscriminate use of viruses and instead are launching targeted attacks against specific organisations or websites.

Staff who visit certain websites, in particular social networking sites, may be placing their organisations at particular risk of a data security breach. It is therefore important to ensure that IT systems are always updated with the latest patches released by the software developer, are regularly scanned for viruses and malware, and that adequate firewalls are in place. Organisations should also consider having emails screened prior to entering their network by their Internet Service Provider to further safeguard their system from being compromised. Having an effective policy in place notifying staff of permitted computer use, and highlighting the dangers of visiting certain sites, will also reduce the risk of breaches. See 'Social *media'* (p.485) and *'Internet and email policies'* (p.271) for more information.

Hacking

Again, no system is foolproof. Any network that has an external connectivity is open to the risk of hacking. Hacking may involve a variety of unacceptable activities, e.g. malicious file destruction, theft of money or intellectual property, or a catastrophic denial of service attack. Additionally, there is an increased used of phishing, which can take a number of guises but is often used as a means of obtaining personal details from individuals, by impersonating a reputable company. For example, this can be done where an email is sent to a user claiming to be from the user's bank, requesting personal details.

Hacking is definitely on the increase, but it is difficult to find accurate figures because, like corporate fraud, most activity is not reported due to the embarrassment and damage to business reputation. For example, the Computer Misuse Act 1990 has been in force for 20 years, but, as there have only ever been a handful of successful prosecutions under this Act, its deterrent effect is questionable.

One of the biggest threats of hacking, however, is from inside a large organisation, and businesses should be particularly wary in times of economic slowdown. Staff that are laid off may become disgruntled and present a real security risk. Difficulties may also arise where ex-suppliers have control of company source codes, passwords and so on.

What do you need to do to protect your data systems and equipment?

Whilst security technology is extremely important, IT security workplace managers should ensure that they also have other security measures in place to prevent or minimise the risk resulting from security breaches through human error, complacency or malice. The precise level of protection in place will require a risk analysis of the data security breaches for the particular organisation against the costs of implementing particular measures, which should be considered at senior management level.

There are many measures that are common sense, which should form part of a company's general security policy. Costs range from minimal, where it is simply a case of more vigorously applying existing procedures, to highly expensive, where the latest technology is implemented.

Physical security

Physical security measures are important to reduce the risk of intruders and theft of equipment. Some physical measures that should be adopted are as follows:

- Control and monitor access to buildings properly, using a record of visitors and badging. Also consider installing CCTV systems, although note that CCTV must be used in a proportionate way and must comply with the DPA (see *'CCTV monitoring,'* p.70).
- Require all staff to take responsibility for security by, for example, challenging 'strangers' out of hours and/or who appear in restricted or non-public areas.
- Make sure that the most important servers are situated in a secure and non-visible part of the premises, or perhaps even at another site.
- If appropriate, consider using biometrics (e.g. retina / iris scans, finger / handprint or facial feature scans, voice pattern scans, keystroke analysis) to identify those authorised to access the most sensitive equipment. However, note that there are data protection issues to consider

with this type of security (see 'Data protection,' p.101).

- Keep an inventory of computer equipment, especially equipment that can be taken from the building, and carry out periodical stock checks. Security tags or other identification methods should be used to ensure that if equipment does go missing, it can be tracked down.

- Staff using laptops and other portable computer equipment, including smartphones and tablets, should be reminded to ensure that they keep the equipment secure at all times and should (along with all other staff) be subject to an IT policy that covers data security inside and outside the workplace.

- Sensitive information and customer data held on laptops, smartphones and other removable media should be encrypted and password protected.

- Draft a policy to staff on what to do if their IT equipment is lost or stolen.

- When staff leave the organisation, or a device is no longer required, data should be deleted (after being backed-up elsewhere, if appropriate). Personal devices such as home computers or smartphones, through which the member of staff might have had access to company data, should also be cleared.

Basic system administration

Basic system administration measures include the following:

- Introduce a system security policy, and require staff to apply it and police it. This should oblige staff to avoid opening emails and attachments when they do not know their origin, and may restrict access to certain websites, such as web-based email services and social networks.

- Oblige staff to follow instructions from their IT managers, such as warnings about current virus attacks.

- Segment the network with appropriate authorisation procedures to limit the number of IT support staff that have entire system access.

- Limit system privileges as much as possible and develop a hierarchy of access.

- Implement an effective password policy and require regular password changes. Do not allow staff to share or otherwise disclose their passwords.

- Keep the system regularly updated with the latest updates from its manufacturer.

Protective software and audit activity

Some of the software protection and audit measures that can be employed are as follows:

- Ensure that anti-virus and anti-malware software is regularly used and updated across the network.

- Carry out regular monitoring of the firewall and general network integrity.

- Use code review software and consider penetration testing, i.e. simulating an attack to see how the system copes (although workplace managers should note that there may be data protection implications if customer or staff data may be accessed during such testing).

Staff issues

Whilst difficult to counter, there are a number of measures that businesses can take in order to protect themselves from fraud or malicious acts by staff members. As noted above, good systems administration plays a major part (for example, effective password protection). It has been found that staff committing fraudulent acts often fail to take time off (presumably for fear that they may be found out in their absence), so it is worth considering checking the leave records of key staff from time to time. Staff access to systems should be carefully controlled from the date of resignation until the person leaves, when access should be immediately terminated.

What should organisations do to limit damage if incidents do occur?

The following procedures and precautions are recommended:

- Ensure staff are aware of the importance of data security, their obligations in respect of it, and know who to contact in the event of a security breach.
- Have a contingency plan in place for restoring / recovering / recreating important data in the event of a disaster, as well as malicious or negligent damage. This could mean regularly backing up data and/or having a Secure Disaster Recovery Site.
- Ensure that forensic evidence is not destroyed in the course of the disaster response as this may deny recourse against the perpetrators or, more importantly, prevent discovery of what went wrong.
- Document IP rights and, where relevant, secure software source code (both sensible business practice) to assist fast remedies in the event of unauthorised use by hackers.

- Ensure that system security obligations are incorporated into employment contracts to avoid disputes over what staff are required to do or not do.
- Consider reporting the breach to the Information Commissioner. Although there is no legal obligation to do so (save in limited circumstances), reporting is encouraged and any enforcement action taken as a result of a breach is likely to be lessened where voluntary reporting has taken place.
- Follow the ICO's Guidance on Data Security Breach Management (see *Sources of further information* below), which recommends a four-step breach management plan:

  1. Containment and recovery.
  2. Assessment of ongoing risk.
  3. Notification of breach.
  4. Evaluation and response.

See also: CCTV monitoring, p.70; Data protection, p.101; Internet and email policies, p.271; Monitoring employees, p.358; Social media, p.485; Confidential waste, p.545.

Sources of further information

ICO – Guidance on data security breach management: http://bit.ly/oFDv3r

Business Link guidance on IT Security: www.businesslink.gov.uk/bdotg/action/layer?topicId=1075408323

Workplace Law's *IT and Email Policy and Management Guide, v.3.0*, is designed to alert employers of the potential problems associated with using computer systems, the internet, and email systems within the workplace, and to provide certain safeguards. For more information visit www.workplacelaw.net.

Jury service

Robert Dillarstone and Lisa Jinks, Greenwoods Solicitors LLP

Key points

- Ensure that you cover jury service and related salary payments in your staff handbook or contract of employment.
- Instruct your employees to claim compensation for loss of earnings from the Court.
- Deduct compensation for loss of earnings from salary payments.
- Plan ahead to cover absences caused by jury service.
- Consider requesting your employee to ask for a deferment if jury service would cause hardship.

Legislation
- Juries Act 1974.

Jury selection
All jurors are selected at random by computer from the electoral register. Anyone on the electoral register between the ages of 18 and 70 may be selected, even if they are not eligible to serve on a jury. Some people never get called; others get called more than once. Jurors usually try the more serious criminal cases such as murder, rape and assault, and are asked to decide on guilt or innocence, although they are sometimes involved in civil cases as well.

Eligibility
Jury service is a public duty and four weeks' notice is usually given. Unless someone is ineligible, has the right to be excused or has a valid reason for discretionary excusal, then they must serve. Individuals who are ineligible to serve as a juror are those who:

- are under 18, or 70 or above, on the date they are due to start their jury service;
- are currently on bail in criminal proceedings;

- have ever been sentenced to imprisonment for five years or more, or have been sentenced to imprisonment or a community order within the last ten years;
- have, or have had in the past, a mental illness, psychotic disorder, mental handicap or severe mental handicap;
- have not lived in the UK, the Channel Islands or the Isle of Man for one period of at least five years since the age of 13; and/or
- are not eligible to vote in parliamentary or Local Authority elections.

Jury service is an average of ten working days but may be longer or shorter than this, depending on which case the juror is put on to when they attend court.

Deferral and excusal
Anyone may apply for discretionary deferment or excusal. Jury service can only be deferred once up to a maximum of 12 months from the original date. The normal expectation is that everyone summoned for jury service will serve at the time for which they are summoned. Only in extreme circumstances will a person be excused. The normal procedure is to defer the individual to a more appropriate

time, e.g. if a holiday is booked or to avoid a shift or night worker attending on a rest day.

Application for excusal could be given on the following grounds:

- Insufficient understanding of English;
- Membership of religious orders whose ideology or beliefs are incompatible with jury service;
- Valid business reason (e.g. if a small business would suffer unusual hardship) – however, application for deferral or excusal cannot be accepted from third parties such as employers;
- Conflict with other important public duties; and/or
- Illness or a physical disability.

Application for excusal could also be given to an individual who has already completed jury service during the two years prior to the current summons.

Loss of earnings and other expenses

With regard to loss of earnings, courts can pay for these, together with travel costs and a subsistence rate. Currently, losses of earnings are paid up to a maximum of £64.95 per day for the first ten days and a maximum of £129.91 for subsequent days. Should the juror be required to serve for over 200 days, loss of earnings will then be paid up to a maximum of £228.06 for subsequent days.

Public transport costs will be paid, although jurors must obtain permission from the court before using taxis. A standard mileage rate (which depends on the form of transport used to get to court) will be paid to jurors who drive to the court, but jurors should seek permission from the court before incurring parking fees. Payment is made directly to the juror

and courts cannot pay third parties such as employers.

Subsistence for food and drink will be paid, currently up to a maximum of £5.71 per day (or £12.17 per day if required to be away from home or work for more than ten hours). Occasionally, jurors are required to stay overnight, in which case the court will arrange accommodation.

As soon as a summons has been received, the employee should forward the juror's loss of earnings certificate provided by the court (Form 5223) to their employer. Employers should note the dates and organise a deduction from salary of the amount representing the value of the allowance for days attended at court. However, unless specified in the contract of employment or staff handbook, there is no legal right to receive regular salary payments while undertaking jury service.

In circumstances where deduction of the jury service allowance results in a nil salary payment, any additional superannuation contributions can be deducted from the next available salary payment to provide continuity of pensionable service.

Employment rights

Jury service will count as part of an employee's continuous employment. This means that an employee will continue to accumulate or keep existing employment rights gained through length of service.

It is not advisable to refuse permission to release your employee for jury service. This could result in contempt of court issues with penalties such as a fine or even imprisonment for the employer. Dismissing your employee may result in a claim against your business for compensation for the loss of employment.

Good planning ahead will help to minimise the impact on the business. Encourage employees to inform you immediately when summoned – and consider having such a clause in your contracts – because this will give you approximately four weeks to make the necessary plans. Alternatively, if you work in a small business, you may consider requesting your employee to apply for a deferment.

See also: Absence management, p.16; Criminal records, p.97.

Sources of further information

Further details can be sought from the DirectGov website:

www.direct.gov.uk/en/CrimeJusticeAndTheLaw/Goingtocourt/DG_072707

Case review

Landmark cases in employment law

Workplace Law

Nicholson v. Grainger PLC (2009)
Tim Nicholson was an executive for the giant property company, Grainger. He was a former Environmental Policy Officer and worked at the time as Head of Sustainability at Grainger. Whilst on a business trip, Nicholson's manager needed him to return to the head office to collect a forgotten phone; however, this required him to take a flight there and back. Nicholson was passionate in his fight against climate change and did not feel that he was able to take the two (what he felt to be unnecessary) flights.

Nicholson refused to take the flights and was made redundant shortly afterwards. Nicholson claimed that this was unfair dismissal as his strong beliefs about climate change put him at odds with the other senior executives, who did not share the same beliefs.

Nicholson took his claim to the Employment Tribunal claiming that, because of his beliefs, he had been targeted for redundancy over the other senior executives who did not hold his beliefs. Grainger's representative claimed that Nicholson was using scientific evidence to form an opinion and that this did not constitute a philosophical belief. Mr Nicholson disputed this by saying that it was more than just an opinion that he held, and that it sculpted the way that he lived his life; he said that he no longer travels by aeroplane, he has renovated his house to make it more carbon neutral, and he only travels by carbon neutral (or as close to as he can get) vehicles.

The judge ruled in favour of Mr Nicholson, claiming that his beliefs went further than that of scientific opinion and that they did constitute a philosophical belief, as he sculpted his whole life around what he felt about the environment and climate change.

workplace law
human resources

Workplace Law's HR and Employment Team provide regular case reviews on historic, landmark and current case law, analysing judgments and giving critical commentary on the outcomes of each case. Visit www.workplacelaw.net for more information, where you can search for cases by subject, name, date or key word, by using our simple case review finder. Each case review details an overview of the facts, the outcome of the case, and expert analysis of the implications of the case, as well as a link to the official judgment. Here we look at a few important cases relating to discrimination.

The ruling in Nicholson's favour paves the way for future claims surrounding the discrimination of people on the grounds of their environmental beliefs. Strong environmental beliefs are now classed as the same as any other philosophical belief and will, therefore, be treated in the same respect as to companies abiding by the Employment Equality (Religion or Beliefs) Regulations 2003. If they do not, an employer can make a claim against the company on the grounds of discrimination.

Heyday Legal Challenge on Age Discrimination (2009)

Shortly following the publishing of the Employment Equality (Age) Regulations, the charities Age Concern and Help the Aged (Age UK) put in complaints about aspects of the Regulations discriminating against the elderly. The charities felt that the UK Government had improperly implemented the EU's 2000 Equal Treatment Directive by including a national default retirement age applicable to all UK workers. They challenged the linked exception of the employment of people near to or aged 65 on the scope for justification of direct discrimination on the grounds of age.

The High Court needed clarification on how the EU Directive should be implemented and so set five questions to The European Court of Justice (ECJ). The ECJ made it clear that the UK Government must present a strong argument and have justified evidence as to why the default retirement age needed to be 65. After reviewing the evidence the ECJ ruled that the UK default retirement age was justified at 65, agreeing with the UK Government.

The ECJ, however, did put forward the strong argument that the default retirement age could be older and agreed that the charities presented a very strong argument

against people being forced out of work aged 65. This ruling was passed on the grounds that the UK Government bring forward the review of the default retirement age to 2010, instead of 2011 to fairly reassess the situation and how people are being affected; if it seems that there is good grounds that the default retirement age should be increased to an older age, then this should be considered with open minds by the UK Government.

From 6 April 2011 the Government started to phase out the default retirement age, and, from 1 October 2011, has been abolished. There is a transition period whereby employers can only enforce retirement to those employees given the correct notice under the Equality (Age) Regulations by 1 April 2011. Enforced retirement outside of this transition period will be deemed as automatically unfair dismissal, unless the organisation has an objectively justified retirement age.

Sharon Coleman v. Attridge Law (2008)

Sharon Coleman was accused by her workplace – Attridge Law – of using her disabled child as a means of manipulating requests for working time and was dismissed. Coleman claimed unfair dismissal on the grounds of the Disability Discrimination Act 1995.

The Disability Discrimination Act 1995 (in force at the time) states that you may only be able to consider yourself discriminated against if the treatment is 'against a disabled person'. Sharon Coleman herself was not disabled; however, her son suffered from bronchomalacia and congenital laryngomalacia from an early age, causing him to require treatment, operations and (from time to time) at-home care from his mother. Subsequently, at the times when her son was at his greatest need, Sharon Coleman requested that she be able to work at home. Attridge Law dismissed her for this reason; when she tried to claim unfair dismissal on the grounds of the Disability Discrimination Act 1995 it spread confusion as to whether this was applicable as the company claimed it was not discriminating against a disability, as Sharon was not disabled and so the Act did not apply.

Sharon Coleman took her claim to the Employment Tribunal; following this it went to the Employment Appeal Tribunal and as far as the European Court of Justice. The EAT admitted it felt it was wrong to say the Act could not be interpreted in line with the Directive; however, it held judgment on the outcome and instead referred it to the European Court of Justice.

In the Advocate General's opinion, Sharon Coleman was directly discriminated against and the law should include all disabled people and those third party people who are primarily associated with their care, for example parents. The European Court of Justice released its judgment that Sharon Coleman had won the suit against Attridge Law. It concluded that the Act applies now to all carers who were not previously protected.

On its return to the Employment Tribunal, the law firm appealed against a preliminary ruling that the Tribunal had Jurisdiction on its claim. The Employment Appeal Tribunal, however, held the view that for an employer to treat an able bodied employee caring for a disabled child less favourably than another employee in a comparable situation was associative discrimination notwithstanding the specific references in the Disability Discrimination Act 1995 to a 'disabled person'. The case has been remitted to the first instance Tribunal for a full hearing. New provisions in the Equality Act 2010 specifically protect employees

from being treated less favourably than others as a result of their association with a person against whom it would be unlawful to discriminate. Previously age, disability, gender reassignment and sex were not covered under association.

Female Council Workers v. Birmingham Council (2010)

In 2010, more than 4,000 female council workers took Birmingham County Council to the Employment Tribunal over sex discrimination and equal pay cases, as they were not getting paid as much as the male workers who were doing equivalent jobs.

Women, in 49 different job roles, complained of being excluded from bonuses, which were worth up to 160% of their basic pay; the bonuses instead were only going to the male workers.

All of the jobs were in predominantly female-dominated roles and included such jobs as cleaning, care and catering and administrative jobs within the council. Men, who were doing the same pay graded jobs as the women were, in some cases, being paid up to four times more.

In one year, a refuge collector took up to 160% of their basic pay in bonuses and earned £51,000; a female worker on the same pay grade took home less than £12,000.

The Employment Tribunal ruled in the female Council workers' favour as it said there had been a clear difference in the way that men and women were being treated by the Council – with men seeming to be favoured.

The Council now faces damage costs of up to £200m to pay back the bonuses that the female workers missed out on.

Leave

Heidi Thompson, Workplace Law

Key points

- Adopting carefully defined policies that formalise practices on compassionate leave, time off for dependants, and sabbatical leave, can help employers promote fair and consistent treatment of their employees.
- Preparing a written policy is also a good opportunity for employers to clarify their attitudes and approach to sensitive issues, which, in turn, should help to increase staff morale and wellbeing.
- Employers should avoid the implication of a contractual right to compassionate leave, sabbatical leave and time off for dependants, unless this is clearly intended.
- The right to time off for dependants is not applicable in all circumstances. A burst boiler or problems with a pet do not count.
- The right to time off under the Employment Rights Act 1996 for unexpected disruptions or the termination of care arrangements for dependants is not limited to last minute unavailability or emergencies.
- Sabbatical leave can be an effective alternative to making an employee redundant.

Legislation

- Employment Rights Act 1996 (Section 57a).
- Equality Act 2010.

Case law

- *Forster v. Cartwright Black* (2004).
- *Royal Bank of Scotland plc v. Harrison* (2009).

Types of leave

- Annual leave (see '*Holiday*,' p.240).
- Compassionate leave.
- Maternity, paternity and adoption leave (see '*Family-friendly rights*,' p.206).
- Sabbatical.
- Time off for dependants.

What is compassionate leave?

Compassionate leave is a term used to describe a period of time off work (either paid or unpaid) that an employer allows an employee who is faced with difficult personal circumstances, such as the death of a family member.

Whilst employees are not legally entitled to compassionate leave as a result of bereavement, employers should take a serious and sympathetic view of requests for time off following the death of a dependant or family member. However, there is a statutory right to take time off for the death of a dependant (Section 57a(1)(c) ERA 1996) (*see below*).

Practical tips

- Define clearly the range of circumstances in which compassionate leave will be granted, and include a list of the family members in respect of whom the right to take leave will apply.
- Define how much compassionate leave may be granted, whilst retaining some discretion and flexibility so as to be able to show consideration

to individual employees in times of difficulty.

- Ensure that policies are applied consistently and fairly to all employees, but consider stipulating a minimum length of service in respect of any paid leave.
- Set out a clear reporting structure in the event that compassionate leave is needed (i.e. supervisor / Head of HR).
- Ensure that bad news affecting an employee is communicated promptly but sensitively to the rest of the team or department, and that workloads are delegated effectively.
- Recognise that employees affected by bereavement may not be able to comply rigidly with a policy (i.e. often death and emergencies will be unexpected, and the employee will not be able to report his/her absence straightaway or may not feel emotionally able to make the call to HR personally).
- Be aware that any compassionate leave granted in relation to an opposite-sex partner should also be granted in relation to a same-sex partner.
- Employees who develop psychological illness following bereavement may find themselves needing to extend their periods of compassionate leave with sickness absence. Employers may therefore wish to offer return-to-work interviews to affected employees to assess their ability to cope with the stresses and strains of the workplace. They may also wish to offer employees a period of free bereavement counselling via Occupational Health.

Time off for dependants

Compassionate leave should be distinguished from an employee's statutory right to take a reasonable amount of unpaid time off during the employee's working hours to deal with certain unexpected or sudden emergencies, such as the death of a dependant (see Section 57a(1)(c) ERA 1996). The right is to 'take action which is necessary,' such as to organise or to attend a funeral.

As well as having the right to time off to deal with the death of a dependant, an employee is entitled to take unpaid time off in the following circumstances, which are set out in Section 57a ERA 1996:

- Where a dependant falls ill, or has been injured or assaulted.
- When a dependant is having a baby (please note that this does not include taking time off after the birth to care for the child, but an employee may be entitled to take maternity, paternity or parental leave for this purpose).
- To make long-term care arrangements for a dependant who is ill or injured.
- To deal with a death of a dependant – this enables an employee to take time off to make funeral arrangements and attend the funeral.
- To deal with an unexpected disruption or breakdown of care arrangements for a dependant.
- To deal with an incident involving the employee's child, which occurs during school hours.

Who counts as a dependant?

A dependant is defined as the employee's spouse, civil partner, child or parent; or a person living in the same household other than by reason of being a tenant, lodger, boarder or employee. This could include, for example, a partner or an elderly aunt or grandparent.

Additional issues to be considered by the employer

Although the statutory right to time off work is unpaid, an employer may want to consider offering its employees paid leave to organise or to attend a funeral. This could improve staff loyalty and retention and help achieve a better work–life balance.

Case studies

Forster v. Cartwright Black (2004)

In this case, the Employment Appeals Tribunal (EAT) considered the scope of qualifying actions for time off work taken in consequence of the death of a dependant. Following the death of her mother, Forster had taken five days' bereavement leave followed by two consecutive periods of sick leave (each lasting two weeks), which her doctor had certified as 'bereavement reaction'. Following receipt of the second sick note, she was dismissed due to her period of absence following her mother's death and her general absence record. The EAT held that the right to time off in consequence of the death of a dependant covered time off to make funeral arrangements, to attend a dependant's funeral and to make necessary practical arrangements, such as registering a death and applying for probate. However, it stated that Section 57a(1)(c) did not cover time off as a result of the emotional consequences and grief associated with the death of a dependant. To avoid any doubt arising, employers should therefore refer to time taken off to grieve the psychological effects of bereavement in a separate compassionate leave policy.

Royal Bank of Scotland v. Harrison (2008)

The right to take time off because of the unexpected disruption or termination of arrangements for the care of a dependant is not limited to emergencies. In this case, the Employment Appeal Tribunal held that the entitlement to dependant leave under the Employment Rights Act 1996 is not limited to last minute unavailability or emergencies. Ms Harrison had two young children. Her childminder told her on 8 December that she would no longer be available on 22 December as previously arranged. Ms Harrison asked her employer for time off and this was refused. Having failed to make alternative childcare arrangements, Ms Harrison did not go to work on 22 December so that she could look after her children and, as a consequence, was issued with a verbal warning that would remain on her record for six months. Ms Harrison was successful in bringing a claim against RBS on the grounds that she had suffered a detriment as a result of staying off work to look after her children.

The EAT upheld the decision of the Tribunal and concluded that the word 'unexpected' in Section 57a(1)(d) ERA 1996 does not involve a time element and that it is not appropriate to seek to incorporate into statute words that are simply not there, such as 'sudden' or 'in an emergency'. The right to time off applies to all employees, namely any individual (male or female, full-time or part-time) who has entered into or works under a contract of employment (whether that is express or implied, written or oral). There is no minimum period of qualifying service required. The case serves as a useful example of the flexibility employers must show when dealing with employees with dependants and requests for time off work in relation to those dependants.

Depending on the composition of an employer's workforce, it may wish to consider extending the application of its policy beyond employees to include other types of worker or to include other emergency situations; such as house fire or flood, etc.

The right to time off for dependants is intended to cover genuine unexpected situations, so the employer should not set a limit on the number of times that an employee can be absent from work under this right. However, employers who are concerned that abuse of the right to time off to care for dependants may become an issue should consider stating that abuse of the right is a specific disciplinary offence that could lead to disciplinary action under its disciplinary procedures.

If a funeral is taking place overseas, an employer should agree a length of absence that is reasonable and fair in all the circumstances. This may mean the employer striking a balance between its own business needs and the needs of the individual employee.

The right to time off does not apply unless the employee tells the employer the reason for his/her absence 'as soon as reasonably practicable' (unless it is not reasonable for the employee to tell the employer the reason for his/her absence until after his/her return to work). Any policy should therefore set out expected timescales for receipt of this information.

An employee who exercises the right to time off for dependants is protected against dismissal or victimisation. This means that it would be unfair to dismiss an employee or to select him/her for redundancy for taking, or seeking to take, time off to exercise this right. Similarly, an employee who is not offered a promotion or an appraisal because he/she has exercised this right would be able to complain that he/she has suffered a detriment. If the dismissed employee is also female, the employer may also be at risk of a claim of indirect sex discrimination.

In order to comply with the requirements of the Equality Act 2010 as concerns religion or belief, employers should, where reasonably practicable, accommodate the requirements of their employees' religions or beliefs when a death occurs. This may mean creating less rigid compassionate leave policies to cater for specific bereavement customs. For example, Hindus believe that cremation must take place as soon as possible following death and it is usual for close relatives of the deceased to remain at home and observe a 13-day mourning period.

Sabbatical leave

Sabbatical leave is a period of leave (usually unpaid), typically lasting between three and six months, which employers allow employees to take in order to spend more time with family, to work on a specific project, to travel, or to merely recharge their batteries. In the current economic climate, sabbaticals can be an effective way for employers to cut costs and be an alternative to making redundancies if demand picks up.

Sabbatical breaks are not officially recognised by law. However, more and more employers are recognising that it is in their best interests to implement well thought out sabbatical schemes.

What are the advantages to employers of offering sabbatical schemes?

■ Adopting a flexible 'can do' approach to sabbatical leave can be an effective way of recruiting and retaining the best talent.

- In demonstrating sensitivity to the work–life balance, employees often return to their former roles feeling more refreshed, motivated, loyal and productive.
- Sabbaticals allow employers to streamline the workforce on a short-term basis with the option of re-integrating the employee back into the organisation at the end of the leave period, without excessive training costs.
- Staff can acquire new skills during their sabbatical, and bring valuable knowledge to the workplace.
- Encouraging a culture of flexibility amongst employees can have a positive effect on staff retention and turnover.
- Sabbaticals can be used by employers to prevent burnout of employees and to assert a progressive approach towards work.

To formalise requests for sabbatical leave, employers are advised to have a formal policy in place. This should help to reduce any potential disputes and give the employer and the employee an agreed procedure to follow. In the absence of any agreement, sabbatical leave can be viewed as a resignation in the hope of later re-engagement.

If this is the case, the employer has no certainty as to whether the employee will return to the organisation at the end of his/her break and the employee has no certainty that there will be a job for him/her upon his/her return. This will rarely be the case and sabbatical leave terms and conditions should be agreed in advance. Any terms regarding the leave should be clearly documented in an agreement. Depending on what is negotiated, employees can return to work at the end of their period of sabbatical leave on the same terms and conditions as before, without having had their continuity of employment broken. However, in the current downturn, the most employers will want to do is offer to conduct a reasonable search for opportunities on the employee's return in what could be a substantially different business a year down the line.

Additional concerns for the employer

Employers should word policies carefully to ensure that the employee has no automatic right to return to the same job or on the same terms and conditions at the end of the sabbatical leave period.

A sabbatical leave package requires careful planning and good communication, so that each party fully understands the implications of any commitments made. It may be useful for individuals to have an obligation to inform employers, by a particular date, of whether they intend to return to the organisation.

In addition, the policy should clearly stipulate the notice required by the organisation where an employee wishes to apply for a sabbatical, as well as what happens to benefits such as accrual of annual leave whilst on sabbatical, so the employee is aware of all such factors.

The needs of the business should determine the length of any period of sabbatical leave granted; although it is advisable to set a minimum and maximum timeframe in the policy. However, a limit of three months may be reasonable, on the basis that it is not long enough for the employee to forget know-how or technical skills, but long enough to have a meaningful break.

See also: Absence management, p.16; Holiday, p.240; Family-friendly rights, p.206; Jury service, p.288; Pregnancy and maternity, p.400; Restrictive covenants and garden leave, p.441; Secondment, p.459; Sickness, p.470.

Sources of further information

For organisations with or without a HR team who require specialist support, advice through hands-on support and/or project management, Workplace Law offer tailored strategic HR support and advice to suit the needs of your organisation.

To enable your organisation to focus on its core business our CIPD qualified and HR specialist team can provide support and advice on a number of strategic HR offerings. Our dedicated HR team can work with you on key HR projects aligned to your HR strategy and business plan, which can include, although are not limited to:

- HR strategy planning;
- Strategic succession planning;
- Site closures;
- Sale of business;
- Acquisitions and mergers;
- Relocation of sites or departments;
- Large TUPE projects; and
- Changing terms and conditions.

All of our HR professionals have 20 plus years of hands-on experience, working in every sector, in small, medium and large organisations. Our HR professionals bring this unique knowledge and experience to provide advice, support and project management to ensure the best fit for your organisation. Visit www.workplacelaw.net for more information.

Mediation

Kelly Barfoot, Kelly Barfoot Mediation Services

Key points

- Mediation is informal, making it much faster to resolve issues.
- Mediation is completely confidential; no notes are kept and nothing is recorded on the individual's HR file.
- Employee or union representation is not appropriate in mediation.
- Mediation is voluntary.
- Using an independent third party for mediation means the internal HR team are not biased should the issue be taken further using the workplace's formal procedures.
- Mediation works well when used as an outcome for disciplinary cases, for example, in situations where people still need to work together afterwards.
- In certain cases it is important for an organisation to prove that they have done all that is reasonably practicable – mediation supports this objective.
- Mediation can be used effectively to resolve conflict within teams as well as between individuals.

Introduction

Disputes, arguments and conflict can have a detrimental impact on an organisation and the employees working within it. It's well known how expensive it can be if an employer is taken to court, but it's not just the monetary costs that need to be considered; it's the long-term effects that can cause the most damage. Conflict can leave an organisation reeling from low morale, high staff turnover, loss of productivity and increased absence due to stress and depression. Many employers now realise that mediation is an effective way of fostering understanding and respect between parties, allowing disagreements to be settled informally to mutual satisfaction.

Times are changing, and in 2009 ACAS released a new code of conduct for discipline and grievance procedures. It urged employers to first try to resolve grievances informally, using mediation, before invoking formal procedures. Looking to the future, alternative dispute resolution is set to play a bigger part in all our lives. The Government has recently instigated changes to bring mediation into family law areas such as divorce and custody issues with the aim of saving the time, stress and money it would cost to get a decision through the courts. Considering our increasingly litigious society, mediation has many benefits to bring to the workplace; after all, even if an employer or employee wins at an Employment Tribunal it is often something of a hollow victory.

What is mediation?

Mediation is a confidential and informal process where an independent third party works with people who have a disagreement. The mediator's aim is to help people find their own solution and reach an agreement to either sort out the problem or improve the situation.

Mediation differs from a formal process because it is voluntary and both parties have to agree to give it a go. Formal processes such as grievance procedures

Facts

- The cost of workplace conflict to UK employers is estimated at £24bn per year.
- 49.4% of employers have increased their use of mediation in the last two years.
- 77% of all disputes at work are because of relationship problems, usually between managers and employees.
- The number of days of management and HR time spent on managing both disciplinary and grievance cases has gone up since 1997, from 13 to 18 days (disciplinary) and from nine to 14.4 days (grievance).
- The number of claims accepted by Employment Tribunals in 2009/10 was 56% higher than for 2008/09.

can force people to take sides and create further divisions. Thisdoesn't help people to continue working together, going forward. Mediation, on the other hand, takes the emphasis away from conflict and places it on restoring the working relationship.

Why mediation works

- Mediation gets people talking, and most importantly working relationships are maintained.
- Mediation is a fast solution and can nip problems in the bud before they escalate.
- It saves money and time. The costs associated with workplace conflict can really add up – for example, wasted management and HR time, stress-related sickness and absence, recruiting and training new members of staff – let alone the huge cost of defending an Employment Tribunal claim.
- Mediation is a lot less stressful than a lengthy, formal procedure and allows your organisation to return to normal quickly.
- It sends out a positive message about dispute resolution and has an impact on the organisation's culture.
- If mediation fails to resolve the issue it doesn't stop individuals litigating, hence parties do not feel like they have to waive their rights.

When should you use mediation?

The vast majority of workplace problems lend themselves to mediation, although it has been proven to be particularly effective in disputes where working relationships have been affected. A 2010 IRS survey found that 77% of workplace disputes are due to poor working relationships. Mediation can be used at every stage of a dispute, for example, before a grievance is even raised, during theprocess, or after as an outcome. Certainly if an organisation was facing an Employment Tribunal claim, mediation could be very powerfuland possibly stop a claim in its tracks. However, if used early on,mediation may prevent an organisation from even getting to a Tribunal in the first place.

Mediation is perfect as a way of clearing the air after disciplinary action. If employment has not been terminated then people do still need to work together after difficult events and this can be very hard if no real way forward has been agreed. It can be made significantly easier for everyone to get back to normal work routines if mediation is used to clear the air.

Mediation does some have limitations. As a general guideline, mediation should not be used where a judgement of right or wrong is essential, such as in a case of gross misconduct or a dispute over employment terms and conditions. A qualified and ethical mediator will let an employer know if the situation is not appropriate for mediation.

The mediation process

The mediator will provide plenty of information before the mediation takes place to ensure all parties completely understand what they are committing to. Once all the parties involved have agreed to mediation, the mediator will usually meet separately with them to get their perspective on the situation. They will then come together in a joint meeting to discuss the issues constructively, with the mediator guiding the process towards resolution. This can take place at the individual's workplace or at a neutral external venue.

A professional mediator has the skills and expertise to control the process and they will agree ground rules for everyone to adhere to in order to keep the discussions productive. It is essential that mediation is conducted in a safe, private and relaxed environment so parties can speak openly and honestly.

The process is completely neutral so the mediator won't take sides or pass any judgement on who is right or wrong. The mediator cannot tell the parties what to do or give any legal advice. The agreement on how to resolve the situation and work together going forward is entirely the decision of the parties involved. Mediation usually takes as little as one day in total; however, it should never be rushed or the results may be put in jeopardy.

At the end of the process the mediator will draw up a written agreement for all who are involved. Whilst the details of the mediation are completely confidential the mediator will let the employer know that the issues have been resolved. Details of

the written agreement can only be shared with the consent of both parties. Because mediation results in a collaborative solution, its effects are usually long-lasting, because the commitment has been secured during the process.

It really is the case that everything stays in the room in mediation. No notes or records are kept by the mediator and nothing is recorded on the individual's HR files, so there has to be trust in the process. Very often the mediation process is the first time that the parties involved have actually had a chance to speak about how they feel. This can be empowering and a real release of tension; many people say it was such a relief to finally get everything out in the open.

Employee or union representation is not appropriate during mediation. This is because mediation is an informal process and works best when just the parties involved and the mediator are present.

What happens if mediation doesn't work?

Before mediation takes place, the mediator makes sure that all parties are committed to resolving the issue. So, in the rare event that agreement cannot be reached, parties can still be referred to their formal grievance or disciplinary procedures. In these cases the mediation process remains confidential and nothing said or produced can be disclosed.

Internal or external mediation?

Many workplaces are now putting internal mediation schemes in place. Key personnel are trained as mediators to resolve disputes internally. Internal mediators benefit from existing knowledge of their organisation and culture,and as such they potentially require less briefing time. This can work very well if the organisation is large enough to overcome the potential issues surrounding confidentiality and bias.

The impartiality of a third party mediator is essential to win the trust of all parties involved and it is this trust that allows the mediator to guide the parties effectively towards a resolution. HR professionals often have the right skills but any conflict of interests or loss of neutrality can damage the process – or any future grievance procedure. Similarly, using someone without the proper mediation qualifications and experience can only serve to make matters worse.

Conclusion

However you see mediation, it is up and coming as a real solution to conflict in the workplace. Many organisations are now offering mediation as an option at each stage of their grievance procedures. The difference with mediation is the emphasis

on the longer term. The outcome of the process deals not only with the present issue but how it can be stopped from happening again.

It must always be remembered that mediation is a voluntary process and people should never be forced or coerced into taking part as this will certainly affect the quality of the outcome. Mediation is an option in any conflict situation and should be given consideration. It is there to be used and should be taken advantage of; after all there is little to lose and so much to gain.

> *See also*: Bullying and harassment, p.58; Disciplinary and grievance procedures, p.121; Employment disputes, p.168; Employment Tribunals, p.179.

Sources of further information

ACAS: Mediation – An Employer's Guide:
www.acas.org.uk/CHttpHandler.ashx?id=949&p=0

ACAS – Code of Practice on Discipline and Grievance:
www.acas.org.uk/CHttpHandler.ashx?id=1041

Employers should have a clear record of the policy and procedures for disciplinary matters to provide clear guidance to employees on the procedure that will be followed by their employer. Workplace Law's **Non-Contractual Disciplinary and Grievance Policy and Management Guide v.4.0** helps employers comply with their obligations and can also act as a checklist for managers, in relation to the steps that should be taken, with a view to minimising procedural irregularities and allegations of unfair treatment. For more information visit www.workplacelaw.net.

Medical records

Lisa Jinks and John Macaulay, Greenwoods Solicitors LLP

Key points

- 'Medical records' encompass any records that may contain information about workers' medical conditions.
- Employers need to be aware of the legal procedure under the Access to Medical Reports Act 1988.
- Employers should be aware of data protection principles as they apply to medical records, and establish who in the organisation is responsible for ensuring compliance.
- Employment contracts should contain provisions allowing employers access to medical information and requiring employees to submit to a medical examination.
- Employers should always bear in mind the principles of disability discrimination under the Equality Act 2010 (which came into force in October 2010), and those under the old Disability Discrimination Act 1995, which will continue to have some relevance.
- Employers also need to be aware of the right to privacy.
- Employers should be aware of the implications of asking pre-employment health-related questions following the implementation of the Equality Act 2010.

Legislation

- Access to Medical Reports Act 1988.
- Disability Discrimination Act 1995 (now repealed).
- Data Protection Act 1998 (DPA).
- Human Rights Act 1998.
- Equality Act 2010.

Background

A major issue for employers is how they can access and use information on workers' medical conditions. This may arise in a variety of situations, for example, where an employee is off on long-term sickness absence, where employers wish to use pre-employment medical questionnaires or where they wish to carry out drugs and alcohol testing etc. They may also need to collate information for insurance schemes, such as private medical insurance or permanent health insurance. Employers need to understand what information they may have access to, and how they may process such information once received.

In addition, employers always need to be careful not to discriminate against employees on grounds of disability.

Access to medical reports

Employers may obtain access to employees' medical records, subject to certain conditions. If they wish to obtain a report from a medical practitioner who has been responsible for the employee's clinical care, they need to comply with the Access to Medical Reports Act 1988 (the Act). Such practitioners would include the employee's GP and others responsible for the employee's care, such as a physiotherapist, psychiatrist or other specialist.

The Act requires that the employer must:

- obtain the employee's express consent in writing before applying to the medical practitioner for a report; and
- notify the employee of their rights under the Act. These include the right to withhold permission from the employer obtaining the report, the right to have access to the report either before it is sent to the employer or afterwards and, on seeing the report, the right to withdraw consent or request amendment of the report.

The medical practitioner will normally have to provide the report within 21 days. One frustration for an employer is that an employee who has stated that they do not want to see the report may subsequently write to their doctor and request to see the report, without informing the employer. If this happens, the employee then has a further 21 days from making the request to make arrangements to have access to the report. If 21 days elapse with no further communication from the employee, the medical practitioner can then release the report to the employer. In this situation it may be sensible for the employer to contact the employee directly to discuss the issue.

The requirements of the Act do not apply if an employer wishes to refer the employee to a medical practitioner who has not been responsible for the employee's clinical care. This means that employers can, subject to having the contractual right to do so, request an employee to be examined by a company-appointed doctor whether from within the organisation or externally without complying with the above procedure (provided that the doctor concerned has not previously treated the employee). In these circumstances, the employee does not have the same rights to see or challenge the report before the employer sees it. Hence the importance of an express provision in the contract of employment stating that the employee consents to be referred to a medical practitioner of the employer's choice at any time.

However, even if such a provision exists, it is always advisable to obtain an employee's *written* consent before carrying out any medical assessment. The issue of consent and the right to privacy are considered below. It is also recommended that any in-house medical adviser should inform the employee of any advice that will be passed to management following a health assessment.

Data protection

It is now more important than ever that employers ensure strict compliance with the DPA as, since April 2010, the Information Commissioner has been able to impose civil fines of up to £500,000 for serious contraventions of data protection legislation.

Medical records amount to 'sensitive personal data' under the DPA. If sickness records are to be 'processed' under the DPA (e.g. obtained, retained, disclosed, disposed of, etc.), then employers must comply with the sensitive personal data rules. Whilst it is worth noting that the DPA only comes into play when such information is held on a computer system or in a 'relevant filing system' (which may include certain structured personnel files) in practice, the DPA is likely to apply to most information held by an employer about its employees.

Under the Data Protection Employment Practices Code, some core principles are set out regarding the processing of information about workers' health. These include:

- the intrusiveness to workers of obtaining information about their health;
- a worker's right to privacy;
- the need for employers to be clear about the purpose of processing such information and whether this is justified by real benefits; and
- the requirement for one of the sensitive data conditions to be satisfied (*see below*).

Workers should be made aware of the extent information about their health is held and the reasons for this. Decisions on workers' suitability for particular jobs are management decisions, but the interpretation of medical information should be left to qualified health professionals.

With regard to the sensitive personal data rules that must be satisfied to process medical information, the following are likely to be the most relevant:

- *Processing is necessary by law.* This condition has quite a wide application in the employment context. Typical examples would be maintaining records of statutory sick pay, maternity pay, ensuring health and safety and preventing disability discrimination.
- *The processing is necessary to protect the vital interests of the worker / some other person.* This would occur when it is vital to access medical records where consent cannot be given/ obtained. An example would be if an employee was involved in a medical emergency and the employee or another person was at risk of harm.
- *The processing is necessary in connection with actual or prospective legal proceedings.* This is most likely to occur when an employer is trying to rely upon medical information to defend a claim for unfair dismissal or unlawful discrimination.
- *Worker's 'explicit' consent.* There are limitations on how far consent can

be relied upon. To be valid, consent must be explicit and freely given. 'Explicit' means the worker must have been clearly told what personal data is involved and informed about the use of this information. The worker must give a positive indication of their agreement, e.g. a signature. 'Freely given' means the worker must have a real choice whether to consent or not and there must be no penalty imposed for refusing to give consent.

'Processing' of medical records

The processing of medical records (e.g. obtaining, holding, disclosing, disposing of, etc.) must comply with data protection principles. Before processing medical information, employers should carry out an impact assessment, i.e. identify the purpose for which the medical information is required and the likely benefits of this, identify any adverse impact on the worker, consider alternative options and judge whether the processing of such information is justified.

It is also advisable that employers identify who within their organisation is authorised to process workers' medical information. In addition, access to medical information by managers / colleagues should be undertaken no more than is necessary. For example, managers should not access information about a worker's medical condition when information is only needed about length of absence. It is also recommended that medical records (giving details of the medical condition) are separated from absence records (which do not have such details) and that medical records are subject to enhanced security, perhaps being password-protected.

Workers' access to records

Workers have a right to access information held about them. This is known as subject access and covers, amongst other information, sickness or absence records held about an individual, whether on computerised files or as part of a 'relevant filing system'.

An employer can charge a fee of up to £10 to provide this information and must respond to a request within 40 days of receipt. The employer must provide the information in a hard copy or other readily readable, permanent electronic form, making clear any codes used and the sources of information. Note, however, that access does not have to be granted where it is likely to cause serious harm to the health / condition of the worker or any other person. In this situation, the employer should consult with an appropriate health professional.

Refusal to consent / right to privacy
Although an employee may refuse to give consent for their employer to access their medical records, the Courts will balance the right to privacy against the rights of the employer. For example, it is possible that a sick employee who claims a right to privacy by consistently refusing access to medical information could still be fairly dismissed on grounds of incapability where it is considered that the employer has followed the appropriate procedures and otherwise done all it could to resolve the matter.

Pre-employment medical questionnaires
The Equality Act targets employers who ask pre-employment health-related questions. Prior to making an offer of employment, employers are permitted to ask candidates questions that:

■ help the employer to determine whether any reasonable adjustments need to be made for the candidate during the selection process;
■ allow the employer to determine whether the candidate can carry out a function that is intrinsic to the job;
■ monitor diversity amongst the applicants;or
■ allow the employer to take positive action in favour of disabled people.

While asking an applicant pre-employment health-related questions other than those that are permitted will not in itself amount to discrimination against a job applicant, acting on the answers may well do. Furthermore, if the candidate were to subsequently bring a discrimination claim against an employer who had asked pre-employment health-related questions, the burden of proof would *automatically* shift to the employer, who would be required to demonstrate that no discrimination took place.

See also: Data protection, p.101; The Equality Act, p.191; Health surveillance, p.231; Occupational health, p.374; Personnel files, p.392; Private life, p.404.

Sources of further information

The Data Protection Employment Practices Code: www.ico.gov.uk

Mental health

Elizabeth Stevens, Steeles Law

Key points

- Employers are subject to a variety of legal obligations in respect of their employees' health and wellbeing. These obligations arise from health and safety legislation, the breach of which is a criminal offence, and also from the law of negligence, contract and discrimination. Injury to an employee's mental health is treated by the law in the same way as injury to physical health.

- The HSE defines 'workplace stress' as 'the adverse reaction people have to excessive pressure or other types of demand placed on them'. According to the HSE, stress is not an illness but a 'state'; it is only if stress becomes too excessive and prolonged that mental and physical illness may develop.

- Employers are not under a duty to eliminate all stress in the workplace, but once an employee has raised the issue of stress, an employer is under a duty to take steps to minimise the risk to the individual. A failure to do so could render the employer liable for a future personal injury claim and/or constructive unfair dismissal claim.

- Employers are also under certain duties in respect of those individuals whose mental health (whether or not impacted by work) amounts to a disability under the provisions of the Equality Act 2010.

Legislation

- Health and Safety at Work etc. Act 1974.
- Protection from Harassment Act 1997.
- Working Time Regulations 1998.
- Management of Health and Safety at Work Regulations 1999.
- Equality Act 2010.

Main cases

- *Sutherland (Chairman of the Governors of St Thomas Beckett RC High School) v. Hatton and others (2002).*
- *Barber v. Somerset County Council (2004).*
- *Essa v. Laing Ltd (2004).*
- *Nottinghamshire County Council v. Meikle (2004).*
- *Hartman v. South Essex Mental Health and Community Care NHS Trust and other cases (2005).*
- *Green v. DB Group Services Limited (2006).*
- *Hone v. Six Continents Retail Ltd (2006).*
- *Majrowski v. Guy's and St Thomas' NHS Trust (2006).*
- *Sayers v. Cambridgeshire County Council (2006).*
- *Intel Corporation (UK) Ltd v. Daw (2007).*
- *McAdie v. Royal Bank of Scotland plc (2007).*
- *Sunderland City Council v. Conn (2007).*
- *Dickens v. O2 PLC (2008).*
- *Cheltenham Borough Council v. Laird (2009).*
- *Veakins v. Kier Islington (2009).*
- *Thaine v. London School of Economics (2010).*

Health and safety legislation

The Health and Safety at Work etc. Act 1974 (HSWA 1974) places a duty on employers to ensure the health,

> **Case study**
>
> *Green v. DB Group Services (UK) Ltd* (2006).
>
> Ms G worked as a company secretary for a commercial bank. During the recruitment process she disclosed to her employer that she had previously been treated for depression. After commencing employment, G alleged that she was being harassed and bullied by a group of four colleagues. She complained to her manager and to the HR department, but no effective steps were taken to deal with her complaints. G subsequently experienced problems with another colleague, who she claimed was conducting a sustained campaign against her, which was designed to undermine and humiliate her. She again complained to her manager and the HR department, but no formal action was taken. Following a holiday, she found that she was unable to walk through the doors of the bank's offices and she was hospitalised with a major depressive disorder. She eventually returned to work for a short period but, following a relapse, she took another period of sick leave and was eventually dismissed.
>
> Her personal injury claim succeeded and she was awarded over £850,000 in damages. The High Court held that G's employer was vicariously liable for the harassment and bullying by G's fellow employees. The bank had failed to take adequate steps to protect her from what was regarded by the Court as a sustained campaign of bullying. The Court considered that a reasonable and responsible employer would have intervened as soon as they became aware of the problem and taken steps to stop the bullying. The defendant knew that the claimant had suffered depression in the past and was therefore more vulnerable than the population at large. The Court was also satisfied that the behaviour of the bank's employees amounted to harassment under the Protection from Harassment Act 1997, for which the defendant was also liable, although a separate award of damages for this was not made.

safety and welfare of their employees as far as is reasonably practicable. This includes taking steps to minimise the risk of stress-related illness or injury to employees. Under the Management of Health and Safety at Work Regulations 1999 employers are obliged to carry out an assessment of the risks to employees' health, including a suitable and sufficient risk assessment for stress. If, after completing an assessment, an employer believes there is a potential risk to employees' health, they should take all reasonable steps to limit this risk and to monitor the situation.

An employer's breach of the statutory duties imposed by the HSWA 1974 is a criminal offence, enforceable by the HSE but not directly actionable by individual employees. However, a breach of health and safety regulations may give rise to a civil liability for damages, where an employee can show that the employer's breach caused illness or injury to the employee. In addition, a failure by an employer to have due regard for the health and safety of its employees may amount to a fundamental breach of contract, entitling an employee to resign and bring a claim for constructive unfair dismissal.

Facts

- Around three in every ten employees will experience stress, depression or some other form of mental health issue in any one year.
- Stress is cited as the biggest cause of long-term sickness absence among non-manual employees, with mental ill health such as clinical depression and anxiety the third biggest cause.
- The top three causes of work-related stress are workload, management style and relationships at work.
- Data collected by GPs indicates that 30.9% of all diagnoses of work-related ill health are cases of mental ill health, with an average length of sickness absence per certified case of 26.8 working days.
- Estimates from the Labour Force Survey indicate that self-reported work-related stress, depression or anxiety accounted for 9.8 million lost working days in Britain in 2009/10, the highest figure across all illnesses and injuries. This amounts to an average absence of 22.6 days of absence for each person suffering from work-related stress.
- Two-thirds of employers (66%) are taking steps to identify and reduce stress, including staff surveys, stress risk assessments and training in stress management.
- The cost of sickness absence resulting from mental health problems that are directly work-related is estimated at £1.26bn a year.

Sources: HSE, CIPD, MIND 2005, Centre for Mental Health.

HSE Management Standards

To assist employers in fulfilling their duties in respect of carrying out risk assessments, and to measure performance in managing work-related stress, the HSE has devised its 'Management Standards'. These are a set of best practice statements of management competencies, to provide a framework for dealing with workplace stress and to help employers meet their legal obligations. It is widely recognised that managers, through their management style and their role as 'gatekeepers' of working conditions, have a significant impact on levels of employee stress, and therefore play a crucial role in identifying and resolving any problems, and preventing unacceptable levels of stress occurring.

The Management Standards are voluntary, but may be used as evidence by the HSE of an employer's failure to comply with their duty to manage stress under the HSWA.

The HSE, in conjunction with the CIPD and Investors in People, has also developed a 'Stress Management Competency Indicator Tool,' to allow managers to assess whether they currently have the behaviours identified as effective for preventing and reducing stress at work. The aim is to help managers reflect on their behaviour and management style. Further tools designed to assist managers and those who train and support them in that role are also being developed. The HSE website has further details.

Working Time Regulations

The Working Time Regulations 1998 implement the European Working Time Directive (93/104/EC), which was adopted by the EC as a health and safety measure and is consistently interpreted as such by the Courts and Employment Tribunals. Long working hours are a recognised contributory factor to the incidence of work-related stress, and an employer's breach of its obligations under the Regulations is actionable by the HSE and in some cases (in relation to rest and leave entitlements) directly enforceable by the individual worker in the Employment Tribunal.

Employers have a duty to take all reasonable steps to ensure that the limits contained in the Working Time Regulations are complied with. This includes a maximum 48 hour average working week (which the employee can voluntarily contract out of) and limits on night working. The Regulations also provide entitlements to daily and weekly rest breaks and paid annual leave, which the employer is under a duty to ensure workers can take but is not obliged to force workers to take.

A failure by an employer to take reasonable steps to comply with the maximum 48 hour average working week is a criminal offence, punishable by a potentially unlimited fine. The HSE is responsible for monitoring compliance and expects employers to maintain records going back at least two years to show that the 48 hour maximum has been complied with in respect of all employees who have not opted out. Employers should bear in mind that the maximum includes time the worker spends working for other employers.

The ability of workers to opt-out of the maximum 48 hour average working week has been the subject of lengthy debate at a European level, with proposals put forward for amendments to be made to the Working Time Directive, which would result in the opt-out being removed. These proposals have, for now, been rejected, and it remains to be seen whether further proposals will be put forward to amend the Directive. (See '*Working time,*' p.564.)

Common law duties

There is a duty implied into all contracts of employment that the employer will take reasonable care for the health and safety of its employees. If an employer breaches this duty and the employee has suffered psychiatric injury as a result, an employee may be entitled to bring a negligence claim against the employer (also known as a claim for personal injury). To do this, the employee must be able to demonstrate that his psychiatric injury was a *reasonably foreseeable* consequence of the employer's breach of duty. Much of the case law has dealt with the issue of whether an individual's psychiatric injury was reasonably foreseeable, as a consequence of bullying suffered by that individual and/or pressures of work.

Reasonable forseeability

Guidance on the issue of reasonable forseeability was given by the Court of Appeal in its landmark judgment in four conjoined stress cases – *Sutherland (Chairman of the Governors of St Thomas Beckett RC High School) v. Hatton and others* (2002). The main points of the guidance are as follows:

- The key question is whether this kind of harm (psychiatric injury) to this particular employee was reasonably foreseeable.
- Forseeability depends upon what the employer knows, or ought reasonably to know, about the individual employee. An employer is usually entitled to assume that an employee can withstand the usual pressures of

the job unless he knows of a particular problem or vulnerability.

- No occupation should be regarded as intrinsically dangerous to mental health.
- An employer is generally entitled to take what he is told by his employee at face value, unless he has a good reason to think to the contrary.
- To trigger a duty on the employer to take steps, the indications of impending harm to health arising from stress at work must be plain enough for any reasonable employer to realise that he should do something about it.
- The employer will only breach the duty of care if he has failed to take the steps that are reasonable in the circumstances, bearing in mind the magnitude of the risk of harm occurring, the gravity of the harm that may occur, the costs and practicability of preventing it, and the justifications for running the risk.
- The size, resources and scope of the employer's operation, and the need to treat other employees fairly, can all be taken into account when deciding what is reasonable.
- An employer can only reasonably be expected to take steps that are likely to do some good.
- An employer who offers a confidential advice service, with referral to appropriate counselling or treatment services, is unlikely to be found in breach of duty.
- If the only reasonable and effective step would have been to dismiss or demote the employee, the employer will not be in breach of duty in allowing a willing employee to continue in the job.

On appeal from the Court of Appeal's decision in *Sutherland v. Hatton* the House of Lords overturned one of the four cases, *Barber v. Somerset County Council* (2004) and in doing so emphasised that the guidelines set out by the Court of Appeal,

whilst 'useful practical guidance,' did not have statutory force.

The key point for employers in order to avoid the risk of a potential claim is to take such action as is reasonable to avoid exacerbating an employee's ill health, as soon as they become aware of any underlying vulnerability an individual may have to stress in the workplace. Possible remedial actions might include allowing the employee to take a sabbatical, redistributing work, extra training and counselling. What is reasonable for the employer to do will depend on factors such as the size of the employer, the resources available, and the impact on other employees.

Sutherland v. Hatton remains the leading case in the area of workplace stress, but subsequent decisions have taken a slightly different stance in relation to some of the guidance set out in that judgment.

Provision of counselling services

In the case of *Intel Corporation (UK) Ltd v. Daw* (2007) the Court of Appeal held that an employee's email to her manager stating that she was 'stressed out' and 'demoralised' and including two references to previous episodes of post-natal depression, was crucial to the issue of reasonable foreseeability. In the circumstances, urgent action should have been taken to reduce the employee's workload. The Court expressly rejected Intel Corporation's submission (following the guidelines in *Sutherland v. Hatton*) that its provision of a counselling and medical assistance service was sufficient to discharge its duty of care. The provision of such services and whether the employer has fulfilled its duty will depend on the facts of the case, and it is for the judge to decide in any particular case which parts of the *Sutherland v. Hatton* guidance are relevant.

This was confirmed by the Court of Appeal in *Dickens v. O2 PLC* (2008), in which the Court held that reference to the employer's counselling service was insufficient in the circumstances of the case. Having explained to her employer the difficulties she was experiencing and the severe effect on her health, the Court was satisfied that management intervention was required and the employee should have been sent home and referred to the employer's occupational health department.

Relevance of the Working Time Regulations

The claimant in *Hone v. Six Continents Retail Ltd* (2006), a pub landlord, claimed that he consistently worked around 90 hours per week, despite not opting out of the maximum 48 hour working week under the Working Time Regulations. He successfully used his employer's breach of the Regulations as part of his argument that his psychiatric injury had been reasonably foreseeable.

However, the High Court in *Sayers v. Cambridgeshire County Council* (2006) made it clear that the fact that an employee is working in excess of the 48 hour per week limit will not in itself render any resulting injury reasonably foreseeable.

Intrinsically stressful jobs

One of the conjoined cases in *Hartman v. South Essex Mental Health and Community Care NHS Trust and other cases* (2005) considered by the Court of Appeal was *Melville v. Home Office*. The employee in this case was a prison officer whose duties included the recovery of bodies of prisoners who had committed suicide. After helping to cut down a body and attempting revival in May 1998, Mr Melville developed a stress-related illness and eventually retired in 1999 on ill health grounds.

Before the Court of Appeal, the Home Office argued that since it knew of no particular vulnerability of Mr Melville it was entitled to assume that he was up to the normal pressures of the job. The Home Office was not successful in this argument and the Court of Appeal held that it was foreseeable that such an injury may have occurred to employees exposed to traumatic incidents. Home Office documents noted that persons whose duties involved dealing with suicides might sustain injuries to their health, and procedures were put in place in relation to post-incident care, which had not been properly implemented.

Discriminatory harassment

Discrimination legislation (since 1 October 2010, the Equality Act 2010) outlaws harassment on the grounds of sex, race, disability, sexual orientation, gender reassignment, religion or belief and age (the 'protected characteristics'). The harassment does not necessarily need to be directed towards the individual who brings a complaint, and the harassment can be based on an individual's perceived characteristic as well as their association with someone who has one of the protected characteristics. The legislation provides that an employer will be liable for workplace harassment based on one of the protected characteristics, carried out by his employees, unless he has taken reasonable steps to prevent this from occurring. Reasonable steps might include, for example, implementing an equal opportunities and anti-bullying policy, and training managers in dealing with complaints of bullying and harassment.

The Equality Act 2010 introduced a harmonised definition of harassment and extends the protection for employees from harassment carried out by third parties. Employers can potentially be liable for the harassment of employees by a third party, if it is aware that such harassment has occurred on two or more occasions and it has not taken reasonably practicable steps to prevent it. *Note: the Government is intending to consult over the removal of the 'unworkable' third party harassment provisions.*

In the case of *Essa v. Laing Ltd* (2004) the Court of Appeal confirmed that personal injury, which includes psychiatric injury, arising from acts of discrimination does not need to be reasonably foreseeable in order for employees to recover damages. The employee only needs to prove that the discrimination caused the injury to occur. In appropriate cases, an Employment Tribunal will discount the award of compensation paid to a claimant where their psychiatric ill health has been caused by a combination of factors, not all of which are the employer's responsibility (see, for example, *Thaine v. London School of Economics* (2010)).

Protection from harassment

The House of Lords confirmed in the case of *Majrowski v. Guy's and St Thomas' NHS Trust* (2006) that employers can be held liable for workplace bullying under the Protection from Harassment Act 1997 (PHA). For this to apply, claimants only need to show they have suffered anxiety or distress as a result of the harassment, rather than a recognisable psychiatric injury in order to bring a negligence claim. It is necessary for claimants to establish a 'course of conduct,' in contrast to a one-off incident of harassment, which can be sufficient to bring a claim under discrimination legislation.

In a subsequent case, *Green v. DB Group Services Limited* (2006), the High Court upheld another claim for workplace bullying under the PHA 1997, but made no separate award of damages, since it had

taken into account the anxiety caused by the harassment in assessing the amount of compensation awarded in respect of the employer's negligence (a figure of over £850,000 – see *Case study*).

More recently, in *Sunderland City Council v. Conn* (2007), the Court of Appeal overturned a County Court decision that a manager's conduct towards an employee amounted to harassment under the PHA 1997. There were only two alleged incidents, the first of which did not 'cross the boundary from the regrettable to the unacceptable' and was not sufficiently serious to be regarded as criminal. There had therefore been no 'course of conduct' necessary to establish a claim under the Act.

In *Veakins v. Kier Islington Ltd* (2009), however, the Court of Appeal concluded that the primary focus should be on whether the conduct is oppressive and unacceptable, as opposed to merely unattractive, unreasonable or regrettable. The County Court in this case had erroneously focused too heavily on whether the conduct would sustain criminal liability. In its judgment, the Court of Appeal observed that since the case of *Sutherland v. Hatton*, it has become harder for employees to succeed in a negligence action based on stress at work and therefore claims under the 1997 Act are more prevalent. However, the Court noted that whilst there is nothing in the language of the Act that excludes workplace harassment, it should not be thought 'from this unusually one-sided case' (*Veakins*) that stress at work will often give rise to liability for harassment. In the great majority of cases, according to the Court of Appeal, the remedy for high-handed or discriminatory misconduct by or on behalf of an employer will be more fittingly in the Employment Tribunal.

Unfair dismissal

Ill health is a potentially fair reason for dismissing an employee, as it relates to their capability to do a job.

In the case of *McAdie v. Royal Bank of Scotland plc* (2007) the employee's stress-related illness was attributed to the conduct of the employer. However, the Court of Appeal agreed with the EAT that the employer could still fairly dismiss the employee for ill health capability in these circumstances. Medical evidence demonstrated that the employee had no prospect of recovery from the illness and she had expressly stated that she would never return to work. There was no real alternative to dismissal.

However, the Court of Appeal accepted that the cause of the employee's incapacity was a relevant factor to take into account and approved of the Employment Appeal Tribunal's suggestion that employers should 'go the extra mile' in finding alternative employment for an employee who is incapacitated by the employer's own conduct, or they should put up with a longer period of absence than they would do in normal circumstances.

Disability discrimination

If an employer is considering dismissing an employee who is suffering from a mental illness they must consider whether the illness may constitute a disability under the Equality Act 2010 (previously the Disability Discrimination Act 1995). The Equality Act protects those with physical or mental impairments from discrimination, provided that impairment satisfies the test for a disability under the Act. Stress itself is not an illness, but a stress-related condition could be an impairment within the meaning of the Act.

Employers are under a duty to make reasonable adjustments where any arrangements made by the employer place a disabled person at a substantial disadvantage compared to non-disabled employees. Where an employee is suffering from a mental impairment, reasonable adjustments might include a phased return to work after sickness absence, a reallocation of duties, reduced working hours, mentoring or counselling.

Disabled employees are not generally entitled to additional sick pay, unless the employer has caused sickness absence to be prolonged as a result of its failure to make reasonable adjustments. This was the case in *Nottinghamshire County Council v. Meikle* (2004), which was not a case dealing with an employee's mental health but could be applied equally to those with stress-related illness whose employer does not take the necessary steps to enable the individual to return to work.

If an employer dismisses an employee for a reason related to their disability they may be guilty of disability discrimination unless they are able to show that the dismissal was justified. A medical report should be obtained in order to establish the employee's likely prognosis and the effectiveness of any potential adjustments before any decision is taken to terminate an individual's employment.

Pre-employment checks

In view of the potential liabilities faced by employers in relation to employees suffering from mental health problems, it might appear prudent to carry out pre-employment checks to establish whether an individual has any pre-disposition to such impairments. This should be done with caution, since a refusal to employ individuals with previous mental health issues is likely to result in successful claims for disability discrimination.

Even greater caution is required following the implementation of the main employment provisions of the Equality Act 2010 on 1 October 2010. Section 60 of the Act restricts the ability for employers to ask questions about an individual's health before an offer of employment is made. Any such questions are permitted for very limited purposes only, including to establish whether any adjustments are required to the recruitment process itself, and in order to ascertain whether the individual can carry out tasks 'intrinsic to the work concerned'. The extent to which health-related questions are permitted has not yet been subject to judicial scrutiny, and case law is awaited to clarify the exemptions.

Questions that do not fall within the permitted exemptions may lead to a presumption of discrimination if a disabled candidate is refused the job. Section 60 does permit health-related enquiries to be made after a job offer has been made, and the offer can be made conditional on satisfactory responses to those enquiries. However, employers should remember that they will be subject to a duty to make reasonable adjustments in respect of any prospective disabled employee, and a decision taken to withdraw a job offer on these grounds runs a high risk of being challenged as discriminatory by the individual.

This provision in the Act relating to pre-employment medical questions is intended to assist disabled people to overcome the well-documented prejudice of some employers towards recruiting those with disabilities, particularly those with a history of mental health issues. In any event, the use of such questionnaires has not always been effective in practice, as demonstrated by the case of *Cheltenham Borough Council v. Laird* (2009) in which the former managing director of the Council had been granted ill health retirement following a depressive illness. The Council subsequently brought proceedings for negligent and fraudulent misrepresentation against Mrs Laird, on the grounds that she had not disclosed her previous episodes of stress-related depression on her pre-employment medical questionnaire. The High Court rejected the Council's claims, on the basis that the answers provided by Mrs Laird had not been false or misleading. The questionnaire was poorly drafted and the wording did not expressly require Mrs Laird to disclose information about her previous history of stress and depression.

NICE guidance

In November 2009, the National Institute for Health and Clinical Excellence (NICE) issued new guidance for employers on promoting mental wellbeing at work. The guidance was developed in recognition of the importance of work in promoting mental wellbeing and is intended to assist employers to meet their legal duties to protect the health of employees. It also recognises that the current financial climate has the potential to increase mental health problems in employees because of worries about job insecurity and unemployment.

The guidance attempts to reduce the number of working days lost due to work-related mental health conditions, including stress, depression and anxiety. It makes a number of recommendations designed to improve the management of mental health in the workplace, including the prevention and early identification of problems. The recommendations, aimed at organisations of all sizes, include the following:

■ Ensure systems are in place for assessing and monitoring the mental wellbeing of employees so that areas for improvement can be identified and risks caused by work and working conditions addressed. This could include employee attitude surveys and information about absence rates, staff turnover and investment in training and development, and providing feedback and open communication.

- If reasonably practical, provide employees with opportunities for flexible working according to their needs and aspirations in both their personal and working lives.
- Strengthen the role of line managers in promoting the mental wellbeing of employees through supportive leadership style and management.

The NICE guidance also states that the HSE Management Standards (*see above*) may provide a valuable tool in implementing the guidance.

Conclusion

To protect themselves, employers should consider the following practical steps:

- Organise and conduct suitable risk assessments of potential stressors.
- Make counselling facilities available.
- Show a receptive and flexible response to complaints.
- Follow the HSE Management Standards and NICE Guidance.

- Be cautious in asking questions about health before making an offer of employment and remember the duty to make reasonable adjustments to prospective employees.
- Provide a written health and safety policy to employees, which includes a section on how to deal with stress.
- Put a bullying and harassment policy in place and ensure employees are aware of their obligations.
- Provide training to managers in dealing with employees suffering from stress and mental health issues, including the requirement to consider reasonable adjustments.
- Ensure sickness absence procedures take into account potential disabilities arising from mental impairments.
- Obtain an up-to-date medical report before considering dismissing an employee with a mental impairment.

See also: Bullying and harassment, p.58; Discrimination, p.126; Equality Act, p.191; Medical records, p.304; Occupational health, p.374; Stress, p.500; Working time, p.564.

Sources of further information

HSE (work-related stress): www.hse.gov.uk/stress

MIND: www.mind.org.uk

Mental health foundation: www.mentalhealth.org.uk

The Shaw Trust: www.tacklementalhealth.org.uk

Centre for Mental Health (formerly the Sainsbury Centre for Mental Health): www.centreformentalhealth.org.uk

NICE: www.nice.org.uk

Migrant and foreign workers

Aliya Khan and Mark Phillips, Tyndallwoods Solicitors

Key points

- It is a criminal offence to employ someone who does not have permission to live and work in the UK.
- A statutory defence is available if employers inspect, take copies of, and keep a record of certain documents.
- Employers must apply for a work permit for employees, if one is needed.
- Employers must not discriminate when recruiting Foreign Nationals.
- Employers must ensure the health and safety of Foreign Nationals.

Legislation

- Immigration Act 1971.
- Asylum and Immigration Act 1996.
- Immigration and Asylum Act 1999.
- Nationality and Immigration Asylum Act 2002.
- Immigration (Restrictions on Employment) Order 2004.
- Immigration, Asylum and Nationality Act 2006.
- UK Borders Act 2007.

General principles

Employers may offer employment to Commonwealth Citizens and Foreign Nationals without a permanent right of residence ('indefinite leave to enter or remain') as if they were a British Citizen if they are:

- a Commonwealth Citizen in the UK as a working holiday-maker (a two-year visa given for Commonwealth Citizens between the ages of 17 and 30);
- a Commonwealth Citizen or Foreign National (excluding EEA Nationals) who have been granted permission to enter or remain in the UK on the basis of marriage (two-year visa or extension);
- an EEA National (including what used to be known as 'A8' Nationals;

- a student who can take employment up to a certain amount of hours a week in term-time or full-time during holidays;
- those granted two years leave to remain under Tier 1 (Post-Study Work);
- in possession of an Immigration Employment Document (IED) from Work Permits (UK), a specialist division of the Immigration and Nationality Directorate (part of the Home Office), which may be given to the individual under Tier 1 or to the company for a specific employee;
- granted permission under Tier 2 to work with a company that has issued them with a Sponsorship Certificate; or
- asylum seekers (those waiting for a decision on their claim to refugee status) with an Application Registration Card endorsed 'Employment Permitted'.

Passports are not generally endorsed with 'Permission to Work'. It is the absence of a 'prohibition on employment' that demonstrates that a person has permission to work. Students have a 'restriction' on employment endorsed on their passports; in other words limited to 20 hours a week during term-time. This may be endorsed

Facts

- In total, around 3.6 million people of working age in Britain were born outside the UK.
- Regionally, London and the South East are host to the largest numbers of migrant workers. In 2000, London was home to 47% of migrant workers (520,000), and the rest of the South East had a further 20% of all migrant workers in the UK. More than two-thirds of Foreign National workers were in this corner of England (compared with only 42% of British workers).
- There were 1.5 million foreign migrants working in the UK in 2005 – 5.4% of the UK employed population.
- A CIPD labour market outlook report showed that few employers hire migrants mainly due to lower wage costs, but that this objective was more important for employers hiring less skilled (9%) than skilled (2%) migrants.
- In the first 80 days of the new migrant workers regime, 137 businesses were issued with notices of potential liability worth almost half a million pounds in fines – contrasted with only 11 successful (criminal) prosecutions in 2008.

on their Biometrics Card. Permission to work is not the same as permission to live in the UK. An employer who obtains a Sponsorship Licence (*see below*) for an employee must also ensure that the individual obtains permission to enter (by obtaining a visa) or remain in the UK (by an application for variation of leave). This is a process of application that the individual must go through before their employment commences.

Someone who has permission to work can continue in their employment (or take alternative employment) whilst waiting for a decision on their application for an extension of stay, providing they applied to extend their leave before their last extension expired. Home Office acknowledgement letters sent in response to extension applications contain the standard wording:

'Provided an Applicant has permission to be in the UK when an application is made, he or she is legally entitled to remain here on the same conditions previously granted until the application has been decided.'

Responsibilities under the Asylum and Immigration Act 1996, the Immigration, Asylum and Nationality Act 2006 and the UK Borders Act 2007

Section 8 of the Asylum and Immigration Act 1996 (the Act) makes it a criminal offence to employ someone who is not entitled to live and work in the UK. Employers and individual managers can face fines of up to £10,000 per employee.

The Act provides a defence if, before the employment commences, the employer checks (Step one), copies (Step two) and retains (Step three) copies of specified documents.

Step one – requesting documents

- Before employment commences, employers must require prospective employees to produce originals of documents from lists drawn up by the Home Office, full details of which can be found on the Home Office Website (see *Sources of further information*).
- To avoid committing the criminal offence, employers should refuse to employ an applicant if the

relevant document or combination of documents cannot be produced.

Step two – checking documents

- Check all details and photos are consistent with the applicant's details and appearance (for example age, gender, race) and that the documents are in date.
- The UK Border Agency (UKBA) advises that if there are any inconsistencies between the documents, the reason for the difference must be proved by documents showing a valid reason.

Step three – record keeping

- Copy the front page and all pages showing any of the employee's details, including photos and signatures.
- Copy pages with an immigration endorsement or stamp.
- The employer must retain the copies.
- If the copies cannot be produced, the defence will not be available.

The defence is not available if the employer knows that the employee is not entitled to live and/or work in the UK – even if they have checked the documents.

Note: These changes apply to employees taken on after 30 April 2004, not for those already in employment at that date. An employer who curtails the employment of Commonwealth Citizens or Foreign Nationals after 1 May 2004 for failure to produce documents specified in the Home Office lists may be liable to a claim for unfair dismissal. Other requirements were in force for employees who were taken on before 1 May 2004.

Compliance

In their employment practices and procedures, employers must avoid discrimination on prohibited grounds, but must also avoid offering or continuing employment to people who are not,

for immigration reasons, permitted to take it. The primary Government tools for prevention of illegal working are the imposition of civil penalties, up to £10,000 per illegal worker, and prosecution of the employer, with fines, forfeiture of cash found, and on indictment up to two years' imprisonment.

In general terms, citizens of the EU have unrestricted access to the labour market; migrants sponsored within the UKBA's Points Based System (PBS) work only for the licensed sponsor; highly skilled migrants within Tier 1 (Post-Study Work) or (General) may work for any employer, as may Foreign Nationals with indefinite leave to remain, or whose limited duration residence permits do not prohibit employment.

Determining whether a Foreign National is entitled to take the particular employment may not be straightforward, even when the passport is carefully examined. It is essential to make the assessment of entitlement to take the employment *before* employment commences.

Where the employment is permitted, it may, for example with students, be limited to 20 hours per week in term-time, or limited to the unexpired duration of a visa or certificate of sponsorship.

The UKBA consequently provides an employers' telephone helpline on 0845 010 677 and assistance with online document verification at www.bia.homeoffice.gov.uk/employingmigrants.

Key documents to establish the right to work must be originals; copies should be retained throughout the employment and for at least two years after it ends. The employment should be monitored to ensure that its terms, conditions and duration coincide with the right to work.

Key documents:

- Passport or EEA Identity Card.
- UKBA Residence Card.
- UK Birth, Adoption, Naturalisation or Registration Certificate.
- UKBA Immigration Status Document or Application Registration Card.
- P45, P60 or National Insurance Card.
- Letter issued by UKBA permitting the employment.

It is essential to consider the comprehensive UKBA guidance on prevention of initial working, which can be downloaded from its website.

Particular categories

Visitors

Visitors to the UK are prohibited from taking employment. Business visitors, including academics, religious workers, sports people and consultants, can undertake only types of activity that are specifically permitted by the Immigration Rules and UKBA Guidance.

Students

Students studying under Tier 4 (General) on a course at NQF 6/QCF 6/SCQF9 or above with a sponsor that is a UK Higher Education Institution or who are studying for a degree are allowed to work up to 20 hours during term-time. The 20 hours per term-time week limitation on student employment applies to PhD students until any application to vary leave (for example into Tier 1 (Post-Study Work)) into a category permitting full-time work is determined by UKBA.

Other students with permission to work include those on a work placement as part of their course, postgraduate doctors and dentists on a recognised Foundation Programme, and a student union sabbatical officer for up to two years.

A student studying a course at NQF 3, 4 or 5/QCF 3, 4 or 5/SCQF 6, 7 or 8 with a sponsor that is a UK Higher Education Institution is only allowed to work ten hours per week.

All students may work full-time whilst on vacation.

A8 Nationals

EEA citizens and any non-EEA dependants are generally entitled to work. What used to be known as A8 Nationals (Czech Republic, Estonia, Latvia, Lithuania, Hungary, Poland, Slovenia and Slovakia) are no longer restricted on taking employment, and have the same entitlements as EEA Nationals.

A2 Nationals

A2 Nationals (Bulgaria and Romania) are freely entitled to undertake self-employment, but their access to the labour market continues to be limited so that they require explicit permission to work within the residual Work Permit Scheme, unless the terms of their Visa / Residence Permit (for example, as a dependant of a person settled in the UK) implicitly allow them to take employment.

Migrants with 'temporary admission'

Migrants with 'temporary admission,' which, confusingly, is not a form of leave to enter or a Residence Permit, will generally have a pending immigration or asylum application. They are usually not permitted to work. In some cases they are permitted, and should have documentation to prove it. Although the online Employer Check-In Service may be helpful, their advice cannot be regarded as authoritative. Such migrants and other Foreign Nationals with pending immigration applications may be unable to produce original documents, as those documents will be in the Home Office with the applications. In such cases, originals may be unavailable for very extensive periods. Original correspondence from the UKBA may then be required to authorise the employment. This may be very slow to arrive.

Extending permission to remain in the UK other than via the Points Based System (PBS)

Nationals of EEA countries

Nationals of EEA countries (except in A2 and Switzerland), may, but are not required to, obtain Residence Cards. Such cards are initially valid for five years. Any non-EEA dependants should be admitted to the UK with family permits endorsed in their passports. Applications for removal of time limits must be supported by original documents. In the case of EEA Nationals, applications may well take over six months to resolve. In the case of non-EEA dependants, the delay may be much greater. Their right to remain in the UK at the date of their in-time application continues by operation of law, until the UKBA decision is received.

It is the *employer's duty* to ensure that they prevent illegal working, but it is the *migrant's obligation* to ensure that their permission to remain in the UK is valid and that they do not conduct themselves so as to breach the terms of such permission. Any such breach could be enforced by curtailment to their leave and/or administrative removal from the UK. Such removal could lead to a mandatory refusal of subsequent application for visa.

Where a migrant has time-limited permission to remain in the UK and/or where their permission is for a purpose now superseded, they must ensure that their application to vary the terms of the permission, or to remove conditions, is received by the Secretary of State before expiry of their valid permission. An application must be on the currently

applicable form, with the appropriate fee, and supported by all relevant documents. Great care must be taken to meet all of these requirements. All the pre-existing terms and conditions of the most recent permission will continue until the application is finally determined. If the application should fail, whether only because an out-of-date form was inadvertently used, or fee payment fails through a dishonoured cheque or refused credit card payment, then the migrant with dependants who lack independent rights to remain, may well have to leave the UK.

Expiry of work permits

If an employee's work permit or visa is due to expire, the employer should apply under the Points Based System for a Sponsorship Licence before the expiry of the old work permit, and the employee should apply for further leave to remain before their current leave expires. This enables an employee to live and work in the UK until a decision is reached by the Home Office – even if in the meantime their permit and/or visa expires.

Changes to the system

Significant changes have taken place in managed migration. Employers are now required to register as sponsors, prove qualifications, and take active responsibility for employees.

Limiting migrants

On 19 July 2010 the UK Border Agency introduced an interim limit to those who will be admitted under Tier 1 (General) and Tier 2 (General). The aim is to limit and achieve an overall reduction of 5% of the number of applicants. From 6 April 2011 to 5 April 2012, the total number of Certificates of Sponsorship (CoS) under Tier 2 (General) for *new* hires earning under £150,000 per year coming to start work from overseas is 20,700. These are known as 'Restricted' jobs. Restricted and Unrestricted jobs are discussed below.

The Points Based System

The UK Border Agency has rolled out the new Points Based System (PBS). The System is based on an 'Australian style' points system where an applicant wishing to work and reside in the UK will be required to obtain the necessary points before being granted permission to do so. The Points System is broken down into the following Tiers:

- *Tier 1* – Highly Skilled Migrants (previously HSMP) – leads to settlement.
- *Tier 2* – Skilled Workers requiring a Sponsorship Licence (previously work permits).
- *Tier 3* – Low Skilled Workers – currently suspended until further notice.
- *Tier 4* – Students with 20 hours' permission to work term-time and full-time permission to work during holidays.
- *Tier 5* – Sponsorship Licence required – temporary leave.

The Scheme combines more than 80 previous work and study routes to the UK into five tiers. Points are awarded according to workers' skills, experience and age and also the demand for those skills in the UK. This allows the UK to respond flexibly to changes in the labour market.

The Immigration rules under Part Six set out the requirements to apply under the Points Based System. Each Tier then has special guidance which is published by the UK Border Agency.

Who should apply?

An applicant does not have to apply under the Points Based System if:

- they are an EEA or Swiss National;
- they are a British overseas territories citizen, unless they are from one of the sovereign base areas in Cyprus;
- they are a Commonwealth citizen with permission to enter or stay in the UK because at least one of their grandparents was born here;
- their spouse or civil partner, unmarried or same-sex partner, or (if the applicant is under 18) one of their parents has permission to stay in the UK under Tier 1 (General) – highly skilled worker of the PBS; or
- they have no conditions or time limit attached to their stay.

Ways of applying

- Entering the UK in a Highly Skilled sub-category.
- Extending a stay in the UK in a Highly Skilled sub-category.
- Switching while in the UK into or out of a Highly Skilled sub-category.

Tier 1 – Highly skilled individuals

Applicants in the Highly Skilled tier will *not* be required to have sponsors. This will make it easy for employers to take on such migrants, without having to issue certificates of sponsorship. The Highly Skilled tier embraces the following categories.

Points

Highly Skilled applicants will need to show that they have enough points to qualify to enter or remain in the UK.

An applicant must score at least:

- 75 points for his/her attributes (age, qualifications, previous earnings and experience in the UK) if they are applying from inside the UK and were last granted leave in Tier 1 (General) Writer, Composer or Artist or as a self-employed lawyer. Set out in Appendix A of the Immigration Rules;
- 80 points from attributes if applying from outside the UK or applying from inside the UK to switch from any other category (Appendix A);

- Ten points for English Language (Appendix B of the Immigration rules); and
- Ten points for maintenance (funds) (Appendix C of the Immigration rules).

If the applicant does not score a minimum of 75/80 points for his/her attributes and ten points for English language and ten points for available maintenance (funds), the application will be refused.

Points will be earned against three seats of objective criteria:

1. Criteria specific to each sub-category.
2. Competence in English language.
3. Maintenance. Migrants must be able to support themselves and their dependants.

The test will be based upon the latest cost of living figures provided in the annual British Council publication, 'Studying and Living in the United Kingdom'.

Maintenance
As with the whole of the Points Based System, the main applicant requires £800 in their bank account for three months, if they are applying from the UK. If the main applicant is applying from abroad then they will require £2,800. If the main applicant is applying from abroad or has been in the UK for fewer than 12 months, they require £1,600 per dependant for three months. However, if the main applicant has been in the UK for 12 months or more, each dependant will require £533 for three months.

Tier 1 (General)
For migrants who qualify for highly skilled employment in the UK. From 23 December 2010, this route closed to overseas applicants.

Applicants who were last granted as a Highly Skilled Migrant, Self-Employed

Lawyer, Writer, Composer or Artist or as a Tier 1 (General) may switch / extend their leave in this category.

Migrants under the rules before 19 July 2010, who have not been granted leave in any category in place since 19 July 2010, must score 75 points. All other migrants must score 80 points.

Those who fall under HSMP ILR Judicial Review Policy Document are not required to score any points.

Points are earned in the following categories:

- Qualifications (Bachelors, Masters or PhD);
- Previous earnings (the 12 consecutive months before the application or 15 months if the applicant was a student);
- UK experience; and
- Age of the applicant at the date of application for the first grant.

Where the migrant was granted leave before 6 April 2010 and has not been granted leave in any other category other than a Highly Skilled Migrant, Self-Employed Lawyer, Writer, Composer or Artist or as a Tier 1 (General) since 6 April 2010, they require 75 points.

No points will be awarded for a Bachelor's degree if:

- the last grant of leave to remain or entry clearance was as a Tier 1 (General) during 31 March 2009 to 5 April 2010; and
- the previous leave to remain or entry clearance before that leave was not as a Highly Skilled Migrant, Self-Employed Lawyer, Writer, Composer or Artist or as a Tier 1 (General).

Others will be granted 30 points for a Bachelors Degree, 35 points for a

Masters, and 50 points for a PhD. Points for previous earnings vary from five points for earnings between £16,000 and £17,999.99, to 45 points for previous earnings of £40,000 or more.

Five points can be earned for UK experience if £16,000 or more of the previous earnings were earned in the UK. Age at the date of application varies from five points (30 or 31 years of age), ten points (28 or 29 years of age) and 20 points (under 28 years of age).

As with all Points Based System applications, the applicant will require ten points for English Language and ten points for maintenance.

Those who require 80 points can earn them as follows:

- 30 points for Bachelors Degree, 35 points for a Masters and 45 points for a PhD.
- Previous earnings range from five points for £25,000 to £29,999.99 to 80 points for those who earned £150,000 or more.
- UK experience attracts five points if £25,000 or more of the previous earnings were earned in the UK.

Points are earned for age between five points for those who are 35 to 39 years old, ten points for those aged between 30 and 34 and 20 points for those under 20 years old.

Tier 1 (Entrepreneur)

A Migrant making an initial application from abroad or switching into this category from a different category must obtain 75 points.

25 points:

- The Migrant must have access to not less than £200,000 of his/her own money. The money can be

shared by an entrepreneurial team of up to two people. Each member of the team may come to the UK as a Tier 1 (Entrepreneur) using the same funds. If the same funds are being relied upon neither one of the applicants must have been previously granted a visa under Tier 1 (Entrepreneur) on the basis of investment and/or business linked in a way other than with each other. Third party contributors who are not applying as Tier 1 (Entrepreneurs) must provide a declaration that the money is available to the applicant or the business with confirmation from a legal representative that the declaration is a valid document. A husband, wife or partner will be regarded as a third party. A third member of an Entrepreneurial team will be considered a third party.

or

- Access to not less than £50,000 from:
  - One or more registered venture capital firms regulated by the Financial Services Authority.
  - One of more UK entrepreneurial seed funding competitions that is listed as endorsed on the UK Trade and Investment website.
  - Entrepreneurs may not mix their own funds with the funding from the venture capital firm/s. If they wish to mix funds then the entrepreneur needs to have no less than £200,000 to invest.

or

- Funding from one or more UK Government Departments, and made available by the Department(s) for the specific purpose of establishing or expanding a UK business. This is where the UK Government Department is providing all or some of the funds.

Evidence of the funding with each body must be provided, together with evidence of the money being available.

25 points:

- The money is held in one or more regulated financial institutions.
- The institution should be regulated by an official regulatory body in the country where the financial institution operates and where the money is held. If the money is located in the UK, then the institution must be regulated by the Financial Services Authority (FSA).

25 points:

- The money is disposable in the UK. The money can be abroad but all of the funds must be freely transferable to the UK and converted into pounds sterling.
- The UKBA will consider if an institution already does business in the UK, if the money is held abroad but in an institution that has a presence in the UK and is regulated by the FSA. In this circumstance, no further evidence will be required to prove the money can be transferred.
- If the money is held abroad by an institution that is not regulated by the FSA, confirmation must be provided that the money can be transferred to the UK.

Ten points:

- The applicant can speak the English Language to the standard required.

Ten points:

- The applicant has the specified amount of funds to support themselves in the UK.

MfB can advise further on the documents that are required and the contents of those documents, including requirements of audited / un-audited accounts and Director's loans.

Applications to extend permission to stay
75 points must be obtained.

20 points:

- The applicant must have invested not less than £200,000 (or £50,000 if, in his/her last grant of leave points were awarded in this category) in cash directly into one or more businesses in the UK.

20 points:

The applicant has:

- registered with HMRC as self-employed;
- registered a new business in which he is a director; or
- registered as a director of an existing business.

The above requirements must have been met if the applicant was last given leave or entry as a Tier 1 (Entrepreneur) within six months of the specified date, which is:

- the date of entry into the UK as a Tier 1 (Entrepreneur) where the Applicant can prove the date they entered;
- the date the visa was granted as a Tier 1 (Entrepreneur) where the Applicant cannot prove when they entered the UK; or
- the date of the grant of leave to remain (for those who switched into this category).

15 points:

- The applicant is engaged in business activity at the time of his/her application. An applicant does not have to remain in the same business as they entered or as self-employed. The applicant may become a director of the business.

20 points:

- The applicant has established a new business or taken over or invested in an existing business creating two new full-time jobs for a person who is settled in the UK.

Ten points:

- Evidence that the applicant can speak English Language to the required standard.

Ten points:

- The applicant has the specified amount of maintenance to support the applicant in the UK.

Tier 1 (Investor)

To apply as a T1 (Investor) a Migrant should either have £1m of their own money or have a loan from the bank for the full £1m and have a personal net value of at least £2m.

Applicants may not mix personal funds and borrowed funds in order to meet the total £1m investment required.

If the money is being borrowed from the bank, the applicant will need to show that their personal net value is worth at least £2m. This is known as Personal Net Worth (PNW). To prove this, an applicant will need to provide a letter from a bank that is a UK regulated financial institution. The letter from the bank must state the following:

- The migrant has not less than £1m for them to borrow; and
- The money is available to the migrant on the date of their letter; and

- The bank is regulated by a UK regulated financial institution; and
- The migrant's personal net worth is at least £2m; and
- The bank will confirm the content of their letter with the UKBA if requested to do so.

Funds must be available, and funds tied up in property will not be accepted unless converted into actual cash in the bank.

To calculate the PNW the bank should consider assets and liabilities. Assets (personal cash, investments and property) will be offset against personal debts (mortgages and loans).

There is no need to satisfy the English Language requirement because while a Tier 1 (Investor) may choose to work in the UK, they do not need to work and therefore do not need to satisfy the English Language requirement.

The period of permission to stay varies for those investing £10m in the UK or £5m or £1m. However, if you invest £1m then the period is five years.

Extension applications and indefinite leave to remain applications

It is a requirement that, after the five years, an applicant has:

- under their control not less than £1m (actual money), in the UK; or
- owns personal assets (minus any liabilities) of not less than £2m; or
- £1m in their control, disposable in the UK, which has not been loaned by a UK financial institute; and
- invested not less than 75% in the UK by way of UK Government bonds, share capital or loan capital in active and trading UK registered companies (excluding off shore companies or trusts, open ended investment companies, companies mainly

engaged in property investment, property management or property development, deposits with banks, ISAs premium bonds and saving certificates and leveraged investment funds) and has invested the remainder balance of the specified invested amount (£1m, £5m or £10m) in the UK by the purchase of assets or by maintaining the money on deposit at HSBC or any other UK regulated financial institution.

An applicant must have spent a specified continuous lawful period in the UK with absence from the UK for no more than 180 days in any 12 calendar months during their leave to remain.

The specified continuous lawful period if you score points varies from three years to five years.

The applicant must have maintained the full specified invested amount (£1m, £5m or £10m) throughout the relevant period (three to five years, except for the first three months).

Tier 1 (Post-study work)

This category aims to retain the most able international graduates who have studied in the UK. Post-study workers are granted a three-year visa if applying from abroad and two years' leave to remain if applying from inside the UK.

Note: Time spent under this category will not count towards settlement. Therefore, post-study workers must switch category either into Tier 1 (General) or under Tier 2 (Sponsorship).

This route is to close in 2012.

Dependants

Successful applicants will be able to bring dependants (children aged under 18, spouses, civil partners, same-sex partners and unmarried partners) into the UK if they can prove that they maintain them.

Challenges to decisions

There are full appeal rights for in-country refusals, though this will be limited with regard to the points-based element. An Appellant cannot submit new evidence. Therefore it is essential to ensure the application is correct first time. Documentary evidence will be rigorously checked. No points will be awarded if there are reasonable grounds to doubt that the evidence is genuine.

There is no substantive right of appeal against refusal of a visa under the PBS.

Tier 2 – Skilled workers

There are four routes within Tier 2:

1. Tier 2 (General).
2. Intra-company transfer.
3. Minister of Religion.
4. Sports people.

In this chapter we will deal with Tier 2 (General) and touch upon Intra-Company Transfers as they are the most common routes.

The main aim of Tier 2 is to enable the UK employer to recruit from outside the European Economic Area (EEA) in jobs that cannot be filled by EEA workers. There must be a genuine vacancy.

The applicant will require 70 points made up of ten points for English Language proficiency, ten points for sufficient maintenance and 50 points for the Sponsorship Licence.

All Tier 2 applicants will require entry clearance or be able to switch into this category. Entry clearance applicants will need to obtain a biometric identity card so the UK Border Agency (UKBA) knows exactly who they are and what they are entitled to do.

As with other PBS Tiers, the employee will need to obtain enough points to qualify.

To employ a migrant worker under Tier 2, employers will be required to obtain a Sponsorship Licence. The UK Border Agency (UKBA) states that there are two fundamental principles as to why it introduced a requirement to obtain a Sponsorship Licence:

1. Employers and education providers who benefit the most from a migrant worker or student should play a part in ensuring the system is not abused.
2. A sponsorship licence ensures that migrant workers are eligible to work and that a reputable employer or education provider genuinely wishes to take them on.

Before a migrant worker can apply under Tier 2, s/he must ensure s/he has a sponsor. The Sponsor is the employer or, as with Tier 4, the education provider. The employer must apply for a Sponsorship Licence online using the UK Border Agency's website and a system called the Sponsorship Management System. The employer will then play two main roles in the migrant's application process:

1. The employer will provide evidence that the migrant is filling a genuine vacancy that cannot be filled by a suitably qualified or skilled, settled worker (someone who already has permission to stay and work in the UK).
2. Pledging that as the employer they accept the duties expected from them.

The sponsor / employer

The Sponsorship Licence itself is worth 50 points. To be granted a licence the employer should apply online,

demonstrating that the job is in the Shortage Occupation List, or the job satisfies the Resident Labour Market Test (RLMT) (that no qualified person can be found from inside the EEA to fill the position), or that the employee would be an intra-company transfer (i.e. is already working with the company in a sister company abroad).

Applying for a licence

To obtain a licence, the employer applies to the UKBA online. Guidance has been published to assist an employer with what documents the UKBA requires. The documents are set out in a separate guidance called Appendix A. Appendix A lists the documents required for the licence. Most applications must be supported by a minimum of four documents from the list. The documents are split into List A, List B and C. List A lists all the mandatory documents (documents that must be provided) for all employers. List B is mandatory for certain types of business or sectors and List C documents are those that can be provided in addition to the mandatory documents but cannot replace the mandatory documents.

Note: The UKBA will not accept a Companies House certificate as one of the four documents required as this document is not listed in Appendix A.

To apply for the licence an employer should:

■ complete the application form online;
■ pay the correct fee. The fee can be paid online; however, if the correct fee is not provided, the application will not be considered;
■ provide proof that the employer is a genuine employer, operating or trading lawfully in the UK by providing specific documents;

Migrant and foreign workers

- provide original or certified copies of those documents;
- meet the suitability criteria – this determines whether an employer is given an A or B rating;
- show the UKBA there is no reason to believe the employer is a threat to immigration control; and
- demonstrate that it agrees to comply with the duties of the Sponsorship.

The online application is sent by the employer only. A legal representative is not authorised to submit the application on behalf of the employer.

Once the application has been submitted, the application form (submission sheet) signed by the Authorising Officer, together with the documents and fee (if not paid online) should be posted to the UKBA within 14 calendar days of submitting the application online. Enquiries can be made to the UKBA with regards to the application by telephone 0300 123 4699 or email at SponsorshipPBSenquiries@ukba.gsi. gov.uk

Once the UKBA approves the licence, the sponsor employer can assign certificates of sponsorship to the migrants wishing to join their employment. The UKBA will set a limit on the number of certificates of sponsorship assigned by the employer for restricted jobs and review the employer's performance after the licence has been assigned. The UKBA may visit an employer's property, whether pre-arranged or not, to check compliance and if it is found that the employer is breaching the illegal working regulations, the UKBA may issue civil penalties or refer the sponsor for prosecution.

Restricted and unrestricted jobs

'Unrestricted' jobs are exempt from the limit and are published by the UKBA.

An 'unrestricted' job will require an 'unrestricted' CoS if they are:

- New hires from overseas but where the migrant will be earning £150,000 or more per annum;
- Extension applications where a migrant is already in the UK working for a company under Tier 2 (General) or has a Work Permit and was granted leave on or before 5 April 2011;
- Changes of Employment applications where the migrant is already in the UK working for a company under Tier 2 (General) or has a Work Permit but wants to change their job to work for a new sponsor; and/or
- Switching into Tier 2 (General) from another category if the Migrant is already in the UK under another category and is eligible to switch into Tier 2.

Once the UKBA agrees the number of unrestricted CoS an employer may assign, they have 12 months in which to assign them. This is known as the 'CoS year'. The CoS year *always* runs from 6 April to 5 April of the next year (this is known as the financial year). However, if the UKBA has granted restricted CoS these must be used within three months, otherwise they will be removed from the employer's account.

Any unrestricted CoS not assigned by 5 April of the next year will be removed from the employer's account.

At the end of the CoS year an employer must advise the UKBA of how many CoS they require for the next year. The UKBA will ask the employer to justify why they require more CoS.

Existing employers with a licence who apply for a new annual allocation under Tier 2 (General) will not be allowed to apply for a CoS if the job is a restricted job. In such circumstances, the Level 1 User must submit an application following the UKBA guidance. A Resident Labour Market Test (where appropriate) must have been conducted.

Shortage Occupation List

The Shortage Occupation List is drawn up by the Migration Advisory Committee (MAC). Previously, if a job title was listed on the Shortage Occupation List then the full points were awarded for the Sponsorship Licence. However, the allocation of points now includes consideration of Appropriate Salary, which can be obtained from the Standard Occupational Classification (SOC) Codes of Practice. A job listed in the Shortage Occupation List will get 30 points but the Appropriate Salary part of the criteria will still need to be satisfied. If a job is not listed on the Shortage Occupation List then the employer must advertise the position and satisfy the Resident Labour Market Test (RLMT) to obtain the 30 points.

To satisfy the RLMT the employer must have advertised the vacancy for at 28 days at Job Centre Plus and the relevant sector-specific Code of Practice. The RLMT does not need to be carried out if the employee is a post-study worker, working for six months or more, as a post-study worker is already considered part of the Resident Labour Market.

All CoS, restricted or unrestricted, must be assigned within six months of the date of the vacancy is first advertised. Therefore, if the advert was submitted in stages then the CoS must be assigned from the date the first advert first appeared.

Resident Labour Market Test (RLMT)

To satisfy the RLMT the employer must have advertised the vacancy at Jobcentre

Plus (or in Northern Ireland, JobCentre Online) for jobs under Tier 2 (General), plus one other advertising method permitted in the relevant Code of Practice. The Codes of Practice can be found on the UKBA website – see *Sources of further information.* If there is no Code of Practice for the job / sector the employer must still advertise in JobCentre Plus.

The time period for adverts to be advertised on or after 14 December 2009 is 28 calendar days. An employer may choose to:

- advertise the vacancy in one single continuous period of 28 calendar days, with the closing date for all applicants 28 days from the date the advert first appeared; or
- advertise the vacancy in two stages. An example may be if an employer advertises a position for 14 calendar days. If he finds a settled person to fill the vacancy then that would end the process there. However, if he finds a migrant who is suitable for the position *he cannot employ that migrant until the advert has been posted for 28 calendar days.* The employer must then re-advertise for a further 14 days and if he genuinely cannot find a settled person (from either the first time or the second time advertising) to fill the position then he may consider the migrant applicant.

The prospective employer must submit the application form themselves electronically and get the support documentation to the UKBA within ten days of submitting the application. This is to verify that the vacancy is a genuine vacancy that cannot be filled by an EEA National and that the sponsor, the employer, will accept responsibilities of sponsorship in respect of the employee.

When advertising, the UKBA states you must always use the advertising methods permitted by the Code of Practice. The advertisement must include:

- the job title;
- the main duties and responsibilities of the job (job description);
- the location of the job;
- an indication of the salary package or salary range or terms on offer;
- skills, qualifications and experience required; and
- the closing date for applications (except for rolling recruitment).

An employer cannot refuse to employ a settled worker if they lack qualifications, experience or skills (including any language skills) that were not specifically requested in the job advertisement.

Minimum skill level

Which applications on or after 6 April 2011 need to be at graduate level and which do not?

If an employer wishes to employ a migrant on or after 6 April 2011, where the migrant is coming to the UK from abroad or if the migrant is switching into Tier 2, the CoS must confirm that the job is at graduate level (either because it is at graduate level or it is in the Shortage Occupation List). The CoS must also confirm that the migrant will be paid the appropriate rate (again this is taken from the Codes of Practice).

Applications made when the migrant is already in the UK and had a visa or leave to remain as a Tier 2 (General) granted under the rules before 6 April 2011, a work permit holder, Representative of an Overseas newspaper, News Agency or Broadcasting Organisation, Member of the Operational Ground Staff of an Overseas-owned Airline or Jewish Agency Employee, the CoS must confirm that the job is at S/NVQ Level 3 unless the migrant was last granted leave as a Senior Care Worker or Established Entertainer. Again, the CoS must confirm the appropriate rate will be paid.

In all other circumstances, when applying to extend leave under Tier 2 (General), the job must be at graduate level.

Minimum salary level

The points claimed for appropriate salary offered by an employer are before tax (gross) and yearly.

The salary may be paid in the UK or abroad. If the salary is paid abroad the salary amount entered on the CoS will be based on the exchange rate published on www.oanda.com on the day the CoS is assigned.

To calculate what the appropriate salary is for a job, the UKBA has published its Standard Occupational Classification (SOC) Codes of Practice. These Codes of Practice will provide information as to what the hourly rate, or wage, for a particular job is.

Points are awarded for up to a maximum of 48 hours a week only. Even if a migrant works more than this, the UKBA will calculate how much a migrant is earning for the 48 hours only.

Table 1 (*overleaf*) sets out the points that can be obtained for the Sponsorship and Appropriate Salary for an Unrestricted CoS.

A Restricted CoS will be scored and prioritised based on Table 2 (*overleaf*). To make a valid application, a minimum of 32 points must be scored from both columns.

Sponsorship	Points	Appropriate salary	Points	Total points
Job in shortage occupation	30	Either £20,000 per annum or the minimum appropriate rate set out in the Code of Practice or Shortage Occupation List, which ever is higher	20	50
Job offer with a salary of £150,000 or more				
Job that passes the Resident Labour Market Test (RLMT)		Worker last had entry clearance / leave to remain as a:	20	
Switching from Tier 1 (post-study worker)		■ Tier 2 (General) before 6 April 2011 ■ Jewish Agency Employee ■ Minister of Religion ■ Representative of an Overseas newspaper ■ Work Permit Holder		
Extension in the same job and the same (or higher) salary (RLMT) not required				
English Language	10			
Maintenance	10			

Table 1: An unrestricted CoS.

Type of job	Points	Salary	Points
Jobs is on the Shortage Occupation List	75	£20,000-£20,999.99	2
Job is at PhD level and is in one of the SOC codes listed in the UKBA guidance	50	£21,000-£21,999.99	3
Resident Labour Market Test conducted (or the job is exempt from the RLMT)	30	£22,000-£22,999.99	4
		£23,000-£23,999.99	5
		£24,000-£24,999.99	6
		£25,000-£25,999.99	7
		£26,000-£26,999.99	8
		£27,000-£27,999.99	9
		£28,000-£31,999.99	10
		£32,000-£45,999.99	15
		£46,000-£74,999.99	20
		£75,000-£99,999.99	25
		£100,000-£149,999.99	30

Table 2: A restricted CoS.

Certificates of Sponsorship

When the UKBA receives an application, up to and including the fifth of each month, that application will be considered on the 11th of the same month. This is known as the Allocation Date. For example, if an application is made between 6 May and 5 June the application will be considered on 11 June.

Applications are prioritised on the highest scores. Those who score the highest points are to be approved first and given a CoS and so forth until there are no more CoS left. If the UKBA receives a number of applications that exceed the number of CoS available, they will grant the CoS to the highest scoring first and consider whether they have a number of applications scoring the same. For example, if the UKBA has given all the highest scoring applications a CoS and there are only 150 CoS left but 250 applications all scoring the minimum of 32 points, the UKBA cannot decide which of these applications is more urgent or worthy of receiving the remainder CoS.

Therefore, the UKBA has stated in such circumstances if it will exceed the limit of CoS to be allocated for that month by 100. If there are more than 100 applications in excess of 32 points then the UKBA will not grant a CoS to any of them but carry forward any remainder CoS to the next month.

Basically, in the above scenario, all the applicants would be granted a CoS as there are 150 CoS remaining, but 250 applicants, but the UKBA can exceed their allocation for the month by 100 and therefore, the number of CoS available is 250. However, if there are 150 CoS remaining and 450 applicants, the UKBA will not grant any of them a CoS but carry forward the 150 unallocated CoS to the next month.

Only in compelling circumstances will a CoS be granted exceptionally outside of the monthly allocation. Such applications will be rare and will only be granted for genuine urgent reasons. The UKBA will *not* accept delays because of absent members of staff as a sufficient explanation.

The Sponsor Management System (SMS) is a system set up by UKBA, which allows an employer to access the system for the purposes of applying for a licence and assigning certificates. Before applying electronically an employer should identify key personnel in the company to play important roles such as accessing the SMS. These key personnel must be based in the UK and must be people of good character. The key personnel are listed below.

Authorising Officer

This person is responsible for the activities of anyone acting on the company's behalf with regard to the sponsorship licence. They ensure the employer meets their duties. They must be an honest, reliable and competent member of staff. Legal representatives cannot act as an Authorising Officer. An un-discharged bankrupt cannot act as an Authorising Officer. The Authorising Officer can have more than one role. The Authorising Officer does not have automatic access to the Sponsorship Management system. If they wish to gain access they must be set up as a Level 1 or Level 2 user. An employer / sponsor must have an Authorising Officer in place throughout the life of the licence. Failure to have an Authorising Officer or failure to advise the UKBA of any change in the Authorising Officer may result in the sponsor's licence being withdrawn, suspended, downgraded to a B-rating (see below regarding ratings), or a reduction in the number of certificates the sponsor is allowed to assign.

Key contact

This person is the main point of UKBA contact and acts as a liaison between the employer and the UKBA. This person is called upon by the UKBA if there is a problem with the application process. The Authorising Officer can act in this role. The key contact does not have automatic access to the SMS unless they are set up as a Level 1 or Level 2 User.

Level 1 User

This person operates the employer's activities on a day-to-day basis via the Sponsor Management System. They will be able to:

■ create and remove other users, such as request an additional Level 1 User and add and remove Level 2 Users from the SMS;
■ amend user details;
■ assign / withdraw certificates;
■ request an increase in certificates;
■ notify the UKBA of minor changes to the employer's details;
■ complete the change of circumstances screen with a view to informing the UKBA to record a bigger change; and
■ report migrant activity.

A legal representative can be appointed to act as a Level 1 User. Only one person can be appointed as a Level 1 User.

After an employer has obtained a licence, they may nominate additional Level 1 Users using the SMS. This depends on the needs of the business; however, as the Authorising Officer is responsible for the actions of users of the SMS, the UKBA advises that the number of Level 1 Users is kept to a minimum.

The Level 1 User must be a paid member of staff or officer holder within the employer's business, or an employee of a third party organisation engaged by the employer / sponsor to deliver all, or part, of their HR function.

Level 2 User

These can be more than one person appointed by the Level 1 User. Legal representatives can act as a Level 2 User. A Level 2 User's duties may include assigning Certificates of Sponsorship to migrants, and reporting migrant activity to the UK Border Agency.

As the Authorising Officer is responsible for *all* users, it is sensible to keep Level 2 users to a minimum and only appoint when absolutely necessary.

The UKBA will do checks on the individuals against the Police National Computer and will as a minimum carry out checks against the Authorising Officer and Level 1 Users.

The UKBA has set out what it calls its overriding principles. The questions it will ask are:

■ Is the employer a bona fide organisation operating lawfully in the UK? In order to prove this, the employer is required to provide certain documents from a list.
■ Is the employer trustworthy? In order to judge this the UKBA will look at the company's previous history and background and that of the key personnel. Any negative findings of previous immigration crimes or dishonesty will be considered and may lead to the refusal of the licence.
■ Is the employer capable of carrying out its duties as sponsor? The UKBA proposes to check a prospective employer's human resources practices to ensure that there is a system in place to enable the employer to carry out his duties.

As a condition of keeping the licence an employer will need to alert the UKBA if their employee does not comply with their immigration conditions.

Suitability criteria

To assess the suitability of an employer the UKBA will consider whether the employer has an effective human resources system in place. It will also consider if any of the key personnel have an unspent conviction. The UKBA will give a score to employers regarding criminal convictions. It will give a score of one for no convictions and a score of three for one or more conviction. If a sponsor or any of its key personnel who have access to the Sponsor Management System is found to have a criminal conviction they are given a score of three.

A score of one, two or three is given to the human resources system, civil penalties and non-compliance. If an employer is selected for a pre-licence visit, the UKBA will score as below:

- *One* – meets all the criteria. This employer is likely to be given an A rating if there are no other reasons for granting a B rating or refuse the application.
- *Two* – meets only some of the criteria. This employer is likely to be given a B rating if there are no other reasons for refusing the application.
- *Three* – does not meet any of the criteria. This employer is likely to be refused.

An employer may obtain an A or B rating if it receives a one or two for civil penalty or non-compliance but receives a three in human resources system. In such cases the UKBA's visiting officer may still recommend an A or B rating with an action plan, which may last for a maximum of 12 months but with review points every three months.

Ratings

The sponsor will be given an A or B rating. If the sponsor meets all the requirements they will be given an A rating. If the sponsor fails to meet either the compliance check or the human resources check they will receive a B rating. If the sponsor does not meet either compliance or human resources checks, the UK Border Agency will refuse to grant a Certificate of Sponsorship.

Transitional ratings

B-rated organisations may be given a short period of time (possibly three months) to improve their performance and obtain an A rating. An action plan will be drawn up that will include steps the sponsor should take to improve. This is a joint project; however, the UK Border Agency will have the final say. After three months the UK Border Agency will check to see if genuine attempts have been made to meet the requirements. If the sponsor does not improve they will lose their licence. However, if there are circumstances outside of the sponsor's control then the sponsor may be put on probation for 12 months.

The UKBA will then review the B rating and possibly grant an A rating. There are certain circumstances where the Sponsorship Licence *will* be refused (or B rating granted) or will *normally* be refused (or B rating granted) or *may* be refused (or B rating granted).

A refusal or B rating will depend on the breach or failure to comply such as:

- not supplying compulsory documents;
- providing forged or false documents;
- when the sponsor / employer does not meet the criteria for a specific tier;
- where one of the key personnel is legally prohibited from becoming a company director;

- any previous convictions for an immigration-related offence or being issued with civil penalty; and/or
- a civil penalty being unpaid with regards to an immigration offence.

The UK Border Agency has the power to cancel a Certificate of Sponsorship and in certain circumstances it will refuse a Certificate. In other situations it may or normally will refuse a licence or award a B rating.

Franchises

If an organisation has a number of franchises that are under its control, each branch may apply for a separate licence or they may apply for one licence covering all the other franchises. If the franchises are separate businesses not under the control of the parent company, each branch will be required to apply separately.

The applicant / employee

Ten points will be granted to the employee (the main applicant) if they can prove they have at least £800 in their bank account for the past three months and a further £600 for each dependant for those applicants in the UK.

The final ten points will be granted to the applicant if they can prove they satisfy the English language requirement.

Once the Sponsorship Licence and the above documentation is to hand, the applicant / employee must then apply for entry clearance or for leave to remain.

Tier 2 Intra-company transfer

This offers multi-national organisations a route to transfer employees to the UK under four sub-categories:

1. Long-term staff.
2. Short-term staff.
3. Graduate trainee.
4. Skills transfer.

Long-term staff

This replaces what was known as 'established staff' – where a vacancy cannot be filled by a settled worker, a skilled employee can be transferred to the UK branch of the employer's organisation.

Under this sub-category an employer may bring a member of staff to the UK for a period of more than 12 calendar months (a maximum of 60 calendar months).

The job must be a graduate level job or above. The salary for the job must be £40,000 per annum (this includes allowances which the UKBA has listed in its guidance). The initial period granted for the member of staff to enter the UK is 36 calendar months with the option of extending it up to 60 calendar months.

Members of staff under the previous Established Staff category (before 6 April 2011) who wish to extend their leave must do so under this category. However, they do not have to satisfy the requirement of a graduate level job or the salary requirement, but they must continue to be employed at S/NVQ Level 3 or above. They will not be limited to 60 calendar months.

Any previous grants of leave granted on 6 April 2011 will not count towards the 60 calendar months. Therefore, if a member of staff spent 12 months under short-term staff and then left the UK, then applied to return to the UK under long-term staff, they will be allowed 60 calendar months under the long-term staff category.

However, if a member staff granted under the long-term staff leaves without spending 60 calendar months in the UK but wishes to return (within 12 months) they will not be granted a further period under the long-term staff category. They will only be allowed to apply under this category again, once 12 months has passed from the expiry date of their original long-term staff visa.

Short-term staff

This also replaces what was known as established staff – with both long-term and short-term staff the employee must have been working for the employer for at least 12 months directly prior to their transfer except when there have been periods of absence due to maternity / paternity / adoption leave, long-term sickness which lasted for one month or longer, the member of staff is a graduate trainee or skills transfer.

This category is used for members of staff who need to come to the UK for a maximum of 12 months.

The job must be at graduate level and the salary must be at least £24,000 per annum. If the member of staff leaves the UK before the 12 calendar months but wishes to return, they must either apply under long-term staff or wait 12 months to lapse from the date of expiry of their original visa.

Graduate trainee

Recent graduates may be transferred to the UK for training. This route must not be used to fill in long-term posts. Graduate trainees must be part of a structured training programme with clearly defined progression towards a managerial or specialist role within the company. The graduate must have been working with the company for at least three months prior to coming to the UK.

The job must be at graduate level and the salary must be at least £24,000 per annum.

This route is not to be used to transfer *all* graduates working at a company but just to accelerate promotion schemes.

A company may only send no more than five graduates per financial year.

A graduate who leaves the UK prior to their period of leave expiring cannot return to the UK in this category unless 12 months have passed from the date of the expiry of their initial visa. They may have to return under the long-term staff sub-category.

Skills transfer

New recruits of the employer abroad may come to the UK to acquire the skills and knowledge that they will need to fulfil their own role overseas or to impart specialist skills or knowledge to the UK workforce. Migrants do not have to be employed by the company for a minimum period under this sub-category.

As with graduates, the job must be at graduate level and the salary must be at least £24,000. As with above, if the migrant leaves the UK, they cannot apply to return until 12 months has passed from the date of the expiry of their initial visa or if they wish to return under the long-term staff sub-category.

Evidence required

All the categories above require evidence that the migrant has been working with the company bringing them to the UK. Evidence should include payslips, bank statements (dated within one calendar month of the application) and Building Society Pass books.

The grant of leave will initially be for three years. A further two years will be given on extension. Settlement can be applied for after five years.

Tier 5 – Sponsorship Licence required

Employers applying under this category are required to have a Sponsorship Licence. The applicant must have sufficient maintenance. This category is designed for temporary workers; each category requires a sponsor and the applicant will be required to satisfy the maintenance requirement. Under this category the applicant requires 30 points for a Sponsorship Licence and ten points for maintenance (funds).

Creative and sporting

Before an employer can assign a certificate, they must have an endorsement from the particular sporting governing body confirming the applicant meets the governing body's requirements. The governing body must be a recognised body. A list of recognised bodies can be found on the UK Border Agency website. Points are granted for sponsorship and maintenance. An applicant may apply from abroad or, if they have already been granted permission to come to the UK as a creative *and* sporting worker, they may extend their leave up to 12 months. If the applicant is already in the UK and wishes to extend their visa as a creative worker *only*, permission may be granted up to 24 months in total. This category is not for people who wish to come or who are already in the UK as sports visitors or entertainers, including for special festivals, which come under Business and Special Visitors.

Charity workers

Charity workers do voluntary unpaid work. The work must be directly related to the work of the sponsoring organisation. The applicant can apply to enter as a charity worker and get a visa for 12 months, or if the applicant is already in the UK as a charity worker but was granted fewer than 12 months, they may extend their visa up to 12 months in total.

Religious worker

The applicant may carry out work preaching, pastoral work and non-pastoral work. This work must be done during a break from the applicant's job overseas. The period of leave granted is 24 months. Dependants of the main applicant are allowed to take up employment. Those who are already in the UK as religious workers but have not been granted the full 24 months may apply for an extension up to the full 24 months.

Government-authorised exchanges

The Government-authorised exchange category is for people coming to the UK through approved schemes that aim to share knowledge, experience and best practice and experience the social and cultural life of the UK. This category must not be used to fill job vacancies or to bring unskilled labour to the UK.

The sponsor for this category will be the overarching body who manages the scheme with the UK. Sponsored researchers are sponsored by the Higher Education Institution they have been sponsored by. All other employers will not be allowed to sponsor an applicant in this category, even if they are licensed as sponsors under other tiers or other categories of Tier 5.

Any work done must be skilled, which means it must be equivalent to NVQ Level 3 or above, unless the work is part of the European Union's lifelong learning programme, where permission is granted to do vocational education and training at a lower skill level.

Applicants are allowed to stay in the UK for up to 24 months under this category.

Avoiding penalties for illegal employment

Criminal and civil penalties

The UKBA website contains an endless stream of reports of arrests, civil penalties and forfeitures of cash. Usually the numbers of arrests are small; the businesses are likewise small. In many cases the businesses are concerned with hot food or food processing, textiles or clothing manufacture, car wash and valeting, or neighbourhood shops. Recent reports appear to be particularly focused in the Midlands, but all parts of the UK are affected. Joint Police and Immigration raids are said to be intelligence led. Sometimes warnings of immigration raids are given. Often publicity will be arranged by UKBA. When 33 'illegal workers' were arrested on 10 June 2011 at Leicester's Imperial Typewriter Building, Immigration Minister, Damian Green, said:

"This operation is one of the largest we have conducted in the Midlands and reinforces our determination to identify and remove more people with no legal right to work in this country."

Simon Excell, Deputy Director Midlands and East UKBA, on 22 June 2011, on the arrest of six people at a Dunstable Bakery said:

"The rules around the employment of foreign nationals are clear and apply to everyone, from the smallest business to multinationals. No one is above the law."

The point should be made that UKBA's conduct is not above criticism. UKBA's Chief Inspector, John Vine, in his February 2011 report on the Croydon Arrest Team 'found significant non-compliance with the Agency's own policy and guidance'.

'Non-compliance' might render a raid unlawful. Raids and arrests are conducted by the 53 Local Immigration Teams around the UK. In January 2011, nationally they conducted 11,913 'visits' and made 6,388 arrests.

Since 27 January 1997 it has been a criminal offence to employ a person in

the UK whose immigration status denies them the right to work. In the first six years, there were only 34 successful prosecutions. Enforcement of the law against illegal employment has been transformed since commencement in February 2008 of sections of the Immigration Nationality Act 2006, which replaced the previous regime with a system of civil and criminal penalties for employers. The key changes were to throw the obligation to defend the legality of employment and the employer, and to create a Documentation Regime to afford employers with a 'statutory excuse' if they are found to be employing people without immigration permission to work. More than 2,500 civil penalty notices were served in the year ending March 2010.

Health and safety

Employers have health and safety obligations towards all employees. For Foreign Nationals, one additional consideration may be whether they can speak English sufficiently for the role and to recognise any safety notices. Employers should consider whether training or assistance can be provided.

Avoiding race discrimination

All checks must be performed in a non-discriminatory way. The Government has issued a Code of Practice on 'Avoidance of race discrimination in recruitment practice while seeking to prevent illegal working' (see *Sources of further information*). The main points are:

- Failure to follow the Code may be considered by an Employment Tribunal.
- All job selections should be based on suitability for the post.
- Make no assumptions based on colour, race, nationality, ethnic or national origins, or the length of time someone has been in the UK.

- Identical checks should be performed for all applicants, although employers may decide to only perform checks on candidates who reach a certain stage.

> *See also*: Discrimination, p.126; International employees, p.259; Recruitment and selection, p.420.

If someone cannot produce the necessary documents, ask them to seek advice.

Sources of further information

Home Office: www.employingmigrantworkers.org.uk

Code of Practice: http://bit.ly/hPmOEx

Immigration and Nationality Directorate: www.ind.homeoffice.gov.uk/applying/eeaeunationals

UK Border Agency: www.bia.homeoffice.gov.uk/

Code of Practice on 'Avoidance of race discrimination in recruitment practice while seeking to prevent illegal working': http://bit.ly/nKMzxu

UKBA Sponsorship and Employers Helpline: 0300 123 4699

Minimum wage

Pinsent Masons Employment Group

Key points

- The National Minimum Wage Act 1998 came into force on 1 April 1999. It provides for a single national minimum wage with no variations by region, occupation or size of company. It covers all relevant workers employed under a contract of employment or any other contract.
- The detailed rules of the national minimum wage (NMW) are contained in the National Minimum Wage Regulations 1999. These are updated annually with new minimum rates.
- All relevant workers must be paid the minimum hourly wage averaged across a 'relevant pay period'.
- Rules exist to say what relevant pay is, and how relevant hours are calculated for different types of workers.
- The NMW applies to gross earnings and is calculated before tax, National Insurance contributions and any other deductions.
- Employers must keep records.
- Employment Tribunals and HM Revenue and Customs inspectors can enforce the duties of employers.
- Not all workers qualify for the NMW. For example, workers attending work experience as part of a course of higher education are excluded.

Legislation

- National Minimum Wage Act 1998.
- National Minimum Wage Regulations 1999.
- Employment Act 2008.

Both the Act and the Regulations came into force on 1 April 1999. They introduced the concept of a national minimum wage, together with employers' obligations and the mechanisms by which workers can enforce these obligations.

Hourly rates

The rate is reviewed annually and from October 2011 the rates are as follows:

- Standard (adult) rate (workers aged 21 and over): £6.08.
- Development rate (workers aged between 18 and 20): £4.98.
- Young workers' rate (workers aged under 18 but above the compulsory school age, who are not apprentices): £3.68.
- Apprentice rate (under 19 or in first year): £2.60.

(see 'Work experience, internships and apprenticeships', p.558).

Entitlement to the minimum wage

According to the Act, the term 'worker' has a specific meaning. It is wider than the term 'employee' and covers a contractor carrying out services personally, unless the employer is the client or customer of the person involved. Truly self-employed people are not 'workers'.

Whether a worker has been paid the requisite minimum wage is determined by reference to his total pay over a relevant period. It is necessary to determine a worker's average minimum pay over a 'pay

---

> **Case study**
>
> A Manchester optician who paid his staff at rates up to 40% less than they were entitled to was successfully prosecuted for National Minimum Wage (NMW) offences and fined £3,696 in June 2010.
>
> Benjamin Gains, proprietor of two optician premises in Liverpool, pleaded guilty to failing to pay four of his employees the NMW. He attempted to hide the fact that he wasn't paying what he should by falsifying employee information and then neglected to produce appropriate documents to HM Revenue & Customs (HMRC).
>
> Trading as 'BG Optical', Gains provided workers with annual contracts based on salaries that appeared to be close to the minimum wage rates but which included a section on paid meal breaks. Following initial checks by HMRC Investigators, Gains altered contracts and other documentation, which he provided to support his claim that he was paying the minimum wage. He had, however, altered the rates of pay by falsifying documents and backdating contracts to show different hours of working and removing staff entitlement to paid meal breaks.
>
> The difference in what staff should have been paid and what they were paid was described as being 'very, very low, literally pence', and Mr Gains offered to pay the staff back if HMRC dropped the case against him.
>
> Mike O'Grady, HMRC Criminal Investigations, said:
>
> "This sentencing sends a clear message to employers, large or small, that HMRC will actively pursue those whom we suspect of flouting National Minimum Wage law. If employers prevent HMRC officers from checking staff records, attempt to alter or falsify pay records and related documents, and refuse to comply with the law they could receive a fine and a criminal record.
>
> "We have a duty to ensure workers receive their salary entitlement. The majority of employers do assist us with our investigations, but if they don't we will pursue cases through the criminal courts. Thankfully the majority of employers know their responsibilities and act within the law."

reference period'. This period is specified in the Act as one month unless the worker is specifically paid by reference to a shorter period (e.g. weekly or fortnightly).

In basic terms, the calculation to determine if the minimum wage has been paid is the total relevant remuneration divided by hours worked in the pay reference period.

The Regulations contain detailed and complicated rules relating to pay reference periods, as well as how to calculate what remuneration actually counts towards assessing whether a worker is being paid the required amount. Further, only certain time will count in the calculation of hours worked – only 'working time' counts.

> **Facts**
>
> - Since its introduction, the number of jobs paid below the NMW has been monitored by the Office for National Statistics. In 1998, a year before the NMW was introduced, nearly 1.3 million employee jobs (5.6%) were paid below the 1999 NMW rate, while in 2008 there were 288,000 (1.1%) paid below the NMW.
> - The impact of the NMW in 1999 can clearly be seen with the percentage of employees being paid below it falling from 5.6% to 2.1% in the year of its introduction. There was a further decrease in 2000, after which the percentage has remained broadly the same, at just over 1%.

For example:

- travelling to and from home is not working time, but travelling for the purposes of duties during work is;
- time spent training at a different location from a worker's normal place of work is working time; and
- deductions from wages due to an advance or overpayment of wages are not subtracted from the total remuneration.

Gross pay figures should be used for the calculation. Also, different types of workers will demand different consideration, particularly where hours vary from week to week. Those types of workers are:

- time workers (paid by reference to the time that a worker works, e.g. hourly paid workers);
- salaried hours (paid an annual salary in instalments for a set number of hours each year);
- output workers (paid according to the productivity of the worker); and
- unmeasured work (no specified hours – all hours worked should be paid for, but the employer and worker can enter into a 'daily average agreement' to clarify the position, although sometimes as with agricultural workers there are specific legal requirements as to what must be included).

Tips and gratuities

Since 1 October 2009, tips, gratuities and service charges can no longer be taken into account when calculating a worker's remuneration. Before October 2009 these could be taken into account if they were 'paid by the employer' through its payroll system.

Other benefits in kind

Benefits in kind such as uniforms, meals and private health insurance do not count. The only benefit in kind that counts is accommodation.

Records

Employers are obliged to keep records that are sufficient to show that they have paid their workers the appropriate minimum wage. It is important that employers maintain sufficient records since it will be presumed that the worker has not been paid the national minimum wage unless the employer can prove to the contrary. A worker has the right to inspect these records if he believes he is being paid less than the required amount and can take a copy. An employer must respond to this request within 14 days (or a later date if one has been agreed between the employer and the worker).

Enforcement

If the employer fails to produce the relevant records, the worker can bring a claim in the Employment Tribunal, which can impose a fine on the employer of up to 80 times the relevant hourly national minimum wage.

The Act implies a right to the NMW into contracts of employment, so a worker who has been underpaid can commence proceedings in an Employment Tribunal to recover the difference between the wages paid and the NMW. It is presumed that the worker has been underpaid unless the employer can prove otherwise.

The Home Secretary can appoint public officers, who have a variety of enforcement powers. These include powers to require employers to produce records to evidence compliance with the NMW, to require any relevant person to furnish them with additional information, and to gain access to premises for the carrying out of these powers.

Inspections and enforcement can be carried out by HM Revenue and Customs inspectors.

The Act also creates a number of criminal offences, based on obligations under the Act. These include:

■ refusing to pay the required minimum wage;

■ failing to keep records proving that the minimum wage has been paid for three years;
■ entering false information into these records;
■ obstructing a public officer; and
■ refusing to answer questions or provide information to a public officer.

The Employment Act 2008 introduced a new method of enforcement, effective from 6 April 2009. The previous separate enforcement and penalty notices were replaced by a single notice of underpayment. Notices of underpayment require the employer to pay a financial penalty to the Secretary of State within 28 days of service. The penalty is now set at 50% of the total underpayment of the minimum wage; the minimum penalty is £500 and the maximum is £5,000. If the employer complies with the notice within 14 days of its service, the financial penalty will be reduced by 50%.

See also: Discrimination, p.126; Employment contracts, p.164; Equal pay, p.184; Expenses, p.200; Work experience, internships and apprenticeships, p.558; Young persons, p.571.

Sources of further information

Guidance on minimum wage: http://bit.ly/cXJZRK

Low Pay Commission: www.lowpay.gov.uk

National Minimum Wage helpline: 0800 917 2368.

Money laundering

Anna Odby, Peters & Peters Solicitors LLP

Key points

- Amongst the recent achievements of the UK's Serious Organised Crime Agency (SOCA), set out in its Annual Report for 2010/2011, was the voluntary withdrawal by UK wholesalers of the €500 note from retail sale in May 2010, after the Agency's analysis showed that there was no credible legitimate use for the note in the volumes it was being supplied in the UK. Over 90% of the demand for the note was found to come from criminals, as it enabled large volumes of cash to be moved effectively. Although possession of the note has not been criminalised, its use is likely to attract the attention of law enforcement.

- The Suspicious Activity Reports Regime Annual Report 2010 confirmed that disclosures of known or suspected money laundering or terrorist financing are routinely used by police departments across the UK. The Metropolitan Police Service matches reports against local intelligence databases and runs searches on reports at the request of other police. Intelligence derived from reports is disseminated to law enforcement and exchanged with financial intelligence units overseas. In 2010 SOCA reviewed over 7,000 reports indicating criminal activity relating to politically exposed persons. In its Annual Plan for 2010/11, the Serious Organised Crime Agency announced its intention to maximise knowledge extracted from SAR data through the use of new Regional Asset Recovery Teams.

- In April 2011 the Treasury issued a revised Financial Sector Advisory Notice on the risk of trading with countries with weak anti-money laundering and counter terrorist finance controls, identifying 15 countries of serious concern due to substantial deficiencies in their anti-money laundering and counter terrorist financing regimes.

- In June 2011 the Office of Fair Trading issued a reminder to businesses supervised under the Money Laundering Regulations 2007 to improve compliance or risk enforcement action, following the publication of results from compliance reviews conducted as part of pilot programmes.

Legislation

- Terrorism Act 2000.
- Proceeds of Crime Act 2002.
- The Proceeds of Crime Act 2002 (Money Laundering: Exceptions to Overseas Conduct Defence) Order 2006.
- Money Laundering Regulations 2007.
- Money Laundering (Amendment) Regulations 2011.

Introduction

In response to a recent Home Office review of the Money Laundering Regulations 2007, the UK Government confirmed its continuing commitment to the effective implementation of the global anti-money laundering and counter-terrorist financing standards agreed by the 36 member states of the supra-national Financial Action Task Force (FATF). Within

Facts

- A 2009 survey by the Financial Action Task Force found that the main sources of money laundered through the global financial system are white collar crimes such as tax offences, fraud, corporate offences, intellectual property offences and corruption; as well as drug-related offences, smuggling and, more recently, 'cyber crime'.
- Terrorist financing was found to derive from a similar variety of offences, ranging from low-level crime to sophisticated and serious organised crime. Although terrorist organisations can also be funded from legitimate activities, a mixture of legitimate and illegitimate sources was found to be more common.
- Finally, the survey suggested that money laundering and terrorist financing operations increasingly rely on internet-based systems and new payment methods in the place of cash and alternative remittance systems, and increasingly involve complex commercial structures and trusts. Money laundering and terrorist financial operations tend also to be global, spanning at least two jurisdictions.
- The UK remained on the list of 'countries of primary concern' published by the US State Department in its 2011 International Narcotics Control Strategy Report, on account of the size, sophistication and reputation of UK financial markets.

the EU, these standards are reflected in the Third EU Money Laundering Directive (Directive 2005/60/EC).

In compliance with these standards a range of duties are imposed on persons who operate in the financial sector, the performance of which is intended to prevent money laundering and terrorist financing. If a person fails to perform these duties they will increase the risk of money laundering or terrorist financing being committed, and will also risk committing a criminal offence themselves.

In the UK the duties are imposed by the Money Laundering Regulations 2007 (the Regulations), which apply to certain identified persons when they conduct business. Persons who are not required to comply with the Regulations must nevertheless be vigilant in order to avoid inadvertently committing one of the money laundering or terrorist financing offences imposed under the general law.

Supervision of compliance with the Regulations is divided between relevant industry regulators who may, in certain circumstances, impose civil penalties for breaches. Sector-specific 'best practice' guidance has been produced by supervisors, enforcement authorities and industry bodies such as the Joint Money Laundering Steering Group (JMLSG).

Courts and regulators may take account of compliance with such relevant guidance as exists when deciding whether an offence has been committed, and are obliged to do so where the guidance has been approved by HM Treasury.

The money laundering offence

Money laundering is criminalised by the Proceeds of Crime Act 2002 (POCA), Part 7, which consolidated and strengthened the previously fragmented anti-money laundering regime in the UK. It provides that a money laundering offence may be committed by dealing with the known or suspected proceeds of any criminal conduct ('criminal property'), however small the amount and in whatever form, in one of the following ways:

- Concealing, disguising, converting, transferring or removing criminal property;
- Entering into, or becoming concerned with, an arrangement known or suspected to facilitate the acquisition, retention, use or control of criminal property; or
- Acquiring, using or possessing criminal property, other than in return for adequate consideration.

All three money laundering offences are punishable by up to 14 years' imprisonment. For a successful money laundering prosecution it is not necessary to prove that the property suspected to be 'criminal property' was, in fact, the proceeds of a crime.

Nor is it necessary to prove the particular type of offence known or suspected to give rise to the 'criminal property', if the circumstances in which the property is handled give rise to an irresistible inference that it can only be derived from a criminal offence (*R v. Anwoir and Others*, 2008).

Exceptions and defences

No money laundering offence will be committed by a person who did not, in fact, know or suspect that the property they dealt with represented the proceeds of criminal conduct (*Athif Sarwar v. HM Advocate*, 2011). The courts have defined suspicion for these purposes as concluding that there is a possibility, which is more than fanciful, that the relevant fact exists (*R v. Da Silva*, 2006).

No money laundering offence will be committed by dealing with the proceeds

of an offence committed abroad which is known, or is believed on reasonable grounds, to have been lawful in the place where it occurred.

However, the Secretary of State has ordered that this exception does not apply to offences that would have been punishable, had they occurred in the UK, by more than 12 months' imprisonment (with the exception of certain offences under the Gaming Act 1968, the Lotteries and Amusements Act 1976 and under Sections 23 or 25 of the Financial Services and Markets Act 2000).

There are special exceptions for lawyers and banks. No money laundering offence can be committed by any steps taken by a lawyer in the course of (genuine) legal proceedings, notwithstanding what the lawyer might have learnt as a result of information they have obtained in their conduct of the proceedings (*Bowman v. Fels*, 2005).

Banks and other deposit-taking bodies will also not be committing a money laundering offence operating an account maintained by them, where the value of the account does not exceed a specified threshold (currently £250, or any higher amount specified by an officer of HM Revenue and Customs or a constable in the course of giving or refusing consent to proceed with an act).

In the absence of a relevant exception, a defence may be obtained by disclosing any known or suspected money laundering to the relevant law enforcement authorities (a so-called 'authorised disclosure'), and obtaining consent to proceed with an act that would otherwise constitute a money laundering offence. Consent to proceed may be sought before, during or even after the act, provided in all cases that it is sought as soon as reasonably practicable.

A defence may still be available even if no authorised disclosure was made at all, if there was a reasonable excuse for not making it. There is as yet no guidance from the courts on what may amount to a 'reasonable excuse' for this purpose.

Terrorist financing offences

The Terrorism Act 2000 (TA) makes it an offence to deal with any property that is likely to be used for the purposes of terrorism (including any resources belonging to a proscribed organisation), and any property that represents the proceeds of acts of terrorism or other acts carried out for the purposes of terrorism. A terrorist financing offence may be committed in one of the following ways:

1. Inviting another to provide property, or receiving property, with the intention that the property should be used for the purposes of terrorism, or with reasonable cause to suspect that the property may be so used, or providing property with knowledge, or with reasonable cause to suspect, that it will, or may, be used for the purposes of terrorism (terrorist fundraising).
2. Using property for the purposes of terrorism, including possessing property with the intent that it should, or with reasonable cause to suspect that it may, be used for the purposes of terrorism (use and possession).
3. Entering into, or becoming concerned in, an arrangement, as a result of which property is made available, or is to be made available, to another, with knowledge or reasonable cause to suspect that the property will, or may, be used for the purposes of terrorism (funding arrangements).
4. Entering into, or becoming concerned in, an arrangement, with knowledge or reasonable cause to suspect that the arrangement facilitates the retention or control of terrorist property by, or on behalf of, another; whether by concealment, removal from the jurisdiction, transfer to nominees or in any other way (terrorist money laundering).

All terrorist financing offences are punishable by up to 14 years' imprisonment. A defence may be obtained by voluntarily disclosing to the relevant law enforcement authorities, as soon as reasonably practicable, any knowledge or suspicion that property is terrorist property, and obtaining consent to proceed with what would otherwise be a terrorist financing offence.

The offence of failing to disclose

Money laundering and terrorist financing are by definition covert activities. To increase the chances of detection there is an obligation to disclose to the relevant law enforcement agencies any knowledge or suspicion that a money laundering or terrorist financing offence is being committed, if the knowledge or suspicion is based on information acquired as a result of carrying on a business in 'the regulated sector'.

For this purpose, the existence of knowledge or suspicion is assessed objectively, i.e. it is satisfied by *reasonable grounds* to know or suspect that a money laundering or a terrorist financing offence is being committed. There is, however, no requirement that the suspicion be based on reasonable grounds as long as it is genuinely held (*Shah v. HSBC Private Bank (UK) Ltd*, 2010).

The activities that are considered to amount to a business in the regulated sector for this purpose are set out in Schedule 9 POCA and Schedule 3A TA, which should be carefully consulted in any cases of doubt. They include acts undertaken in the course of business conducted by:

- credit and financial institutions;
- auditors, insolvency practitioners, external accountants and tax advisers;
- legal professionals and notaries, when participating in financial or real property transactions;
- trust or company service providers;
- estate agents;
- high value dealers, when receiving total cash payments in excess of €15,000; and
- casinos.

There is also a wider obligation to disclose any belief or suspicion that a terrorist financing offence has been committed that is based on information obtained in the course of a trade, profession, business or employment.

A failure to make these disclosures, when required, is a criminal offence punishable by up to five years' imprisonment. There is no need to prove that a money laundering offence, or a terrorist financing offence, has in fact taken place.

Defences

The obligation to disclose does not apply to legally privileged information. Legal professional privilege protects any information passing between relevant professional advisers (appropriately regulated lawyers, accountants, auditors or tax advisers and any persons they employed, or working in partnership) and their clients in connection with the seeking or provision of legal advice, as well as information that passes between relevant advisers and any other persons in connection with legal proceedings.

However, legal professional privilege will not protect information that is communicated or provided with the intention of furthering a criminal purpose. Case law suggests that legal professional privilege will be defeated even if the criminal purpose is unknown to the adviser

or their client (*R v. Francis and Francis*, 1989). A reasonable excuse will also provide a defence to a failure to disclose known or suspected money laundering or terrorist financing. There is no statutory definition of what would constitute a reasonable excuse for this purpose, which has yet to be interpreted by the courts.

Guidance produced by the Crown Prosecution Service (CPS) suggests that the defence of reasonable excuse will be available to a professional adviser who forms a genuine, albeit mistaken, belief that information is privileged (see *Sources of further information*).

Further defences are available where the knowledge or suspicion (or reasonable grounds to suspect) relates to money laundering. There is no obligation to disclose information that does not identify the money launderer or the location of the laundered property, unless it is reasonable to expect that the information in question will assist in revealing these details.

A specific defence may be available to employees who fail to disclose reasonable grounds for knowledge or suspicion of money laundering, if their employer has not provided them with the training specified in the Regulations (Regulation 21). This defence will not, however, be available if the employee in question had *actual* knowledge or suspicion of money laundering.

Suspicious Activity Reports

Disclosures made in good faith, whether made in furtherance of an obligation to disclose or for the purpose of obtaining a defence to a money laundering or terrorist financing offence, are 'protected' in the sense that they will not be taken to breach any restrictions on disclosure, however imposed.

In the majority of cases, disclosures will take the form of a Suspicious Activity Report (SAR) made in accordance with the internal policies and procedures operated by a business for this purpose. Internal SARs are received by a nominated officer or Money Laundering Reporting Officer (MLRO) who, in their turn, must consider whether to make an external SAR to the Serious Organised Crime Agency (SOCA).

A separate offence of failing to disclose will be committed by a nominated officer or MLRO who fails to pass on to SOCA any internal money laundering SAR received when required to do so.

SOCA is the UK's designated Financial Intelligence Unit (FIU). SOCA will store any SARs received on a secure database, accessible only by appropriate law enforcement and government agency staff. SARs are to be kept confidential, to the extent possible. Concerns about breaches of confidentiality can be reported to a SAR Confidentiality Hotline operated by SOCA (by telephone to 0800 234 6657).

Where a disclosure is made for the purpose of obtaining consent to proceed with an act which may otherwise be a money laundering or terrorist financing offence, consent can be presumed if SOCA does not respond within seven days.

If SOCA does refuse consent, the proposed act cannot be undertaken for a moratorium period of 31 days (which, unlike the seven-day notice period, includes weekends and public holidays).

In the majority of cases, SOCA should only refuse consent when a criminal investigation involving restraint proceedings is likely to follow or is already underway (Home Office Circular 029/2008). SOCA must not refuse consent without good reason, and must keep any decision to refuse consent under continuous review (*UMBS Online Ltd v. SOCA*, 2007).

There is as yet no prescribed format for disclosures, but SOCA has produced preferred forms for the submission of manual and electronic disclosures. Detailed guidance on how to submit a SAR is available from SOCA's website (see *Sources of further information*).

Tipping off and prejudicing an investigation

It is an offence for a person who learns, in the course of a business in the regulated sector in the regulated sector, that a SAR has been made (whether internally, within an organisation, or externally, to SOCA or another law enforcement agency) to pass this information on to anyone else, if this is known or suspected to prejudice any existing or future money laundering or terrorist financing investigation. The offence of 'tipping off' is punishable by up to two years' imprisonment.

It is an offence for anyone, regardless of whether or not they obtained the information in the course of a business in the regulated sector, to inform another person that a money laundering or terrorist financing investigation is underway, or in contemplation.

It is also an offence to falsify, conceal, destroy or otherwise dispose of documents that are known or suspected to be relevant to a money laundering investigation, or to cause or permit another to do so, unless there was no intention to conceal any facts from the investigation. The offence of prejudicing a money laundering investigation is punishable by up to five years' imprisonment.

The prohibition against tipping off and prejudicing an investigation does not extend to disclosures made to the supervisory authorities, made in support of the detection, investigation or prosecution of a criminal offence, or the enforcement of a court order made under POCA or TA.

The restrictions created by the 'tipping off' offence have caused problems in practice. Persons who have made a SAR for the purpose of seeking consent to act on their client's or their customers' instructions may find it difficult to provide a credible reason for any delay in execution. The courts have confirmed that there is no risk of legal action for breach of contract in circumstances where it would be a criminal offence to honour a customer's mandate (*K Ltd v. National Westminster Bank Plc*, 2006).

Compliance with anti-money laundering and terrorist financing obligations do not, however, completely exclude any duty of care owed to customers and clients, which may, in principle, be breached by delay in seeking consent to proceed (*Shah and another v. HSBC Private Bank (UK) Ltd*, 2010).

A series of exceptions to the tipping off offence have also been introduced to permit SARs to be discussed between the following parties, if they are situated within the EEA or in a country or territory imposing equivalent anti-money laundering and counter-terrorist financing obligations:

- Employees, officers or partners who are members of the same undertaking or group.
- Credit or financial institutions belonging to the same group.
- Lawyers and other specified professional advisers within different undertakings that share common ownership, management or control.

- Counterparties of the same kind (i.e. credit institutions, financial institutions, lawyers and other specified professional advisers of the same kind) who are subject to equivalent duties of professional confidentiality and personal data protection, but only if the information in question relates to a client or former client and to a transaction or provision of a service involving them both, and it is disclosed for the purpose of preventing a money laundering or terrorist financing offence.

In assessing the equivalence of anti-money laundering and counter terrorist financing obligations in another jurisdiction for this purpose, regard should be had to the recent Common Understanding between EU Member States on third country equivalence under the Third Money Laundering Directive (see *Sources of further information*).

There is also a limited exception that permits professional advisers to discuss a SAR or a money laundering or terrorist financing investigation with their clients, for the sole purpose of dissuading them from engaging in criminal conduct.

The Money Laundering Regulations 2007

The Regulations apply to largely the same category of people who are considered to carry out a business in the regulated sector for the purposes of POCA and TA. There are limited exceptions for some types of businesses, who may fall outside the scope of the Regulations if the regulated business does not form part of their main activity and they conduct financial activity only on an occasional or very limited basis.

The Regulations also apply to foreign branches and subsidiaries of regulated persons, who must ensure that the

Regulations are complied with to the extent permitted by local law. If there is doubt about the application of the Regulations, the detailed provisions in Regulation 3 should be consulted carefully.

In order to enable effective supervision of compliance with the Regulations, consumer credit institutions and estate agents must register with the Office of Fair Trading (OFT). High value dealers, money service businesses and trust or company service providers must register with HM Revenue and Customs (HMRC).

Money service businesses and trust and company service providers must also satisfy HMRC that the person who makes the application to register the business, any person who effectively directs or will effectively direct the business, any beneficial owner and the MLRO are all 'fit and proper' persons who have not been convicted or made the subject of a court order relating to money laundering, terrorist financing, fraud, tax evasion or insolvency.

The purpose of the Regulations is to increase awareness of money laundering and terrorist financing risk, and to ensure that information that may assist money laundering or terrorist financing investigations is collected and stored. For this purpose, regulated persons are required to 'know' their customers by conducting 'customer due diligence' (CDD).

Standard CDD involves three main steps. Firstly, identification evidence must be obtained, and verified by reliable and independent information. Secondly, the identity of any beneficial owner must be established. Where the customer is a legal entity, this will require an understanding of the ownership and control structure. To assist in this exercise, the Regulations set out context-specific definitions of beneficial ownership in Regulation 6. Finally, information must be obtained about the stated purpose and intended nature of a proposed business relationship.

CDD should ordinarily be performed before any business relationship is entered into, or any occasional transaction is carried out. It may, however, be delayed if necessary so as not to interrupt the normal conduct of business, provided there is little risk of money laundering and terrorist financing and CDD is completed as soon as practicable after first contact.

If CDD cannot be performed properly, a business relationship cannot be entered into or continued, and no transaction can be carried out with, or for, the customer or client in question. There is a limited exception to the requirement to cease acting for professional advisers in the course of ascertaining the legal position for a client, or defending or representing a client in, or concerning, legal proceedings; which includes advice on the institution or avoidance of proceedings.

Depending on the specific circumstances, an inability to perform CDD may in itself give rise to sufficient knowledge or suspicion that a money laundering or terrorist financing offence is being committed, so as to trigger disclosure obligations under POCA or TA (discussed above). A refusal to enter into a business relationship, or the termination of an existing business relationship, does not extinguish an obligation to disclose.

The extent of CDD required in any one instance is to be determined by adopting a risk-based approach. Customers or clients who are considered to pose a low risk of money laundering or terrorist financing may be subjected to simplified CDD, and in limited circumstances the obligation to conduct CDD may be excluded altogether. The categories of customers or clients potentially eligible for simplified CDD are, subject to specific conditions, credit or financial institutions, listed companies, UK and EU public authorities and lawyers operating pooled accounts.

Simplified CDD may also be applied in certain circumstances to transactions that relate to specified types of products such as life insurance, insurance contracts, pensions, superannuation or similar schemes and electronic money. A further exception for junior ISAs has recently been added by the Money Laundering (Amendment) Regulations 2011.

Conversely, CDD must be applied on an enhanced basis in any situation that by its nature presents a higher risk of money laundering or terrorist financing. This includes customers or clients who are not physically present for identification purposes, or who are politically exposed persons (PEPs).

The Regulations define a PEP as an individual who is, or has at any time in the preceding year, been entrusted with a prominent public function by a state other than the UK, by an institution of the European Community or by an international body. Immediate family members or known close associates of such persons will also be PEPs. In these circumstances, the Regulations require additional CDD measures.

The risk presented by a customer or client, or their activities, may also increase as a result of the particular jurisdiction involved, particularly if the country or territory in question has been identified by HM Treasury as having deficiencies in their anti-money laundering and counter terrorist financing systems. In these circumstances, specific and adequate

measures must be taken to compensate for the higher risk of money laundering or terrorist financing. A separate requirement to cease acting arises where HM Treasury issues a direction to any regulated person, requiring them not to continue or enter into a business relationship, or carry out a transaction, in respect of a person to which the FATF has applied 'counter-measures'.

Due to the particularly high risk of money laundering and terrorist financing presented by shell banks and anonymous accounts, credit and financial institutions are prohibited from entering into or maintaining a correspondent banking relationship with a shell bank, and must not set up any new anonymous accounts or passbooks.

In certain limited circumstances, the Regulations permit reliance on CDD already performed by other regulated persons. However, any person relied on to perform CDD must undertake to make available, on request, and as soon as reasonably practicable, any information relating to CDD. Ultimate responsibility for compliance with the Regulations can never be delegated.

Regulated persons are required to constantly monitor their business relationships in order to ensure that CDD information is kept up to date and transactions undertaken on behalf of a customer or client are consistent with what is known about them.

Regulated persons must also be able to demonstrate to their supervisory authority that the CDD measures they have taken have been appropriate to the money laundering and terrorist financing risk, taking into account the type of customer or client and the nature of the business relationship, product or transaction. For this purpose, and to ensure that information potentially relevant to any investigation is available to the law enforcement authorities, CDD records must be kept for five years from the end of the business relationship or the completion of an occasional transaction.

Finally, regulated persons must adopt and operate appropriate compliance systems. The essential elements of such systems must include the appointment of a nominated officer or MLRO and the establishment of internal reporting procedures to enable compliance with statutory disclosure requirements. Employees must regularly be provided with appropriate training on how to recognise and avoid money laundering and terrorist financing.

A breach of the Regulations is a criminal offence, punishable by a maximum of two years' imprisonment, regardless of whether any money laundering or terrorist financing has actually taken place. Enforcement of the Regulations is entrusted to the Financial Services Authority (FSA), the HMRC Commissioners and the OFT, which have been provided with a range of investigatory powers for the purpose of detecting breaches.

As an alternative to a criminal prosecution, these authorities also have the ability to punish breaches by means of civil penalties. In addition, persons who are required to register with their supervisory authorities can be de-registered as a result of compliance failures.

However, no prosecution can be brought or civil penalty imposed where there are reasonable grounds for the designated authority to be satisfied that the regulated person or entity had taken all reasonable steps and exercised all due diligence to ensure compliance.

Practical guidance

The combined effect of POCA, TA and the Regulations is that persons who operate businesses in the financial sector are subject to a wide range of extensive, and often onerous, obligations. A common complaint is that the 'burden' of compliance does not outweigh its benefits.

Although a recent Government review of the operation of the Regulations concluded that they were proportionate and effective overall, a number of adjustments have been proposed in order to reduce the burden on business, including the exclusion of very small business and non-lending credit institutions from the scope of the application of the Regulations, and the removal of criminal penalties for certain breaches.

However, compliance is expected to remain a complex exercise. The risk-based approach adopted by the Regulations means that the extent of the steps required are likely to vary considerably as between different industries, sizes of business and types of clientele. Considerable care should be taken to identify and assess the money laundering and terrorist financing risk specific to a business for this purpose.

Relevant guidance produced by supervisors and industry organisations should be consulted and regularly monitored for updates. The Treasury maintains a list of approved anti-money laundering and counter terrorist finance guidance, which is published on its website.

Reasons for any departure from relevant guidance, particularly Treasury-approved guidance, should be compelling and should be recorded. Steps taken in compliance with the obligations and any compliance-related decisions should also be documented wherever possible and these records can then be relied on to demonstrate compliance if necessary. Compliance policies and training materials should be regularly revised to reflect internal compliance reviews and any changes in the obligations themselves or related guidance.

The role played by the nominated officer or MLRO in securing compliance within an organisation is crucial, and the performance of this role must not be impeded by reason of a lack of independence, lack of cooperation or lack of access to information.

See also: Criminal records, p.97; Whistleblowing, p.551.

Sources of further information

Financial Action Task Force (FATF) – 40 Recommendations and nine Special Recommendations on Terrorist Financing: www.fatf-gafi.org/

CPS – 'Proceeds of Crime Act 2002 Part 7 – Money Laundering Offences', Legal Guidance, 6 May 2010: www.cps.gov.uk/legal/p_to_r/proceeds_of_crime_money_laundering/index.html

HM Treasury – Anti-money laundering and counter terrorist finance: www.hm-treasury.gov.uk/fin_money_index.htm

Detailed guidance on how to submit SARs: www.soca.gov.uk/about-soca/the-uk-financial-intelligence-unit/completing-a-suspicious-activity-report-sar

Common Understanding between Member States on third country equivalence under the Anti-Money Laundering Directive (Directive 2005/60/EC) (June 2011): www.hm-treasury.gov.uk/d/fin_eu_third_countries_equivalence_list.pdf

Monitoring employees

Lisa Jinks and John Macaulay, Greenwoods Solicitors LLP

Key points

- The monitoring of staff at work, such as computer use and telephone calls, is a sensitive subject that has become highly topical.

- Many organisations have a legitimate need to monitor their workers' actions, whether to record commercial transactions, to monitor the quality of service being provided, or to monitor personal activities to ensure electronic communication systems are not misused.

- Increasingly, organisations have at their disposal a range of technologies and methods for carrying out such monitoring, for example, keystroke logging, monitoring of sent and received emails and internet usage, and the use of software applications to track general computer use. There are also a range of technologies with application outside the office, for example, GPS technology to track companies' vehicles and drivers.

- Organisations that undertake monitoring must be aware of their legal obligations when doing so, and must also bear in mind the rights of monitored workers, as well as third parties (e.g. customers) who might also be affected by such monitoring. The consequences of implementing monitoring incorrectly include:

  - breaches of human rights and other legislation, including potential criminal liability;
  - adverse publicity;
  - complaints of breaches of data protection rights to the Information Commissioner, who has the power to impose fines of up to £500,000; and
  - Employment Tribunal and court claims by employees.

This chapter should be read in conjunction with those on 'CCTV monitoring' (p.70), 'Data protection' (p.101) and 'IT security' (p.282).

Legislation

- Data Protection Act 1998.
- Human Rights Act 1998.
- Regulation of Investigatory Powers Act 2000.
- Telecommunications (Lawful Business Practice) (Interception of Communication) Regulations 2000.

Human Rights Act 1998

Under Article 8 of the Human Rights Act 1998 (HRA) everyone has 'the right to respect for his private and family life, his home and correspondence'.

The right of workers to keep personal matters private, even when these intrude into the workplace, has been confirmed by the European Court of Human Rights (*Copland v. United Kingdom* (2007)). In this case, the monitoring by her employer of Ms Copland's telephone calls, emails and internet use for a period of 18 months without her consent was found to be a violation of her Article 8 rights.

Regulation of Investigatory Powers Act 2000

The Regulation of Investigatory Powers Act 2000 (RIPA) lays down the legal basis for

> **Facts**
> ■ 65% of organisations monitor usage of the internet, rising to 86% in local government and 88% in the police.
>
> *Source: Chartered Management Institute Survey 2008.*

monitoring, which involves 'the interception of a communication in the course of transmission', setting out provisions for authorising surveillance and specifically addressing the legality of surveillance over some private networks.

RIPA applies to public and private telecommunications systems, and public postal services; so in the same way as it is an offence to open an individual's letter before it is delivered to them, an email sent from an internet service provider must not be intercepted. However, because it only covers communications 'in the course of transmission', it does not cover, for example, opening emails that have already been opened by the intended recipient.

For a communication to be lawfully intercepted under RIPA, employers must obtain the consent of both the sender and the recipient. In practice, while the consent of workers may be relatively easily obtained, gaining the consent of both the sender and recipient in external emails will be considerably more difficult. It is against this background that the Telecommunications (Lawful Business Practice) (Interception of Communication) Regulations 2000 (LBPR) were introduced.

The LBPR authorise employers to intercept communications without consent in order to:

■ establish the existence of facts relevant to the business;

■ ascertain compliance with relevant regulatory or self-regulatory practices and procedures;
■ quality check work done;
■ prevent or detect crime;
■ investigate or detect unauthorised use of telecommunications system; and
■ ensure the communication system's security and effective operation.

However, in order to obtain the protection of the LBPR, the employer must also make all reasonable efforts to inform the system users that communications may be intercepted. This is most commonly done through inclusion in IT and electronic communications policies, employment contracts and general notices around the workplace. 'Users' has been interpreted not to include those external to the organisation (for example, those phoning in or sending incoming emails), making the requirement to give notice under the LBPR considerably less onerous than the equivalent requirement for consent under RIPA.

RIPA also imposes additional restrictions on public sector employers' ability to carry out covert monitoring (i.e. surveillance that is carried out in a manner calculated to ensure that persons who are subject to the surveillance are unaware that it is or may be taking place).

Data Protection Act 1998
Where monitoring of employees involves the processing of personal data, the Data Protection Act 1998 (DPA) also applies

(see also 'Data protection', p.101). It is rare that monitoring will not constitute processing for the purposes of the DPA, and employers should ensure that they comply with their obligations under this Act. For example, where monitoring is automatic (e.g. the automatic recording and monitoring of telephone calls, emails and internet access) or where staff are recorded on CCTV, data will be processed. Similarly, data will be processed if monitoring is not automatic but paper records are created that are then entered on to a computer system or filed in a structured filing system. Even where there is no technical 'processing' – for example, if a line manager listens into a call but makes no written record of it, employers are advised to follow the procedures required under the DPA.

The DPA has eight enforceable 'data protection principles', which provide, amongst other things, that personal data may only be collected where (i) it is necessary for one of the lawful bases for processing, (ii) it is relevant and (iii) it is not excessive for the purpose for which it is collected. It must also not be retained longer than is necessary and must be kept safe from accidental loss and unauthorised viewing.

In addition, processing must be fair and transparent, so individuals about whom personal data is collected must be informed of that fact, told why it is being collected and given a chance to view what data is held about them (and to correct it if it is inaccurate).

Organisations should be particularly careful if it is possible that sensitive personal data – such as information about an individual's health – could be captured by monitoring, as there are stricter requirements for the processing of such data (including normally requiring the individual's explicit consent).

The DPA gives the individual the right to claim compensation and rectification, blocking, erasure and destruction of personal data. The Information Commissioner may take action against organisations that do not comply with their obligations under the DPA, including the ability to levy a fine of up to £500,000 (see 'Data protection' (p.101) for more information).

Employment Practices Code

The Information Commissioner has issued an Employment Practices Code for the use of personal data in an employment relationship. The Code has no specific legal status and there are no set sanctions for failing to comply with the provisions of the Code. However, it provides an indication as to how the Commissioner will apply the DPA, and Employment Tribunals and courts should take the provisions of the Code into account where monitoring issues come before them.

It is in the interests of both the employer and their staff to comply with the Code. The Code encourages transparency about monitoring, which increases trust in the workplace, and helps the employer meet its legal requirements under the DPA and RIPA, reducing the risk of legal action.

Part 3 of the Code deals with employee monitoring, which is defined as 'activities that set out to collect information about workers by keeping them under some form of observation, normally with a view to checking their performance or conduct... either directly, indirectly, perhaps by examining their work output, or by electronic means'.

The Code covers various types of monitoring that would be expected, for example:

- using automated software to check whether a worker is sending or receiving inappropriate emails;
- checking emails to detect evidence of malpractice;
- examining logs of websites or telephone numbers to check for inappropriate use; and
- using CCTV in the workplace (see also 'CCTV monitoring, p.70).

The Code also covers some more unexpected activities, for example, collecting information through checkout terminals to monitor the efficiency of checkout operators, and videoing workers to collect evidence of malingering. The Code is also intended to cover information obtained through credit reference agencies to check that workers are not in financial difficulty.

The key message in the Code is that monitoring is intrusive, that workers have a legitimate expectation of privacy – even at work – and therefore if monitoring must take place, it should be balanced and proportionate.

The Code provides employers with detailed guidance to help them ensure that monitoring is proportionate. Employers are encouraged to carry out and record the results of impact assessments, which involves considering:

- the purpose of the monitoring arrangement and the benefit likely to result;
- whether it would have an adverse impact on the worker(s);
- whether there are any alternatives to achieve the identified purpose;
- the obligations arising from the monitoring; and
- whether the monitoring can be justified.

Other recommendations cover:

- notifying employees with a sufficient level of detail that monitoring is being carried out;
- ensuring that information collected through monitoring is only used for the purpose for which it was collected;
- ensuring that information collected through monitoring is stored in a secure way and access is limited;
- ensuring that individuals can gain access to monitoring information if requested in a subject access request (see 'Data Protection,' p.101);
- providing monitored individuals with an opportunity to make representations about the collected data; and
- having a person responsible for checking that the organisation's policies and procedures comply with the DPA – a 'data protection manager'.

Of course, the extent to which these will all be carried out will depend on a range of factors, including the size of the organisation, the regularity of monitoring and the data being recorded. However, where any type of monitoring takes place – even where limited and occasional – those involved should be given appropriate training so they are fully aware of their obligations under the DPA.

The Code contains guidance concerning specific types of monitoring, such as the monitoring of electronic communications, video and audio monitoring, and covert monitoring. The Code suggests that organisations should adopt a policy in relation to electronic communications, setting out acceptable and unacceptable use of email, internet and telephone and the monitoring that will be carried out of such use (see 'Internet and email policies', p.271).

The Code also provides guidance on how an organisation can meet the requirements of RIPA and LBPR, and the interaction between those pieces of legislation and the DPA. In essence, it does not necessarily follow that lawful collection under RIPA or LBPR will comply with the DPA and, likewise, even DPA-compliant collection may be unlawful under either or both of those statutes. Each statute needs to be considered for its own particular requirements.

Conclusion

The monitoring and recording of workers' activities is legally and politically sensitive, and if carried out incorrectly or unchecked can leave an employer open to significant penalties and legal action.

Employers that intend to carry out monitoring should first undertake the following steps:

- Become familiar with the legal obligations under RIPA, the LBPR and the DPA, and ensure that the intended monitoring is lawful under these statutes.
- Read and implement the recommendations of Part 3 of the Employment Practices Code, as well as any other available guidance, such as that published by Business Link and ACAS.
- Discuss, at a high level in the organisation, the need for monitoring and, if agreed that this is a justified course of action, draft and implement a comprehensive monitoring policy setting out the reasons for such monitoring, and the protections in place.
- Communicate the existence of monitoring to staff, and third parties who may also be affected. Where possible, obtain explicit consent from such persons.
- Bear in mind individuals' rights under the HRA at all times.

See also: CCTV monitoring, p.70; Data protection, p.101; Human rights, p.248; Internet and email policies, p.271; IT security, p.282; Personnel files, p.392; Social media, p.485.

Sources of further information

The Employment Practices Code can be found at http://bit.ly/1HLK49

ACAS advice leaflet on internet and email policies: www.acas.org.uk/media/pdf/d/b/AL06_1.pdf

Business Link guidance on monitoring in the workplace: www.businesslink.gov.uk/bdotg/action/layer?topicId=1074452663

Workplace Law's *IT and Email Policy and Management Guide v.3.0* has been designed to alert employers of the potential problems associated with using computer systems, the internet and email systems within the workplace and to provide certain safeguards. For more information visit www.workplacelaw.net.

Music licensing

Christine Geissmar, PPL, and Barney Hooper, PRS for Music

Key points
- Just about every workplace in the UK where music is played can find itself covered by wide-ranging copyright laws.
- Most businesses are aware of the benefits of music, but many are unaware of the legal requirements relating to its use in the workplace.

Legislation
- Copyright, Designs and Patents Act 1998.

PPL and PRS for Music

Copyright protects music in different ways and under the Copyright, Designs and Patents Act 1988, two separate licences are usually required whenever you play recorded music in public – one from PPL and one from PRS for Music.

PPL provides music licensing solutions for businesses that play recorded music in public. Established in 1934, PPL carries out this role on behalf of tens of thousands of performers and record companies, without retaining a profit. PPL's licensing of the public performance of recorded music enables businesses to lawfully use millions of recordings for very little effort.

PRS for Music carries out a very similar role, but collects for the songwriters, composers and music publishers, in respect of the rights in the musical compositions embodied in recorded music. Also a not-for-profit company, the society has 80,000 members and has been operating since 1914.

PPL and PRS for Music are two separate companies. Whilst carrying out similar functions, the two licensing organisations operate independently, represent different

rights holders and have separate tariffs, terms and conditions.

Why does a workplace need a music licence?

Like any other aspect of business, music has to be paid for. Under the Copyright, Designs and Patents Act 1988, if recorded music is 'played in public' (i.e. played in any context other than a domestic one) every play of every recording requires the permission of the record company that controls the copyright in the recording and the permission of the creator of the music in that recording.

If PPL and PRS for Music did not exist, businesses that wanted to use music would be required to contact potentially thousands of record companies, writers, composers and music publishers to individually obtain their permission, before being able to play music lawfully.

'Playing music in public' has a wide legal meaning. It is not limited to playing music at business premises where members of the general public have access (such as pubs, shops and gyms) but also such premises such as offices, factories and warehouses where music is being played to staff.

It is the legal responsibility of the proprietor to ensure that all their business premises

> **Facts**
> - Music can increase profits – research shows that more than a third of customers would be willing to pay 5% more for products and services from businesses that play music.
> - Music means more customers – 81% of customers that visited hair salons said that they would like to hear music. 70% would pay more to go to a restaurant that plays music.
> - Music can improve customer service – over a quarter of callers who were left holding in silence for one minute thought they had been holding for over five minutes on the phone, compared to 0% of callers who listened to on-hold music.
> - Music works for your staff – 66% of employees believed that music made them feel more motivated at work, with over a quarter stating they would be less likely to take sick time if music was played at work. 77% said they were more productive when good music was played, and this rises to an overwhelming 83% among warehouse workers.
> - In 2010 the size of the UK music industry was estimated at £3.8bn.

are appropriately licensed for playing recorded music in public. The proprietor is liable for any acts of infringement within the premises; therefore it is their duty to ensure that the premises are accurately licensed and that staff do not use recorded music within unlicensed premises.

Penalties for infringing copyright laws

Where a business or organisation requires a licence but does not obtain one, it is infringing copyright by playing recorded music in public. PPL and PRS for Music each regularly visit premises around the country to assess licensing requirements and ensure their information is up to date and complete.

Businesses requiring a music licence should contact both PPL and PRS for Music to ensure they have what they need. Both licensing organisations can help explain the requirements and ensure companies get the licences that are right for their business.

If a business continues to use music without having the correct licences then they could be taken to court; however this is always a last resort and both PPL and PRS for Music will work with a business to ensure they are licensed correctly.

If a case did go to court, then a business could be ordered to stop playing music until it has paid for the relevant music licences, and they may also have to pay legal costs.

Exemptions

A PPL licence is not required where a business or organisation does not play recorded music, or only does so in a domestic context (which would include closed family events such as weddings or birthday parties).

Where only live music is played, a PPL licence is not needed (as the recording is not being used) but a PRS for Music licence will be needed to cover the use of the compositions being performed live.

The process of obtaining a licence

The process of obtaining a licence from both PPL and PRS for Music is quick and easy.

To apply for (or find out more about) a PPL licence, you can either ring the PPL New Business Team on 0207 534 1070 or visit www.ppluk/en/Music-Users and click on the 'apply now' button. Licence fees must be paid in full before a licence is issued.

PRS for Music can be reached on 0800 0684828 or by visiting its website: www.prsformusic.com.

The cost of a licence

The cost of both a PRS for Music and PPL licence depends on the kind of business, what the size of the business premises is (which is measured in different ways depending on the business type), and how music is being played.

When introducing and revising tariffs, PPL seeks to charge a fair and reasonable fee. PPL and PRS for Music regularly consult with trade bodies and users in the affected business sectors as part of the tariff review process.

If, within the first year of having a PPL licence, a company's circumstances change, they can contact the PPL New Business Team to discuss. If a company has had a PPL Licence for longer than a year, they should contact the PPL switchboard on 0207 534 1070.

For more information on the benefits a licence can bring to a business, please visit www.musicworksforyou.com.

See also: Intellectual property, p.252.

Sources of further information

PPL: www.ppluk.com

PRS for music: www.prsformusic.com

www.musicworksforyou.com

Night working

Pinsent Masons Employment Group

Key points

Night workers attract special protection limiting their shifts and requiring the completion of regular health assessment; therefore it is important for employers to ascertain whether they employ workers who would be classified as night workers. If so, they should check:

- how much working time night workers normally work;
- if night workers work more than eight hours per day on average, whether the amount of hours can be reduced and if any exceptions apply;
- how to conduct a health assessment and how often health checks should be carried out;
- that proper records of night workers are maintained, including details of health assessments; and
- that night workers are not involved in work that is particularly hazardous.

Legislation
- Working Time Regulations 1998.
- Management of Health and Safety at Work Regulations 1999.

Working Time Regulations
The Working Time Regulations provide basic rights for workers in terms of maximum hours of work, rest periods and holidays. Night workers are afforded special protection by the Regulations. Depending on when they work, workers can be labelled 'night workers'.

Night workers
A 'night worker' is any worker whose daily working time includes at least three hours of night time:

- on the majority of days he works; or
- sufficiently often that he may be said to work such hours as a 'normal course', i.e. on a regular basis.

Employers and workers can agree a proportion of annual working time that must be worked during night time in order to qualify as a night worker in a collective or workforce agreement. However, the agreement cannot exclude workers who would otherwise count under the 'normal course' test.

Night time
In the absence of any contrary agreement, night time is defined as the period between 11 p.m. and six a.m. Another definition of night time hours can be determined in a relevant agreement, provided it lasts at least seven hours and includes hours between midnight and five a.m.

Night work limits
An employer must take all reasonable steps to ensure that the normal hours of a night worker do not exceed an average of eight hours for each 24 hours over a 17-week reference period (which can be extended in certain circumstances).

The average eight-hour limit applies to the 'normal hours of work' performed by the worker, not the hours actually worked.

> **Case study**
>
> *R v. Attorney General for Northern Ireland ex parte Burns* (1999)
>
> This case discussed the definition of 'night worker' and, in particular, the meaning of 'normal course'.
>
> The claimant was asked to change to a shift system, which would involve some night work, which she agreed to. She started on the new shift system but when the night work starting causing her some health problems she insisted on moving to a day shift and subsequently was dismissed.
>
> The UK had not implemented the Working Time Directive at the time, despite the fact that it should have done. The claimant brought judicial review proceedings against the Government for its failure to implement the Directive in time, since its failure left her unable to claim compensation against her employers.
>
> As part of the proceedings, the Northern Ireland High Court had to determine whether the claimant was a 'night worker' for the purposes of the Directive. The claimant worked the night shift one week in every three and in that one week of night shifts she worked three hours during night time. The Government argued that the claimant did not work nights in the 'normal course of her employment'.
>
> The court held that the words 'as a normal course' of employment meant no more than as 'a regular feature' of employment. Since the Directive had contemplated that a worker may work only three hours in the night time to be classified as a night worker, the definition of night worker should not be limited to only those workers who work in the night time exclusively or even predominantly.
>
> 'Normal course' therefore means 'on a regular basis', and is a wide definition. However, occasional or ad hoc work at night does not make a person a night worker.

Overtime was originally excluded from the calculation of normal hours but it has been included since 2003 where it is obligatory and guaranteed or regularly worked.

Therefore, normal hours includes contractual hours plus any compulsory or regular overtime, but not ad hoc overtime or a reduction in hours because of holidays, sickness, maternity or other reasons.

The average is calculated over a 17-week rolling reference period but a collective or workforce agreement may be used to stipulate fixed successive periods.

The other provisions in the Regulations relating to rest breaks and holidays apply equally to night workers.

Special hazards

Where a night worker's work involves special hazards or heavy physical or mental strain, there is an absolute limit of eight hours on any of the worker's working days. No average is allowed. Work involves a 'special hazard' if either:

- it is identified as such between an employer and workers in a collective agreement or workforce agreement; or
- it poses a significant risk as identified by a risk assessment that an employer has conducted under the Management of Health and Safety at Work Regulations 1999.

Health assessment

All employers must offer night workers a free health assessment before they begin working nights, and thereafter on a regular basis. Workers do not have to undergo a health assessment, but they must be offered one.

All employers should maintain up-to-date records of health assessments. A health assessment can comprise two parts – a medical questionnaire and a medical examination. It should take into account the type of work that the worker will do and any restrictions on the worker's working time under the Working Time Regulations. Employers are advised to take medical advice on the contents of a medical questionnaire.

Recent evidence has emerged linking night working and cancer, especially breast cancer amongst female night workers. A number of possible theories for why this might be have been put forward, including artificial light that night workers are regularly exposed to, and the fact that their body clock is out of sync with the environment. Employers should be alert to this and ensure that their workers know that drugs are available to help shift workers adjust to the time changes and to promote sleep.

New and expectant mothers

New and expectant mothers have certain special rights in relation to night work. See 'Pregnancy and maternity' (p.400).

See also: Occupational health, p.374; Pregnancy and maternity, p.400; Working time, p.564.

Sources of further information

Guidance on night working is available from the DirectGov site: www.direct.gov. uk/en/Employment/Employees/WorkingHoursAndTimeOff/DG_10028519

Notice periods

Mike Cummins, Cummins Solicitors

Key points

- In an employment law context, a contract (whether express or implied) will have a period of notice to end the relationship.
- There is a statutory minimum level of notice that has to be given, but the parties can contract to give a greater period of notice.
- The notice period will be determined either by law or by the terms of the contract, but it can be varied in some circumstances.
- Employees intending to take maternity, paternity, adoption or parental leave must give notice to the employer.

Legislation

- Section 86, Employment Rights Act 1996.
- Section 4, Section 11, Maternity and Parental Leave Regulations 1999.
- Schedule 2, Regulation 16 Maternity and Parental Leave Regulations 1999.
- Fixed-Term Employees (Prevention of Less Favourable Treatment) Regulations 2002.
- Paternity and Adoption Leave (Amendment) Regulations 2002.
- Work and Families Act 2006.

Contractual and statutory notice

In employment law, when the parties to an employment relationship want to bring the relationship to an end, they will have to serve notice.

Section 86 of the Employment Rights Act 1996 provides that employees with between one month and two years' continuous service are entitled to at least one week's statutory notice and, thereafter, to a further one week's notice for each complete year of continuous employment, up to a maximum of 12 weeks' notice after 12 years. Employees with periods of continuous employment of 12 years or more are entitled to at least 12 weeks'

notice. The minimum period of notice given by an employee after one month's employment is one week. A longer period of notice may be expressly agreed.

Garden leave

Many contracts of employment provide an employer with the option of not allowing an employee to attend the workplace during the notice period. The employee is paid and receives the same benefits. This is known as 'garden leave'. It means that an employee is unable to commence any new role.

The reason behind such a clause is clear. It allows an employer to keep an employee on notice, out of circulation and away from confidential information and/or trade secrets in the business. The clause has to be inserted into the contract in order that the employer is not acting in breach of the contract. See 'Restrictive covenants and garden leave' (p.441) for more information.

Payment in lieu of notice (PILON)

A PILON clause gives the employer the right to terminate an employee's contract of employment with immediate effect and to pay in lieu of the notice period that would have been worked. This means that the employer is not terminating the employee's contract in breach of contract and can still enforce post-termination restrictive covenants if applicable.

The inclusion of a PILON clause in a contract of employment means that the payment will be fully taxable.

If a PILON clause is included in the contract and is not discretionary, an employee does not have an obligation to mitigate their loss in the event that they are dismissed without notice or pay in lieu in circumstances where the employer is not entitled summarily to terminate the contract. Therefore the employee will have a claim as a debt for pay in lieu of notice in relation to the notice period, even if the employee succeeds in finding another job on identical terms and conditions of employment immediately.

Fixed-term contracts (FTC)

Employees recruited on contracts to complete specific tasks that are expected to last three months or less have a right to receive a minimum notice period of one week if their contracts are terminated before the expected expiry date and they have completed at least one month's continuous service.

If an FTC is for a period of four weeks or less, but owing to circumstances the employer allows the employee to continue in post for three months or more, the contract stops being an FTC and in a sense becomes a permanent contract with statutory notice periods applying.

If an employee has been employed on an FTC that has expired and then enters into a further FTC with the same employer, provided the gap between the two contracts is not more than one clear week (measured from Sunday – Saturday) the interval between the contracts will not break the continuity of employment. There are certain exceptions that provide for a longer period of time to lapse between consecutive fixed-term contracts. These include where the employee is incapable of work through illness or injury, where the break is due to a 'temporary cessation of work', or where continuity is preserved by arrangement or custom.

Subject to the above, statutory notice periods do not apply to a FTC. There is nothing to prevent an employer from including a notice period in a FTC that allows earlier termination of employment as a contractual term, if the employer wishes to have this facility.

It is actually considered sensible to do this as, without an early termination clause, an employer may be committed to pay for the full term of the FTC, even if circumstances change such that the employee is no longer required. The reason why the employer ends a contract early should, in any event, be a fair reason and be reasonable in all the circumstances.

Notice periods of maternity, paternity, adoption or parental leave

An employee intending to take maternity or paternity leave must give notice before the end of the 15th week before the expected date of birth. They must state the expected week of childbirth and the date of the start of the leave. An employee taking paternity leave should also state how much leave is being taken. An employee taking maternity or paternity leave is able to change their mind about when they want to start maternity / paternity leave, providing they inform the employer at least 28 days in advance.

Employees intending to take adoption leave must notify the employer within seven days of confirmation that they have been matched for adoption, the date the child is expected, and the date leave will commence.

Employees, unless it is otherwise collectively agreed, must provide their employer with 21 days' notice of when they will take parental leave.

Employees returning from maternity or adoption leave do not have to give any notice to their employer if they are returning at the end of their entitled leave. The employer is responsible for informing the employee of when the leave expires.

In the event that an employee wants to return early, eight weeks' notice must be given to the employer. Failure to do this means an employer can postpone the return until this has run out or until the date when the leave would have ended. Should the employee not wish to return at the end of a period of leave, normal contractual notice must be given to the employer. There is no requirement for an employee to state in advance whether she intends to return after maternity or adoption leave.

Retirement

The default retirement age (DRA) of 65, together with all of the associated statutory requirement procedures, were phased out from 6 April 2011 and abolished altogether from 1 October 2011. This means that employers can no longer automatically retire employees at 65 by giving at least six months' notice. Retirement dismissals will now have to be dealt with on an individual basis and the notice period that will apply will be governed by the employee's contractual entitlement, or statutory minimum notice if that is greater.

See also: Dismissal, p.146; Employment contracts, p.164; Fixed-term workers, p.218; Leave, p.252; Pregnancy and maternity, p.400; Restrictive covenants and garden leave, p.441; Retirement, p.445.

Sources of further information

For organisations with or without a HR team who require specialist support, advice through hands-on support and/or project management, Workplace Law offer tailored strategic HR support and advice to suit the needs of your organisation. To enable your organisation to focus on its core business our CIPD qualified and HR specialist team can provide support and advice on a number of strategic HR offerings. Our dedicated HR team can work with you on key HR projects aligned to your HR strategy and business plan.

All of our HR professionals have 20 plus years of hands-on experience, working in every sector, in small, medium and large organisations. Our HR professionals bring this unique knowledge and experience to provide advice, support and project management to ensure the best fit for your organisation. Visit www.workplacelaw.net for more information.

Comment ...

Whither the pendulum?

Peter Browning

The recent call by the CBI for a review of employment legislation suggests the thought that the pendulum has swung too far toward the employee, and thus ceases to be fair to employers. Yes, I know, it all depends upon your point of view, and how you interpret the concept of fairness. At the one extreme are the Victorian employers – those who built the Empire (and their fortunes) on the backs of the workers. At the other extreme, there are those who believe that the world, and their employer if they have one, owes them a comfortably effortless living.

Between those two extremes, there is a vast range of good employers and good employees, peppered sadly with perhaps too many 'bad apples' in both barrels to allow that the world of employment could be unfettered by law, even if that was today an option within European legislation.

Bad apples do require legislation, but one might reasonably argue that any logical concept of fairness in employment law has simply died as a result. Employment law is today almost unique in jurisprudence because, perhaps in too many instances, the employer is required to prove his innocence. Innocent until proven guilty? No, guilty until proven innocent! That might reasonably be regarded as a direct contravention of the Magna Carta, and of the freedoms for which so many have given so much, but it is these days a very real and sometimes very costly element of employment law.

 Peter Browning is now at the 'wrong' end of his 50+ year career, begun in a design drawing-office and, through seven years in banking, into retail distribution. Taking up his first management job in 1956, just when the Suez crisis began, his job grew over the next 14 years to the control of a large retail network from the Severn to the Thames. After three years at an FE College, Peter returned to his native Cornwall where, eventually, he was able to take up self-employment in a business which, before he retired, had grown to employ nearly 200 people, spread over five locations. The thing he now misses most is the 15 years he spent as a lay member of Employment Tribunals.

Perhaps the best approach to deciding what is fair, and what is unfair, is to begin with the common law on contract. In simple terms, I walk into a bar, and order a pint of Guinness. The 'pint' is duly delivered, but with an over-abundance of froth. Having ordered and paid for a pint, should I not have my pint glass properly filled? But what happens in the world of employment? I wish to buy 40 hours of labour per week, and every hour (at the current rate) must cost £6.08. No it doesn't, it must cost all of that, £243 every week, plus National Health Insurance, statutory sick pay, statutory holidays, maternity and paternity pay, together with the cost of compliance with a huge raft of employment, health, safety, discrimination and disability laws, and I must also reserve against future redundancy and notice pay entitlements.

But then we get to the really daft bit. At law, even if he wins his case, an employer always loses – not only the cost of representation but also the costs of attendance and preparation. Extremely rarely, these costs may be awarded, but the law is now so complex that Tribunals (although headed by lawyers) too often get things wrong.

There must then be an Appeal (at even more cost) to the Employment Appeal Tribunal and, again too often, to the Higher Courts. And then the learned judges will dance on the head of a pin whilst trying to interpret the intention of Parliament. This begs the question: If lawyers cannot agree upon how the law should work, how on earth is the lay employer expected to be able to cope with this degree of complexity, whilst simultaneously having to succeed in an increasingly competitive national and international marketplace?

> "Bad apples do require legislation, but one might reasonably argue that any logical concept of fairness in employment law has simply died as a result. Employment law is today almost unique in jurisprudence because, perhaps in too many instances, the employer is required to prove his innocence. Innocent until proven guilty? No, guilty until proven innocent!"

There will of course be those who thoroughly disagree with me, but I submit that the source of any such disagreement can only arise from a basic presumption that one has an absolute right to be employed, and that the employer is solely responsible for all that then follows – good or bad. He must also collect taxes, and he must account for and remit those taxes entirely at his own expense.

But there is no law that says that an employee must give value for money, so that the employer can only rely upon mutual trust and confidence. There is nothing in employment legislation that requires that my metaphorical half-hourly pint of Guinness shall be fairly frothed, and this, I believe, is where the imbalance presently lies.

Dare we go back to the Victorian drawing board? Mr Thomas Carlyle, a Scottish Calvinist, made very clear his view – 'A fair day's wages for a fair day's work', but he could usefully have added that 'fairness is a two-edged sword'. If it doesn't cut both ways then, whatever else, it sure ain't fair.

Occupational health

Greta Thornbory, Occupational Health Consultant

Key points
- 'Work is generally good for your health and wellbeing.' The authors of this statement, Waddell and Burton, added several provisos in that there are various physical and psychological aspects of work that are hazardous and can pose a risk to health and work should do the worker no harm.
- Conversely, employers want to employ people who will give them good service, who have the knowledge, skills and understanding to take on the roles and tasks required of them. Occupational health (OH) services are designed to support and help employers meet these requirements.
- This chapter will cover:
  - What is Occupational health (OH)?
  - How OH can help employers to fulfil their legal requirements.
  - The financial implications of health and safety at work whilst ensuring business viability.

Legislation

There is a great deal of legislation that employers are required to consider and comply with regarding the health, safety and welfare of employees; not only health and safety legislation but also that which comes under employment law, all of which affects the health of the employee. All the health and safety legislation is under review by the present Coalition Government at the time of writing.

The Health and Safety at Work etc. Act 1974 (HSWA) is an overarching piece of legislation in that it sets out the duty of the employer to take care of the health, safety and welfare of their employees, and of others who may be affected by his work undertaking – so far as is reasonably practicable. It is from this main Act that most secondary health and safety legislation is derived, and singularly the most important is the Management of Health and Safety at Work Regulations, which charges employers with the duty to undertake a risk assessment in relation to the health and safety of employees.

What is OH?

In 1950 the Joint ILO (International Labour Organisation) / WHO (World Health Organisation) issued the first definition of OH, which was updated in 1995 to these three objectives:

1. The maintenance and promotion of workers' health and working capacity.
2. The improvement of working environment and work to become conducive to health and safety.
3. The development of work organisation and working cultures in a direction that supports health and safety at work and in doing so promotes a positive social climate and smooth operation and may enhance the productivity of the undertaking.

Defining 'health'

The most accepted definition is from the World Health Organisation, which defines health as 'a state of complete physical, mental and social wellbeing and not merely the absence of disease or infirmity'.

> **Case study**
>
> At an Employment Tribunal, when Dundee City Council was found in breach of the Management of Health and Safety Regulations, its Personnel Manager admitted that he did not understand the meaning of OH and the Tribunal itself struggled to define it during the course of the hearing. It would probably have been better if they had asked for an OH expert from one of the OH bodies to give an explanation and to demonstrate the business case. The HSE has said that the appropriate use of OH expertise and resources is necessary to comply with statutory duties and will help with reducing work-related sickness absence.

Why occupational health?

OH has been and is promoted on all levels; the international perspective is supported by the WHO/ILO. In turn OH has been, and is, supported at a national level by all UK governments to a greater or lesser extent, although to date there is no legal requirement for employers or employees to have access to OH it is strongly recommended in much of the guidance issued from government departments.

OH also figures clearly in the Government strategies for health at the beginning of the 21st Century. Various government departments, together with the HSE, have produced a plethora of strategies and plans over the years. Today much of this is based on the work of Dame Carole Black from the recommendations in her report published in 2008. The report and all the up-to-date strategies can be found at the website www.dwp.gov.uk/health-work-and-well-being/. Health, work and wellbeing is a cross government initiative that promotes the positive links between health and work. Companies can even download a tool that enables them to assess and help improve the health and wellbeing of their employees.

Key to the health, work and wellbeing initiatives is the management of absence from work by supporting employees with ill health, chronic conditions by enabling return to work and rehabilitation. This is where occupational health professionals can help and support both employers and employees as they have the specialist knowledge and skills to do this. The Government is in the process of piloting a number of projects with regard to return to work and rehabilitation following the introduction of the new 'fit note' which GPs are required to indicate what special considerations should be given to an employee returning to work after sickness absence. The mantra today being 'not work can't you do but what can you do'.

Small employers who are not in a position to employ dedicated occupational health professionals can now use a free Occupational Health advice line. However, to companies who have access to occupational health professionals there remains no change to their remit except to embrace the concept of public health and the setting up of a new Council for Work and Health. This council is chaired by Diana Kloss and its members are from all the branches of the professions that make up occupational health and health and safety. The Council is in its early days of work. For more details and up-to-date information on occupational health and health at work, visit the Health, Work and Wellbeing website.

The legal aspect

One legal requirement for employers is Employer Liability Compulsory Insurance (ELCI) and this is often quoted when challenging employers about their health, safety and wellbeing provision for employees. However, there are many costs not covered by the insurance. The issue here is that it is the cost of the insurance that is the problem, not that it is a compulsory legal requirement. OH professionals offer sound advice on how to comply with applicable legislation to reduce the adverse effects of work on health and to reduce the risk of prosecution and legal liability. This is particularly relevant where health surveillance is required or where health is likely to be affected, resulting in costly long-term sickness absence. It is known that work-related stress-related conditions and MSDs are the two main causes of long-term sickness absence.

Financial aspects

If employers want 'maximum output for minimum outlay' then they need to appreciate the financial benefits of considering the health and wellbeing of employees, particularly the ill health that is caused or made worse by work. OH professionals advise organisations on health assessment, health surveillance and monitoring, managing absence and general health and lifestyle issues. Every employer pays a premium for employers' liability compulsory insurance. This is to cover injuries and ill health experienced by employees whilst at work. It does not cover the whole scenario. For every £1 of insured costs of an accident or ill health there will be another £10 of uninsured costs. The HSE describes ELCI as the tip of the iceberg. As the founder of easyJet said after being cleared of the death of five people in a tanker accident and a subsequent 11-year lawsuit: "If you think safety is expensive, try an accident".

OH professionals

OH professionals are mainly doctors and nurses who have undertaken specific training in the field of OH, usually to first degree or higher degree level. The Faculty of Occupational Medicine has developed an accreditation scheme for Occupational Health Services and employers. It is still in its early stages of development and over 200 organisations are going through accreditation at time of writing. This service can be accessed via www.seqohs.org

See also: Absence management, p.16; Health surveillance, p.231; Mental health, p.308; Pregnancy and maternity, p.400; Sickness, p.470; Smoking, p.478; Stress, p.500.

Sources of further information

World Health Organisation (WHO): www.who.int/en/

Working for Health: www.dwp.gov.uk/health-work-and-well-being/

Workplace Law's **Occupational Health 2008: Making the business case – Special Report** addresses the issues of health at work, discusses the influence of work on health and highlights the business case for occupational health services at work. For more information visit www.workplacelaw.net.

Outsourcing

Louise Smail, Ortalan

Key points

Before outsourcing:

- Have clear objectives and understand the implications of outsourcing.
- Consider issues, aside from cost, that the outsourcing will bring.
- Is there a commitment from the organisation to manage the relationship?
- How will key people be affected by the outsourcing?
- What impact will it have on the organisation?
- Have a clear understanding about what services are to be provided.

Supplier selection:

- Guarantee to meet specific service levels in the contract.
- Has a proven track record in the service being outsourced.
- Issues around conflict of interest with other clients.
- Has intellectual property been considered?
- Ongoing training of staff and staff development.

Contract:

- Supplier's performance – KPIs.
- Flexibility for introducing contract variations.
- Flexibility to accommodate new services and projects.
- The means of resolving day-to-day problems.

Legislation

UK law does not specifically regulate outsourcing arrangements, but the following should be considered.

Public sector

Public sector outsourcing may be subject to UK Regulations that implement EC public procurement directives. Where this is the case, the awarding authority may be required to use the *Official Journal* of the EU to advertise the intention to outsource and ensure that all bidders are treated equally. The EU public procurement rules are likely to impact on the timing of the pre-contract procedure and influence the award criteria adopted.

Even if the outsourcing by public organisations is outside the public procurement legislation, the awarding authority should still generally seek to comply with the spirit of the legislation (*OJ C179/2,1 August 2006*). The UK private finance initiative (PFI) legislation applies to certain public sector outsourcing arrangements. Notice should also be taken of other laws and guidance such as:

- detailed guidance published by the Office of Government Commerce: www.hm-treasury.gov.uk/d/ managingrisks_deliverypartners.pdf
- Human Rights Act 1998.
- Local Government Acts 1999 – 2003.
- Freedom of Information Act 2000.

Financial services

The main piece of legislation regulating financial services is the Financial Services and Markets Act 2000 (FSMA). The statutory regulator is the Financial Services Authority (FSA) under the FSMA and issues rules and guidance. An FSA-regulated firm cannot delegate or contract out of its regulatory obligations when outsourcing, and must give advance notice to the FSA of any proposal to enter into an outsourcing arrangement and of any changes to such arrangements. There are specific FSA rules on outsourcing. There are additional requirements where firms outsource portfolio management for retail clients to a supplier in a non-EEA state.

There are no additional regulations related to IT, telecommunications, or business processes. It is important that any prospective supplier or customer should ensure that any proposed outsourcing is not subject to additional regulatory requirements in other sectors.

Benefits of outsourcing

Outsourcing has been an issue for many businesses for some time, both in the private and public sector. The current economic crisis has seen many businesses who previously may not have considered this looking closely at it as an option, and it may now form a new model for businesses during the foreseeable future. Outsourcing and partnering arrangements have the potential to deliver value well beyond cost savings, by opening access to talent and capabilities, whilst maximising business model flexibility. However, this is not without its challenges. Many companies are held back by cost benefit justification and their own lack of experience. Often when the projects involving outsourcing fail, the organisation's first inclination is to blame the service providers, with the service providers thinking that the main cause of failure is poor collaboration with customers.

Many of the disadvantages can be avoided if organisations research the service provider and do not regard outsourcing simply as a money saving scheme, as this is not always the case. As a consequence, organisations should be certain that they have a valid reason for outsourcing and that they intend to liaise regularly with the service provider to avoid losing all control of the process.

The current economic downturn is a large concern for a lot of organsiations who are looking to protect their profit margins by reducing cost. Some consider restructuring their business or divesting loss-making assets. Many companies are considering or have already decided to outsource certain of their business processes, which should allow them to reduce costs, refocus core activities and to help transform their business.

When an organisation is thinking about outsourcing, they need to carry out a due diligence exercise, looking carefully at what it is they are going to outsource. They need to look closely at the internal costs and make sure that all the tax, legal and commercial issues have been fully explored. Then an organisation can go into the process with a full understanding of all the issues that they need to address. It may also be possible that at the end of this exercise outsourcing is no longer an attractive option and isn't taken up.

Processes that can be outsourced

- *IT functions* – most IT functions can be outsourced, including:
    - network management to project work;
    - website development; and
    - data warehousing.

- This can provide benefits by providing the latest technology and software upgrades without having expensive investments.
- *HR and business processes* – this can include activities such as recruitment, payroll and secretarial services and can provide access to specialist skills that you only pay for when they are used.
- *Finance* – auditing is usually outsourced anyway, but this can be the entire accounting function, including bookkeeping, tax management and invoicing.
- *Sales and marketing* – an agency can be used to handle marketing communications.
- *Health and safety* – there are consultants who specialise in health and safety compliance.
- Fire and security.
- Legal advice.
- Logistics.
- Installations and service.

Non-business-critical tasks can also be outsourced, such as cleaning, catering and facilities management.

Types of outsourcing

- *Direct outsourcing* – contract between outsourcing organisation and supplier.
- *Multi-sourcing* – outsourcing organisation contracts with many different suppliers – important to indirect outsourcing wherethe outsourcing organisation appoints a supplier who then immediately sub-contracts to a different supplier, possibly outside the UK.
- *Joint venture or partnership* – the outsourcing organisation and the supplier set up a joint venture company, partnership or contractual joint venture. These maybe as an off-shore entity.
- *Captive entity* – the outsourcing organisation outsources its processes to a wholly owned subsidiary.

- *Build operate transfer* – the outsourcing supplier contracts with a third party to build and operate a facility. This facility is then transferred back to the outsourcing organisation.

Choosing your outsourcing partner

It is important to investigate not just the references offered by the potential partner but ensure that they are not so popular and in such demand that they are overstretched and won't be able to supply the right staff. When interviewing and selecting your partner, make sure that the key staff who are suggested are actually the ones that will be part of your arrangement with them.

Legal issues and contract matters

Contracts will necessarily focus on ensuring the key performance indicators, to ensure that the service is provided in the way that the organisation expects. There are other issue that also need to be considered – maintenance agreements, software licenses, any assets – and that can include employees who are needed to provide the service and details of their ownership.

How long is the outsourcing contract for? What break points are included? It is important to have a point in the contract so that if it isn't working the contract can be broken without penalties.

Where the outsourced service is critical to the operation of the business, any losses that may be suffered if the supplier fails may be significant. Any liabilities that are imposed in the contract should be proportionate to the value of the contract. It is important to identify any areas where the outsourcing organisation's liability should not be subject to any limit. This could be in relation to indemnity in relation to intellectual property rights or TUPE issues, which are often unlimited because they represent the organisation's protection for unquantifiable third party liabilities, which the outsourcing organisation is able to prevent or control.

Privacy, confidentiality and intellectual property

It is important that there is a non-disclosure agreement and privacy clause as part of the contract. Employees of the organisation would be subject to this and so should the outsourcing organisation. It is also important to make sure that the organisation outsourcing the work has a clear understanding and contractual arrangement to ensure that its intellectual property is protected. Transfer of employees to the new provider is an important consideration. It is also important to consider obligations to the employees and also the liabilities for these employees at the end of the contract. The contract also needs to look at how assets that are used by the outsourcing organsiations are managed, and also what will happen to these at the end of the contract.

Consideration needs to be given to how any new intellectual property rights are to be dealt with, and who owns them. Some of this will depend on negotiation, how much is paid for the services, and which of the services are a bespoke solution. The organisation may have to consider granting a license.

- Identify confidential information and specify the type of security that is expected.
- List applicable privacy laws and regulations.
- Require the outsourcer to limit access to authorised personnel.
- Specify that the outsourcer shall be liable for complying with applicable laws and regulations.
- Exercise access and control over the information; impose restrictions on how information may be used,

transferred, or shared; and ensure the right to audit the outsourcer's security procedures.

Business continuity

Organisations whose business continuity plan has relied upon their own resources will now need to make sure that the outsourcer is also part of this process. They should be part of any arrangements and fully informed about their part in it and also take part in any exercises.

Managing the contract performance

Any service description in the contract should be legally enforceable. There needs to be a detailed description of the services to be provided and all the obligations on the outsourcing organisation should be clearly identified and what the organisation expectsof the outsourcing organisation (key performance indicators).

Terminating an outsourcing arrangement

Any outsourcing arrangement needs to include a mechanism for management of the relationship and procedures to be followed when problems arise. If these remedies are not successful then there should be an exit plan that considers the provision of the services for the duration of the notice period and any period including cooperation with the new outsourcer. There also needs to be a system for the return or transfer back of assets and software and the licences of intellectual property and the provision of information and know-how to the organisation or new outsourcer. Consideration will also have to be made about the treatment of employees and any obligations under TUPE and other relevant regulations.

Whatever organisations decide to do, they need to remember that although the work is outsourced, the risk and liability issues arising still need to be managed as it remains with them.

Ten things to avoid

1. Selecting the wrong vendor.
2. Outsourcer's people do not understand the organisation – make sure that you get the staff that were promised, or equivalent experience and competence.
3. Stuck with only one vendor and a contract that doesn't work – ensure that the question is asked before outsourcing – what happens if this doesn't work?
4. Creeping specification – starting with a neat and easily understood set of services and then widening it to include many other issues and therefore making the contract limits and performance difficult to understand.
5. Security breaches and confidentiality arrangement.
6. Failure of the business continuity – disaster recovery system.
7. Employees not engaged with the process.
8. Difference governance models – make sure these are aligned before you start.
9. Increased costs – ensure that increases in costs, both for employees and services, are covered in the contract.
10. Misaligned reporting systems.

See also: Agency and temporary workers, p.25; Contract disputes, p.90; Contractors, p.93; Employment contracts, p.164; Facilities management contracts, p.204; Intellectual property, p.252; IT security, p.282; Secondment, p.459; TUPE, p.523.

Sources of further information

National Outsourcing Organisation www.noa.co.uk

Complying with health and safety law – and looking after the health, safety and welfare of everyone connected with your organisation – can be time-consuming and complicated, diverting precious resources and attention away from your main focus – your core business. Workplace Law can help, because managing the health and safety of an organisation, like yours, is *our* core business.

The Workplace Law **Health and Safety Support Contract** provides you with total support, 365 days of the year, regardless of how many people you employ. Since every organisation is unique, so is our support contract – tailored to meet the specific needs of your business, your people, and the sector you operate in.

The level of support can be designed to either assist your health and safety team, or act as your competent person, as required under the Management of Health and Safety at Work Regulations 1999. We offer sensible, pragmatic advice concentrating on practical action to control significant risks – not over-responding to trivial issues. Visit www.workplacelaw.net for more information.

Part-time workers

Pinsent Masons Employment Group

Key points

- It has always been risky to treat part-time workers less favourably than comparable full-time workers, owing to the potential for a claim of sex discrimination or equal pay.
- Regulations introduced in 2000 now also provide protection for part-time 'workers' (wider than the term 'employees'), irrespective of sex discrimination.
- Part-time workers can request a written statement from their employers if they suspect discrimination, requiring their employer to provide an explanation for their treatment.
- Employers should review their practices and procedures to ensure that they are compliant with legislation.
- There is no exemption for small businesses.
- The Part-Time Working Regulations are untouched by the Equality Act 2010 and will remain in force.

Legislation

- Part-time Workers (Prevention of Less Favourable Treatment) Regulations 2000.
- Part-time Workers (Prevention of Less Favourable Treatment) Regulations 2000 (Amendment) Regulations 2002.

Overview

The Part-time Workers (Prevention of Less Favourable Treatment) Regulations 2000 (the Regulations) came into force on 1 July 2000 to provide a basic right for part-time workers not to be treated less favourably on the grounds of their part-time status than comparable full-time workers, unless this can be justified on objective grounds. This means part-time workers are entitled, for example, to:

- the same hourly rate of pay;
- the same access to company pension schemes;
- the same entitlements to annual leave and to maternity and parental leave on a pro rata basis;
- the same entitlement to contractual sick pay; and
- no less favourable treatment in access to training.

Who do the Regulations apply to?

The Regulations apply to 'workers' and not just to 'employees'. This wider definition includes part-time workers who may not be employees, such as homeworkers and agency workers. They apply to men as well as women.

A part-time worker is someone who is 'paid wholly or partly by reference to the time he works and, having regard to the custom and practice of the employer in relation to workers employed by the worker's employer under the same type of contract, is not identifiable as a full-time worker'.

A part-time worker must therefore be identified by reference to the particular circumstances of each employer.

Facts

- According to the latest statistics, 7.82 million people work part-time in the UK. This represents the highest since records began in 1992, and accounts for more than a quarter of the workforce.
- Overall the number of people in part-time employment was 7.82 million in the three months to May 2010, up 148,000 from the three months to February 2010. Of this total, 1.94 million were men and 5.87 million were women.
- In April 2009 hourly rates for men were £12.97 for full-timers, £7.71 for part-timers and £12.42 for all employees. For women, hourly rates were £11.39 for full-timers, £7.86 for part-timers and £9.68 for all employees.
- When calculated using the mean rather than the median, women's hourly pay was 16.4% less than men's pay for full-time employees, and 13.2% less than men's pay for part-time employees.
- 79% of women who work part-time state that they do not want a full-time job, and of these, 74% say that children or domestic family responsibilities are their reason for working part-time.
- Only 7% of managers and senior officials work part-time, compared to 33% of those in administrative and secretarial occupations.
- Only 8% of those in skilled trades occupations work part-time, compared to 52% of those in personal service jobs and 57% in sales and customer service jobs.

'Less favourable treatment'

A part-time worker has the right not to be treated less favourably than the employer treats a comparable full-time worker as regards the terms of their contract or by being subjected to any other detriment by any act, or deliberate failure to act, by their employer.

The Tribunal must be satisfied that the treatment was on the ground that the worker is a part-time worker. Where less favourable treatment is alleged, the burden is on the employer to show that the reason was objectively justified, i.e. was something other than that they were a part-time worker. Less favourable treatment cannot be offset or cancelled out by more favourable treatment of a different kind – the 'term by term' approach.

The employer is permitted to treat the part-time worker differently where it can objectively justify the difference in treatment. Less favourable treatment will only be justified on objective grounds if it can be shown that the less favourable treatment is to achieve a legitimate objective (e.g. a genuine business objective), that it is necessary to achieve that objective, and that it is an appropriate way to achieve the objective.

Discrimination at all stages of employment – recruitment, promotion, terms of employment and dismissal – is potentially unlawful.

Promotion is an area where employers have often in the past favoured full-time staff over part-timers. Previous or current part-time status should not form a barrier to promotion to a post, whether the post itself is full-time or part-time. Part-time employees must also not receive a lower basic rate of pay than comparable full-time employees, unless this can be 'objectively justified' (e.g. by a performance-related pay scheme).

The same hourly rate of overtime pay should be paid to part-timers as to comparable full-time employees, once they have worked more than the normal full-time hours. The Regulations do not provide part-time workers with an automatic right to overtime payments once they work beyond their normal hours. However, part-timers working beyond their contracted hours should be paid the same as a full-timer would be paid for working the same number of hours, otherwise there is a risk of an equal pay claim.

The Regulations allow part-time workers to participate in the full range of benefits available to full-timers, such as profit-sharing schemes, unless there are objective grounds for excluding them. Any benefits should be pro rata to those received by comparable full-time workers. Also, employers must not exclude part-time workers from training schemes as a matter of principle. They should take great care to ensure that part-timers get the same access to training as full-time workers.

Part-time workers must be given the same treatment in relation to maternity leave, parental leave and time off for dependants as their full-time colleagues, on a pro rata basis where this is appropriate. Similarly, career break schemes should be made available to part-time workers in the same way, unless their exclusion is objectively justified.

Comparators

To assert less favourable treatment, a comparison must be made with an appropriate full-time worker. The Regulations only allow part-time workers to compare themselves with actual full-time

workers working for the same employer in the same or similar work and with a similar level of qualifications and experience. They must also be employed under the same type of contract. Unlike claims under discrimination legislation, claimants under these Regulations are not allowed to base a claim on how the employer would have treated a hypothetical comparator.

Written reasons

The Regulations provide that in certain cases the worker is entitled to a written explanation for their difference in treatment.

Where a worker believes that they have been treated less favourably by their employer because of their part-time status they can make a request in writing for a written statement of particulars of the reasons for the treatment. The employer must reply to the request within 21 days. If the employer deliberately and without reasonable excuse omits to provide a written statement, or the statement is evasive or equivocal, the Tribunal can make an inference. Any written statement that is provided is admissible in evidence in any subsequent proceedings brought under the Regulations.

If the employee is submitting an unfair dismissal claim, a written statement can be requested under Section 92 of the Employment Rights Act 1996 (ERA), and therefore a written statement cannot also be requested under the Regulations. As with written statements issued under the Regulations, a written statement issued under the ERA is admissible as evidence in proceedings. Note, however, there is no specific provision in the ERA allowing Tribunals to draw inferences as to the reason for dismissal from the lack of a written statement or an unequivocal response. The burden is on the employer to prove the reason for dismissal though, and there is no reason why a Tribunal should not draw an inference if the employer is evasive. In addition, where the employer has not reasonably provided the statement or where it is inadequate or untrue, the Tribunal can award two weeks' pay.

Dismissal

There are certain situations in which a dismissal by an employer for a specific reason will be treated as being automatically unfair. For example, where someone is dismissed for bringing proceedings against the employer under the Regulations, this will be deemed automatically unfair. No qualifying period of employment is required for such a claim.

Where someone is dismissed as a result of his part-time status and a comparable full-time worker was not dismissed, this will be a form of less favourable treatment and the employee may make a complaint to a Tribunal under the Regulations, as well as bringing an ordinary unfair dismissal claim.

If there is a redundancy situation, then part-time workers should be treated just as favourably as full-timers, unless this difference in treatment can be objectively justified. Part-time status should not be a criterion for selection for redundancy.

Sex discrimination, equal pay and changing to part-time work

Part-time workers who are treated less favourably in relation to full-time workers may also be able to bring an indirect sex discrimination claim. For example, it can be argued that a refusal to consider part-time workers for promotion amounts to indirect sex discrimination because most part-time workers are women. They may also have an equal pay claim. For example, the payment of a bonus to full-time workers without a pro rata bonus being paid to part-time workers may

breach the principle of equal pay for equal work.

Before the Regulations came into force, these claims were often the only recourse that part-time workers had, and there remains a large overlap between the Regulations and the sex discrimination and equal pay provisions in the Equality Act 2010. It is now relatively common to find claimants submitting claims under both the Regulations and the Equality Act 2010 in Tribunal proceedings. However, using the Regulations avoids a lot of the expense and complexity associated with equal pay and sex discrimination claims. For more information see *'Discrimination'* (p.126).

Note, also, that the Regulations do not give full-time workers the right to switch to part-time working. An indirect sex discrimination claim is still the avenue of redress for claimants whose employers have refused to allow a woman to switch to part-time hours due to childcare responsibilities or after a period of maternity leave.

Flexible working

Employees of either sex with children under 17 may have the right to request a change in working patterns (such as a change in hours) under the flexible working provisions. However, these provisions do not afford a positive right to switch to part-time working. An employer simply has an obligation to consider requests and must follow certain procedural requirements. These provisions do, however, augment the sex discrimination rules by providing a framework to employees to put forward their case for flexible working, requiring an employer to consider the merits of their case.

Practical points

Employers will find it useful to take note of the following points:

- They should review periodically when they can offer posts on a part-time basis. If an applicant wishes to work part-time, the employer should ascertain whether a part-time worker could fulfil the requirements of the job.
- Employers should look seriously at requests to change to part-time working and, where possible, explore how this can be carried out.
- They should review how individuals are provided with information on the availability of part-time and full-time positions.
- Employers are encouraged to keep representative bodies informed about certain aspects of the business' use of part-time workers.
- Benefits that cannot be pro-rated should be identified. Unless there are objective reasons for not providing them to part-time employees, consider providing a cash alternative.
- Managers should amend their handbooks (e.g. pay, bonuses, sick pay, maternity pay, pensions, holidays, etc.) to include a section on part-time workers and the consequences of breaching the Regulations.
- Disciplinary procedures should be amended to make it a disciplinary offence to discriminate against part-time workers.

- Awareness of the rights of part-time workers may need to be raised, and training provided on the subject.

Enforcement

Workers can bring a number of claims under the Regulations.

They can bring a claim of less favourable treatment or detriment within three months of the relevant act or omission by the employer. Where the Tribunal upholds the claim it can make a declaration as to the rights of the parties, order the party to pay compensation, or recommend that the employer take action to obviate or reduce the adverse effect on the claimant of any matter to which the claim relates within a specified period.

Where the worker is dismissed as a result of their part-time status the employee may bring an unfair dismissal claim in addition to a claim for less favourable treatment.

See also: Benefits schemes, p.44; Discrimination, p.126; The Equality Act, p.191; Family-friendly rights, p.206; Fixed-term workers, p.218.

Sources of further information

BIS Guidance on Part Time Workers: http://bit.ly/qVpguP

Pensions

Alice Hill, Taylor Wessing

Key points

- Pension provision in the UK falls into two categories – state benefits and private arrangements.
- State pensions comprise basic state pensions and state second pensions (S2P). Contributions are collected from employees and employers via National Insurance Contributions (NICs). The amount of state pension that an individual will receive will depend on the NICs paid or credited over an individual's working life.
- Private pension arrangements may take the form of either occupational pension schemes or personal pensions.
- Occupational pension schemes are schemes established by an employer, for the benefit of employees. Different occupational pension schemes operate different arrangements. These are commonly known as defined benefit schemes or defined contribution schemes.
- Employers with five or more relevant employees, who do not offer an occupational or personal pension scheme that meets certain criteria, must provide employees with access to a stakeholder pension. This is usually a type of personal pension scheme and is one to which both employers and employees may contribute.
- The current stakeholder regime will be superseded by auto-enrolment from 2012.

Legislation

- Income and Corporation Taxes Act 1988 (as amended by the Income Tax (Earnings and Pensions) Act 2003).
- Social Security Contributions and Benefits Act 1992.
- Pension Schemes Act 1993.
- Pensions Act 1995.
- Welfare Reform and Pensions Act 1999.
- Child Support, Pensions and Social Security Act 2000.
- Civil Partnership Act 2004.
- Finance Act 2004.
- Pensions Act 2004.
- Pensions Act 2007.
- Pensions Act 2008.

Overview

This chapter provides a brief overview of the two types of pension provision in the UK – state benefits and private pension arrangements. The chapter is aimed at helping those involved with workplace pension provision.

State benefits

State pensions are provided by the Government on the basis of contributions made or credited to the National Insurance Fund over an individual's working life. These contributions are compulsory and are effectively part of the general taxation and benefits system.

There are two tiers of state benefits – the Basic State Pension and the State Second Pension (S2P). From April 2011, the Government committed to restore the link to earnings with a triple guarantee that the state pension will rise by the highest of average earnings, prices or 2.5%.

Basic State Pension

An individual is entitled to receive the Basic State Pension if they meet the following criteria:

- They have reached State Pension age; and
- They (or their husband, wife or civil partner) have enough qualifying years' employment based on National Insurance Contributions (NICs).

The State Pension Age (SPA) is currently 60 for women and 65 for men. From April 2010, the SPA for women started rising gradually and currently the plan is that, by 6 April 2020, it will be 65 for both men and women. The Coalition Government has accelerated the timetable, such that the SPA will be 66 for men and women by April 2020. Further increases to 68 are being considered.

From 6 April 2010 the number of years required in order to qualify for a full Category A Basic State Pension was reduced to 30, and any number of qualifying years will give entitlement to at least some Basic State Pension.

There are NIC credits available for individuals who care for children or severely disabled people. An employee with a full NIC record is currently (2011/12) entitled to receive £102.15 a week if they are a single person and £163.35 week if part of a pensioner couple.

State Second Pension (S2P)

Until April 2002, the additional state pension for employees was called the State Earnings-Related Pension Scheme (SERPS). The amount of SERPS pension that an employee received was based on a combination of the amount of NICs that they had paid and their salary.

In April 2002 SERPS was reformed and the additional state pension is now known as the State Second Pension (S2P). This provides a more generous additional pension than SERPS for low and moderate earners, and certain carers and people with long-term illness or disability.

Currently, employers (in relation to occupational pension schemes) and employees (in relation to personal pension arrangements) may choose to 'contract-out' of S2P. This means that employees can divert their NIC payments to a private pension scheme but will receive a smaller benefit from the State as a result. It will no longer be possible to contract out under a personal pension scheme or under an occupational defined contribution scheme from April 2012.

Private pension arrangements

Private pension provision in the UK is highly regulated, both by the Government and other regulatory bodies. In recent years there has been much reform of the pensions industry and this has served to increase the powers of regulatory authorities, including the Pensions Regulator.

Other than in respect of stakeholder pensions (*see below*) employers and employees are not currently compelled to set up or contribute to private pensions. The Government is aware that this is likely to result in long-term problems for individuals who have failed to provide sufficiently for their retirement.

From 1 October 2012 new laws are due to start coming into force which will affect all employers with at least one employee in the UK. Each employer will be issued with a 'staging date' by the Pensions Regulator on which the auto-enrolment requirements will apply to it, with larger employers being given an earlier date. The staging date is based on the number of employees in the employer's PAYE scheme as at 1 April 2012. From the staging date, employers will be required to automatically enrol 'eligible jobholders" into a qualifying pension scheme. Eligible jobholders are those aged between 22 and state pension age, working, or ordinarily working, in the UK and earning above a certain level (currently £7,475).

Employers will be able to use their own existing occupational pension scheme or personal pension scheme if it meets statutory quality requirements. Both occupational defined benefit and defined contribution schemes can be qualifying schemes. As an alternative, the Government has set up a central scheme called the National Employment Savings Trust (NEST). For a defined contribution scheme to be a 'qualifying scheme', minimum contributions must be made as shown in the table below. The contribution percentages are based on a specified band of earnings (£5,035-£33,540).

Date	Minimum employer contribution	Minimum total contribution
From staging date until Sep. 2016	1%	2%
Oct 2016 – Sep. 2017	2%	5%
Oct. 2017 onwards	3%	8%

Jobholders will be free to opt out of either type of scheme once they have joined, but while they remain active members their employers will be required to pay a

minimum level of pension contributions. Those workers who are not eligible do not need to be auto-enrolled but may choose to opt in to a pension scheme. If they opt in, employer contributions do not need to be made in respect of them unless they have earnings of at least £5,035 and are aged at least 16 but under 75, in which case they must be treated in the same way as eligible jobholders.

Taxation
Although there is currently no element of compulsion for employers or employees to contribute to a private pension there are significant tax benefits if they choose to do so. In return for complying with specific requirements laid down by legislation, private schemes registered with HMRC can enjoy generous tax relief, both for employees and employers.

Under the current pensions regime, implemented from 6 April 2006, there is a maximum amount of savings on which a member of a registered pension scheme can receive tax relief. It is tested against a standard lifetime allowance, which for 2010/11 is set at £1.8m. If the total value of a member's benefits from all registered schemes exceeds this limit, a tax charge is payable. From 2012, the lifetime allowance will be reduced to £1.5m.

There is also a limit on the annual increase in value in savings from all registered schemes. For 2010/11 it was set at £255,000. From April 2011, the annual allowance was reduced from £255,000 to £50,000 for tax privileged saving. This change is instead of the previous Government's proposal to apply a high income excess relief charge to contribution and accruals to registered pension schemes by individuals whose income exceeded £150,000. The amount of contributions that can be made by an individual, whether employed or self-employed, is restricted to the greater of 100% of UK earnings (subject to the £50,000 limit mentioned above) or £3,600 per annum.

Occupational pensions schemes

Occupational pension schemes are usually established under trust and operated in accordance with the scheme's trust deed and rules. A group of people will be appointed as trustees of the scheme and are responsible for running the scheme and have a duty to act in the best interests of the members of the scheme. Legislation requires that at least one-third of the scheme's trustee board must be nominated by the members but it is possible that this fraction may be increased to one-half in the future. Previously, employers were able to suggest alternative arrangements, which meant they could opt-out of the member-nominated trustee requirements, but this is no longer possible. The trustee board must also consult advisers (where appropriate) such as actuaries, administrators and solicitors when reaching its decisions.

Traditionally, most occupational pension schemes were established on a defined benefit (DB) basis, meaning that the pension payable at retirement was calculated by reference to a salary-related formula set out in the scheme's rules. DB schemes involve employees making contributions during their working life and the employer guaranteeing that the final pension will be at a specific level. The advantage of this type of arrangement for employees is that, in the absence of employer insolvency, it provides certainty. The problem for employers is that they bear the risk of poor investment returns, inflation, salary increases, members living longer and similar risk factors.

Many employers have chosen to close their DB schemes and now offer employees admission to a defined contribution scheme (DC). DC schemes do not guarantee members a specific level of final pension but instead provide a promise to contribute a given percentage of employee salary and invest this, together with any employee contributions. The actual pension payable at retirement is dependent upon the investment return achieved during the period of membership of the scheme and the cost of securing a pension on the annuity market on retirement.

When an employee leaves a company that operates an occupational pension scheme they may leave their benefits in the scheme until they reach retirement age (during this time they will be referred to as 'deferred members') or they may transfer the benefits they have built up under the scheme to:

- a new pension scheme operated by their new employer;
- a personal pension scheme; or
- an insurance company by way of a deferred annuity (i.e. a promise to pay a pension when the employer reaches a specific age).

Personal pension schemes

Personal pensions are a contract between an individual and a provider other than the employer, usually an insurance company or a bank. All personal pensions operate on a DC basis. Personal pensions are often used by individuals without access to an occupational scheme, employees who do not wish to join their occupational scheme, the self-employed or employees who have access to an employer's group personal pension scheme (a GPP).

Employers frequently offer GPPs as an alternative to an occupational pension scheme. GPPs are simply a collection of personal pension schemes provided by one provider, with each employee having his own personal pension operating within this arrangement. The employer is not obliged to make contributions, although most do. If an employer contributes less than 3% of an employee's salary to a GPP or a personal pension scheme they must ensure that they also designate a stakeholder pension scheme (*see below*). Because a personal pension scheme is provided by an organisation other than the employer, an employee's ability to continue to contribute to his or her pension should not be affected if the employee leaves service (although any reduced commissions / charges negotiated by the employer may not continue).

Stakeholder pensions

The stakeholder pension is usually established as a personal pension scheme and was an initiative introduced by the Government in 2001. The Government realised that the basic state pension and S2P was unlikely to provide sufficient benefits for people who were not also contributing to an occupational or personal pension. There is no compulsion on employees to join a stakeholder pension but employers are obliged to make it available in certain circumstances.

Employers' obligations are:

■ to designate a stakeholder pension for their staff (having consulted with employees about the introduction of the stakeholder); and

■ to allow employees to have their contributions to the stakeholder deducted from their salaries and passed directly to the insurance company operating the stakeholder.

There is no obligation upon employers to contribute anything towards stakeholder pensions, although this option is available. Employers who fail to comply with their obligations risk civil penalties of up to £50,000 from the Pensions Regulator. Some employers are exempt from the legislation governing stakeholder pensions, for example:

■ employers with fewer than five 'relevant' employees (this is broadly dependent on the length of an employee's contract and the amount that he or she earns); or

■ employers who operate an alternative occupational or personal pension scheme for their employees which meets certain criteria.

The stakeholder regime will be superseded by auto-enrolment from 2012 onwards.

Life assurance

Occupational pension schemes may provide members with life assurance. Generally, a life assurance scheme will provide a tax-free lump sum defined as a multiple of salary in respect of employees who die while in the employer's service.

See also: Benefits schemes, p.44; Retirement, p.445.

Sources of further information

HMR&C pension schemes: www.hmrc.gov.uk/pensionschemes

HMR&C stakeholder pensions: www.hmrc.gov.uk/stakepension

The Pensions Regulator: www.thepensionsregulator.gov.uk

Personnel files

Amy Bird, CMS Cameron McKenna LLP

Key points
- Accurate and easily accessible personnel records assist employers in many ways. They improve the efficiency of recruitment, training and promotion of staff, help identify problems such as performance, sickness absence or labour turnover, provide information for the purposes of equal opportunity monitoring, assist in compliance with legal requirements and help provide a defence to claims by employees and third parties.
- Data protection principles are likely to apply to information recorded in personnel files.

Legislation
- Data Protection Act 1998.
- National Minimum Wage Act 1998.
- Working Time Regulations 1998.
- Immigration, Asylum and Nationality Act 2006.
- Criminal Justice and Immigration Act 2008.
- Coroners and Justice Act 2009.
- Equality Act 2010.

What information should be held in personnel files?

Operating a business involves keeping information about each of the organisation's workers. Employers collect, record and maintain information about their workers during every stage of the employment relationship; for example, during recruitment and through appraisals, training records, fit notes, disciplinary records and the administering of benefits. There is no definitive list of what information should be contained in a personnel file. However, examples of information that are likely to be held in personnel files are:

- Personal details, such as name, date of birth, address, telephone number, emergency contact details, qualifications, National Insurance number, details of any disability.
- Details of employment within the organisation, such as job description(s), job application(s), date employment commenced, job title, promotions, shift allocations, pay reviews, secondments.
- Terms and conditions of employment, such as statement of employment particulars, remuneration, notice period, hours of work, holiday entitlement.
- Benefits, such as insurances, private medical cover, share options, company cars, loans, nursery care schemes.
- Training and development activities.
- Performance reviews or appraisals.
- Sickness or injury records.
- Absences, such as holiday, lateness, maternity / paternity / adoption / dependants' leave, compassionate leave, sabbatical.
- Work-related accidents.
- Disciplinary action.
- Grievances raised.
- Record of termination of employment, such as garden leave, post-termination restrictive covenants, payments made on termination, reasons for leaving.

> **Facts**
> ■ The Data Protection Act 1998 sets out principles to which employees need to have regard in keeping personnel files.
> ■ According to a survey carried out for Navigant Consulting by YouGov in 2007, one million employees have admitted to losing confidential data.
> ■ The Information Commissioner's Office annual report 2010/2011 showed that 603 data security breaches were reported in that time (almost one-third in the private sector).

Why do employers keep personnel files?

Some information is required to fulfil legal requirements. For example, employers need to keep records of:

■ their workers' pay (including payments of Statutory Sick Pay, statutory maternity, paternity and adoption pay) for the purposes of complying with tax and National Insurance obligations and to meet the requirements of the National Minimum Wage Act 1998;

■ hours worked by most workers and holidays taken, to comply with the requirements of the Working Time Regulations 1998;

■ accidents, injuries and diseases, to comply with health and safety rules and regulations;

■ disciplinary action taken and grievances raised, to provide evidence of compliance with the ACAS Code on Disciplinary and Grievance Procedures and any relevant company procedures; and

■ proof of identity and other documents obtained to comply with the Immigration, Asylum and Nationality Act 2006, to show an employee has the right to work in the UK.

Keeping accurate personnel files also helps organisations to operate efficiently and remain competitive. Good personnel records can help organisations:

■ treat staff fairly and properly, for example in accordance with legislation (*see above*);

■ use their staff resources effectively, for example, appraisals or details of a worker's qualifications and experience can help an employer assess whether a worker would be suitable for promotion;

■ develop or amend employment policies and procedures and implement such policies and procedures fairly and consistently. For example, records of disciplinary action can help employers to ensure consistency in the application of the disciplinary procedure;

■ improve the efficiency of their recruitment, training and development of staff. For example, a record of a worker's qualifications and experience can help an employer assess whether a worker has any training needs and can also be useful evidence in Tribunal. Performance reviews or appraisals can help to assess a worker's performance and decide whether there are needs for training;

■ more accurately detect, monitor and control problems, such as in relation to performance, discipline, sickness, lateness, absenteeism and high turnover of staff. For example, individual absence records can be used to monitor an individual's absence levels. Statistics on absence levels across the organisation may help employers detect and monitor problems across the workforce and take corrective action. Exit interviews can provide information to help employers deal with high labour turnover;

■ reduce the risk of discrimination on the grounds of, for example, sex, race, disability or age, by providing the information necessary to implement and monitor equal opportunity policies. For example, sickness records can be useful when considering making reasonable adjustments to the job or the workplace for the purpose of complying with the Equality Act 2010;

■ provide important evidence if an employee makes a claim to an Employment Tribunal. For example, Employment Tribunals would expect organisations to hold records of an employee's termination to show what payments have been made to the employee (e.g. notice pay, redundancy pay, outstanding holiday pay, etc.). Records of disciplinary action and dismissal are vital if an organisation is faced with complaints about, for example, unfair dismissal or discrimination; and

■ provide information that may be required in the context of corporate transactions; e.g. making it easier to comply with requirements to provide 'employee liability information' under Regulation 11 of TUPE.

What considerations do employers need to think about when recording information?

Employers need to understand that the personnel files they keep contain information that is personal and can be sensitive. The Data Protection Act 1998 (DPA) lays down both legal obligations and standards that aim to balance an employer's need to keep information about its workers against a worker's right to respect for his or her private life.

The DPA places legal responsibilities on organisations to register under the DPA and process (e.g. obtain, record, retain, use, disclose or dispose of) personal data in a fair and proper way. The DPA is concerned with personal data that can be processed by equipment operating automatically or which is recorded, or intended to be recorded, in a 'relevant filing system' (*see below*).

Everything from workers' personnel files to customer lists may be covered by the DPA. The DPA gives special protection to personal data that is 'sensitive'. Sensitive personal data is information concerning an individual's racial or ethnic origin, political opinions, religious or other beliefs, trade union membership, health, sexual life and any actual or alleged criminal offence. Sensitive data can only be processed under strict conditions.

The Data Protection Act

Personal data

Personal data is any information that relates to an identified or identifiable living individual. An individual's name and address can be personal data, and other information about an individual – for example, an individual's employment history or job title – would also be personal data if the individual could be identified from that information and/or from other information in the possession of the person controlling the processing of that information. Personal data also includes any expression of opinion about an individual and any indication of the intentions of the person controlling the processing of the information, or any other person, in respect of that individual.

In August 2007 the Information Commissioner, who is responsible for the enforcement of the DPA, issued a guidance note on what constitutes personal data for the purposes of the DPA. The guidance includes a flowchart, comprising a series of questions together with illustrative examples, to assist in determining what is personal data. See *Sources of further information*.

Relevant filing systems

A relevant filing system contains information within a system that is structured and/or indexed by reference to either individuals, or to criteria relating to individuals, that is readily accessible (i.e. the information is stored in a similar way to a computerised filing system).

The Information Commissioner has given guidance on when manual files are deemed to be a relevant filing system. For example, manual files will only be covered if they are sufficiently structured so the searcher can retrieve the personal information without leafing through the contents.

To help identify whether a relevant filing system is in place, use the 'temp test':

If you employed a temporary administrative assistant (a temp), would they be able to extract specific information about an individual without any particular knowledge of your type of work or the documents you hold?

If the temp could easily locate the relevant information, the information will be held in a relevant filing system.

A paper personnel file, relating to an individual and indexed internally by subject matter, for example, by reference to personal details, sickness, absence, disciplinary record, etc. is likely to be organised in a relevant filing system for the purposes of the DPA.

Name dividers within a file on a particular topic are likely to be deemed to be a

relevant filing system, but files that are organised chronologically are unlikely to be covered by the DPA.

For full guidance details, visit the Information Commissioner's website: www.ico.gov.uk.

Data protection principles

Anyone who processes personal information must comply with the eight data protection principles. In summary, these principles state that data must be:

1. fairly and lawfully processed;
2. processed for limited purposes;
3. adequate, relevant and not excessive;
4. accurate and up to date;
5. not kept for longer than is necessary;
6. processed in accordance with the data subject's (e.g. the employee's) rights;
7. secure; and
8. not transferred to other countries without adequate protection.

In June 2009, The Chartered Institute for IT (formerly known as the British Computer Society) launched the Personal Data Guardianship Code, aimed at promoting best practice in following these principles. It also sets out five principles of good data governance:

1. Accountability.
2. Visibility.
3. Consent.
4. Access.
5. Stewardship.

For more information about the DPA, see *'Data protection'* (p.101).

How to establish and operate an effective personnel records system

It is important to ensure that the system operates effectively for the needs of the organisation, and, where relevant, complies with the DPA. The employer should take into account the following points when setting up and managing a personnel records system.

Purpose

Be clear about the purpose(s) for which any personal information is collected about workers. The information collected should meet the needs of the organisation.

Keep staff informed

It is not necessary to seek workers' prior consent to keep most employment records about them; however, employers should explain to staff the purposes for which they intend to process personal data. Employers could include this information in a staff handbook, intranet site or employment contract, or draft a separate data protection policy, to inform workers about the records that are being or are likely to be kept about them and why, the uses to which they are likely to be put, where the records will be kept and for how long, who will have access to the records and the circumstances in which they might be disclosed.

Keep personal information stored securely

Employers are responsible for the security of personal information collected and must take appropriate measures to prevent unauthorised access or unlawful processing, accidental loss, destruction or damage to the employment records. Records may be kept:

- *Electronically (on a computer)* – there are a number of advantages to storing records electronically; for example, the speed of the provision of information and the flexibility of the information available makes updating and analysing data easier. Password protection, or similar security measures, should be implemented to limit unauthorised access to computerised records.

- *Manually* – a simple and effective approach for smaller organisations might be to keep paper personnel records using a card index system. Manual files that contain personal information should be securely locked and only those who should have access retain the key.

- *In a combination of the above systems.* Employers should restrict information that is taken outside the workplace to what is necessary and put in place rules and procedures that deal with, for example, the information that may be taken off site, and keeping that information secure. In November 2007, following the loss of child benefit records by HM Revenue and Customs, the Information Commissioner's Office issued a recommendation that, amongst other things, portable and mobile devices used to store or transmit personal information should be protected by encryption software designed to safeguard against unauthorised access to the information stored on the device. In April 2008 the Information Commissioner published two Good Practice Notes on management and notification of breaches of data security, which give guidance on some of the things that an organisation needs to consider where a security breach occurs and on the notification of breaches to the Information Commissioner's Office. The Coroners and Justice Act 2009 increased the Information Commissioner's powers to deal with potential breaches of the DPA by a government department or a designated public authority. It introduced a new right from April 2010 for the Information Commissioner to serve assessment notices on a data controller who is suspected of violating the data protection principles contained in the DPA. In addition, the Information Commissioner now has the power to enter and inspect any premises named in an assessment notice where a data controller has failed to comply with a requirement imposed by the assessment notice.

Consider which staff should have access to which records

In July 2008 the European Court of Human Rights ruled that the European Convention on Human Rights imposes an obligation on public bodies and governments to implement measures to keep private data confidential.

Ensure that information is easily accessible

It is useful if the system (whether computerised or manual) is designed so that important information on each subject is easily accessible (e.g. visible on one screen or one side of a card) as this makes locating and updating information easier. However, structuring personnel files in this way is likely to be deemed to be a relevant filing system and thus within the scope of the DPA.

Differentiate between sickness or injury records and absence records

Because sickness and injury records contain sensitive personal data (details of the illness, condition or injury responsible for a worker's absence) they should be kept separately from absence records (which note the incidence of absence but do not include details of the illness or specific medical condition), where possible. For example, sickness and injury records could be kept in a sealed envelope or subject to additional password protection on an electronic system. This helps to ensure that information on workers' health is not accessed when only information regarding a worker's absence is required. For more information about health information, see *'Medical records'* (p.304).

Keep personal data accurate and up to date

Workers should be asked to check for accuracy and to update information held on their personnel files that is likely to be subject to change, such as their home address, for example, on a yearly basis. It is important that the personnel records system is set up to limit access to individuals' records, so that each worker can only access his or her own record, before asking workers to check and update their records. It is also useful for organisations to review personnel records regularly to check that all the information stored is useful and necessary and that there is no unnecessary duplication of records. Information that is not relevant, out of date or for which there is no genuine business need or legal duty to keep, should be destroyed.

Comply with the provisions of the DPA when passing data to third parties or across national borders

Unless certain conditions are satisfied, personal data should not be transferred to a third party outside the European Economic Area unless contractual or other guarantees have been put in place to ensure an adequate level of data protection for workers.

Check the effectiveness of the personnel records system regularly

It is useful for organisations to know whether the system is providing the information it requires quickly and accurately and to determine whether any improvements can be made.

For further guidance on how to comply with the DPA, 'The Employment Practices Code' provides some good practice recommendations for employers at www.ico.gov.uk.

How long should records be retained for?

It is up to each employer to decide how long to retain their personnel records, as there are no specific document retention periods specified in the DPA. Employers should:

- establish and adhere to retention periods for recruitment records that are based on the business needs of the organisation;
- ensure that no recruitment record is held beyond any relevant professional guidelines or statutory period (for example, three to six months for most Employment Tribunal claims, six years for County Court claims, three years for an accident, and six years for wage / salary records);
- destroy information obtained by a vetting exercise as soon as possible or in any case within six months. A record of the result of vetting or verification can be retained;
- as far as possible, set standard retention times for categories of information held in employment records. Consider basing these on a risk analysis approach;
- anonymise any information about workers and former workers where practicable, especially if it is to be held longer than the period necessary for responding to claims; and
- if possible, establish a computerised system that flags information retained for more than a certain time as due for review or deletion.

Employers must therefore strike a balance between ensuring that employment records are not kept for longer than is necessary but are not destroyed where there are business needs to retain them.

When deciding which records should be retained, it is advisable to:

- treat pieces of information individually, or in logical groupings, to prevent all the information in a record being retained just because there is a need to keep part of it; and
- consider the principle of proportionality; i.e. records about many workers should not be kept for a long time on the basis that one of the workers might possibly query some aspect of his employment in the future.

Where records are to be disposed of, they should be effectively destroyed; for example, by shredding information recorded on paper and completely and permanently deleting information stored in a computerised format. See 'Confidential waste' (p.545).

Recent developments

In November 2010, the European Commission adopted a strategic communication on EU data protection. This was consulted on until January 2011, and draft legislation is expected to be put forward in 2011. This is expected to include measures to strengthen individuals' personal data protection.

Since April 2010, as a result of the Criminal Justice and Immigration Act 2008 introducing a new Section 55A into the DPA, employers can now face fines of up to £500,000 where they commit a serious breach of the DPA. The Information Commissioner has produced guidance on when such monetary penalties may be imposed. The first two monetary penalties were served against A4e (a £60,000 fine following an unencrypted laptop containing sensitive personal data of 24,000 individuals being stolen from an employee's home) and Hertfordshire County Council (a £100,000 fine after details of a live court case concerning sexual abuse of a child were passed to a member of the public).

In late 2009 / early 2010 the Government consulted on introducing custodial sentences for knowing or reckless misuse of personal data. A response to the consultation has not yet been provided.

See also: Data protection, p.101; Medical records, p.304; Confidential waste, p.545.

Sources of further information

ACAS – 'Personnel data and record keeping': www.acas.org.uk/index.aspx?articleid=717

The Information Commissioner's Office – 'Technical Guidance – Determining what is Personal Data,' the 'Employment Practices Code,' and 'Quick Guide to the Employment Practices Code': http://bit.ly/qoN1Jd

ICO – Notification of Data Security Breaches to the Information Commissioner's Office: http://bit.ly/3yp37O

ICO – Guidance on data security breach management: http://bit.ly/2Ok6gv

ICO – Guidance about issue of monetary penalties: http://bit.ly/5byF1f

European Commission: http://bit.ly/9KUfHY

It is vital that employers familiarise themselves with their obligations under the Data Protection Act and ensure that the appropriate procedures are put in place to ensure compliance. Workplace Law's *Data Protection Policy and Management Guide v.4.0* has been published to help employers understand and meet those obligations and to provide clear guidance for employees on their responsibilities when handling sensitive personal data. For more information visit www.workplacelaw.net.

Pregnancy and maternity

Mandy Laurie, Dundas & Wilson

Key points

- Employment legislation provides new and expectant mothers with special rights and protection, including the right to:
  - take time off for antenatal care;
  - maternity leave and pay;
  - return to work to the same job (or another that is suitable and appropriate, depending upon the length of maternity leave);
  - request flexible working; and
  - protection from suffering a detriment or dismissal on the grounds of her pregnancy.

Legislation

- Sex Discrimination Act 1975.
- Workplace (Health, Safety and Welfare Regulations) 1992.
- Employment Rights Act 1996.
- Working Time Regulations 1998.
- Maternity and Parental Leave etc. Regulations 1999.
- Management of Health and Safety at Work Regulations 1999.
- Flexible Working (Procedural Requirements) Regulations 2002 (Procedure Regulations).
- Flexible Working (Eligibility, Complaints and Remedies) Regulations 2002 (Eligibility Regulations).
- Work and Families Act 2006.
- The Statutory Pay, Social Security (Maternity Allowance) and Security (Overlapping Benefits) (Amendment) Regulations 2006.
- The Maternity and Parental Leave etc. and Paternity and Adoption Leave (Amendment) Regulations 2006.
- The Maternity and Parental Leave etc. and Paternity and Adoption Leave (Amendment) Regulations 2008.
- The Flexible Working (Eligibility, Complaints and Remedies) (Amendment) Regulations 2009.

- The Additional Paternity Leave Regulations 2010.
- The Agency Workers Regulations 2010.
- The Equality Act 2010.

Key employment issues

Time off for antenatal care

Provided the employer has been made aware of the pregnancy, expectant mothers are entitled to paid time off to attend antenatal appointments (where the appointment has been made or recommended by their doctor, midwife or a registered nurse).

The right to time off:

- is during working hours;
- includes not just the appointment time but travelling and waiting time; and
- should be paid.

If an employer unreasonably refuses time off, or allows time off but does not pay for it (either in whole or in part), the employee can make a complaint to an Employment Tribunal within three months of the date of the antenatal appointment concerned. If the complaint is justified, the Employment

---

Case study

Blundell v. Governing Body of St Andrew's Catholic Primary School (2007)

Ms Blundell was a teacher in a primary school. When she told her employer she was going off on maternity leave, she was asked if she would accept 'floating duties' when she returned; i.e. she would not be assigned to a particular class. She resisted this request. When she returned from maternity leave, she was given a different class from the one she was teaching before her leave. She made a complaint of sex discrimination against her employer on the ground that she had been treated less favourably because of her pregnancy. She also claimed she had not returned to 'the job in which she was employed before her absence' as provided by Regulation 18 of the Maternity and Parental Leave etc. Regulations 1999.

The EAT said that she had suffered a detriment and less favourable treatment on the ground of her sex in that she had lost the opportunity of putting forward her choice, and thereby possibly securing, her preferred class. However, she had returned to a role in accordance with her contract. Her contract said she was a 'teacher' and in a normal year she could have been asked to return to a different class, regardless of her maternity leave.

It is recommended that communications should be maintained with employees on maternity leave so that they are aware of opportunities in the workplace. As a general guide, an employee on maternity leave should only return to a different role if that new role is one which is similar in nature to the previous role. Again, generally any change in roles should be in keeping with the history of such changes in that place of work.

Tribunal must make a declaration to that effect and if the refusal to allow time off is unreasonable, the employer will be ordered to pay the expectant mother an amount of pay equal to the pay she would have received for the period of time off requested. This may also constitute unlawful pregnancy and maternity discrimination under the Equality Act 2010.

Maternity leave

All new mothers (irrespective of length of service):

- *must* take two weeks' maternity leave (four if they work in a factory) after the birth of their baby. It is prohibited to deduct the two-week period of compulsory maternity leave from any calculation of a discretionary bonus.

- *may* take 52 weeks' statutory maternity leave (SML), providing they inform their employer in writing (no later than the end of the 15th week before their expected week of childbirth (EWC)) that they are pregnant, the date of their EWC and the date they intend their maternity leave to start.

Maternity pay and benefits

A new mother is entitled to 39 weeks' Statutory Maternity Pay (SMP) if, by the end of the 15th week before the EWC:

> **Facts**
>
> - According to a major piece of research carried out in 2005 by the Equal Opportunities Commission (one of the organisations that was replaced by the Equalities and Human Rights Commission (EHRC)), every year around 440,000 women continue to work during their pregnancy. Nearly half of these women experience some kind of disadvantage at work, and around 30,000 are actually forced out of their jobs.
> - Each year, pregnant women forced to leave their work lose out on approximately £12m in statutory maternity pay. However, the cost to employers of replacing these women actually amounts to some £126m every year.
> - A report by the National Childbirth Trust (NCT) found that one in three new mothers returning to work felt the experience had been 'difficult' or 'very difficult'.
> - The same NCT survey revealed that 31% of mothers felt that, since becoming pregnant and returning to work, their relationship with their boss had deteriorated.

- she has been continuously employed for 26 weeks; and
- her normal weekly earnings for the previous eight weeks were not less than the lower earnings limit for the payment of primary class I National Insurance contributions.

SMP will start on any day of the week, concurrently with SML.

During maternity leave, an employee has a statutory right to benefit from the terms and conditions that would have applied to her had she been at work, except for the terms providing for her remuneration. Therefore, all benefits, such as private health insurance and childcare vouchers, will continue. New mothers accrue paid holiday throughout the entire period of SML. This can raise issues regarding carry-over of holiday into the next leave year.

Keeping in Touch (KIT) days
New mothers can return to work for up to ten days during their SML without losing their right to leave or SMP, provided both parties agree. As a minimum, a new

mother must be paid any SMP she is due for each KIT day worked. Whether she has any additional entitlement to payment at her contractual rate of pay for KIT days will depend upon what has been agreed with her employer.

Return to work
Following SML, new mothers are entitled to return to the same job as if they had not been absent. If this is not reasonably practicable, following return from any period of SML that is greater than 26 weeks, the new mother should return to another suitable and appropriate job within the employer's organisation. If a new mother wants to return early from SML she must notify her employer eight weeks in advance.

Right to request flexible working
A mother who has been continuously employed for 26 weeks has the right to formally apply in writing to her employer to request a change in hours, times or location of work for the purpose of enabling her to care for her child (provided the child is under 17 or under 18 if the

child is disabled). An employer may refuse such a request, but only if they are justified by certain business reasons. Requests should follow the formal flexible working process (see *'Flexible working'*, p.221).

Unfair dismissal

Dismissals relating to the right to take time off for antenatal care, maternity leave and pay, return to work and pregnancy-related dismissals will be automatically unfair, irrespective of the new or expectant mother's length of service. This is covered in *'Family-friendly rights'* (p.206).

Discrimination

Pregnancy and maternity is one of the 'protected characteristics' covered by the Equality Act 2010. This means that although some maternity rights apply only to employees, there will be wider protection for other individuals (such as job applicants and agency workers) to ensure that they cannot be discriminated against on the grounds of pregnancy or maternity. The Act also provides specific protection for women on maternity leave in relation to pay, ensuring they are entitled to receive any pay rises or bonuses that they would have received had they been at work.

Fertility treatment

Under the Equality Act 2010, pregnant employees are protected against discrimination on the grounds of their pregnancy during a 'protected period'. In 2009, the Employment Appeal Tribunal

(*Sahota v. Home Office and Pipkin*) held that employees undergoing fertility treatment will be deemed to be pregnant when fertilised ova are implanted but the 'protected period' will be extended beyond the usual limits to allow for various steps of the IVF process to be taken into account.

Agency workers

The Agency Workers Regulations 2010 come into force on 1 October 2011. Amongst other things, the Regulations extend the right to paid time off to attend antenatal appointments to agency workers who have completed the requisite 12-week qualifying period.

Additional Paternity Leave

Under the Additional Paternity Leave Regulations 2010, for children born on or after 3 April 2011, if a mother returns to work before the end of her SML entitlement, the mother's spouse, civil partner or partner may take the balance of the leave (up to 26 weeks) as additional paternity leave, provided he does so before the child's first birthday.

See also: Childcare provisions, p.75; Dismissal, p.146; The Equality Act, p.191; Family-friendly rights, p.206; Flexible working, p.221; Leave, p.252.

Sources of further information

Electronic template maternity, paternity and adoption policies and management guides are downloadable from www.workplacelaw.net.

HSE – Expectant mothers: www.hse.gov.uk/mothers/faqs.htm

Private life

Mark Kaye, Berwin Leighton Paisner LLP

Key points

- It is reasonable for workers to have a legitimate expectation that they can keep their personal lives private, and workers are entitled to a degree of privacy in the workplace.
- Interference in a worker's private life is justifiable in certain circumstances. However, disciplining or dismissing without proper justification could give rise to an unfair dismissal claim, and special protections are in place to ensure workers are not discriminated against because of issues in their home life.
- Employers have an obligation to take into account a worker's human rights. The use of personal data by an employer, in particular 'sensitive data', is strictly regulated in the UK, principally under the Data Protection Act 1998.
- A large proportion of all complaints made to the Data Protection Information Commissioner relate to subject access requests not being complied with and a significant percentage of all complaints arise out of the disclosure of personal data.
- Claims in the Employment Tribunal for both sexual orientation and religious discrimination continue to rise year on year.

Legislation

- Access to Medical Reports Act 1988.
- Employment Rights Act 1996.
- Data Protection Act 1998.
- Human Rights Act 1998, Schedule 1.
- Equality Act 2010.

General rules

Most employees have an expectation that what they do in private or in their own time is their own affair. It is reasonable for workers to assume that they can keep their personal lives private, and workers are entitled to a degree of privacy in the workplace. However, the right to respect for privacy is not absolute. Sometimes it is fair and reasonable, because of the impact that the individual's private activities have on either his work or the workplace, for the employer to interfere.

Generally, dismissal for outside conduct will only be fair if it has a material impact on either the employee's suitability to continue in his role, or the employee's business (e.g. reputation or adverse customer reaction etc.). Before dismissal, alternative positions might have to be considered (e.g. an employee-driver facing a temporary driving ban might be able to undertake alternative work in the short-term or perform his driving duties by alternative means).

Where an employer is, in principle, justified in probing into an employee's private life, the law protects an employee in a number of respects. The employer must ensure that it is not contravening these protections if any disciplinary action or dismissal is going to be fair.

Where disciplinary action or dismissal for outside conduct is contemplated, general principles of fairness require an investigation, and a proper disciplinary process should be followed.

Case studies

Post Office v. Liddiard (2001)

Mr Liddiard was arrested during the 1998 World Cup in France for hurling bottles at Tunisian fans and assaulting a police officer. He was sentenced to 40 days in jail. Mr Liddiard's actions attracted widespread press coverage, which included condemnation by the Prime Minister. As a result, the Post Office summarily dismissed Mr Liddiard for gross misconduct on the grounds that his conduct in France brought the Post Office into disrepute. Mr Liddiard brought a claim for unfair dismissal against the Post Office, which was successful in the Employment Tribunal and the Employment Appeal Tribunal. It was held that he had been dismissed for reasons beyond his control (including the press coverage and the Prime Minister's comments) and that the dismissal was unfair because various background issues had not been considered by the dismissing manager. The Post Office appealed.

The Court of Appeal upheld the appeal and sent the claim back to the Employment Tribunal to be reheard, as the original Tribunal had not properly considered whether the Post Office had acted reasonably by treating Mr Liddiard's conduct as a sufficient reason for dismissal that fell within the range of reasonable responses of a reasonable employer. In particular, the Court of Appeal felt that the press coverage and political pressure were evidence that Mr Liddiard's actions had brought the Post Office into disrepute, rather than being the cause of the disrepute. As such, the Post Office should have been entitled to take this evidence into consideration.

This case does not offer guidance on when it would be appropriate to dismiss someone for conduct such as hooliganism, but the decision does imply that such circumstances exist, as long as the dismissal falls within the range of reasonable responses. However, it appears that such a response would only be reasonable where the employee's conduct directly affects the employer's business.

T Doherty v. Consignia and *M Doherty v. Consignia*

These two cases show that those circumstances (in which a dismissal is deemed to be a reasonable response) are few and far between. In these cases, Mr Doherty and his brother (both Arsenal fans) were involved in violence during the UEFA Cup Final in Copenhagen in 2000, where both were caught on camera kicking a Galatasaray fan. The brothers' actions made it into the tabloid press, where it was made clear that they worked for Consignia. As a result of their conduct they were both subjected to Consignia's disciplinary procedures and subsequently dismissed.

The Employment Tribunal held that there had been various procedural errors in the disciplinary process, including:

Case studies – *continued*

- a failure to consider the brothers' previously clean employment records;
- a failure to sufficiently consider and rely on the brothers' statements throughout the disciplinary process;
- placing too much of an emphasis on media coverage; and
- inconsistencies between the treatment of the brothers and other Consignia workers accused of being involved in hooliganism at the same Cup final.

The Tribunal also found that there was insufficient evidence to suggest that there had been a substantial effect on Consignia's business as a result of the brothers' actions. The outcome of all these findings was that the decision to dismiss the brothers was outside the range of reasonable responses of a reasonable employer. The dismissals were, therefore, unfair. Unusually, the Tribunal ordered reinstatement.

From these cases it is clear that an employee's involvement in hooliganism will not automatically mean that employers can dismiss him or her for gross misconduct. In fact, the *Doherty* cases suggest that even negative press for the employer will not, on its own, be sufficient to justify dismissal.

Relying on a criminal conviction to justify dismissal will not necessarily be fair. The employer must generally conduct its own investigation and satisfy itself that dismissal is reasonable and appropriate.

Care needs to be taken with regards to respect for private life, not just during employment but at the recruitment stage as well. Principal protections for workers are given in the legislation discussed below.

Human Rights Act 1998

The relevant parts of the Human Rights Act 1998 (HRA) for these purposes are the right to respect for private and family life (Article 8) and the right to freedom of expression (Article 10). It is possible to interfere with a worker's human rights where this can be justified in a work context.

While the rights of employees under the HRA are only directly enforceable against a public sector employer, all employers must be aware of these rights to ensure that their treatment of employees is fair. As Tribunals have to take account of the HRA, if an employee's human rights have been disregarded in a disciplinary investigation leading to dismissal, for example, it could result in the Tribunal finding the dismissal unfair.

Data Protection Act 1998

Information about a worker's private life will involve personal data and, in many cases, sensitive personal data. The Data Protection Act 1998 (DPA) regulates the use of personal data by an employer and covers data contained in some manual records, as well as all computerised records.

The Employment Practices Code issued by the regulatory body, the Information Commissioner, assists employers in complying with the DPA. It emphasises the need, when intruding into a worker's privacy, to carry out an impact assessment, which balances the employer's objectives against any adverse impact of the intrusion for the employee. An area where impact assessments are especially relevant is workplace monitoring.

Sensitive personal data includes information about a person's ethnic or racial origins, political opinions, religious or other beliefs, trade union membership, health, and criminal record. Before using 'sensitive personal data', it may be necessary to obtain explicit consent from the employee. Consent is not necessary where the data is to be used for, among other things:

■ ensuring a safe system at work or otherwise to comply with health and safety rules; or
■ preventing or detecting crime.

Therefore, where an employer suspects that an employee has been involved in a criminal offence outside work, which is relevant to the job that he performs, or within the workplace, intrusion into the employee's privacy may well be justified under the DPA.

Discrimination legislation

The rules governing discrimination most likely to be relevant to a worker's private life are found in the Equality Act 2010 (formerly the Employment Equality (Sexual Orientation) Regulations 2003 and the Employment Equality (Religion or Belief) Regulations 2003). They make it unlawful for employers to discriminate on grounds of actual or perceived sexual orientation, religion or belief.

Sexual orientation covers orientation towards persons of the same sex, of the opposite sex, and of the same sex and the opposite sex. Religion or belief

covers religion, religious belief or similar philosophical belief.

The Equality Act 2010 prohibits:

■ *direct discrimination* – e.g. dismissing someone because he frequents gay clubs or bars;
■ *indirect discrimination* – e.g. inviting only spouses of employees to a work social event, or holding all social events on a Friday, or catering only for employees of a Christian belief;
■ *victimisation* – e.g. not promoting someone because he has made (or intends to make) a complaint about being discriminated against on sexual orientation or religious grounds; and
■ *harassment* – being unwanted conduct that has the purpose or effect of violating a person's dignity or creating an intimidating, hostile, degrading or offensive environment.

Care needs to be taken at the recruitment stage as well as during employment. Questions about the prospective worker's private life during the recruitment stage could give rise to other forms of discrimination, notably discrimination on the grounds of sex or disability. For example, asking a job applicant or existing employee about their plans to have children could give rise to a sex discrimination claim, or asking about serious medical ailments during an interview could create exposure to a disability discrimination claim.

Tribunal cases

As noted above, the general rule is that off-duty conduct can be a valid reason for dismissal if it is relevant to the person's employment and makes that employee unsuitable for the job, or risks damaging the employer's business.

Examples of past Tribunal cases include the following:

- A teacher of teenaged pupils was fairly dismissed after having allowed others to grow cannabis in his garden, in view of the position of responsibility and influence that he held.
- A manager was fairly dismissed after having smoked cannabis in front of subordinates at a work party, because the employer decided that her conduct had undermined her authority at work.
- A teacher was fairly dismissed after his conviction for an offence of gross indecency with a man.
- An air traffic controller was fairly dismissed for use of drugs outside work, because of a need to maintain public confidence in the safety of the air traffic control system. While there were no signs of the employee being anything other than fully capable at work, dismissal was a proportionate response in the circumstances.
- A probation officer (whose duties included supervising sex offenders) was fairly dismissed for participation outside work in activities involving bondage and sado-masochism. The Court decided that the individual's human right to respect for his private life had not been infringed because his activities were public knowledge (via a website on the internet), and although his right to freedom of expression was infringed, the employer was entitled to protect its reputation and maintain public confidence in the probation service.
- An employee was unfairly dismissed when banned from driving, because he had offered to perform his duties using public transport, at his own expense, which was, in the circumstances, a workable alternative.
- A postman was unfairly dismissed after a conviction for football hooliganism, because the 'Post Office could not show that its reputation had been damaged by the conduct (see *case study*).

- An employee was fairly dismissed after it was discovered he had been cautioned by the police for engaging in sexual activity with another man in a public toilet. The Court of Appeal found that as the activity had taken place in a public place, the employee's right to respect for his private life had not been engaged.
- An employee was fairly dismissed for falsifying timesheets where the employer had obtained evidence through covert surveillance of the employee's home. The employer was found not to be in breach of Article 8 and its actions were justified as it was investigating criminal activity.

Social networking

The recent increase in social networking sites, business or non-business related, are having an impact on blurring the boundaries between employees' private and working lives. The case of a teenaged girl who was sacked from her job for describing it as 'boring' is an example, as is the case of *Hays Specialist Recruitment (Holdings) Ltd and Another v. Ions and Another*, an interesting example of how the use of social networking websites can lead to potential issues for employers and employees. Mr Ions was encouraged by his employer, Hays, to join LinkedIn (a business-oriented social networking website). Hays alleged that he had deliberately transferred details of Hays' contacts from its confidential database to his personal account at LinkedIn. Despite Mr Ions' argument that this was done with Hays' consent and that, once the business contact had accepted the invitation to join his network, the information ceased to be confidential as it could be seen by all his contacts, the High Court held that Hays had reasonable grounds for considering that it might have a claim against Mr Ions in relation to the transfer of confidential information to his LinkedIn account while still employed by Hays.

Recruitment considerations

Employers often ask prospective workers questions that relate to their private life, particularly during the interview process. Recording the answers gives rise to data protection principles. Employers do not have complete freedom to ask any question they like about a job applicant's private life, as this could result in potentially damaging evidence against them (e.g. asking a woman whether she is pregnant or has children).

Drug / alcohol testing

The extent to which employers have the right to require workers to undertake random drug or alcohol testing is limited, as such testing is likely to entail an invasion of personal privacy that breaches Article 8. However, testing is justified where it is in the interests of, among other things, ensuring safety at work and public safety. The Information Commissioner's Employment Practices Code provides helpful guidance on alcohol and drug testing.

Workplace relationships

Although workplace relationships are commonplace, many employers are uneasy about relationships formed between work colleagues – especially if one is the direct report of the other. The risks include claims by other employees of favouritism and fallout when the relationship ends (e.g. sexual harassment claims).

Some employers require the employees to make a 'relationship declaration' (at the beginning and the end of the relationship). Others introduce a complete ban or a ban on relationships between a supervisor

and his/her direct or indirect report. Such bans can risk infringing the right to privacy under Article 8.

An employer needs to be very careful if it seeks to resolve the issue by dismissing an employee for breaking a rule on workplace relationships, or asking one of the employees to leave. Such action carries a high risk of exposure to unfair dismissal, and discrimination, claims.

Practical steps for employers

- Have clear rules on what amounts to acceptable conduct both in and outside work.
- Communicate the rules to employees.
- Ensure that the rules are followed, consistently, in practice.
- Ensure that any allegations of inappropriate off-duty conduct are properly investigated and that, where relevant, the requirements of the HRA and the DPA are taken into account.
- Be satisfied that the off-duty conduct makes the employee unsuitable for the job.
- Check whether there is any alternative to dismissal.
- Do not automatically assume that a criminal conviction will justify an employee being dismissed.

> *See also*: CCTV monitoring, p.70; Data protection, p.101; Human rights, p.248; Monitoring employees, p.358; Personnel files, p.392; Social media, p.485.

Sources of further information

The Employment Practices Data Protection Code can be found at the Information Commissioner's Office: www.ico.gov.uk/

Comment ...

Coming out at work

Kevin McCavish, Shoosmiths

Employers faced with an employee who comes out as gay at work for the first time may be unsure how they should react: there is little guidance available for organisations.

An employee's sexual orientation is clearly something private, which they should not be required to share with colleagues if they do not wish to do so. Other than in respect of equality monitoring, which should be anonymous, there is no reason why an employer needs to enquire into the sexual orientation of its employees.

However, work is a significant part of most people's lives; it can be an important source of social support and leisure as colleagues form friendships and even relationships in the workplace. Consequently, employees may wish to be open with their colleagues about their personal life, not least to avoid the stress caused in trying to maintain secrecy.

As the ex-Chief Executive of BP, Lord Browne, and ex-Cabinet Minister, David Laws, discovered, a lack of transparency about their private lives can cause particular issues for more senior employees.

More recently, cricketer Steven Davies was in the news because he told his England team mates he was gay. The revelation had the great and the good of the sporting world lining up to show their support.

But coming out undoubtedly takes courage, and could be a difficult process

Kevin McCavish is a Partner and Head of Shoosmiths National Employment Law Team. Kevin advises on all areas of employment law from redundancies and contractual variations to sale and purchase of businesses and senior executive severances. As a former barrister, Kevin has considerable contentious employment law experience and regularly represents clients in Employment Tribunal proceedings, dealing with issues ranging from unfair dismissal and redundancy claims to lengthy and complex discrimination cases.

for the employee concerned if they are unsure how colleagues will react, or how it may affect their careers; they are likely to need support and understanding.

When an employee comes out to colleagues there is the potential for an employer to fail to manage the situation properly and, in the worst case scenario, to incur legal liability if, for example, an employee was bullied by colleagues as a result of coming out and a manager failed to deal effectively with that.

Employers need to understand what the law expects of them in a situation where they become aware an employee is gay, and think about how best to manage staff and others to create a harmonious culture in their workplace.

Under the Equality Act 2010, sexual orientation is one of nine protected characteristics. Sexual orientation includes orientation towards people of the same sex, the opposite sex and either sex.

Employees and others are protected against direct and indirect discrimination because of their sexual orientation. The Act also protects against harassment. Harassment occurs where there is:

"unwanted conduct related to" [sexual orientation] which has "the purpose or effect of violating [the victim's] dignity, or creating an intimidating, hostile, degrading, humiliating or offensive environment for [the victim]."

A person does not have to have a particular protected characteristic themselves to bring a complaint of harassment. The conduct in question need only be related to a relevant protected characteristic. For example, a heterosexual female employee who overheard derogatory comments directed at a gay male colleague may be able to bring a claim of harassment herself if the comments created an offensive environment for her.

Importantly, under the Act, employers are liable for any unlawful discrimination or harassment by their employees which is committed in the course of employment, whether or not the employer knows or approves of their actions.

This is known as 'vicarious liability' and means that an individual can bring a claim against their employer based on the actions of their colleagues.

An employer does have a defence if it can show that it took all reasonable steps to prevent the unlawful conduct.

An employer can, in certain more limited circumstances, also be liable for the unlawful actions of third parties such as customers and contractors.

> "Coming out undoubtedly takes courage, and could be a difficult process for the employee concerned if they are unsure how colleagues will react, or how it may affect their careers; they are likely to need support and understanding."

Claims for discrimination on the grounds of sexual orientation are on the rise: in 2009-2010 the number of claims issued in England and Wales was 710, an 18% increase on the year before.

Given that compensation for breach of the Act is potentially unlimited, it is in employers interests to ensure that they do as much as they can to prevent any unlawful discrimination or harassment of their employees (on all the protected grounds, not just sexual orientation) in the workplace.

When managing a diverse workforce, responding sensitively to a gay employee who comes out is likely to be the most effective way to avoid legal liability.

Probationary periods

Gareth Edwards, Veale Wasbrough Vizards

Key points

- A probationary period is a trial period at the beginning of a new employment relationship, which usually lasts for three to six months.
- Details of the period should be set out in the contract of employment.
- The employee will commonly be subject to assessments and reviews during and at the end of the probationary period, in order to assess whether s/he is capable of undertaking the role to which s/he was appointed.
- At the end of the probationary period, the employee may be confirmed as a permanent employee if s/he has successfully completed the period, or if his/her performance is considered unsatisfactory s/he may then be dismissed. If his/her employment is unsatisfactory but there is hope of some improvement, the probationary period may be extended to continue to assess suitability.
- It is advisable for the probationary period to end well within the first year of employment to minimise the risk of unfair dismissal claims.

Legislation

- Employment Rights Act 1996.

Introduction

A probationary period is a trial period of normally about three to six months, sometimes longer, at the beginning of an employment relationship. During the probationary period the employer will assess the employee's suitability for the position and at the end of the period decide whether or not the individual should be confirmed as a permanent employee. The contract of employment may set out terms and conditions that only apply during probation, for example a shorter notice period.

When should a probationary period be used?

It is usually sensible and advisable for employers to use a probationary period when appointing a new employee. Although interviews and assessments are a useful way of assessing applicants, they cannot fully reveal whether an employee

is suitable for the position. Usually this can only be done by observing the employee in the role. Accordingly, a probationary period allows an employer to assess whether the employee is capable of performing the job and whether s/he fits into the team.

However, there may, of course, be circumstances where a probationary period may not be appropriate – for example, if an employee is going to be employed on a short, temporary contract, or if the employee is an existing employee who has simply moved to a different post.

Length of period

Normally, a probationary period will last for between three and six months. However, the length of the period should be determined by the industry sector and how long the employer needs to assess the employee's suitability for the specific role. Some roles may require a longer probationary period in order to properly assess an employee's capabilities.

However, it should be borne in mind that, generally speaking, an employee cannot bring a claim for unfair dismissal until s/he has 12 months' continuous service. This is the reason why most probationary periods will allow the employment to end well before the first anniversary of the start of the employment.

It is usually prudent to include a provision allowing for the extension of the probationary period if the employer considers that this is appropriate in the circumstances. However, before deciding whether or not to extend the probationary period, consideration should be given to whether an extension is likely to lead to an improvement in performance or whether there are specific issues to be addressed. If performance has generally been poor and there is no further training or guidance that could be offered that would be of benefit and lead to a significant improvement, then it may not be worthwhile extending the period. Consideration should also be given to whether the employee has been unable to work during some of the period, for example due to sickness. As mentioned above, when considering extending the period, the employer should bear in mind the date upon which the employee will acquire one year's service.

During the probationary period

Statutory entitlements and protections are unaffected by the existence of a probationary period. However, during the probationary period employees may only have limited contractual rights. For example, there is commonly a reduced notice period and restricted access to employee benefits.

The terms of the probationary period should be set out in the employee's contract of employment. It is also prudent for employers to have a probationary

policy that clearly sets out the purpose of the period and how it is operated. The main purpose of the probationary period is to assess the employee's suitability for the role by monitoring and reviewing performance. Regular reviews allow the employer to consider if further supervision or training is required, or whether steps should be taken to dismiss the employee prior to the end of the probationary period.

Any concerns with the employee's performance or capability should be brought to the attention of the employee as soon as possible, in order to give him/her the opportunity to rectify the situation. Employers should keep a record of these discussions and ensure that all employees who have similar roles, or who undertake substantially the same role, are subject to the same length of probationary period and the same rules.

Expiration of the probationary period

At the end of the period (whether or not extended) the employer must decide whether to dismiss the employee, or confirm the employee in post. If it is the latter situation, the employer should clearly notify the employee that s/he has successfully passed the probationary period and that s/he is now a permanent employee on permanent contractual terms. If the employee is to be dismissed, it is good practice for the dismissal to follow the procedure in the ACAS Code, which has replaced the statutory dismissal procedure. Although many employees will not have one year's service at the end of their probationary period and therefore will be unable to bring a claim for unfair dismissal, they may still be able to bring claims that do not require a year's service, such as unlawful discrimination. By following a formal procedure the employer will be better placed to show that the reason for the dismissal was for failing to perform to the required standard during the probationary period. See 'Disciplinary and grievance procedures' (p.121).

Best practice, regardless of length of service, would be for the employer to set out in writing that it is considering dismissal and inviting the employee to a meeting to which s/he has the right to be accompanied by a work colleague or trade union representative. The meeting should be held and the employee given the opportunity to make representations. The employee should be informed of his/her right to appeal.

When dismissing employers should take care to ensure they can take advantage of any shorter notice provisions that may be applicable. This will mean checking the wording of the employment contract and acting in good time. Delay in notifying the employee of the outcome of the probationary period may result in the employee believing they have passed the probationary period and are therefore entitled to longer notice.

See also: Disciplinary and grievance procedures, p.121; Dismissal, p.146; Employment disputes, p.168; Interviewing, p.275; Recruitment and selection, p.420.

Sources of further information

For organisations with or without a HR team who require specialist support, advice through hands-on support and/or project management, Workplace Law offer tailored strategic HR support and advice to suit the needs of your organisation.

To enable your organisation to focus on its core business our CIPD qualified and HR specialist team can provide support and advice on a number of strategic HR offerings. Our dedicated HR team can work with you on key HR projects aligned to your HR strategy and business plan, which can include, although are not limited to:

- HR strategy planning;
- Strategic succession planning;
- Site closures;
- Sale of business;
- Acquisitions and mergers;
- Relocation of sites or departments;
- Large TUPE projects; and
- Changing terms and conditions.

All of our HR professionals have 20 plus years of hands-on experience, working in every sector, in small, medium and large organisations. Our HR professionals bring this unique knowledge and experience to provide advice, support and project management to ensure the best fit for your organisation. Visit www.workplacelaw.net for more information.

Psychometric testing

Tar Tumber, Workplace Law

Key points

- Psychology is the science of behaviour and mental processes.
- Psychometrics is the study concerned with the theory and technique of psychological measurement, which includes the measurement of knowledge, abilities, attitudes, personality traits, and educational measurement.
- Psychometric or psychological testing is an assessment procedure designed to provide objective measures of one or more psychological aspects.
- Companies spend millions of pounds a year on psychometric tests that measure personality types, learning styles and the personal preferences of their employees and potential recruits.

Legislation

- Equality Act 2010.

Introduction

Psychometric testing is an assessment procedure designed to provide objective measures of one or more psychological characteristics. The important feature of psychometric tests is that they produce measures obtained under standardised assessment conditions that have known reliability and validity (i.e. they provide a reliable and appropriate way of comparing a person's performance against that of others in a comparator group).

There is growing evidence indicating that the use of psychometric tests for selection purposes has increased in recent years. Recruitment agencies may ask their candidates to complete one of the tests before offering them temporary or permanent job positions with their clients. More directly, all types of organisations are using tests and are using more of them. The results of a survey conducted in 2009 across a wide range of organisations are shown below.

There are two main types of psychological test – those that measure ability, aptitude or attainment, and those designed to assess personal qualities such as personality, beliefs, values or interests, motivation or drive.

There are no specific rules and different tests will measure different things for different roles, so tests for management consultancy roles will be different to those for a sales manager.

	Main reason	Additional reason
To predict candidates' performance	41%	73%
To assess whether candidates will fit in	34%	67%
To obtain information prior to interview	25%	48%

Facts

- In 2003, tests were used in most of the public sector and for selection in more than 70 of the FTSE 100 companies.
- In 2008, this figure increased to 85% of the FTSE 100.
- In 2010, this figure was defined at 95% of the FTSE 100 using psychometric tests for selection purposes.
- In addition to the FTSE 100, the police, the civil service, airlines and even football clubs such as AC Milan have been reported to use profiling techniques to understand what motivates their employees.

Reasons for using psychometric tests

There are several reasons why there has been an increase in the number of organisations using tests as part of the recruitment or development strategy.

Adding some 'fact' to the subjective recruitment process

Psychometric testing offers some 'scientific' credibility and objectivity to the recruitment process, which otherwise can be seen as highly subjective.

Feedback from the various tests also provide an indication of areas to be discussed in more detail at the interview, thereby enhancing the value of the interview by generating more interesting and productive discussions within interviews, concentrating on areas that have been identified.

There are several theories used in the processing of the test results, such as taking a humanistic approach, a psychodynamic approach, or a social learning approach. These theories add 'scientific' value and also help to narrow down the personality and psychological traits of the candidate in a way that makes the information usable for the company's particular situation.

Increased regulation and legislation

Tests are seen to have more reliability, validity and generally deemed more objective a means of selecting candidates when used alongside other forms of selection such as interviews or other exercises. Tests can be seen as an objective way to measure a candidate's skills to the required competencies for the post in question. Competency profiles themselves are perceived as linked to the promotion of opportunity to all, as well as reflecting the skill requirements of the organisation. As the majority of psychometric tests are proven not to have a negative impact on minority groupings, they can be promoted alongside an organisation's equal opportunity policy. It is not surprising, therefore, that the single most widely given reason to apply psychometric tests during recruitment/promotion processes is that they are deemed to increase the validity of the selection process against any legal challenges.

In addition, the difficulty of dismissing staff means that the costs of getting it wrong at the recruitment stage are perceived as increasingly high – hence the view that psychometric tests are more reliable and valid has significantly increased their value with employers. Furthermore, organisations may view the process of using qualifications as a criterion for selection as creating a barrier to access, thereby contravening the organisation's published equal opportunities policies.

Loss of confidence in academic qualifications

Research suggests there has been a loss of confidence in school-based formal qualifications and/or the standard of degrees. Many managers now accept tests as providing up-to-date information on skills such as quantitative reasoning, which complement qualification-based evidence. In addition, ability / aptitude tests are also seen as providing data on a variety of skills that are not suited to formal certification.

Testing costs have decreased

As well as the higher validity and reliability of using psychometric tests, increased test use may also be a response to the decreasing cost of testing relative to other methods of selection. With several credible test providers on the market, the cost of 'buying in' to psychometric testing has fallen in the last few years. This is due to the increased use of technology, particularly the internet, in administering tests and assessing the results. Net based tests provide more or less immediate scoring / feedback to the nominated recruiting managers and this therefore reduces the need to have trained assessors available to score and feedback results into the selection process quickly enough to be useful.

Increased costs of training staff

Given the current climate, it comes as no surprise that the cost of training and developing staff has increased. Research suggests that organisations with larger training expenditures use psychometric testing more than those with smaller training expenditure. This is likely because the cost of staff development increases the value of all relevant selection information,

and in particular justifies the additional cost of testing.

Dealing with candidate numbers

Psychometric tests are a quick and relatively cheap way of eliminating large numbers of unsuitable candidates very early on in the recruitment process, for example if used at the milkround when undergoing graduate recruitment. Screening out these candidates as soon as possible means companies can focus more time and effort on the candidates who are deemed more suitable. Therefore, from an HR perspective, psychometric testing can reduce the workload considerably as it can replace initial screening interviews, which were traditionally used to shortlist candidates for a more rigorous second interview.

Types of test

There are two main types of psychometric tests used by employers as part of their selection processes: personality questionnaires and aptitude / ability tests.

Personality questionnaires

Personality questionnaires can be used to determine how people are likely to behave under various conditions, i.e. preferred style of working. There are no right or wrong answers, and the questionnaires are usually completed in the candidate's own time.

Candidates are advised to approach personality questionnaires as honestly and straightforwardly as possible, whilst thinking of themselves in a work environment. The information derived from such questionnaires can then be used to assess how well the candidate may fit into certain team or working environments.

The format of questionnaires can be a series of statements that the candidate must agree or disagree with, or the candidate is presented with a number of statements and asked to choose which are the most and least like them. It is important for candidates to answer honestly, as some questionnaires incorporate linked questions later in the questionnaire to assess whether the candidate provides a similar response to the previous linked questions. This is not a way to 'catch out' the candidate, but more a method to understand the candidate's consistent responses.

Personality questionnaires can also be used as self-assessment tools to help an existing employee to understand their preferences and how these relate to their strengths and possible areas for development whilst in the workplace.

Aptitude / ability tests

The second main type of test used within the workplace is the aptitude or ability test – these are proven methods for assessing critical qualities for job success, such as problem solving, effective communication, as well as innovation and creativity; however, they do not test intelligence or general knowledge. It is for these reasons that employers use these tests so widely.

Often presented in a multiple-choice format, the questions have definite right and wrong answers. They are usually strictly timed and increasingly computerised. In order to be successful, the candidate is advised to work as quickly and as accurately as possible through the test questions.

There are several different types of ability test. Some of the more widely used are defined below:

- *Verbal reasoning tests* – designed to test the candidate's ability to comprehend written information and

then evaluate arguments about this information.
- *Numerical reasoning tests* – designed to assess understanding of numerical and statistical data (often displayed in a table format) and then make logical deductions about this data.
- *Accuracy tests* – designed to assess the candidate's ability to accurately and quickly detect errors in various forms of information. For example, these may be used when selecting for clerical posts.
- *Inductive reasoning tests* – designed to assess how well a candidate can cope with unfamiliar information and provide solutions. Those who perform well in such assessments have a greater capacity for analytical/conceptual thought processes.

Other forms of ability tests can be used when staff are already in place as part of a career development programme i.e.:

- *Motivation questionnaires* – these can be used to understand what situation or factors cause an increase or decrease in the employee's motivation levels. By using this information, management can then look to increase job satisfaction, thereby increasing longevity in a role. As with personality questionnaires, there are no right or wrong answers, and the candidate is asked to complete the questionnaire as honestly as possible.
- *Situational judgement tests* – these are designed to measure ability to make good judgements when presented with several responses to workplace situations. A situation is detailed and the candidate is asked to select the most effective response in dealing with that situation. Such tasks may be used in recruitment campaigns, but also when undertaking promotional processes.

Conclusion

Factors such as the above are likely to encourage further growth in psychometric testing in the immediate future. Nothing additional is required for this to happen: simply the continuing influence of HR departments in a highly regulated labour market, plus an increasing number of managers comfortable with test results/ feedback should continue this trend.

All of the surveys of psychometric testing produced over the past ten years consistently suggest that use has been increased steadily and that test use for recruitment is now very common and supports a substantial commercial sector of test creation and processing. This has led directly to more and more specific tests being produced for use within particular organisations, settings, or for particular jobs. As more of these tests gain recognition and acceptance it is inevitable that psychometric testing will continue to increase.

See also: Interviewing, p.275; Personnel files, p.392; Recruitment and selection, p.420; References, p.434; Screening, p.453.

Sources of further information

British Psychological Society: www.bps.org.uk

Workplace Law is licensed to purchase, administer and feedback to you on the most appropriate and valid tests for your purposes:

- using ability tests that measure ability to perform different tasks; and
- personality and motivation questionnaires, to understand a candidate's preferred behavioural style at work.

Working with Workplace Law, you can be confident that you are matching skills to job requirements in a way that is objective and fair to all candidates. Workplace Law's qualified and trained testers can administer tests online or offline (onsite) to suit your requirements. In both instances, tests can be administered quickly and efficiently with feedback provision based on your reporting requirements.

The team will work with you to ensure the test suits your needs and helps you predict effective performance in the role.

All tests are used from the SHL inventory banks – with more than 30 years' experience of psychometric assessment, SHL is a world leader in people performance solutions. See www.workplacelaw.net for more details.

Recruitment and selection

Anna Youngs, Mills & Reeve

Key points

- Carefully and clearly define the job description of the vacant post(s).
- Carefully draft the advertisement for the job vacancy and consider where the advertisement is to be placed.
- Limit the information requested on the application form to that which is relevant to the post.
- Prepare questions to be asked at interview in advance and keep score sheets to record answers given during the interview.
- Data collected during the recruitment process must be used in accordance with the Data Protection Act 1998.
- Ensure compliance with the Equality Act 2010.
- Confirm any offer of employment in writing and clearly set out any attached conditions – offers of employment should be conditional on the relevant conditions and employment checks (OH, references, CRB, etc).
- Keep a paper trail recording your processes, decisions and reasons.

Legislation

- Rehabilitation of Offenders Act 1974 and the Rehabilitation of Offenders Act 1974 (Exceptions) Order 1975 (as amended).
- Data Protection Act 1998.
- Equality Act 2010.

Some employment rights start on the first day of employment. However, discrimination legislation offers protection throughout the recruitment process, starting when the job advertisement is placed. Equally, an employer must ensure that all documentation relating to a job is accurate to ensure that misrepresentations are not made. Prospective employees / workers can bring claims against a prospective employer regarding the recruitment process, including advertising, shortlisting and what happened at interview.

Key principles of the Equality Act 2010

When undertaking a recruitment process, employers should be aware of the key principles of the Equality Act 2010, which provides that an employer (A) must not:

1. Discriminate against or victimise a person (B):
    - in the arrangements A makes for deciding to whom to offer employment;
    - as to the terms on which A offers B employment;
    - by not offering B employment.
2. Harass a person (B) who has applied to A for employment.

There are further requirements in relation to pre-employment health questions, which are discussed below.

Please note that the Equality and Human Rights Commission has produced the Employment Statutory Code of Practice, part two of which sets out recommended practice for employers. Chapter 16 in part two specifically considers recruitment issues.

'Arrangements' in the recruitment process in the context of the Equality Act 2010 covers a wide spectrum of matters, and examples are likely to include:

- application forms (appearance, format, contents);
- arrangements in relation to interviews (timing, location, tests); and
- job descriptions and person specifications.

Job description

Once a vacancy has arisen and there is a need to recruit, the initial step should be to clarify the role and the employer's requirements within a job description. The vacancy may be a new role within an organisation or a vacancy caused by a person leaving or reducing their working hours (for example, working part-time). In any case, careful consideration should be given to the job description, including necessary skills, expertise and qualifications.

The job description will become an important contractual document because it will define the job and be useful if there are any disputes over the nature and requirements of the job. Also, it will give focus to those involved in the recruitment process, making them aware of the requirements of the organisation.

It is not necessary to list every task the employee would be required to carry out within the job description, as maintaining some flexibility can be beneficial to both an employer and an employee. The job description should instead contain the main duties and responsibilities, reporting structure, place of work, and objectives. Other details such as pay and working hours do not need to be included as these will be contained within the contract of employment.

In addition to the job description, a person specification can be used to detail the type of person and competencies required to perform the job. The document would list those qualifications, training, skills, experience, knowledge and personal skills that are either essential or desirable criteria. Like the job description, these should be relevant to the job, such as the ability to manage a team. Consideration should be given to how necessary these criteria are and whether any alternatives are equally as acceptable, such as equivalent qualifications to GCSEs (to avoid age or race discrimination, for example).

Some positions may require someone of a particular race or sex, for example, to undertake the post. Employers can consider whether the post to be filled falls within an exemption to the general requirement for equality of opportunity in the Equality Act. Exempt positions will be few and far between. A common example is the race and sex of the actor chosen to play Othello. Generally speaking, employers are likely to require legal advice if they think that such an exemption may apply.

Positive action

Where persons who have a protected characteristic suffer a disadvantage connected to the characteristic, have particular needs or are disproportionately under-represented, employers can take certain actions to address these problems. This is called 'positive action' and it applies in relation to recruitment and promotions.

- Employers are not *obliged* to take positive action.
- Positive action will be allowed if:
  - it is a proportionate means of addressing needs or disadvantages shared by members of a protected group; or

- it will encourage wider take-up in activities where the participation of members of a protected group is disproportionately low; and (in either case)
- the person with the relevant characteristic is 'as qualified as' those others and the employer does not have a policy of treating such people more favourably (and must not routinely do so). The employer must therefore ensure that the candidate is of equal merit – query whether effectively only their protected characteristic should distinguish them from another candidate.

- Employers will need evidence of under-representation in the workforce, or at a particular level.
- In practice, it is likely to be very hard to establish that one candidate is 'as qualified as' another, as it is unlikely that two candidates will have the same level of qualifications, experience, etc. Positive action could well breed claims from unsuccessful candidates, so advice should be sought before making a decision on recruitment or promotion based on positive action.

Advertising

The next step in the recruitment process is to advertise the vacant post. Not only must the advert be accurately drafted so as to not misrepresent the job vacancy, but also an employer must be aware of their duties under the Equality Act 2010. When drafting the advertisement, certain phrases should be avoided that may be perceived as discriminatory, such as gender-specific words like 'salesman' and the use of phrases such as 'young and dynamic' or 'fit and healthy'. It is advisable to state within the advert that the organisation is an Equal Opportunities Employer.

Not only must care be taken over the wording of the advert but also where the advert is placed. If adverts are publicised in limited places, it could be argued that it limits the types of people who will be aware of the vacancy; for example, only placing the advert on the internet could be considered to discriminate against older people who are less likely to have access to the internet, or if a job is only advertised internally or by word of mouth, there is a risk that an employer will continue to recruit people of a certain race, sex, religion, etc. (albeit that in some circumstances, this would be justifiable).

If the advertiser subscribes to the 'Two Ticks' (guaranteed interview) scheme, this should be referred to in the advert.

Application forms

Certain questions should be avoided on the application form and placed on a separate equal opportunities monitoring form, which should then only be used by Human Resources / Senior Management and not those directly involved in selecting applicants.

The following questions should not be placed on the application form:

- The applicant's marital status or previous names;
- The applicant's race or religion;
- The applicant's National Insurance number or passport number;
- The applicant's nationality;
- The applicant's sexual orientation;
- The applicant's date of birth;
- The level of sickness absence taken by the applicant; and
- Whether the applicant has a particular health condition.

It is legitimate for an employer to ask whether or not an applicant requires a work permit.

It is also permissible to ask about past criminal convictions. However, an applicant is not required and should not be asked to provide details of spent convictions unless an exemption applies under the Exceptions Order to the Rehabilitation of Offenders Act 1974. In certain cases, such as where an employee will be working with a vulnerable group of people, an employer is entitled to information about spent convictions.

The Equality Act 2010 specifically addressed the issue of health questions asked prior to offering employment. Whereas previously health questions were common in application forms, Section 60 of the Equality Act prohibits employers from asking about the health of applicants:

■ before offering work to an applicant; and
■ before including the applicant in a pool of applicants from whom the employer intends to offer work to in the future, unless the question falls within an exemption within the Act.

Perhaps confusingly, the Act goes on to say that asking about an applicant's health will not in itself contravene the Act, but rather the way in which such information is used may do so. However, if 'inappropriate' questions are asked, applicants will be able to use this as prima facie evidence of discrimination. In addition, if an employer acts in breach of Section 60, it may face an investigation by the Equality and Human Rights Commission and possible enforcement action, including fines of up to £5,000.

The exemptions enabling employers to ask questions about health are:

■ Establishing whether any reasonable adjustments will be required to ensure that the applicant can participate in interviews and other forms of assessment.

■ Establishing whether the applicant will be able to carry out a function that is intrinsic to the work concerned.
■ Monitoring diversity in the range of people applying for employment (although this should be on a separate monitoring form).
■ If the vacancy has a requirement for applicants to have a specific disability.
■ To take 'positive action' under Section 158 of the Equality Act. For example, some employers subscribe to the Two Ticks (guaranteed interview) scheme, where disabled people are guaranteed interviews if they meet the minimum criteria for the role.

Essentially, 'one size fits all', generic health questions should not be asked prior to offering an applicant the job. However, offers can still be made conditional upon a successful medical examination or questionnaire (subject of course to the possible inference of discrimination where such questions are asked, which existed even prior to the Equality Act).

What is not clear is how far an employer will need to go to evidence that it is asking a question in order to establish whether the applicant will be able to carry out an intrinsic aspect of the job. Certainly questions will have to be tailored for the specific job and certainly in the majority of cases it is highly unlikely that asking questions about past health issues will be deemed relevant to the applicant's ability to carry out the job. It is likely, therefore, that these new provisions will create litigation, particularly in relation to whether a question was necessary to establish whether the applicant could carry out an intrinsic function of the work.

Shortlisting
When considering which applicants to shortlist for interview, only the information provided on the application forms should be considered (as well as any

accompanying documents provided by the applicant such as their CV). The equal opportunities monitoring form should not be considered by those carrying out the shortlisting exercise.

Applicants should be selected for the next stage of the recruitment process after a comparison of the details provided on the application form with the job description and person specification. If an applicant is to be rejected, the reason should be recorded and kept for at least six months to assist in providing feedback to unsuccessful applicants and to explain any decisions should a claim be brought at an Employment Tribunal.

Some employers may choose to use selection and aptitude tests as part of their selection process. Any such tests should be carefully considered to ensure that the tests are evaluating skills relevant to the post. Adjustments should be made to any such tests if an employer is aware that an applicant has a certain condition(s) that may hinder their ability to perform in the test.

Interviews

It is important that those employees who are to carry out interviews should be trained in equal opportunities and aware of their employer's equal opportunities policy. Records should be kept to evidence that they have attended such training.

At the interview, questions should centre around the job description and person specification. To ensure consistency, questions should be prepared prior to the interview and a score sheet used during each interview. If, during the interview, the applicant discloses information about themselves, such as they have children under the age of five or require certain adjustments to be made to their workplace, the information should be noted as well as the response given by those conducting the interview. Notes of the interview should be kept for at least six months after the decision is fed back to the applicants, again to provide feedback and to allow any decision not to offer the job to be justified. There are certain questions that should not be asked of an applicant during the interview and these are the same as set out above in the section on application forms.

Retention of recruitment records

Throughout the recruitment process an organisation will collect a great deal of personal data about an applicant, and the Data Protection Act 1998 will apply to these records. The Information Commissioner has issued the Employment Practices Code. Part one of the Code provides guidance on how to remain within the remit of the Data Protection Act during recruitment and selection.

The The Code does not specify how long an organisation should retain information obtained during the recruitment process, but states that it should only be retained for such periods as are necessary to complete the recruitment process and suggests that any data obtained during a recruitment process should be retained for no more than six months, although as the time limits for bringing discrimination claims can be extended at the discretion of the Employment Tribunals (if it is just and equitable to do so), a longer period may be justifiable. Any information obtained during the recruitment process must be stored securely until it is destroyed.

Documents that should be retained in case of litigation include:

- relevant policies, job descriptions, etc.;
- interview notes and scorecards; and
- notes of discussions about candidates – including all handwritten notes from each panellist.

In relation to the successful applicant, once claims in relation to the recruitment process are unlikely to be made, an employer should only retain information that is relevant to the continuing employment relationship.

Making a job offer

Once the successful applicant has been identified, an offer of employment should be made in writing and should set out comprehensively the terms of employment to avoid any uncertainty at a later stage, such as salary, job description and start date. The letter should state a date by which the offer of employment is to be accepted and whether or not there are any conditions that must be fulfilled, such as pre-employment checks. Employers are entitled to make an offer of employment

subject to receiving a health report, satisfactory criminal records bureau report, proof of qualifications and satisfactory references. If employers are making conditional offers, the offer letter needs to be entirely clear that this is the case.

See also: Criminal records, p.97; Data protection, p.101; Disability legislation, p.116; Discrimination, p.126; Equal pay, p.184; The Equality Act, p.191; Interviewing, p.275; Migrant and foreign workers, p.318; Personnel files, p.392; Vetting, barring, blacklisting and social engineering, p.534.

Sources of further information

ACAS: Advisory booklet – *Recruitment and induction*:
www.acas.org.uk/index.aspx?articleid=744

Information Commissioner: The Employment Practices Code – Part 1:
http://bit.ly/mP949B

Age Concern: www.ageconcern.org.uk

Equality and Human Rights Commission: www.equalityhumanrights.com

Workplace Law Career Network is a professional services recruitment agency specialising in human resources, health and safety, property and facilities management. We provide permanent recruitment and interim management solutions for employers. A division of market-leading law firm, Workplace Law, we are able to draw on a wide range of resources to offer enhanced support to candidates and clients. Candidates have access to CIPD-accredited training and updated information through the award-winning Workplace Law Network service.

Enhanced services for clients include psychometric testing, assessment centres and advice on employment law, including fair recruitment, TUPE and restructuring and redundancy support. We operate nationally from offices in Cambridge and London – visit http://recruitment.workplacelaw.net/ for more details.

Comment ...

Agent for change

Neil McDiarmid, Workplace Law Career Network

The biggest change in recruitment in the last year has been the launch of a niche recruitment consultancy that can offer an expert service above and beyond that offered by more 'traditional' recruitment agencies. The name of this consultancy? Workplace Law Career Network. Launched and managed by recruitment expert (guru!) Neil McDiarmid, Workplace Law Career Network offers recruitment and consultancy services in the areas of premises and facilities management, building services, health and safety and human resources. Our aim is to add value to the service provided to both existing and new clients of Workplace Law by providing full-time and interim staffing solutions, using the experience gained over the last 15 years as a leading law firm, providing training and consultancy in these sectors.

The biggest change in recruitment next year will undoubtedly be the Agency Worker Regulations (AWR). They come in to place in October of this year and agencies have to ensure compliance by 1 January 2012. The intention of the Regulations is to protect temporary workers by ensuring they have the same pay and working conditions as their comparable permanent employee. There are two categories to consider:

- Week one rights – from the first week of employment the temporary worker can have access to the same shared facilities as their permanent equivalent. Compliance here is the sole responsibility of the hirer.

Neil McDiarmid is Managing Consultant of Workplace Law Career Network, the specialist recruitment division of Workplace Law that focuses on the recruitment of permanent and interim staff in the field of Facilities Management, Building Services, Health and Safety and Human Resources. Neil has nearly a decade of recruitment industry experience and launched Workplace Law Career Network in January 2011 returning to the Group following a previous spell as Business Development Manager.

- Week 13 rights – once a temporary worker has spent 12 weeks in the same assignment with the same hirer, he/she should receive at least the same pay and working conditions as the comparable permanent employee. This covers salary (including any overtime and bonus), days of holiday entitlement and hours of work. Responsibility for this falls to the hirer, agency and service provider.

The fear amongst those recruitment agencies largely reliant on temporary worker income is that this will affect their profit margins greatly, particularly those providing unskilled workers such as labourers or care workers, for example. In these cases agencies tend to pay the minimum amount possible to the temp worker and are able to pass the benefit of that on to their client by keeping their fees relatively low. What the introduction of the Agency Worker Regulations means is that agencies are now going to need to pay their temp workers significantly more and will have to pass that cost on to their clients.

Clients, however, are likely to use this as an opportunity to renegotiate agency rates, with a view to reducing profit margins for the agencies in order to keep their costs on a par with what they had been previously paying. The impact for agencies providing qualified workers shouldn't be as significant, as 'skilled' workers choosing to work on a temporary / contract basis are often earning a higher hourly / daily rate than their peers to compensate for the risk of working without the security of full-time employment.

It's not just recruitment agencies that this will impact upon, though, and a recent report by law firm, Allen & Overbury, estimates that the change could cost UK businesses £1.3bn a year to provide equal benefits to agency workers – an average cost per worker of between £1,755 and £3,722, or £90,000 per business per year, compromising the benefit of using a flexible workforce during the current economic climate.

"I wish I had a pound for every time someone asked me...

'...what's the market like at the moment?' I'm asked that question by nearly every client and candidate that I speak to, so if someone was prepared to give me a pound per question it could prove to be a lucrative side line!"

This year has been a year of positives rather than negatives, although part of being a recruitment consultant is handling the disappointment of being let down by the clients or candidates you represent.

The best thing to happen to me professionally this year is the best thing to ever happen to me professionally – the opportunity to launch Workplace Law Career Network. Leaving the security of Randstad CPE, the second largest recruitment company in the world, to launch a recruitment division for a company that had never 'done' recruitment before was a huge gamble, but presents me with career progression opportunities that no other employer could. With our existing HR consultancy division it also presents clients of Workplace Law with innovative recruitment solutions unique to Workplace Law Career Network.

On a personal level, the thing I'm most proud of this year has to be the birth of my daughter, Elsie. I'm hugely, perhaps overly, proud of both her and her big brother, Seth. If pushed on the matter I would have to say that Elsie is the prettiest, most intelligent baby in the world, although I accept my views on this matter may not be impartial!

I'm going to be employing two to three trainee recruitment consultants over the course of the next year, so my role will have a greater managerial bias as I look to mentor and educate these new employees. Taking on additional staff will allow us to work in more defined sectors with all of Workplace Law Career Network employees focusing on one area and becoming trusted experts in their field. I have always intended Workplace Law Career Network to be seen as a consultancy service with employees knowing more about the clients, candidates, legislation and trends in their sector than any competitor. Whilst Workplace Law's 15-year history of providing training and consultancy services puts us in a unique position to be able to achieve this goal, my ability to impose the belief of fair and ethical recruitment into new employees is equally important. I can't wait for the challenge!

The part of the job that I look forward to most is placing staff. The success or failure of any recruitment agency hinges on the number of staff that they place with their clients, so this should be the biggest buzz for anybody working in recruitment. No matter how big Workplace Law Career Network becomes, every placement should be greeted with the same enthusiasm as the first. I've got huge aspirations for the division and every placement we make moves us a step closer to matching those ambitions.

Neil McDiarmid

@WLCareerNetwork

Redundancy

Lisa Gettins, Sarah Lee and John Turnbull, BPE Solicitors

Key points

- Section 139 of the Employment Rights Act 1996 defines redundancy as the dismissal of an employee from employment wholly or mainly due to:
    - his employer ceasing or intending to cease carrying on business for the purposes for which the employee was employed, either completely or in the place that the employee was employed (known as the place of work redundancy); or
    - the requirements of the employer's business to carry out work of a particular kind having ceased or diminished or are expected to cease or diminish. whether that is across the business or where the employee is employed (known as type of work redundancy).

- Section 195 of the Trade Union and Labour Relations (Consolidation) Act 1992 (TULRCA) also includes a definition of redundancy when used for assessing eligibility for redundancy payments. Section 195 defines redundancy as a dismissal for a reason not related to the individual concerned.
- Collective consultation must take place where an employee intends to make 20 or more employees redundant in any 90-day period. As a result of the ACAS guidelines, employers should follow a basic procedure for consultation, regardless of the number of employees involved.

Legislation

- Trade Union and Labour Relations (Consolidation) Act 1992 (TULRCA).
- Employment Rights Act 1996 (ERA).
- Employment Act 2002.

Redundancy payments

To be eligible for a statutory redundancy payment an employee must have at least two years' continuous service. The lower and upper age limits (18 and 65) on the right to claim redundancy payments no longer apply as a result of age discrimination legislation that came into force on 1 October 2006. Statutory redundancy payments are calculated in accordance with the employee's age, length of service and the rate of the employee's weekly pay (subject to a statutory cap, which is currently £400 per week but traditionally increases on 1 February each year). The employee's weekly pay is multiplied by their complete years' service and age multiples as follows:

- By 1.5 for every year in which the employee was 41 years old or older;
- By one for every year in which the employee was aged between 22 and 40; and
- By 0.5 for every year in which the employee was between 18 and 21.

The maximum payment is 30 weeks' pay (including the 1.5 multiplier) or £12,000. A redundancy ready reckoner is available on the BERR website to calculate statutory redundancy payments due.

Case study

A typical situation may involve a business that needs to restructure, whether to be more efficient or to avoid financial catastrophe, in tough economic trading conditions. In this hypothetical case, you have a Customer Services Department, an Export Department, an IT Department and a Reception, all at one site.

You propose to reduce headcount at varying levels across those departments, which will involve 40 proposed redundancies.

Given that the proposal is to dismiss 20 or more employees within a short period of time at one site, a collective consultation will take place, with notice not starting to run until after this 30-day period has expired. Form HR1 will also need to be sent to the Secretary of State (for Business, Innovation and Skills).

It would be sensible to draw diagrams of the current structure, together with diagrams of the proposed new structure (detailing the roles as opposed to individual staff names), so that it is clear which departments will be affected.

Employees will need to elect representatives and the collective consultation period should commence once those representatives have been elected. Failure to follow collective consultation procedures could result in a penalty of 13 weeks' pay per employee.

Stand-alone roles should be identified, as should those roles where a skills matrix will be required, in order to make a number reduction. Skills matrices should be consulted on with the representatives and on an individual level. The skills matrices should also be as objective as possible and include clear definitions so that if different managers were to score the 'at risk' staff against those criteria, those two managers would arrive at the same scores.

Suitable alternative employment and 'bumping' should also be considered, together with any other suggestions the employees or representatives may have.

It may also open a window of opportunity for voluntary redundancy, albeit reserving the right to retain key skills within the workforce.

At the end of the process, those staff remaining at highest risk should be invited to a meeting, in writing, with the right to be accompanied by a work colleague or Trade Union representative. All details of redundancy pay, notice pay, accrued holiday and any other enhanced payments, should be provided to the employee, in writing, together with the right of appeal.

Penalties

Failure to carry out a proper procedure (whether the ACAS guidelines or collective consultation procedure) may result in substantial claims. Getting the collective consultation wrong can result in claims for protective awards in the value of 90 days' full pay per employee.

Claims for unfair dismissal in relation to any aspect of the redundancy process can also be brought if there is a fault in the process. Employees usually need one year's continuous employment to make such a claim unless they link it to discrimination.

The current statutory maximum compensatory award for unfair dismissal is £68,400. There is also potential liability for a basic award, which is calculated on the same basis as the redundancy payments. Therefore, if they are paid the redundancy pay, only the compensatory award will be made.

Failure to follow the ACAS guidelines will allow an Employment Tribunal to increase a compensatory award by up to 25% depending on the circumstances and will also make the dismissal automatically unfair. Any uplift will not take an award beyond the statutory maximum.

Redundancy process checklist

Below is a checklist of the most important issues to be considered in a redundancy process. Please note it is not a comprehensive guide and individual circumstances may vary. It is not intended to be a substitute for legal advice, which should be sought regarding individual circumstances.

Step one – Planning

As soon as the possibility of redundancy has been identified as an option, document the reason for the proposed redundancies and plan the redundancy process.

Step two – Redundancy policy

Does your company have a redundancy policy in place, which has been communicated to the employees, or is

there an implied policy in place through custom or practice? If so, check that those policies are compatible with the statutory procedures and then follow your own policy. If you have no policy or it does not follow the ACAS guidelines the following steps should be taken.

Step three – Collective consultation

If you are proposing to dismiss 20 or more employees from one establishment over a 90-day period, you are required to enter into collective consultation with appropriate representatives. This may be a Trade Union representative or an elected employee representative. Your collective consultation should set out the framework for redundancy selection and who will be in the pool of selection. You will also have to carry out individual consultation after the collective consultation.

If you are proposing to make 100 or more employees redundant at one establishment within a 90-day period, consultation must take place in 'good time' and at least 90 days before the first of the dismissals.

If you are proposing to dismiss at least 20 but fewer than 100 employees at one establishment within a 90-day period, collective consultations must begin in 'good time' and at least 30 days before the first dismissal.

Collective consultation should start as soon as redundancies are proposed. The employee representatives can assist in the planning stage of the selection process and reduce the risk of claims being brought for failure to follow proper procedure. There is an obligation for employers to inform the Secretary of State (for Business, Innovation and Skills) of proposed large-scale redundancies using form HR1, a copy of which should be sent to the appropriate representatives.

Collective consultations should include discussions about avoiding dismissals, reducing the number of employees to be dismissed, and mitigating the consequences of dismissal.

Consultation should also be undertaken with a view to reaching agreement. Regardless of whether or not agreement is possible, the next step is individual consultation.

Step four – Individual consultation

To follow a fair procedure in accordance with the ACAS guidelines, all employees should be invited to a meeting in writing, informing them of the potential redundancy situation.

Employees are entitled to attend meetings with a fellow employee or a Trade Union representative of their choice.

Inform each employee of the reason for the redundancy and the selection process that is going to take place. Inform them of the reason why they are potentially at risk of redundancy and ask them to consider whether they are in the correct pool for selection. If they do not consider they are in the correct pool, consider their reasons for this.

After the meeting, confirm whether or not the employee is in the pool of selection and provide them with details of the redundancy selection criteria (e.g. length of service, skills and qualifications, disciplinary record) taking care not to unlawfully discriminate against the affected employees.

Hold a second meeting where you discuss the selection criteria and any alternatives to redundancy you or the employee may have, including alternative employment or job sharing.

Step five – Confirm the options in writing

If appropriate, apply the selection criteria and provisionally select the redundant employees. Write to those selected employees to confirm this. Do not state that they will be made redundant but do inform them that a possibility of the full and final meeting will be their dismissal.

Inform the employee at the final meeting the reason as to why they have been selected for redundancy and explain the consequences of this. Invite the employee to comment on the selection. After the meeting consider any points raised by the employee and then confirm to them in writing their selection for redundancy. Be sure to offer the employees the opportunity to appeal to a higher level of management.

Consider whether there is any suitable alternative employment within the company or group of companies that can be offered to the employees, and if they accept it decide whether a trial period should be given in their new role.

Redundant employees will be entitled to notice payments, redundancy payments and payment of accrued but untaken holiday pay.

Write to the affected employees and invite them to a final meeting. Inform them of their dismissal and then write to them offering them an appeal against their dismissal on grounds by reason of redundancy.

See also: Dismissal, p.146; Employee consultation, p.160; Employment disputes, p.168; Notice periods, p.369.

References

Pinsent Masons Employment Group

Key points

- The subject of employee references will usually arise when offering a prospective employee a contract of employment or when providing a reference for a current or former employee.

- An employer is under no obligation to provide a reference for a current or former employee, unless a term in the contract of employment compels it, or, as in some regulated industries such as financial services, it is obliged to provide a reference under the regulations of a relevant body.

- If a reference is given, the referee must take great care in compiling it and must use all reasonable skill and care to ensure the accuracy of the facts contained in the reference and the reasonableness of the opinions contained within the reference as the referee may be liable as a consequence of a defective reference.

- Employers should be aware that if the reference results in the former employee suffering a loss or failing to be employed by the new employer then the content of the reference will be made known to the individual.

Legislation

There is no legislation that sets out what must be included in references or the form they should take. There are, however, data protection issues, and employers should have regard to the Data Protection Act 1998 when giving references and responding to employees' requests for access to information (including references) that the employer holds.

Offering a prospective employee a contract of employment

When recruiting new staff it is common for a prospective employer to make a job offer expressly conditional on receiving satisfactory references from the prospective employee's previous employer.

If the prospective employer's decision to employ is conditional upon receipt of a satisfactory reference, this must be made clear in the offer letter. To avoid dispute, it should be made clear that it is for the employer to determine what is satisfactory.

Providing a reference for a current or former employee

An employer is under no obligation to provide a reference for a current or former employee. However, employers must be careful to ensure that their policy on references is consistent or it could lead to allegations of discrimination or breach of the implied term of mutual trust and confidence.

There are some exceptions to the general rule that there is no obligation to provide a reference such as where a term in the contract of employment compels it, or, as in some regulated industries such as financial services, it is obliged to provide a reference under the regulations of a relevant body. In addition, a manager may have assured an employee he will get a reference or one is provided under the terms of the compromise agreement.

However, if a reference is given, the referee must take great care in compiling it, for he may be liable as a consequence of a defective reference.

Duties are owed by the employer to recipients of references and to the subject of those references.

When giving a reference about an existing employee who is seeking employment with another employer, there are a number of points that an employer must consider:

- An employer must use all reasonable skill and care to ensure the accuracy of the facts contained in the reference and the reasonableness of the opinions contained within the reference. Failure to do so may amount to a breach of the implied term of trust and confidence, entitling the employee to resign and claim constructive dismissal.
- Even if the reference is factually accurate, the employer must be careful not to give an unfair impression of the employee concerned. Therefore the employer should not include a disproportionate amount of negative facts and exclude those that are to the credit of the employee (e.g. stating that he always took long lunches, but not stating that he always worked late in the evening).
- Where an employee has been the subject of disciplinary action, this should only be referred to in the reference being provided where the employer:
  - genuinely believes the statement being made to be true;
  - has reasonable grounds for believing that the statement is true; and
  - has carried out as much investigation into the matters referred to in the statement as is reasonable in the circumstances.
- It would accordingly not be appropriate for an employer to refer

to a disciplinary incident where the employment was terminated before a full investigation was conducted.
- Other than in certain circumstances (e.g. where industry rules or practice require full and frank references), references do not have to be full and comprehensive. The employer's obligation is to provide a true, accurate and fair reference that does not give a misleading impression overall. Some employers will limit the reference to basic facts such as the dates of employment and the position held. Employers are entitled to set parameters within which the reference is given, e.g. by stressing their limited knowledge of the individual employee.
- Care should be taken to comply with data protection requirements because personal and sensitive data will be involved.
- Mark the reference 'private and confidential: for the addressee only'.

A practical danger

References could be used in evidence where the dismissal of an employee is the subject of litigation, so employers should take care in giving a reference in such circumstances. It is not unusual for employers to give positive references to employees who have been dismissed for poor performance, as part of a negotiated settlement in such circumstances. Should they choose to do so in terms that are misleadingly favourable to the employee, the referee may find himself liable to a subsequent employer who relies on the references.

Employees' claims

The most common action for an employee who is the subject of an inaccurate reference is a damages action in respect of any economic loss that may flow from a carelessly or negligently prepared reference.

In order to establish that an employer is in breach of its duty to take reasonable care in the preparation of a reference, the employee must show that:

- the information contained in the reference was misleading;
- by virtue of the misleading information, the reference was likely to have a material effect upon the mind of a reasonable recipient of the reference to the detriment of the employee;
- the employee suffered loss as a result (for example, the withdrawal of a job offer); and
- the employer was negligent in providing such a reference.

Unsatisfactory references

If a reference is received that is unsatisfactory or causes concern, the employer can terminate the employment provided the job offer or employment contract allows for this. If not, notice to terminate the contract will have to be given and the employer will be liable to the individual for notice monies due under the contract of employment.

See also: Employment contracts, p.164; Interviewing, p.275; Recruitment and selection, p.420; Screening, p.453; Vetting, barring, blacklisting and social engineering, p.534.

Sources of further information

For organisations with or without a HR team who require specialist support, advice through hands-on support and/or project management, Workplace Law offer tailored strategic HR support and advice to suit the needs of your organisation. To enable your organisation to focus on its core business our CIPD qualified and HR specialist team can provide support and advice on a number of strategic HR offerings. Our dedicated HR team can work with you on key HR projects aligned to your HR strategy and business plan, which can include, although are not limited to:

- HR strategy planning
- Strategic succession planning
- Site closures
- Sale of business
- Acquisitions and mergers
- Relocation of sites or departments
- Large TUPE projects
- Changing terms and conditions

All of our HR professionals have 20 plus years of hands-on experience, working in every sector, in small, medium and large organisations. Our HR professionals bring this unique knowledge and experience to provide advice, support and project management to ensure the best fit for your organisation.
Visit www.workplacelaw.net for more information.

Resignation

Suzanne McMinn, Workplace Law

Key points

- Make sure that the employee's resignation is confirmed in writing.
- Do ensure that you acknowledge in writing their resignation.
- Understand the reasons why the employee is leaving.
- Be clear about the notice period of the employee who is leaving, whether they have provided you with right length of notice, and if you need them to work their notice.
- Ensure all company property is returned and any work is handed over promptly.

Legislation

- Employment Rights Act 1996.

Introduction

Even during these difficult economic times, resignation rates are on the increase. In the last year resignations have risen from 1.8 to 2%, showing that there is still some level of movement within the labour market. Although not always welcomed by managers, resignations do allow a company the opportunity to review the current organisation structure, working practices and skills needed for particular roles.

To ensure that the resignation process runs smoothly, make sure that you follow a few key steps. Look to understand why the employee has decided to resign. If it's a key employee you may wish to look to see if you are able to change their mind! If it's a resignation that you have been hoping for for some time, act professionally throughout the exit process, and don't celebrate the employee's decision to leave!

Once an employee has decided to leave your organisation you will need to assess if there is any risk to the employee working their notice. If they are leaving to work with a competitor you may not wish them to work their notice and offer payment instead, or you may consider placing them on garden leave. You will need to consider what approach you will take based on the risks involved. Where someone leaves with immediate effect, it often means you need an immediate replacement. You need to consider what effect that will have on the business and the morale of the remaining employees.

Although a verbal resignation is acceptable, always try and get the employee to confirm their resignation in writing. This way it corroborates both parties' understanding of when the actual resignation date is, and this will help you calculate when the notice period needs to commence.

Acknowledge the resignation

Once the employee has tendered their resignation you need to respond to this, confirming to the employee that you have accepted their decision to resign. Outline their notice period to them and that they will or will not be required to work it. Where you have decided that the employee is not required to work their notice period you will be required to make a payment in lieu of the contractual notice that they are entitled to. You should ensure that the employment contract allows you to make payment in lieu of the notice period prior to confirming this to the employee.

In your acknowledgement letter confirm to the employee the process for handing in any company equipment, confirm any accrued outstanding holiday and if they are required to take this or will be paid for it, and outline to them when any final payments are due to be made, for example a bonus or commission that is due.

Where it is appropriate you may wish to outline in the letter any handover that is required in light of outstanding projects, work or client commitments. In this way it focuses the employee's attention on the areas that need to be closed off before they leave your organisation. Take the opportunity to confirm in writing the hard work and commitment that they have given to the organisation, and thank them for it.

Rescinding resignations

There is the odd occasion where an employee will submit their resignation and then look to rescind it. This could be down to any number of reasons, for example the next job opportunity may have fallen through or there may have been a change in personal circumstances. Whatever the reason, once an employee has submitted their resignation it cannot be rescinded without the employer's agreement. There is only one exception to this, and that is where the resignation has been offered in the heat of the moment.

Other than this one exclusion, employers are not legally bound to accept an employee who wishes to claim their job back. Employers may wish to consider requests and look at the previous service of the employee and consider whether

or not they would be a loss to the organisation and then make their decision accordingly.

Heat of the moment

Dealing with resignations that occur after conflict within the office, or where an employee has undue pressures at home that lead them to make knee jerk decisions, can be tricky. Where a resignation has occurred after a heated discussion within the workplace, allow the employee some time to cool off and think seriously about their decision to resign. Often a little time away from the situation will ensure that the employee gives consideration to their actions and thinks through the consequences of their immediate resignation. The employee often concludes that resignation is not the route that they want to consider and in these instances you can allow them to rescind their resignation.

Ambiguous resignations

There may be a situation in the workplace where tempers flare and an employee is heard to shout, "That's it, I've had it with this place!" and off they flounce. On the face of it, have they resigned? In such instances the resignation can be ambiguous and rather than make an assumption you should follow up in writing to confirm if the employee wishes you to accept their comments as a verbal resignation, and, as stated above, you should look to ask them to confirm their intention in writing.

If the employee states that it is not the case you should then expect them to return to work forthwith.

Resignations during a disciplinary process

It is sometimes the situation where you commence the disciplinary process against any employee and during this they decide to resign from your organisation. Do you have to cease the disciplinary process that has already started?

Where the employee still has a notice period to serve you can look to conclude the disciplinary process during their notice period. They are still employed by the organisation during this time so you are within your rights to look to conclude the hearing and apply the appropriate sanction.

Where the disciplinary outcome is to dismiss on the grounds of gross misconduct you would apply this sanction and it would supersede any resignation. Therefore the employee would have been dismissed rather than resigned.

Resignations and constructive dismissal

Where an organisation has looked to make fundamental changes to an employee's contractual benefits without their agreement, for example, removal of a bonus or commission scheme, or a reduction in salary, an employee could exercise their right to resign from the organisation.

Where an employee resigns under this situation they could claim constructive dismissal, as through the actions of the employer there has been a fundamental breach of their employment contract.

Other examples that would constitute constructive dismissal would be where the employer has failed to provide a safe working environment or where the employee has been forced to relocate to a different location and there is no contractual provision to do this.

Having outlined the risks of constructive dismissal, this does not mean to say that employers are not able to change an

employee's employment contract. But to do so they should consult regarding the change, the change should have come about due to a significant business reason, and most importantly they should look to gain the employees' agreement to the contractual change. Failure to do so, where the change is implemented, could give rise to claims of constructive dismissal.

Non acceptance of TUPE transfers

Where a TUPE (Transfer of Undertakings (Protection of Employment) Regulations) situation occurs an employee may assert that they do not wish to transfer to the new employer.

Under TUPE, all employees in the business entity, who are subject to the transfer, automatically move across to the new employer on their existing employment terms and conditions.

During the TUPE consultations an employee may raise objections to the transfer that is taking place. In most cases any objections can be discussed and settled during the consultation process. However, there are some situations where this is not the case and the employee may refuse to transfer. Where this occurs the employee is deemed to have resigned from the organisation effective from the date of the transfer. There is no dismissal, no redundancy and no obligation on the new employer to enforce the transfer of their contract. The role still exists with the new employer under the same employment terms and conditions, it has become the employee's choice not to follow the transfer and therefore it is deemed that they have resigned.

Leaver's checklist

Once you have received and accepted an employee's resignation there are a number of areas that you need to ensure are followed from an administrative perspective so that your own systems and procedures are closed properly and there is no risk to the organisation.

These can include such areas as:

- Removal from your organisation's IT systems;
- Calculating final payments and raising a P45;
- Conducting an exit interview;
- Arranging the return of all company equipment, security passes, laptops, etc.; and
- Cancelling fuel cards and mobile phone contracts.

Finally, where appropriate, you may wish to organise a leaving party or gift to thank the employee for their commitment and service to your organisation.

Once you have reviewed your leaver's arrangements, consider if you need a replacement in the role. Take the opportunity to look at the organisation's structure – are the same key skills required and have the duties changed? A resignation is a great chance to review exactly what your business needs, rather than replace like for like.

See also: Discrimination, p.126; Dismissal, p.146; Health surveillance, p.231; Redundancy, p.429.

Sources of further information

Direct Gov Website www.direct.gov.uk/en/Employment

The Workplace Law website has been one of the UK's leading legal information sites since its launch in 2002. As well as providing free news and forums, our Information Centre provides you with a 'one-stop shop' where you will find all you need to know to manage your workplace and fulfil your legal obligations.

It covers everything from the latest Employment Tribunal cases to redundancy law, as well as detailed information in key areas such as equality and diversity.

You'll find:

- quick and easy access to all major legislation and official guidance, including clear explanations and advice from our experts;
- case reviews and news analysis, which will keep you fully up to date with the latest legislation proposals and changes, case outcomes and examples of how the law is applied in practice;
- briefings, which include in-depth analysis on major topics; and
- WPL TV – an online TV channel including online seminars, documentaries and legal updates.

Visit www.workplacelaw.net for more information.

Restrictive covenants and garden leave

Anna Youngs, Mills & Reeve

Key points

■ Restrictive covenants operate to protect the employer's business after an employee has left employment.

■ They are prima facie void as a restraint of trade.

■ To enforce a covenant, the terms must be no wider than necessary to protect a legitimate business interest.

■ Restrictive covenants are enforced by the Courts.

Introduction

An employee must observe certain restrictions that are implied by law into a contract of employment (e.g. fidelity, obedience, working with due diligence and care, not to use or disclose the employer's trade secrets or confidential information during employment). However, these implied terms are of a limited nature and, save in respect of highly confidential information, do not apply after termination of the contract.

Restrictions that apply to employees after the employment relationship ends either take the form of a garden leave clause or a restrictive covenant.

What are restrictive covenants and when do employers need them?

Restrictive covenants are contractual post-termination obligations (commonly incorporated into an employee's contract of employment) that seek to prevent employees from doing certain things that may be damaging to the employer's business when they leave the employment.

The main types of restrictive covenants are:

■ Non-solicitation of staff (to prevent ex-employees from recruiting key employees of the business).

■ Non-solicitation of customers and non-dealing covenants (to protect the client base of the business by preventing employees from dealing with and soliciting customers).

■ Non-competition (to prevent the ex-employee from taking up employment in competition with the business).

■ Protecting confidential information acquired by the ex-employee during the course of employment.

These covenants can be used in isolation, or together in order to bolster the protection provided to the employer.

However, the employer's need to protect its business must be balanced against the employee's right to earn a living and take up work in their area of expertise.

The legal approach to restrictive covenants

The starting point in law is that restrictive covenants are void as being a restraint of trade and are therefore unenforceable unless the employer can show that it is a justifiable covenant, which will only be the case where:

- the employer has a legitimate interest to protect, which will vary depending on the nature of the business (examples include business connections, stability of the workforce, confidential information, etc.); and
- the covenant goes no further than is reasonably necessary for the protection of the legitimate interest.

There can never be any certainty as to the enforceability of restrictive covenants because to enforce any restriction the employer has to obtain a court order, which is granted at the discretion of the court by reference to what it regards as reasonable in the circumstances.

When will a restrictive covenant be enforceable?

Even if there is a legitimate interest to protect, the restriction can be no wider than reasonably necessary to protect that interest. This is achieved by limiting the scope of the covenant by reference to the restricted activities, the length of the period of restraint and, where appropriate, the geographical area to which it applies (e.g. the duration of the restricted period should be no longer than necessary to protect the business interest). The following factors are useful pointers:

- *Non-solicitation of staff.* Consider which groups of employees need to be protected and the time period necessary for the influence over these staff to diminish.
- *Non-solicitation of customers.* In respect of current customers,

the covenant should be limited to customers with whom the employee had contact, and the time period should be limited by considering the amount of time it would take for the employee's successor to build up a relationship with these customers. The general customer base and prospective customers can also be protected in certain circumstances.

- *Non-dealing covenants.* A blanket ban on dealing with any customer should be avoided, and therefore consideration should be given to which key contacts are at risk because of the relationship with the employee.
- *Non-competition.* The restriction must be for a limited time and may need to be limited in terms of geographical area. Consider how long it will be until competitive activities by the individual are no longer a material threat to the legitimate business interest, as well as the area of activities of the employee and the size of the restricted area.
- *Protecting confidential information.* The key to confidentiality clauses is to carefully define what is 'confidential information'.

As well as considering what the legitimate business interest is, the employer must consider what level of protection is reasonably necessary in respect of any given employee at the time that they enter into the covenant. What is enforceable against one employee may not be against another. For example, a senior employee would have very different contacts to someone at a trainee level, and even employees at the same level may have different access to customers and confidential information. Therefore employers should not impose heavy restrictions on junior employees on the basis that they may be promoted, as the status of the employee at the time of entering into the covenant is what will be considered. Instead, if an employee is promoted, the employer should take the opportunity to revisit the restrictions and issue a new contract.

In almost all cases, the length of the restrictive period will be a key factor.

What if the clause is too wide-ranging?

If a clause is too wide-ranging, it will not be enforceable. The court will not re-write the clause, but they may sever unenforceable clauses and 'blue pencil' restrictions, leaving enforceable restrictions intact.

The court, in deciding whether unlawful provisions may be severed from the rest of the terms, will consider whether:

- the provisions can be removed without needing to amend the remaining wording;
- the remaining terms are supported by adequate consideration; and
- deleting the unenforceable wording changes the character of the contract.

Note: If an employer commits a repudiatory breach of contract, or terminates the employment in breach of contract, it is highly unlikely that any restrictive covenants will be enforced.

Garden leave

The need for garden leave normally arises where employees hand in their notice in order to work for a competitor, although these clauses can also be used where the employer gives the employee notice of termination. The aim of garden leave is to keep the employee away from confidential information long enough for the information to become out of date, and from customers long enough to enable customer relationships to be forged with an alternative contact. This can be done either by changing the employee's duties during their notice period, or by requiring

the employee to stay at home (whilst enjoying normal pay and benefits) on 'garden leave' during all or part of their notice period. During garden leave the employee remains employed and therefore the employer must continue to perform all terms of the contract, including paying all pay and benefits under their contract.

Putting an employee on garden leave is still a restraint of trade, and therefore the same principles as with restrictive covenants apply, such as having a period no longer than is reasonably necessary to protect a legitimate business interest. Therefore, even where, for example, 12 months' notice is required, in the first six months the employee could be assigned alternative duties (provided the contract allows for this) and then only the latter six months would be garden leave.

If the employee's contact does not give the employer the right to put the employee on garden leave (for example, by including a clause allowing the employer to assign no or different duties during the notice period) then the employer should be aware that in some circumstances the courts will say that the employee has the right to work. A likely example is where the employee's work is skilled and they need to undertake work in order to retain their skills.

Employers are advised to take legal advice if they are considering taking action that may not be permitted within the terms of the contract of employment. Particular care should be taken if the employer hopes to rely on post-termination restrictions and/or other rights contained within the contract, as a breach of contract by the employer can release the employee from their contractual obligations.

Enforcing restrictive covenants

Restrictive covenants are enforced by the courts. An employer may seek an injunction to prevent an employee from breaching the terms of the covenant. If this is not possible, there is a claim against the employee for damages for breach of the covenants, provided that the covenant is enforceable (i.e. not an illegal restraint of trade) and provided that any breach of the covenant has caused the employer loss.

Enforcing breaches of restrictive covenants is difficult and expensive, so employers need to think carefully about whether their 'legitimate business interest' warrants the time and expense of litigation. Perhaps negotiation and persuasion is a sensible first step, but bear in mind that litigation must be commenced swiftly if there is to be any hope of enforcing a restrictive covenant.

> *See also*: Dismissal, p.146;
> Employment contracts, p.164;
> Leave, p.252; Redundancy, p.429.

Sources of further information

The Workplace Law website has been one of the UK's leading legal information sites since its launch in 2002. As well as providing free news and forums, our Information Centre provides you with a 'one-stop shop' where you will find all you need to know to manage your workplace and fulfil your legal obligations.

It covers everything from the latest Employment Tribunal cases to redundancy law, as well as detailed information in key areas such as equality and diversity.

You'll find:

- quick and easy access to all major legislation and official guidance, including clear explanations and advice from our experts;
- case reviews and news analysis, which will keep you fully up to date with the latest legislation proposals and changes, case outcomes and examples of how the law is applied in practice;
- briefings, which include in-depth analysis on major topics; and
- WPL TV – an online TV channel including online seminars, documentaries and legal updates.

Content is added and updated regularly by our editorial team who utilise a wealth of in-house experts and legal consultants. Visit www.workplacelaw.net for more information.

Retirement

Heidi Thompson, Workplace Law

Key points

- The Default Retirement Age, under the Equality (Age) Regulations 2006, has been abolished from 1 October 2011.
- There is a transition period whereby employers can only enforce retirement to those employees given the correct notice under the Equality (Age) Regulations by 1 April 2011.
- Enforced retirement outside of this transition period will be deemed as automatically unfair dismissal, unless the organisation has an objectively justified retirement age.

Legislation

- The Employment Rights Act 1996.
- Employment Equality (Age) Regulations 2006.
- The Equality Act 2010.

The Age Discrimination Regulations

Under the Equality Act 2010, which replaces the previous regulations, less favourable treatment on the grounds of age, whether direct or indirect, is unlawful unless it can be justified. This applies throughout the sphere of employment.

From 6 April 2011 the Government started to phase out the default retirement age (DRA). From this point employers were no longer able to issue notifications of retirement using the DRA procedure, and all default retirement ages will no longer be enforceable going forward.

Where notification has already been given prior to 6 April 2011 in accordance with the procedures set out in the previous Employment Equality (Age) Regulations 2006 (which would have been a minimum of six months and no more than 12 months' notice), employers can continue with the retirement process as long as the employee is aged 65 – or the company's retirement age, if higher, before 1 October 2011.

In accordance with the previous DRA procedures, those employees will be able to request to work on beyond their notified retirement date, and companies will be able to agree an extension to their employment. If the employer wishes to give an extension that still ends with dismissal under the DRA, the extension must be for a fixed period of six months or less and the employee's retirement on or before 5 October 2012. As such, the employee's right to request to work beyond retirement ceases on 5 January 2012.

Other than these transitional arrangements, employers will not be able to rely on the DRA any longer. As a result an employer cannot compulsory retire their employees, unless the retirement can be objectively justified.

In what circumstances can a company enforce an objectively justified retirement age?

In some instances it may be possible to retire an employee lawfully at a set age, provided that the retirement age can be objectively justified, which means that it is

Case study

Rob is asked by his manager during an appraisal meeting where he sees himself in the next few years. Rob, who is 64, advises his manager that he would like to work for another year and then draw his company pension in order to go travelling with his wife.

It is important that the manager notes Rob's plans and discusses with him how they can best retain his considerable knowledge and experience and agree that they will meet regularly to plan for Rob to offer training and mentoring when appropriate to other employees.

As the DRA is no longer in place, Rob can change his mind and as such the manager should advise him of this and state that he is required to give notice in line with his contract of employment and that the resignation would only become final at this stage.

Josie is 25 and works in the sales team of a large IT company. Josie has struggled to meet her targets this year due to the downturn in the market. Josie has a meeting with her manager who advises her that he is unimpressed with her performance and unless it improves formal action would be taken, which could result in her dismissal.

Josie later finds out that her colleague, Janet, who is 67, has lower sales than her, but has not been given the same warning by their manager.

In this situation it is possible that Josie could claim direct age discrimination as she is clearly being treated differently to Janet, particularly if Josie is subsequently dismissed and no action is taken against Janet.

It is also possible that in this case the employer is making allowances for Janet and not taking the same action against her due to her age. The employer cannot rely on the DRA to remove Janet from the organisation and as such Josie and Janet should both be performance managed if it is considered that their sales figures are unacceptable.

a proportionate response to a legitimate aim. The justification will be of paramount importance in the event that such a policy is challenged in an Employment Tribunal.

Generally such a justification would only be used in exceptional circumstances and the majority of companies will not be able to reply on this. In the main these will be in posts where the employer already has a retirement age under the age of 65. An example would be the emergency services where a certain level of physical fitness is required, or posts involving exceptional mental fitness such as air traffic controllers. They are also used where the DRA Regulations do not apply, such as for partners in a law firm.

Organisations must think carefully before implementing such a policy. It will be essential that this meets a legitimate

> **Facts**
> - By 2020, nearly 50% of the UK population will be over 50.
> - Government estimates for the UK show that life expectancy for people aged 65 in 2008 will be around 82 for men and around 85 for women.
> - The Government estimates that the scrapping of default retirement ages will cost employers collectively £3m per year in unfair dismissal claims.
>
> *Sources: Age Concern, ONS, Government Actuary's Department.*

aim and that by enforcing a compulsory retirement age it is a proportionate means of achieving it.

It is likely that we will see case law around this area in the coming months, which will give a clearer indication of the test of justification. Ultimately, employers must take time to consider their policy and ensure they have clear evidence to support the proposal, providing clarity that there is no less discriminatory alternative, and remembering that justification must be objective and not subjective.

If an organisation does establish a justified retirement age, any such dismissal will be considered as a dismissal for some other substantial reason. It is also necessary to follow a fair procedure, giving adequate notice of the impending retirement (in line with contractual notice). Employers can still consider requests for an extension to retirement in these circumstances, but care must be taken that this does not undermine the justification for the retirement age or create inconsistency between employees that make such a request.

In what circumstances will a retirement amount to unfair dismissal?

Previously the Regulations amended the unfair dismissal provisions in the Act. There is no age cap for unfair dismissal claims but, where the correct procedure was followed the employee was unable

to challenge the reason for dismissal. In cases where notification was given to an employee prior to 6 April 2011, and the correct procedure under the Employment Equality (Age) Regulations 2006 followed, this will remain the case.

However, the removal of the DRA from 6 April 2011 will mean that retirement will no longer be a fair reason for dismissal going forward, unless an employer has an objectively justified retirement age. As such, outside of the transition arrangements detailed above, any such dismissal would be deemed automatically unfair and the employee could claim unfair dismissal and direct age discrimination.

How can employees retire with the removal of the DRA?

The removal of the DRA does not mean that employees will be required to work indefinitely, but rather that employers can no longer force employees to retire at a set age, unless where a justified retirement age is in place.

Employees can voluntarily opt to retire when they choose to do so and draw any pension they are entitled to under the scheme rules. To invoke this, employees would be required to give notice in line with their contract of employment. It is recommended that employers have open discussions with employees regarding their future plans to aid transition between work and retirement. It is important to remember that where an employee has stated that they are considering retiring, they can change their mind, and as such organisations should await for formal notice from the employee of their intention to retire before taking any action.

Where an employee has indicated their intention to retire and subsequently changes their mind it is important to discuss this with the employee to establish why. Ultimately an organisation cannot compulsory retire them but they can understand the reasons for the decision and in some circumstances be able to assist the employee to overcome any such problems from preventing them from retiring.

What should employers do now the DRA has been removed?

The removal of the DRA will be a significant change for many organisations and should prompt reviews of their practices and processes for managing employees.

As employers can no longer rely on a DRA they will need to ensure their processes for managing performance are clear, non-discriminatory and consistently applied across the organisation. It is important that managers are aware of any updated procedures and are fully trained in dealing with employee performance.

It will be important to hold regular discussions with all employees (regardless of their age) to review their performance, clarify expectations of them and to discuss their future plans within the organisation. It will not be discriminatory to ask employees of their future plans and aspirations, providing you do not single out older workers for such discussions. These meetings should be held in an open and honest manner, but must not include questions that could be deemed

as discriminatory, such as implying that an older worker is 'surely ready for retirement'.

The appraisal process is an ideal time to have such discussions with all employees and this will assist with setting objectives, reviewing performance, clarifying expectations and understanding future plans. This will enable employers to plan for the future and ensure succession planning. In addition to the appraisal process, these discussions can take place as frequently as is deemed appropriate for the organisation, but certainly good practice would be to hold them annually.

Employers do not have to treat all employees exactly the same but must ensure fairness and consistency and that there is not more favourable treatment of an employee because of their age unless it can objectively justify the treatment.

Where an employee is performing badly this must be addressed and the cause identified. Employers will not be able to rely on the DRA to effectively remove such performance issues for older workers. Likewise, failing to address poor performance in older workers may also be discriminatory. Employers must also avoid the stereotype that older workers are likely to be associated with poor performance. As such, all performance issues must be dealt with promptly through the correct procedures and any such dismissal would be on the grounds of capability.

It is also important to consider that as employees get older, in some circumstances they may acquire more impairments than younger employees. As such, employers must consider the Equality Act 2010 when making decisions with respect to their employment and ensure that they do not discriminate.

How should employers manage benefits for older workers?

In the majority of cases employers cannot treat employees with less favourable treatment due to their age as this would amount to direct age discrimination, unless such treatment can be objectively justified, i.e. the employer has a sound business reason for it.

However, upon abolishing the DRA the Government's Regulations set out a small number of exemptions around 'insurance and financial benefits' which would include private health care, life and accident insurance and death in service. As it is accepted that such benefits become more costly with age, the Government's aim was to encourage employees to not remove such benefits for all employees and rather allow them to remove the benefits for employees at the age of 65 (or state pension age) and as such give an exemption to equal treatment on the grounds of age.

However, there are some concerns and uncertainties around the wording of the Regulations, and employers must take care when implementing such policies and carefully word their contracts of employment to take full advantage of the exemption.

Points to bear in mind are:

- The Regulations only cover 'employers', which means others who may also provide insured benefits to employees, such as the trustees of a pension scheme, are unlikely to be exempt.
- The Regulations refer to 'insurance or a related financial service', which is not defined and as such there may be uncertainty about what exactly is, and is not, covered.
- The Regulations do not cover pension contributions made by the employer.
- It is important to remember that the Regulations only apply to age discrimination claims and not breach of contract. Organisations that propose to change terms for existing employees will need to consult accordingly to remove the benefit.
- The Regulations only apply when an employer stops the benefit at 65 (or the state pension age) and so cannot apply where an employer opts to cease benefits before 65 or later.

See also: Discrimination, p.126; Dismissal, p.146; Health surveillance, p.231; Redundancy, p.429.

Sources of further information

Business Link: www.businesslink.gov.uk/employingpeople

Age and the workplace: Putting the Employment Equality (Age) Regulations 2006 into Practice: www.acas.org.uk/index.aspx?articleid=1044

Guidance for employers – Working without the default retirement age: http://bit.ly/jTgPps

Case review

Compulsorily retiring employees

Alan Chalmers, DLA Piper

Fuchs v. Land Hessen (2010)
Fuchs was employed by the state of Hessen as a prosecutor until he reached the age of 65. German law allowed compulsory retirement of civil servants, and Hessen's retirement age was 65. A further requirement was that continued employment should always be in the interests of the service and Fuchs' application to continue working beyond 65 was rejected as not meeting this criterion.

The ECJ decided that the legitimate aims of Hessen's compulsory retirement law were:

- establishing a balanced age structure in order to encourage the recruitment and promotion of young people;
- improving personnel management; and
- thereby preventing possible disputes concerning employees' fitness to work beyond a certain age.

The law may therefore be legitimate provided it allows these aims to be achieved by appropriate and necessary (i.e. proportionate) means, which is a matter for the German courts to assess. Given that posts in the relevant part of the civil service were limited, the ECJ said that it would 'not appear unreasonable' for the German authorities to consider that the compulsory retirement measure could secure the aims pursued.

The ECJ also said that an employer's need to keep costs down could be a legitimate aim justifying a compulsory retirement age.

Alan Chalmers is head of the Employment, Pensions and Benefits group in Sheffield. He has considerable experience in all aspects of employment law, both contentious and non-contentious. He acts for high-profile clients in both public and private sectors and across a range of industries including retail, manufacturing and brewing. Alan advises clients on senior executive severance, contract issues and large-scale reorganisation and redundancy programmes. He also manages industrial relations issues. Alan is a member of the Equality and Diversity group and provides training and advice to clients on compliance and best practice relating to discrimination legislation.

However, it remains unclear to what extent cost alone can justify age discrimination, although recent UK decisions have suggested that this may be possible.

Seldon v. Clarkson, Wright and Jakes (2008)
The EAT said that law firm Clarkson, Wright and Jakes (CWJ) was not entitled to force one of its partners, a Mr L J Seldon, to retire at the age of 65 just because of a general assumption that people's performance deteriorated at that age.

The EAT accepted CWJ's argument that it had a retirement age to avoid undermining the collegiate atmosphere of the firm by resorting to specific performance measures to oust partners. It said, though, that it had not shown that that age should be 65.

'The collegiality objective does justify the adoption of a compulsory retirement rule, but ... the Tribunal was not entitled to form the view that this objective itself justified fixing that age at 65,' said the EAT's ruling.

The EAT supported two other reasons used by CWJ to force Seldon's retirement. Those were that the firm had to have a definite retiring age so that it could plan properly for the future and so that it could offer more junior lawyers the realistic prospect of promotion to partner.

The end of the DRA

1 October 2011 marks a significant employment law milestone, as no employee who reaches age 65 on or after that date can be retired relying on the statutory default retirement age. For those reaching 65 before 1 October, retirement under the statutory provisions is only possible if notice of retirement was given prior to 6 April 2011.

Without doubt, the removal of the default retirement age has occasioned a policy shift, and many employers are no longer relying on retirement as a reason for terminating employment. However, the demise of the default retirement age does not mean that employers may never retire employees. It is permissible to operate a compulsory retirement age provided that this can be objectively justified as a proportionate means of achieving a legitimate aim. So when will compulsory retirement be objectively justified?

To date, the courts have accepted a variety of legitimate aims for the use of a compulsory retirement age, including:

- using the prospect of future promotion to replace senior staff to facilitate recruitment and retention of younger employees;
- workforce planning;
- maintaining diversity by having an age-balanced workforce, which shares job opportunities amongst the generations;
- avoiding an adverse impact on pensions and benefits;
- ensuring service of a high quality or ensuring continued competence; and
- protecting the dignity of older workers by avoiding the need to undertake capability reviews of their performance.

As well as having the purpose of achieving one or more legitimate aim, use of a compulsory retirement age must be proportionate. Evidence will be required to show that implementation of a retirement age corresponds to and achieves a real business need, that it goes no further than necessary to achieve that need, and that alternative ways of meeting that need do not exist. As this is assessed on a case by case basis, it is difficult for employers to be sure their retirement policy will be found to be lawful.

Fuchs v. Land Hessen is the latest ECJ decision to take a fairly relaxed view of what is needed to justify a compulsory retirement age. The case adds a new potential legitimate aim that employers may be able to rely on to justify compulsory retirement; the aim of seeking to avoid legal disputes with older employees over their fitness for service. However, employers wanting to make compulsory retirements are advised to seek additional legitimate aims as it is unclear whether this aim alone will be sufficient justification.

It also remains unclear the extent to which individual private employers will be able to objectively justify retaining a compulsory retirement age. *Fuchs* concerned public sector employment and the comments about legitimate aims must take account of that background. UK employers also need to bear in mind that the abolition of the statutory default retirement age means they can no longer argue that having a compulsory retirement age is consistent with national employment policy. The case of *Seldon v. Clarkson, Wright and Jakes* will be heard by the Supreme Court in the autumn and this may provide more guidance on the extent to which a compulsory retirement age can be justified in the UK.

Screening

Suzanne McMinn, Workplace Law

Key points

- Screening can be carried out on current as well as prospective employees.
- Whether screening is voluntary, advisory or mandatory will depend on the nature of the role.
- Unless a statutory exception applies, employees' spent convictions are not relevant and do not need to be disclosed by them.
- Criminal records checks are centrally administered, and their scope is determined by the nature of the role in question.
- Employers must take great care in how they handle information obtained through criminal records checks.
- Jobs involving work with children or vulnerable adults are subject to specific statutory screening requirements.
- Centrally maintained 'barred lists' must be checked to ensure that there is no known reason why an individual should not be allowed to work with vulnerable groups.
- It has been recommended that a registration system for those wishing to work with vulnerable groups should be developed. Registration was due to begin across the UK in 2010, but plans are on hold in England, Wales and Northern Ireland while the Government remodels the proposal. From February 2011 in Scotland the protection of vulnerable groups scheme went live, which ensures that people are held on a register.

Legislation

- Rehabilitation of Offenders Act 1974 (and associated exceptions orders).
- Police Act 1997.
- Data Protection Act 1998.
- Financial Services and Markets Act 2000.
- Police Act 1997 (Criminal Records) Regulations 2002.
- Safeguarding Vulnerable Groups Act 2006.
- Protection of Vulnerable Groups (Scotland) Act 2007.

What is employee screening?

Employee screening (or vetting) is the carrying out of background checks on current or prospective employees to verify information they have put forward and/or to assess their suitability for a particular role.

Employee screening is most commonly used in recruitment. In the absence of a pre-existing relationship with a candidate, employers are well advised to independently verify matters such as employment history, skills, and qualifications. For that reason, job offers are often conditional upon receipt of satisfactory references, and criminal records checks.

Employers may also wish to carry out checks on their existing employees. This may be done as part of an internal recruitment process, for example where an employee is being promoted or is taking on new responsibilities, or it may be done at regular intervals where the circumstances of the individual's employment justifies that approach.

The extent to which employee screening is required (if at all) is almost always driven by the nature of the job that the individual is being employed to do. For example:

- An employer seeking to hire a shop assistant *may* ask about criminal record history because it does not wish to employ anyone with a conviction for fraud or dishonesty.
- Employers in the financial services sector *should* (according to the Financial Services Authority) carry out criminal records checks on employees seeking 'approved person status' under the Financial Services and Markets Act 2000.
- Where an employee will be working with children or vulnerable adults, the employer *must* carry out criminal records checks beforehand.

This chapter will focus on employee screening in the form of criminal records checks, particularly in relation to employees who work with children and/ or vulnerable adults. Although the chapter refers to the screening of employees, the same principles apply to organisations engaging volunteers or licensees.

How much can screening uncover?

Employee screening involves balancing two competing interests. The employer will want to know as much about the individual as possible so that it can make a fully informed decision. The individual, on the other hand, will be concerned about any unreasonable invasion of their privacy.

This balancing act is at the core of the Rehabilitation of Offenders Act 1974 and associated legislation. That Act provides that where a person with a criminal conviction does not re-offend within a specified period from the date of conviction, he will be considered to have been rehabilitated and his conviction will be 'spent'. The time it takes for a conviction to become spent depends on the length of the sentence that is imposed, rather than on the nature of the offence. Convictions that are accompanied by custodial sentences of more than two-and-a-half years never become spent.

In the context of employee screening, the practical effect of a conviction becoming spent is that the individual will not normally need to disclose it to a current or prospective employer. This is the case even if the person is placed by the employer under a contractual obligation to disclose all convictions, or if they fail to disclose convictions in response to a direct request from the employer. An employer cannot rely on an individual's failure to disclose a spent conviction as the reason for dismissing or refusing to hire or promote that individual.

However, there are exceptions to this rule. Where an individual is being considered for an occupation that is listed in a statutory Exceptions Order, the employer will be able to ask them (through the disclosure procedure outlined below) about spent and unspent convictions. If the individual has been told that they are obliged to reveal spent convictions, their failure to do so will amount to valid grounds for refusing to hire or promote them, or for dismissing them. The Exceptions Orders list too many excepted occupations to go through here, but they focus on positions of trust (doctors, solicitors, accountants, teachers, police, etc.). Full details can be found on the website of the relevant government agency (*see below*).

Criminal records checks

Information about spent and unspent convictions is centrally controlled. Employers can access information from the appropriate government agency (each set up under Part V of the Police Act 1997) as follows:

- In England and Wales, the Criminal Records Bureau (CRB), an executive agency of the Home Office;
- In Scotland, Disclosure Scotland, an executive agency of the Scottish Government; and
- In Northern Ireland, Access NI, a joint programme between the Northern Ireland Office, the Department of Health, Social Services and Public Safety, the Department of Education and the Police Service of Northern Ireland.

There are three levels of checks that can be carried out in the UK:

1. Basic disclosure.
2. Standard disclosure.
3. Enhanced disclosure.

Basic disclosure

Basic disclosure certificates are currently only available from Disclosure Scotland and Access NI (not the CRB). They will only reveal details of unspent convictions. Anyone can apply for a basic disclosure in their own name, and the disclosure certificate will be sent directly to them.

Standard disclosure

Standard disclosure checks reveal details of:

- spent and unspent convictions registered on the Police National Computer;
- police cautions; and
- police reprimands and warnings.

Enhanced disclosure

An enhanced disclosure is the highest level of check available. It will cover the information accessible via a standard disclosure and also:

- any relevant information held by local police forces that the chief police officer of the relevant force decides should be disclosed (for example,

allegations in respect of which charges were never brought); and
- where requested, a check of the statutory lists containing details of people considered unsuitable to work with children or vulnerable adults (*see below*).

Whereas anyone can apply for a basic disclosure in their own name, standard and enhanced disclosures are only available to bodies that are registered with the CRB, Disclosure Scotland or Access NI. This ensures that employers can only access details of unspent convictions where the Exceptions Orders mentioned above apply, and the nature of the role means the information is relevant.

It is also possible to obtain standard and enhanced disclosures through umbrella bodies, which act as an intermediary between the employer and the CRB, Disclosure Scotland or Access NI. This might be a professional association, regulatory body or a commercial venture set up to provide the service.

Handling the information

Employers that carry out criminal records checks need to put appropriate systems in place to handle the information they obtain. If disclosure certificates reveal details of offences, allegations, proceedings, convictions or sentences, that information will be sensitive personal data for the purposes of the Data Protection Act 1998. This means the employer must ensure the information is processed fairly, and that it is kept secure. Employers should:

- make it clear to the relevant employees / candidates in advance that the checks will be carried out;
- ensure that the information is only accessible by those who absolutely need to see it in the course of their duties;

- keep a record of who has seen the information;
- ensure that the information is held in secure conditions;
- not retain the information for any longer than is necessary (generally information collected for recruitment decisions should not be kept for longer than six months); and
- use secure methods to destroy the information once it is no longer required.

Making decisions

If an employer puts the appropriate systems in place, employee screening should be a relatively straightforward process. Much more difficult is actually processing the information that is obtained through screening, and using it to make a decision.

In some cases, the employer's hands will be tied. For example, if an enhanced disclosure reveals that a person is on a barred list (*see below*) the employer must not employ them in a post that involves working with a vulnerable group.

In other cases, the employer will need to make a judgement and there may not necessarily be a right or wrong answer. However, if checks reveal a criminal conviction, it will usually be relevant to ask:

- How closely related is the conviction to the job being considered?
- How serious is the underlying offence (in the eyes of the law and the employer and any other interested parties)?
- How long ago was the conviction obtained (and whether it is spent or unspent)?
- Is it one of a series of convictions (especially if there are other related convictions)?
- What has the individual done since the conviction to remedy any concern the employer might otherwise have?

- Are there any mitigating circumstances or further context offered by the individual?

Protection of vulnerable groups

Whereas employee screening for most jobs is at the employer's discretion, the vetting of those who work with children or vulnerable adults has been mandatory for some time. Statutory lists of individuals considered unsuitable for such work have been in operation for many years.

The effectiveness of the vetting system in this field was called into question in 2002, when school caretaker, Ian Huntley, murdered Soham school children, Holly Wells and Jessica Chapman. Huntley had come to the attention of Humberside Police in relation to allegations of eight separate sexual offences from 1995 to 1999, and had been investigated in relation to one other allegation. This information had not emerged in the vetting check requested by his employer at the time of his appointment to Soham Village College late in 2001 and carried out by Cambridgeshire Constabulary.

Sir Michael Bichard led an independent inquiry into the matter, and his report set out a number of recommendations aimed at improving employee screening in this area. The main recommendations, and the progress made in implementing them, are discussed below. The relevant implementing legislation for these purposes is the Safeguarding Vulnerable Groups Act 2006 (which applies in England, Wales and Northern Ireland) and the Protection of Vulnerable Groups (Scotland) Act 2007.

It was recommended that all posts (including those in schools) that involve working with children or vulnerable adults should be subject to the enhanced disclosure regime. Previously, standard disclosures were sufficient for those who did not have direct contact with children or vulnerable adults. Since 12 October 2009, enhanced disclosures have been mandatory for all new recruits seeking to work with these groups.

The Report also recommended that one central body should control the statutory lists of individuals barred from working with vulnerable groups. Before 30 January 2009, three separate lists were maintained and there was a fair degree of overlap and administrative complexity.

Independent Safeguarding Authority

The Safeguarding Vulnerable Groups Act 2006 set up the Independent Safeguarding Authority (ISA), which from 30 January 2009 took control of these lists. From 12 October 2009, the three existing lists were replaced by two new ones: the ISA Children's barred list, and the ISA Vulnerable Adults barred list. The system in Scotland follows the same format, with the Protection of Vulnerable Groups (Scotland) Act 2007 setting up a children's list and an adults' list. This has now been revised and a new membership scheme commenced in February 2011. The plan is that the lists will dovetail, so that an individual who is barred in one jurisdiction will be barred throughout the rest of the UK.

In each jurisdiction, checks of these two lists will form part of an enhanced disclosure. It is a criminal offence for individuals who appear on a barred list to apply to work with children or vulnerable adults in the specified posts. Employers also face criminal sanctions if they knowingly employ a barred individual in such a post.

Registration schemes

More difficult to implement has been the recommendation that arrangements should be introduced requiring those who wish to

work with children or vulnerable adults to be registered. The Bichard Inquiry Report said that this register – perhaps supported by a card or licence – would be able to confirm to employers that there is no known reason why an individual should not work with these groups.

The registration scheme proposed in England, Wales and Northern Ireland is the Vetting and Barring Scheme, whereas the scheme in Scotland is termed the Protecting Vulnerable Groups Scheme.

Vetting and Barring Scheme

The Vetting and Barring Scheme envisaged by the Safeguarding Vulnerable Groups Act 2006 would impose registration requirements on employees and workers engaged in a 'regulated activity'. Regulated activities include teaching, training, instruction, supervision, advice and treatment, or any activities that are carried out at places like schools, nurseries and care homes and provide for the opportunity of contact with vulnerable groups.

It was envisaged that individuals would be able to apply for registration with the ISA on a voluntary basis from 26 July 2010. Registration was to be compulsory from November 2010, and from that date organisations providing regulated activities would be prohibited from taking on individuals who were not ISA-registered.

However, on 15 June 2010 it was announced that registration with the Vetting and Barring Scheme would be halted "to allow the Government to remodel the scheme back to proportionate, common sense levels".

There is a clear concern in the new Coalition Government that the compulsory registration scheme in its proposed form would dissuade law-abiding individuals from working with vulnerable groups.

The Children's Minister, Tim Loughton, has said that "we shouldn't be driving a wedge between children and well-meaning adults, including people coming forward to volunteer with young people". At the time of writing, the scope of the remodelling process has yet to be finalised.

The halting of the registration scheme does not affect other screening measures such as the barred lists (*mentioned above*) and the duty to refer.

Protecting Vulnerable Groups Scheme

The Scottish Government launched its own registration scheme on 28 February 2011. The Protecting Vulnerable Groups Scheme will take four years to fully phase in, and will be managed and delivered by Disclosure Scotland. According to Disclosure Scotland, the scheme will:

- help to ensure that those who have regular contact with children and protected adults through paid and unpaid work do not have a known history of harmful behaviour;
- be quick and easy to use, reducing the need for registered members to complete a detailed application form every time a disclosure check is required; and
- strike a balance between proportionate protection and robust regulation and make it easier for employers to determine who they should check to protect their client group.

The important distinguishing factor from the Vetting and Barring Scheme is that the Scottish scheme will not be compulsory.

Conclusion

Employee screening is a complex area, and the consequences of getting it wrong can be extremely serious. Employers should carefully plan any recruitment or promotion process, giving due consideration to how much information will need to be obtained via screening. Proper procedures need to be put in place to ensure that the individual candidates and the decision-makers understand the screening process, and to ensure that the information is handled appropriately.

The law on employee screening for work with vulnerable groups is evolving, and close attention must be paid to the governmental guidance as it develops.

See also: Criminal records, p.97; Data protection, p.101; Monitoring employees, p.358; Personnel files, p.392; Private life, p.404; Recruitment and selection, p.420; References, p.434; Vetting, barring, blacklisting and social engineering, p.534.

Sources of further information

Criminal Records Bureau: www.crb.homeoffice.gov.uk

Disclosure Scotland: www.disclosurescotland.co.uk

Access NI: www.accessni.gov.uk/home.html

Independent Safeguarding Authority: www.isa-gov.org.uk

Secondment

Suzanne McMinn, Workplace Law

Key points

- Different types of secondment (intra-company, intra-group and external) throw up different types of legal issues.
- Secondments can be of enormous benefit in deploying an employer's resources in the most effective manner.
- The human aspects of secondment are as important as the legal aspects.
- Secondments between employers must be documented carefully, with the secondee's employment status being the key issue.
- Secondments need to be carefully managed as they progress.

Legislation

There are no statutes or regulations that focus specifically on secondments, but general employment legislation will impact on secondment arrangements. For example, discrimination legislation can be engaged in respect of actions or omissions during the secondment. General contract law will also impact on interpretation of any secondment agreement and/or disputes as to the employment status of the secondee.

What is secondment?

Put simply, a secondment is the temporary loan of an employee. This covers a number of possible scenarios:

- *Intra-company secondment.* This is where an employee is asked to work in a different department for a set period of time. There may be sufficient flexibility in the employee's terms and conditions of employment to require such a move, and in any event these switches can often be easily agreed on a relatively informal basis, with little prospect of legal issues arising.
- *Intra-group secondment.* This is where an employee is asked to work for another employer in the same group of companies. Again, a switched-on employer that is part of a group will already have catered for this possibility in contracts of employment. The terms of the secondment also tend to be easier to agree when the seconding and host employers are related undertakings.
- *External secondment.* This is where an employee is sent to work for an external employer, such as a client or customer of his normal employer. These arrangements tend be put on a more formal footing. Depending on the nature and length of the secondment, disputes can often arise further down the line where the seconding and host employers have divergent commercial interests.

The common theme is the temporary nature of the arrangement. The Employment Appeal Tribunal in *Capita Health Solutions v. BBC and another* said that a secondment "connotes a temporary assignation, regarded, at least at its outset, as being on the basis that the employee will return to work directly for the seconding employer". Secondments may lead to resignations and transfers, but they are in themselves merely temporary loans. The ability to revert to the status quo after a period of time, or on completion of a specific task, is one of the most attractive features of secondments for employers.

The benefits for employers

Every employer faces difficulties from time to time in deploying resources effectively. Being able to control the assignment of tasks and temporarily manipulate headcount through secondments is therefore a significant benefit. This is especially the case where the employer's business needs to react quickly to ever-changing demands.

An employer that experiences an upsurge in work in one of its departments may be reluctant to commit resources to it by recruiting new personnel on a temporary or permanent basis. Where the existing workforce has sufficiently transferable skills, and where quieter departments can spare the staff, intra-company secondments may be the perfect solution. This allows the employer to meet the spike in demand and resume normal service when it subsides. The same logic can apply to more predictable business needs, such as cover for maternity absence.

Conversely, secondments can be used to tackle a downturn in work. If an employer considers that a drop off in work is just a temporary blip, it may be wary of implementing redundancies that leave it unprepared when demand picks up. An external secondment, where the host employer picks up some or all of the secondee's salary costs, can be an ideal solution for the struggling seconding employer.

Whether or not there are upsurges and downturns, secondments can also be a good way to develop the skills and contacts that an employer has at its disposal. Opportunities for growth within a particular department or company may be limited, and an intra-company, intra-group or external secondment can unlock an employee's potential. This has obvious benefits for the employee in terms of personal and career development, but is also a relatively easy way for the employer to invest in its people.

Similarly, secondments can help the seconding employer develop good relationships with the host employer, who in turn gets manpower and an external perspective on its business. External secondments to customers and suppliers can be an excellent business development tool, and can encourage valuable secondments in the other direction.

The disadvantages for employers

Moving staff around can be challenging, and secondments are no exception. Whilst a secondment might look like a neat solution on paper, employers need to consider the human aspect and the effect the arrangement will have on the workforce.

From the seconding employer's perspective, the main pitfalls are to be found in selecting the secondee and filling the vacuum. In some cases the host employer will request a particular secondee, which simplifies matters if the request can be accommodated. If it is up to the seconding employer whom to send, care needs to be taken. Which employee will make the best impression? Who will manage to cope with the upheaval, flitting from one working environment to another and then back again? If you let them go, are you confident they will come back at all?

The seconding employer also needs to be careful how it deals with the impact of the secondment on the employees who stay behind. It is likely that some of those employees will need to take on extra tasks and responsibilities, and perhaps for no extra reward. Add to the equation that they may already be disaffected due to having been overlooked for the secondment opportunity, and the neat solution on paper has the potential to be an employee relations time bomb in the office. In addition, where the secondee is a key member of the team, it is worth asking whether the seconding employer really can afford to let them go at all, even for a short time. There is often a careful balancing act between accommodating secondment requests from important clients and ensuring the stability of the team from which the secondee would be drawn.

From the host employer's perspective, the value of the secondment needs to outweigh the difficulty of merging the secondee into the business. Any new recruit can upset the balance of a team, and problems can be exacerbated where the new recruit remains employed by someone else. The secondee needs to get up to speed with the host employer's ways of working and follow the day-to-day instructions of its management, but ultimate responsibility should remain with the seconding employer. That is a line that many employers (and secondees) find difficult to tread.

As well as these practical employee relations issues, there are a number of difficult legal problems thrown up by secondment.

Documenting the arrangement

Any secondment, even if just to another role within the same company, is a departure from the normal employment relationship, and so it is important to document it properly.

The first step is to review the prospective secondee's contract of employment. It may be that it contains specific provisions about accepting secondments,

or mobility provisions that allow the necessary flexibility in role or location. If the contract is silent on those points, it might be necessary to vary it before the secondment can start.

Intra-company secondments, involving only one employer, are generally easy to document. Where the secondee's contract of employment is sufficiently flexible, often all that is needed is a simple letter to deal with the practical aspects of the secondment (start date, duration, allowances, etc.). With intra-group and external secondments it is advisable to have a more detailed secondment agreement that caters for at least some of the following thorny issues.

Employment status

As already stated, secondments are loans and not transfers, so the intention is that the secondee remains employed by the seconding employer for the duration of the secondment. However, matters are often not so clear cut and disputes can arise about employment status, especially where the secondment is allowed to drift on beyond its initial term.

When deciding who actually employs a secondee, the Tribunal or Court will first of all examine the contracts that are in place. One of the main aims of a secondment agreement is to put it beyond doubt that the secondee is to remain an employee of the seconding employer. Some ways the agreement can do that include stating that:

- the parties agree that the secondment arrangement is not intended to create any kind of employment relationship between the secondee and the host employer;
- if the secondee is deemed to become an employee of the host employer at any point, the host employer may terminate that employment and the seconding employer will re-engage the

secondee on the terms and conditions that existed previously;

- the secondee will remain subject to the terms of their contract of employment with the seconding employer;
- the seconding employer will remain liable for the payment of contractual salary and benefits to the secondee;
- the seconding employer will retain responsibility for management issues such as performance appraisals, pay reviews, sick leave, allocation of holidays and disciplinary and grievance matters;
- the host employer may request a replacement secondee at any time;
- the seconding employer may provide a substitute of its choosing at any time; and
- the secondment will terminate in the event that the secondee's employment terminates.

Performance, discipline and grievance

It should be decided at the outset who will take responsibility for supervising the secondee's performance, and handling any disciplinary and grievance issues that arise during the secondment. This will depend to a large extent on how important it is to the host employer that it gets a particular named secondee, as opposed to just one of the seconding employer's members of staff.

Some secondments are designed to tap in to the specialist skills or knowledge of a particular individual. In that case the host employer may want to take a hands-on approach to performance management, to ensure it gets the service it needs. Other secondments are just about getting bodies in to do some work. In that case the host employer may want the seconding employer to take charge, or even just send a different secondee if the first one gets into trouble.

Whatever the underlying rationale for the secondment, host employers need to bear in mind that becoming overly involved in the day-to-day management of the secondee might (in the absence of other factors) create a presumption of a direct employment relationship.

Data protection

Employers need to process personal and sensitive personal data relating to their employees, and for secondments to work properly some of those data will need to be shared with the host employer. This means that both employers will need to comply with the terms of the Data Protection Act 1998.

If the secondment is to a host employer based outside the European Economic Area, the seconding employer should take steps to ensure that any of the secondee's personal data it shares with the host are adequately protected. It may be necessary to include specific provisions on this topic in the secondment agreement.

Confidentiality and intellectual property

Depending on the seniority of the secondee, the contract of employment is likely to give the seconding employer some measure of protection over its confidential information, and also intellectual property created during the individual's employment. In many cases, though, it will want to increase that protection by including robust provisions in the secondment agreement itself.

Equally, the host employer is likely to want to impose confidentiality obligations on the secondee in respect of sensitive information obtained about its business during the course of the secondment. A distinct confidentiality agreement between host and secondee is advisable, providing a direct contractual undertaking from the individual.

If there is a prospect of the secondee creating intellectual property during the secondment then it should be decided at the outset who will own the rights to that property. The seconding employer would typically retain ownership of the intellectual property, given the terms of the individual's contract of employment. But the host employer may stake a legitimate claim based on the fact that the secondee created the property using its equipment, materials or information.

Whatever the levels of trust between seconding employer, secondee and host employer, and whatever 'understanding' the parties think they have, clear and comprehensive confidentiality and intellectual property obligations are always a good idea.

Restrictive covenants

A common worry about sending valued employees on secondment to a client or customer is that the host employer will persuade the secondee to jump ship and join it on a permanent basis. To address that concern, seconding employers will often insist on the secondment agreement containing restrictive covenants, prohibiting the host employer from poaching the individual.

There is often a delicate balancing act to perform here. The secondment probably wouldn't have happened if the seconding employer did not genuinely value its relationship with the host employer, so only the prospective departure of a particularly valuable employee is likely to justify litigation.

As well as non-solicitation covenants, the seconding employer may insist on

provisions prohibiting the host employer from acting in competition with it, for example by utilising the secondee's knowhow or contacts to influence business relationships.

Apportionment of liability

The seconding and host employers may reach agreement as to how certain liabilities relating to the secondee should be apportioned. For example, the host may insist that the secondment agreement states that the seconding employer remains vicariously liable for the actions of the secondee during the secondment (particularly where the secondee has professional skills), whereas the host employer may be expected to assume responsibility for the secondee's health and safety whilst on the host's premises.

In some cases, the seconding employer will require the host employer to maintain appropriate insurance to cover any loss, injury or damage caused by or to the secondee during the course of the secondment. The secondment agreement can set out the minimum level and coverage of such insurance.

TUPE

Given that a secondment is essentially the transfer of an employee's services from one employer to another for a period of time, there is a risk that it could be deemed to be subject to the Transfer of Undertakings (Protection of Employment) Regulations 2006 (TUPE). Where the secondee's services can in themselves be classed as an 'undertaking' within the meaning of TUPE, or (perhaps more likely) where it can be said there has been a service provision change, the secondee's employment may transfer to the host employer. For TUPE to apply, it needs to be the case that the individual's employment would otherwise be terminated by the transfer. That will not be the case in a genuine secondment, but host employers might nonetheless want some protection against the potential inheritance of employees under TUPE.

It is now established law that it is not open to employers to use secondments to circumvent the effect of TUPE. In *North Wales Training and Enterprise Council Ltd (t/a Celtec) v. Astley and others* a number of civil servants employed by the Department of Employment agreed to be seconded to Celtec when it took over some vocational training services in 1990. All parties proceeded on that basis until three years later, when the employees formally resigned from the Department of Employment and joined Celtec. The House of Lords (now the Supreme Court) ruled that there had been a TUPE transfer in 1990, and the secondment arrangement did not displace that.

Conclusion

Managed properly, secondments can be of great benefit to all concerned, and it is no wonder that secondments have proved a popular tactic for businesses in the recent recession. They can offer much needed flexibility for employers when recruitment of permanent staff is not viable either due to cost or lack of supply. Seconding and host employers who invest enough time in planning a secondment and managing its progression should each reap significant rewards – and so should the secondee.

See also: Data protection, p.101; Disciplinary and grievance procedures, p.121; Discrimination, p.126; Employment contracts, p.164; Employment status, p.174; Intellectual property, p.252; Restrictive covenants and garden leave, p.441; TUPE, p.523.

Sources of further information

CIPD: www.cipd.co.uk/subjects/lrnanddev/secondment

Self-employment

Lisa Gettins, Sarah Lee, Rachel Stephens and John Turnbull,
BPE Solicitors LLP

Key points

- One of the most important, yet most frequently overlooked, issues is contracts / terms of business that your business will trade under.
- You will need public liability insurance and probably occupier's liability insurance.
- Your business premises will have to comply with all aspects of health and safety legislation and fire regulations.
- If you hold or use personal data, which includes information about any staff on your books, customers or clients, you must comply with the eight principles contained within the Data Protection Act.
- If you employ staff, you will have to provide contracts of employment and consider implementing appropriate policies and procedures.

Legislation

- Health and Safety at Work etc. Act 1974.
- Data Protection Act 1988.
- Employment Rights Act 1996.
- Employment Act 2002.

Overview

The purpose of this chapter is to help direct the minds of those who are considering 'jumping ship' and setting up their own business.

We look first at the legal differences between employed and self-employed status. We then look at the issues to be addressed in starting up and running a business of your own successfully. Finally, we look at the implications for existing businesses in engaging the services of a self-employed individual or employing staff.

Employed versus self employed – what is the difference?

The chapter on employment status (p.174) sets out the necessary considerations in addressing the question of 'Who is

employed and who is self-employed?' In short, where:

- an individual is obliged to provide services personally; and
- there is mutuality of obligation between the two parties (the giving and receiving of work); and
- the individual is subject to 'sufficient' control at the hands of the person for whom he works,

the individual is likely to be an employee and thus benefit from unfair dismissal protection, redundancy payment, statutory notice, equal pay, maternity rights, not to be discriminated against on the grounds of gender, age, disability, race, gender orientation, religion and belief and sick pay, to name but a few. Assuming, however, that an individual is not or would rather not be an employee, what are the considerations / implications for them?

Why might you want to become self-employed?

There are many reasons why an individual may consider becoming self-employed.

For example, they may find a niche in the market or they may have been made redundant recently or indeed some time ago and are struggling to find work. Alternatively, an individual may be seeking more flexibility or control in terms of their work and, in particular, in terms of their working hours.

What are the immediate and obvious concerns to being self-employed?

Although there are many benefits to being self-employed there are also a number of risks. For example, you will have to accept that:

- you will not necessarily earn a regular income;
- in practice, it is likely you will end up working long hours;
- you won't get paid when you are on holiday;
- you will be responsible for your own tax returns / accounts;
- you will have to make your own arrangements in terms of pension; and
- you will have to arrange adequate cover for sick leave and, from a personal perspective, you will also have to accept the lack of social contact with other employees, a transition that some people find very difficult.

Practical issues

Below are some considerations you will have when setting up your own business.

What kind of business will you operate and how will you trade?

You will need to decide whether you are going to trade as a sole trader, a partnership, as a limited company, buying a franchise or an existing business. There are pros and cons to each option as well as financial and legal considerations. Consequently, it is worth taking advice as to which format best suits your needs.

What about the finances?

You will need to register with HM Revenue and Customs on a self-employed basis. From this, your income tax and National Insurance position will become clearer. A reputable accountant will help you through the registration process and the daunting regime of self assessment and payments on account (if relevant). Your accountant will also help with VAT registration as and when your turnover reaches (currently) £70,000. If you need funding you will need to devise a strategy dealing with who you will ask, when, and produce relevant presentations for each potential investor.

Depending on the nature of the business, you may have to address the issue of money laundering. You will have to consider suitable processes to address money laundering at the outset of any relationships and have suitable documentary evidence of compliance with the necessary regime.

Once you are up and running you will need to establish a credible system for record keeping and decide how you will invoice clients, e.g. weekly, monthly, or at the end of a project. You will need to produce budgets, cash flows and so forth and ensure that you can pay your invoices and liabilities as and when they fall due for payment.

Where will you trade?

It may be that you intend to operate your business from your premises at home. Alternatively, you will need to find appropriate premises from which to operate. This may be an outright purchase or a rental property. Whichever option you choose you will have to establish whether you are required to pay business rates. You may also have to consider whether planning permission is required in terms of the use of the building or indeed whether any permits are necessary.

Marketing

To be successful, people will need to know about your business. You will, therefore, have to give serious consideration to how you will advertise your business. Options vary from flyers through the door to adverts in newspapers and appropriate trade journals or indeed on television. Much will depend on what you can afford and your target area. In any event, you may wish to utilise the expertise of external marketing / PR experts.

Contracts and terms of business

One of the most important, yet most frequently overlooked, issues is contracts / terms of business that your business will trade under. Without them, your business is left open to unlimited liability. If you will be working for other companies, they are likely to impose their terms of business or a service agreement on to you. You should consider whose equipment you will use, whether you need insurance, whether you will be able to provide a substitute if you are unable to attend, etc.

For businesses that do not, you will need to have your own terms and conditions. It is worth taking advice on the specific contents of your terms and conditions but the most important terms are likely to be identifying the scope of your liability under any contracts, payment terms, any exclusions of liability from breaches of contract / duty, notice periods and dispute resolution (provisions such as mediation or arbitration rather than expensive court proceedings). Also it is advisable to state in your terms what country (legal jurisdiction) any disputes will be heard.

Insurance

This is an important area and you should obtain quotes before making the decision to set up on your own as, for some, this cost will be prohibitive. You will need public liability insurance and probably occupier's liability insurance. Whatever the situation, you are likely to need insurance for your premises both in terms of the building itself and the contents. If you have vehicles for use in connection with the business, they will have to be insured for business use. If you begin employing others, you will need Employers' Liability Insurance.

Licences and intellectual property

Your needs will depend on the nature of the business you are operating but you will need to check whether any licences are needed. You should also consider whether any protection is needed for your businesses name, logo or the products in terms of their intellectual property.

Health and safety

Your business premises will have to comply with all aspects of health and safety legislation and fire regulations. The Environmental Health department of your Local Authority will be able to provide all of the information you require, and external health and safety consultants will conduct the necessary risk assessments for you and implement the necessary policies and procedures. Breach of health and safety law carries very serious penalties including, in some cases, imprisonment. It is a vast area of the law in which you should not seek to compromise.

Data protection

The Data Protection Act applies to all organisations, no matter how small or large. Its purpose is to prevent the abuse of an individual's personal data. If you hold or use personal data, which includes information about any staff on your books, customers or clients, you must comply with the eight principles contained within the Data Protection Act. As a rule of thumb, you should appoint an individual with responsibility for ensuring that your business adheres to the Data Protection Act. In addition, you may be required to register with the Data Protection Commissioner, for which a small fee is payable.

Employing others

It may well be that you need to employ or engage other staff from the outset. Alternatively, this may become a necessity as and when your business expands. If so, you need to consider the capacity in which you wish to engage others, e.g. as employees, as consultants, as casuals and, whatever their status, you need to look at the implications of it. For example, ensuring they are lawfully entitled to work in the UK by checking their passports, visas and work permits and keeping copies of the paperwork.

If they are consultants, you should agree terms and conditions setting out who is responsible for what, ensure that they have adequate insurance, and setting out how you will pay them.

If you employ staff, you will have to provide contracts of employment and consider implementing appropriate policies and procedures, in particular disciplinary and grievance procedures, a health and safety policy, and an equal opportunities policy. You should address health and safety issues and fire regulations in the workplace, even if the workplace happens to be the individual's home. You should also make yourself familiar with employment law in terms of how and when you can dismiss an employee fairly, treating employees equally, holidays, sickness, pension rights, family friendly policies, etc.

Implications for other business of having self-employed individuals on the premises

A common 'nuisance value' Employment Tribunal claim relates to alleged 'self-employed' consultants who, on termination of their contract for services, argue that they were actually an employee of the organisation to whom they provided their services. In light of this potential claim, steps should be taken to ensure parties are clear from the outset as to what the nature of the relationship will be. Thereafter, the contract must reflect this intention and the practices adopted should not deviate from the contractual position.

As a business, you will be responsible for certain actions of consultants, contractors and indeed some visitors whilst they are on your premises. It should be made clear at the outset, therefore, what your policy is in relation to health and safety, fire safety and discrimination.

Conclusion

This chapter gives a flavour of the considerations to be addressed in relation to self-employed status. It can, by no means, address all of the issues but should help address your mind to the various concerns / implications that you will need to consider before launching on your own.

Sources of further information

HMRC: www.hmrc.gov.uk/selfemployed/

The Workplace Law website has been one of the UK's leading legal information sites since its launch in 2002. As well as providing free news and forums, our Information Centre provides you with a 'one-stop shop' where you will find all you need to know to manage your workplace and fulfil your legal obligations.

It covers everything from the latest Employment Tribunal cases to redundancy law, as well as detailed information in key areas such as equality and diversity.

You'll find:

- quick and easy access to all major legislation and official guidance, including clear explanations and advice from our experts;
- case reviews and news analysis, which will keep you fully up to date with the latest legislation proposals and changes, case outcomes and examples of how the law is applied in practice;
- briefings, which include in-depth analysis on major topics; and
- WPL TV – an online TV channel including online seminars, documentaries and legal updates.

Content is added and updated regularly by our editorial team who utilise a wealth of in-house experts and legal consultants. Visit www.workplacelaw.net for more information.

Sickness

Sarah Barratt, Berwin Leighton Paisner LLP

Key points

- Contracts of employment and statements of terms must state whether or not the employer makes payments for periods of absence due to sickness and, if so, upon what terms.
- Certain qualifying employees are entitled to Statutory Sick Pay (SSP), in respect of which, for a specified period, employers are responsible.
- When terminating the employment of those who are absent due to sickness (whether for conduct, capability or some other substantial reason), consideration must be given to (a) the fairness of the decision and the procedure followed; (b) the existence of permanent health insurance schemes; and (c) the question of disability discrimination.

Legislation

- Health and Safety at Work Act 1974.
- Social Security Contributions and Benefits Act 1992 (as amended).
- Disability Discrimination Act 1995 (as amended).
- Employment Rights Act 1996 (as amended by the Employment Act 2008).
- Access to Medical Reports Act 1998.
- Data Protection Act 1998.
- Working Time Regulations 1998.
- EC Working Time Directive (2003/88/EC).
- Employment Act 2008 (6 April 2009).
- Equality Act 2010.

Sick pay

Most employees have an entitlement (either contractual or statutory) to be paid sick pay from their employer while absent from work due to ill health.

In practice, most employers operate company sick pay schemes that expressly outline each employee's contractual entitlement. However, the position may also be affected by company policies or custom and practice. Provided the employer pays to the employee the minimum level of remuneration he would be entitled to under the Social Security Contributions and Benefits Act 1992 (as amended) (SSCBA), the employer can opt out of the SSP scheme.

The legislative provisions dealing with payment of Statutory Sick Pay (SSP) are lengthy and technical. Broadly speaking, the SSCBA provides that all employees, subject to certain specified exceptions, are entitled to receive SSP from their employer. This entitlement is limited to 28 weeks in a three-year period. The weekly rate of SSP for days of sickness from 6 April 2011 is £81.60.

To qualify for SSP, certain prerequisite conditions must be satisfied. Essentially these are as follows:

- The individual must be an 'employee', not a worker, during the 'period of incapacity for work' (PIW).
- The employee must have four or more consecutive days of sickness (including weekends and holidays) during which he is too ill to be capable of doing his work.

Case study

What to do if…

Jane Wright has been off sick since she was told by her manager, Nick Tate, that she has the highest levels of sickness absence in the company. Nick has been trying to contact Jane daily, but she is not returning his calls. He has a friend who is a doctor who has told him that Jane cannot possibly be too sick to contact him. Nick wants to know if he can get rid of Jane, or at the very least not pay her while she is off.

The company is entitled to keep a comparative table of sickness absence. This can be a useful tool for identifying issues such as bullying or poor management in a particular part of the business. The comparative table of employees' sickness absence should, however, be made anonymous for Data Protection Act reasons.

Nick would be able to compare Jane Wright's levels of sickness absence against others in the company. As Jane's levels of absence are the highest in the company, it may be legitimate for Nick to raise the issue with Jane, but this should obviously be done sensitively.

Nick should ascertain whether or not Jane has a recurring or ongoing medical issue or disability. If appropriate, Jane should be sent to a doctor so the company has up-to-date medical advice about her condition, its effects and prognosis. The company will then be in a position to assess risk factors under the Equality Act 2010 and its duty to make reasonable adjustments.

As a starting point, the company should stay in regular contact with Jane while she is absent on long-term sick leave and this contact should be handled sensitively.

Importantly, the company should not make Jane feel pressured to return to work or criticised for being off sick. Jane should be kept abreast of any relevant developments in the workplace and asked about her state of health.

Care should also be taken to ensure that the person making contact with the employee is suitable. In this case, Nick's conduct appears to be one of the reasons why Jane is off sick so it may not be appropriate for him to be the point of contact. Ideally, the point of contact should be someone who has received absence management training. Once the point of contact has been chosen he/ she should establish an acceptable method of contacting / communicating with Jane (phone or email) and then try to arrange meetings, which could be home visits or at a neutral venue. The company should be careful not to exacerbate Jane's condition.

It is common for employees to claim they are too sick to have contact with work. This issue needs to be dealt with sensitively. The company could arrange

Case study – *continued*

to have contact with a friend or family member of the employee, with the employee's permission, or perhaps the employee's medical advisor, again with the employee's permission. Employees also have obligations to stay in contact with their employers whilst they are on sick leave and in the absence of medical reasons why this is not possible a refusal to do so could be a disciplinary matter. In this case, however, Jane is likely to have an explanation for not speaking to Nick. Nevertheless, it should be explained to her that she is obliged to keep in contact with her employer whilst she is absent.

Nick should not have discussed Jane's case with his friend who is a doctor and he should certainly not rely on his friend's advice. It is important for the company to seek current and up-to-date medical advice about Jane's absence. This should be done in conjunction with Jane in order to obtain information about her condition, a prognosis on her ability to return to work and also to assess what adjustments may be needed to assist her return to work. Medical advice should be obtained formally and a written record kept.

Provided that Jane has been off sick for four or more consecutive days (and meets the other qualifying requirements) she should be entitled to Statutory Sick Pay.

Depending on the terms and conditions of her employment contract and the company's policies and customs and practice in relation to sickness absence, Jane may also be entitled to company sick pay.

Stopping any entitlement to sick pay would almost certainly give rise to claims of unlawful deductions from wages, breach of contract and potentially disability discrimination and constructive unfair dismissal (if Jane resigns as a result).

Dismissing Jane at this stage is premature and would almost certainly give rise to liability for unfair dismissal and, potentially, disability discrimination. As outlined above, it is essential to get up-to-date medical evidence before even considering dismissal. Once such evidence has been obtained, the employer will be in a position to assess how long Jane is likely to be off work and whether this can be accommodated. The company will also be able to assess whether there is anything it can do to facilitate her return to work.

If the company forms the view that it may have no alternative but to consider dismissing Jane on the grounds of her capability, it will need to ensure that Jane has been warned of this possibility. Consultation should take place with the employee before any decisions are taken and a fair dismissal procedure should be followed.

Note: The ACAS Code does not apply where the reason for the proposed dismissal is ill health but the employer should nevertheless adhere to normal principles of natural justice.

Facts

- According to a 2010 CIPD annual absence survey, employees take on average 7.7 sick days leave a year, with public sector employees taking an average of 9.6 days.
- Research published by the Department for Work and Pensions reveals that almost half (48%) of respondents reported taking some sick leave in the previous 12 months and the average number of days' sickness absence was 4.5, while 42% reported that they had gone to work in the previous 12 months when, in their opinion, they should have taken sick leave.
- Only 10% of respondents said they were not aware of their organisation's sick pay policy, while 65% reported that sick pay was paid at their normal rate of pay during their first seven days of absence.

- The employee must have had average weekly earnings of not less than the current Lower Earnings Limit (LEL) within the previous eight weeks. The current LEL 2011/2012 is £102 per week.
- The employee must notify his employer of his sickness leave (subject to certain statutory requirements and any agreement between them).
- The employee must provide evidence of his inability to do his normal job. This is usually done by self-certification (days one to seven inclusive) and a doctor's certificate ('fit note') (day eight onwards).

Those who do not, or no longer, qualify for SSP may be entitled to other social security benefits, e.g. incapacity benefit, statutory (and/or contractual) maternity pay, etc.

All employers have a statutory obligation to keep (and retain for at least three years after the end of the relevant tax year) records for SSP purposes. As a minimum, for each employee, an employer must record the dates of any PIWs over the four or more consecutive days of absence and the payments made in respect of the PIWs and details of payments not made, with reasons.

Fit notes

'Fit notes' (or, to give them their proper title, Statements of Fitness for Work) replaced sick notes with effect from 6 April 2010.

Instead of certifying that an employee is sick (after seven days' sickness), a doctor will now issue a fit note. This will state either that the employee is 'not fit' for work, or that he or she 'may be fit' for work. Where an employee may be fit for work, the doctor can make recommendations as to what adjustments may need to be made so as to enable the employee to return to work. There are specific boxes that the doctor can tick to indicate which adjustments may be appropriate – a phased return to work, amended duties, altered hours or workplace adaptations – together with a comments section for more details. If the employer cannot make the adjustments suggested by the doctor, the employee will be deemed to be not fit for work.

As well as indicating the length of time the fit note will last (not more than three months initially), it will also indicate whether the employee needs to be seen by the doctor again before he or she can return to work.

Fit notes should help employers to manage long-term sickness absence, if utilised properly by doctors. This is because they may encourage both the employer and employee to consider whether there are any aspects of the job that the employee can undertake, despite the sickness or injury.

Given an indication of possible workplace adjustments by the doctor, employers may be well advised to seek the early involvement of occupational health advisers after even a relatively short sickness or injury period of seven days, which is likely to increase the administrative burden for employers. A failure to deal with recommendations made by the doctor in a fit note may lead to claims for personal injury (foreseeability may be easier to establish); or possibly even unlawful deductions from wages (without those adjustments the employee cannot earn their remuneration by working).

Sickness leave

When dealing with sickness leave, a distinction should always be made between absences on grounds of longer periods of medically certificated illness (capability issues) and those bouts of persistent short absences caused by unconnected minor illnesses that may call for disciplinary action if no valid reason is given for the absence or there is a failure to comply with the attendance procedure (conduct issues). In both dismissal scenarios, a potentially fair reason must exist and the employer must act reasonably in all the circumstances, and adopt a fair procedure before taking the decision to dismiss as a consequence of the reason. Further, what may be considered fair and reasonable will vary according to the particular circumstances of each individual case.

Conduct

A dismissal on the grounds of conduct owing to persistent periods of absences from work should be fair, provided the employer:

- believed the employee to be guilty of misconduct;
- has reasonable grounds to believe the employee is guilty of misconduct;
- before any disciplinary meeting, investigates the extent of and reasons for the employee's absences (thereby allowing the employee an opportunity to explain);
- informs the employee of the level of attendance he is expected to attain, of the time within which he should achieve it, and that he may be dismissed if there is insufficient improvement;
- thereafter monitors the situation and offers support or assistance, if appropriate, for a reasonable period prior to dismissal; and
- follows a fair dismissal procedure which is compliant with the ACAS Code of Practice (where appropriate).

Capability

Dismissal on the grounds of incapability due to ill health is a potentially fair reason to dismiss for unfair dismissal purposes but the employer must be able to demonstrate it acted reasonably in treating the employee's absence or attendance record as a sufficient reason for dismissal.

The employer should:

- investigate the employee's true medical position and prognosis for recovery (e.g. by obtaining a medical report with the employee's consent);
- after considering the requirements of the business, the possibility of adjustments or alternative employment and the likelihood of the employee returning to work in the foreseeable

future, conclude there is no alternative but to dismiss;

- consult with the employee about the possibility of his employment being terminated prior to dismissal; and
- follow a fair dismissal procedure that is compliant with the principles established by case law.

The ACAS Code on Discipline and Grievance does not apply to dismissals where the reason for dismissal is ill health or capability. However, for general unfair dismissal purposes the employer is still obliged to follow a fair dismissal procedure.

This will involve:

- providing the employee with reasonable notice of meetings, advance notice of matters to be discussed at the meeting, and an undertaking of the potential outcomes of the meeting;
- undertaking adequate investigation;
- allowing an opportunity for the employee to make representations; and
- a right of appeal.

Only when an employer obtains a clear prognosis of the employee's state of health will it be able to adequately assess the requirements of the business and what other alternative positions may be offered to the particular employee.

Dismissals and permanent health insurance (PHI) schemes

Where an employee has a right to receive permanent health benefits, the grounds on which an employer can dismiss are considerably restricted. In short, an employer may act unlawfully when it dismisses an employee who is in receipt of benefit under a PHI scheme. This is because there is an overriding implied term that an employer should not dismiss the employee solely to deprive him of the very benefit that it is the primary purpose of PHI schemes to provide.

In limited circumstances, an employer may be able to lawfully dismiss for good cause such as for gross misconduct or for some other form of fundamental breach by the employee or for capability or where a genuine redundancy situation exists, as long as nothing in the contract prohibits them from doing so and a proper consultation process is undertaken.

Dismissals and disability discrimination

Any worker who is dismissed in the light of his illness could potentially bring a claim under the Equality Act 2010. To do this he would need to show that, by reason of the dismissal, the employer treated him less favourably because of his illness and that the illness constitutes a disability as defined by the legislation, i.e. 'a physical or mental impairment which has a substantial and long-term adverse effect upon a person's ability to carry out normal day-to-day activities'. Certain conditions, including HIV, cancer and MS, are automatically treated as a disability under the legislation.

Whether an employee is 'disabled' for the purposes of the legislation may be straightforward but, where it is not, the employer may need a medical report to establish disability and what 'reasonable adjustments' might then be required. If proven, the ultimate question then becomes whether the employer can be expected to wait any longer for the employee. To help avoid a finding of discrimination and unfair dismissal, the employer will need to be able to justify the reason for dismissing the employee and show that it made all reasonable adjustments as are practicable in the circumstances.

Notice rights

Where an employee who is incapable of work because of sickness or injury has his employment terminated with the statutory minimum period of notice, and his contract of employment or statement of terms specifies normal working hours, he is entitled to receive a minimum hourly rate of pay during that notice period for any period during normal working hours in which he is too ill to be capable of doing his work.

Where an employee who is incapable of work because of sickness or injury has his employment terminated with the statutory minimum period of notice, and his contract of employment or statement of terms does not specify normal working hours, he is entitled to a week's pay for each week during that notice period when he is too ill to be capable of doing his work.

Under statute, where an employee who is incapable of work because of sickness or injury has his employment terminated by contractual notice of at least a week more than the statutory notice period, there are statutory provisions in place which disapply the employee's (otherwise protected) right to be paid statutory notice pay. In such circumstances, where the employee's sick pay entitlement has ended, he will not be entitled to any pay for his notice period.

Accrual of holiday

For some time, there has been a controversial issue as to whether workers on indefinite sick leave are entitled to accrue paid holiday under the Working Time Directive. The European Court of Justice's and the House of Lords' decision in *Stringer and Schultz-Hoff* held that employees will continue to accrue the four weeks' statutory minimum holiday entitlement under the Working Time Directive (but not the additional 1.6 weeks

provided for under the UK law) whilst on sick leave.

The practical implications of this decision are as follows:

- Employees accrue annual leave whilst on sick leave and employers must allow employees to take such leave.
- Currently, under the Working Time Regulations 1998, employees may not carry over accrued holiday from one holiday year to the next whilst still in employment.
- On termination of employment, employees are entitled to payment for annual leave accrued in their final year.
- On termination of employment, in some circumstances where the employer has repeatedly failed to pay, employees can also claim for unpaid holiday pay from previous holiday years.
- Additional issues arise for consideration where an employee has the benefit of PHI cover, in particular, whether employees who take annual leave whilst receiving PHI benefit will be treated by the PHI insurer as returning to work.

The ECJ case of *Pereda v. Madrid Movilidad* held that employees who cannot take their accrued annual leave because of sick leave must be allowed to take it on their return, even if it means holiday is carried over. The principle in *Pereda* arguably only applies to public sector employees at the moment as they can directly rely on the Working Time Directive.

> *See also*: Absence management, p.16; Discrimination, p.126; Dismissal, p.146; The Equality Act, p.191; Fit notes, p.214; Leave, p.252.

Sources of further information

ACAS: www.acas.org.uk

HSE: www.hse.gov.uk

HSE – Guidance for employers:
www.hse.gov.uk/sicknessabsence/guidancehome.htm

HMRC – Employer help book for statutory sick pay:
www.hmrc.gov.uk/helpsheets/e14.pdf

HMRC – Statutory sick pay – an overview:
www.hmrc.gov.uk/paye/employees/statutory-pay/ssp-overview.htm

ACAS – Code of Practice on Disciplinary and Grievance Procedures (2009):
www.acas.org.uk/index.aspx?articleid=2179

ACAS – Health, work and wellbeing guidance booklet (April 2010):
www.acas.org.uk/CHttpHandler.ashx?id=854

Smoking

Hayley Overshott, Kennedys

Key points

- Smoking in prescribed places is against the law throughout the British Isles. Since 2004, Regulations have been phased in for each country within the UK, with the ban slowly taking effect at different dates across the different countries. The Republic of Ireland was the first to introduce the ban in 2004, whilst England was the last to follow suit, and has now been 'smoke-free' since July 2007.

- For all of the UK, it is therefore now against the law to smoke in virtually all 'enclosed' and 'substantially enclosed' public places and workplaces, meaning that previously designated indoor 'smoking rooms' have now been outlawed. The ban also applies to public transport and work vehicles used by more than one person.

- Employers and managers of smoke-free premises and vehicles have legal responsibilities to prevent people from smoking, namely to:
  - take reasonable steps to ensure staff, customers, members and visitors are aware that the premises and vehicles are legally required to be smoke-free;
  - display 'no smoking' signs in smoke-free premises; and
  - ensure that no one smokes in smoke-free premises or vehicles.

Legislation

The Health Act 2006 requires workplaces to be smoke-free. At the present time, the nuts and bolts of the 'smoke-free' legislation in England is set out in the following Regulations:

- The Smoke-free (Premises and Enforcement) Regulations 2006 set out definitions of 'enclosed' and 'substantially enclosed' places and the bodies responsible for enforcing smoke-free legislation.
- The Smoke-free (Exemptions and Vehicles) Regulations 2007 set out the exemptions to smoke-free legislation and vehicles required to be smoke-free.
- The Smoke-free (Penalties and Discounted Amounts) Regulations 2007 set out the levels of penalties for offences under smoke-free legislation.

- The Smoke-free (Vehicle Operators and Penalty Notices) Regulations 2007 set out the responsibility on vehicle operators to prevent smoking in smoke-free vehicles and the form for fixed penalty notices.
- The Smoke-free (Signs) Regulations 2007 set out the requirements for no-smoking signs required under smoke-free legislation.

Similar legislation exists for Scotland, Wales and Northern Ireland. The Scottish position is set out briefly below, but the focus of this chapter is on the application of the smoke-free legislation as it applies in England and Wales.

The Health Act 2009, which contains provisions to ban the display of tobacco products and regulate tobacco vending machines, received Royal Assent on

Case studies

A man who was dismissed for smoking 'an inch or so' within his workplace failed in his unfair dismissal claim at an Employment Tribunal.

A supervisor spotted Mr Smith smoking beside an open fire door in a locker room. There was a 'no smoking' sign on the door, and the factory had become 'smoke-free' in March 2006 when the Scottish Executive introduced a smoking ban. Smith had previously attended a staff presentation about the new no-smoking policy, and signs were put up warning that breaching the policy could lead to dismissal.

At the hearing, Mr Smith – who described his smoking as 'an addiction' – said he was under pressure and feeling depressed about working 12-hour shifts and had lit a cigarette without thinking. The Tribunal acknowledged that Smith's dismissal had had a 'devastating' effect on him and his family. However, it ruled that the dismissal had not been unfair when weighed against the importance his employers placed on 'preserving their business, their property and, more importantly, the lives of their other staff'. The Tribunal also noted that if Smith had walked 'just an inch or so beyond the door' and smoked outside, then he would not have been breaching company policy.

A taxi driver was fined in March 2010 after he was repeatedly caught smoking in his cab. Paul Dalgleish, who drives a hackney carriage, was spotted smoking in October 2009 by an enforcement officer. There were no passengers on board.

Dalgleish had received two previous written warnings about smoking in his cab. He did not pay a £50 fixed penalty notice issued after the latest offence and the matter was brought before Carlisle Magistrates' Court. Dalgleish did not attend and the case was proven in his absence. He was fined £200 and ordered to pay £75 costs plus a £15 victim surcharge.

Manchester City Council successfully prosecuted a business for allowing smoking on its premises in February 2008. The prosecution – for failing to prevent smoking in a smoke-free area – was made against the owners of a shesha bar, which allowed customers to smoke Middle Eastern water pipes (known as shesha pipes) in the first floor premises. The company was fined £1,500 with full costs of £1,028.12 awarded to the Council, for flagrantly breaking the ban.

The owners thought they could carry on allowing smoking by introducing a door entry system, in an attempt to stop council officers gaining evidence. Officers visited the premises but were delayed entrance for around five minutes. The owner was warned that the officers suspected this was to remove evidence of smoking, and he could face prosecution if any evidence was found. He was also warned in writing.

12 November 2009. The Tobacco Advertising and Promotion (Display) (England) Regulations 2010 ban the display of tobacco products at the point of sale and came into force for large retailers (over 280 square metres of floor space) on 1 October 2011, and for smaller retailers from 1 October 2013. The ban on tobacco vending machines came into force on 1 October 2011.

Scotland

On 30 June 2005, the Scottish Parliament passed the Smoking, Health and Social Care (Scotland) Act 2005, which introduced a complete ban on tobacco smoking in enclosed public places in Scotland from 26 March 2006. The Act makes it an offence for those in charge of 'no-smoking premises' to knowingly permit others to smoke there. It is also an offence to fail to display 'no-smoking' signs in such premises. The Act provides that culpable managers may also be prosecuted, as well as their employer companies.

The Prohibition of Smoking in Certain Premises (Scotland) Regulations 2006 add flesh to the Act's bones and contain provisions relating to the provision and display of no-smoking signage, giving effect to Schedule 1 of the Act, which lists the types of premises that are prescribed to be no-smoking premises, defining key expressions such as 'premises' and 'wholly enclosed,' and setting out the levels of the relevant fixed penalties and other administrative matters.

The Scottish Parliament passed the Tobacco and Primary Medical Services (Scotland) Act 2010 on 27 January 2010, ending the display of tobacco in shops and banning cigarette vending machines in Scotland. This Act also contains provisions to ban proxy purchasing, introduce a register for tobacco retailers and making it an offence for under-18s to purchase tobacco.

Common law

Prior to the ban, in an employment law context, the Courts and Tribunals had tended to imply a right to protection for employees in the workplace, stating that there was a term implied into employment contracts that the employer would provide and monitor for his employees, so far as is reasonably practicable, a working environment that was reasonably suitable for the performance by them of their contractual duties. Applying this formula, it was held that a non-smoker was constructively dismissed (i.e. there was a fundamental breach of his/her employment contract) as a result of being required to work in a smoke-affected atmosphere, despite his/her protests. The smoking ban has reinforced this implied right.

Having said this, employers who choose to introduce anti-smoking measures that go beyond the requirements set out in the smoke-free legislation, for example by banning smoking anywhere on the premises, whether inside or out, must take care that by doing so they are not seen to

> **Facts**
>
> - Smoking in a smoke-free premises or vehicle can attract a fixed penalty notice of £50 or a fine up to £200.
> - Failure to display no-smoking signs in smoke-free premises and vehicles can attract a fixed penalty notice of £200 or a fine up to £1,000.
> - Failure to prevent smoking in a smoke-free premises or vehicle can lead to a fine up to £2,500.

be victimising smokers who may for many years have enjoyed an unfettered right to smoke in the workplace, in order to avoid the possibility of antagonism and ill feeling.

The best way to avoid this problem is to have introduced a reasonable and carefully considered smoking policy, with the smoke-free legislation at its heart, and to have consulted employees on its introduction. This is discussed in further detail below.

What is the effect of the smoke-free legislation in England?

As indicated above, employers and managers in charge of premises and vehicles to which the legislation applies should:

- take reasonable steps to ensure staff, customers, members and visitors are aware that the premises and vehicles are legally required to be smoke-free;
- display 'no-smoking' signs in smoke-free premises; and
- ensure that no one smokes in smoke-free premises or vehicles.

Premises

Premises:

- that are open to the public;
- that are used as a place of work by more than one person; or
- where members of the public might attend to receive or provide goods or services,

are to be smoke-free in areas that are enclosed or substantially enclosed.

Premises are 'enclosed' if they have a ceiling or roof and, except for doors, windows and passageways, are wholly enclosed either permanently or temporarily. Premises are 'substantially enclosed' if they have a ceiling or roof but there is an opening in the walls or an aggregate area of openings in the walls that is less than half the area of the walls.

The ban, therefore, includes offices, factories, shops, pubs, bars, restaurants, private members clubs and workplace smoking rooms. A 'roof' also includes any fixed or movable structure, such as canvas awnings. Tents, marquees or similar are also classified as enclosed premises if they fall within the definition.

Vehicles

'Enclosed vehicles' are to be smoke-free at all times if they are used 'by members of the public or a section of the public (whether or not for reward or hire)'; or 'in the course of paid or voluntary work by more than one person, even if those people use the vehicle at different times, or only intermittently'.

For example, a delivery van used by more than one driver, or which has a driver and passenger, must be smoke-free at all times. It should be noted that the

Regulations do not extend to vehicles used for non-business purposes.

Signs

All smoke-free premises must display a no-smoking sign in a prominent position at each entrance that:

- is the equivalent of A5 in area;
- displays the international no-smoking symbol in colour, a minimum of 70mm in diameter; and
- carries the words, 'No smoking. It is against the law to smoke in these premises,' in characters that can be easily read.

In addition, any person with management responsibilities for a smoke-free vehicle has legal duties to display a no-smoking sign in each enclosed compartment that can accommodate people.

What penalties can be imposed?

Smoking in a smoke-free premises or vehicle can attract a fixed penalty notice of £50 or a fine up to £200. Failure to display no-smoking signs in smoke-free premises and vehicles can attract a fixed penalty notice of £200 or a fine up to £1,000.

Failing to prevent smoking in a smoke-free premises or vehicle can lead to a fine up to £2,500.

The smoke-free legislation is enforced by a number of bodies, but primarily by district councils. There is no provision in the legislation for smoke-free offences to result in a review of a pub's licence. Councils are encouraged to approach enforcement by supporting businesses and the public to comply with the smoke-free law in the first instance, by providing advice, support and information. Formal enforcement action should only be considered where the seriousness of the case warrants it.

Exemptions

There are some limited exemptions:

- Private dwellings (with particular exceptions such as a communal stairwell).
- Designated bedrooms in hotels, guest houses, inns, hostels and members clubs (if they meet conditions set out in the Regulations).
- Designated bedrooms / rooms used only for smoking in care homes, hospices and prisons (if they meet conditions set out in the Regulations).

Compliance with the ban

Recent statistics confirm that there is an ongoing high level of compliance with the legislation, and this trend has continued over the four years since the legislation came into effect, with the overall compliance rate for the four years since implementation standing at 98.3%.

Between January and June 2010, authorities in England carried out over 70,000 premises and vehicle checks for compliance with the ban and signage requirements. 98.4% of those inspected were found to be compliant in terms of the ban itself, whilst 97% appeared to comply with the obligations regarding signage.

During that same period of inspection, 371 written warnings were issued by the authorities upon premises / vehicle owners for failing to prevent smoking – equating to 0.5% of all premises / vehicles inspected. Enforcement against individuals smoking in smoke-free areas was higher, however, with 400 fixed penalty notices served, and with 28 Court hearings relating to contravention of the legislation being held in the first six months of the year alone.

Statistics released by the Department of Health in 2010, following a study conducted by the University of Bath, confirmed that the number of heart attack admissions to hospital fell by 2.4% in the first 12 months of the ban. The study suggested that the fall in emergency admissions may be linked to the general decrease in exposure of the public to second-hand smoke since the ban was introduced. Whilst the study only monitored the change in trends between 2000 and 2008, it is thought that it demonstrates a clear association between the smoking ban and a reduction in the rate of hospital admissions for smoking-related afflictions, thus lending further support to the Government's decision not to interfere with what appears to be an effective means of regulation.

Introducing a smoking policy

All employers should by now have taken action to comply with the statutory smoking ban. In terms of the introduction of new or revised smoking policies to supplement or reinforce such action, an employer should consider both the form of the policy and the manner of its introduction. Whether a policy is reasonable or not will be a question of fact. However, as well as considering the implications of smoking bans, a prudent employer should take account of:

- the practicalities of the workplace;
- the nature of the business, including whether clients will be regularly visiting the building and whether employees are visiting clients at their homes;
- workplace opinion;
- assistance to smokers in adapting to the new policy;
- consultation with individuals and/or their representatives;
- ensuring that employees are fully aware of the possible sanctions for breach of the policy, including cross-references to the disciplinary procedure; and
- regular reviews of the policy for ongoing effectiveness.

A smoking policy could be incorporated into an existing employee handbook or a health and safety policy. It is advisable that the policy is in writing; however, a verbal understanding could also be implemented.

When introducing a smoking policy it is advisable for employers to give employees plenty of notice and to train managers on the operation of the policy. The policy, including the consequences of breaching it, should be notified to staff, perhaps via a staff intranet or by letter, and reference should be made to where the policy can be found.

Once a policy is in place it must be consistently enforced. It would, however, be sensible to support smokers during the early period of the policy and perhaps to avoid overly harsh sanctions during those early stages.

Disciplining employees who breach the ban

Disciplinary procedures should be updated to include a breach of a no-smoking policy as an act of misconduct and possibly gross misconduct. Having publicised the alterations, employers should make good on the promise to use them when there are reasonable grounds for doing so.

When considering sanctions for breach of a no-smoking policy, dismissal will not always be an appropriate sanction. For a first time breach, a more reasonable response would be to issue a written warning. The nature of the sanction will depend on the facts of the individual case. While in most cases dismissal would not be an appropriate sanction, in one case in 2007, where the employee breached a no-smoking policy in a factory using highly flammable materials, an Employment Tribunal found the dismissal to be within the reasonable range of responses due to the danger attached to such an action.

Smoking areas and breaks

Employers may wish to designate specific areas outside their premises as smoking areas. This may be appropriate to prevent employees from smoking too close to the premises' windows and entrances. It would be advisable to set out in the smoking policy where employees can and cannot smoke.

Employers could consider imposing limits on the amount of time or number of breaks that employees are allowed to take, in order to prevent resentment arising on the part of non-smoking employees. While employees are entitled to smoke during any lunch break or other break permitted under the Working Time Regulations 1998, employers are not, however, required by law to give employees who smoke additional breaks. If an employer does decide additional breaks should be provided to smokers, the details of this should be set out clearly in the smoking policy.

Assisting employees in giving up smoking

It is advisable when implementing a no-smoking policy to consider offering support to employees to give up smoking. NICE has provided guidance – *Workplace smoking: what you can do to encourage your employees to stop smoking* – which can be found at www.nice.org.uk/PHI005.

This guidance is not legally binding, but is provides some practical suggestions for employers to consider. It suggests that employers should publicise information on local stop-smoking support services. It also recommends that consideration should be given to providing on-site stop-smoking support for employees or to allow employees to attend smoking cessation services during working hours without loss of pay.

> *See also*: Discrimination, p.126; Driving at work, p.156; Occupational health, p.374; Staff handbooks, p.494.

Sources of further information

Helpful guidance, including downloadable signage, can be accessed at the following websites:

England – www.smokefreeengland.co.uk

Wales – www.smokingbanwales.co.uk

Scotland – www.clearingtheairscotland.com

Northern Ireland – www.spacetobreathe.org.uk

Social media

Roger Byard, Cripps Harries Hall LLP

Key points

- Employers face a constant risk that the actions and comments of employees on the internet will have a negative impact on their business if they are seen by customers or potential customers, suppliers or current and prospective employees.
- There is a danger that employees will disclose confidential trade secrets, business information and client contacts via the internet.
- Some employers prohibit all access to social networking sites and personal emails whilst employees are at work. However, employees are still able to access these sites in their free time and so employers remain exposed to the problems associated with these sites.
- To help to protect both their reputation and confidential business information, employers should devise and implement a social media policy for their employees.
- The policy should define unacceptable online behaviour and provide guidelines to employees on their use of the internet for both personal and business purposes.
- Employers should make it clear in any disciplinary rules that acts that breach the social media policy could lead to dismissal for gross misconduct.

Legislation

- Employment Rights Act 1996.
- Human Rights Act 1998.
- Employment Practices Data Protection Code.
- European Convention on Human Rights.

Introduction

Social media sites enable users to establish links with others, interact with them, publish photos and videos of themselves and establish an online existence. Social media is being increasingly used across all areas of life and most recently by businesses as a tool for promoting themselves (through what can amount to free advertising) and for assisting the recruitment process through the information about candidates that can be obtained online. A recent survey by Microsoft revealed that in 2009 already 41% of UK recruiters were rejecting candidates based on information available about them online.

The extraordinarily rapid development of social media, which spans the generations of internet users and the conventions that have become associated with its use, has created a virtual environment that carries risks for both individuals and businesses. Statements that might be acceptable if made in private can become very damaging when they go 'viral' either on a social media site like YouTube or through email.

Understanding what is acceptable behaviour when using social media sites both in and out of work is an important area for all employers to address.

> **Facts**
> - Facebook has over 500 million users.
> - YouTube is viewed by over two billion people each day.
> - There are 181 million blogs and in 2010 there were over 50 million tweets.
> - Every second a new member joins LinkedIn, which boasts membership of at least one executive from every Fortune 500 company.
> - To watch all of the videos currently on YouTube would take a person 1,000 years.
> - 25% of search results for the world's top 20 brands are linked to user-generated content on social networking sites.
>
> *Source: www.socialmediatoday.com.*

Types of social media

There are various types of social media.

- A weblog (blog) enables users to publish information and opinions on any topic and to invite comment.
- Social and business networking sites allow individuals and organisations to generate links with each other, creating lists of contacts that can be viewed by other members.
- Digital media sharing sites enable users to upload videos and photos that can be viewed by others.
- Online encyclopaedias provide web pages on an extraordinarily wide range of topics, which anyone can create and edit.
- Some social media websites enable users to operate in a virtual world, creating 3D personas that can interact with others.

The advantages of social media from the business perspective

Companies are able to use social networking sites to expand and build on existing contacts, which can lead to future business opportunities. These sites provide easy access to a list of contacts in a wide variety of sectors. When businesses make new contacts they can then search the contact lists of these organisations, creating ever wider networks of professionals with a mixture of skills.

It has been suggested that a keenness to try new forms of technology may be attractive to prospective employees. It has certainly been confirmed that an increasing number of employers use the internet, and in particular social media, to research job applicants. The enormous range of information that individuals post on the internet can be of great interest to potential employers.

For existing employees, social media can help to develop relationships between colleagues. Social networking sites are an easy way for members of an organisation to make contact outside business hours and to develop a rapport and a sense of community within the business.

Social media provides new ways to develop and promote a company's business. Many companies are using specially trained individuals within the establishment to compose blogs and write comments regarding the company's goods and services. This can generate interest in an item and can effectively equate to free marketing for the company and its business. Social networking sites have tools that enable a limited form of market research to be undertaken (for example to determine how many users might view an advertisement).

Some companies have used sites like 'Second Life', in which users create a three-dimensional persona that exists in a virtual world, to sell products online. Users are willing to pay for items available on the site which can only be used by their 'virtual' characters.

Social media technology provides an effective method of sharing information and knowledge with others in similar organisations. Businesses can easily connect with other companies in the same sector and learn new ideas and ways of working.

The limitations and risks to an employer arising from the use of social media

People are often unaware that comments made on social networking sites can be accessed and viewed by a large number of people very easily. Users are often ignorant about security settings and how to limit access to what they post online.

Once a comment, video or photo has been posted it can then be copied and forwarded around the world. It is difficult to retract and delete any of this material once it has been published. From an employer's perspective, there is the potential to find themselves, at one extreme, just mildly embarrassed, to facing at the other such serious financial and/or reputational damage that the business is put in jeopardy.

Employers are vicariously liable for the unlawful discrimination of their employees against a co-worker, even if the discriminatory acts do not take place on the company's premises (*Jones v. Tower Boot Co Ltd*). An employee who publishes a discriminatory comment about a colleague on a social networking site will expose their employer to potential liabilities. It is important to note that the employer will have a defence to such a claim if they can show that the employee was not acting 'in the course of employment', or that the employer took all reasonably practicable steps to prevent the harassment.

It is likely that employers may see the risks to reputation posed by social media as far greater than the risk of claims that they may face. Employees can publish derogatory or disparaging remarks about the business, and unless employers have appropriate safeguards in place there is little action that can be taken. If these comments are seen by individuals from outside the business it can damage significantly the employer's reputation in the wider world.

If employees are permitted to use social networking sites for personal use during business hours, there is the possibility that overuse may lead to a decrease in efficiency and have a negative impact on business activities.

There is a real possibility that employees will publish confidential information about the company, its activities, staff and clients online, which in itself could be commercially damaging. Employers should ensure that their employees are aware how the use of confidential data is restricted. Their contracts of employment should state expressly how the use of such material is regulated.

The social networking site, LinkedIn, whilst providing a useful list of all business contacts, can pose a problem for a business once an employee has left the

Case studies

In *Grant and Ross v. Mitie Property Services UK Limited* two employees were dismissed for overuse of the internet. At the hearing of their subsequent claim in the Employment Tribunal it was held that the dismissals were unfair because the employer's rules regarding internet use were vague. This case illustrates the importance of having clear guidelines on internet use during office hours for both business and personal reasons and ensuring that employees comply with them.

In *Taylor v. Somerfield* an employee was dismissed for bringing the company into disrepute, after posting a video on YouTube showing two members of staff hitting each other with plastic bags. The Employment Tribunal held that this dismissal was unfair because there was insufficient evidence to prove significant damage to the reputation of the company. The Tribunal was persuaded by the argument that the video had only received eight 'hits' and had not been viewed by a large number of people.

In *Pay v. United Kingdom* (2009), an employee worked as a probation officer for sexual offenders. He was dismissed when photos were posted on the internet, without his permission, of him involved in sado-masochistic activities. Pay had argued that the photographs were private and that Article 8 of the European Convention on Human Rights applied. However his dismissal was viewed by the Employment Tribunal as proportionate and fair because of the nature of Pay's role within the organisation.

In *Preece v. JD Wetherspoons plc*, an employee of a pub chain posted offensive messages about customers on Facebook. It was held by the Tribunal that this was a fair dismissal because the employee had breached both the company's electronic communications and social media policy. Breach of the social media policy was specifically cited in the company's disciplinary procedure as an example of gross misconduct.

A dismissal was held to be fair in *Gosden v. Lifeline Project Ltd* (2009) where an employee sent an offensive email from their home computer to a colleague. The email instructed recipients to pass it on, which eventually led to it entering the employer's email system. The employee's argument that the email was intended to be private was rejected.

organisation. There is nothing to prevent the ex-employee from getting in touch with business contacts that they made through their employment. Companies can guard against this by imposing restrictive covenants in employment contracts.

Companies face a risk that negative comments will be posted about it or its products or services by unconnected third parties. It is difficult to take action against this but businesses should try and monitor the appearance of the name of their organisation across the internet.

Company social media policy

All employers should have a social media policy included either in their employee handbook or as an individual document that is provided to new members of staff. Equally important is the need to implement and monitor the policy to help minimise the risks that arise from the use of social media. Further, it is evident from recent cases that it is important employers will be able to justify a dismissal for breach of the policy only where that policy is clear and adhered to.

The policy should include rules regarding access to the internet and social media sites during office hours. If the employer permits limited personal use, then clear guidelines as to how long and when employees will be allowed access should be provided. The employer should undertake monitoring of internet use and view random samples of emails sent. Employees should be informed that this will take place and what may happen with any results obtained.

The policy should set out guidelines for the responsible use of social media. These guidelines would include prohibiting employees from posting disparaging, derogatory or discriminating comments about their employer or any group company, its customers, potential customers, suppliers and employees. Employees should be advised that they should make it clear in any posting that they may make that any comments about the business reflect their own views and not those of the company. The policy should emphasise that it applies to actions carried out both inside and outside the business. Employees should also be prohibited from revealing confidential information relating to the business, its activities, clients or customers, referrers of business, suppliers and colleagues on social networking sites. They should be reminded that business contacts made during the course of their employment should not be added to personal social networking accounts.

A company may want to include a section in the policy explaining what action employees should take if they are contacted with a request for a comment regarding their employer that will be published in any form of media. Employers can provide that any business contacts that employees make through social networking are the property of the employer. These contacts could be further protected through the use of restrictive covenants in employment contracts.

An increasing number of businesses are actively using social media as a means of promoting their activities. Many businesses employ people specifically to ensure that the business has a visible presence online. It is important that these employees receive proper training and understand any guidelines in place for use of social media in a business context. This should detail what the company would like to achieve through the use of social media and the rules governing how employees should behave online and the 'tone' and language they should adopt.

Finally, it is important that the disciplinary rules should be linked to the social media policy by stating that breach of the policy will result in disciplinary action and could lead to dismissal for gross misconduct.

Other safeguards for employers

For employers to ensure compliance with data protection rules, they should ensure that employees are reminded that it is not appropriate to disclose personal data or information about colleagues on social networking websites. This should be included in the section on data protection in employment contracts.

Conclusion

The rapid development of social media in recent years has provided businesses with many new and innovative ways to expand and advertise. However, it is important that employers are aware of the pitfalls involved with this new technology and the risks and dangers that the actions of employees can provoke. Employers should ensure that they have in place an appropriate social media policy covering employee behaviour online.

See also: Bullying and harassment, p.58; Data protection, p.101; Intellectual property, p.252; Internet and email policies, p.271; IT security, p.282; Monitoring employees, p.358; Private life, p404; Screening, p.453; Staff handbooks, p.494; Vetting, barring, blacklisting and social engineering, p.534.

Sources of further information

ACAS: www.acas.org.uk

Technological advances in the field of information technology have resulted in many positive benefits for employers. However, the increase in technological advances has also brought with it many employment-related issues. These include harassment, discrimination, and breach of contract issues. Workplace Law's *IT and Email Policy and Management Guide v.3.0* has been designed to alert employers of the potential problems associated with using computer systems, the internet, and email systems within the workplace and to provide certain safeguards. For more information visit www.workplacelaw.net.

Keep up to date with what's going on at Workplace Law via our social media channels:

Twitter: http://twitter.com/WorkplaceLawNet

LinkedIn: www.linkedin.com/groups/Workplace-Law-Network-3960478

Facebook: www.facebook.com/workplacelaw

YouTube: www.youtube.com/user/WorkplaceLaw

Comment ...

The social network

Gavin Bates, Workplace Law

My second year as Community and Communications Manager at Workplace Law has been a year of building foundations for some major changes that will come to fruition fully in 2012.

Conveniently, at the same time as ACAS released its cyber guide, I created our own social media strategy, looking at the involvement of Workplace Law and its consultants on platforms such as Facebook, Twitter, LinkedIn and YouTube.

Writing and developing the strategy was the easy part, but implementing the strategy has been a major challenge. Whilst social media appears to have taken over the world, there are still plenty of people who are unfamiliar or uncomfortable with it.

As a company that began as a publisher printing newsletters, shifting to these new forms of media has at times seemed as daunting a prospect as any major change in life. But once familiarity has been introduced, tweeting, for instance, is not really that much different than more traditional forms of communication. The format may have changed but the audience still remain as human as ever.

As Erik Qualman says:

"We don't have a choice on whether we DO social media, the question is how well we DO it."

I'm sure there are plenty of companies that have struggled to implement this

Gavin Bates is the Community and Communications Manager at Workplace Law. Before joining the WPL team he had written for the award-winning student newspaper, Concrete, Indian music magazine, Rave, and local Cambridge-based fanzine, R*E*P*E*A*T. With a degree in English Literature and Philosophy from the University of East Anglia, he continues to maintain an avid interest in sociology and politics, as well as regular gigging in both a covers and original band. Gavin regulates the lively Workplace Law forum, oversees community fundraising events and has for the past year been building the new Workplace Law website – watch this space!

cultural shift, as was probably the case when the internet was born, as well as the associated complications of staff using these channels outside of the businesses' commercial strategy. We have really benefited from having a clearly worded strategy from the start, and training staff on creating and maintaining social media accounts. Whilst these are early days for us, I'm confident we have the basis with which to engage and connect with a growing number of people who will benefit from our knowledge and expertise.

As well as seeing and hearing more from our consultants and experts on LinkedIn and Twitter, in the next year you will also be able to read regular blogs on the Workplace Law website, which will not only help our customers get to know the people behind Workplace Law, but also provide important insights and advice in their chosen industries.

Moving away from more traditional forms of media will also see us producing more films in 2012. In the past year we have begun to create documentaries and online seminars, but as of autumn 2011 we introduced a more regular schedule to tie in with our other online strategies. As well as monthly online seminars and legal updates for our premium members covering health and safety, human resources and the environment, I also have the pleasure of presenting free weekly news updates, which we hope will keep our members fully up to date with the latest changes in a more concise and modern format.

Tied in with this – and probably the biggest change next year – will be the launch of our new website. Our business has changed a great deal since the last site was launched, and given how quick change can be, our new platform has been developed to help us adapt more easily. As well as the design being brought fully up to date, users will also find a big shift in the navigation and structure of the site, which we are confident will make it much more usable and accessible for everyone. We'll be adding a lot more features and functions – some of you may have noticed that we have already been updating your details and requesting preferences from you so that we can start to tailor content to your needs and requirements.

It promises to be a very exciting year for us in terms of our online presence and use of digital media, and I'm sure our customers will benefit greatly.

> "I wish I had a pound for every time someone asked me...
>
> ...What are you collecting money for now, Gavin?!"

Many see community involvement by organisations as something nice to do, but not essential when compared with the day-to-day challenges of keeping a business afloat. Aside from the obvious, possibly cynical, benefit of receiving great PR, I can't see how doing even the tiniest bit for others less fortunate is anything but essential. David Cameron's 'big society' may have become a laughing stock but, in principle, there is something innately rewarding about 'doing your bit'.

I have organised Workplace Law's team for the London to Cambridge bike ride for the past two years. As well as the enormous sense of pride at seeing so many staff, associates, clients, family and friends overcome the testing 60-mile route, the fact that we have been able to raise over £12,000 has been a great achievement.

What makes raising this money even more special, however, is the fact that the majority of it has gone directly to Exhall Grange Specialist School and Science College in Coventry.

One of our previous employees, Ciaron Dunne (who has since gone on to build his own business), saw his sister attend the school and his mum act as a governor for a period, and ever since then we have maintained close ties.

I have been lucky enough to attend Exhall Grange twice now, once to deliver 2010's fundraising money during a school assembly, and once to join in the celebrations for their Diamond Jubilee anniversary.

The first thing that hits you about the school is the overriding sense of calm – very different from what I remember of school – and when it does come to life it is impossible not to find a smiling face amongst pupils and staff. It really is an amazing place to visit, and makes me very proud that we can support them.

Some of the money we raised last year has, rather appropriately, already been used to purchase some specialised and expensive bikes, and I am looking forward to presenting them with another cheque again this Christmas. Seeing the results of our fundraising efforts is a great reward for us at Workplace Law.

@GavinBatesWPL

Staff handbooks

Heidi Thompson, Workplace Law

Key points

- Ensure that staff handbooks are easy to read.
- Use a format that is easy to update.
- Reduce printing costs by publishing on your company intranet site.
- Ensure that all staff have access to the staff handbook.
- Ask new starters to sign to confirm they have read and understood the contents of the staff handbook.
- Build time into induction training to read the staff handbook.
- Clarify whether or not the contents are contractual.
- Review and amend policies regularly to reflect legislative changes and best practice.

Legislation

- Employment Act 1989.
- Trade Union and Labour Relations (Consolidation) Act 1992.
- Employment Rights Act 1996.
- National Minimum Wage Act 1998.
- Working Time Regulations 1998.
- Employment Relations Act 1999.
- Part-time Workers (Prevention of Less Favourable Treatment) Regulations 2000.
- Employment Rights Act 2002.
- Fixed-term Employees (Prevention of Less Favourable Treatment) Regulations 2002 and 2008.
- Information and Consultation of Employees Regulations 2004.
- Employment Act 2008.
- Equality Act 2010.

Purpose

Employers increasingly issue their staff with staff handbooks. Staff handbooks are an essential employee management tool, which can be adapted to suit all organisations. They provide an essential element of good communication and can put in place a system of best practice for the employer and employee to follow throughout the course of an employment relationship.

Staff handbooks can vary considerably in terms of scope and length and, to this extent, can be tailored to suit the employment circumstances.

Once a staff handbook is assembled, employees can refer to one central source in order to clarify the employer's position with regards to any number of policies (including, for example, pay structures, holidays and absences, training, equal opportunities, disciplinary and grievance matters, redundancy, health and safety and so on).

Staff handbooks are also a very convenient way of inducting new members of staff to the structure and culture of an organisation.

Importantly, they can also be instrumental to employers in successfully defending Employment Tribunal claims.

Legal position

There is no legal requirement for an employer to publish a staff handbook. A Contract of Employment and/or a Section 1 Statement can adequately set

---

Case study

Keeley v. Fosroc International Ltd (2006)

In this case the Court of Appeal held that it is well established that where a contract of employment expressly, or impliedly, incorporates a document such as a collective agreement or staff handbook, some, but not necessarily all, of the specific provisions of that document may acquire the status of contractual terms. The issue in this case was whether or not an employee had a contractual entitlement to an enhanced redundancy payment pursuant to a provision set out in the staff handbook that was incorporated into his employment contract.

Mr Keeley was denied an enhanced redundancy payment and issued High Court proceedings claiming that he was contractually entitled to one, either expressly or impliedly. Although the High Court rejected the claim, the Court of Appeal concluded that the redundancy provision was suitable for incorporation as a contractual term. In reaching this decision it was influenced by factors such as the 'language of entitlement' and the provision's inclusion in the 'Employee benefits and rights' part of the staff handbook where other arguably contractual entitlements, both redundancy-related (such as paid time off to look for work) and otherwise (for example, entitlements in respect of parental and paternity leave) could also be found.

The lesson for employers is to ensure clarity in the staff handbook regarding which provisions are merely aspirational or an expression of current policy, and which are intended to form part of the contract of employment.

out an employee's terms and conditions. However, certain terms and conditions are often too lengthy and cumbersome to include in the Contract / Section 1 Statement. Staff handbooks therefore provide an ideal solution to set out additional contractual information, together with other, non-contractual, information, which may be of key importance to both the employer and the employee.

Broadly speaking, a staff handbook will be made up of four sub-categories:

1. *Contractual issues*. These may include, for example, individual pay rates or enhanced redundancy provisions (over and above the statutory position) which are deemed to form part of an employee's terms and conditions of employment.

2. *Non-contractual issues*. These will encompass provisions that fall within the general statutory entitlement (such as statutory sick pay or maternity leave), together with more general company policies that are not considered to be part of the terms and conditions of employment (for example, use of the internet at work).

3. *Company-specific information*. Including the hierarchy of the management structure, mission statements or company history.

4. *Industry data*. This might include information about money laundering policies or quality standards within that field of work.

Crucially, employers must be careful when drafting Contracts of Employment / Section 1 Statements and staff handbooks to be absolutely clear about which parts of the staff handbook are contractual (by explicitly saying so in the Contract / Section 1 Statement) and which are not. For example, if a contract makes reference to the disciplinary and grievance procedures being set out in the staff handbook, wording should also be inserted in the contract to clarify that, for the avoidance of doubt, these policies do not form part of the employee's terms and conditions of employment. This means an employer will be free to raise and update policies and procedures.

This method also offers greater protection to the employer. For example, an employee should be prevented from successfully claiming breach of contract where the employer fails to complete a grievance investigation within the desired timeframe set out in its policy, provided that policy expressly states that the contents of the policy do not form part of the employee's contract of employment.

That said, recent developments in case law (see *Case study*) have shown that Tribunals are prepared to interpret disputed handbook provisions as creating contractual rights in favour of the employee, particularly where those provisions relate to remuneration (such as enhanced redundancy payments). It is therefore advisable for employers to separate contractual from non-contractual rights, or to expressly state the position (including a denial where provisions do not have contractual force) in order to eliminate any scope for ambiguity or dispute.

At various times, an employer may seek to rely on the policies set out in a staff handbook, for example during an Employment Tribunal claim. In order to do so successfully, it will be vital that the employer can demonstrate that the employee had access to, and full knowledge of, the contents of the staff handbook / relevant policy (including the latest version). One way to achieve this would be to ensure that all staff sign a document acknowledging that they have seen and/or have access to the staff handbook as amended from time to time.

Format

For staff handbooks to be effective, they must be easily accessible to all employees. The format in which the staff handbook is published will therefore depend on the type of organisation.

Some employers prefer to issue all staff with a hard copy of the staff handbook. This way, it is easy to monitor who has or has not received a copy. Employees can be asked to sign a document to acknowledge receipt of the hard copy as evidence of this. It is advisable for hard copies to be produced in binders so that out-of-date sections can be removed and replaced as and when required. However, hard copy staff handbooks can be costly for the employer to produce, particularly where there are a large number of employees. Updating the sections can also be more onerous as new hard copy sections will need to be distributed, clearly identifying that they replace the previous section in order to avoid confusion.

Alternatively, employers are more often favouring intranet-based staff handbooks, which are particularly useful in large organisations, provided that all employees have unlimited access to the information they contain, as and when required. Internet policies can be updated more easily and the information is available to employees instantaneously, without the need for costly or onerous distribution. However, employers must be careful to ensure that their employees are informed as and when changes are made to the staff handbook. Intranet-based staff handbooks are also preferred in paper-free office environments, although it is helpful to provide a facility whereby relevant sections of the staff handbook can be printed off if an employee prefers to refer to a paper-based format. As above, it is also worth ensuring that members of staff sign a document to acknowledge that they are aware of the contents of the staff handbook and that they have access to this (as amended).

Employers should also be aware of their obligations under the Equality Act 2010 and be ready to provide employees with the contents of the staff handbook in formats such as large type, Braille or audio, where it is reasonable to do so.

Updates

Given the fact that employment legislation is in a constant state of flux, staff handbooks and the policies within them can easily become out-of-date, reflecting bad practice or, at worst, unlawful provisions. It is therefore essential that each employer has in place a system that monitors and reviews the policies contained within their staff handbook, ideally before April and October each year, to reflect the changes in legislation and case law developments. In this way, any necessary amendments can be made ahead of / at the time of changes to the law.

To the extent that staff handbooks incorporate terms and conditions for employees, any changes made to these terms and conditions should not be undertaken until consultation and agreement has been reached with the employees (or, where appropriate, employee representatives) as unilaterally imposed changes to terms and conditions are not enforceable.

Similarly, it is also considered best practice to consult with recognised trade unions / employee representatives whenever significant changes are made to any (non-contractual) policies set out by employers. This helps to maintain good employment relationships and can also support an employer in defending an Employment Tribunal claim if it can show that the employee was not only aware of the change but was consulted about, and agreed to, the change in a particular policy.

It is also important for employers to ensure, in particular, that managers have the necessary level of understanding and awareness to manage staff in line with the terms and policies agreed.

Key advantages

Staff handbooks can be crucial in ensuring that a consistent approach is taken across the board in dealing with any number of employees. This can avoid feelings of unequal treatment or discontent, and can also significantly limit the likelihood of Employment Tribunal claims being brought. For the employer, staff handbooks can bring harmonisation to a workforce that, previously, may have worked under different terms, conditions and policies.

Similarly, employees find staff handbooks user-friendly and know where to look in order to obtain specific information relating to their employment. In turn, this provides an additional advantage to the employer, who is not left to deal with queries that would otherwise crop up time and time again.

Drafting the handbook

Some employers will produce their staff handbooks internally, within the human resources / personnel department. The same internal department would also then be responsible for updating the staff handbook as and when required.

Alternatively, some employers seek legal advice in drafting and/or reviewing existing staff handbooks, in order to ensure that the policies are compliant with the latest legislative changes and views on best practice.

There is also widespread use of external guidance sources available to assist with the drafting of staff handbooks. Certain industries publish model documents and contracts as precedents. Advice can also be sought from the BIS website and the ACAS Code of Practice. Various policies can also be viewed and downloaded from the internet, although employers should be cautious of adopting such general-purpose policies without at least considering whether they meet the needs of the individual employer and are consistent with any terms contained within the contracts of employment, as well as the extent to which they are compliant with current legislation.

Content checklist

Essential:

- Absence / sick leave and pay (see p.16 and p.470).
- Collective agreements (if any).
- Deductions from wages (including recovery of overpayments).
- Disciplinary and grievance procedure (see p.121).
- Equal opportunities / equality and diversity (see p.184 and p.191).
- Family-friendly policies, including maternity, paternity and adoption leave, emergency time off for dependants and parental leave (see p.206 and p.400).
- Health and safety policy (this could be published as a separate document or handbook).
- Holiday leave and pay (see p.240).
- Hours of work.
- Information and consultation arrangements (if any).

- Notice periods (see p.369).
- Pay and benefits (including overtime pay).

Optional:

- Bank holiday working.
- Bereavement / compassionate leave (see p.252).
- Bullying and harassment (see p.58).
- Change of personal details.
- Communications.
- Company car.
- Company equipment (mobile phones, laptops, tools, etc.).
- Dress code (see p.152).
- Drugs and alcohol (see p.36).
- DSE eyesight policy.
- Expenses procedure (see p.200).
- Flexible working arrangements (see p.221).
- Forms for in-house use.
- Gifts and hospitality (especially important in light of the new Bribery Act 2010 – see 'Bribery', p.49).
- Housekeeping and building security.
- Incapacity and capability.
- Induction.
- Internet and email policy (see p.271).
- Introduction to the organisation.
- Jury service (see p.288).
- Organisation chart / management structure.
- Organisation products and services.
- Performance management / appraisals.
- Redundancy (see p.429).
- Reference policy (see p.434).
- Retirement and pension benefits (see p.445).
- Smoking (see p.478).
- Stress (see p.500).
- Termination of employment.
- Time off for trade union representatives (if applicable).
- Training and promotion.
- Travel policy.
- Whistleblowing (see p.551).

Checklist of dos and don'ts

Do:

- ensure that you are familiar with current employment legislation and how this affects your policies and procedures;
- use bullet points, short sentences and paragraph subheadings;
- write confidently, concisely and directly;
- write formally;
- choose a format that is easy to update – loose-leaf or ring binders are helpful;
- try to make your handbook attractive to encourage staff to read it;
- think about including a frequently asked questions section (FAQs);
- consult senior managers and staff representatives (if applicable) when drafting new policies and procedures;
- get the contents checked from a legal perspective before publishing; and
- get it proofread to reduce errors or typing mistakes.

Don't:

- use scene-setting, padding or long lead-ins;
- use long paragraphs;
- use foreign phrases or Latin;
- use jargon, clichés or humour;
- be vague – this can lead to misinterpretation resulting in disputes with your employees; or
- ignore current employment legislation or best management practice.

See also: Alcohol and drugs, p.36; Bribery, p.49; Bullying and harassment, p.58; Disciplinary and grievance procedures, p.121; Employment contracts, p.164; Employment Tribunals, p.179; Holiday, p.240; Redundancy, p.429; Restrictive covenants and garden leave, p.441; Smoking, p.478; Whistleblowing, p.551.

Sources of further information

ACAS guidelines on drawing up handbooks are available at www.acas.org.uk

Comprehensive, accurate and up-to-date policies and procedures are required by all employers to ensure that they comply with the latest employment law and health and safety legislation. Unfortunately, however, most of us don't have time to keep policies updated, or simply don't have the expertise to know what the policies and procedures should cover.

That's why Workplace Law's team of expert editors and advisors has drafted a series of 21 complete and updated policies and procedures templates, covering all the major areas of risk to employers. All documents are issued electronically in MS Word format so that you can customise them for your organisation, and are accompanied by extensive guidance on the subject matter. The templates are written in the plain-English, jargon-free style you will find in all Workplace Law publications. Each template is downloadable, giving you instant access upon purchase. For more information visit www.workplacelaw.net.

Stress

Heidi Thompson, Workplace Law

Key points

- All employers owe a legal duty of care to their employees. Injury to mental health is treated in the same way as injury to physical health.
- Sixteen general propositions for bringing any civil claim for compensation for stress were provided by the Court of Appeal and approved as general guidance by the House of Lords. These are listed below (see '*Criteria for civil cases*').
- A successful claim must show that, on the balance of probabilities, an employer had knowledge or deemed knowledge of the foreseeability of harm to a particular employee, so that the lack of his taking reasonable steps to, as far as is reasonably practicable, alleviate the risk of or prevent that harm occurring constituted a breach of duty of care to the employee, and that this caused the injury or loss.
- The HSE has urged employers to carry out risk assessments and implement measures to eliminate or control workplace stress or risk criminal prosecution. The HSE's Management Standards on stress (a web-based toolkit to help businesses comply with their duties) were published on 3 November 2004. Employers will need to take on board this HSE guidance in order to provide best practice in health and safety.

Legislation

- Health and Safety at Work etc. Act 1974.
- Management of Health and Safety at Work Regulations 1999.
- The Equality Act 2010.

Main cases

- *Stokes v. Guest Keen and Nettlefold (Bolts and Nuts) Limited* (1968).
- *Walker v. Northumberland County Council* (1995).
- *Katfunde v. Abbey National and Dr Daniel* (1998).
- *Sutherland v. Hatton* (2002).
- *Barber v. Somerset County Council* (2004).
- *Hartman v. South Essex Mental Health & Community Care NHS Trust* (2005).
- *Mark Hone v. Six Continents Retail Limited* (2005).
- *Edward Harding v. The Pub Estate Co. Limited* (2005).
- *London Borough of Islington v. University College London Hospital NHS Trust* (2005).
- *Dickens v. O2 (2009).*

Legal aspects of stress claims

All employers owe a legal duty of care to their employees. Injury to mental health is treated in the same way as injury to physical health.

Criteria for civil cases

A successful civil claim must show that, on the balance of probabilities, an employer had knowledge or deemed knowledge of the foreseeability of harm to a particular employee, so that the lack of his taking reasonable steps to, as far as is reasonably practicable, alleviate the risk of or prevent that harm occurring, constituted a breach of duty of care to the employee, and that this caused the injury or loss.

Facts

- In 2009/10 an estimated 435,000 individuals in Britain, who worked in the last year, believed that they were experiencing work-related stress at a level that was making them ill.
- Around 16.7% of all working individuals thought their job was very or extremely stressful.
- The annual incidence of work-related mental health problems in Britain in 2008 was approximately 5,126 new cases per year. However, this almost certainly underestimates the true incidence of these conditions in the British workforce.
- An estimated 230,000 people, who worked in the last 12 months, first became aware of work-related stress, depression or anxiety in 2008/09, giving an annual incidence rate of 760 cases per 100,000.
- In 2009/10, an estimated 9.8 million working days were lost through work-related stress. Every person experiencing work-related stress was off work for an estimated average of 22.6 days, which equates to 0.42 days per worker.
- The incidence rate of self-reported work-related stress, depression or anxiety has been broadly level over the years 2001/02 to 2008/09, with the exception of 2001/02 where the incidence rate was higher than the current level.

Source: HSE.

A stress injury is not as immediately visible as, for instance, a broken leg, and the 16 propositions put forward by Lady Justice Hale in the Court of Appeal judgment of *Sutherland v. Hatton* (and related cases) are still regarded as the best useful practical guidance as to whether or not a stress claim may be successful. (These propositions are listed in full at the end of this section.)

Nonetheless, every case does still depend on its own facts and in the later House of Lords case of *Barber v. Somerset County Council* Lord Walker preferred as a statement of law the statement of Swanwick J in *Stokes v. Guest Keen and Nettlefold (Bolts and Nuts) Ltd* that "the overall test is still the conduct of the reasonable and prudent employer, taking positive thought for the safety of his workers in the light of what he knows or ought to know".

State of knowledge

Knowledge of the employee and the risks they are facing is key in both leading House of Lords cases on workplace stress. Lord Walker went furthest in the *Barber* case and stated that, where there was developing knowledge, a reasonable employer had a duty to keep reasonably abreast of it and not be too slow to apply it. Where the employer has greater than average knowledge of the risks, he may be obliged to take more than the average or standard precautions.

Knowledge is critical in the area of what is or is not 'reasonably foreseeable' in a civil claim. This was reinforced by the Court of Appeal case of *Mark Hone v. Six*

Continents Retail Limited. In this case it was brought to the employer's attention that long hours were being worked and the employee was tired. It was held that it did not matter that the employer did not accept the level of the recorded hours as accurate as the fact the employee had been recording those hours was sufficient to indicate that he needed help and contributed to the "sufficiently plain indications of impending harm to health".

This may be contrasted with another Court of Appeal case of *Edward Harding v. The Pub Estate Company Ltd* where, as manager, the claimant's hours were within his own control, no reduction in hours was requested, nor additional staff; complaints concentrated on working conditions. In this case, the Court of Appeal overturned judgment at first instance because they found no sufficient message was ever passed to the employers of a risk to the employee's health. This was reinforced through the recent case of *Dickens v. O2*, where the claimant was entitled to damages for psychiatric injury caused by work-related stress. The injury was reasonably foreseeable from the point at which the claimant described her severe symptoms to the employer and said she did not know how long she could continue before taking sick leave. Thereafter the employer breached its duty of care by failing to send her home and refer her immediately to its occupational health service.

On deciding if a psychological injury was reasonably foreseeable after the event, it has been held that this is "to a large extent a matter of impression" (*London Borough of Islington v. University College London Hospital NHS Trust*). Therefore, all factors that would go to make up such an impression should be monitored, such as working hours, increased workload, time off sick etc. as well as specific indications

of stress from employees. This is therefore a matter to be considered on the individual facts of each case.

Part-time workers

However, time actually spent at work may well be a crucial factor in some cases. It was held in the Court of Appeal case of *Hartman v. South Essex Mental Health and Community Care NHS Trust* that it would only be in exceptional circumstances that someone working for two or three days a week with limited hours would make good a claim for injury caused by stress at work.

Confidential advice / health service

There are a number of precautionary measures outlined at the end of this chapter for employers to protect themselves against workplace stress claims and, in particular, the provision of a confidential advice service was thought likely to provide a good defence in the *Sutherland* case.

It was confirmed in *Hartman* that the mere fact that an employer offered an occupational health service should not lead to the conclusion that the employer had foreseen risk of psychiatric injury due to work-related stress to any individual or class of employee. An employer could not be expected to know confidential medical information disclosed by the claimant to occupational health. However, there may be circumstances where an occupational health department's duty of care to an employee requires it to seek his or her consent to disclose information that the employer needs to know, if proper steps are to be taken for the welfare of the employee.

Stress in other civil claims

Stress now raises its head more often in claims involving bullying and harassment, disability, discrimination and constructive dismissal. Failure to recognise and address stress issues in the context of these types of claim could result in significant liability for an employer. For instance, where an employee may establish that he falls within the definition of a disabled person under the Equality Act 2010 and an employer fails to make reasonable adjustments to the workplace for this disability, compensation would also be payable for the psychiatric or physical injuries occurring from stress suffered as a result of this.

Sixteen propositions for stress claims

A summary of the 16 propositions stated in *Sutherland v. Hatton* is provided below.

General
1. The ordinary principles of employers' liability apply.
2. There are no occupations that should be regarded as intrinsically dangerous to mental health.

Reasonable foreseeability
3. The threshold question to be answered in any workplace stress case was stated as: 'whether this kind of harm to this particular employee was reasonably foreseeable'. This has two components: (a) an injury (as distinct from occupational stress) that (b) is attributable to stress at work (as distinct from other factors).
4. Foreseeability depends upon what the employer knows (or ought reasonably to know) about the individual employees.
5. Factors likely to be relevant in answering the threshold question include:
   ■ the nature and extent of the work done; and
   ■ signs from the employee of impending harm to health.
6. The employer is generally entitled to take what he is told by his employee at face value, unless he has good reason to think to the contrary.

7. To trigger a duty to take steps, the indications of impending harm to health arising from stress at work must be plain enough for any reasonable employer to realise that he should do something about it.

Duty of employers
8. The employer is in breach of duty only if he has failed to take steps that are reasonable in the circumstances.
9. The size and scope of the employer's operation, its resources and the demands it faces are relevant in deciding what is reasonable; these include the interests of other employees and the need to treat them fairly (e.g. in any redistribution of duties).
10. An employer can only be expected to take steps that are reasonable in the circumstances.

Guidelines for employers
11. An employer who offers a confidential advice service, with referral to appropriate counselling or treatment services, is unlikely to be found in breach of duty.
12. If the only reasonable and effective step would have been to dismiss or demote the employee, the employer will not have been in breach of duty in allowing a willing employee to continue in the job.

(However, in light of the lead judgment of Lord Walker in *Barber* that there is a requirement for 'drastic action' if an employee's health is in danger, it may be said that in the absence of alternative work, where an employee was at risk, ultimately the employer's duty of care would not preclude dismissing or demoting the employee at risk.)

13. In all cases, it is necessary to identify the steps that the employer both could and should have taken before finding him in breach of his duty of care.

14. The claimant must show that the breach of duty has caused or materially contributed to the harm suffered. It is not enough to show that occupational stress alone has caused the harm; it must be attributable to a breach of an employer's duty.

Apportionment

15. Where the harm suffered has more than one cause, the employer should pay only for that proportion of the harm suffered that is attributable to his wrongdoing, unless the harm is truly indivisible. It is for the defendant to raise the question of apportionment.
16. The assessment of damages will take account of pre-existing disorders or vulnerability and of the chance that the claimant would have succumbed to a stress-related disorder in any event.

It is not the case that one or other of the tests is more important; all 16 have to be looked at in respect of each individual case.

Criteria for criminal liability

There is no specific statute or other regulation controlling stress levels permitted in the workplace; therefore broad principles of health and safety at work will be applied as set out in the Health and Safety at Work etc. Act 1974 (HSWA) and the Management of Health and Safety at Work Regulations 1999 (MHSWR).

Where no action is taken by an employer on stress, he may be deemed to have fallen short of his duty to take all reasonably practicable measures to ensure the health, safety and welfare of employees and others sharing the workplace and to create safe and healthy working systems (HSWA).

Additionally, there is the requirement to undertake risk assessments of stress and put in place appropriate preventive and protective measures to keep the employees safe from harm (MHSWR).

Any breach of an employer's statutory or regulatory duties under health and safety legislation towards his employees giving rise to criminal liability may also be relied upon by a civil claimant as evidence of the employer's breach of duty in a negligence action and, indeed, in support of a claim for constructive dismissal.

Risk assessments

West Dorset Hospitals NHS Trust was the first organisation to have an improvement notice issued against it with the requirement that it assessed and reduced the stress levels of its doctors or other employees or face court action and a potentially unlimited fine. More recently, Liverpool Hope University has been served with an improvement notice on similar grounds. The HSE has urged employers to carry out risk assessments and implement measures to eliminate or control workplace stress or risk criminal prosecution.

It is therefore important that risk assessments for stress are undertaken, regularly reviewed and recommended actions implemented. Unlike civil litigation, any criminal prosecution carries with it the threat of an unlimited fine and/or imprisonment.

A general risk assessment of potential 'stressors' at work should be sufficient for most businesses but should additionally take into account any discrete categories of employees, such as night workers, the young, and expectant mothers. But if an employer becomes aware of an employee at specific risk or who has raised any concerns, an individual risk assessment should be carried out for them, recommendations implemented and regularly reviewed.

Health and safety policy

It is further recommended that an employer's health and safety policy sets out guidance on how stress should be dealt with and a clear complaints-handling procedure. In this way a company can show that it has followed its own procedures in dealing with any complaints and implementing any actions.

Conclusion

In order to protect themselves against enforcement action as well as employee claims, employers are advised to organise risk assessments of potential stressors, to make facilities such as counselling and grievance procedures available to employees, and to show a receptive and flexible response to complaints. In addition, compliance with the HSE Management Standards / Guidance will assist in showing that an employer has met the reasonable standard of duty of care required.

Combating stress: an employer's checklist

- No employer has an absolute duty to prevent all stress, which can be as a result of interests outside work. However, once an employee has raised the issue of stress, an employer is under a duty to investigate properly and protect the employee as far as is reasonably practicable.
- Health monitoring – both through a confidential advice line and/or regular company medicals.
- Counselling – an employer who offers a confidential advice service, with referral to appropriate counselling or treatment services, is unlikely to be found in breach of duty. This is of course relative to the problem and the service provided but is a good indication that a proactive approach by an employer can protect him from stress claims and enforcement action.

- Regular medicals – these are a useful tool in alerting employers of any risks. However, medical confidentiality has to be observed and express consent given by employees for their clinical information to be shared with employers.
- Dismissal – in the absence of alternative work, the employee deemed at risk should be dismissed or demoted.
- Written health and safety policy – clear guidance in a company's health and safety policy on how stress should be dealt with shows that the company is complying with the health and safety regulations to provide a safe working environment for employees and enables staff to follow a set procedure. It would also stand as a defence where an employee fails to disclose that he is suffering from stress because of ignorance of a company's procedures.
- Equally, a bullying and harassment code should be in force and there should be a clear complaints-handling procedure.
- Risk assessments should cover all workplace risks and should therefore include stress. HSE guidance on risk assessment can be found at www.hse.gov.uk/pubns/indg163.pdf.
- Risk assessments should be regularly reviewed and recommended actions implemented.
- Working time – employers can combat stress by monitoring and recording employees' working time with action being taken if the benchmark set out in the Working Time Regulations 1998 is breached.
- Implementation of HSE Management Standards / Guidance will assist in showing that an employer has met the reasonable standard of duty of care.

See also: Discrimination, p.126;
The Equality Act, p.191; Medical
records, p.304; Mental health,
p.304; Occupational health, p.374;
Working time, p.564.

Sources of further information

As part of the general duty to keep abreast of developing knowledge and practice, employers should be aware of the HSE's stress page at www.hse.gov.uk/stress/index.htm. This includes example stress policies and the HSE's Management Standards for workplace stress.

Additional HSE guidance includes an action pack (*Real Solutions, Real People* (ISBN: 0 7176 2767 5 priced at £25.)). The pack includes a guide for employers and employees alike and an introduction to the Management Standards. Other HSE guidance in the form of free leaflets include the following: *Tackling stress: the management standards approach – a short guide*; *Making the Stress Management Standards work: How to apply the Standards in your workplace*; and *Working together to reduce stress at work: A guide for employees.* These are available at the publications section of the HSE stress web page.

The Management Standards look at six key areas (or 'risk factors') that can be causes of work-related stress: 'demands,' 'control,' 'support,' 'relationships,' 'role,' and 'change'. The standard for each area contains simple statements about good management practice that can be applied by employers.

HSE guidelines such as these are voluntary and as such are not legally binding. They do, however, have evidential value. They assist the court in the interpretation of legislation and what the reasonable standard of duty of care owed may be. Therefore, compliance with these Management Standards / Guidance will assist in showing the court that an employer has met the reasonable standard of duty of care required.

Strikes

Pam Loch, Loch Associates Employment Lawyers

Key points

- There is no formal right to strike in the UK; however, legislation provides limited protection for trade unions from liability for the economic torts committed when a strike is organised and takes place.

- Industrial action does not, of itself, incur criminal liability either on the part of the organiser or the participator.

- If the employee was taking part in unofficial industrial action at the time of his or her dismissal, then, subject to limited exceptions, he or she has no right to complain of unfair dismissal.

- A person is not entitled to be paid for the period while he or she was on strike.

- There has been a rise in the use of injunctions to halt strikes on procedural grounds, although recent case decisions may lead to a reverse of this trend.

- In recent years there has been a marked increase in strikes and other industrial action. The recession has contributed to the situation as employers have been compelled to make cost savings and unions have sought to protect their members. It is likely that this trend will continue due to job cuts and pay freezes in both the public and private sectors.

- Collective disputes between an employer and its workforce or trade union are normally resolved through existing consultative or dispute procedures. Strikes and other industrial action are usually a last resort.

Legislation

- Trade Union and Labour Relations (Consolidation) Act 1992.

Right to strike

The right, or freedom, to strike in civil law is heavily restricted. It is not a right in itself and rather it is in effect a right to stop work after giving due notice. There are other forms of industrial action short of a strike, such as an overtime ban, go slow or work to rule. The right to organise is generally limited to a right to organise primary, but not secondary, industrial action; that is action taken against an employer directly involved in the dispute, about pay or other terms and conditions of employment or about other specified employment-related matters. Article 11 of the European Convention on Human Rights confers no express right to strike – see *Ministry of Justice v. Prison Officers Association* (2008).

Recent cases have focused on the stringent requirements placed on trade unions by the law when it comes to arranging strike action. In particular, where industrial action is organised by, or in the name of a trade union, then the union must ballot its members, and give the employer formal notice of intention to take industrial action.

Criminal law

Industrial action does not, of itself, incur criminal liability either on the part of the organiser or the participator. Criminal offences committed in connection with a strike, such as threatening behaviour, assault etc., are not subject to any special rules as compared with such acts committed otherwise than in connection with a strike.

Contractual liability

Industrial action does not normally incur liability in contract at collective level, but is often a breach of contract at the individual level; that is between employer and worker. For example, in the case of a strike, the worker has withdrawn his labour and this will leave him open to a claim for breach of contract. This can have the effect of making the organiser, usually a trade union, liable in tort, generally for one or more of the following 'economic torts':

- Inducing a person to break a contract;
- Interfering with business by unlawful means;
- Indirectly interfering with a contract by unlawful means;
- Intimidation; and/or
- Conspiracy.

In relation to liability in tort there is a statutory defence available under Section 219 of the Trade Union and Labour Relations (Consolidation) Act 1992 that the act was done in 'contemplation or furtherance of a trade dispute'. The issue of whether industrial action is a breach of the contract of employment depends on the terms of the contract, express or implied, upon the nature of the acts done or omitted to be done, and the circumstances in which the industrial action took place. However, in Case C-438/05 *Viking Line* (11 December 2007) and Case C-341/05 *Laval un Partneri* (18 December 2007) the European Court of Justice held that the free movement provisions of the EC Treaty, here Articles 43 (freedom of establishment) and Article 49 (freedom to provide services), impose obligations on trade unions which may make collective action unlawful.

Unfair dismissal

This is probably the most important area of the law relating to strikes. The Trade Union and Labour Relations (Consolidation) Act 1992 differentiates between unofficial industrial action (Section 237) and official industrial action (Section 238) and within official action gives special treatment to 'protected' industrial action (Sections 238(2b) and 238a). If the employee was taking part in unofficial industrial action at the time of his or her dismissal, then, subject to limited exceptions, he or she has no right to complain of unfair dismissal.

The exceptions are where the reason for dismissal is related to any of the following:

- Jury service;
- Family related rights, e.g. maternity leave, time off for dependants, etc;
- Certain health and safety issues;
- Employee representative negotiating a workplace agreement relating to flexible working or working time; and/or
- Whistleblowing (this is only automatically unfair during unofficial action).

Dismissal takes place on the date the employment actually ends, unless the contract is terminated by notice, in which case the date of the dismissal is the date when notice is given (Section 237(5)).

Industrial action is unofficial unless:

- the employee is a member of a union and his union has authorised or endorsed the action; or
- the employee is not a member of a union but among those taking part in the action there are members of a trade union by which the action has been authorised or endorsed; or
- none of the employees taking part in the action are members of a union.

The question of whether a person was a member of a union is to be determined as at the time he or she began to take part in the industrial action, but the union membership is to be disregarded if it is unconnected with the employment in question (Section 237(6)). A union will have authorised or endorsed industrial action if it has done so:

- in accordance with the union's rules; or
- by the union's executive committee, president or general secretary; or
- by some lesser union official or committee, provided that the union's executive committee, president or general secretary have not repudiated the industrial action in accordance with Section 21.

Pay

As industrial action, including striking, normally constitutes a breach of the employment contract by the employee, employees are not entitled to be paid for the period when they are on strike. The correct amount to be deducted is the pay for the period of the strike, not the loss to the employer – see *Cooper v. Isle of Wight College* (2007). It depends on how the employee is paid as to what can be deducted. Unless the contract of employment specifies otherwise, if the employee is paid a salary, then the usual permitted deduction will be one calendar day per day of striking.

Where an employee has been involved in non-strike industrial action which did not constitute a breach of contract, the employee is entitled to be paid in full. Where there is only partial performance of the contract of employment, the employer is entitled to make an appropriate deduction from salary – see *Spackman v. London Metropolitan University* (13 July 2007), where a 30% deduction was upheld by the County Court.

Where an employee has had salary deducted for taking part in industrial action, they are prevented from bringing an authorised deduction of wages claim in the Employment Tribunal. This is regardless of whether or not there was a breach of contract committed by the employee by taking part in industrial action. If an employer has deducted more than it should, the employee's recourse would be in the civil court for breach of contract or an action for debt, or if no longer employed they could bring a breach of contract claim in the Employment Tribunal.

Injunctions

The union balloting requirements for industrial action have been criticised because a simple majority can result in lawful strike action, even if only a small proportion of those eligible actually voted. Also, notification of a ballot may not necessarily lead to a strike. Conversely, the balloting and notice requirements are strict and any small error or omission made by a union has resulted in employers successfully obtaining injunctions against industrial action.

There are three key areas that unions must get right: notification of intention to ballot; the process for the ballot itself; and the way in which the outcome is communicated to members. Over the last couple of years a number of high profile employers have sought injunctions to halt strikes based on technical failures of the unions in complying with the obligations placed on them.

Unions must state the total number of employees who will be entitled to vote in a ballot or could be eligible to take part in industrial action and the categories of workers involved, with an explanation of how numbers were arrived at.

Alternatively, where some of the relevant employees have union membership fees deducted from their salary, the union must provide information that will allow the employer to work out the numbers, categories and workplaces of relevant employees. In 2010, EDF prevented a planned London Underground strike because the union had wrongly categorised some of its members as 'technicians / engineers' rather than 'test room fitters' and 'shift testers' (*EDF Energy Powerlink Ltd v. National Union of Rail Maritime and Transport Workers* (2009)).

There have been a series of highly publicised injunctions sought by British Airways (BA) against Unite. BA successfully sought an injunction against Unite before Christmas 2009, halting a proposed 12-day strike. The High Court upheld BA's claim that the strike would be unlawful due to Unite including in the ballot and strike notices, and balloting process, several hundred employees who it knew would leave BA before the strike (due to voluntary redundancy). The legislation requires only those employees due to take part in the industrial action to be balloted and identified in the relevant notices.

Unite defended its position on the basis that the information it provided was 'as accurate as… reasonably practicable' for the purposes of the relevant Act. The Court rejected this argument, stating that Unite was, or should have been, aware that the ballot notice would include a large number of members that Unite could not reasonably believe would actually have been entitled to vote, and in fact Unite gave the opposite advice on its website. The Judge also took into account the timing of the planned strike, stating that it would be more damaging to BA, and the wider public, than if it were to take place at any other time of the year.

There was a further ballot by Unite of BA's workers in January and February of 2010. Initially BA was successful in obtaining another injunction from the High Court, only to have this decision overturned three days later by the Court of Appeal. This time, Unite had complied fully with the elements it previously fell down on, but the question for the Court of Appeal was Unite's alleged failure to comply with the statutory provisions on communicating the result of the ballot to its members. With one Judge dissenting, the Court decided that Unite did not have to ensure a personal communication to each member in order to comply with the requirement to 'inform'. The Court reviewed the various methods of notification Unite used and ruled that it had complied with the legislation. Another factor that swayed the Court toward this decision was that in the previous action, BA had not complained of inadequate 'informing', even though the same methods of communication had been used.

This more relaxed stance taken by the Court of Appeal is reflected in another decision which overturned a strike injunction. In *RMT v. Serco Ltd and another case* (2011), the Court of Appeal overturned the High Court's very strict application of several features of the rules including relating to when balloting failures are 'accidental' and the 'reasonably practicable' accuracy of figures.

The Court of Appeal's recent decisions may well lead to fewer applications, or successful applications, for injunctive relief against strike action. Where employers could previously rely on technical points to quash strike action, recent decisions may encourage unions to successfully use the threat of strike action to their tactical advantage.

See also: Dismissal, p.146; Trade unions, p.516.

Sources of further information

Trade Union and Labour Relations (Consolidation) Act 1992:
www.workplacelaw.net/news/display/id/32539

Department for Business, Innovation and Skills
www.bis.gov.uk/policies/employment-matters/rights/trade-unions

Direct Gov: www.direct.gov.uk/en/employment

Advisory, Conciliation and Arbitration Service (ACAS): www.acas.org.uk

Terminal illness

Pam Loch, Loch Associates Employment Lawyers

Key points
- This chapter looks at the protection afforded to terminally ill employees. It seeks to provide guidance to employers on how to manage the working relationship and how to minimise exposure to Tribunal claims.
- It also considers the effect of terminal illness generally on the employer and work colleagues.
- Employers need to be aware of their responsibilities and obligations regarding employees with terminal illnesses under various employment-related laws.
- Key areas of the working relationship that terminal illness affects are benefits, the production of medical evidence, adjustments to working conditions, time off and dismissal.
- There is a *positive* duty on employer to make reasonable adjustments for disabled employees.
- HR management is of fundamental importance as it will naturally be an acutely distressing time for the terminally ill employee and their family.

Legislation
- Employment Rights Act 1996.
- Data Protection Act 1998.
- The Equality Act 2010.

The Equality Act came into force in October 2010 and brought together and amended existing discrimination legislation concerning sex, race, disability, sexual orientation, religion or belief and age.

Disability discrimination
An employee (or applicant for employment) will qualify as disabled for the purposes of the Equality Act if they have a physical or mental impairment that has a substantial and long-term adverse effect on their ability to carry out normal day-to-day activities. Cancer, HIV infection and multiple sclerosis are deemed disabilities under the Equality Act from the point of diagnosis, irrespective of whether the worker displays any symptoms. As a general rule, however, any employee who has been medically diagnosed with a terminal illness is likely to be covered by the Equality Act.

An employer must be careful not to discriminate because of disability against an employee, either by:

- treating them unfavourably because of something arising in consequence of their disability, without objective justification (discrimination arising from disability);
- treating them less favourably than others because of their disability (direct discrimination);
- applying a provision, criterion or practice that disadvantages those with a shared disability without objective justification (indirect discrimination);
- failing to comply with a duty to make reasonable adjustments for their disability where it places them at a substantial disadvantage;
- victimising them;
- subjecting them to harassment; or
- asking them pre-employment health questions other than for a prescribed reason.

There is legal protection from discrimination to cover the whole working relationship, from the recruitment stage (e.g. interviews) to post-termination discrimination (e.g. in the course of providing references).

There is no minimum qualifying period under the Equality Act. There is also no financial cap on the awards made for discrimination claims, and compensation can take account of a likely prolonged period out of the workplace. Additional awards can be made for injury to feelings.

Associative discrimination
It is sufficient that disability is the reason for the treatment; the disability may be that of the claimant or some other person. Furthermore, there is no requirement to prove any 'association' between the claimant and the disabled person.

Discrimination by perception
Where an employee isn't actually disabled, but an employer perceives them to be disabled and treats them less favourably because of that perception, this will constitute unlawful discrimination.

Reasonable adjustments
An employer is under a positive duty to make reasonable adjustments to working conditions once it becomes aware, or ought reasonably to be aware, that an employee has a disability under the EA. This could include time off for treatment such as chemo- or radio-therapy, re-allocation of certain work duties to others/a reduction in hours to relieve the ill employee of duties and reduce stress, adjustments to the employee's job description or work location, and the provision of specialist equipment.

The Disability Discrimination Act set out factors that had to be taken into account when determining whether an adjustment was reasonable. The Equality Act does not do this but the Equality and Human Rights Commission (EHRC) Code of Practice does replicate (apart from one) the list that was contained in the DDA. The EHRC Code, however, states that ultimately the test of reasonableness is objective and that these factors only 'might' be taken into account:

- The extent to which the adjustment would ameliorate the disadvantage;
- The practicability of taking the step;
- The financial and other costs that would be incurred by the employer, and the extent to which the step would disrupt any of its activities;
- The financial and other resources available to the employer;
- The availability of external financial or other assistance (for example, assistance from the Access to Work scheme run by Jobcentre Plus); and/or
- The nature of the employer's activities and the size of the undertaking.

Adjustments may have an impact on other employees who, for example, have to increase their workload to make up for the ill employee's reduction in hours. These effects should be monitored and considered carefully at all times by the employer.

Unfair dismissal (including constructive unfair dismissal)
Employees who have accrued a year's service will have the right not to be unfairly dismissed. An employer can only defend a claim of unfair dismissal successfully if it can establish that the reason for the dismissal is one of five potentially fair reasons and that dismissal for that reason was fair in all the circumstances (*see below*).

An employee may be able to treat themselves as having been constructively dismissed if, for example, the employee resigns as a result of detrimental treatment or harassment by their employer by reason of their illness.

Sickness and financial relief

The employment contract should stipulate how long an employee is entitled to receive any enhanced sick pay (for example, there may be entitlement to full pay for a certain length of time and a right to half pay for a further period after that).

An employer should consider whether an individual off sick is likely to return to work in the foreseeable future. If the employee asserts that they are unable to work and unlikely to return, the employer may wish to consider whether they would qualify under any permanent health insurance (PHI) or ill health pension provisions, and facilitate the employee contacting the relevant provider.

An employer also needs to ensure that an employee receives their correct pay entitlement, including holiday pay under the Working Time Regulations.

It is widely considered unlawful to dismiss an employee before they have exhausted their right to contractual sick pay or are about to commence, or are in receipt of, PHI. This is because it is possible to imply a term into an employee's contract of employment stating that they are entitled to receive the full benefit of the employer's sick pay scheme/PHI before being dismissed by reason of their illness.

Where appropriate, an employer should have frank discussions about ways in which it can assist and support the employee, and alleviate any particular concerns they may have. For example, it may be helpful to draw the employee's attention to any early retirement due to ill health options, medical insurance

(including palliative care) availability and any life assurance schemes in operation (which may pay off the employee's mortgage after death for example).

Medical evidence and testing

An employer should request and keep confidential records of all medical certificates as evidence of the employee's illness and up to date prognosis.

Employers should always obtain the employee's consent (which must be freely given and not given under duress) particularly before seeking a medical report from the employee's own medical practitioner.

Dealing with sickness absences

An employer should consult regularly with any terminally ill employee, especially in relation to medical evidence received and before making adjustments, identifying an alternative position and certainly before taking a decision to dismiss.

Any disclosure by an employee relating to their medical condition and any test results must be treated in strictest confidence. Employers should always respect the right to privacy.

It is important for employers to maintain appropriate contact with employees on sick leave and to ensure they remain included in any work-related issues where possible (including social event invitations and work-related consultations), without being intrusive or overbearing.

When dealing with a terminally ill employee, particularly as part of a capability procedure, it is essential to ensure that accurate and legible records are kept of all meetings and correspondence.

Data protection

Medical information is protected under the Data Protection Act 1998 and is classified as 'sensitive personal data', requiring a stricter level of care and more onerous obligations by the employer than for other personal data. The 'processing' of medical information includes obtaining, holding and disclosing such data.

Dismissals and following a fair procedure

Dismissal by an employer of a terminally ill worker is generally a last resort.

An employer needs to rely on one of five potentially fair reasons to dismiss an employee with over a year's service. If an employer needs to terminate the employment of a terminally ill employee, it will usually seek to rely on 'incapacity' or 'some other substantial reason' as the substantive ground for dismissal. In addition, an employer must follow a fair procedure when dismissing an employee.

Operating a fair procedure can be onerous. It should include, as a minimum:

- Investigating the cause and likely length of the absence;
- Keeping in contact with the employee;
- Obtaining medical evidence;
- Meeting and consulting with the employee regarding medical evidence;
- Considering reasonable adjustments or alternative employment; and
- Following a fair and reasonable dismissal process, including giving the employee the right to appeal any dismissal decision.

Early retirement on the grounds of ill health may be an option for employees who are unable to continue working. Some occupational pension schemes allow members to retire and claim their pension before their normal retirement age if they are suffering from ill health or incapacity.

In practice, an employer will often try to negotiate the termination of an employee's employment by way of a settlement agreement.

Checklist

- Review contracts of employment to ensure terms and conditions (e.g. those relating to sickness) are clear and compliant with current law.
- Review and update policies and procedures.
- Consider delivering training to managers as to how to deal with issues concerning terminal illness and disabilities generally.
- Ensure the right balance is struck between the needs of the business and care for employees.
- Avoid dismissing an employee who is in receipt of income protection insurance as a benefit of their employment.

See also: Absence management, p.16; Disability legislation, p.116; Discrimination, p.126; The Equality Act, p.191; Health surveillance, p.231; HIV and AIDS, p.234; Medical records, p.304; Occupational health, p.374; Personnel files, p.392; Sickness, p.470.

Sources of further information

Office for Disability – HM Government: www.officefordisability.gov.uk/

Department for Work and Pensions: www.dwp.gov.uk/directgov/

Trade unions

Pinsent Masons Employment Group

Key points

- A trade union is an organisation consisting of workers whose main purpose is the regulation of relations between workers and their employers.
- Employers are prevented from offering inducements to their employees not to be a member of a trade union, not to take part in the activities of a trade union, not to make use of the services of a trade union and not to give up the right to have their terms and conditions of employment determined by a collective agreement.
- Further protection is provided to ensure that employees should not suffer detrimental actions for being a union member or using a union's services.

Legislation

- Trade Union and Labour Relations (Consolidation) Act 1992.
- Trade Union Reform and Employment Rights Act 1993.
- Employment Relations Act 1999.
- Employment Relations Act 2004.

Trade unions and collective agreements

In some industries, negotiated collective agreements exist relating to pay and terms of employment, and in some circumstances those agreements can also form part of the workers' contracts of employment.

A collective agreement may not always be enforceable between the union and the employer. However, the terms of a collective agreement may become incorporated into an individual employee's contract of employment, and so themselves become terms and conditions of employment.

Collective agreements can be incorporated if the employment contract expressly says so, or if the custom and practice in the industry is that the collective agreements are impliedly incorporated. However, some parts of collective agreements are not appropriate for incorporation.

Generally, once the terms of a collective agreement are incorporated into a contract of employment, they become terms of the contract and in some cases can remain in force even if the original collective agreement terminates.

Trade union recognition

The Employment Relations Act 1999 (ERA) created rules for trade unions to be recognised by employers on a statutory basis as long as certain conditions are fulfilled (*see below*).

In general terms, however, 'recognition' of a trade union is important in a number of ways. If a union is recognised, employers will have certain duties, for example:

- to consult with the union and its representatives on collective redundancy situations;
- to disclose information for collective bargaining purposes; and
- to allow time off to employees engaged in trade union activities or duties.

In addition, employers are under a duty to provide information to and consult with recognised trade unions concerning TUPE transfers.

Statutory recognition

In certain circumstances, even outside the provisions of the ERA, trade union recognition can take place voluntarily. An employer can voluntarily recognise a trade union, either expressly by stating so or by clear conduct that shows an implied agreement to recognise that union.

Accordingly, an employer that actually enters into negotiation with a trade union about terms and conditions of employment, conditions of work, employee discipline, trade union membership, etc., may be deemed to recognise the union voluntarily.

However, the statutory procedure also allows the trade union to apply for recognition so that it can conduct collective bargaining regarding pay, hours and holidays. The procedures are complex and are set out in Schedule A1 to the Trade Union and Labour Relations (Consolidation) Act 1992 (TUL(C)RA),

the legislation containing the recognition machinery introduced by Schedule 1 to ERA. To trigger the statutory procedure, the trade union must apply to the employer in respect of the workers who wish to constitute a bargaining unit (BU). A BU is determined by a number of factors that may result in a sector of the workforce being identified as a BU even though they may not have been the subject of separate negotiations in the past or even where the employer wishes to negotiate with the whole workforce.

The request to the employer must:

■ be in writing;
■ identify the relevant trade union and the BU; and
■ state that the request is made under paragraph eight of Schedule A1 to TUL(C)RA.

Further, the trade union must be independent and the employer must employ at least 21 workers.

Negotiation

The employer should, within ten working days of receiving the written request from the trade union, accept the request, reject it, or offer to negotiate.

If the parties agree on the BU and that the trade union should be recognised in respect of the BU, that is the end of the statutory procedure.

However, if the employer rejects the trade union's request outright or fails to respond, the union can apply to the Central Arbitration Committee (CAC).

The employer or the trade union may request the Arbitration, Conciliation and Advisory Service (ACAS) to assist in conducting negotiations. If the employer proposes that ACAS assistance be requested, and the union fails to respond within ten working days of the proposal or rejects such a proposal, no application to the CAC can be made. This is provided that the proposal is made by the employer within ten working days of having informed the union of its willingness to negotiate.

The trade union may approach the CAC if no agreement is reached between the parties, and if the employer fails to respond to the request within the ten-working-day period. If the employer informs the union within ten working days that it does not accept the request but is willing to negotiate, then there is an additional 20 days for negotiation, starting the day after the first ten-day period ends. If no agreement is reached at the end of the additional 20-day period, or if the parties agree a BU, but do not agree that the trade union is to be recognised, the trade union may apply to the CAC. On a practical note, if the employer reaches an agreement with the trade union that a ballot on recognition can take place, it may wish to include an undertaking by the trade union that the latter will not make another request for recognition for a period of time.

The CAC may accept the request if the initial request for recognition was valid and is on the face of it 'admissible'. The CAC will normally decide within ten working days of it receiving the request whether it may accept the claim. The CAC decides if the application is admissible by asking whether the trade union has 10% membership and whether the majority is likely to be in favour of recognition.

If the CAC accepts an application, but the BU has not been agreed, the employer must, within five working days, supply certain information about his workforce to the union and the CAC. If the BU has not been agreed by the parties, the CAC will try to help the parties to agree a BU within 20 working days of it giving notice of its acceptance. If the claim is not accepted by the CAC, this is an end to the statutory procedure.

If an agreement is reached between the parties, or if the CAC determines the BU, and this BU is different from the one originally proposed, then the validity test must be applied again.

If the CAC is satisfied that more than 50% of the workers constituting the BU are members of the trade union, it must usually issue a declaration that 'the trade union is recognised as entitled to conduct collective bargaining on behalf of the workers constituting the BU', but may hold a ballot if any of the following three factors apply:

1. It is in the interests of good industrial relations; or
2. A significant number of the trade union members within the BU informs the CAC that they do not wish the trade union to conduct collective bargaining on their behalf; or
3. Evidence leads the CAC to doubt whether a significant number of trade union members really want the trade union to conduct collective bargaining on their behalf.

If any of these conditions apply, or if the CAC is not satisfied that the majority of the workers in the BU are members of the union, then the CAC must arrange to hold a secret recognition ballot in which the workers constituting the BU are asked whether they want the trade union to conduct collective bargaining on their behalf.

Within ten working days of receiving the CAC notice, the trade union, or the trade union and the employer together, may notify the CAC that they do not want a ballot to be held. If a ballot is held in any event or if no objection is made, the ballot will be conducted by a Qualified Independent Person (QIP), who is appointed by the CAC. A QIP can, for example, be a practising solicitor.

The ballot must take place within 20 working days from the day the QIP is appointed, or such longer period as the CAC may decide. It may be conducted at a workplace, by post, or by a combination of these two.

The CAC must inform the employer and the trade union of the result of the ballot as soon as it is reasonably practicable after it has itself been so informed by the QIP.

If a majority of the workers voting in the ballot, and at least 40% of the workers constituting the BU, vote in favour of recognition, the CAC must issue a declaration that the trade union is recognised as entitled to conduct collective bargaining on behalf of the BU.

The parties will then have a 30-working-day negotiation period in which they may negotiate with a view to agreeing a method by which they will conduct collective bargaining. If no agreement is reached, the employer or the trade union may apply to the CAC for assistance.

If an agreement still cannot be reached, the CAC must take a decision.

The Code of Practice, 'Access and Unfair Practices during Recognition and Derecognition Ballots' (see *Sources of further information*), gives guidance regarding the union's access to workers during the period of recognition ballots and the avoidance of unfair practices whilst campaigning during that period. Whilst the Code imposes no legal obligations, its provisions are admissible in evidence and will be taken into account by any Court, Tribunal or the CAC where relevant.

See also: Employee consultation, p.160; Strikes, p.507; TUPE, p.523.

Sources of further information

Central Arbitration Committee (CAC): www.cac.gov.uk/

ACAS: www.acas.org.uk

DTI: Code of Practice 'Access and Unfair Practices during Recognition and Derecognition Ballots': www.bis.gov.uk/files/file14418.pdf

Training

Lizzy Campbell, Anderson Strathern

Key points

- Well-trained staff can help businesses retain a competitive edge.
- Training staff in basic employment law and equality and diversity issues will help reduce risk to the business.
- There is a statutory defence open to employers in discrimination legislation and, although it is a difficult test to meet, training in equality and diversity is one of the things that businesses can do to help them meet their obligations.

Legislation

- Equality Act 2006.
- The Apprenticeships, Skills, Children and Learning Act 2009.
- Equality Act 2010.

Why train your staff?

A business' most important resource is its employees. Giving employees the tools to enable them to excel is one way of making sure that they remain highly motivated and committed. Well-trained staff can be key to businesses achieving improved quality and increased productivity. This appears to have been recognised by the Government in the Apprenticeships, Skills, Children and Learning Act (2009), which gives employees the right to request time off to undertake training (subject to meeting certain conditions).

Well-trained staff will give a business that competitive edge. Proper staff training will, of course, also help businesses manage risk. So, in terms of workplace law, what are the key areas where training will be of greatest benefit?

Basic employment law for managers

The increasing complexity of employment law can leave employers exposed if managers do not have a basic understanding of the main requirements of current employment legislation. The absence of such knowledge can lead to a decision to discipline or dismiss being made, which may not stand up to scrutiny in an Employment Tribunal. There are therefore certain key areas where training for managers is required if a business is going to avoid exposure to possible claims.

In the first instance, managers need to be aware of the importance of the contract of employment and the basic statutory rights of an employee.

The procedures adopted by an employer are vital to the fairness of any decision made to discipline or dismiss an employee, so every manager should be trained in the nature and application of the business' grievance and disciplinary procedures and should understand the basic requirements for conducting a fair and reasonable disciplinary process (see 'Disciplinary and grievance procedures', p.121).

Managers should also be aware of the potentially fair reasons for dismissal. They need to know what they can or should take into account when considering an appropriate sanction and what evidence they require to justify the decision that is taken.

It is also useful for managers to be aware of the potential costs to the business – in terms of money, time and damage to reputation – of not complying with current employment law requirements.

Equality and diversity

Increasingly, employers are becoming aware of the benefits of training their staff at all levels in equality and diversity issues. Included in this should be a basic grounding in discrimination law.

A key time of risk for employers can be during recruitment and selection where a lack of sound reasoning or inconsistent practices may leave a business exposed to accusations of bias. As the number of discrimination claims continues to rise, many organisations already make it compulsory for staff to attend recruitment and selection training. Part of this should be to ensure that all staff – not just managers – have a general awareness of the nine protected characteristics under the Equality Act 2010, which came into force in October 2010, replacing and consolidating the previous separate pieces of discrimination legislation.

Under the Equality Act 2010, there is a statutory defence open to an employer accused of discrimination. However, in order to establish such a defence, the employer has to be able to say that it took 'such steps as were reasonably practicable' to prevent its employee doing whatever discriminatory act is being complained of. The bar for this test is set high. To have any prospect of being able to clear it, the employer will, at the very least, be required to:

- have well drafted policies and procedures, which are clearly communicated to its staff;
- ensure that staff are trained in the application of those policies and

procedures; and that managers know how to spot potential problems as they develop and take appropriate action to remedy these; and
- train in equality and diversity issues more generally.

This training should include the provision of up-to-date sessions to ensure that knowledge and understanding is kept current.

All of this needs to be in place and operating consistently before an employer has any prospect of successfully making out a statutory defence.

Public sector duties

All Public Authorities have duties in terms of Section 149 of the Equality Act 2010 to eliminate discrimination, harassment and victimisation, to promote equality of opportunity and to foster good relations between those who share a protected characteristic and those who do not. These provisions came into force in April 2011 and build on the existing public sector duties. The new duties, however, now cover all the protected characteristics (except pregnancy and maternity) so those organisations that had previously focussed on disability, sex and race have had to incorporate the new characteristics into their equality considerations.

Many organisations have made training of their staff a key element of meeting their public sector duties. Having committed themselves to such a course of action, it is vitally important that those in the public sector meet their obligations. A failure to do so may lead to an Employment Tribunal being invited, in any discrimination claim, to consider that a lack of regard for equal opportunities has been shown. This could then lead to the establishment of an evidential basis for inferring discrimination.

Many public sector organisations also use their procurement processes to meet their statutory duties to promote equality of opportunity. Those who tender to provide services to such organisations may now be asked to demonstrate their own anti-discrimination practices and policies. It is therefore not unusual for those tendering to be asked, for example, if all managers undergo compulsory training in equality and diversity. Apart from the obvious downside to the business of not providing such training, a negative answer can now also mean a lost business opportunity.

It is therefore becoming increasingly important for businesses looking for new opportunities to make sure they retain the competitive edge by putting such training in place.

See also: Absence management, p.16; Bullying and harassment, p.58; Disability legislation, p.116; Discrimination, p.126; The Equality Act, p.191; Recruitment and selection, p.420; Stress, p.500.

Sources of further information

Employment legislation changes frequently and it is imperative that managers keep up-to-date with the latest changes. The implications of handling a situation incorrectly can be significant, as employees (past and present) and job applicants can make a claim at an Employment Tribunal.

Training can give managers and supervisors a practical understanding of key areas of employment law, and give them more confidence when dealing with day-to-day management issues, as well as an understanding of the implications of their actions.

Workplace Law offer bespoke training to suit the needs of your employees, culture and organisation and will provide them with the confidence to take an active and committed role within the process.

All of our trainers are experienced HR professionals with hands-on experience working in every sector in small, medium and large organisations. Our HR professionals bring this unique knowledge and experience to ensure our training courses provide best practice and commercial advice with real life experiences. Visit www.workplacelaw.net for more information.

TUPE

Pinsent Masons Employment Group

Key points
- One of the biggest employment law issues for workplace managers is the impact of the Transfer of Undertakings (Protection of Employment) Regulations 2006 (TUPE 2006) on the sale of a business or on a change of service provider.
- TUPE 2006 came into force in April 2006 and repealed and replaced the Transfer of Undertakings (Protection of Employment) Regulations 1981 (TUPE 1981).
- Where TUPE 2006 applies, it provides that contracts of employment and associated liabilities transfer by operation of law from the outgoing employer or service provider to the incoming employer or service provider.

Legislation
- Acquired Rights Directive 2001.
- Pensions Act 2004.
- Transfer of Undertakings (Protection of Employment) Regulations 2006.

Does TUPE apply?
TUPE 2006 applies to 'a transfer of an undertaking, business or part of an undertaking or business situated immediately before the transfer in the UK to another person where there is a transfer of an economic entity which retains its identity (a 'business transfer')'. Whether there has been a business transfer is not always straightforward.

The key questions are:

- Is there any undertaking or entity?
- Does the undertaking retain its identity after the transfer?
- Has there been a change in employer?

The law in this area is notoriously uncertain, but there will ordinarily be a business transfer if there is a transfer of significant assets from the old employer to the new employer, or where a substantial proportion of the workforce transfers in terms of skill and number. Case law suggests that the incoming employer cannot simply refuse to take on staff to avoid the application of TUPE.

TUPE does not generally apply to a transfer of shares.

In each case a general review of a number of key indicators is necessary to determine whether there has been a business transfer. These include:

- the type of undertaking being transferred;
- whether tangible assets (such as buildings, property, etc.) are transferred;
- whether intangible assets (such as goodwill) are transferred;
- whether the majority of employees are taken on by the new employer;
- whether customers are transferred;
- the degree of similarity between the activities carried on before and after the transfer; and
- the period for which activities cease (if at all).

Case study

Kimberley Housing Group Ltd v. Hambley and others (2008)

Leena Homes had a contract with the Home Office to provide accommodation and related services in the Teeside area for asylum seekers. In 2006 it lost the contract, which was instead awarded to two contractors – Kimberley and Angel. Kimberley and Angel both denied that TUPE applied and Leena's employees lost their jobs. Six of them brought Employment Tribunal claims. The questions for the Tribunal were:

- Does TUPE apply where there is not just one transferee?
- Which of the two transferees did each claimant transfer to if TUPE did apply?

The Employment Tribunal held that there had been a service provision change, TUPE applied, and the liabilities under the contract could be split between the two service providers. The EAT agreed and ruled that the correct approach was to consider which aspect of the activities the employee was assigned to. The Tribunal needed to establish which transferee had, following the service provision change, taken up the activities to which each claimant was assigned. In this case, all six claimants transferred to Kimberley, which had taken up the vast majority of the activities previously performed by Leena.

There have been other recent Tribunal decisions that have found there was no service provision change on a re-tendering exercise where contracts were lost and awarded to a number of new contractors. This was because it was not possible to identify which of the new contractors was performing the activities previously performed by each outgoing contractor, and it was not therefore possible to say to which contractor any particular employee had transferred. The EAT recognised that there may be circumstances where a service provided by one contractor to the client is so fragmented that a service provision change has not taken place.

TUPE also applies on a service provision change. A service provision change covers situations where a contract to provide a client (public or private sector) with a business service, e.g. office cleaning, workplace catering, etc., is:

- awarded to a contractor ('contracted out' or 'outsourced');
- re-let to a new contractor on subsequent re-tendering ('reassigned'); or
- ended with the bringing 'in house' of the service activities in question ('contracted in' or 'insourced').

There will not be a service provision change where:

- the contract is wholly or mainly for the supply of goods for the client's use;
- the activities are carried out in connection with a single event or task of short-term duration;

- there is no identifiable grouping of employees providing the service; or
- any organised grouping does not have, as its principal purpose, the provision of services to a particular client, e.g. where employees provide services to a number of clients.

The original employer or service provider is known as the 'transferor', whereas the new employer or service provider to whom the business or contract is transferred is known as the 'transferee'.

Cross border transfers

There has been debate about whether TUPE applies to overseas transfers. The case of *Holis* ruled that TUPE has the potential to apply to a transfer of a business from the UK to another country, although careful analysis about whether TUPE applies will be needed in each case.

Implications of TUPE 2006

A summary of the principal implications of TUPE 2006 is as follows:

- Employees who were assigned immediately before the transfer to the relevant business / service become employees of the transferee.
- The terms and conditions of their employment transfer to the transferee. All contractual terms transfer, including certain rights relating to occupational pension schemes.
- In broad terms, liabilities in relation to the transferring employees transfer to the transferee.
- Changes to terms and conditions of the transferring employees will be void if the sole or principal reason for the change is the transfer itself, or a reason connected with the transfer which is not an economic, technical or organisational reason (an 'ETO reason') entailing a change in the workforce.
- Any employee dismissals will be automatically unfair where the sole

or principal reason for the dismissal is the transfer itself, or a reason connected with the transfer which is not an ETO reason entailing a change in the workforce.

- Collective agreements and trade union recognition in respect of transferring employees usually transfer to the transferee.
- Obligations exist for both parties to inform and (in certain circumstances) to consult with employee representatives. Both transferor and transferee are jointly and severally liable for any failure by the transferor to inform and consult.
- There is an obligation on the transferor to provide the transferee with certain specified information about the transferring employees (e.g. their identity and age), known as employee liability information, at least 14 days before completion of the transfer (*see below*).
- There is the right to make permitted variations to terms and conditions of employment on the transfer of an insolvent business, provided the changes are designed to safeguard employment opportunities by ensuring the survival of the undertaking, and the changes are agreed with appropriate representatives of the employees.

Which employees transfer?

Only those assigned to the business or service that is subject to the relevant transfer will transfer under TUPE 2006.

The key questions will be the amount of time they spend working for the business or providing the service, whether they are part of the organisational framework, the nature of their responsibilities and reporting lines.

Also, only those employed 'immediately before the transfer' will transfer, or those who would have been employed immediately before the transfer if they had not been otherwise unfairly dismissed for a reason connected to the transfer.

There is nothing to prevent the transferor from inserting employees into the business just before the undertaking is transferred. Only proper investigation and due diligence on the part of the transferee can sort out whether such potentially undesirable employees have been 'dumped' into the business.

Employees have the right to object to transferring to a new employer. However, if they exercise this right, their employment terminates immediately. There will be no dismissal and no resignation and accordingly they will have no right to claim compensation as a result. An exception is that the employee would still have the right to claim constructive dismissal if the employer commits a repudiatory breach of contract or because of actual or planned detrimental changes to his terms and conditions.

The worker must be an employee of the transferor (not a self-employed contractor).

Changing terms and conditions

Changes to terms and conditions are void (i.e. ineffective) if the sole or principal reason is the transfer itself, or a reason connected with the transfer that is not an ETO reason entailing changes in the workforce.

Changes to terms and conditions are potentially effective (i.e. effective, subject to being agreed between the parties) if the sole or principal reason is not the transfer itself but is a reason connected with the transfer that is an ETO reason entailing changes in the workforce. One of the predominant reasons for changing terms and conditions is to harmonise terms and conditions; in normal circumstances this will not qualify as an ETO reason.

There is no particular time period following which a change will no longer be connected to the transfer. It will simply be a matter of fact as to whether the causal link has been broken.

One way of circumventing this difficulty is to terminate employment and to re-engage on revised terms. If an employee is dismissed for a reason connected to the transfer, that dismissal is automatically unfair. The employee would then have the right to claim unfair dismissal. So this route is only viable with the consent of the employee.

Legal advice should be sought to manage any change to terms and conditions, the reason for which could be considered to relate to the transfer.

Information and consultation

Both the transferor and the transferee must provide information and, if necessary, consult with 'appropriate representatives' (i.e. trade unions if they exist, or elected employee representatives) of any employees affected by the transfer.

The transferor and transferee must provide the following information in writing to the appropriate representatives of their respective affected employees:

- Confirmation that the transfer is to take place;
- When it will take place;
- The reasons for it;
- The 'legal, economic and social implications' of the transfer;
- Any 'measures' that the transferor envisages taking towards the affected employees (if there are no such measures, that should be made clear); and
- Any 'measures' that the transferee envisages taking towards the affected employees (again, if there are no such measures, that should be made clear).

The transferee is under a duty to give information to the transferor about the measures it intends to take in relation to the affected employees.

If there are no 'measures' then there is no need to consult. Given the wide interpretation of 'measures' it is rare that there will be no need to consult. The information must be given sufficiently in advance of the transfer to enable proper consultation to take place if necessary. The consultation must be with a view to seeking agreement.

If either employer fails to inform and consult in compliance with TUPE, the representatives may present a complaint to an Employment Tribunal within three months of the completion of the transfer.

If the Tribunal finds that the complaint is well founded, it may order the employer who has failed to comply with the duty to pay appropriate compensation to affected employees. The amount of compensation will be that which the Tribunal considers just and equitable having regard to the seriousness of the failure of the employer in question to comply with their duties, and will not exceed an amount equal to 13 weeks' gross pay (uncapped) per employee.

The transferor and transferee are jointly and severally liable for any award of compensation made by an Employment Tribunal for failure by the transferor to comply with the information and consultation requirements. The rationale on making the two parties jointly and severally liable is that, if such a liability were to pass wholly to the transferee, there would arguably be little or no incentive for the transferor to comply with the relevant information and consultation requirements.

Employee liability information

The 1981 TUPE Regulations did not require a transferor to provide a transferee with any details whatsoever about the transferring workforce.

However, in standard business sales details of the transferring employees were, and still are, generally provided as part of the due diligence process, backed up by warranties and indemnities in the sale agreement which enable the transferee to sue on those contractual provisions if undisclosed liabilities materialise post-transfer. However, under TUPE 1981, where there was no direct contractual relationship between the transferor and transferee (say, in the context of outsourcing) the transferee faced greater risk of unexpected liability.

TUPE 2006 introduced a new duty to provide 'employee liability information' to address this issue, contained in Regulation 11. It is important, as failure to comply could lead to the transferor having to pay a large amount of compensation to the transferee. However, in most business sales (or classic transfers) due diligence will already have been conducted by the transferee before completion to gain information about the employees. In those circumstances the liability created by TUPE 2006 will often be secondary to any contractual assurances. The statutory obligation is more relevant in contracting-out arrangements where there is no direct contractual relationship between the outgoing and incoming service provider, or where the respective bargaining positions are such that the transferor might have managed to close the deal without giving warranties.

Under Regulation 11 of TUPE 2006 the transferor has a duty to provide 'employee liability information' to the transferee not less than 14 days in advance of the transfer in respect to each employee assigned to the transferring business or service.

Employee liability information means:

- the identity and age of the employee;
- the information that would be contained in a Section 1 statement of particulars of employment under the Employment Rights Act 1996;
- disciplinary and grievance proceedings taken by or against an employee within the previous two years in circumstances where the ACAS Code of Practice on Disciplinary and Grievance Procedures applies;
- legal action that has been brought by an employee within the past two years or that the transferor has reasonable grounds to believe that the employee might bring; and
- details of collective agreements that will have effect in relation to the employee after the transfer.

This is wider than simply providing information about employees who will actually transfer. Transferees will also need to know about employees whose claims they may be liable for, for example, employees dismissed before the transfer, because of the transfer, or for a reason connected to the transfer.

If the transferor fails to comply with its duty to provide employee liability information, the transferee can apply to the Employment Tribunal for compensation, which will be assessed with regard to the losses suffered with a minimum award of £500 per employee.

See also: Contractors, p.93; Dismissal, p.146; Employee consultation, p.160; Employment Tribunals, p.179; Outsourcing, p.377; Redundancy, p.429; Trade unions, p.516.

Sources of further information

Workplace Law's **TUPE Transfers 2007: Rights and Responsibilities Special Report** is aimed at people who have to deal with TUPE issues on a regular basis, and sets out what the Transfer of Undertakings (Protection of Employment) Regulations (TUPE) 2006 legislation is intended to do, what it actually does and how the process may be managed. The Report defines exactly what and who is transferred in a TUPE transfer (and what isn't), what the roles and responsibilities are of the transferor and transferee, and how the whole process should be managed.

Using case law examples, the report highlights what can and does go wrong, how TUPE relates to contractors and service providers, whether union membership transfers and is recognised, and other issues ancillary to protecting employees and employers during a business transfer or takeover. For more information visit www.workplacelaw.net.

BIS Guidance – Employment rights on the transfer of an undertaking: www.berr.gov.uk/files/file20761.pdf

VAT

Richard Woolich, DLA Piper

Key points
- Value Added Tax (VAT) is a tax charged on most goods and services that VAT-registered businesses provide in the UK, or that businesses supply in the UK. It is also charged on goods and some services that are imported from countries outside the European Union (EU), and brought into the UK from other EU countries.
- VAT is charged when a VAT-registered business sells to either another business or to a non-business customer, and the place of supply is in the UK.
- When VAT-registered businesses buy goods or services they can generally reclaim the VAT they have paid, although there are some exceptions, e.g. for businesses in financial services, charities, educational and health establishments.

Legislation
- Employment Agencies Act 1973.
- Value Added Tax Act 1994.

Introduction
There are three rates of VAT in the UK, depending on the goods or services the business provides:

1. Standard – 20%.
2. Reduced – 5%.
3. Zero – 0%.

There are also some goods and services that are exempt from VAT and outside the UK VAT system altogether.

Businesses add VAT to the price they charge when they provide goods and services to:

- *business customers* – for example a clothing manufacturer adds VAT to the prices they charge a clothes shop; and/or
- *non-business customers* – members of the public or 'consumers' – for example a hairdressing salon includes VAT in the prices they charge members of the public.

If you're a VAT-registered business, in most cases you:

- charge VAT on the goods and services you provide; and
- reclaim the VAT you pay when you buy goods and services for your business.

If you're not VAT-registered then you can't reclaim the VAT you pay when you purchase goods and services.

If you're a business and the goods or services you provide count as what's known as 'taxable supplies' you'll have to register for VAT if either:

- your turnover for the previous 12 months has gone over a specific limit – called the 'VAT threshold' (currently £73,000); or
- you think your turnover will soon go over this limit.

You can choose to register for VAT if you want, even if you don't have to, if you are below the threshold above, or if you have started a business. This will enable you to recover VAT on costs.

VAT

Employees and consultants

The services of an employee (which includes a director) are not subject to VAT. Article 10 of the EU Council Directive 2006/112/EC (EU Directive) states that persons are excluded from carrying on an economic activity independently 'in so far as they are bound to an employer by a contract of employment or by any other legal ties creating the relationship of employer and employee as regards working conditions, remuneration and the employer's liability'. Accordingly, employers do not have any direct VAT costs in hiring employees. The tests as to whether an individual is an employee (as opposed to a self-employed consultant) follow case law, including the degree of control over the individual, whether the individual can dictate his own hours, uses his own equipment and whether the individual can genuinely appoint a substitute.

A self-employed consultant does, however, potentially make taxable supplies of service and where a consultant is resident or established in the UK and supplies its services to a UK based business, the place of supply will be in the UK and it must generally charge UK VAT. This would not be a concern for most businesses in retail or manufacturing, which would be able to reclaim the VAT, assuming they hold a valid VAT invoice. But VAT is a real cost for banks, insurance companies, hospitals, charities and educational establishments, which make principally exempt supplies. Where the consultant is not registered for VAT and is trading below the VAT threshold, currently £73,000, no VAT would be charged. If the business receiving the consultant's services has its only business establishment outside the UK, or the fixed establishment of the business most closely connected with the receipt of the services is outside the UK, then the business would be liable

for VAT in the relevant jurisdiction under the reverse charge where its relevant establishment is located in the EU, and depending on local VAT law, there may be no VAT if the business' relevant establishment is outside the EU.

Supplies of staff

The supplies by a company or other entity of its staff (e.g. a personal service company that employs a consultant, or an employment agency that employs staff) is similarly liable to VAT. The value of the supplies will include any fee and staff costs such as salary, NICs and pension contributions. Businesses in exempt and partially exempt sectors, which rely heavily on temporary staff, and the supply of staff by employment bureaux, have a choice of structuring their arrangements on a principal or agency basis. Under the employment agency basis, the customers would receive an introduction to temporary staff, and simply pay VAT on the commission, not on the full salary costs, thereby lessening the VAT cost. But they would then need to employ the staff and take on employment law and regulatory obligations.

Alternatively, the employment business would provide a supply of staff and take on all the employment law obligations, but the downside is that VAT would be due on the full value of the services, including the salary costs. The VAT implications of the principal model were modified until 1 April 2009 by the Staff Hire Concession, whereby HM Revenue & Customs (HMRC) agreed that, subject to certain conditions, where the employment business acted as principal, the salary cost would be excluded from the value of the supply, but this has since been abolished for employment businesses.

The recent First Tier Tribunal decision in *Reed Employment v. HMRC* seems at first sight to be very good news for exempt and partially exempt businesses, as it seems to offer the benefits of a lower VAT cost and not having to take on employment obligations. In this case, it was held that the employment business was providing introduction services, rather than a supply of staff, and should only charge VAT on its profit margin above the salary cost, and exclude the salary costs themselves. The critical issues were that there could not be a supply of staff if the bureau never passed control of the workers to the recipient business and, furthermore, as a matter of economic reality, because the recipient business bore the economic cost of the staff, the salary could not form part of the value of the supply for VAT.

But HMRC has rejected the approach taken in *Reed*, and attempted to restrict it to its facts, perhaps in an attempt to limit the number of claims for wrongly paid VAT. However, it gives no reasons for rejecting the technical reasoning of the First Tier Tribunal and it seems inevitable that further litigation will be initiated to clarify whether this analysis can be maintained in other cases. In the meantime, it seems prudent to see if arrangements can be structured similarly to constitute introductory services where the business customer is exempt or partially exempt. Employment businesses should make protective claims for a repayment by HMRC in the meantime, pending clarification of this issue.

There are, however, certain supplies of staff that are treated as not made in the course of a business and are outside the scope of VAT. These include secondments between and by government departments, secondment between National Health bodies, and some secondments between local authorities.

There is still a staff hire concession for businesses that are not employment

businesses within the meaning of the Employment Agencies Act 1973. Where a member of staff is seconded to another business that exercises exclusive control over the allocation and performance of the employee's duties during the secondment, and is responsible for paying the employee's remuneration directly to the employee or discharges the employer's obligations to pay any third party PAYE, NICs or pension contributions, then such payments are excluded from the value of the supply, but this is subject to conditions and must not be done with a view to financial gain by the employer.

Joint employment and paymaster concessions

In cases of genuine joint employment by two or more separate entities there is no taxable supply between the joint employers in accordance with the concession in VAT Notice 700/34/05 (see *Sources of further information*), subject to the conditions stipulated in the VAT Notice.

Furthermore, the VAT Notice provides a concession that paymaster arrangements are outside the scope of VAT. These occur where staff are jointly employed and one entity pays the salaries and recharges to the other employer, or staff are separately employed by different associated companies and one entity pays the salaries and recharges the others.

New exemption for cost sharing

A new VAT exemption for cost sharing is also being consulted upon by HMRC. The principle is that VAT exempt and non-business entities will be able to form and become members of a cost-sharing group, and share certain costs, without charging VAT on recharges. This should even be capable of operating cross-border. This exemption will be beneficial to exempt businesses and non-business organisations and is anticipated to be enacted as part of the UK legislation in April 2012, even though it is already contained in the EU Directive at Article 132(f). It will be necessary for the costs to be recharged at cost, and the costs must be 'directly necessary' for exercising the VAT-exempt or non-business activities. The cost-sharing exemption should facilitate VAT-efficient structures for cost-sharing, but may not be available for costs such as back office outsourcing for accounting, finance, IT services, HR and procurements as they are not 'directly necessary'. Furthermore, charities may only be able to take advantage of the exemption if the costs are incurred for their non-business activities. It is expected to be of interest, for example, to universities sharing research equipment and resources.

Business entertainment expenditure

The basic rule for VAT purposes is that input tax cannot be reclaimed on business entertainment expenses. However, input tax on staff entertainment can be reclaimed, unless staff are attending the event as well as non-staff and the staff's function is to act as hosts.

Where directors attend staff events, then the input VAT on the event can be reclaimed in full. However, where directors attend events that do not include staff members, none of the input tax can be reclaimed.

Salary sacrifice

Where an employee has a choice of accepting a contractual reduction in salary in return for a benefit, for example, a pension contribution, then that is known as a salary sacrifice.

The case of *Astra Zeneca UK Ltd v. HMRC* held that salary sacrifices could have VAT implications. In this case, the employer gave its employees face value vouchers in return for a reduced salary. The employer claimed it could recover the VAT on the purchase of the vouchers, but was not making a supply of services in providing the vouchers. The Court ruled that the provision of the vouchers, in return for the employees giving up part of their cash remuneration, was a supply of services. Accordingly, the employer could recover the input VAT incurred on acquiring the vouchers but had to account for VAT on the consideration received from its employees by way of the salary sacrificed.

In the past it was HMRC policy to make a distinction between an employer supplying goods and services to an employee in return for the employee agreeing to 'deduct' part of his salary in return (whereby the employer would be able to deduct input tax, and there would be a taxable supply by the employer), and goods and services provided to an employee as part of a 'salary sacrifice', involving an amendment to the employee's contract (whereby input tax would be deductible by the employer, but there would be no taxable supply). HMRC now considers, following *Astra Zeneca*, that there is no distinction between cases involving deductions from salary and salary sacrifices. In both cases, the amount of salary foregone is consideration for supplies of benefits, and in both cases input tax will be recoverable by the employer in accordance with the normal rules and output tax will be due from the employer on the provision of the goods or services, depending on the VAT status of those goods and services.

The new policy for salary sacrifices will be applied from 1 January 2012.

The employer will have to account for output VAT on the amount of salary foregone by the employee, or the cost to the employer of the benefit (if greater). This raises some valuation issues. The new policy will affect arrangements such as the cycle to work scheme and home computers, but may also include food and catering, as well as the provision of vouchers. Many organisations that suffer a restriction on their VAT recovery, including charities, universities and financial institutions, will now benefit from VAT recovery on these goods and services, but non-VAT registered businesses will need to be aware that salary sacrifice schemes will count towards the VAT registration threshold, and the potential requirement to register for VAT. There are some uncertainties as to how the new practice will work in relation to cars, where in some circumstances there is partial VAT recovery by the employer.

See also: Agency and temporary workers, p.25; Pensions, p.387; Self-employment, p.465.

Sources of further information

HMRC: VAT Notice 700/34/05: http://bit.ly/q2zOcg

Value Added Tax Act 1994: www.workplacelaw.net/news/display/id/35935

Vetting, barring, blacklisting and social engineering

Pinsent Masons Employment Group

Key points

- Section 144 of the Criminal Justice and Immigration Act 2008 gave the Information Commissioner (the privacy regulator) a new power to impose monetary fines of up to £500,000 in respect of breaches of the Data Protection Act 1998. This power has been in operation since 6 April 2010.

- Under Section 77 of the Criminal Justice and Immigration Act 2008, the Secretary of State may introduce a custodial sentence in respect of knowingly or recklessly obtaining personal data or the information contained within such data without the consent of the data controller (i.e. the person in lawful control of the relevant database).

- There are legal obligations on employers acting as data controllers under the Data Protection Act 1998 to ensure that they procure personal data about prospective and current employees in a fair and lawful manner.

- Section 55 of the Data Protection Act 1998 makes it a criminal offence to knowingly or recklessly obtain personal data or the information contained within such data without the consent of the person in lawful control of the relevant database.

- Once in force, Section 56 of the Data Protection Act 1998 will make it a criminal offence for a data controller, in connection with employment or prospective employment, to compel individuals to use their right of subject access to seek access to specified data (e.g. criminal records).

- The Government introduced the Employment Relations Act 1999 (Blacklists) Regulations 2010 to outlaw the compilation, dissemination and use of employment blacklists. This chapter does not deal with the Regulations but looks primarily at the impact of the Data Protection Act 1998 on pre-employment vetting.

Legislation

- Police Act 1997.
- Data Protection Act 1998.
- Human Rights Act 1998.
- Criminal Justice and Immigration Act 2008.
- Employment Relations Act 1999 (Blacklists) Regulations 2010.

Background

The unlawful obtaining of the personal data of prospective employees hit the headlines in March 2009 when the media widely reported an investigation by the Information Commissioner's Office into the use of a database run by Mr Ian Kerr, trading as The Consulting Association. It was reported that the database contained details of construction workers' trade union activity and employment history. It had allegedly been used by 40 construction companies, without the knowledge of the individuals, to vet potential employees.

There were subsequent calls to strengthen the law by introducing new Regulations to prohibit blacklisting. Draft Regulations were introduced in 2003 but were never implemented. These draft Regulations have now been revised and went before Parliament for approval in early 2010 and came into force on 2 March 2010. Along with the Data Protection Act 1998 (DPA) this is the key legislation that applies in relation to pre-employment vetting.

Notwithstanding the blacklisting controversy, it is important not to lose sight of the fact that vetting can often be an important part of the recruitment process. In some cases, employers are legally obliged to vet, for example, for certain posts that involve working with children / vulnerable adults. In other situations, there may be good reasons to vet, where there are particular risks to the employer, customers or others if vetting is not undertaken. The crucial point is that vetting should be done lawfully and fairly.

Legal obligations on employers

The DPA sets out eight data protection principles. A number of those principles have an impact on how employers should obtain information about prospective employees.

This chapter looks at the relevant principles and what these principles mean in practice for employers who wish to undertake pre-employment vetting in a way that complies with the DPA. For these purposes, vetting involves the employer undertaking investigations about the employee using third party sources.

Some key questions that arise in this context are as follows:

- Do you have a good reason to vet?
- When should you carry out the relevant checks?
- What have you told applicants? Is consent required?

- What have you told the Information Commissioner?
- What sources will you use? Are they reliable?
- Do you use third party recruitment agents? If so, what obligations are imposed on them in relation to obtaining personal data?

First data protection principle

Personal data must be processed fairly and lawfully

Employers have an obligation to process personal data about applicants fairly and lawfully. This obligation requires employers to:

- provide applicants with an appropriate data protection notice including:
  - the identity of the employer;
  - the purpose or purposes for which the data are intended to be processed; and
  - any other information that is necessary to make the processing fair (e.g. disclosure to third parties).
- satisfying one of the conditions for processing the personal data, as set out in Schedule 2 of the DPA; and
- if the vetting involves processing sensitive personal data (e.g. conviction data), satisfying a sensitive data condition, as set out in Schedule 3 of the DPA.

In practical terms, the cornerstones of the first data protection principle are transparency and proportionality.

Transparency

The Information Commissioner's Data Protection Employment Practices (the 'Code') is a good source of information about what the data protection principles mean in practice. It is clear from the Code that recruitment forms should set out that vetting will take place and what will be involved in the vetting exercise.

In particular, applicants should be told what sources will be used and what information will be revealed to those sources as part of the vetting exercise.

The Code also makes clear that applicants should be told at the outset that their application is likely to be rejected if the vetting exercise reveals particular information about them.

Another aspect of transparency is the notification provided to the Information Commissioner. Under the DPA, except in limited circumstances, a data controller is required to notify the Information Commissioner of the types of processing of personal data undertaken by such data controller. If applicable, it is advisable to check that the notification is up to date and covers use of personal data for vetting purposes.

Proportionality

As indicated above, data controllers who undertake pre-employment vetting must satisfy one of the conditions for processing the personal data collected, as set out in Schedule 2 of the DPA. The condition that is likely to apply is that the processing is necessary for the purposes of legitimate business interests pursued by the employer and is not unwarranted by reason of prejudice to the rights and freedoms or legitimate interests of the applicant. In order to satisfy this condition, employers must be able to demonstrate that they have acted in a way that it is proportionate to the risks that they are seeking to address.

Proportionality demands that employers consider whether the vetting is justified by reference to the advertised job. The Code suggests that vetting is likely to be justified if it is undertaken to reduce particular and significant risks to the employer, to the employer's customers or to others.

However, while certain types of vetting may be justified for employees holding particular positions of trust within the business, comprehensive vetting is unlikely to be justified for all employees. The Code suggests that employers should also consider whether there is a less intrusive way to get the information that they need, for example, by getting the relevant information from the applicant and then verifying it.

Based on the Code, it seems that acting fairly or proportionately is also about carrying out any necessary checks at the appropriate point in the recruitment process and ensuring that detailed checks are only carried out in relation to applicants who are chosen for the job. If the vetting involves processing sensitive personal data (e.g. conviction data), employers must comply with one of the additional conditions set out in Schedule 3 of the DPA for processing such sensitive personal data. In many cases, employers will need the explicit consent of the individual.

While consent is not always necessary to undertake vetting, in practice, it is a good idea to provide a data protection notice in writing and to ask applicants to provide consent at the same time (e.g. in the relevant application form). In any event, as indicated in the Code, it is important to secure the consent of an applicant if it is required to obtain information or documents from a third party.

Third data protection principle

Personal data must be adequate, relevant and not excessive in relation to the purpose or purposes for which they are processed

In order to be fair and lawful, the collection of personal data must comply with the other relevant principles of the DPA, including the third data protection principle. Even where vetting is justified, employers often make the mistake of using the vetting process as a general 'fishing expedition' to gather as much information as possible about applicants. The Code makes clear that, once employers have identified a justifiable objective for vetting, they should seek only such information as is necessary to achieve that objective. The Code also suggests that employers should only look for information where they are likely to find it and should not ask for information from the applicant's family or close associates unless there are exceptional reasons for doing so.

For these reasons, indiscriminate vetting exercises using social networking sites raise a number of data protection concerns. It is certainly arguable that this type of vetting amounts to general intelligence-gathering and is comparable to approaching the family and friends of the applicant. Use of information obtained as part of a vetting exercise must also take account of anti-discrimination laws.

Fourth data protection principle

Personal data shall be accurate and, where necessary, kept up to date
The source from which personal data is obtained is often the key to ensuring its accuracy and reliability. Consequently, another principle that is relevant to obtaining personal data is the fourth data protection principle.

So, how does this requirement translate into what employers should do in practice? Clearly, any recruitment decision should be based on accurate data. A key point outlined in the Code is that employers should take into consideration the reliability of the source of the information before deciding what weight to attach to it. The Code makes clear that employers must

not base a recruitment decision solely on information obtained from an untrustworthy source and should ensure that there is a process by which applicants can comment on information unearthed by the vetting exercise. Such process should also allow the feedback from the applicant to be taken into account in deciding whether the applicant should be selected for the job.

The requirement to ensure accuracy raises further concerns about the practice of referring to social networking sites as a means of vetting prospective employees. There are serious questions about the reliability of information obtained from such sources as the basis for a recruitment decision. In any event, individuals should be given the opportunity to make representations regarding information that will affect such a decision.

Seventh data protection principle

Appropriate technical and organisational measures shall be taken against unauthorised or unlawful processing of personal data and against accidental loss or destruction of, or damage to, personal data
This data protection principle is likely to have a bearing on the collection of personal data to the extent that employers must put measures in place to ensure the security of personal data submitted by applicants. For example, if applicants are invited to submit personal data via the employer's website, the employer should ensure that security measures such as encryption-based software are in place to protect the personal data while it is in transit.

In addition, security is an important issue if employers will be using a third party to obtain personal data on their behalf. For example, if a recruitment agency is engaged to undertake recruitment checks on behalf of an employer, a robust contract should be put in place to address the specific data protection risks.

The contract with a third party service provider must meet the minimum requirements set out in the DPA to govern a data processing relationship, which include, requiring the third party to put in place appropriate technical and organisational measures to protect the data being processed, a requirement to take steps to ensure the reliability of staff who have access to the data, an obligation on the third party to act only on instructions from the employer.

Due diligence should also be carried out on the third party service provider both prior to appointment and during the term of the contract. The contract with the third party service provider should include audit rights for the employer or another equivalent means in order to check whether the third party is complying with the contract and particularly whether the appropriate technical and organisational measures have been put in place.

Other data protection principles

This chapter focuses in particular on the data protection principles that are likely to have an impact on how personal data is obtained, i.e., the first, third, fourth and seventh data protection principles. However, all of the eight data protection principles outlined in the DPA will be relevant to the ongoing storage and processing of the relevant personal data. See 'Data protection' (p.101) for more information.

New power to fine

So what happens if employers procure personal data in a way that breaches the DPA? Historically, the enforcement powers available to the Information

Commissioner in respect of a breach of the data protection principles were quite limited. However, Section 144 of the Criminal Justice and Immigration Act 2008 introduced powers whereby the Information Commissioner may impose monetary fines in respect of breaches of the DPA. The new powers are contained in Sections 55a-e of the DPA and have been in force since 6 April 2010 (but do not apply retrospectively).

Essentially, the new Section 55a allows the Information Commissioner to serve a monetary penalty notice on a data controller if satisfied that:

■ there is a serious failure to comply with the data protection principles;
■ the failure was of a kind likely to cause substantial damage or distress; and
■ the failure was either deliberate or the controller knew or ought to have known of the risk of contravening the data protection principles and failed to take reasonable steps to prevent such contravention.

Guidance issued by the Information Commissioner indicates that the penalty will be used as a sanction as well as a general deterrent, but reserved only for the most serious cases. As such, the penalty will only be imposed when it is 'reasonable and proportionate,' given an assessment of all the facts, with particular attention paid to the level of fault, the likelihood of substantial damage, the nature of the data and the number of individuals affected.

The maximum penalty (set out in the Data Protection (Monetary Penalties) (Maximum Penalty and Notices) Regulations 2010) is set at £500,000. The level of fine within this limit will be determined with reference to a range of factors including:

- the seriousness, duration and effect of the contravention;
- any procedures to avoid the contravention and steps taken once the contravention is brought to the data controller's attention;
- the role of senior figures in the contravention; and
- the impact the penalty would have on the data controller (including concession for genuine financial hardship).

Since the new powers came into force, the Information Commissioner has issued a number of monetary penalty notices, some of which are set out below.

ACS Law

ACS Law used IP addresses to accuse people of illegal file sharing. The ICO would have fined ACS Law £200,000 but because the firm was a sole practitioner and had ceased trading, the individual, Andrew Crossley, was fined £1,000 due to his limited means.

A4e Limited

A4e Limited had an unencrypted laptop used by an employee for home working. The laptop contained personal data of 24,000 customers and was stolen during a burglary. A4e Limited was fined £60,000

Hertfordshire County Council

Employees in the childcare litigation unit accidentally sent two faxes to the wrong recipients on two separate occasions. The first misdirected fax was meant for a barristers' chambers but was sent instead to a member of the public. The second misdirected fax, sent 13 days later, contained information relating to the care proceedings of three children, the previous convictions of two individuals, domestic violence records and care professionals' opinions on the cases. Hertfordshire County Council was fined £100,000.

What is also known is that the Information Commissioner will consider its objective to maximise the deterrent effect of fines by setting an example to other data controllers, where it is necessary to do so to counter the prevalence of such breaches. Therefore, it is within the Information Commissioner's power to make an example of household brands or major organisations that breach the DPA to promote compliance by sending a clear message to other organisations that serious compliance failures, not necessarily limited to security breaches, will attract a fine. Therefore, the market status of an organisation could also be a factor in determining whether or not a fine will be levied by the Information Commissioner.

Section 55 Data Protection Act 1998 – 'Social engineering'

As well as the data protection principles, there are a number of other provisions of the DPA that have a bearing on the procurement of personal data. Section 55 of the DPA (referred to as 'social engineering') makes it a criminal offence knowingly or recklessly to obtain or disclose personal data or the information contained within such data without the consent of the data controller. The example given in the Code is of an employer who misleads another data controller into disclosing information by indicating untruthfully that the applicant had agreed to such information being disclosed.

Consequently, not only must personal data relating to prospective employees be procured by an employer in accordance with the data protection principles, but employers may also be guilty of a criminal offence if they try to obtain personal data about such prospective employees in an underhand way, i.e. without the consent of the data controller of the relevant data.

Under Section 77 of the Criminal Justice and Immigration Act 2008, the Secretary of State may make an order to introduce the following custodial sentences in respect of a breach of Section 55:

- On summary conviction, up to 12 months' imprisonment; and
- On conviction on indictment, up to two years' imprisonment.

Before making such an order, the Secretary of State must consult the Information Commissioner and such media organisations or others as he considers appropriate. Fines can apply in the alternative or together with imprisonment.

Employers should also remember that there is a possibility that a director or officer of a company could be vicariously liable under Section 55 as a result of the actions of one of their employees. Consequently, it is important to put in place policies and procedures to ensure that employees understand their data protection responsibilities, not only in respect of personal data relating to prospective employees but also in respect of personal data relating to colleagues, customers and other third parties.

Section 56 Data Protection Act 1998 – 'Enforced subject access'

Under Section 7 of the DPA, individuals can apply for access to information held about them – this right is known as the right of subject access. Enforced subject access occurs where an employer compels an individual to use their right of subject access to obtain personal details to be used by the employer for the purposes of making a recruitment decision.

For example, an individual may be forced to access and supply his medical information by a potential employer as part of the recruitment process.

Section 56 makes it a criminal offence for an employer, in connection with employment or prospective employment, to require an individual to produce 'relevant records'. 'Relevant records' are essentially criminal records and include records showing convictions or cautions where the data controller is a chief officer of police or the Secretary of State.

In general, the practice of enforced subject access in this area is considered to be in conflict with the Rehabilitation of Offenders Act 1974. This is because the information provided in response to a subject access request for 'relevant records' will usually include information about spent convictions, and most employers are not entitled to ask for this information under the Rehabilitation of Offenders Act. However, Section 56 has not yet been implemented and is not due to be brought into force until certain provisions of the Police Act 1997 (i.e. those dealing with certificates of criminal records) have been brought into force.

Enforced subject access to health records does not give rise to a criminal offence. However, any term or condition in a contract is void to the extent that it requires an individual to supply or produce to any other person a 'health record' or a part or copy of such 'health record' that has been or is to be obtained by an individual through exercising their right of subject access. 'Health record' is defined in Section 68(2) of the Data Protection Act.

Practical guidelines

- Application forms / recruitment materials should set out all information necessary to ensure the fairness of any pre-employment vetting, i.e. the nature of the vetting, the purpose of the vetting etc. – generally it is a good idea to obtain consent to the relevant vetting at the same time the information is collected.

- Employers should check that their notification with the Information Commissioner is up to date and covers vetting if applicable.
- Vetting must be proportionate to the perceived risks to the employer or to the employer's customers / third parties.
- Information collected should be relevant to the objectives of the vetting exercise.
- When making a recruitment decision, employers should take account of the reliability of the sources from which the relevant information was obtained, should allow the individual to provide feedback, and should take that feedback into consideration.
- Employers should ensure that they have a written contract in place with third parties who will be carrying out recruitment checks on their behalf, that the contract meets the DPA minimum security requirements and that they undertake appropriate due diligence in relation to such third parties.
- Employers should have a policy that sets out employees' responsibilities in relation to the handling of personal data.

> *See also*: Criminal records, p.97; Data Protection, p.101; Medical records, p.304; Personnel files, p.392; Private life, p.404; Confidential waste, p.545.

Sources of further information

Information Commissioner's Data Protection Employment Practices Code: www.ico.gov.uk

Comment ...

Super-injunctions – to tweet or not to tweet

Kate Smith, Shoosmiths

The identities of a number of celebrities said to have taken out 'super-injunctions' to prevent the media reporting their private lives were, in the summer of 2011, revealed on Twitter and shared with thousands of users. A super-injunction is a form of injunction under which the media cannot report the existence of said injunction, or its details – in effect, a 'gagging order'. The media storm surrounding the alleged relationship between a married Premier League footballer and an ex-Big Brother contestant is one of several recent injunctions of this

Type, and came under scrutiny as a result of social networking site, Twitter. However, in a victory for irony, it then became discussed at length by the media.

This, combined with the fact that an MP circumvented the injunction by way of parliamentary privilege and named the footballer alleged to have taken out the injunction, has led to wild speculation about what will happen next in this area of law. Surely reform has to be high on the agenda?

Intrinsically related to the current debates about super-injunctions and their tenability in the ever-developing world of online communication, is what may happen if false allegations are made online, be that via social media sites or otherwise. If such allegations are made, then various parties risk becoming embroiled in accusations of 'online libel', with potentially severe

Kate Smith is a solicitor in Shoosmith's commercial litigation team, based in Milton Keynes. She acts primarily for international and UK-based companies, together with partnerships and individuals in commercial disputes. Kate studied Environmental Geology at the University of Leeds before completing the Graduate Diploma in Law, followed by the Legal Practice Course at The College of Law in York. Kate joined Shoosmiths as a newly-qualified solicitor in September 2008.

consequences. With the Government's draft Defamation Bill currently the subject of public consultation, together with the fact that injunctions and privacy laws are maintaining a continuous presence in the UK media, England's controversial libel laws are yet again the source of debate.

However, whilst the law in this area may receive something of a makeover, it is doubtful whether the legal system can stay ahead of the game when it comes to the role of technology in defamation cases.

There is no universally accepted definition of what makes a statement defamatory. Viewed broadly, though, a defamatory comment is one that is untrue and likely to damage the reputation of the subject in the eyes of 'right-thinking' people.

As communication technology advances, the law of defamation has been in danger of becoming obsolete. The law has emerged slowly over time to deal predominantly with traditional forms of publication and has struggled to adapt to new forms of social media, which are developing at something like breakneck speed.

The first known case of libel via Twitter was recently heard by the High Court in Wales, and is a good example of how the casual act of posting on a website can have serious and expensive consequences.

In the Twitter case, it was possible to identify the defendant with ease. More difficult, however, are situations in which defamatory material is posted online by anonymous website users. In situations where the main defendant may be 'person or persons unknown', a claimant will seek to pursue against the website host as well as the person making the defamatory statement.

The so-called 'publication rule' in English law poses particular concerns for website hosts and moderators. The rule states that every time a defamatory comment is viewed there is a new publication of that comment. Website hosts may be guilty of 'secondary publication' whereby they

> "As communication technology advances, the law of defamation has been in danger of becoming obsolete. The law has emerged slowly over time to deal predominantly with traditional forms of publication and has struggled to adapt to new forms of social media, which are developing at something like breakneck speed."

facilitate the publication of defamatory material by a third party.

The publication rule is particularly unfortunate for website hosts who, by the nature of their service, may end up publishing a defamatory comment thousands of times. The matter is further complicated by the ease with which foreign parties can sue one another in the English courts.

Generally speaking, as long as the defamatory statement has been published in England and the claimant has some sort of reputation in England, then they can sue there. Of course this rule was developed before the internet made it possible to publish anything, anywhere in the world, at the push of a button.

Internet Service Providers (ISPs) are generally protected from proceedings by the Electronic Commerce (EC Directive) Regulations 2002. Where ISPs act merely as conduits and remove defamatory information upon request they are unlikely to be liable for publication. Comparable rulings have been made concerning the role of search engines.

For those who run sites that allow the posting of user generated content, the decision of whether or not to moderate users' postings amounts to a dilemma. The more responsibility that is accepted for moderating a site, the more likely it is that the site's owners or moderators will be held liable for defamatory comments, especially if they are not taken down swiftly once a complaint has been made.

However, allowing entirely unmoderated postings may have an equally detrimental effect on the site's reputation. Even if legal liability is avoided, hosting a site that allows users to post unsavoury or defamatory comments may not be a wise decision from a public relations perspective.

Is change afoot with the draft Defamation Bill? The draft Bill proposes the introduction of a 'single publication' rule, which would mean only one publication would be deemed to take place when material is posted online, rather than a new one every time the information is viewed.

There is also a proposal to make it more difficult for foreign parties to sue one another in the English courts (so-called 'libel tourism'), because of England's relatively claimant-friendly regime.

What does this mean? The Government's new Bill may relieve some of the risks in respect of multiple publications and libel tourism for website hosts. However, the Bill is still the subject of public consultation and so its contents will not be confirmed for some time. These changes, if confirmed, may reduce the potential burden on website hosts and moderators to some extent but the courts are still likely to consider how widely a defamatory posting was viewed when calculating damages. If a moderator knew about a defamatory posting and left it available for viewing by large numbers of people they will struggle to avoid liability.

In relation to privacy injunctions in their myriad forms, there have been numerous recent suggestions that the law in its present form simply is inadequate and that reform is required. In particular, there has been a recent referral to the Joint Committee of Peers and Members of Parliament to investigate the use of privacy orders. It is probable that substantial changes may be made in the near future – watch this space!

Confidential waste

David Flint and Valerie Surgenor, MacRoberts LLP

Key points

- Confidential waste includes any record that contains personal information about a particular living individual, or information that is commercially sensitive.

- Examples include correspondence revealing contact details, personnel records, job applications and interview notes, salary records, Income Tax and National Insurance returns, contracts, tenders, purchasing and maintenance records and sensitive industrial relations negotiation material.

Legislation

- Official Secrets Act 1989.
- Data Protection Act 1998 (DPA 1998).
- Freedom of Information Act 2000 (FOIA 2000).
- Freedom of Information (Scotland) Act 2002 (FOISA 2002).
- Waste Electrical and Electronic Equipment (WEEE) Directive (2002/96/EC).
- The Landfill Regulations 2002.
- The Landfill (Scotland) Regulations 2003.
- Waste Electrical and Electronic Equipment Regulations 2004 (WEEE Regulations).
- The Waste Electrical and Electronic Equipment (Amendment) Regulations 2009.
- Data Retention (EC Directive) Regulations 2009.
- The Public Records (Scotland) Act 2011.

Implications of the Data Protection Act 1998

The DPA 1998 does not set out a standard way in which confidential waste should be disposed of; however, businesses must ensure that the steps they are taking meet with the intention of the DPA 1998.

The DPA 1998 covers all computer records, information held in a relevant filing system, discs and CDs (and in the case of public authorities all other information that is not held on computer records or a relevant filing system).

Companies have several responsibilities under the DPA 1998. They must ensure that data is not kept for longer than is necessary and also that when data is finished with it is destroyed in a safe and secure manner. Throwing files away into office bins in the hope that they will be adequately destroyed is not sufficient. Companies must take appropriate technical and organisational measures to prevent against unauthorised or unlawful processing of personal data and against accidental loss or destruction of, or damage to, personal data. The Act specifically states that in deciding the manner in which to destroy data, consideration must be given to the state of technological development at that time, the cost of the measures, the harm that might result from a breach in security, and the nature of the data to be disposed of.

The issues that must be addressed with regards to confidential waste in a paper environment are different to those that must be addressed in an electronic environment. Special care must be taken when destroying electronic records as these can even be reconstructed from deleted information. Erasing or reformatting computer disks (or personal computers with hard drives) that once contained confidential personal information is also insufficient.

Although the DPA 1998 does not prescribe an exact method by which confidential records should be destroyed, employers should consider the following:

- Procedures regarding the storage and disposal of personal data including computer disks, pen drives, USB memory sticks and print-outs should be reviewed.
- Waste paper containing personal data should be placed in a separate 'confidential' waste bin and shredded by a reputable contractor, who meets the new EN15713:2009 standard on securely destroying confidential waste and is registered and audited to ISO 9001:2008. It is also advisable to ensure that the contractor's employees are screened in accordance with BS 7858:2006.
- If sub-contractors are used as data processors, a sub-contractor who gives guarantees about security measures and takes reasonable steps to ensure compliance with those measures should be chosen. Furthermore, a contract should be drawn up with the data controller, and certificates of destruction (and recycling of equipment) of documents by the sub-contractor should be issued as proof that the process has been completed.
- A standard risk assessment should be completed in order to identify threats to the system, the vulnerability of the system, and the procedures that can be put in place in order to manage and reduce the risks.

Penalties for non-compliance

Contravention of the DPA 1998 is a criminal offence and the Information Commissioner has the discretion to impose financial penalties of up to £500,000 for serious breaches of the DPA 1998 on the issuance of a monetary penalty notice.

The ICO has recently published draft guidance on its powers to impose financial penalties. The guidance is not yet in force, as a consultation process is being carried out to allow businesses to comment on the guidance and request any further information which they would find helpful.

The guidance, in its draft form, provides that the ICO will consider the following when deciding the level of fine to be imposed:

- The level of harm individuals have suffered;
- Whether the breach has caused substantial damage or distress;
- Whether the contravention was deliberate; and
- Whether the organisation at fault knew there was a risk but didn't take any steps to prevent the breach.

It is possible for a single breach to attract the maximum penalty of £500,000 if that breach is serious enough, for example, losing customer data due to inadequate security.

Audits

Government departments found guilty of serious breaches of the DPA 1998 may find themselves the recipients of a compulsory audit notice. The purpose of audits is to allow the ICO to assess whether organisations are acting in compliance with the DPA 1998 and identify their strengths and weaknesses. Whilst the ICO hopes that government departments will consent to audits, if they do not, and the ICO takes the view that an audit is necessary, they can issue a compulsory audit notice and thereafter conduct an audit of a department. Whilst compulsory audits only apply to government departments at present, this may be extended to other organisations in the future.

The ICO has issued guidance that deals with both compulsory and voluntary audit notices. The guidance provides that an audit will be deemed necessary where:

- a risk assessment has been conducted and the result indicates that it is probable that personal data is not being processed in compliance with the Act;
- there is likelihood of damage or distress to individuals; and
- the organisation has unjustly refused to consent to an audit.

The risk assessment will take into account factors including, for example, compliance history, business intelligence, and the volume and nature of the personal data being processed.

The ICO has confirmed that a penalty will not be imposed in relation to a breach discovered whilst carrying out an audit. This may offer some comfort and encouragement for organisations to consent to an audit. A further incentive for cooperation is that the ICO has said it will, where appropriate, publicly identify organisations that do not offer a reasonable level of cooperation.

Individuals who suffer damage as a direct result of a contravention of the Data Protection Act by a data controller are entitled to be compensated for that damage. Prosecutions under the DPA 1998 are becoming increasingly common.

There is also a strong commercial incentive for businesses to protect personal data following the publicity of the Sony and Epsilon data breach scandals in 2011. A security hack of Sony's playstation network and user database resulted in the theft of information of what has been estimated to be around 100 million online gaming users. The information taken included names, email addresses, dates of birth, phone numbers, and debit and credit card details. Sony then had to contact all customers to warn them that their information had been taken and that they may receive correspondence, requesting personal information, which claimed to be from Sony. It is considered to be one of the biggest data loss incidents ever to occur.

US company Epsilon suffered data theft in respect of a significant (but undisclosed) number of customers. Epsilon is a marketing company that builds and hosts customer databases for about 2,500 companies, including major retail companies such Marks and Spencers and Play.com. Epsilon refused to disclose the full extent of the breach, but insisted that the data stolen only included email addresses and not credit card details. However, an email address is of significant value to hackers as it allows them to target customers by launching phishing attacks.

The above cases are just a couple of examples of a long line of security breaches in recent years.

Additional responsibilities for Public Authorities

FOISA and FOIA

Section 61 of the FOISA 2002 and Section 46 of the FOIA 2000 place additional responsibilities on Public Authorities regarding the management and disposal of their records. Section 61 and Section 46 respectively state that it is desirable for Public Authorities to follow the Code of Practice on Records Management (the Code). The Code sets out various practices regarding the creation, keeping, management and disposition of their records. The implications of the FOISA 2002 and the FOIA 2000 are very far-reaching as the Code is applicable to all records in all formats, including paper, electronic, video and microfilm. It should be noted that the ambit of this definition is wider than that under the DPA 1998, and extends to all personal data.

The issues discussed in the Code affecting the disposal of confidential information can be summarised as follows:

- The disposition of records must be undertaken in accordance with clearly established policies that have been formally adopted by authorities and are enforced by properly authorised staff. Authorities should establish a selection policy that sets out in broad terms the function for which records are likely to be selected for permanent preservation and the periods for which other records should be retained.
- Disposal schedules should be drawn up for each business area. These schedules should indicate the appropriate disposition action for all records within that area.
- A permanent documentation of any records destroyed, showing exactly what records were destroyed, why they were destroyed, when they were destroyed and on whose authority they were destroyed, should be kept. The record should also provide some background information on the records being destroyed, such as legislative provisions, functional context and physical arrangement.
- Records should be destroyed in as secure a manner as is necessary for the level of confidentiality they bear.
- Authorities must have adequate arrangements to ensure that before

a record is destroyed they ascertain whether or not the record is the subject of a request for information under the FOISA 2002 or the FOIA 2000. If a record is known to be the subject of a request under either the FOISA 2002 or the FOIA 2000, the destruction of the record should be delayed until either the information is disclosed or the review and appeal provisions have been exhausted.

Public Records (Scotland) Act 2011

The Public Records Act received Royal Assent on 20 April 2011 and is expected to enter into force towards the end of 2011.

The Act was introduced following a general review of the public records system by the Keeper of Records for Scotland in 2009, which found that individuals were not easily able to access their personal records due to inadequate record management. This review was in response to the Historical Abuse Systemic Review (the Shaw Report) of 2007, which revealed that individuals who had attended residential schools or stayed at children's homes had struggled to trace their personal records for medical, identity or family purposes as a result of poor record keeping.

The Act aims to improve record keeping across a range of public authorities, and prevent confidential records being misplaced or accidently destroyed by requiring public authorities to implement a records management that will create transparency and accountability. The Keeper of Records will have the authority to approve these plans and will issue guidance to assist authorities.

Once approved and implemented, Authorities must ensure that they undertake regular reviews of their records management plan. The Keeper will have the authority to schedule reviews.

If an Authority has failed to comply with the Act, under Section 7 of the Act, the Keeper can issue a notice requiring the Authority to take action within a certain timescale. If the Authority does not comply with the requirements of the action notice, the Keeper may take appropriate steps to publicise the failure of the organisation.

Only public authorities that are named in the Act will be subject to its provisions, including, for example, the Scottish Government, local authorities, the Scottish courts and the NHS. However, if private organisations carry out functions on behalf of any of these authorities, records created by private organisations in respect of those functions will be covered by the Act.

Public authorities, who are subject to the provisions of this legislation, must take action to ensure they implement an appropriate records management plan in order to avoid negative publicity, which could be severely damaging.

Disposal of IT equipment
Companies, when disposing of their IT equipment, must act with extreme care in order to ensure that personal data is completely erased. Despite the fact that contravention of the DPA 1998 is a criminal offence, a study published by the University of Glamorgan's Computer Forensics Team revealed that around half of second-hand computers obtained from various sources contained sufficient information to identify organisations and individuals. This clearly illustrates that businesses are failing properly to delete highly sensitive information stored on their computers before they are sold on, and failing to meet the requirements of the DPA 1998.

There are various ways a business may dispose of its IT equipment responsibly. Shredding disks is considered to be the most effective way to destroy a disk and all the personal data that it contains. Where businesses wish to reuse a disk, unless they can adequately delete the files themselves, refurbishers or recyclers should be used.

The European Waste Electrical and Electronic Equipment (WEEE) Directive seeks to regulate the disposal of electronic equipment by requiring that member states of the European Union ensure that approximately 20% of their WEEE (around four kilograms per person in the UK) is collected and recycled. The Directive received effect in the UK on 1 July 2007. Manufacturers and importers of electrical and electronic equipment (EEE) are responsible for financing the producer compliance regimes for the collection, treatment, recycling and recovery of WEEE. Such schemes are monitored by the relevant environmental agency.

Retailers, on the other hand, must either offer customers a free exchange (or 'take-back') of WEEE for EEE, or help to finance public waste WEEE recycling services. The Regulations are reasonably specific about the sort of equipment that falls under their ambit and the sort of equipment that does not. Replacement peripherals and components, such as hard disk drives, are not considered WEEE under the Regulations except where they are inside equipment that is within their scope at the time of disposal.

Failure to comply with the WEEE Regulations may result in a breach of the DPA 1998, as well as considerable bad publicity.

The Data Retention Regulations
The new Data Retention (EC Directive) Regulations 2009 came into force in April 2009. These Regulations require that public communications providers

(defined as providers of a public electronic communications network or service) retain communications data for a specific period, beginning at the date of the communication. This period is 12 months in the UK. The data to be retained includes telephony and internet data stored or logged in the UK, such as who sent the data, where it was sent from and when. For example, telecommunications services will involve retaining data relating to the name and address of the subscriber, the calling telephone number and the date and time of the start and end of the call. This information is subject to data protection and data security. Although the Regulations specify that the data held should be destroyed at the end of the period of retention, there is no specific guidance on how this should be done. The Regulations simply require the data to be deleted 'in such a way as to make access to the data impossible'.

It is therefore important that such public communications providers, and indeed any organisation that processes personal data, create their own successful methods of destruction of confidential waste in order to avoid any loss and any potential security breach.

Official Secrets Act 1989

Under Section 8 of the Official Secrets Act 1989, government contractors and crown servants will be guilty of an offence if they fail to comply with official direction to return or dispose of documents or articles which it would otherwise be an offence under the Act to disclose. Prohibited disclosures include, for example, information in relation to security and intelligence, international relations, and information which could result in the commission of a crime. If Section 8 of the Act is breached then individuals may face a prison sentence of three months, a £5,000 fine, or both.

See also: Data protection, p.101; IT security, p.282; Personnel files, p.392.

Sources of further information

Information Commissioner: www.informationcommissioner.gov.uk

Information Commissioner Guidance on Monetary Penalties:
www.ico.gov.uk/upload/documents/library/data_protection/detailed_specialist_
guides/ico_guidance_monetary_penalties.pdf

Information Commissioner Guidance on Audit Notices:
www.ico.gov.uk/upload/documents/library/corporate/detailed_specialist_guides/
assessment_notices_code_of_practice.pdf

British Security Industry Association: www.bsia.co.uk

Whistleblowing

Pinsent Masons Employment Group

Key points

- The Public Interest Disclosure Act 1998 protects workers from detriment as a consequence of disclosing wrongdoings on the part of their employer.
- To fall within the protection, the employee's disclosure must have been made in a certain way, about certain matters, to certain people.
- The definition of those protected under the Act goes beyond employees and includes contractors.

Legislation

- Employment Rights Act 1996.
- Public Interest Disclosure Act 1998.
- Public Interest Disclosure (Prescribed Persons) Order 1999.
- Public Interest Disclosure (Prescribed Persons) (Amendment) Order 2003 and 2005.

Protection

The Public Interest Disclosure Act 1998 has become known as the 'Whistleblowers' Act' because it protects workers who suffer detriment or are dismissed as a result of 'blowing the whistle' – disclosing wrongdoing – on their employers, provided that the informer goes through the correct channels. The provisions of the Act are now incorporated into the Employment Rights Act 1996. To be protected, the worker must be able to show that:

- in his reasonable belief the disclosure relates to one of a list of specified wrongdoings; and
- the disclosure is made by one of six specified procedures to specified people.

List of wrongdoings

A protected disclosure is a disclosure made by a worker which, in the reasonable belief of the worker, tends to show that:

- a criminal offence has been, is being or is likely to be committed;
- a person has breached, is breaching or is likely to breach a legal obligation;
- a miscarriage of justice has occurred, is occurring or is likely to occur;
- the health and safety of an individual has been, is being or is likely to be endangered;
- the environment has been, is being or is likely to be endangered; or
- there is an attempt to cover up one of the above.

Procedures for disclosure

In order to be protected, the disclosure must be made only to the category of persons set out in the Act, not any person.

Any one of six methods of disclosing will be protected so long as the worker can show that he was justified in choosing that method. The six methods are:

1. Disclosure to employer / third party.
2. Disclosure to legal advisor.
3. Disclosure to ministers.
4. Disclosure to prescribed persons.
5. Other external disclosure.
6. Exceptionally serious failures.

Disclosure to employer / third party

The disclosure must be in 'good faith' (i.e. honestly, even if it is careless or negligent) and can be to the employer (e.g. telling the chairman that a director is fiddling expenses) or to a third party if one is involved (e.g. a supplier).

A policy may also exist allowing workers to complain to a particular person (e.g. an external accountant).

Disclosure to legal advisor

A disclosure made 'in the course of obtaining legal advice' will be protected, even if it is not made in good faith.

Disclosure to ministers

A disclosure can be made 'in good faith to a Minister of the Crown' if the employer is one appointed by an Act of Parliament (e.g. an NHS trust and statutory tribunals). The worker is not required to first make a disclosure to the employer.

Disclosure to prescribed persons
The current list of 'prescribed persons' (see Employment Rights Act 1996, Section 43f) is given in the Public Interest Disclosure (Prescribed Persons) (Amendment) Order 1999.

Specific persons are listed for particular purposes or industries including the HSE, Financial Services Authority, HM Revenue and Customs and Serious Fraud Office. The worker must reasonably believe that the information disclosed is substantially true and that it falls within the remit of the prescribed person. There is no need to alert the employer first.

Other external disclosure

Wider disclosures are possible to persons such as the media, police and MPs, but to remain protected the worker must pass a number of tests.

The worker must:

- make the disclosure in good faith and not for personal gain;
- reasonably believe that the information disclosed and allegations are substantially true; and
- show it is reasonable to make the disclosure, and that one of the following reasons is true:
  - The worker reasonably believes at the time of making the disclosure that he will be subjected to a detriment by the employer if disclosure is made to the employer or to a prescribed person; or
  - The worker reasonably believes that evidence will be concealed or destroyed if disclosure is made to the employer; or
  - The worker has previously made disclosure of the same information to the employer or to certain prescribed persons.

There is a list of considerations governing whether the disclosure is 'reasonable' or not. These are:

- the identity of the person to whom the disclosure is made;
- the seriousness of the wrongdoing;
- whether the wrongdoing will or is likely to continue or recur;
- whether the disclosure is made in breach of a duty of confidentiality that the employer owes to any other person;
- if the employee has previously disclosed substantially the same information to the employer, or to a prescribed person, whether they have taken action and what action they have taken or might have taken; and
- if a previous disclosure is made to the worker's employer, whether the worker complied with any whistleblowing procedure authorised by the employer.

> **Case study**
> *Goode v. Marks and Spencer plc* (2010)
>
> In this case, the Employment Appeal Tribunal (EAT) discussed the meaning of a 'qualified disclosure' and ruled that an expression of opinion does not attract protection under the whistleblowing legislation.
>
> When the employer proposed some changes to its discretionary enhanced redundancy scheme the claimant told his line manager that he thought the changes were 'disgusting'. He then sent an email to *The Times*, attaching a copy of the proposals. He was quickly identified as the source of the email and, following disciplinary proceedings, was summarily dismissed.
>
> The Tribunal held that the disclosures were not 'qualifying disclosures' for the purposes of the whistleblowing legislation and the EAT agreed.
>
> The EAT found that the Tribunal had been entitled to conclude that what had been disclosed to the line manager was a statement of the claimant's state of mind (that he was 'disgusted' with the proposals). In addition, there was nothing in his statement that anyone could reasonably believe tended to suggest that the employer would fail to comply with any legal obligation in respect of the redundancy scheme.
>
> This decision supports a distinction between facts amounting to information which may be protected, and allegations, statements of position and opinions, which will not be.

Exceptionally serious failures

Where the wrongdoing is 'exceptionally serious', the other methods of disclosure can be overridden. However, the employee takes clear risks. He must:

- make the disclosure in good faith and not for personal gain;
- reasonably believe that information and allegations are substantially true;
- show that the wrongdoing is of an 'exceptionally serious nature' – this is a matter of fact (the worker could be mistaken, even if he believes it is serious – if wrong, he loses protection); and
- show it is reasonable for the worker to make the disclosure, bearing in mind the identity of the person to whom the disclosure is made.

What can the worker claim?

Legal protection is given to workers who make a protected disclosure in certain specified circumstances (*see above*). They will have the right not to be subjected to any detriment by their employer on the ground that they have made a protected disclosure, and not to be dismissed and not to be selected for redundancy for this reason.

'Detriment' does not technically include dismissal. However, a dismissal will be regarded as automatically unfair if it is due to the worker making a disclosure, and no qualifying period of service is needed for a worker to bring such a claim of unfair dismissal. There is no limit on the amount of compensation that can be awarded.

Passing details of claims to Regulators

Since 6 April 2010, Employment Tribunals have been able to pass on details about whistleblowing allegations to relevant regulatory authorities so that the substance of the allegations can be investigated. The ET1 has been amended to allow claimants to tick a box to indicate whether they would like the details passed on. Revised guidance accompanying the claim form makes it clear what happens if the box is ticked. If the claim is accepted, the Tribunal's administrative staff (not employment judges) will identify and contact the relevant regulator. The Tribunal will write to both parties to confirm that a regulator has been contacted. It will be for the regulator to decide whether the underlying issue contained in the claim form requires investigation.

Practical issues

Employers should consider introducing a whistleblowing policy, separate from disciplinary and grievance procedures, in order to encourage such matters to be resolved within the organisation and in a regulated manner. New and existing policies will also need to be reviewed in light of the Bribery Act 2010, which came into force in July 2011. Employers are responsible for ensuring that bribery does not occur within their organisation and whistleblowing policies can help with this by providing an appropriate procedure for reporting suspected bribery. Whistleblowing procedures should therefore be updated to make it clear that they can be used for reporting suspected bribery (see 'Bribery,' p.49).

Further, any provision in a contract of employment purporting to prevent a worker from making a protected disclosure will be void.

See also: Bribery, p.49; Discrimination, p.126; Dismissal, p.146; Employment Tribunals, p.179; Money laundering, p.346.

Sources of further information

ACAS: www.acas.org.uk

Financial Services Authority: www.fsa.gov.uk

Public Concern at Work: www.pcaw.co.uk

Comment ... ''

After Wikileaks

Shonali Routray, Public Concern at Work

In early 2011, the whistleblowing website Wikileaks hit the headlines, exposing and embarrassing world-leading companies and public figures with information meant to be kept confidential. What are the lessons to be learned from Wikileaks, and the role of whistleblower protection in the UK? What should employers do to make sure that their whistleblowing arrangements work and there is a safe alternative to silence?

In his interview for the American TV show '60 Minutes', Julian Assange, the founder of internet media organisation, Wikileaks, stated in the context of there not being any whistleblower protection that:

"If [employees] who say that there is some abuse going on and there's not a proper mechanism for internal accountability and external accountability, they must have a conduit to get that out to the public. And we are the conduit."

In amongst the drama of Wikileaks this statement focuses the mind on the question: Where there are dangers and real risks to the public, how do we ensure that those who spot them are able to raise a concern effectively and early with minimum risk to ourselves?

When we travel to work on the train, we rely on it being ok for the track engineer to raise a concern about a signal failure. We want to know that when we go the hospital, the nurse who is looking after our mother or father is able to raise a concern about wrongdoing or malpractice early,

Shonali Routray is the Legal Director at PCaW. Public Concern at Work is an independent, self-funding whistleblowing charity. It runs a free confidential helpline on 020 7404 6609 for people with whistleblowing concerns; promotes the public interest through its policy work; and advises public bodies, business, regulators and unions on how to create more open and accountable cultures.

even if they only have a suspicion. Most, if not all of us, would agree that we would rather that the nurse and the engineer raise their concerns than keep quiet. But how do we ensure that this is the case?

And, when reflecting on our own workplaces, are we given messages that say that it is safe to speak up?

The Public Interest Disclosure Act in the UK 1998 (PIDA) has been in place in employment law for over a decade, providing an important backstop for workers who have raised a concern about wrongdoing or malpractice in the workplace, and have been victimised or dismissed for having done so. PIDA covers a wide range of wrongdoing, from breaches in health and safety, dangers to the environment, criminal offences, miscarriages of justice and a breach of a legal obligation. The wrongdoing could be about to occur, have occurred, or be recurring, and even extends to wrongdoing overseas.

PIDA is unusual for UK employment law, as it goes beyond the normal scope of employees and covers workers, including temporary or agency workers, GPs, student nurses and doctors. There is no qualifying period for protection and this means that PIDA applies from the very start of employment. In addition, there is no cap in compensation under PIDA. The thinking behind this was that PIDA should apply to all workers, including city bankers and senior professionals at the top of the ladder. The highest compensation award to date in the private sector has been £5m, made to two city bankers in the case of *Backs and List v. Chesterton plc*, who raised concerns about a takeover.

PIDA readily protects individuals who raise their concern internally. For an individual to be protected for raising a concern internally they need to show they have a reasonable belief of information tending to show that wrongdoing is occurring and have raised this in good faith. Similarly, there is a low hurdle for protection for individuals who raise a concern in good faith with regulators such as the Financial Services Authority, National Audit Office, Serious Fraud Office and the Care Quality Commission. An individual need only show

that they have reasonable belief and the information is substantially true.

Finally, PIDA provides protection for individuals who in good faith make a wider disclosure to the media, the police or even a MP. In order to be protected, individuals would have to show that they have a valid cause to go wider: they are not doing it for personal gain, they have raised their concern already either internally or with a regulator; or if they have not raised a concern they had reasonable grounds to believe that they would be victimised or there would be a cover up if raised internally or with a regulator.

A Tribunal would also consider whether the disclosure is reasonable in the circumstances, such as the identity of the person disclosed to, whether there was breach of confidence, whether there was a whistleblowing policy and what the organisation's response was if the matter was raised with them at an earlier stage. Furthermore, an individual can be protected for raising a concern wider, if that concern is exceptionally serious.

> "When PIDA was first enacted, Lord Nolan, one of its prominent supporters, praised it for "so skilfully achieving the essential but delicate balance between the public interest and the interest of the employers". It is this balance that will be effective in the post-Wikileaks age, for it promotes open and confidential whistleblowing."

When PIDA was first enacted, Lord Nolan, one of its prominent supporters, praised it for "so skilfully achieving the essential but delicate balance between the public interest and the interest of the employers". It is this balance that will be effective in the post-Wikileaks age, for it promotes open and confidential whistleblowing. In order to be protected, an individual must show that they have raised a concern and then been victimised, and if someone raises a concern anonymously it will be extremely hard to gain protection. PIDA also emphasises internal accountability and regulatory oversight, by enabling an individual to be readily protected should they raise a concern either internally or with a regulator.

Additionally, PIDA acknowledges the role of wider public accountability and provides protection. Moreover, the PIDA framework encourages employers and organisations to deal with a concern responsibly and if they do not, it means that the individual is more likely to be protected. Despite its balancing framework, many individuals do not know about the protection offered in the UK. Nor do they realise that the protection in the UK is considered one of the best in the world. In a whistleblowing survey conducted by YouGov for our ten-year review of whistleblowing protection in the UK, only 22% of adults surveyed knew that there was protection for people raising concerns.

It is worth noting that the USA has a piecemeal approach to whistleblower protections, offering only limited protections for federal employees and employees of listed companies. It is in this environment, where there is no clear whistleblower protection or routes for individuals to raise a concern either internally or externally, that individuals are more likely to turn to raising a concern anonymously with an organisation such as Wikileaks. The Enron whistleblower, Sherron Watkins, has expressed that she would have used Wikileaks because of the lack of protection.

Employers may be concerned about whether in the post-Wikileaks age employees will start to leak information anonymously. It is highly unlikely that there would be floods of information leaked to outside organisations. From our analysis of Employment Tribunal judgments, we found that eight out of ten claimants have raised a concern internally. We find this figure is mirrored in our helpline. Therefore employers have a big opportunity to capture information at an early stage.

From the perspective of giving advice day in and day out to whistleblowers across all sectors, we would recommend that employers need to give their workers clear routes and options for raising a concern. Employers also have to understand that there are times, where in the public interest, a worker will go outside an organisation and perhaps raise their concern with a regulator. In addition, while PIDA does not prescribe whistleblowing arrangements, it is clear when considering wider disclosures to the media, Tribunals will consider the arrangements of the organisation. PIDA also makes it clear that any confidentiality agreements that prevent individuals from raising a concern that is covered by PIDA (aka a public interest concern) will be void in law.

Thus employers would be well advised to consider their arrangements and in particular the messages they are giving to staff. The PIDA framework balances the interests of both employers and their workers, and despite being drafted before Wikileaks, it will continue to provide protection to whistleblowers throughout the UK who have acted honestly and reasonably.

Work experience, internships and apprenticeships

Pam Loch, Loch Associates Employment Lawyers

Key points
- At a time when the level of unemployment is continuing to increase at an alarming rate, students and recent graduates are finding it much harder to gain a foothold on the first rung of the career ladder.
- Employers have the pick of a large group of well-qualified potential employees, and will be looking for individuals who stand out from the crowd.
- One way of doing this is for students and graduates to gain valuable work experience in industry. A well-prepared and managed work experience placement could also prove to be of great benefit to an employer.

Legislation
- Employment Rights Act 1996.
- National Minimum Wage Act 1998.
- Public Disclosure Act 1998.
- Working Time Regulations 1998.
- Apprenticeships, Skills, Children and Learning Act 2009.
- Equality Act 2010.

Introduction
Work experience students can provide the perfect resource for carrying out research, tackling projects placed on the back burner or freeing up permanent staff. The National Council for Work Experience (NCWE) cites typical projects carried out by students as:

- marketing and market research;
- design and implementation of databases;
- research and development; and
- reviewing work processes and efficiency.

Work experience placements, managed and monitored effectively, provide an opportunity to identify the most able candidates as potential recruits; effectively you 'try before you buy,' thus saving on recruitment costs.

In the summer of 2009 the Government launched an official internship scheme, known as the Graduate Talent Pool, aimed at improving the employability of graduates. It was intended the scheme would support around 5,000 internships of up to three months on a rolling programme.

The Department for Business, Innovation and Skills (BIS) facilitates applications from graduates and matches them with internships placed on the website by employers. Graduates from 2008, 2009, 2010 or 2011 UK universities are eligible to apply.

The Graduate Talent Pool website encourages employers to pay their interns at least the minimum wage and highlights that employers could be at risk where an intern is classed as a worker and is unpaid. The website goes on to say that it is only in limited circumstances that employers will want to offer unpaid internships. Some employers do offer unpaid work experience or volunteer schemes and graduates receiving Jobseekers Allowance for six months or more will be able to do an unpaid internship for up to 13 weeks whilst still claiming an allowance.

The Chartered Institute of Personnel and Development (CIPD) recommends that companies offering internships should adhere to the 'Internship Charter', a voluntary code of practice produced in 2009. This provides six principles for an employment to consider which are recruitment, payment and duration, induction, treatment, supervision, reference and feedback, each of which are given their own dedicated section in the CIPD guide.

Good practice

When considering taking on a work placement student, your first steps should include:

- Consider what you are looking for in a work experience student.
- Establish exactly what gaps you have in the organisation that a student may be able to fill. Ensure there is real work for placements to do and offer a variety of tasks to make the work experience more worthwhile for both parties.
- Consider how much time and resources (both human and financial) can be devoted, whether the placement is paid or voluntary and whether you will be paying expenses. The CIPD suggests that reasonable travel expenses should be paid as a minimum.
- Allocate responsibility for induction and management. Supervisors need to be clear about their roles and what is expected of them.
- As with any other new recruit, it is important a job description is in place; this ensures that you will get applicants who are right for the job.
- Consider what access (if any) the student will require to the organisation's IT systems and what

security measures need to be put in place.
- Decide how long you will need the work placement to last.

The placement should be managed effectively throughout. It would be prudent to provide a short induction during the first day to brief on the ethos of the company, housekeeping issues and what is expected of the work placement.

It is also recommended that if paid work experience is provided, a contract of employment is in place setting out clearly the student's working hours, obligations, responsibilities and what is expected of them during the placement (although not all work experience placements will give rise to an employment relationship – *see below*).

Towards the end of the placement, gather feedback from the student, so that if necessary you can make any appropriate changes to your work placement scheme. It is also helpful to the student to provide feedback on their performance, in order for them to learn from the experience and to further develop their skills.

Confidentiality

An employer should consider any confidentiality issues associated with a potential work placement. There may be some posts to which it would be preferable not to assign students, or there may be particular aspects of the work with which a student should not be involved. In these circumstances, an employer should try to plan around this. Alternatively, it might be necessary for the student to sign a confidentiality agreement prior to starting the placement.

Supervision

Proper supervision of the work placement is important, to ensure the work is being carried out to the correct standard and to identify potential problems at an early stage. Arranging for an experienced team member to act as the intern's mentor would be best practice. In 2008 it was reported that a teenager on a work placement at a large city law firm was jailed for five months after stealing £13,500 and attempting to steal a further £46,500 while working in the firm's accounts department. This is an extreme example, but mistakes made by a work experience student could prove costly, or at least embarrassing, to the company.

Legal considerations

There are several potential areas of liability to bear in mind when considering offering work experience placements.

Status of work experience staff

An employer may offer individuals workplace experience or, as now more commonly the case, an internship. The latter is a more formalised programme of work, usually over the summer holidays with candidates being picked after an interview process.

Whichever term is used, it is important to determine whether an individual will fall into the category of a worker, employee or simply a volunteer to determine what, if any, employment rights will follow from their status.

Worker

A work experience student is likely to fall within the wide statutory definition of a 'worker'. A worker is essentially an individual who undertakes to personally perform work or services for another party and is not a client or customer of that party. Thus, if a student is personally obliged to do certain tasks and there is an obligation to work set hours, they will probably be a 'worker' for certain statutory purposes.

A worker has fewer rights than an employee, but will have certain statutory employment rights under the Employment Rights Act 1996 (ERA), including the right to be accompanied at grievance and disciplinary hearings, not to be discriminated against on the grounds of sex, race, disability, etc., and whistleblowing rights. Generally, they will also be subject to the rules under the Working Time Regulations 1998 (WTR) and National Minimum Wage Act 1998 (NMWA).

Employee

If an individual on a work placement has taken on responsibilities normally undertaken by an employee of the organisation, they may be deemed to be 'employed'. This means that they may be entitled to claim unfair dismissal and maternity leave, along with other rights given to employees under the ERA.

In practice, the right to claim unfair dismissal is unlikely to arise, given the requirement for 12 months' continuous service. However, there are exceptions to this general rule.

For example, if the dismissal was for a discriminatory reason, no period of service is required to bring a claim. It will also be automatically unfair to dismiss an employee for certain inadmissible reasons, e.g. health and safety reasons, or seeking to enforce rights under the WTR. An employee dismissed in these circumstances does not need any qualifying period of continuous employment in order to bring a claim for unfair dismissal.

There is no single test to determine if an individual is an 'employee'. However, both parties must be under an 'irreducible minimum of obligation'. In other words, the employer is obliged to provide work, usually for remuneration, and exercise sufficient control over the individual, who is obliged to personally perform the work required.

Volunteer

A volunteer will not enjoy any rights under the ERA, provided they are a genuine volunteer. Volunteers on work experience would probably spend all their time work shadowing (i.e. observing employees going about their normal activities) rather than carrying out set tasks independently. It also encompasses those who provide their time and effort without any contractual obligation to do so and individuals engaged by a charity or voluntary organisation, who receive no monetary payment or only money for expenses.

Apprentice

Apprentices undertake specific training usually for a fixed term of years or until a set qualification is achieved. Whilst apprentices are 'employees' under the ERA, they have greater rights. An apprentice cannot be dismissed in the same way as an ordinary employee, nor can they be made redundant unless there has been a fundamental change in the employer's business. If an apprentice is dismissed in breach of contract, any damages awarded may take into account wages and training lost under the fixed term of the contract and loss of future employment prospects.

Government-backed apprenticeships, where there is a tripartite agreement in which the employer provides the opportunity for work experience, and the training is carried out under the auspices of a training provider, can result in apprenticeship contracts.

The Apprenticeships, Skills, Children and Learning Act 2009 received Royal Assent on 12 November 2009. Among

other things, the Act creates a new apprenticeships structure which, through apprenticeship frameworks, facilitates the creation of apprenticeship agreements between the employer and apprentice. Such an agreement is treated as a contract of service, rather than a contract of apprenticeship, which makes the scheme more attractive to employers.

Working time

The number of hours a work experience placement works will be generally down to agreement. However, the limits on working hours contained in the WTR apply to 'workers' and therefore may apply to those on work experience.

Employers should bear in mind the main provisions of the WTR, namely:

- the 48-hour limit on average weekly working time;
- the right to daily rest breaks of at least 20 minutes when working more than six hours and rest periods of 11 consecutive hours in any 24-hour period; and, if applicable
- the specific provisions relating to night time working;

unless the specific exclusions or derogations contained within the WTR are applicable.

An employer should also note that there are special provisions relating to young workers (those who are over 15 and under 18 and who are over the compulsory school age). In these cases:

- the working time limit must not exceed eight hours a day or 40 hours a week;
- rest breaks of at least 30 minutes must be taken where daily working time is more than four-and-a-half hours, as well as a rest period of at least 12 consecutive hours in any 24-hour period; and

- young workers are prohibited from working between ten p.m. and six a.m. or, where contractually required to work later than ten p.m., 11 p.m. to seven a.m.

Again, the WTR provide for a number of exceptions and derogations.

National minimum wage

Employers should bear in mind that paid work experience staff are likely to be entitled to receive the national minimum wage (NMW). The NMW stipulates all workers are entitled to be paid NMW provided they are of school-leaving age or ordinarily work in the UK.

The current rates (as of 1 October 2011) are £6.08 for workers aged 21 and over, £4.98 for 18-20 year olds, £3.68 for 16-17 year olds and £2.60 for apprentices, and increase on 1 October each year.

Genuine volunteers are not workers and are therefore not entitled to the NMW, but, for this exception to apply, the relationship must be properly voluntary in nature and not merely labelled as such in order to circumvent the requirements of the NMW. Entitlement to NMW would depend on the circumstances under which the individual is engaged and even if not a worker for some purposes, it may be the case that they would still be considered a worker for national minimum wage purposes.

However, if the individual is under no obligation to carry out work and has no contract or formal agreement, then the person may be considered a volunteer and therefore not be covered by national minimum wage legislation.

As well as volunteers, there are other circumstances when a work experience placement will not be entitled to the NMW. These include:

- individuals who undertake work experience resulting from government work placements and schemes funded by the European Social Fund;
- students carrying out work experience under the European Union's Leonardo da Vinci programme; and
- workers on a higher education course where part of the course is work experience, provided this experience does not exceed one year and is required by the course.

HM Revenue and Customs (HMRC) Compliance Officers can carry out inspections at any time to determine entitlement to the NMW and the level of pay received by workers. The Employment Act 2008, which came into force in April 2009, has changed how the NMW is enforced. Notices of underpayment now require an employer to pay a financial penalty within 28 days of service. The penalty is set at 50% of the total underpayment (the minimum penalty is £100, the maximum £5,000). If the employer complies with the notice within 14 days, the financial penalty is reduced by 50%.

The Act has also changed the way that criminal offences under the NMW are enforced. The most serious cases are triable in the Crown Court. This means that employers who deliberately fail to pay the NMW may now face stiffer penalties.

The Government White Paper, *Opening Doors, Breaking Barriers: A Strategy for Social Mobility* (April 2005), encourages that the appropriate NMW should be paid.

Discrimination

Discrimination legislation, which prohibits both harassment and discrimination on grounds of race, sex, disability, religion or belief, sexual orientation and age, applies to workers, prospective workers and also those seeking or undergoing vocational training. The Equality Act 2010 retains this protection from discrimination for workers and those in vocational training.

However, in early 2011 the Court of Appeal ruled that a Citizen's Advice Bureau (CAB) volunteer who had no contract with CAB could not pursue a claim under the DDA. This decision applies equally to the Equality Act and unless an unpaid worker has a legally binding contract 'personally to do work' or they are carrying out work experience or vocational training, they will not be protected by discrimination legislation.

From a practical viewpoint, employers should extend their equal opportunity policies to work placements and make copies accessible to applicants. All applicants for work experience should be considered on an equal basis without reference to any potentially discriminatory factors, and a thorough and transparent selection process should be followed.

Whistleblowing

There are specific provisions within the ERA introduced by the Public Disclosure Act 1998 (PIDA), protecting workers who make disclosures about certain types of malpractice in the workplace, otherwise known as 'whistleblowing'.

Essentially, protected disclosures relate to breaches of criminal or civil law, miscarriages of justice, and risks to health and safety or the environment.

Workers who blow the whistle are protected from detriment and dismissal. Employers should be aware that under PIDA the definition of 'worker' is a lot wider than the definition contained within the ERA and will include those who undertake work experience as part of a training course or are provided with training for employment (except in cases where the course is run by an 'educational establishment'). Thus, most individuals operating within the workplace will fall within the scope of the whistleblowing provisions.

See also: Children at work, p.80; Discrimination, p.126; Employment status, p.174; National minimum wage, p.342; Whistleblowing, p.551; Working time, p.564; Young workers, p.571.

Sources of further information

The NCWE has issued guidelines to help businesses get the most out of work experience placements: www.work-experience.org

Graduate Talent Pool: http://graduatetalentpool.bis.gov.uk

The Chartered Institute of Personnel and Development: www.cipd.co.uk

HM Government – *Opening Doors, Breaking Barriers: A Strategy for Social Mobility:* http://download.cabinetoffice.gov.uk/social-mobility/opening-doors-breaking-barriers.pdf

Working time

Pinsent Masons Employment Group

Key points
- The Working Time Regulations 1998 (which implement the EC Working Time Directive into UK law) limit working hours and provide for rest breaks and holidays.
- The Business Link website (see *Sources of further information*) provides further information on the Regulations.
- Employees can opt out of the 48-hour week, and other rights can be softened or extended in 'special cases' or by agreement.
- The Regulations do not apply to some sectors, or to time that is not 'working time'.

Legislation

The Working Time Regulations 1998 came into force on 1 October 1998.

The Regulations limit working hours and provide for rest breaks and minimum paid holiday rights. Night workers have special rights that are covered in the Regulations – see *'Night Workers'* (p.366).

Workers

The Regulations apply to 'workers' – this includes employees, temporary workers and freelancers, but not individuals who are genuinely self-employed. Young workers are also covered by the Regulations and are protected by special rights such as greater rest break entitlements – see *'Young Persons'* (p.571).

Some types of workers are excluded from the Regulations altogether, and some are subject to separate regulation or partial exemption. The Regulations were amended from 1 August 2003 to extend working time measures in full to all workers in road transport (other than those covered by the Road Transport Directive), non-mobile workers in road, sea, inland waterways or lake transport, to workers in the railway and offshore sectors and to all workers in aviation who are not covered by the Aviation Directive.

Since 1 August 2004 the Regulations have also applied to junior doctors, with some exceptions and special rules.

Working time

'Working time' is defined as any period during which a worker is 'working, at his employer's disposal and carrying out his activity or duties'; any period during which the worker is receiving 'relevant training'; or any additional period that is agreed in a relevant agreement to be 'working time'. This can lead to uncertainty in some cases, but it is clear that working time will not usually include time spent travelling to and from the workplace and time during rest breaks. Time spent on call has been the subject of much debate in case law, which has concluded that 'on call' time constitutes working time if the employee is required to be in the workplace rather than at home, even if the worker is asleep for some or all of that time.

Unmeasured working time

The provisions relating to the 48-hour week (*see below*), night work, and minimum rest

Case study

Rawlings v. The Direct Garage Door Company Ltd (2009)

The non-payment of holiday pay to a worker who has been on sick leave can amount to an unlawful deduction from wages even where the worker has not actually requested to take the leave in question.

The claimant was employed at a company where the holiday year ran from 1 January to 31 December. He was absent on sick leave throughout the whole of 2004 and remained on sick leave until his employment was terminated on 5 April 2006. In 2004 he exercised his right to take his statutory holiday, despite being on sick leave, and received holiday pay for the 2004 period, but he failed to follow the same process for 2005 and 2006.

The claimant commenced proceedings under the Working Time Regulations (WTR), seeking holiday pay for 2005 and for 2006 (up to his resignation in April). He brought the claim as an unlawful deduction from wages claim.

The Employment Tribunal relied on the ECJ judgment in *Stringer* (*see below*) to uphold the claimant's unlawful deduction claim for holiday pay for those periods. The Tribunal found that the claimant had been unable to take annual leave during 2005 and 2006 due to illness and he was entitled to be paid holiday pay, as there had been a series of unlawful deductions from wages.

This case is one of the first Employment Tribunal decisions that has tried to deal with the conflict between the WTR, which provide that statutory holiday may only be taken in the holiday year in which it accrues, and ECJ case law, which provides that workers who are off sick and cannot take their holiday in any holiday year must be allowed to carry it over to a later date. Other cases have the opposite view. Although Employment Tribunals decisions are not binding, the Tribunal in this case decided that the employee could not take his 2005 statutory holiday entitlement as he was off sick. On this basis it allowed him, in effect, to carry it over into 2006 and to be paid in lieu on termination. There have been no Employment Appeal Tribunal decisions dealing with this issue.

periods will not apply where a worker's work is not measured or predetermined or can otherwise be determined by the worker himself.

Examples are managing executives or other persons who have discretion over whether to work or not on a given day without needing to consult the employer.

48-hour week

An employer is expected to take all reasonable steps in keeping with the need to protect health and safety, to ensure that in principle each worker works no more than 48 hours on average in each working week. Young workers may not work more than eight hours a day or 40 hours a week and, unlike the working hours of adult workers, there are no averaging provisions for young workers.

The average working time is calculated across a 17-week rolling reference period immediately prior to the calculation date. This reference period can be extended in certain circumstances such as where the worker is a new starter; where there is a relevant agreement replacing the rolling 17-week periods with fixed successive periods of 17 weeks; under a collective or workforce agreement; and where special case provisions apply to the worker.

The time spent working for any employer is included as working time, so care is needed if an employer knows or should know that an employee has more than one job. A worker cannot be forced to work more than these hours if the hours constitute 'working time'.

The Regulations allow a worker to opt out of the 48-hour week restriction by written agreement in a number of ways, including by way of an amendment to the individual's contract of employment, but it must be in writing. The opt-out agreement can last for a fixed period or indefinitely. Any opted out worker can cancel the opt-out by giving at least seven days' notice, unless the opt-out agreement provides for longer notice, which cannot exceed three months in any event. Even if a worker has agreed to opt out, he cannot be required to work excessively long hours if this creates a reasonably foreseeable risk to health and safety.

Where a worker has contracted out of the 48-hour week, the employer no longer needs to keep records showing the number of hours actually worked by the opted-out individual.

In these circumstances only a list of those who have opted out is necessary.

See below for the current position on the continued availability of the opt-out.

Rest periods

Under the Regulations, workers are entitled to regular breaks in the working day and rest periods between working days.

Employers must provide that rest periods can be taken, but there is no need to ensure they are actually taken. The rest period is in addition to annual leave and can be paid or unpaid.

The provisions can be summarised as follows:

- There should be a minimum rest period of 11 uninterrupted hours between each working day.
- Young workers are entitled to 12 hours' uninterrupted rest in each 24-hour period.
- There should be a minimum weekly rest period of not less than 24 uninterrupted hours in each seven-day period.
- Days off can be averaged over a two-week period.
- Workers who work for six hours are entitled to a 20-minute break.
- There should be adequate rest breaks where monotonous work places the worker at risk.

Special cases

Workers can be asked to work without breaks in a number of 'special cases'.

The basis of the special cases is that, if they exist, there is a reasonable need

for work to be carried out quickly in a confined period. If because of one of the 'special cases' a worker is not able to take a rest break when he would ordinarily be entitled to do so, he should be allowed to take an equivalent rest break as soon as reasonably practicable thereafter.

Also, where special cases exist, the 17-week average period for the 48-hour week can be extended to 26 weeks. These include:

- where there is a 'foreseeable surge of activity';
- where 'unusual and unforeseeable circumstances beyond the control of the worker's employer' exist;
- where continuity of service or production is needed (e.g. hospital care, prisons, media, refuse and where a need exists to keep machines running);
- where permanent presence is needed (e.g. security and surveillance); and
- where there is great distance between the workplace and an employee's home, or between different places of work.

Annual leave

Subject to certain exceptions, workers have a statutory right to a minimum of 5.6 weeks' paid annual leave. This rose from 4.8 weeks on 1 April 2009. A part-time worker is entitled to 5.6 weeks' holiday reduced pro-rata according to the amount of days they work. Where a worker begins employment part-way through a leave year, he is entitled in that leave year to the proportion of the 5.6 weeks' annual leave that is equal to the proportion of the leave year for which he is employed.

There is no statutory right under the Regulations to time off on bank holidays. The October 2007 and April 2009 increases in annual leave gave full-time workers a further eight days' holiday to address the fact that because the Regulations did not provide an entitlement to bank holidays, many employers were counting the eight public holidays against the then four-week annual leave entitlement. Note, however, there is no right to time off to be taken on bank holidays, and whether a worker can be required to work on a bank holiday is a matter for the employment contract or managerial prerogative.

Contractual holiday provisions should be checked to ensure enough holiday is given, and can also be used to fill in gaps in the Regulations, including, for example, in relation to the clawback of overpaid holiday pay when an employee leaves.

For the purposes of the statutory leave entitlement, workers are entitled to be paid a 'week's pay' for each week of annual leave. The exact way in which payment is calculated depends on a number of factors but, effectively, where a worker is paid an annual, monthly or weekly amount to which he is contractually entitled, his holiday pay will be the weekly equivalent of that amount. However, where a worker receives a varying amount of pay each week, which is not contractually provided for or agreed, a 'week's pay' must be calculated in accordance with the average amount of pay the worker received in the 12-week period prior to the date of payment. Specific pro rata rules apply to untaken holiday when an employee leaves.

The Regulations provide a right to stipulate when a worker can take his leave entitlement, including notice provisions for the employer and the employee.

Annual leave and sickness

The interaction of holiday rights and sick leave was in a state of uncertainty for some time. The issues were resolved (in part) by the ECJ decision in *Stringer v.*

HMRC. Very generally, the position now is that:

- a worker on sick leave accrues statutory holiday;
- a worker can take statutory paid holiday during sick leave; and
- if a worker falls sick during a period of pre-booked statutory holiday, they can choose whether to take the period when they are sick as sick leave or as statutory holiday.

This is a very complex area and the law is in a state of flux in certain areas.

The Government has launched a consultation to amend the Working Time Regulations to ensure that UK legislation is consistent with the Working Time Directive, as interpreted in a number of judgments of the ECJ, relating to the interaction of annual leave with sick pay, maternity pay and parental leave.

For more information see *'Holiday'* (p.240) and '*Sickness*' (p.470).

Agreements

Various parts of the Regulations can be disapplied or softened by specific agreements. This can be done by using a 'collective agreement' between an employer and trade union, a 'workforce agreement' between an employer and its workers or trade union, or 'individual agreements' between an employer and a worker.

Records

Employers must keep adequate records to show in particular whether the limits in the Regulations dealing with the 48-hour week and night work are being complied with.

The courts will expect employers to be able to show they are complying with the Regulations and policing working time.

Officers of the HSE are entitled to investigate an employer's working time practices, and can demand to see copies of its records.

Employers are not required to keep records of annual leave taken by workers and therefore there is no penalty if records are not retained. However, it is advisable for employers to keep records to ensure that there are no disputes over a particular worker's entitlement.

Enforcement

The Regulations provide a wide range of sanctions, depending on the breach in question. The limits on working time and the record-keeping requirements are enforced by the HSE or Local Authority Environmental Health Departments. They can issue 'improvement' or 'prohibition' notices, which attract unlimited fines and up to two years' imprisonment for directors if such a notice is not complied with.

Workers may present a complaint to an Employment Tribunal in connection with any failure by their employer to provide them with the relevant protections afforded by the Regulations. Where a worker is also an employee, and is dismissed as a result of exercising a right under the Regulations, his dismissal will be deemed to be automatically unfair. Employees may present a claim to an Employment Tribunal regardless of length of service.

EC proposals for change

The European Commission was obliged to review certain aspects of the European Working Time Directive, which the Working Time Regulations implemented in the UK. In June 2008, the EU Council published proposed wording for a directive to amend the Working Time Directive. The agreed position was that the opt-out would remain, but the following restrictions would apply:

- Workers will have to renew the opt-out in writing annually.

- Workers will be able to opt back in with immediate effect during the first six months of employment or up to three months after the end of any probationary period, whichever is longer. This means that the notice period for opting back in will be two months rather than the current three months.
- An opt-out will be void if signed at the same time as the employment contract.
- An opt-out will be void if signed within four weeks of starting work. (This provision will not apply to workers who work for an employer for fewer than ten weeks in a 12-month period.)
- No worker can work for more than 60 hours a week, averaged over three months, unless permitted in a collective agreement or agreement. (This provision will not apply to workers who work for an employer for fewer than ten weeks in a 12-month period.)
- Working time plus inactive on-call time cannot exceed 65 hours a week, averaged over three months, unless permitted in a collective agreement. (This provision will not apply to workers who work for an employer for fewer than ten weeks in a 12-month period.)

In addition:

- The reference period for calculating the 48-hour week may be extended to six months, 'for objective or technical reasons, or reasons concerning the organisation of work'.
- There will be a new category of time called 'inactive part of on-call time', which counts as neither working time nor a rest period.
- Compensatory rest may be given after a 'reasonable period', rather than straight after the shift to which it relates.

However, the amended Directive is not yet in force because agreement could not be reached. In particular, several member states wanted to end the opt-out altogether, which faced fierce opposition from other member states, including the UK. In April 2009, negotiations in Europe came to an end without any agreement having been reached on the proposals. The Commission effectively recommenced the process in March 2010 by launching a fresh consultation on proposals to comprehensively review the legislation.

The legal framework in this area therefore remains largely unchanged and the opt-out system remains. However, talks are expected to resume at some point in the future.

See also: Holiday, p.240; Dismissal, p.146; Flexible working, p.221; Night working, p.366; Sickness, p.470; Stress, p.500; Young persons, p.571.

Sources of further information

Business Link – Working Time: http://bit.ly/qHUOeK

Young persons
Pinsent Masons Employment Group

Key points
- A young person is a person who is over compulsory school age, which is currently 16 years, and who is under the age of 18 years. A child is a person not over compulsory school age.
- Young workers have particular rights under the Working Time Regulations 1998, particularly relating to rest breaks and night work assessments.
- Particular hourly rates apply to young workers for minimum wage purposes.

Legislation
- Children and Young Persons Act 1933 (as amended).
- Employment Rights Act 1996 (as amended).
- National Minimum Wage Act 1998.
- Working Time Regulations 1998.
- Working Time (Amendment) Regulations 2002.

Working time

Daily rest
Young workers are entitled to a break of at least 12 consecutive hours in any 24-hour period.

Weekly rest
Young workers are entitled to a weekly rest period of at least 48 hours in each period of seven days (i.e. two days off each week). In addition, if owing to the nature of the work and because of technical or organisational reasons a young worker cannot take two days off per week, then the rest can be spread across 36 hours in a week.

Rest breaks while at work
If a young worker is required to work for more than four-and-a-half hours at a stretch, he is entitled to a rest break of at least 30 minutes. A young worker's entitlement to rest breaks can be changed or excluded only in exceptional circumstances. If a young worker is working for more than one employer, the time he is working for each one should be added together to see if he is entitled to a rest break in a total four-and-a-half-hour period of work.

A young person's entitlement to breaks can be changed or not taken in exceptional circumstances only. The circumstances and 'special cases' are narrower than those for older workers and include the situation where no adult is available to do the work. Where this occurs, the worker should receive compensatory rest within three weeks. Compensatory rest is a period of rest of the same length as the period of rest that a worker has missed.

Annual leave
Young workers have the same entitlements as adult workers in respect of annual leave. Under the Working Time Regulations 1998, all adult employees are entitled to at least 5.6 weeks' paid annual leave in each year.

Time off for study and training
Young persons who are not in full-time secondary or further education are entitled to take time off during working hours for the purposes of study or training leading to an external qualification (academic or vocational) which 'enhances the young

person's employment prospects'. The length of time that can be taken is that which is reasonable in the circumstances, and the young person should be paid for the time taken off at his normal hourly rate.

National Minimum Wage

The National Minimum Wage Act 1998 came into force on 1 April 1999 and provides for the minimum level of pay to which almost all workers in the UK are entitled. Since 1 October 2004, most workers over 16 years of age have been covered by the Act. The rates are reviewed in October each year, and the current rate is £3.68 as of October 2011. Although the National Minimum Wage rates discriminate on grounds of age, they are specifically exempted from the Equality Act 2010. See 'Minimum wage' (p.342)

Practical points

If a company employs young workers, managers should check how many rest periods and breaks they are receiving.

If young workers are not receiving the correct rest periods, consider:

- how these can be given; and
- whether the amount of hours worked can be reduced.

Managers should always ensure that:

- proper records of young workers are maintained, including details of health assessments;
- young workers are not involved in work that is particularly hazardous; and
- young workers are receiving the National Minimum Wage.

See also: Discrimination, p.126; Minimum wage, p.342; Working time, p.564.

Sources of further information

The Workplace Law website has been one of the UK's leading legal information sites since its launch in 2002. As well as providing free news and forums, our Information Centre provides you with a 'one-stop shop' where you will find all you need to know to manage your workplace and fulfil your legal obligations.

You'll find:

- quick and easy access to all major legislation and official guidance, including clear explanations and advice from our experts;
- case reviews and news analysis, which will keep you fully up to date with the latest legislation proposals and changes, case outcomes and examples of how the law is applied in practice;
- briefings, which include in-depth analysis on major topics; and
- WPL TV – an online TV channel including online seminars, documentaries and legal updates.

Content is added and updated regularly by our editorial team who utilise a wealth of in-house experts and legal consultants. Visit www.workplacelaw.net for more information.

The contributors

Suzanne McMinn, HR Consultant
suzanne.mcminn@workplacelaw.net

Suzanne McMinn is a Chartered Member of the CIPD, with over 15 years' experience in HR. She is also a Specialist Paralegal Practitioner in Employment Law and is experienced in dealing with Employment Tribunal claims. Suzanne has worked in both the private and public sector, advising clients at strategic and operational level covering a broad range of HR issues. Suzanne was in a Business Partner role for five years, prior to joining Workplace Law as a HR Consultant. Suzanne has devised and delivered training on a variety of HR issues to senior and junior managers in a variety of business environments. She is able to translate the complex subject of employment law into language that managers can relate to and can provide interesting real life examples. She is also a course tutor for Workplace Law's accredited CIPD certificate level courses.
@SMcMinnWPL

Heidi Thompson, HR Consultant
heidi.thompson@workplacelaw.net

Heidi Thompson is an HR Consultant at Workplace Law. She is a Chartered Member of the CIPD, with a Masters Degree in HR Management with over 17 years' experience working in both the private and public sector for a variety of different companies including manufacturing, investment banks, Government bodies, schools and healthcare. Heidi advises clients at strategic and operational level covering a broad range of HR issues over the entire employment relationship. Heidi worked as an outsourced HR Consultant for a number of years as well as an internal HR Manager for a large oil and gas company. As a consultant at Workplace Law she is charged with advising senior and junior managers on all areas of HR and employment law issues.
@HThompsonWPL

Tarvinder Tumber, HR Consultant
tar.tumber@workplacelaw.net

Tarvinder Tumber is an HR Consultant at Workplace Law. She is a Chartered Member of the CIPD and a Member of the British Psychological Society, with over 12 years' experience working in HR. Tar has been advising clients in both the private and public sector for a number of years, including healthcare companies, schools, publishing houses, banks and manufacturing organisations. This has been at both strategic and operational level, covering a broad range of HR issues spanning the entire employment relationship. Tar has worked both in internal HR as an HR Business Partner and also has several years' experience as an outsourced consultant where she has adapted her communication to suit the needs of the individual audience. She has delivered training to customers and is also trained in the delivery of SHL psychometric tests.
@TarTumber

ANDERSON STRATHERN
SOLICITORS

Anderson Strathern LLP is a dynamic and progressive full service law firm. The firm is focused on its clients' needs and achieving excellence in terms of the quality of advice and its overall service. Anderson Strathern's impressive client base includes commercial, heritage and public sector clients.

The firm has recognised strengths in all aspects of property, corporate services, dispute resolution, employment, discrimination and private client management. Its parliamentary and public law team provides a unique service and is relevant to many areas of business. The firm has the largest number of Accredited Specialists of any Scottish law firm and was the only new appointment to the Scottish Government Legal Framework Agreement Panel. Anderson Strathern is a member firm of the Association of European Lawyers. While much of its client work has a Scottish focus, a significant number of the firm's solicitors are dual qualified in England as well as Scotland and the firm acts on behalf of clients in transactions throughout the UK, while the firm's Employment Unit represents employer clients in Employment Tribunals in Scotland, England and Northern Ireland.

www.andersonstrathern.co.uk

Lizzy Campbell, Senior Solicitor
lizzy.campbell@andersonstrathern.co.uk

Lizzy Campbell is a Senior Solicitor in the Employment Unit. Lizzy advises both employer and employee clients on a wide range of employment issues including unfair dismissal, TUPE and performance management as well as negotiating Compromise Agreements. Lizzy is also involved in representing clients in the Employment Tribunal. Lizzy regularly delivers training on employment law topics, including, most recently, sessions on performance management and managing disciplinary / grievance investigations. Lizzy recently obtained the CIPD Certificate in Training Practice.

Debbie Fellows, Associate
debbie.fellows@andersonstrathern.co.uk

Debbie Fellows is an Associate in the employment unit and is accredited by the Law Society of Scotland as a specialist in employment law. She has experience advising both employers and employees across a wide range of employment issues, including unfair dismissal, redundancy, TUPE, contracts of employment, service contracts and discrimination (in particular equal pay), as well as representing clients at Employment Tribunal. Debbie regularly provides interactive training to clients on employment and discrimination issues and through this is committed to working with clients to ensure their compliance and understanding of employment law.

Chris McDowall, Associate
chris.mcdowall@andersonstrathern.co.uk

Chris McDowall is a Senior Associate in the Employment Unit. He deals with all aspects of employment law and advises a wide variety of clients on issues that are both individual and collective in nature. Chris has designed and delivered in-house training sessions to the HR teams of clients as well as training for their managers, including a practical guide to employment law as part of an induction-training programme for new line managers. He has also tutored at the University of Edinburgh and is a member of the Employment Lawyers Association and the Scottish Discrimination Lawyers Association.

*berwin leighton paisner

Berwin Leighton Paisner LLP is a leading law firm based in the City of London and with offices in various jurisdictions around the world. We pride ourselves on our superb client base, including many leading companies and financial institutions. We strive to lead the market in the excellence of our service delivery. We are well known for our extraordinary success in developing market leadership positions within the employment, pensions, real estate, corporate and finance areas. We distinguish ourselves by working with our clients in creative and innovative ways to achieve commercial solutions.

www.blplaw.com

Kirstie Allison, Associate
kirstie.allison@blplaw.com

Kirstie Allison advises a variety of clients on a broad range of employment matters. She conducts litigation (both in the High Court and Employment Tribunal) and advises on employment law issues arising in relation to business and share acquisitions and disposals. Kirstie's experience also includes drafting employment documentation, including service agreements and HR policies, guiding clients through redundancies and TUPE transfers, advising in relation to compromise agreements and providing advice on day-to-day employment law matters.

Sarah Barratt, Associate
sarah.barratt@blplaw.com

Sarah Barratt has experience in both contentious and non-contentious aspects of employment law, acting for a range of public and private sector clients. She has handled Employment Tribunal cases on a variety of issues including unfair dismissal, discrimination, TUPE and equal pay. She also has experience of drafting and advising on employment contracts, consultancy and compromise agreements and HR policies and procedures, as well as providing advice on day-to-day employment law matters. Sarah also has experience of business sales and acquisitions and due diligence reporting.

Ian De Freitas, Partner
ian.defreitas@blplaw.com

Ian De Freitas is a Partner in the Intellectual Property Group. His practice splits into three main areas: all forms of intellectual property disputes; media and crisis management; and technology and outsourcing disputes. He is best known for his work in the technology and new media sectors, but he also acts for a number of clients in the financial services, publishing and hotels sectors. He is a regular contributor of comments on legal issues to the broadcast and print media. Ian also deals with public relations and crisis management issues. This has involved work across a broad spectrum, including investigative broadcast and print journalism; pressure groups; shareholder activists; foreign governments; hate websites; and harassment of directors and employees. Ian is a partner in the firm's Crisis Management Team and has close links with professionals in the PR industry.

Marc Hanson, Head of Commercial Construction
marc.hanson@blplaw.com

Marc Hanson is Head of the Commercial ConstructionTeam, specialising in all aspects of facilities management law, from contract drafting to dispute resolution. He has extensive experience of advising property owners, contractors, institutions and public authorities in connection with major domestic and international projects.

Toby Headdon, Senior Associate
toby.headdon@blplaw.com

Toby Headdon specialises in contentious and non-contentious aspects of all intellectual property law. This includes advising on the protection, enforcement, acquisition, disposal, and exploitation of all types of intellectual property rights. Toby has considerable experience in negotiating IP licences and advising on IP ownership strategies. He has worked on a number of complex acquisitions, disposals and licensing arrangements, which have involved tracing ownership and intra-group restructuring of IPR for tax-driven purposes. He also has considerable experience in advising on avoiding IPR infringement and enforcing IPR against infringers (including in relation to software), including the conduct of court proceedings to full trial.

Mark Kaye, Senior Associate
mark.kaye@blplaw.com

Mark Kaye advises on a broad range of employment matters with a particular emphasis on advisory work and non-contentious corporate finance and PFI transactions, including frequently advising in relation to the application or otherwise of TUPE.

Lizzie Mead, Junior Associate
lizzie.mead@blplaw.com

Lizzie Mead advises in all aspects of employment law. She has experience in a wide range of areas including preparing cases for the Employment Tribunal and High Court, involving discrimination, whistleblowing and post-termination restrictions, drafting service agreements and contracts of employment, advising on TUPE issues, unfair dismissal and employment status. Lizzie advises a range of clients across various industries but is experienced within the financial services, retail and recruitment sectors. Lizzie regularly presents at seminars, provides in-house training and writes articles and chapters for leading legal and personnel publications on a wide range of employment law issues.

Jackie Thomas, Associate Director
jackie.thomas@blplaw.com

Jackie Thomas specialises in all aspects of employment law, and advises on both contentious and non-contentious employment law issues, including executive service contracts, discrimination and issues arising from the termination of employment.

Solicitors

Law firm BPE is based in Cheltenham, and clients range from private investors, to dynamic entrepreneurs, high street chains, public institutions, blue chip multi-nationals, and a foreign Government. Legal services supplied range from corporate, company commercial, commercial property, commercial litigation, insolvency, employment, tax / trusts and wills, PI for Insurers and volume residential property.

www.bpe.co.uk

Pav Clair, Solicitor
pav.clair@bpe.co.uk

Pav Clair trained and qualified with BPE and carries out contentious and non-contentious work. He has impressed clients with his professionalism and analytical skills. A natural communicator, he advises employers on all aspects of employment law, and high value Employment Tribunal claims, particularly supporting senior members of the team.

Lisa Gettins, Partner and Head of Employment
lisa.gettins@bpe.co.uk

Lisa Gettins has 14 years' experience specialising in employment law and advises on all aspects of contentious and non-contentious work. During this time, Lisa has worked in-house in manufacturing, for a firm specialising in public sector work and for an international law firm. She has extensive experience advising private and public sector employers, particularly in relation to TUPE, defending high value discrimination claims, strategic advice on business restructuring, and trade union issues, ranging from recognition to strike action.

She is an experienced Tribunal advocate in both Tribunal and the EAT and has also dealt with a number of Court of Appeal cases, including reported cases in the fields of whistleblowing, constructive dismissal, sex discrimination and TUPE. Lisa is also CIPD qualified, regularly dealing with policy and consultation papers on behalf of CIPD.

Sarah Lee, Solicitor
sarah.lee@bpe.co.uk

Before joining BPE Solicitors LLP, Sarah Lee worked for an international law firm based in Birmingham. She is a very down-to-earth lawyer, who quickly gains the confidence of senior executives with her excellent communication and client handling skills. Sarah is well versed in all aspects of employment law and has successfully defended national clients in a wide range of Tribunal claims, including complex whistleblowing, discrimination and unfair dismissal.

Her first class negotiation skills have also facilitated a number of successful commercial settlements. Sarah is equally at home providing practical advice to clients on day-to-day employment issues and more strategic advice, such as redundancy and restructuring.

Cripps Harries Hall.

Cripps Harries Hall LLP is a leading law firm based in the South East. In addition to having a national reputation for the legal services it provides to individuals and for commercial property work the firm has particular strengths in the house building, education retail shopping centre and charity sectors. The firm advises many high-profile clients from individuals to plcs including financial institutions, local and national government and charities. Our core values of being Distinctive, Open and Committed underpin all that we do to provide the highest quality of service to our clients.

Our employment team, led by Roger Byard, advises on all employment issues and has particular expertise in the employment problems encountered by people who work in the education retail and charity sectors.

www.crippslaw.com

Camilla Beamish, Solicitor
camilla.beamish@crippslaw.com

Camilla Beamish is a Solicitor who specialises in employment law. Camilla advises on a wide range of contentious and non-contentious employment issues and has particular expertise in the management of grievance, disciplinary and dismissal proceedings (including redundancy programmes) and discrimination claims. Her clients include fully listed plcs, private companies, charities and high net worth individuals.

Roger Byard, Partner
roger.byard@crippslaw.com

Roger Byard is a recognised leader in the practice of employment law and has extensive experience acting for both employers and employees. He has particular expertise relating to the employment problems arising on the outsourcing of services and the appointment and where necessary the dismissal of senior executives and managers especially those who work in the retail education and charity sectors. He regularly advises individuals in the legal and other professions in relation to employment and partnership difficulties and has built a reputation for giving wise counsel.

GREENWOODS
SOLICITORS LLP

Greenwoods Solicitors LLP is a commercial law firm providing top quality legal advice and pragmatic solutions to our local, national and international clients. Whilst not one of the largest regional firms, we have been successful in identifying the market in which we are best placed to operate. By knowing who we want to work for and having the right lawyers we have been able to focus and develop our strengths to give those clients the very best service. We know the importance of building strong working relationships with our clients. We seek to understand their objectives, the commercial environment within which they operate and their need for practical legal advice. We are proactive, we look for solutions (rather than just problems) and adopt a 'can-do' attitude. We are committed to drafting legal documents in plain English and to communicating with our clients in a straightforward way.

www.greenwoods.co.uk

Robert Dillarstone, Director
rdillarstone@greenwoods.co.uk

Robert Dillarstone is Greenwoods' Managing Director. He has acted in cases both before the Court of Appeal and the House of Lords. His strength lies in his commercial, practical and personable approach to delivering solutions to clients. Robert has received consistently strong reviews from the legal directories over many years which independently analyse legal service provision. Past reviews have referred to the team's 'excellent reputation as far afield as the City' (*Legal 500*) and to Robert as 'talented and effective' and 'never ducking an issue' (Chambers and Partners' *A Client's Guide to the Legal Profession*).

Kathryn Gilbertson, Director
kgilbertson@greenwoods.co.uk

Kathryn Gilbertson heads Greenwoods Solicitors LLP's nationally renowned Business Defence team advising on all aspects of regulatory law, including corporate manslaughter, health and safety issues, food safety and trading law matters. Kathryn, with the support of her team, has represented numerous companies in trials and inquests concerning fatal accidents, major workplace incidents and safety issues. She has a reputation for an innovative approach to regulatory compliance issues and for her astute commercial awareness.

Lisa Jinks, Associate
ljinks@greenwoods.co.uk

Lisa Jinks has substantial experience in all aspects of employment law, having qualified in 1992. Her all-round expertise includes corporate immigration advice, an area that Lisa built up since joining Greenwoods Solicitors LLP. One of Lisa's key responsibilities is employmentlaw@work, Greenwoods' up-to-the minute email update service which has been a great success since 2002.

John Macaulay, Director
jmacaulay@greenwoods.co.uk

John Macaulay has specialised in employment and discrimination law since qualifying in 1991 and has a wealth of experience in advising on all aspects of employment law, including spending significant time 'at the sharp end' and arguing clients' cases at Tribunal. *Chambers UK 2009/10* reports 'John Macaulay draws praise for showing excellent commitment to his clients' and that his team 'impresses clients with its client-focused employment advice.'

EMPLOYMENT LAWYERS

Loch Associates Employment Lawyers provides commercial employment legal advice and HR services to employers and executive employees. Based in the south-east with offices in London and Tunbridge Wells, we act for clients right across the UK in a variety of sectors. Our specialist knowledge and skills in this complex legal area and our commercial approach provide our clients with a valuable insight to make the right decisions.

At Loch Associates Employment Lawyers, we believe the diversity of our experience gives us the edge over our competitors, as our legal know-how is complemented by our team's experience gained in businesses outside the legal world. Clients benefit from our ability to apply legal advice effectively to the commercial environment at competitive rates.

We provide advice to companies and executive employees in a wide range of sectors, including professional services, manufacturing, outsourcing, leisure, PR and marketing, financial services and IT, acting for small businesses and charities through to companies employing many thousands of employees. Together with HR consultants from our sister company, Enablise Limited, we help our clients on all aspects of employment law and HR, providing practical and accurate advice with the bigger picture in mind.

www.lochassociates.co.uk

Sophie Applewhite, Associate
sophie@lochassociates.co.uk

Sophie Applewhite is an Associate Employment Lawyer and advises on both contentious and non-contentious employment law issues and represents clients at Employment Tribunals. Her experience includes advising both employers and employees on unfair dismissal, discipline and grievance issues, redundancy, compromise agreements and employment contracts. Sophie has also been involved in a number of complex, high value discrimination claims and has experience of mediations as an alternative means to negotiating settlements.

Chloe Harrold, Associate
chloe@lochassociates.co.uk

Chloe Harrold is a dual qualified English Employment Lawyer and New York Attorney. Chloe's employment law experience includes advising both employers and employees on a variety of employment law areas such as redundancy, restructuring, unfair dismissal and discrimination and also includes advising employers in relation to incentive and benefit arrangements.

Pam Loch, Managing Partner
pam@lochassociates.co.uk

Founder of Loch Associates Employment Lawyers, Pam Loch is a dual qualified Scottish and English Employment Lawyer with extensive experience in contentious and non-contentious employment matters, having acted for employers and employees advising on all aspects of employment law in England and Scotland. She advises plcs, private companies, charities and individuals. Her experience is extensive but includes acting for law firms, football clubs and in sectors including manufacturing, media, advertising, financial institutions, technology and leisure. As well as conducting her own advocacy in Employment Tribunals, she has also acted for clients in proceedings in the Employment Appeal Tribunal and the High Court. Pam is an Associate of the Chartered Insurance Institute, a member of the Employment Lawyers' Association and she is also an accredited mediator. She appears regularly on national television and radio shows as well as being widely published.

maCROBERTS

MacRoberts LLP, one of Scotland's leading commercial law firms, prides itself on being highly-attuned to clients' needs. Over many years, a huge range of leading British and international businesses, banks and other financial institutions have continued to trust MacRoberts' lawyers to lend a clear insight to the commercial and legal issues that face them. In an increasingly frantic world there is no substitute for a commercial partner on whom you can rely.

Our full service offices in Glasgow and Edinburgh, combined with the extensive experience of over 40 partners, means that we are able to offer clients innovative and cost effective solutions based solidly in commercial practice. We provide a comprehensive range of legal services across all sectors and our commitment to the success of our clients remains at the core of everything we do.

www.macroberts.com

David Flint, Partner
david.flint@macroberts.com

David Flint specialises in all aspects of non-contentious intellectual property, with particular emphasis on computer-related contracts and issues. He is acknowledged as a leading expert in intellectual property law, computer / IT law, and European law. He has also specialised in corporate insolvency for almost 30 years, is a licensed insolvency practitioner and has an extensive practice in competition law. He is a member of the CBI Competition Panel and the Joint Working Party on Competition Law of the UK Law Societies and Bars and the Chair of an American Bar Association Committee on Intellectual Property law.

Siobhan O'Neil, Solicitor
siobhan.o'neil@macroberts.com

Siobhan O'Neil joined MacRoberts in 2009 and specialises in Employment law. She is involved in a wide range of contentious and non-contentious work. She provides advice to clients on a range of issues in an uncomplicated and commercial manner. Siobhan is part of the Employment Law Group's Equal Pay Team.

Valerie Surgenor, Partner
valerie.surgenor@macroberts.com

Primarily practising in non-contentious intellectual property, information technology and compliance and regulatory matters, Valerie Surgenor has a keen interest in the areas of information management and data security, having particular experience in the carrying out of European- and UK-wide Data Protection Compliance Audits. As a member of the MacRoberts Compliance and Regulatory Group, Valerie advises on the areas of anti-corruption and the new UK Bribery Act and related compliance issues.

MILLS
— & —
REEVE

What really sets Mills & Reeve apart from other law firms is the way we work with our clients. We understand that they no longer want a traditional law firm in the 21st century – they want one that embraces forward thinking approaches to service, billing, commercial know-how, innovation, people management and community engagement. We have the resources available for large transactions but we are small enough to retain a distinct culture to provide clients with flexibility and personal attention.

We are a full service law firm, with accessible specialists for immediate contact. We advise some of the UK and the world's most successful and innovative businesses and public sector organisations as well as individuals. This distinctive blend of clients adds to our experience and expertise, which gives us additional insights and ideas to help our clients fulfil their ambitions.

Some things you should know about Mills & Reeve:

- We are a top 50 UK law firm.
- Our commercial clients include global and UK based businesses, FTSE and AIM listed organisations, private companies and start-ups.
- We advise more than 70 universities and colleges, over 100 healthcare large healthcare organisations, 65 local authorities as well as leading international insurers.
- We have the largest private tax team outside of London and one of the largest family teams in the world.
- Around 800 people work in the firm (including 98 partners and over 350 other lawyers) from offices in Birmingham, Cambridge, Leeds, London, Manchester and Norwich serving clients throughout the country and internationally.
- We use our network of firms across the globe to support our clients' international requirements.
- Ranked in *Financial Times*' Innovative Lawyers special 2010 report as a 'stand-out' firm for our focus on post-recession efficiency.
- We have been listed in *The Sunday Times*' 100 Best Companies to Work For 2011 and hve been since 2004, and have held the Investor in People accreditation since 1998.

www.mills-reeve.com

Anna Youngs, Associate
anna.youngs@mills-reeve.com

Anna Youngs is an Associate at Mills & Reeve in the Birmingham office, specialising in Employment Law. She works for a range of commercial clients and public sector bodies. Anna has a particular interest in TUPE issues and her recent work includes advising on the employment implications of a merger and the subsequent restructuring process, acting on complex disability claims , advising on the TUPE implications of transfers from the public sector to the private sector, and advising in relation to director / shareholder disputes. Anna carries out advocacy at the Employment Tribunal and undertakes client training on all aspects of employment law.

Pinsent Masons LLP is an international law firm with over 270 partners and more than 1,000 lawyers, who provide a full range of corporate and commercial services. Internationally, it works in alliance with Salans. The firm operates in the major commercial and financial centres of the UK as well as the Middle-East and Asia Pacific. In the UK, it has offices in London, Birmingham, Leeds, Manchester, Edinburgh, Glasgow and Bristol. Internationally, the firm is based in Hong Kong, Beijing, Shanghai, Singapore and Dubai. Clients benefit from the depth of industry knowledge of the firm's teams of specialist lawyers who provide a comprehensive service in health and safety, employment, PPP / PFI projects, dispute resolution (property and commercial), commercial property, planning, environment and sustainability, corporate and commercial, data protection, pensions, insolvency and taxation. With over 80 lawyers, the firm has one of the largest teams of employment specialists of any UK law firm and a recent Chambers survey confirmed the Group as employment law adviser of choice to the FTSE 250.

www.pinsentmasons.com

Other contributors

Bond Pearce: Dale Collins, Dan Fawcett and Karen Plumbley-Jones
www.bondpearce.com

Bond Pearce LLP is a leading national business law firm providing commercial, corporate, real estate, dispute resolution and employment services to some of the UK's pre-eminent corporate and public sector organisations.

The firm advises in excess of 40 FTSE 350 companies, making it one of the leading FTSE advisors outside of London. Bond Pearce is a national leader in energy, retail, real estate and insurance and is also recognised for having one of the largest dispute resolution practices in the country, a heavyweight property, planning and environment team and full service corporate, finance and commercial capability.

The firm's growth has been based on forging strong client relationships, delivering effective business solutions and recruiting high-calibre people across the firm. Clients have access to more than 440 legal professionals, 72 of whom are recognised as 'Leaders in their Field' in the 2012 edition of *Chambers* with best of the UK status in areas such as Retail, Insurance, Energy, Local Government and Health and Safety specialisms.

Dale Collins is a Solicitor-Advocate and is recognised in the legal directories for his experience and expertise in the field of health and safety law. He has been a criminal advocate for over 22 years and has extensive advocacy experience in the criminal courts and before other tribunals, both from a prosecution and defence perspective, having dealt with everything from pollution of watercourses to corporate manslaughter. Dale also has an MA in Environmental Law and is an experienced lecturer.

Dan Fawcett has specialised in employment law since qualifying with Bond Pearce in October 2008. He advises clients on a wide range of contentious and non-contentious employment matters, from defending Tribunal claims to reviewing policies and providing ad hoc employment advice. Recently Dan's work has focused on defending a wide range of discrimination, unfair dismissal and whistleblowing claims and Dan conducts his own Employment Tribunal advocacy.

Karen Plumbley-Jones is a Practice Development Lawyer specialising in employment law. She has wide experience of advising employers and employees on employment law and has a particular interest in the employment aspects of corporate transactions. She delivers seminars and training for clients and the CIPD. She is a member of the Employment Lawyers Association.

Butler & Young Group: Dave Allen and Steve Cooper
www.byl.co.uk

The Butler & Young Group of companies provides professional, practical advice and support on a wide range of construction projects. Its development has seen it grow to a company with over 150 professional staff in all disciplines and over 15 offices nationwide.

Building on its success, the Butler & Young Group now has a family of companies providing a multi-disciplined construction consultancy, comprising building control, fire engineering, health and safety, DDA auditing, environmental engineering and asbestos surveys through to structural design and party wall surveying.

The Butler & Young Group provides an effective and efficient service with experts in all fields of the building industry. This enables it to provide completed schemes, which are on budget, on time, and satisfy all statutory obligations.

Dave Allen is the Head of Quality and Standards at Butler & Young Group and is responsible for setting technical policy in the group and ensuring a quality service is maintained through technical and procedural auditing.

He has 25 years' experience in Building Control, dealing with projects as diverse as towers in Canary Wharf and listed barns in Herefordshire. He is actively involved in national building control working groups and has recently been involved in the implementation of a new IT system at Butler & Young.

Steve Cooper is the Standards and Warranty Manager for Butler and Young Group and is a member of the Association of Building Engineers. He has over 20 years' experience in the construction industry having spent most of that time in Building Control.

During this time he has been employed in both the private and public sector and has experience in dealing with the full spectrum of building work from the refurbishment of historic buildings to modern methods of construction.

Recently the Government has placed a great deal of emphasis on reducing carbon emissions in Building Regulations and they are likely to be used as the driver for the move to the Code For Sustainable Homes. Steve has been providing training on this subject.

Charles Russell: Nicola McMahon and Susan Thomas
www.cr-law.co.uk

Over 100 years of Charles Russell's diligent client service has given it a unique position as a firm which successfully combines traditional values with the progressive practices of a modern commercial firm.

The result is a firm which enjoys a refreshing diversity of work. Through the quality, intelligence and commitment of our staff, we have achieved a balance which offers real benefits to our clients whether they are seeking legal advice for themselves, their family, or on behalf of their business.

We increasingly find that clients require a full range of legal services and so we are committed to providing legal services to both commercial and private clients. After all, where there is commerce there are people.

Having qualified into the Charles Russell Employment and Pensions Service Group in 2008, Nicola McMahon advises on all aspects of employment law, both contentious and non contentious, and corporate immigration matters.

Nicola has delivered Charles Russell seminars and internal client training sessions and has written various articles for national newspapers and employment publications.

Susan Thomas qualified in September 2005 and became an Associate in 2010. She primarily advises corporate clients and not-for-profit organisations on all aspects of employment law, both contentious and non-contentious, including business reorganisation and transfers, discrimination, employment policies and procedures, parental rights and grievance and disciplinary issues.

She is experienced in drafting employment policies, handbooks, contracts and service agreements. She has spoken to the Chartered Institute of Personnel and Development, speaks regularly at client training programmes and seminars, and is involved in organising training for the Employment Lawyers Association.

CMS Cameron McKenna: Amy Bird and Rupert Choat
www.cms-cmck.com

CMS Cameron McKenna is a full service international law firm, advising businesses, financial institutions, governments and other public sector bodies. The firm has over 130 partners and employs around 700 legal and tax advisers in total. CMS Cameron McKenna has a strong network of offices throughout the UK, CEE and beyond. Our lawyers have strong expertise in many legal areas including facilities management, construction, health and safety, projects and project finance, real estate, environment, financial services, corporate, energy and natural resources, insurance and reinsurance, technology, life sciences, intellectual property, human resources, pensions, competition, European law, arbitration and litigation.

Amy Bird graduated from King's College London with first class honours in Law and completed her legal practice course at BPP, obtaining a distinction. After training with CMS Cameron McKenna LLP, she qualified as a solicitor into the firm's employment team in August 2007.

She has worked with clients across a wide range of sectors, including completing post-qualification secondments to the in-house legal teams of two FTSE 100 companies, market-leaders in the telecoms and energy sectors. She supports clients by formulating service agreements and negotiating board-level exits, drafting staff handbooks and policies, advising on individual disciplinary issues, and advising on TUPE and other employee aspects of corporate transactions.

Rupert Choat has specialised in facilities management and construction for 13 years. Originally an Atkin Chambers barrister, he often appears as advocate. *Legal 500* says that "ex-barrister Rupert Choat is 'very bright and patient'" and he "is praised for his 'succinct and well-explained advice'". He was the winner of the International Law Office's Client Choice Award for Construction 2010. *Chambers & Partners UK* says Rupert is "'a gifted intellectual and good manager of a team'" and "Clients highlight that Rupert Choat 'can certainly hold his own almost anywhere – he's cool, calm and collected with a deep knowledge of the relevant matters.'"

Rupert regularly writes for *Building* magazine, RICS Journals and CMS' market leading Law-Now alert service.

Cummins Solicitors: Michael Cummins
www.cummins-solicitors.com

Cummins Solicitors is a niche firm of employment solicitors which began in business at the beginning of 2011. The firm advises on the whole range of employment law issues, mainly for employers ranging in size from small owner-managed business to national household names. The firm also acts for a small number of senior employees. The firm offers advice on the whole range of employment law issues, but with particular experience in representing clients at the Employment Tribunal and in providing training.

All of our lawyers have worked at large national practices and have significant experience in the field of employment law along with a true passion for what they do. Our clients tell us that, as well as providing excellent advice, they enjoy working with us because we are practical and down to earth. We believe that what matters to clients is the success of their business. That philosophy drives the way we give advice – with practical solutions, telling clients what we would do in any given situation in the best interest of their business. We don't sit on the fence.

Mike Cummins is a Director of Cummins Solicitors. Mike qualified in 1998 and has specialised in employment law since qualification, enjoying significant experience of the whole range of employment issues including advising on large and small acquisitions as well as personally representing clients at several hundred tribunal hearings and at the Employment Appeal Tribunal. Mike particularly enjoys providing training on all aspects of employment law. He is regularly asked to contribute articles for leading journals, legal publications and trade magazines and to present at public forum seminars.

DLA Piper: Jonathan Exten-Wright and Richard Woolich
www.dlapiper.com

With more than 3,700 lawyers located in 29 countries and 67 offices throughout Asia, Europe, the Middle East and the US, DLA Piper is positioned to help companies with their legal needs anywhere in the world. The group advises on all areas of employment, trade union and employee relations, discrimination and diversity management, pensions, equal pay and job evaluation, employee benefits and reward legal issues. It has a specialist employment law training team called Advance, which delivers training on a commercial basis.

Jonathan Exten-Wright practises employment law on behalf of public and private companies. He is experienced in senior executive issues and board room disputes, injunctive proceedings, in central and local government transactions, contracting-out / outsourcing, private finance initiatives, mergers and acquisitions, and sales of businesses, trade union recognition and negotiations, works councils and collective consultation, redundancy and change programmes, contract variation, and discrimination. In addition Jonathan advices on partnership and LLP disputes. Jonathan is also involved in pan-European labour law support. Clients include various well known financial service organisations; hoteliers; telecom and media organisations and public sector bodies.

Richard Woolich is a Partner in the tax group, based in the London offices. Richard focuses on leading the international VAT practice and on real estate transactions, joint ventures and funds.

Richard advises entrepreneurs and institutions on all types of property transactions, corporate real estate work and VAT in general. Richard has spoken at conferences (Henry Stuart, CLT, IIR and Jordans). He is a chartered tax adviser and an associate member and director of the Institute of Indirect Taxation. Richard sits on the VAT and Property Liaison group and the Stamp Taxes Practitioners group.

Dundas & Wilson LLP: Mandy Laurie
www.dundas-wilson.com

Dundas & Wilson is a commercial law firm highly rated by clients as well as by *Chambers* and *Legal 500* directories. Our clients value our determined focus. They rely on the quality of our advice and instruct us to oppose, work with or on panels alongside major London firms. They choose us time and again because we work tirelessly to deliver the right results at the right value.

Mandy Laurie is a Partner in Dundas & Wilson's employment team and has considerable experience in representing both private and public sector clients throughout the UK. She is described as an inspirational solicitor, a unique 'all-rounder', who has an incredibly engaging manner with clients. Excellent in advocacy, she is viewed as being very practical and commercially focused. Mandy regularly gives advice on potentially contentious issues and problems with an international aspect, and has a particular interest in discrimination and equality issues.

Greta Thornbory, Occupational Health Consultant
www.gtenterprises-uk.com

Greta Thornbory is an Occupational Health and Educational Consultant with over 30 years' experience in OH practice and teaching. During that time she has worked with government departments, professional bodies, pharmaceutical, educational and other companies, including several multi-nationals, on a variety of occupational health and safety projects. She also worked for the Royal College of Nursing for 12 years as a senior lecturer and programme director of both occupational health and continuing professional development, during which time she was responsible for many of the 95 Nursing Update programmes for the learning zone on BBC TV and was the RCN representative on the UN Environment and Development Round Table on Health and Environment.

She is now Consulting and CPD Editor of *Occupational Health* and is responsible for commissioning and editing the monthly multidisciplinary CPD articles and resources for professional updating purposes. She is the co-author with Joan Lewis of *Employment Law and Occupational health: a practical handbook* first published in 2006 (2nd ed. 2010) and edited *Public Health Nursing*: a textbook for health visitors, school nurses and occupational health nurses, published in July 2009.

Kelly Barfoot Mediation Services: Kelly Barfoot
www.kbmediationservices.co.uk

Kelly Barfoot is the Director of Kelly Barfoot Mediation Services and works within the organisation as a Senior Mediator. Based in Grantham, Lincolnshire, the business provides specialist employment mediation to organisations locally and nationally with the aim of resolving workplace conflict simply and effectively. Kelly is committed to common sense dispute resolution and wants to keep employers out of court and working relationships on track. Kelly is a Myers Briggs Type Indicator practitioner and also has Counselling qualifications, making her the ideal person to tackle some of the sensitive issues that come up during mediation. Kelly has a strong background in learning and development and HR, having worked for high profile organisations such as Travelex and IKEA, so has a full appreciation of the challenges faced in today's workplaces.

Kennedys: Hayley Overshott
www.kennedys-law.com

Kennedys is known primarily as an insurance-driven commercial litigation practice, although the firm is also recognised for skills in the non-contentious commercial field, particularly within the insurance, construction and transport industries. Kennedys has a fast-growing reputation for its work in employment law and the healthcare and insolvency sectors.

Kennedys' approach in all matters is recognising that the 'product' required by clients is the economic resolution of the claim, not merely the legal services necessary along the way. The firm looks at the commercial issues relevant to each case. All Kennedys' fee earners work with this philosophy in mind. Having acted for individuals and organisations involved in many of the major cases in this area, including the trial resulting from the Hatfield rail crash, Kennedys' Health and Safety team is widely recognised as a leader in its field.

Hayley Overshott advises and assists companies and individuals under investigation by the authorities in connection with health and safety and environmental incidents and issues. She also has experience of complex commercial litigation, with a specialism in the rail industry.

Metis Law: David Sinclair
www.metislaw.com

Metis Law LLP is a new style of regional law firm with a strong property and construction base. Metis acts across the public and private sector, providing businesses with tailored services and innovative products. The firm has a reputation for delivering solutions to a range of property, facilities and construction organisations.

David Sinclair is one of a few dual-qualified Solicitors and safety practitioners in the UK, who have achieved Chartered Health and Safety Practitioner status. Trained originally as a mining engineer, David has a BSc Honours degree in Occupational Health and Safety and a Durham University postgraduate diploma in Environmental Management.

Ortalan: Louise Smail
www.ortalan.com

Louise Smail has extensive experience in the field of risk management with a wide range of organisations, including local government, emergency services, railways and process industries.

Louise acted as Advanced Works Safety Manager for Union Railways Limited, looking at the issues of environment and consents associated with the works. Louise now runs her own consultancy, Ortalan, where she works on high profile projects looking at business risk evaluation, business continuity and performance and the impact of changes in legislation in both the UK and Europe.

Peters & Peters Solicitors LLP: Dr Anna Odby
www.petersandpeters.co.uk

Peters & Peters Solicitors LLP specializes in Fraud and Regulatory Litigation, Commercial Fraud Litigation and Compliance. Key practice areas include asset recovery, commercial litigation and alternative dispute resolution, competition regulation including cartels and price fixing, regulatory and financial services compliance including money laundering and financial sanctions compliance, extradition and mutual legal assistance, corruption, corporate risk and fraud prevention, financial crime and tax investigations.

Dr Anna Odby is an Associate in Peters & Peters' Fraud and Regulatory Department. She specialises in business crime and regulatory advice, with particular expertise in money laundering regulation and compliance. A former university lecturer in Public Law and Human Rights Law, Anna holds a Doctorate in anti-money laundering law. She joined Peters & Peters in 2005 where she trained in civil and criminal fraud before qualifying.

Pitmans LLP: Amanda Trewhella
www.pitmans.com

Pitmans LLP is the largest law firm in the Thames Valley, with offices in Reading and in the City of London. With national expertise, regional leadership and the ability to deliver on both a local and a national level, the company has been established for over 150 years. As a founder member of InterAct Europe, Pitmans is part of a powerful international network, with offices in 17 European cities. Rated highly in the influential *Legal 500* and *Chambers Directories*, the company continues to be industry award-winners.

Amanda Trewhella is a Solicitor who has been part of Pitmans LLP's employment team since 2009. Amanda is an employment law specialist with experience of advising on all aspects of the employment relationship from recruitment and the drafting of HR policies and employee handbooks through to advising on business reorganisations, disciplinary and grievance procedures and drafting and negotiating compromise agreements and severance packages. She has advised on the bringing and defending of a variety of Employment Tribunal claims including unfair dismissal, breach of contract, flexible working, whistleblowing and discrimination claims.

PPL: Christine Geissmar
www.ppluk.com

PPL is the UK-based music licensing company which licenses recorded music for broadcast, online and public performance use. Established in 1934, PPL carries out this role on behalf of thousands of record company and performer members. If recorded music is played in public – including offices, factories and general workplaces – music licences are legally required.

PRS for Music: Barney Hooper
www.prsformusic.com

PRS for Music represents 80,000 songwriters, composers and music publishers in the UK. As a not-for-profit organisation it ensures creators are paid whenever their music is played, performed or reproduced; championing the importance of copyright to protect and support the UK music industry. The UK has a proud tradition of creating wonderful music that is enjoyed the world over and PRS for Music has been supporting the creators of that music since 1914.

PRS for Music provides business and community groups with easy access to over ten million songs through its music licences. Barney Hooper is Head of PR and Corporate Communications at PRS for Music.

Rochman Landau: Howard Lewis-Nunn
www.rochmanlandau.co.uk

As you would expect, this firm is committed to excellence. Legal acumen, precision, efficiency and pragmatism all form part of the services we provide. However, there is more to our practice than the key factors that clients require from their lawyers as a matter of course. Our business can only be as strong as our relationships with clients and we know that we will be judged on our understanding of value, speed and communication. We are a highly regarded firm and very proud of our reputation.

Howard Lewis-Nunn qualified as a barrister in 1994 and has practised in law firms in the City and West End since 1997. He has extensive experience in all aspects of employment law including executive contracts, dismissals, discrimination claims, injunctions, advising on employment issues on transactions, data protection issues, and executive service agreements. With a background as a barrister, Howard has particular expertise in advocacy. He also gives presentations to clients and external organisations on employment issues. Howard's clients include retailers, professional service companies, employment agencies, manufacturers and individuals. Howard is a member of the Employment Lawyers' Association.

Steeles Law: Tina Maxey and Elizabeth Stevens
www.steeleslaw.co.uk

Steeles Law is a medium-sized, multi-disciplinary law firm with offices in London, Norwich (HQ) and Diss, providing legal services to a diverse mix of clients, from corporate organisations and institutions to public sector bodies, charities and individuals. The firm is particularly recognised for the strength of its specialist employment practitioners, who provide practical and commercially sensible advice across the full range of employment law and HR issues and who have experience of handling the most complex and sensitive workplace disputes.

Tina Maxey qualified in 2005 and advises clients on a wide range of contentious and non-contentious employment law issues. She is experienced in preparing tribunal cases on behalf of employers and also drafts employment documentation, including directors' service agreements and compromise agreements. She deals with regular queries from employers relating to the ongoing employment relationship, including performance management, long-term absences, disciplinary matters and employee grievances. She has also delivered in-house training for clients. Tina is a member of the Employment Lawyers Association.

Elizabeth Stevens is a Professional Support Lawyer in the employment team of Steeles Law. She regularly writes articles on employment law for publication, as well as designing and delivering seminars and training programmes for clients.

Taylor Wessing: Rachel Farr, Alice Hill and Lorraine Smith
www.taylorwessing.com

Taylor Wessing is a powerful source of legal support for organisations doing business in or with Europe and is based primarily in the UK, France and Germany, with further offices in Brussels, Alicante, Dubai and Shanghai. A market leader in advising IP and technology-rich industries, Taylor Wessing boasts a strong reputation in the corporate, finance and real estate sectors alongside indepth experience across the full range of legal services including tax, commercial disputes and employment.

Rachel Farr is a Professional Support Lawyer in the Employment and Pensions Group, focusing on UK employment law. She was previously an Associate in the Group, advising both employers and employees on both contentious and non-contentious issues. Rachel joined the firm in 2003.

Alice Hill is a Professional Support Lawyer in the pensions group. She was previously an Associate with the group, having trained and qualified with the firm in 2002. Alice has experience in matters arising from the administration of occupational pension schemes and the winding up of such schemes and has advised both sponsoring employers and trustees on these matters. Alice has also worked on a number of contentious matters, including various complaints to the Pensions Ombudsman on behalf of both complainants and respondents. Alice is an Associate Member of the Association of Pension Lawyers.

Lorraine Smith is a Professional Support Lawyer. She focuses on analysing the latest legal and market practice developments in corporate law and their impact for our clients and the transactions we advise on. She also organises and updates Taylor Wessing's corporate legal know-how resources, prepares bulletins for clients and provides internal legal training for our lawyers. She trained at Herbert Smith, and came to Taylor Wessing after a period at Lovells (now Hogan Lovells). She draws on transactional and advisory experience in private M&A, group reorganisations and corporate governance.

Tyndallwoods Solicitors: Aliya Khan
www.tyndallwoods.co.uk

Tyndallwoods is a Birmingham Legal Practice undertaking a wide range of contentious and non-contentious work. Our Immigration Team, while undertaking a very wide range of advice and advocacy has in the past mainly focused on human rights. We have now launched a tailored business unit within the Immigration Team, Migration for Business – MfB. Our highly experienced and specialist team has provided immigration services for more than 25 years and we are regularly cited as one of the leading firms in this area. The law relating to migrant workers changed in 2008/09 when a new type of relationship between employer and employee rolled out by the Government in tandem with a points-based objective qualification system. The system assesses applicants against a wide range of criteria and brings significant additional responsibilities for those involved in migration which, if not complied with in full, can have serious consequences.

Aliya Khan is a Legal Executive and a senior caseworker in the Migration for Business unit – MfB. She has been working with Tyndallwoods since 2003. She undertakes various applications and reviews such as Skilled Migrants under Tier 1 and Tier 2 Sponsorship, Work Permits for Romanian and Bulgarian nationals, Tier 1 Post Study Workers, student applications and EEA nationals. Her main focus of work is with those who wish to seek employment in the UK or who are already working in the UK.

Veale Wasbrough Vizards: Gareth Edwards
www.vwv.co.uk

Veale Wasbrough Vizards (VWV) acts nationally for clients in the Education and charities, Healthcare, Private wealth, Public and Family owned business sectors. The firm also offers a dedicated service to individuals. The firm's combination of specialist expertise, genuine teamwork and client commitment sets it apart. VWV is recognised for excellence in specific sectors and for its established commitment to training, teamwork and approachability. One goal is to help clients succeed, through high standards, technical expertise, a creative approach, and commitment to staff.

Gareth Edwards is a Partner and Head of the employment team at Veale Wasbrough Vizards. Gareth advises on the full range of both contentious and non-contentious employment law and labour relations issues. He has a wide range of experience managing complex and sensitive issues in the workplace, together with managing Employment Tribunal disputes. He is also an experienced Employment Tribunal advocate. Gareth advises on industrial relations issues and non-contentious issues, such as executive severances, business reorganisations, TUPE and outsourcing issues, plus the employment aspects of corporate transactions. Gareth regularly conducts in-house training seminars and also speaks at external conferences.

Directory of information sources

Access Association
0113 2478102
www.access-association.org.uk

Action on Smoking and Health (ASH)
020 7739 5902
www.ash.org.uk

Advisory, Conciliation and Arbitration
Service (ACAS)
08457 474 747
www.acas.org.uk

Age UK
0800 1698787
www.ageconcern.org.uk

Alcohol Concern
020 7264 0510
www.alcoholconcern.org.uk

Association of British Insurers (ABI)
020 7600 3333
www.abi.org.uk

Association of Chief Police Officers (ACPO)
020 7084 8950
www.acpo.police.uk

Association of Sustainability Practitioners
www.asp-online.org

Blind in Business
020 7588 1885
www.blindinbusiness.co.uk

British Association of Occupational
Therapists (BAOT) / College of Occupational
Therapists (COT)
020 7357 6480
www.cot.co.uk

British Automatic Fire Sprinkler Association
01353 659187
www.bafsa.org.uk

British Chambers of Commerce (BCC)
020 7654 5800
www.britishchambers.org.uk

British Institute of Facilities Management
(BIFM)
0845 058 1356
www.bifm.org.uk

British Occupational Health Research
Foundation (BOHRF)
020 7034 3420
www.bohrf.org.uk

British Occupational Hygiene Society (BOHS)
01332 298101
www.bohs.org

British Retail Consortium (BRC)
020 7854 8900
www.brc.org.uk

British Standards Institution (BSI)
020 8996 9001
www.bsi-global.com

Business in the Community
020 7566 8650
www.bitc.org.uk

Cadw
01443 336 000
www.cadw.wales.gov.uk

Customer Contact Association (CCA)
0141 564 9010
www.cca.org.uk

Central Arbitration Committee (CAC)
020 7904 2300
www.cac.gov.uk

Centre for Accessible Environments (CAE)
020 7840 0125
www.cae.org.uk

Centre for Effective Dispute Resolution
(CEDR)
020 7536 6000
www.cedr.co.uk

Chartered Institute of Arbitrators
020 7421 7444
www.ciarb.org

Chartered Institute of Personnel and
Development (CIPD)
020 8162 6200
www.cipd.co.uk

Chartered Management Institute
01536 204222
www.managers.org.uk

CIFAS (the UK's Fraud Prevention Service)
www.cifas.org.uk

Civil Contingencies Secretariat (Cabinet
Office)
0207 276 1234
www.cabinetoffice.gov.uk

Criminal Records Bureau (CRB)
0870 9090811
www.crb.gov.uk

Crown Prosecution Service (CPS)
020 3357 0000
www.cps.gov.uk

Department for Business, Innovation and
Skills (BIS)
020 7215 5000
www.berr.gov.uk

Department for Communities and Local
Government (DCLG)
0303 444 0000
www.communities.gov.uk

Department for Work and Pensions (DWP)
www.dwp.gov.uk

Department of Health (DH)
020 7210 4850
www.dh.gov.uk

Direct Gov
www.direct.gov.uk

Employee Assistance Professionals
Association
01993 772 765
www.eapa.org.uk

Employers and Work-Life Balance
020 7976 3565
www.theworkfoundation.com

Employers' Forum on Age (EFA)
0845 456 2495
www.efa.org.uk

Employers' Forum on Disability
020 7403 3020
www.efd.org.uk

Employment Appeals Tribunal
020 7273 1041
www.employmentappeals.gov.uk

Employment Lawyers Association
01895 256972
www.elaweb.org.uk

Employment Tribunal
0845 795 9775
www.employmenttribunals.gov.uk

English Heritage
0870 333 1181
www.english-heritage.org.uk

ENTO (formerly Employment NTO)
0116 251 7979
www.ento.co.uk

Equality and Human Rights Commission
0845 604 6610
www.equalityhumanrights.com

Ergonomics Society
01509 234904
www.ergonomics.org.uk

Facilities Management Association (FMA)
07960 428 146
www.fmassociation.org.uk

Federation of Small Businesses
(FSB)
01253 336000
www.fsb.org.uk

Financial Services Authority (FSA)
020 7066 1000
www.fsa.gov.uk

Forum of Private Business (FPB)
0845 130 1722
www.fpb.org

Gangmasters Licensing Authority
0845 602 5020
www.gla.gov.uk

Her Majesty's Treasury
020 7270 4558
www.hm-treasury.gov.uk

HM Revenue & Customs
www.hmrc.gov.uk

Home Office
020 7035 4848
www.homeoffice.gov.uk

Information Commissioner's Office
0303 123 1113
www.ico.gov.uk

Institute of Alcohol Studies (IAS)
01480 466 766
www.ias.org.uk

Institute of Customer Service (ICS)
01206 571716
www.instituteofcustomerservice.com

Institute of Directors (IoD)
020 7766 8866
www.iod.com

Institute of Environmental Management and
Assessment (IEMA)
01522 540069
www.iema.net

Institute of Hospitality
020 8661 4900
www.instituteofhospitality.org

International Facilities Management
Association (USA)
+1 713 623 4362
www.ifma.org

International Stress Management
Association UK (ISMA UK)
01179 697284
www.isma.org.uk

Investors in People
020 7467 1900
www.investorsinpeople.co.uk

Kelly Barfoot Mediation Services
0845 643 7355
www.kbmediationservices.co.uk/

Knowledge-Counsel
01344 779438
www.knowledge-counsel.com

Legislation Gov UK
0870 600 55 22
www.legislation.gov.uk/

Low Pay Commission
020 7215 8459
www.lowpay.gov.uk

Mind
0845 7660163
www.mind.org.uk

National Association for the Care and
Resettlement of Offenders (Nacro)
020 7840 7200
www.nacro.org.uk

National Association of Pension Funds
(NAPF)
020 7601 1700
www.napf.co.uk

National Register of Access Consultants
(NRAC)
020 7735 7845
www.nrac.org.uk

Northern Ireland Committee of the Irish
Congress of Trade Unions (NIC.ICTU)
02890 247940
www.ictuni.org

Office of Communications (Ofcom)
020 7981 3000
www.ofcom.org.uk

Office of Public Sector Information (OPSI)
See Legislation.Gov.UK

Patent Office
0300 300 2000
www.ipo.gov.uk

The Pensions Regulator
0870 6063636
www.thepensionsregulator.gov.uk

PPL
020 7534 1000
www.ppluk.com

PRS for Music
www.prsformusic.com

Public Concern at Work
020 7404 6609
www.pcaw.co.uk

Recruitment and Employment Confederation
(REC)
020 7009 2100
www.rec.uk.com

Remploy
0800 155 2700
www.remploy.co.uk

Royal Association for Disability and
Rehabilitation (RADAR)
020 7250 3222
www.radar.org.uk

Royal National Institute of the Blind (RNIB)
020 7388 1266
www.rnib.org.uk

Royal National Institute for Deaf People
020 7296 8000
www.rnid.org.uk

Scottish Trades Union Congress (STUC)
0141 337 8100
www.stuc.org.uk

Sign Design Society
020 8776 8866
www.signdesignsociety.co.uk

Stress Management Society
0800 327 7697
www.stress.org.uk

Telework Association (TCA)
0800 616008
www.tca.org.uk

The Stationery Office
0870 600 5522
www.tso.co.uk

Trades Union Congress (TUC)
020 7636 4030
www.tuc.org.uk

United Kingdom Accreditation Service
(UKAS)
020 8917 8400
www.ukas.com

Wales Trades Union Congress (TUC Cymru)
020 7636 4030
www.tuc.org.uk

Work Foundation
020 7976 3565
www.theworkfoundation.com

Working Balance
0161 217 2500
www.workingbalance.co.uk

Working Families
020 7253 7243
www.workingfamilies.org.uk

Working Well Together (WWT)
0113 283 4269
www.wwt.uk.com

Workplace Law
0871 777 8881
www.workplacelaw.net

Index